MODERN HUMANITIES RESEARCH ASSOCIATION
TUDOR AND STUART TRANSLATIONS
VOLUME 18

THOMAS MAY, LUCAN'S *PHARSALIA* (1627)

MODERN HUMANITIES RESEARCH ASSOCIATION
TUDOR AND STUART TRANSLATIONS

General Editors
Andrew Hadfield (University of Sussex)
Neil Rhodes (University of St Andrews)

Associate Editors
Guyda Armstrong (University of Manchester)
Fred Schurink (University of Manchester)
Louise Wilson (Liverpool Hope University)

Advisory Board
Warren Boutcher (Queen Mary, University of London);
Colin Burrow (All Souls College, Oxford);
A. E. B. Coldiron (Florida State University)
Patricia Demers (University of Alberta)
José Maria Pérez Fernández (University of Granada)
Robert S. Miola (Loyola College, Maryland)
Alessandra Petrina (University of Padua)
Anne Lake Prescott (Barnard College, Columbia University)
Quentin Skinner (Queen Mary, London)
Alan Stewart (Columbia University)

texts.mhra.org.uk

Thomas May,
Lucan's *Pharsalia* (1627)

Edited by
Emma Buckley and Edward Paleit

Modern Humanities Research Association
Tudor and Stuart Translations 18
2020

Published by

*The Modern Humanities Research Association
Salisbury House
Station Road
Cambridge CB1 2LA
United Kingdom*

© *Modern Humanities Research Association 2020*

Emma Buckley and Edward Paleit have asserted their right under the Copyright, Designs and Patents Act 1988 to be identified as the authors of this work. Parts of this work may be reproduced as permitted under legal provisions for fair dealing (or fair use) for the purposes of research, private study, criticism, or review, or when a relevant collective licensing agreement is in place. All other reproduction requires the written permission of the copyright holder who may be contacted at rights@mhra.org.uk.

First published 2020

*ISBN 978-1-78188-995-4 (HB)
ISBN 978-1-78188-008-1 (PB)*

CONTENTS

General Editors' Foreword	vi
Acknowledgements	vii
Introduction	1
Further Reading	29
Abbreviations	31
Note on Editorial Practice	33
Frontispiece	36
Dedication to William, Earl of Devonshire	38
The Life of Marcus Annaeus Lucanus	40
Dedicatory Poem: Ben Jonson to Thomas May	43
Dedicatory Poem: H. V. to Thomas May	44
Dedicatory Poem: J. Vaughan to Thomas May	45
Lucan's *Pharsalia*: The First Book	47
Lucan's *Pharsalia*: The Second Book	82
Lucan's *Pharsalia*: The Third Book	115
Lucan's *Pharsalia*: The Fourth Book	147
Lucan's *Pharsalia*: The Fifth Book	181
Lucan's *Pharsalia*: The Sixth Book	218
Lucan's *Pharsalia*: The Seventh Book	254
Lucan's *Pharsalia*: The Eighth Book	291
Lucan's *Pharsalia*: The Ninth Book	333
Lucan's *Pharsalia*: The Tenth Book	378
Appendix	405
Textual Notes	406
Glossary: Most Important Names and Places	420
Bibliography	441
Index	450

GENERAL EDITORS' FOREWORD

The aim of the *MHRA Tudor & Stuart Translations* is to create a representative library of works translated into English during the early modern period for the use of scholars, students and the wider public. The series will include both substantial single works and selections of texts from major authors, with the emphasis being on the works that were most familiar to early modern readers. The texts themselves will be newly edited with substantial introductions, notes, and glossaries, and will be published both in print and online.

The series aims to restore to view a major part of English Renaissance literature which has become relatively inaccessible and to present these texts as literary works in their own right. For that reason it will follow the same principle of modernisation adopted by other scholarly editions of canonical literature from the period. The series will have a similar scope to that of the original *Tudor Translations* published early in the last century, and while the great majority of the works presented will be from the sixteenth century, like the original series it will not be rigidly bound by the end-date of 1603. There will, however, be a very different range of texts with new and substantial scholarly apparatus.

The *MHRA Tudor & Stuart Translations* will extend our understanding of the English Renaissance through its representation of the process of cultural transmission from the classical to the early modern world and the process of cultural exchange within the early modern world.

Andrew Hadfield
Neil Rhodes

ACKNOWLEDGEMENTS

This project has been a collaborative effort undertaken with the institutional support of City University and the Universities of St Andrews and Exeter. We are grateful for the chance to have shared work-in-progress, jointly or as individuals, at research seminars or workshops in Yale, Durham, St Andrews, Exeter and Aberdeen. Particular thanks are due to Nora Goldschmidt, who allowed us to see her unpublished but forthcoming work on Lucanian 'biofiction'. Several cohorts of St Andrews Honours students worked with draft versions of this text and without fail provided energetic and pointed critique of both Lucan and this modern edition.

More general thanks are owed to Neil Rhodes and Andrew Hadfield, who have patiently supported this project, and we are very grateful to Simon F. Davies for his scrupulous copy-editing: he has not only saved us from many errors, but also encouraged us to provide a much clearer and comprehensible guide to May's Lucan. We are, of course, responsible for any errors which remain.

INTRODUCTION

Thomas May's *Lucan's Pharsalia* is a translation into rhyming couplets of the Latin poet Lucan's ten-book narrative on the Roman civil wars, now usually called the *Bellum Ciuile* ('Civil War'). May was not the first to translate Lucan into English. Barnaby Googe and George Turberville had contemplated doing so in the 1560s and 1570s. Christopher Marlowe translated the first book into blank verse before his death in 1593. In 1614 Arthur Gorges, a cousin of Sir Walter Raleigh, published a version in octosyllabic couplets. May's translation was more well-known and culturally influential than its predecessors, however. It was republished three times during his lifetime, as well as afterwards, and was a major reason for his high (if not uncontested) literary standing during the mid-seventeenth century. The work's impact may have been partly to do with its associations with Ben Jonson, one of the dominant voices of early Stuart literature. It also capitalized on a fascination among English writers of the early seventeenth century with the late republican and early imperial period of Roman history, and with Roman Stoicism. Lucan's subject, the doomed struggle to preserve republican liberty, was especially topical in the England of the late 1620s: May's work frequently implies analogies between English and Roman political experience. Finally, his was and remains an accomplished translation of a sometimes challenging Latin text, and an important moment in the history of Lucan's English reception. It remained the standard English translation until Nicholas Rowe's of 1718.

This is a modernized edition of the first complete (1627) edition of the translation. In this introduction we offer a brief summary of May's career and an overview of the work he translated, as it was read and understood in the early seventeenth century. We then give an account of the translation itself, including its political and literary context and some of May's habits as a translator.

1. Thomas May

Thomas May was born in or just after 1596 in Mayfield, Sussex into a family of middle-ranking gentry.[1] He studied at Sidney Sussex College, Cambridge, matriculating in 1609 at the age of fourteen and proceeding BA in 1613, the year after he published his first poem, an elegy on the death of the Prince of Wales.[2]

---

[1] For discussions of May's career, see Allan Griffith Chester, *Thomas May: Man of Letters, 1595–1650* (Philadelphia, PA: University of Pennsylvania Press, 1932); David Norbrook, 'May, Thomas (b. in or after 1596, d. 1650)', *ODNB*.

[2] University of Cambridge, *Epicedium Cantabrigiense* (Cambridge: Cantrell Legge, 1612), sig. O3ʳ; STC 4481. May's poem is untitled.

In 1615 he registered at Gray's Inn, although there is little evidence that he practised law. His city comedy *The Heir* was performed in 1620 and published two years later with a dedicatory poem by the poet and wit Thomas Carew.[3] May also wrote the verse translations for Kingsmill Long's English version of John Barclay's *Argenis* (1625), an Arcadian romance allegorizing European politics and originally written in Latin.[4]

May turned to Lucan in the mid-1620s as part of a shift towards Roman subjects and literary models. This 'Roman turn' included drama: May's *The Tragedy of Cleopatra* was performed in 1626 and *The Tragedy of Julia Agrippina* two years later, although it is unknown where or by whom. *The Tragedy of Cleopatra* contains characters, lines and phrases borrowed from Lucan. The first three books of May's translation were published in 1626 and the full work in 1627, under the title *Lucan's Pharsalia, or the Civil Wars of Rome between Pompey the Great and Julius Caesar*. He followed it up with further translations of Latin poetry, Virgil's *Georgics* (1628) and a selection of Martial's *Epigrams* (1629). In 1630 he published a seven-book *Continuation* of Lucan's narrative, a work he dedicated to Charles I. The early 1630s were a productive literary period for May. He composed an adaptation of Sophocles' *Antigone*, with scenes of witchcraft indebted to Lucan, and a translation of John Barclay's *Icon Animorum*, a description of the different characteristics of European peoples (both published in 1631). New editions of his translation of Lucan appeared in 1631 and 1635, and of the *Continuation* in 1633. He also turned to writing English historical poetry, producing works on the reigns of Henry II (1633) and Edward III (1635). Like his *Continuation*, each were in seven books and dedicated to Charles.

During this period May was friendly with Ben Jonson, who had written a commendatory poem for the 1627 edition of the translation, and with other lawyers and writers later remembered as part of a circle of friends by Edward Hyde, the future Earl of Clarendon. Besides May, Jonson and Hyde, this group included Carew, John Vaughan (who also wrote a poem for May's translation), John Selden, Charles Cotton and Sir Kenelm Digby, later Jonson's literary executor.[5] In 1636 May's comedy *The Old Couple*, later printed in 1658, was

[3] For Carew's poem, see Thomas May, *The Heire* (London: Bernard Alsop for Thomas Jones, 1622), sigs A3^{r-v}; STC 17713. The second 1633 edition (STC 17714) claims the date of 1620 on its title page. See G. E. Bentley, *The Jacobean and Caroline Stage*, 6 vols (Oxford: Oxford University Press, 1956), IV, p. 836.

[4] *Barclay his Argenis: or the Loves of Poliarchus and Argenis*, trans. by Kingsmill Long (London: George Purslowe for Henry Seile, 1625); STC 1392. May's authorship of the verses is recorded in the Stationers' Register entry for 19 June 1625: see *A Transcript of the Registers of the Company of Stationers of London, 1554–1640 AD*, ed. by Edward Arber, 5 vols (London: privately printed, 1875–1894), IV, p. 106. Barclay's work was first published in Paris in 1621.

[5] Edward Hyde, *The Life of Edward Earl of Clarendon ... Written by Himself*, 2 vols (Oxford: Clarendon Press, 1827), I, pp. 34–41 (comment on May, I, pp. 39–40). Hyde dated

performed at court; it may have been written earlier.⁶ After Jonson's death in 1637 May contributed a poem to the memorial collection *Jonsonus Virbius*, comparing his friend and mentor to a dead Lucan mourned by lesser poets.⁷ It was later alleged that he was disappointed at not inheriting Jonson's 'laureate' pension, bestowed instead on William Davenant, and thereafter soured in his attitude to the monarchy.⁸ May dedicated the first edition of *The Tragedy of Cleopatra*, in 1639, to Digby.

In 1640 May's *Supplementum Lucani*, a Latin translation of his *Continuation*, was published in the Dutch city of Leiden, and included commendatory poems by members of the university as well as the English writers Joseph Rutter and Richard Fanshawe. May seems to have written it while in the Netherlands, although it is unclear why he was there.⁹ Reprinted in London and Leiden in 1646, May's *Supplementum* had a much longer publication history than his translation, remaining in print until the nineteenth century. Samuel Johnson thought it superior to Cowley or Milton's neo-Latin poetry.¹⁰

During the conflicts of the 1640s May sided with Parliament. In 1642 he published a caustic historical analysis of the dangers of protracted parliaments when faced with over-bearing monarchs: it was republished several times under different titles.¹¹ After civil war broke out he became a paid Parliamentary writer, and his authorial or editorial hand may lie behind a number of publications.¹² In 1647 he produced *The History of the Parliament which began November the Third MDCXL* (i.e. the Long Parliament), an official pro-Parliamentary history of the period's political and military struggles. It makes a number of pointed analogies with Lucan. He followed it up in 1650 with the terser *Historiae Angliae Parliamenti Breviarium*, which was translated into English as the *Breviary of*

---

this acquaintance to the late 1620s, while 'he was only a student of the law' (ibid., I, pp. 34).

⁶ *The Old Couple, A Comedy. By Thomas May, Esq. London* (London: J. Cottrel for Samuel Speed, 1658); Wing M1412. See Norbrook, 'May, Thomas'.

⁷ Thomas May, 'An Elegie Upon Beniamin Johnson', in *Jonsonus Virbius*, ed. by Brian Duppa (London: E. P. for Henry Seile, 1638), sig. D3ʳ.

⁸ This charge is levelled by Hyde, *The Life*, I, p. 40, and repeated by Anthony à Wood, *Athenae Oxonienses*, ed. by Philip Bliss, 4 vols (London: for F. C. and J. Rivington, 1813-1820), III, p. 810.

⁹ For the *Supplementum*, see David Norbrook, *Writing the English Republic: Poetry, Rhetoric and Politics, 1627-1660* (Cambridge: Cambridge University Press, 1999), pp. 225-28; Edward Paleit, *War, Liberty, and Caesar: Responses to Lucan's 'Bellum Ciuile', ca. 1580-1650* (Oxford: Oxford University Press, 2013), pp. 285-96. For a modern edition, see *Das Supplementum Lucani von Thomas May: Einleitung, Edition, Übersetzung, Kommentar*, ed. by Birger Backhaus (Trier: Wissenschaftlicher Verlag, 2005).

¹⁰ Samuel Johnson, 'Cowley', in *Selected Poetry and Prose*, ed. by Frank Brady and W. K. Wimsatt (Berkeley: University of California Press, 1977), p. 343.

¹¹ Thomas May, *A Discourse Concerning the Success of Former Parliaments* (London: for I. H. and H. White, 1642); Wing M1404.

¹² See Norbrook, 'May, Thomas'.

the History of the Parliament of England and covered events up to 1649. Around this time May was almost certainly involved in the government's orchestrated campaign against the Leveller John Lilburne.[13] 1650 also witnessed further editions of his translation and *Continuation*.

May died in December 1650 and was buried at the Council of State's expense in Westminster Abbey, his tombstone — apparently composed by the republican pamphleteer Marchamont Nedham — celebrating him as 'champion of the English Commonwealth [or republic]'.[14] May's political choices were vigorously and sometimes viciously criticised by royalist writers who felt he had betrayed his former loyalties, an animus clearly revealed in the posthumous rumour that he was an atheist who died after a drunken binge.[15] This anti-portrait is fixed forever in Andrew Marvell's satire 'Tom May's Death': it may owe something to May's rumoured association with republican libertines like Henry Marten and Thomas Chaloner.[16] His tomb was broken up after the monarchy was restored in 1660, and he was re-buried with many other Parliamentarians in an un-marked grave in the precincts of St Margaret's Church, next to the Abbey.

2. Lucan and the *Bellum Ciuile*

Giving an account of Lucan and his text risks prejudicing a reader's encounter with May's translation. Nonetheless, for the benefit of those unfamiliar with the *Bellum Ciuile*, or who have approached it with a different frame of reference, we here give a short account of the text, before moving to consider elements of its early modern reception that are particularly relevant for considering May's engagements.

2a. Lucan's Text

Save for a few scraps, the *Bellum Ciuile* is Lucan's only surviving work.[17] Written during the early 60s AD in ten books of dactylic hexameters, the meter of Virgil and Homer's epic poems, its subject is the civil war of the 40s BC between Julius

---

[13] Cuthbert Sydenham, attrib., *An Anatomy of Lieut. Col. John Lilburn's Spirit and Pamphlets* (London: John Macock for Francis Tryton, 1649), sigs A2^r–A4^r (preface addressing parliament by 'T. M.'). John Lilburne, *The Innocent Man's First Proffer* (London: printer unknown, 1649), believed the whole pamphlet was May's, and furiously attacked its accusations.

[14] 'Quem Anglicana Resp. habuit vindicem': Wood, *Athenae Oxonienses*, III, p. 811.

[15] John Aubrey, *Brief Lives*, ed. by John Buchanan-Brown (London and New York: Centaur Press, 1972), p. 196; cf. Wood, *Athenae Oxonienses*, III, p. 811.

[16] Norbrook, 'May, Thomas'.

[17] Lucan also apparently composed prose works, epigrams, a *Medea* (unfinished), as well as the poems *Iliaca*, *Saturnalia*, *Catachthonion* and *Siluarum X*. For the few remains we have, see Edward Courtney, *The Fragmentary Latin Poets* (Oxford: Oxford University Press, 1993), pp. 352–56.

Caesar and the armies of the Roman Senate initially commanded by Pompeius Magnus — 'Pompey the Great' — which resulted in Caesar's victory and the *de facto* end of the Roman republic. The main action of the poem begins with Caesar's invasion of Italy in January 49 BC by crossing the river Rubicon. Lucan pursues the story through many different battles and military theatres. The climactic battle of Pharsalus in Thessaly is treated in the seventh book, Pompey's murder at the mouth of the Nile in the eighth. The tenth and final book breaks off with Caesar trapped in Ptolemy's palace in Alexandria (47 BC). It is shorter than the others and most early modern readers thought Lucan's narrative incomplete. The work's unfinished state forms the pretext for May's own brief narrative supplement to the tenth book, which we reprint in this edition, as well as his more substantial *Continuation* of 1630.[18]

As its modern title reveals, much of Lucan's work is about the horrors of civil war — its agony, nihilism, savagery and futility. The text's opening image, of a people sticking a sword into their own bowels, establishes the warped moral and political coordinates of a civil war world, where even language turns against itself. It also continuously underlines the historical and ideological significance of the war and its outcome, for Lucan a turning point in Rome's history: her last moment of genuine freedom and republican self-government before Caesar's dictatorship and the dynastic rule of his imperial successors. The narrative is haunted by the tragedies and triumphs of Rome's past, to many of which it repeatedly refers: for example, Rome's origins in fratricidal conflict, her victory over her ancient enemy Carthage (and the rot that set in at Rome afterwards), or the period of competition and unrest in Italy in the generations before Caesar and Pompey, sometimes known as the 'Social Wars'. It is equally haunted, however, by later events of the civil wars and the reality of monarchy at Rome. The poet's own present is forced on the reader by an ostensibly flattering opening address to Nero, the then emperor, as the true patron (so Lucan declares) of any Roman poem (I. 33–66; 1. 35–72).[19] Many Renaissance commentators considered this passage bitterly ironic, given not only Nero's reputation as a vain and capricious tyrant, but also Lucan's sustained hostility to Caesar, Nero's ancestor, and repeated attacks on regal government within his text.

The *Bellum Ciuile* thus gives voice to the profound tensions that constituted Roman political experience. Its geographical scope is equally broad. Lucan frames the civil war as a global event, drawing in races and peoples from the

---

[18] Several intended endings have been conjectured to Lucan's epic: the suicide of Cato at Utica 46 BC; the assassination of Julius Caesar in 44 BC (the choice of May's own *Continuation*); or possibly Octavian's defeat of Antony and Cleopatra in 31 BC at the Battle of Actium.

[19] References to Lucan's Latin text use Roman numerals for book numbers; those to May's translation, Arabic numerals. See further the 'Note on Editorial Practice', below.

far western limits of Roman power and from beyond the river Euphrates in the east, while often referring to lands far to the south, in Africa, or north across the Rhine and Danube. This world-historical context accentuates the disaster of the war. Given the vast roll-call of enemies still to conquer (above all the Parthians, inhabitants of modern Iran and Iraq, who had inflicted a shocking defeat on Rome shortly before the conflict began), a central problem within the text is Rome's failure to fulfil her imperial destiny, indeed the nightmarish possibility that civil war is the logical conclusion of her citizens' conquering drives.

The narrative is built around three major characters. Julius Caesar is presented programmatically in the first book as a lightning bolt, a combination of dynamic daring and all-destructive monomaniac ambition (I. 143–67; 1. 156–72). In his way stands Pompey, chosen by the Senate as general of the republic's armies, whom Lucan depicts as a strategically indecisive elder statesman, content to rest on past glories, who only achieves heroic status in death. Set apart from this mis-matched duo is the severe Stoic Cato (Cato the Younger), a significant republican voice in the text who deplores Rome's loss of liberty and warns that both sides are implicated in guilt. Cato's major opportunity for heroism is not in battle, but through a punishing march across the Libyan sands, where the Roman troops are harried not just by desert heat but also an army of snakes (IX. 587–949; 9. 677–1072). This arena provides the perfect backdrop for the ascetic and self-controlled general to offer an example of self-denial, toughness and Stoic constancy to his men, while avoiding implication in the wickedness of civil conflict. Other lesser but important roles are played by a cast of historical characters, including Caesar's future assassin Marcus Junius Brutus; king Juba of Numidia, a prominent ally of Pompey; Gaius Scribonius Curio, the tribune of the plebs who joined Caesar and according to Lucan started the war; and L. Domitius Ahenobarbus, another ancestor of Nero's and among several Pompeian generals (including Afranius, Petreius, Varus and Scipio) mentioned during the action. Lucan's range of reference includes great heroes and villains not just of Roman history (e.g. Crassus, Catiline, the Gracchi) but of the ancient world more generally, for example Cyrus of Persia, Hannibal of Carthage and Alexander the Great.

Lucan's exploration of public, male-oriented power systems does not leave much space for female characters. Women nonetheless play a significant, if limited, role in *Bellum Ciuile*. The narrative is book-ended by Caesar's encounter with two female figures: the image of *Roma*, a matron in mourning who begs him in a dream not to cross the Rubicon, and the alluring but dangerous Cleopatra, who seduces him in order to regain political power in Egypt (I. 185–94, 1. 199–229; X. 53–171, 10. 63–200). Pompey is literally haunted by his dead wife Julia, the daughter of Caesar, while his relationship with

Cornelia provides a sense of emotional heart and pathos absent from the other relationships of the epic. Cato's sterile wedding to Marcia, in book two, provides pointed counterbalance. And at the centre of *Bellum Ciuile* is the terrifying night-witch Erictho, whose horrific necromancy thrilled many early modern readers.

Lucan clearly relied on various sources when writing his text, and his treatment is broadly chronological. Nonetheless his is not straightforwardly an 'historical' narrative: rather it causes us to ask questions of what is meant by 'history', especially in relation to other modes of narration.[20] Certainly Lucan is not above outright invention. He imagines, for example, a moment at the battle of Pharsalus when Brutus, disguised as a plebeian, nearly kills Caesar five years before he is 'fated' to do so (VII. 586–96; 7. 666–77). Later Pompey is portrayed proposing an alliance with the Parthians, Rome's major enemy, after defeat at Pharsalus — again unhistorically, as far as we know (VIII. 262–330; 8. 303–80). The leader of a mass-suicide of troops surrounded at sea, Vulteius, is not found in any independent account of the civil war (IV. 415–581; 4. 455–642). And while another Caesarian centurion, Scaeva, is historical, Lucan's fantastical account of his single-handed war against the Pompeian army at Dyrrachium abandons verisimilar credibility (VI. 140–262; 6. 153–294). There are also supernatural moments in the text — most obviously when the god Apollo possesses the priestess of Delphi in book five, or when the ghastly witch Erictho reanimates the corpse of a Roman soldier in book six (v. 64–236, VI. 419–830; 5. 78–270, 6. 472–946).[21] These episodes are conscious reworkings of the reassuring scenes of prophecy and positive encounters with the underworld found in earlier epic poetry.

One of Erictho's boasts, that she possesses the kind of supernatural power that makes the whole cosmos fear her, discloses another important aspect of Lucan's design (VI. 730–49; 6. 831–54). Unlike his predecessors in the epic or historical-epic tradition, Homer, Virgil and Ennius (a Roman writer of the second century BC), the *Bellum Ciuile* does not embed human action within a larger scheme of anthropomorphic divinity presided over by an Olympian Zeus/Jupiter in charge of fate. Such refusal to mythologise historical forces is part of a running battle against the monarchical ideology of the imperial

---

[20] Andrew W. Lintott, 'Lucan and the History of the Civil War', *The Classical Quarterly*, 21 (1971), 488–505; Jan Radicke, *Lucans poetische Technik. Studien zum historischen Epos. Mnemosyne Supplement 249* (Leiden: Brill, 2004).

[21] On Lucan's treatment of the traditionally 'divine' elements of epic, see esp. David Feeney, *The Gods in Epic: Poets and Critics of the Classical Tradition* (New York: Oxford University Press, 1991), pp. 250–301; Elaine Fantham, 'The Angry Poet and the Angry Gods: Problems of Theodicy in Lucan's Epic of Defeat', in *Ancient Anger: Perspectives from Homer to Galen*, ed. by Susanna Braund and Glenn W. Most (*Yale Classical Studies 32*) (Cambridge: Cambridge University Press, 2004), pp. 229–49.

principate, and especially its major poetic exponent Virgil, whose *Aeneid* aligns the victory of his patron Augustus with cosmic design and purpose.[22] In the *Bellum Ciuile*, the idea of worshipping emperors as gods (a practice Augustus had inaugurated for his adopted father Julius Caesar) is greeted with sarcastic verses about swearing by *umbras* — empty shadows or ghosts (VII. 455–59; May translates *umbras* as 'men's souls', 7. 522). In place of epic's standard divine machinery, the text promotes a conflicted picture of historical causality. There are frequent references to the relatively impersonal forces of 'fate' or 'the fates', along with personified 'Fortune' and the 'Parcae', female representations of destiny rendered by May as 'the Fates'; sometimes Lucan does mention 'those above [*superi*]', although often with a rather ironic edge. Lucan sometimes alludes to, without necessarily fully adopting, the doctrines of Stoic providentialism. Caesar often seems to have a special relationship with Fortune, and Rome's fall into slavery under the emperors is represented as malignantly fated.[23] All these imply some idea of a bleak historical pattern or even determinism, as May's thematized use of the term 'fatal', not always invited by the Latin, also registers.[24]

At other moments, however, Lucan denies that there is any principle let alone divinity ruling events: everything is pure chance.[25] He sometimes intervenes rhetorically into the historical action, appealing to the participants to act differently. These moments are not simply imaginative rebellions against the inevitability of civil war, bloodshed and imperial despotism. They sanction the possibility, however remote, that what he describes as an eternal struggle between 'Caesar and Liberty' (VII. 695–96; 7. 790–91) might eventually boast a different outcome, and success be reconciled once more — for a time — with virtue.

[22] Philip Hardie, *Virgil's 'Aeneid': Cosmos and Imperium* (Oxford: Clarendon Press, 1986); Richard F. Thomas, *Virgil and the Augustan Reception* (Cambridge: Cambridge University Press, 2001).

[23] On the apparent interchangeability of fate (*fatum*) and fortune (*fortuna*) in Lucan's text, see Friedrich Wolf-Hartmut, 'Cato, Caesar, and Fortune in Lucan', in *Lucan: Oxford Readings in Classical Studies*, ed. by Charles Tesoriero, assisted by Frances Muecke and Tamara Neal with an Introduction by Susanna Braund (Oxford: Oxford University Press, 2010), pp. 369–410; Bernard F. Dick, '*Fatum* and *Fortuna* in Lucan's *Bellum Civile*', *Classical Philology*, 62 (1967), 235–42; Christine Walde, '*Fortuna* bei Lucan — Vor- und Nachgedanken', in *Götter und menschliche Willensfreiheit von Lukan bis Silius Italicus*, ed. by Thomas Baier (*Zetemata* 142) (München: C. H. Beck, 2012), pp. 57–74; on malicious fate, Thomas Gärtner, 'Objektives Fatum und Subjektive Fatumsgläubigkeit im Bürgerkriegsepos des Lucan', *Acta Antiqua*, 45 (2005), 51–84. In the translation, May sometimes uses 'fortune' for Lucan's *fatum*, and 'fate' (or equivalents) for his *fortuna*, perhaps implying that he thought the precise schema of causality unimportant: see e.g. 7. 285.

[24] See, below, e.g. 1. Arg. 1, 1. 43, 1. 94, 6. 458, 10. 61. May's *A Continuation of Lucan's Historicall Poem till the death of Julius Caesar* (London: J. Haviland for James Boler, 1630) also uses 'fatal' to describe the battles of Thapsus, Mutina and Munda; Caesar finally meets his end when the assassins brandish 'fatall ponyards' (sig. L2^v).

[25] For example at 7. 505–06.

Lucan's life, which was short but eventful, has always been an important accompaniment to his text, shaping how its rhetorical manoeuvres are perceived and understood right up until the present day. As it is difficult to give a wholly neutral account of it, we here consider primarily how it was used and understood by early modern readers. There was no shortage of biographies of Lucan in May's time. At least one, and sometimes many more, could be found in most editions of his work. Some of these Lives dated back to antiquity, while others were compiled by Renaissance scholars.[26] May drew on a number of these sources for his own version, 'The Life of Marcus Annaeus Lucanus', which he printed before his translation. These accounts varied in length, emphasis and degree of approval, but certain features were common to nearly all of them. Marcus Annaeus Lucanus was born in 39 AD in Cordoba, Spain, into an upper-class Roman family; he was a nephew of Seneca, the statesman and Stoic philosopher. He spent most of his short life in Rome. His literary abilities were recognised while still a young man, prompting the admiration of the emperor Nero. The latter led to inclusion in the emperor's literary coterie and the promise of a political career.[27] Nero, however, soon became jealous of the younger man's talents, and prohibited public recitation of his verses. Most accounts, including May's, saw this as the key factor which prompted Lucan to join the so-called 'Pisonian Conspiracy' to depose the ruler. The coup was a failure, and he was ordered to commit suicide. According to some sources he slit his veins in his bath and died reciting verses from the *Bellum Ciuile*. This scene, suggestively combining Stoic defiance of pain with political defiance of tyranny, was a point of fascination for early modern readers. It was pictorially represented on the title page of May's 1627 translation and favourably described in his 'Life' as an act of undaunted virtue.[28] It also undoubtedly strengthened, and strengthens, a reader's sensitivity to the anti-Caesarian and anti-tyrannical aspects of Lucan's text.

2b. Lucan in Early Modern Culture

Lucan was well-known and widely read during the mediaeval and early modern periods. The first printed text appeared in 1477; by May's time there had been over one hundred editions, albeit only two in England, as well as

---

[26] Nora Goldschmidt, 'Lucan: A Guide to Selected Sources', in *Living Poets* (Durham, 2015) <https://livingpoets.dur.ac.uk/w/Lucan:_A_Guide_to_Selected_Sources?oldid=4787> [accessed 29 October 2019]; ibid., *Afterlives of the Roman Poets: Biofiction and the Reception of Latin Poetry* (Cambridge: Cambridge University Press, 2019), pp. 85-129.

[27] For a modern assessment of the literary and cultural milieu of Neronian Rome, see *A Companion to the Neronian Age*, ed. by Emma Buckley and Martin T. Dinter (Oxford: Wiley-Blackwell, 2013).

[28] May pointedly does not include the less flattering detail from Tacitus that Lucan implicated his own mother Acilia in the conspiracy before dying (*Annales*, ed. by C. D. Fisher (Oxford: Clarendon Press, 1906), XV. 49).

several commentaries.[29] Early modern readers were divided as to the work's merits. One point of controversy was its style: some considered it lofty or indeed sublime, while others regarded it as fustian. The famous Renaissance literary theorist Julius Caesar Scaliger, for example, remarked, 'I think Lucan doesn't sing: he barks' (*mihi latrare, non canere, uidetur*).[30] Lucan's historical or quasi-historical method of narration was another focus of debate. During the mid-sixteenth century a number of literary theorists influenced by Aristotle's *Poetics* had argued, somewhat pejoratively, that Lucan was more historian than poet.[31] This verdict was concerned mostly with which narrative mode was most effective at communicating normative forms of truth, rather than principles of historical inquiry. In England it led to Lucan becoming a model for a number of poets seeking to write historical narratives in verse, such as Samuel Daniel, whose *The Civil Wars* (c. 1595–1609), a work on the Wars of Roses, imitates Lucan closely in places. May, too, was to write works in this genre. A third area of contestation was Lucan's knowledge and by extension that of his time. The *Bellum Ciuile* contains a great many passages that are dense in astronomical, geographic and ethnographic lore. In the late sixteenth century the great textual scholar Joseph Scaliger (son of Julius Caesar Scaliger) used these episodes as examples of antiquity's manifest 'errors'.[32] This was an assault on Lucan's truth-value from a somewhat different angle than that of poetic theory. More positively received, on the other hand, was Lucan's potential as an authority on Roman military technology or tactics. His battle narratives, which many modern scholars read as blood-drenched burlesque, had several admirers.

By the early seventeenth century scholars and writers were paying increasing attention to the Stoic elements of Lucan's text, thanks in part to the labours of the Flemish scholar Justus Lipsius in reconstructing ancient Stoicism as a coherent body of doctrine.[33] One of Lipsius's protégés, Hugo Grotius, published an edition

---

[29] On translation and creative imitation of the *Bellum Ciuile* in early modern Europe (including but not limited to Italy, France, Spain, the Low Countries, Poland and England), see e.g. Walter Fischli, *Studien zum Fortleben der Pharsalia des M. Annaeus Lucanus* (Luzern: E. Haag, 1944); several essays in *Lucans Bellum Civile. Studien zum Spektrum seiner Rezeption von der Antike bis ins 19. Jahrhundert*, ed. by Christine Walde (Bochumer Altertumswissenschaftliches Colloquium, 78) (Trier: Wissenschaftlicher Verlag Trier, 2009); Yanick Maes, 'Translating Lucan in the Early Seventeenth Century', in *A Companion to the Neronian Age*, ed. by Buckley and Dinter, pp. 405–24.
[30] Julius Caesar Scaliger, *Poetices Libri Septem*, ed. by Gregor Vogt-Spira and Luc Deitz, 6 vols (Stuttgart: Frommann Holzboog, 1994–2011), v, p. 270. For humanist attitudes to Lucan, see Paleit, *War, Liberty, and Caesar*, pp. 29–52 (pp. 45–46 on Scaliger).
[31] See Paleit, *War, Liberty, and Caesar*, pp. 54–90; and on the antecedents of the history/poetry question in the Middle Ages, Peter von Moos, 'Lucain au Moyen Âge', in *Entre histoire et littérature: Communication et culture au Moyen Âge*, ed. by Peter von Moos (Millennio medievale, 58) (Firenze: Sismel, 2005), pp. 89–204.
[32] See Paleit, *War, Liberty, and Caesar*, pp. 83–84.
[33] For Lipsius and neo-Stoicism, see Mark Morford, *Stoics and Neostoics: Rubens and the*

of Lucan in 1614.[34] It is clear, too, that many readers were drawn to Lucan's traumatized account of civil war as well as his passionate commemoration of republican liberty and undoubted antagonism to Julius Caesar and his imperial successors. The text became a way of meditating on or coming to terms with European readers and writers' own unsettling political experiences.[35] Amongst such responses can be found Ercilla's *La Araucana* (1586), an epic poem on the conquest of Chile, the Lucan-centos of Pierre Chrétien (1588) on the Dutch uprising, and Agrippa D'Aubigné's *Les Tragiques*, a poem on the sufferings of Huguenots during the French civil wars. In England, besides the verse histories of Samuel Daniel and his imitators already mentioned, this approach was to find expression in Abraham Cowley's (incomplete) *The Civil War*, an attempt to wrestle with England's own descent into strife, written in Oxford during the summer and autumn of 1643.[36]

Finally, Lucan's commemoration of a non-monarchical system of government we term 'the Roman republic', which overlaps with the Latin concept of *res publica* but is not identical to it, was an attraction for many early modern readers, writers and translators, not least in England. This partly reflects the influence of Renaissance classical republicanism — an amalgam of ideas about virtuous citizenship, liberty and the mixed constitution — which had a marked influence on English culture and discourse from the late sixteenth century onwards.[37] After the regicide of 1649, in fact, a number of English writers took the Roman republic as a model for the country's new system of government, and began to articulate a 'neo-Roman' or republican theory of liberty.[38] This republican 'moment' of the early 1650s intersects with the afterlife of May's translation and we discuss it further below. Such contexts have persuaded some scholars to argue or assume that Lucan's text typically had a republican identity

---

Circle of Lipsius (Princeton: Princeton University Press, 1991); Adriana McCrea, *Constant Minds: Political Virtue and the Lipsian Paradigm in England, 1584–1650* (Toronto: University of Toronto Press, 1997); John M. Cooper, 'Justus Lipsius and the Revival of Stoicism in Late Sixteenth-Century Europe' in *New Essays on the History of Autonomy*, ed. by Natalie Brender and Larry Krasnoff, (Cambridge: Cambridge University Press, 2004), pp. 7–29.

[34] See Maes, 'Translating Lucan'. Grotius's 'Notes' at the back of his text, while mostly devoted to textual matters, also draw attention to Stoic elements in Lucan's text.

[35] For an overview of the Continental Lucan, see Maes, 'Translating Lucan'.

[36] Philip Hardie, 'Lucan in the English Renaissance', in *Brill's Companion to Lucan*, ed. by Paolo Asso, (Leiden: Brill, 2011), pp 491–506; Maes, 'Translating Lucan'.

[37] Markku Peltonen, *Classical Humanism and Republicanism in English Political Thought, 1570–1640* (Cambridge: Cambridge University Press, 1995).

[38] Blair Worden, 'English Republicanism', in *The Cambridge History of Political Thought*, ed. by J. H. Burns with Mark Goldie (Cambridge: Cambridge University Press, 1991), pp. 443–78; Quentin Skinner, *Liberty before Liberalism* (Cambridge: Cambridge University Press, 1998); J. G. A. Pocock, *The Machiavellian Moment: Florentine Political Thought and the Atlantic Republican Tradition*, 2nd ed. (Princeton and Oxford: Princeton University Press, 2003), pp. 361–422.

in early modern England, and that there was a specifically, or exclusively, republican 'tradition' of reading it.[39] It is doubtful, however, that — at least before the English Civil War — republicanism can be considered a coherent ideological package in which virtues, constitutional arrangements, political commitments and identities, and views of the shape of English or Roman history were all similarly configured and motivated. May, as we discuss below, was undoubtedly sympathetic to Lucan's political outlook, but what he took (or made out) that outlook to be was specific to his own personal and historical circumstances. Meanwhile, even the broadest definition of republicanism does not account for everything about his response, including for example the ways he softens and heroizes Julius Caesar's portrait.

3. May's Translation

3a. The 1626 and 1627 Editions

May must have begun the translation by late 1625 or early 1626. Books one to three were completed by 18 April 1626, when they were entered for publication in the Register of the Stationers' Company, and duly published later that year.[40] The remaining seven presumably followed by 12 March 1627, when the publication rights for the whole translation were registered.

It's somewhat of a mystery why the first three books appeared separately. The 1626 volume contains no paratextual materials, which suggests it was printed in haste. An attempt at political timeliness is possible, as we discuss further below. Commercial incentives may also have been a factor.[41] In early modern England the sales risk of a publication typically rested with publishers. John Norton and Augustine Matthews, however, owned the publication rights as well as printing the first, 1626 version. The rights to the 1627 edition, on the other hand, were entered to different Stationers, John Marriot and Thomas Jones, on the condition that the original printer-publishers were 'to have the printing' at a specified rate of fifteen shillings per 1500 sheets.[42] This arrangement, transferring the financial risk to Marriot and Jones, suggests Norton and Matthews wanted or needed a guaranteed cash flow (they may already have

---

[39] For this argument, see David Norbrook, 'Lucan, Thomas May, and the Creation of a Republican Literary Culture' in *Culture and Politics in Early Stuart England*, ed. by Kevin Sharpe and Peter Lake (London: Macmillan, 1994), pp. 45–66; Norbrook, *Writing the English Republic*, pp. 23–62. See also Andrew Hadfield, *Shakespeare and Republicanism* (Cambridge: Cambridge University Press, 2005); Patrick Cheney, *Marlowe's Republican Authorship: Lucan, Liberty and the Sublime* (London: Routledge, 2009).
[40] Arber, ed., *A Transcript*, IV, p. 159.
[41] Cf. Norbrook, 'Lucan, Thomas May', p. 57.
[42] Arber, ed., *A Transcript*, IV, p. 174.

paid May for the translation, and made other outlays). Similar incentives may have lain behind the decision to publish the first three books early.

Perhaps May had worked slower than expected. There are signs that he sped up later on: the ratio of English to Latin lines of text is impressively tight for the first three books of the translation, between 107% and 108%, but is typically around 115% for the remaining seven, suggesting a looser and thus probably faster rate of translation. It is difficult to be sure about just how fast he worked. The gap between the two dates in the Stationers' Register implies a rate of just under seven weeks per book for books four to ten, or about eighteen lines of Latin text per day: however, this assumes no pre-existing drafts and ignores time spent arranging fair copies and/or devising paratextual matter. Aside from pace, May's translation practice does not seem to have changed very much. The verbal differences between the first three books of the 1627 edition and the 1626 volume are very slight. Both editions adopt the same basic format, whereby each book is fronted by a verse argument explaining its narrative contents, and followed by a series of explanatory historical notes, a layout repeated in May's 1628 translation of the *Georgics* and also his 1630 *Continuation* of Lucan.

The 1627 edition is in octavo format and, at roughly 15 x 10 cm, not a large or handsome text: there were more lavishly produced classical translations in the period. This may reflect the commercial aims of the publication and, relatedly, May's need to make money from his work.[43] On these grounds as well as others it is important to differentiate a (relatively) mass-market publication like *Lucan's Pharsalia* from, say, Hobbes's translation of Thucydides (1628), printed in prestigious and expensive folio. Nonetheless, May and his publishers took some care in devising the form and look of the publication for potential buyers. Commendatory poems were sourced from John Vaughan and the prestigious figure of Ben Jonson, as well as the unknown 'H. V.'. The various paratexts present Lucan and his text in a consistently positive way, emphasising his personal virtue and nobility, praising his stylistic 'height', and commending him for commemorating republican liberty and earning a tyrant's hatred. A title page engraving, showing Pompey and Caesar facing each other on a plinth on which is a scene from the battle of Pharsalus, and topped by a tableau of Lucan committing suicide, is reinforced by May's poem on the facing page, suggesting collaboration between the author, engraver and printer-publishers. The engraver was a Dutchman, Friedrich Hulsen (1580–1635). Although he worked for most of his career abroad, in 1627 he produced engravings for a series of English publications that year celebrating the country's Protestant traditions and identity.[44]

---

[43] May's relative poverty is emphasised by Hyde (*The Life*, I, p. 40).
[44] Sidney Colvin, *Early Engraving & Engravers in England (1545 — 1695): A Critical and Historical Essay* (London: British Museum, 1905), pp. 117-18; Syrithe Pugh, *Herrick*,

Finally, books two to nine were prefaced by poetic dedications to individual English aristocrats, who were carefully chosen to suit the subject of each book but also to develop the themes of virtuous nobility, military heroism and stewardship of liberty already highlighted in May's introductory materials. These dedications have been defaced or cancelled in most surviving copies for reasons we discuss below; they did not appear in later editions of the translation.[45] One of these dedicatees, William Cavendish, second Earl of Devonshire, was also chosen as the dedicatee for May's whole work. The choice may have had a political motivation — there is nothing to suggest any other connection between the two men — although the subject matter of the single-book dedication concentrates on Lucan's literary qualities as opposed to political content. Cavendish died in early 1628; May's later works were dedicated to different figures, although not later editions of the translation.

3b. Latin Text, Other Sources and Style

Lucan's text, in the early seventeenth century, differed considerably from the one Latin readers know today. It had yet to benefit from the contributions of Richard Bentley in the eighteenth century, or A. E. Housman in the twentieth, or the development of systematic textual criticism in nineteenth-century Germany. Early modern editors of Lucan tended to rely on the texts of their predecessors and on their own Latinity and critical judgment, only occasionally (and eclectically) drawing on manuscript witnesses. As well as sometimes being differently worded, their editions were differently punctuated from modern ones, which can lead the Latin to have different meanings or connotations. Lucan's lines were not always in the preferred modern order, and certain passages which editors now omit or consider spurious were regarded as unproblematic.

May's translation is largely reliant on Thomas Farnaby's edition and accompanying commentary, published in London in 1618.[46] Farnaby was a well-known London schoolmaster and wit, and a former friend of Ben Jonson; probably therefore May knew him personally. May's dependence is exhibited in various ways. Firstly, he usually follows Farnaby's text of Lucan, which is modelled on Hugo Grotius's edition of 1614 (his translation incorporates some of Grotius's lections), although he sometimes chooses the variant

Fanshawe and the Politics of Intertextuality: Classical Literature and Seventeenth-Century Royalism (Farnham/Burlington, VT: Ashgate, 2010), pp. 151–74; Maes, 'Translating Lucan', pp. 410–11.

[45] On these 'almost' dedications, see Norbrook, *Writing the English Republic*, pp. 44–49; Paleit, *War, Liberty, and Caesar*, pp. 234–35.

[46] Marcus Annaeus Lucanus, *M. Annaei Lucani Pharsalia*, ed. by Thomas Farnaby (London: Richard Field, 1618). We refer to this edition throughout as F. Farnaby's edition was reprinted in Frankfurt in 1624; in theory May could have used this instead.

readings recorded in Farnaby's commentary. These choices reveal a certain autonomy, within the constraints of the method: in the space of a few short lines, for example, May can be found accepting one of Grotius's conjectures but rejecting another, reversing Farnaby's own preferences.[47] When translating some of Lucan's more intricate or opaque passages, especially in the areas of astronomy, geography or ethnography, he often prefers Farnaby's explanations or paraphrases to Lucan's original wording.[48] Occasionally he uses Farnaby to correct Lucan's apparent mistakes, particularly with regard to historical events or his understanding of the natural world.[49] Once or twice he incorporates Farnaby's rare suggestions of an equivalent English idiom.[50] Finally, his historical 'annotations' to each book are mostly translations or paraphrases of Farnaby's comments, which in turn tend to reprise and summarize passages of classical historiography.

May did not only use Farnaby's edition, however. 'The Life of Marcus Annaeus Lucanus' draws on classical or Renaissance biographies he would have had to find elsewhere, most probably other editions of Lucan. His verse arguments to each book adapt those of the fifteenth-century commentator Giovanni Sulpizio, which were often reprinted in sixteenth-century editions of the *Bellum Ciuile*, but aren't by Grotius or Farnaby; his narrative continuation of the translation, appended in italics to the final book, is also inspired by a similar but shorter set of verses by Sulpizio. It is not easy to pinpoint, however, what precise edition (besides Farnaby's) May used. This is partly because Renaissance commentaries on Lucan absorb and repeat their predecessors. On the rare occasions where May seems to agree with another commentator there remains the possibility that he was simply following his own interpretation: for example, when he thinks that Ptolemy's *satelles* ('attendant') is Pompey's murderer Achillas, as Lambertus Hortensius did in his commentary of 1578.[51] A few passages read as if they were translated without a commentary at all.[52]

Besides editions and commentaries May probably utilised a number of Latin or English reference works. A catalogue of English plants in book nine, for example, suggests access to an upmarket herbal containing both English and Latin plant names.[53] A particularly interesting feature of May's translation practice is his conscious appropriations of previous English literary engagements with the *Bellum Ciuile*. Lines Ben Jonson appropriated from Lucan for his *The Masque of Queenes* (1609) and his Roman tragedy *Sejanus*

---

[47] See e.g. 7. 658 and 7. 664.
[48] See e.g. 1. 588, 2. 149, 6. 12–20, 7. 177n, 8. 185–90, 490–95.
[49] See e.g. 2. 716, 724–25, 10. 236.
[50] See e.g. 6. 221.
[51] See 9. 1148n.
[52] See e.g. 4. 461ff, 6. 843–46.
[53] See 9. 1045–50.

(1603), for example, reappear in May's translation of the relevant passages.[54] May also recycled some of John Marston's adaptations of Lucan in the latter's tragedy *Sophonisba* (1605), as well as certain borrowings from the *Bellum Ciuile* in Fletcher and Massinger's play *The False One*.[55] Finally, May's translation of book one is clearly influenced by Marlowe's vivid verbal choices.[56] Aside from these conscious intertextual instances, there are occasional echoes of important English literary figures such as Spenser, Sidney or Shakespeare. The final book, which depicts Caesar in thrall to Cleopatra's oriental opulence, overlaps with the tone and register of Marlovian tragedy, as well as the anonymously authored *The Tragedie of Caesar and Pompey, or Caesar's Revenge* (published 1607, but probably written *c.* 1595), itself deeply indebted to Lucan and other ancient historical sources on the period directly after the battle of Pharsalus.

It is debatable how much these individual examples affect the translation's *overall* feel. At times, May clearly favours early modern literary idiom and abandons Lucan's. When it is hot, for example, 'summer is in her pride'. The sea is 'Thetis's lap' and the 'wat'ry main'. The woods are alive with 'amorous silvans and wanton nymphs'. Women are 'fair' or 'poor' and display 'snowy' arms and breasts; men have 'forward spirits', 'hazard war' and are capable of 'strange cruelty'. Occasionally Roman cultural reference points are overridden with contemporary ones. When May's Caesar imagines his own future should he lose the war, he invokes the fate of a seventeenth-century traitor, rather than Lucan's description of Roman punishments (the cross or chains, or his own head placed on the *rostra* in the Roman *forum*):

> Think upon Caesar's chains,
> His racks and gibbets; think you see this face,
> These quartered limbs stand in the marketplace.
> (7. 344–46; VII. 304–06)

May introduces contemporary military techniques like wildfire and sulphur balls to his battle narratives, and painted fore-decks and ship's ensigns to his descriptions of Roman ships. At the same time, the graphic and gruesome displays of gore found in Lucan are frequently toned down into something less savage or shocking. The Latin's language of battle-madness, characterized by terms like 'rage [*furor*]' and 'frenzy [*rabies*]', are softened into an idiom of 'woe' and 'valour', suggestive of chivalric romance. This practice is evident in the two set-piece heroic combat-narratives of the text, involving the soldiers Vulteius and Scaeva, which are a more brutal and morally compromised affair in Lucan than in May (IV. 415–581, 4. 455–642; VI. 140–262, 6. 153–294). May's rendition of Vulteius, who counsels suicide, echoes the heroizing strategy of a previous

---

[54] See 6. Ded. 14n, 6. 528, 9. 656–57n, 673.
[55] See e.g. 6. 576n, 585n, 8. 562n, 582n.
[56] See e.g. 1. 42, 199, 205, 483 and notes.

translator, Arthur Gorges, and is noticeably less hostile than more orthodoxly Christian judgments such as Sir William Alexander's (in 1614) that Vulteius was 'of Fame too greedy, prodigall of Life'.[57] The same strategy is also, significantly, visible in the translation's representation of Caesar. While much of Lucan's hostility remains, Caesar's cruelty (*saeuitia*), rage (*ira*) and extreme ruthlessness are less glaring in May's version. The extremity of Caesar's emotions — which in both classical and Renaissance culture imply tyrannical servitude to passion — also undergo corrective modification (see e.g. 5. 418–29, 10. 83–96, 10. 509 ff.). Some of the sting in Lucan's account of Pompey is also drained, not least through May's frequent use of the epithet 'majestic' to describe him.[58]

Nonetheless, May's is far from a fully domesticated translation: in fact, it is one of the least obviously anglicizing classical translations of the early seventeenth century. This is partly reflected in May's vocabulary, which frequently resorts to Latin import words, particularly when dealing with set-piece descriptions from astronomy, geography, and the material and natural world. The Latinate character of May's text is apparent in its very opening lines, with May following the lead of Arthur Gorges in making the 'pile' his habitual translation for the *pilum*, the Roman legionary spear, a choice he sustains virtually throughout and took care to defend in an historical note. In English 'pile' normally means something quite different: the effect is to jolt an English reader out of their semantic comfort zone. The few vernacular neologisms May creates are built from Latin: 'parentation' (4. 867) to describe 'funeral rites', deriving from the Roman festival of mourning the Parentalia; the flaming-javelin weapon, the 'phalaric', from the Latin *phalarica* or *falarica* (VI. 198, 6. 221); 'devex', deriving from the Latin *devexa*, which May was the only English writer ever to deploy as a noun (X. 39, 10. 47).[59]

As important as individual verbal choices, however, is May's Latinate approach to sentence construction. His translation often aims at the sententious severity, compressed hyperbole and elliptical syntax associated not only with Lucan but with other early imperial Latin poets like Martial and Persius or Seneca. The results, in an uninflected language like English, are sometimes

---

[57] Sir William Alexander, *Doomes-Day, or, the Great Day of the Lords Judgement* (London: Andro Hart, 1614), sig. O1ʳ; for Gorges' account, see Paleit, *War, Liberty, and Caesar*, pp. 191–92.
[58] See e.g. 2. 565, 7. 772, 8. 15, 780, 887, 1003. The term 'majestic' has of course possible political implications, although May often seems to mean simply 'venerable' or 'impressive'.
[59] Although the *OED* attributes the first use of 'parentation' to May, it also appears in John Selden, *The Duello, or Single Combat* (London: George Held for I. Helm, 1610), p. 9. Before May, Joshua Sylvester used *Phalariks* in the final section of his translation of du Bartas's *Bartas his Divine Weeks and Works Translated* (London: Humphrey Lownes, 1608), sig. Iii6ᵛ. Sylvester's term, however — which he explains in the margin as 'instruments of war wherein wild fire is put' — comes from the French *phalarique* rather than from Latin (cf. *OED*, s.v. 'phalaric, n.').

obscure. Here for example are Caesar's troops mounting a steep hill in close formation:

> Piles guide their falt'ring steps;
> Hold, as they climb, they catch on shrubs and slips;
> Their swords serve not to fight, but cut their way.
>
> (4. 45–47)

In Lucan, it is clear that the soldiers plant their spears in the ground to aid their footing, grab at the shrubbery with their hands and cut a path with their swords (IV. 41–43). May's emulation of Lucan's inflected word order, however, means that he fails to distinguish a new subject. It is therefore less easy to discern in his version that it is the soldiers, not their spears, who 'catch hold on shrubs and slips'. More generally, May's fidelity to Lucan's ellipses often results in sentences whose exact structure is impossible to ascertain: they consist of long lists of clauses in untethered apposition, without a controlling verb or indeed emphatic end-point. In such passages the reader must work hard to identify continuities of thought that might counteract the discontinuities in syntax and occasionally grammar. An influence on Milton's later blank verse style should not be discounted.

In some ways it can even be argued that May is stylistically *plus quam Lucanus*: more Lucanic than Lucan himself. Alert to Lucan's sustained interest in paradox and contrast, he often supplements it with reduplication and repetition, thus hammering home the point (see e.g. 6. 553, 8. 971 ff., 10. 469–70). A text hardly free of gnomic moralizing — Lucan's *sententiae* have always been a well-known feature of his style — receives additional aphoristic freight. For example, the Egyptian counsellor Pothinus' bold decision to assault Caesar in the tenth book of the narrative is attributed by Lucan to personal over-confidence: 'His (Pothinus') crimes gave him such determination [*tantum animi*] that he [ordered Caesar's death]' (x. 347). May cannot resist the opportunity for moral commentary:

> By open force
> A most unconquered captain he assaults:
> So much are minds emboldened by their faults.
>
> (10. 396–98)

This closing generalisation is not found in Lucan. Yet it is not entirely unfaithful: paradox and irony are part of how Lucan expresses a world whose ethical foundations have been ruptured beyond repair. One of May's achievements as a translator is to give the reader a sense of the political and moral argument being made through the Latin text's compressed, ironic, hyperbolical style. It allows an English reader contact with parts of Lucan's voice obscured by the coldly powerful, near-contemptuous onward thrust of Marlowe's translation, or the false balance and ordered closure of Rowe's couplets, let alone Gorges' uneven jingles. It would be wrong, however, to say that May developed such a style unaided: it owed a great deal to the pioneering efforts of his mentor Ben Jonson in domesticating post-Augustan poetic syntax and diction. It is to Jonson's influence, as well as the wider literary and political context informing May's debts to him, that we now turn.

3c. Literary and Political Context

May's *Lucan's Pharsalia* belongs to a group of writings of the early seventeenth century which dwell on the late republican and early imperial period of Roman history. This literature explored the causes of the republic's failure and the experience of the loss of liberty, while also examining political conditions under the ensuing tyrannies of Tiberius, Caligula, Nero and Domitian. Intellectually informed by the cult of Tacitus, neo-Stoicism, and theories of sovereignty and reason of state, it acquired topical urgency from the growth of regal absolutism in contemporary Europe, and was often infused with a dystopian analysis of courtly politics.

In England such literature was given a major impetus by the works of Ben Jonson, in particular his Roman tragedies *Sejanus* (published 1605) and *Catiline* (1611) and the philosophy of virtuous neo-Roman nobility espoused in many of his *Epigrams* (1616), which are, in part, modelled on those of Martial, a poet writing under Domitian. Jonson's writings helped adapt and disseminate for an English readership the neo-Stoic moral and political philosophy of Justus Lipsius, which attempted to unite an ideal of constancy, or courageous indifference to external misfortune, with a prudential conception of absolute monarchy.[60] They also contain a number of borrowings from or adaptations of Lucan, a writer whose 'parts' (or episodes) and 'high' style Jonson valued more than the *Bellum Ciuile* as a whole.[61] The literary influence of Jonson's Roman tragedies was considerable, and from the late 1610s a younger generation of dramatists began to turn to them as models, often repeating Jonson's habit of appropriating Lucan. In 1619, for example, John Fletcher and Philip Massinger collaborated on *The False One*, a play about the Roman takeover of Egypt in the aftermath of the civil war between Caesar and Pompey. This play contains a number of Lucanian borrowings. In 1624 *The Tragedy of Nero* represents Lucan himself as an aristocratic patriot compelled to oppose a tyrannical

---

[60] For Lipsius, see above (note 33). For Jonson's indebtedness, see Blair Worden, 'Ben Jonson Among the Historians', in *Culture and Politics in Early Stuart England*, ed. by Lake and Sharpe, pp. 67–90 (pp. 88–89); Robert C. Evans, *Jonson, Lipsius, and the Politics of Renaissance Neo-Stoicism* (Durango: Longwood, 1992); McRea, *Constant Minds*, pp. 138–70.
[61] For further discussion (including Jonson's engagements with Lucan), see Paleit, *War, Liberty, and Caesar*, pp. 63, 128–29, 162–65.

prince; it too alludes to the *Bellum Ciuile*, although more obliquely.[62] Finally, in 1626 Massinger wrote *The Roman Actor*, a tragedy dramatizing the horrors of Domitian's reign; May later wrote a commendatory poem for its first edition of 1629, describing Massinger as 'my most deserving friend'.[63]

May's turn to Lucan and to Roman history continues this line of writing. His *The Tragedy of Cleopatra*, performed in 1626, places Egypt's loss of independence in the context of the loss of Roman liberty and the rise of single rule in the person of 'Caesar' (here meaning Octavian), whom he presents as a cynical opportunist rather than the virtuous peace-bringer of Augustan literature. This historical framing of the play draws heavily on Lucan's poem, which May was translating at the same time, but is also coloured by the dramatic style of Jonson's *Sejanus*. His translation of Lucan exhibits similar emphases and motifs. Its introductory epistle and single-book dedications thematize Lucan's work as dealing with the death of Roman liberty and her fall into a monarchy 'but heavy and distasteful', while upholding the 'virtue' of the republic's last champions as demonstrating noble endurance in a climate of external jeopardy.[64] Some of the single-book dedications (whose immediate political context we discuss below) are clearly modelled on Jonson's *Epigrams*, while the translation as a whole owes a stylistic debt to the sententious, hyperbolical style of *Sejanus* and *Catiline*. The influence of Jonson can also be detected in May's attitude to Lucan's disputed generic status. In his dedicatory epistle to William Earl of Devonshire, he advances a distinctly hybrid position, arguing that the work's 'matter' or subject — as distinct from its style — was a 'true history adorned and heightened with poetical raptures, which do not adulterate nor corrupt the truth, but give it a more sweet and pleasant relish'.[65] Terminologically speaking, this appraisal is indebted to Horace's doctrine of the *dulce* and *utile* but also to conventional celebrations of historiography, following Cicero, as the 'light of truth'.[66] When applied to Lucan's text, however, it tries to blend two quite separate literary appraisals. On the one hand it gives invented or fictional passages an intoxicating, potentially sublime quality ('raptures'). May has Lucan's gruesome account of the Thessalian witch Erictho in book six particularly in mind here, echoing Jonson in the *Masque of Queenes* in the latter's own praise of the book as Lucan's 'most poetical' on

---

[62] For further discussion of these plays, see Paleit, *War, Liberty, and Caesar*, pp. 140–62.
[63] Philip Massinger, *The Roman Actor* (London: Bernard Alsop and Thomas Fawcett for Robert Allot, 1629), sig. A3ᵛ.
[64] See below, pp. 38–39.
[65] See below, p. 38.
[66] Horace, *Ars Poetica*, 343–44 in *Opera*, ed. by Edward Wickham and H. Garrod (Oxford: Clarendon Press, 1901); Cicero, *De Oratore, Books I–II*, trans. by E. W. Sutton, ed. by H. Rackham, Loeb Classical Texts (Cambridge, MA: Harvard University Press, 1948), II. 36.

account of Erictho's 'horrid height'.[67] But on the other it echoes earlier English engagements with Lucan by the likes of Samuel Daniel or Arthur Gorges, who had likewise identified truth with historical narrative as opposed to poetic fiction. This programmatic position, however, conceals May's discomfort at Lucan's *actual* departures from historical 'truth', which he sometimes silently corrected.[68] An historical note added in the second, 1631 edition states baldly that Lucan's account of the sea battle at Massilia 'is not rightly related' and 'differs much from the relation of true histories'.[69]

Such debts may reflect Jonson's personal guidance as well as general literary influence: as we have mentioned above, he was a friend of May's in the late 1620s and 1630s, and the younger poet may well have considered him a mentor, judging by his decision to commemorate him posthumously, in 1637, as a dead Lucan. It is from Jonson, too, that May is likely to have absorbed the vein of neo-Stoic sentiment that runs through his translation. Seventeenth-century neo-Stoics were fascinated by the topos of suicide, especially as a response to political disaster or misfortune. In *Sejanus*, Jonson had dramatized the self-slaughter of the virtuous citizen Silius in front of the assembled Roman Senate, borrowing one or two doctrines from Lucan's Cato in book nine of the *Bellum Ciuile* to emphasise Silius's indifference to death. It is probably significant that May reuses Jonson's renditions in his own translation of Cato's speech.[70] Likewise Hulsen's engraving of Lucan's suicide, on the translation's title page, may owe something to the *Death of Seneca*, a famous painting by Sir Peter Paul Rubens (another Lipsius protégé), although admittedly Hulsen's Lucan, unlike Rubens' Stoic sage, sports seventeenth-century moustaches. May was to carry his fascination with suicide into his *Continuation*, which makes that of Cato at Utica, in 46 BC, into a set-piece.[71] The translation's repeated emphasis on the 'secure' character of Stoic virtue, in the sense of indifference to external jeopardy or *apatheia*, typically has an approving register.[72] That said, there is a trace of antagonism in the epithet 'sour' May's translation applies to Cato and indeed 'Cato's sect'.[73] When other writers of the period applied 'sour' to Stoicism, the tone is often clearly critical.[74] Unsurprisingly the usage may

---

[67] See 6. Ded; Ben Jonson, *The Complete Masques*, ed. by Stephen Orgel (New Haven & London: Yale University Press, 1969), pp. 527, 535; cf. Paleit, *War, Liberty, and Caesar*, p. 163.
[68] For example at 2. 716–17, 724–25.
[69] See below, 'Annotations on the Third Book', note 'h' (to 3. 541).
[70] See below, 9. 656–57, 673.
[71] May, *Continuation*, sigs F4ʳ–7ʳ. For Cato's exemplary status to May's contemporaries, see Freya Cox Jensen, '"Creating" Cato in Early Seventeenth-Century England', in *Concepts of Creativity in Seventeenth-Century England*, ed. by R. Herissone and A. Howard (Cambridge: Boydell and Brewer, 2013), pp. 233–52.
[72] See below, 2. 303–04, 306, 314, 9. Ded. 3 and note, 9. 476.
[73] See 2. 357, 2. 402; the second translates L.'s *dura*, 'hard, unyielding'.
[74] Traiano Boccalini, *The new-found politicke*, trans. by John Florio et al. (London: Eliot's

once again derive from Jonson, who has Catiline describe Cato as 'your sour austerity'.[75]

Early modern neo-Stoicism often went hand in glove with a preference for absolute monarchy.[76] Despite his strong moral aversion to courtly corruption and tyranny, and dislike of flattery, Jonson himself relished his role as masque-writer for the early Stuart court. The ideological slant encouraged by May's translation of a pro-republican text seems ostensibly quite different. In the later seventeenth century, John Aubrey was to remark that May's 'translation of Lucan's excellent Poeme made him in love with the Republique, which tang (*odorem*) stuck by him'.[77] This comment aligns with other, mostly royalist perspectives, which read his Parliamentary allegiances as subversive of England's firmly monarchical political culture. Such was certainly the charge animating Andrew Marvell's 'Tom May's Death', in which Ben Jonson's ghost charges May's 'most servile wit, and mercenary pen' for presuming too direct an analogy between English and Roman political experience:

> Go seek the novice statesmen, and obtrude
> On them some Roman-cast similitude,
> Tell them of liberty, the stories fine,
> Until you all grow consuls in your wine.[78]

The 'novice statesmen' here are the rulers of England during the Commonwealth (1649–1653) and their literary supporters, a number of whom had reached for classical and especially Roman constitutional models to legitimise the post-regicidal regime. Marchamont Nedham for example, a friend of May's, used his translation of Lucan to sketch out ideas of republican citizenship in a number of issues of the government newsletter *Mercurius Politicus* during 1650–1651.[79] Marvell's Jonson is also criticising the regular comparisons, usually via Lucan, May had made between the fall of the Roman republic and England's slide towards Catholicism and absolutism under the Stuarts in his *The History of*

Court Press for Francis Williams, 1626), sig. B3ᵛ, 'certain wilfull sowre *Stoicks*'; Thomas Jackson, *A Treatise Concerning the Original of Unbelief, Misbelief or Mispersuasions* (London: John Dawson for John Clark, 1625), sig. Cc4ᵛ (STC 14316), 'any dull sowre Stoicks devotion'.

[75] Ben Jonson, *Catiline his Conspiracy*, III. 1. 207 (in *The Cambridge Edition of the Works of Ben Jonson*, ed. by David Bevington, Martin Butler and Ian Donaldson, 7 vols (Cambridge: Cambridge University Press, 2012), IV, p. 87).

[76] As argued, most famously, by Gerard Oestreich, *Neostoicism and the Early Modern State* (Cambridge: Cambridge University Press, 1982).

[77] Aubrey, *Brief Lives*, p. 196.

[78] Andrew Marvell, 'Tom May's Death', lines 43–46, in *The Poems*, ed. by Nigel Smith, revised ed. (Edinburgh: Pearson, 2007).

[79] See Blair Worden, *Literature and Politics in Cromwellian England* (Oxford: Oxford University Press, 2007), pp. 95–97; Paleit, *War, Liberty, and Caesar*, p. 253.

the Parliament (1647).[80] His and similar post-regicidal accounts reflect distaste not only for May's political choices but a desire to paint the English Revolution as an act of reckless subversion by people who had spent too much time with classical texts.

How accurate was this antagonistically motivated portrait of May? An admiration for quasi-republican government certainly did exist in the 1620s, even among May's friends: in Hyde's *Life* John Vaughan is said to have looked 'most into those parts of the law which disposed him to least reverence to the crown, and most to popular authority'; he is quick to insist that Vaughan's inclinations remained purely intellectual.[81] He does not suggest that May shared such beliefs — at least not at the time. Certainly, May's translation seems less concerned with precise institutional contrasts between republican or monarchical systems of government — let alone the benefits of 'popular authority', which does not chime with his often aristocratic emphasis[82] — but rather with the loss of a symbolic political order of virtue, nobility and freedom in the aftermath of Caesar's victory, a theme he highlights repeatedly in both his translation and other works.

Such emphases arose in part from contemporary political crisis.[83] The mid- to late 1620s were dominated by the attempt of Charles I and his favourite the Duke of Buckingham to prosecute a war against Catholic Spain; from 1627 England was also at war with France. Both policies encouraged a climate of aggressive Protestant patriotism, to which many writers responded: a good example is Michael Drayton's *The Battle of Agincourt* (1627), a narrative of Henry V's famous military campaign to which Ben Jonson and John Vaughan contributed dedicatory poems, as they did, the same year, for May's translation.[84] The domestic political consequences were more contentious. During the parliament of 1626 (2 February to 15 June; May must have been composing his translation during the period), which was summoned to agree subsidies for military expenditure, many MPs blamed Buckingham, whose control of patronage and office-holding had aroused considerable resentment, for a poor start to the war. Exercised also by his and the king's apparent anti-Calvinist sympathies — often interpreted as proto-Catholic by Protestant hardliners — they tried to impeach him. Forced to dissolve the parliament to protect Buckingham, Charles decided

---

[80] See e.g. May, *The History of the Parliament of England: which began November the third, M.DC.XL.* (London: Moses Bell for George Thomason, 1647), pp. 4, 21.
[81] Hyde, *The Life*, I, p. 37.
[82] For May's tendency to suppress mention of 'the people' as a political agent, or associate it with fickleness or sedition, see e.g. 1. 2, 119, 174, 297, 4. 881.
[83] For discussions of the context, see Paleit, *War, Liberty, and Caesar*, pp. 224-28; Norbrook, *Writing the English Republic*, pp. 43-50.
[84] Michael Drayton, *The Battaile of Agincourt* (London: Augustine Mathews for William Lee, 1627), sigs a^r-a2^{v}A3^{r-v}.

during the winter of 1626–1627 to try to raise money solely on the basis of his royal prerogative. The measure was fiscally successful but politically divisive. Many leading gentry and noblemen refused to pay the so-called Forced Loan, which seemed to threaten an absolutist style of government without consent, in the style of the major Catholic monarchies against whom England was supposedly fighting. A number of these refusers were imprisoned without trial, raising further questions over the 'liberties of the subject'. In the meantime, a fleet under Lord Willoughby was sent to the coast of Spain: damaged by October storms and lack of proper funding, the expedition was soon forced to return embarrassingly to port.[85]

In this climate, perennial fears of popery — never far from the surface in early modern England — merged with concerns for the preservation of English laws, liberties and indeed sometimes 'liberty' against royal encroachment. Animosity towards Buckingham's control of royal patronage stoked further animosity towards his 'ambition' and cultivation of 'faction'. This context is addressed in many of May's poetic dedications of books two to nine of the translation to English aristocrats, and must indeed have been a reason for choosing the latter as dedicatees. Several of these noblemen had military experience fighting against the Catholic powers abroad, a fact the dedications invariably underline and celebrate.[86] Many were Puritan in sympathy and/or opponents of Buckingham's ascendancy or Charles's proto-absolutist style. One or two who survived to the Civil War ended up fighting for Parliament.[87] These addressees are typically compared with the champions of Rome's doomed republic, although the astonishing, suicidal bravery of two Caesarian leaders, Vulteius and Curio, constitute the models May proposes for the Earl of Essex in book four.[88] Five of the addressees were known or suspected refusers of the Forced Loan: one, Theophilus Clinton, Earl of Lincoln, had been thrown in the Tower for encouraging resistance to it in his locality.[89] May's dedication to Clinton lays pointed stress on his ability to rise above misfortune, comparing his conduct to Pompey's heroic imperturbability in the face of defeat and death.[90] Only one of May's dedicatees was a known supporter of Buckingham, and this is Lord Willoughby, to whom he dedicates book five, in which Caesar suffers a mutiny and makes a failed attempt to sail to Italy because of storms. The analogy with Willoughby's own failed expedition to Cádiz in October 1627 is not difficult to identify. Collectively the single-book dedications align

[85] For more on this episode, see below, 5. Ded. and notes.
[86] For details on these figures, see our notes to the individual dedications.
[87] Namely the earls of Essex and Warwick, dedicatees of books four and nine.
[88] See 4. Ded. 8–14 and notes.
[89] Norbrook, *Writing the English Republic*, p. 44; Paleit, *War, Liberty, and Caesar*, p. 234 and notes.
[90] See 8. Ded. and notes.

heroic English Protestantism with a neo-Stoic conception of virtuous nobility proved in hardship, while allowing a reader to infer an analogy between Rome's doomed *libertas* — a consistent theme of May's paratextual materials — and the 'laws and liberties' of England's parliamentary monarchy. Analogy is not, of course, identity, particularly at a philosophical level. There is no evidence to suggest that May thought English and Roman liberty were conceptually identical or even that he had fully theorized the idea. The point of comparison, for May, was less the nature of freedom than the experience of losing it.

Most copies of May's 1627 text show these dedications mutilated or their pages excised. It seems likely that someone — whether May or the printer-publishers — decided at some point to suppress them. That they survive at all suggests this happened after the first copies had been sold. We don't know whether the move was voluntary or enforced. There is no documentary evidence for *why* they were removed. A mistake in the name and title given to one dedicatee, the Earl of Sheffield, seems an unlikely reason to eliminate them all.[91] The most probable explanation is a change in the political climate around the time of the text's publication, presumably the spring and early summer of 1627. At this point Buckingham was preparing an expedition to relieve the siege of French Protestants at La Rochelle, a venture that was greeted with enthusiasm even by his critics; May wrote a supportive poem for the occasion.[92] Divisions in England's tight-knit political elite also showed signs of healing, with the favourite being reconciled to his most powerful antagonist on the Privy Council, the Earl of Pembroke (dedicatee of book two). Charles was sufficiently persuaded of his critics' goodwill to summon another parliament, which met in early 1628 and started relatively harmoniously, although things soon went south. In this context May's dedications may have seemed untimely, overblown and unnecessarily divisive. They disappear from later editions. Later publications were dedicated to courtly figures and his *Continuation* to Charles I.

The pro-war but constitutionally anxious atmosphere of the late 1620s colours May's tactics as a translator. It almost certainly lies behind the idioms of chivalric heroism or military camaraderie which infuse some of his battle descriptions (for example at 3. 723 ff.), or his allusions to seventeenth-century maritime practice. The translation's consistent emphasis, already discussed, on a neo-Stoic ideal of virtuous nobility that stretches to defiant suicide, shaped by Lucan's own fate under the tyrannical Nero, is juxtaposed with un-Lucanian references to ambition, faction or even 'treason' that align the destruction of the Roman republic by military magnates like Sulla, Caesar, Pompey or Crassus with the ascendancy of the Duke of Buckingham, and the defenders of the

---

[91] A possibility raised (but treated critically) by Norbrook, *Writing The English Republic*, p. 48n. See 3. Ded, and note.
[92] See PRO, SP 16/68/74: for a transcript, Paleit, *War, Liberty, and Caesar*, p. 237n.

republic with Protestant patriots.[93] The formula 'laws and liberties' makes a few contextually significant appearances.[94]

It would be a mistake to think that all May's decisions as a translator can be traced to a single political context. Nor is the perspective necessarily that of a partisan 'republican', a paid-up advocate of a coherent ideological programme, as opposed to a sceptical or concerned commentator. For one thing, the analogy between Lucan's subject matter and English political experience depends on an essentially lapsarian master-narrative which tells of the collapse of an idealized political order of aristocratic virtue and liberty — an order therefore that already exists — rather than any kind of revolutionary commitment to overturn existing traditions, as implied in many royalist or Restoration retrospectives. Nonetheless, the Marvellian charge of a 'Roman-cast similitude' is not entirely false. May's work has an ideological edge and topical urgency that distinguishes it from other classical translations of the 1620s, and looks forward to the often heavily partisan versions of Roman literature produced during the Civil War, Commonwealth and Protectorate.

3d. Later Editions and Afterlife

May's translation was well known and widely read until at least the 1660s. It is frequently quoted by writers during this period, often appreciatively — a good example is John Weever's *Ancient Funerall Monuments* (1631), which cites it repeatedly — and it exercised an idiomatic influence on much literature of the 1630s and 1640s. The work's praise for Lucan's suicide and resistance to tyranny appears to have been particularly famed. In Aston Cokain's *A Chain of Golden Poems*, for example, one poem — purportedly sent with May's translation to a mistress — contrasts the poet's erotic self-sacrifice with Lucan's self-slaughter: the jokiness as well as the occasion testifies to the translation's cachet in ways that more straightforward responses might not.[95] While May's political allegiances attracted hostility from royalist writers, as already noted, this did not necessarily affect his esteem as a translator. Even Hyde, who thought May himself 'deserves to be forgotten', had good words for the translation.[96] Thomas Fuller, in his *The History of the Worthies of England* (1661), stated that Lucan was to many 'judicious' readers 'an excellent poet, and losing no lustre by Mr. May's translation'.[97] Over the longer term it was May's *Continuation* — and

---

[93] For 'ambition', see e.g. 1. 95n, 3. 255, 7. 435–36; 'faction', e.g. 2. 398n; 'treason' e.g. 9. 330.
[94] See e.g. 9. 644; for M.'s attitude to *libertas* more generally, see 7. 399, 422.
[95] Aston Cokain, 'To My Mrs., before Mr. Mayes Lucan that I sent her', in *A Chain of Golden Poems* (London: William Godbid, 1658), pp. 44–45.
[96] 'His parts of nature and art were very good, as appears by his translation of Lucan (none of the easiest work of that kind)': Hyde, *The Life*, I, pp. 39–40.
[97] Thomas Fuller, *The History of the Worthies of England* (London: J. Grismond, W. Leybourne and William Godbid for Thomas Williams, 1662), sig. Ooo3^r.

especially its Latin translation as the *Supplementum Lucani* — which was to have greater durability. But as late as 1675 Milton's nephew Edward Phillips — who preferred the latter texts — still writes of May, somewhat grudgingly, as the 'vulgarly admired translator of *Lucan* into Latin verse'.[98]

Evidence for the work's immediate literary success is also found in the publication of a second and third edition within eight years (in 1631 and 1635). Each was undertaken by different combinations of printer-publishers, perhaps (again) to spread the financial risk. Each also claimed that May had revised the text and enlarged his historical annotations. In fact such adjustments, which we record in our Textual Notes, are relatively few and fail to correct some very obvious mistakes; they were probably undertaken simply to refresh the work's sales value and beyond correcting printing errors seem aimed mainly at rendering misconstrued Latin more accurately, or (selectively) clarifying prosody and pronunciation. Very little else about the work was changed, besides the removal of the single-book dedications discussed above. The addition of new 'covering' title pages — Hulsen's title page engraving was preserved on an inner leaf, along with May's facing-page poem — necessitated the removal of another page from the first quire; the rather abysmal commendatory poem by 'H. V.' duly disappeared. The dedication to William Earl of Devonshire was, however, repeated. The original dedicatee had died in early 1628; later readers may have assumed his son — who was identically named and titled — was intended.

The publication of May's *A Continuation of Lucan's Historical Poem* in 1630 raises some interesting questions about May's perception of his text. In seven books, it takes the story forward as far as Julius Caesar's assassination in March 44 BC, dealing along the way with the defeat and deaths of many of the remaining republican leaders. It adopts the same textual format as the translation, and there are also many clear borrowings and imitations as well as a sustained idiomatic resemblance. Indeed, May appears to have consciously and deliberately quoted his earlier translation, and in particularly freighted ways, for example using similar words to describe the defiantly dying Caesar as Lucan does of Pompey.[99] This pattern of self-quotation, which can also be found in his *The History of the Parliament*, and which he shares with other classical and English poets, seems not simply an unconscious habit but a means of consciously fashioning his career as a 'Lucanic' writer. Did this deliberately constructed continuity mean that he also conceptualised his two Lucanic narratives as a single work? Intriguingly, the choice of seven books may have been influenced by the seventeen-book *Punica* of Silius Italicus, the historical epic with which

---

[98] Edward Phillips, *Theatrum Poetarum, or a Compleat Collection of the Poets, especially the most eminent, of all ages* (London: for Charles Smith, 1675), sig. Hh6^r.
[99] See 8. 719–46; May, *Continuation* (1630), sigs K6^v–7^r.

Lucan's work (in ten books) was often paired by Renaissance literary critics. That said, May could simply have liked a seven-book narrative, which he also used for his English historical poems of the 1630s. *The Continuation* was not published together with the translation until 1650, the last year of May's life, when political and literary circumstances had changed considerably.

The fourth, 1650, edition of May's translation also claimed alterations and additions by the author, while undertaking very few actual changes to the text. Yet in other ways it differed more substantially from its predecessors. It replaced Hulsen's engraving and May's accompanying poem with a new title page and a facing-page engraving of Lucan's bust in a Roman landscape by the prolific contemporary engraver Thomas Cross. This edition was almost certainly intended to be sold together with the third edition of the *Continuation*, which also appeared in 1650; both works are bound together in many surviving copies. William Sheares, the publisher of both 1650 texts, had printed the 1635 edition of the translation. He went on to print another edition of the *Continuation* in 1657 and in 1659 both works in one volume, entitled *Lucan's Pharsalia ... being an historical poem until the death of Julius Caesar*. The final edition of the translation appeared in 1679, during the Exclusion Crisis, when a number of writings recalling the Civil War and Commonwealth were reprinted. This may, in its way, be fitting: May's translation is the product and expression of the decades-long turbulence engendered by Charles I's accession to the English throne in 1625. The expulsion of Charles's son, James II, in 1688 was to take English politics and literature in a different direction.

FURTHER READING

Lucan

More detailed advice will follow below, but a good place to start is Philip Hardie, 'Lucan's *Bellum Civile*', in *A Companion to the Neronian Age*, ed. by E. Buckley and M. T. Dinter (Oxford: Wiley-Blackwell, 2013). Some of the most influential articles of the twentieth century on Lucan are collected in *Oxford Readings in Classical Studies: Lucan*, ed. by Charles Tesoriero (Oxford: Oxford University Press, 2010). A thorough reading list on Lucan and his reception up to 2009 is available in S. Braund, 'Lucan', in Oxford Bibliographies in Classics: see https://www.oxfordbibliographies.com.

Lucan, always a divisive and dividing force, was in critical disfavour for much of the early twentieth century. His fates revived with important modern readings in the 1970s, including *Lucan*, ed. by Werner Rutz (Wege der Forschung, 235) (Darmstadt: Wissenschaftliche Buchgesellschaft, 1970); Frederick Ahl, *Lucan: An Introduction* (Ithaca and London: Cornell University Press, 1976); Emanuele Narducci, *La provvidenza crudele. Lucano e la distruzione dei miti augustei* (Pisa: Giardini, 1979); J. C. Bramble, 'Lucan', in *The Cambridge History of Classical Literature ii: Latin Literature*, ed. by E. J. Kenney and W. V. Clausen (Cambridge: Cambridge University Press 1982), pp. 533–57; W. R. Johnson's *Momentary Monsters: Lucan and His Heroes* (Ithaca and London: Cornell University Press, 1987); and John Henderson's, 'Lucan/The Word at War', *Ramus*, 16 (1987), 122–64. Important monographs in the wake of this surge in interest include Jamie Masters, *Poetry and Civil War in Lucan's 'Bellum Civile'* (Cambridge: Cambridge University Press, 1992); Shadi Bartsch, *Ideology in Cold Blood: A Reading of Lucan's Civil War* (Cambridge, MA: Harvard University Press, 1997); and Matthew Leigh, *Lucan: Spectacle and Engagement* (Oxford: Oxford University Press, 1997).

The ideologically complex *Bellum Ciuile* has attracted sustained attention in the twenty-first century, with more than ten monographs, especially in English and German, published since 2012. For work in English see esp. Martin T. Dinter, *Anatomizing Civil War: Studies in Lucan's Epic Technique* (Ann Arbor: University of Michigan Press, 2012) (on poetics and the body); Jonathan Tracy, *Lucan's Egyptian Civil War* (Cambridge: Cambridge University Press 2014) (on politics and culture). Ethics and aesthetics have attracted particular attention: see R. Sklenár, *The Taste for Nothingness: A Study of Virtus and Related Themes in Lucan's 'Bellum Ciuile'* (Ann Arbor: University of Michigan Press, 2013), Francesca D'Alessandro Behr, *Feeling History: Lucan, Stoicism, and the Poetics of Passion* (Columbus, OH: Ohio State University Press, 2007), and H. J. M. Day, *Lucan and the Sublime: Power, Representation and Aesthetic Experience* (Cambridge: Cambridge University Press, 2013).

The results of two major recent conferences on Lucan and his reception may be found in *Letture e lettori di Lucano: Atti del Convegno internazionale di studi, Fisciano, 27–29 marzo 2012*, ed. by P. Esposito and C. Walde (Pisa: ETS, 2015) and *Présence de Lucain*, ed. by F. Galtier and R. Poignault (Clermont-Ferrand: Centre de Recherches A. Piganiol-Présence de l'Antiquité, 2016).

Reception of Lucan

A useful starting point is Christine Walde, 'Lucan (Marcus Annaeus Lucanus), *Bellum Civile*', in *The Reception of Classical Literature: Brill's New Pauly Supplements I*, ed. by Walde, vol. v (Leiden: Brill, 2012). This can be read online, with appropriate access.[1] For general overviews of Lucan's English reception, see Philip Hardie, 'Lucan in the English Renaissance', and Susanna Braund, 'Violence In Translation' in *A Companion to Lucan*, ed. by Paulo Asso (Leiden: Brill, 2011), pp. 491–506 and 507–24; and Edward Paleit, *War, Liberty, and Caesar: Responses to Lucan's 'Bellum Ciuile', ca. 1580–1650* (Oxford: Oxford University Press, 2013), which offers detailed discussions of May's translation and his *Continuation* (pp. 215–311).

Modern discussion of the political contexts animating May's translation and other seventeenth-century responses to Lucan was initiated by David Norbrook: see 'Lucan, Thomas May and the Creation of a Republican Literary Culture', in *Culture and Politics in Early Stuart England*, ed. by Kevin Sharpe and Peter Lake (Stanford: Stanford University Press, 1993), pp. 45–66; *Writing the English Republic: Poetry, Rhetoric and Politics, 1627–1660* (Cambridge: Cambridge University Press, 1993), esp. pp. 1–62. In Norbrook's wake, Andrew Hadfield, *Shakespeare and Republicanism* (Cambridge: Cambridge University Press, 2008), pp. 23–59, and Patrick Cheney, *Marlowe's Republican Authorship: Lucan, Liberty and the Sublime* (Basingstoke: Palgrave Macmillan, 2008), seek to identify 'republican' aspects of Shakespeare and Marlowe's engagements with Lucan. May's translation also figures in Yanick Maes, '*Haec Monstra Edidit*: Translating Lucan in the Early Seventeenth Century', in *A Companion to the Neronian Age*, ed. by Buckley and Dinter, pp. 405–24. The reaction of other seventeenth-century poets, especially Andrew Marvell, to May's work and career, is discussed in Andrew Shifflett, '"By Lucan Driv'n About": A Jonsonian Marvell's Lucanic Milton', *Renaissance Quarterly*, 49 (1996), 803–23,

---

[1] <https://referenceworks.brillonline.com/browse/brill-s-new-pauly-supplements-i-5/alphaRange/Lo%20-%20Lu/L> [accessed 15 October 2019]. English edition by Matthijs H. Wibier (2012).

and, selectively, in the middle chapters of Blair Worden, *Literature and Politics in Cromwellian England: John Milton, Andrew Marvell, Marchamont Nedham* (Oxford: Oxford University Press, 2007).

For Lucan's vexed status in Renaissance debates about poetic and historical narrative, and his consequent importance to English historical poetry, see Clarke Hulse, *Metamorphic Verse: The Elizabethan Minor Epic* (Princeton: Princeton University Press, 1981; now available as a legacy imprint), pp. 195–241, and Gerald Maclean, *Time's Witness: Historical Representation in English Poetry, 1603–1660* (Madison: University of Wisconsin Press, 1990), pp. 15–63; see also Paleit *War, Liberty, and Caesar*, ch. 2.

For Nicholas Rowe's 1719 translation of Lucan, which finally displaced May's, see the edition by C. A. Brown and Charles Martindale (London: Everyman, 1998), and more recently volumes IV and V of *The Plays and Poems of Nicholas Rowe* (London: Routledge, 2016), edited by Stephen Bernard and Robin Sowerby.

Abbreviations

KJV: *The Bible* [The King James Version] (London: Robert Barker, 1611)

LFB: Christopher Marlowe, *The First Book of Lucan Translated into English*, in *The Complete Works*, ed. by Fredson Bowers, 2 vols, 2nd ed. (Cambridge: Cambridge University Press, 1981), pp. 273–306

L&S: *A Latin Dictionary*, ed. by Charlton T. Lewis and Charles Short (Oxford: Clarendon, 1879)

New Pauly: *Brill's New Pauly: Encyclopaedia of the Ancient World*, ed. by Hubert Cancik Helmuth Schneider, Manfred Landfester and Christine F. Salazar (Leiden: Brill, 2005).

OCD: *Oxford Classical Dictionary, Third Revised Edition* (Oxford: Oxford University Press, 2005)

ODNB: *Oxford Dictionary of National Biography* (Oxford: Oxford University Press, 2004)

OED: *Oxford English Dictionary, Third Edition* (Oxford: Oxford University Press, 2005)

OLD: *Oxford Latin Dictionary*, 2nd ed. (Oxford: Oxford University Press, 2012)

PRO: Public Record Office, State Papers

STC: *A Short-Title Catalogue of Books Printed in England, Scotland and Ireland 1475-1640*, ed. by A. W. Pollard and G. R. Redgrave (London: The Bibliographical Society, 1976–1991)

TLL: *Thesaurus Linguae Latinae (TLL) Online* (Berlin & Boston: De Gruyter, 2009)

NOTE ON EDITORIAL PRACTICE

This is an edition of May's translation as first published in full in 1627 (STC 16887). Four others were published during his lifetime, in 1626 (the first three books only), 1631, 1635 and 1650. In each case they were undertaken by different combinations of London printer-publishers. The full titles are as follows.

STC 16886: *Lucan's Pharsalia, or the civill warres of Rome, betweene Pompey the Great and Julius Caesar. The first three bookes. Translated into English by T. M. London: Printed by I N & A M and are to be sold by Math: Law at the signe of the Fox nere Saint Austens gate*, 1626.

STC 16887: *Lucan's Pharsalia: or The ciuill warres of Rome, betweene Pompey the great, and Iulius Cæsar. The whole ten bookes. Englished, by Thomas May. Esquire. London: printed for Thomas Iones. and Iohn Marriott*, 1627.

STC 16888: *Lucans Pharsalia: or The ciuill warres of Rome, betweene Pompey the great, and Iulius Cæsar. The whole tenne bookes, Englished by Thomas May, Esquire. The second edition, corrected, and the annotations inlarged by the author. London: printed by Aug. Mathewes, for Thomas Iones, and are to be sold at his shop in St. Dunstanes Church-yard*, 1631.

STC 16889: *Lucans Pharsalia: or, The civill vvarres of Rome, between Pompey the great, and Iulius Cæsar. The whole ten bookes, Englished by Thomas May, Esquire. The third edition, corrected by the author. London: Printed by A M and are to be sold by Will: Sheares at his shop, in Britaines Bursse, and neere Yorke House*, 1635.

Wing L3387: *Lucans Pharsalia: or, The civil-wars of Rome, between Pompey the great, and Julius Cæsar. The whole ten books, Englished by Thomas May, Esquire. The fourth edition, corrected, and the annotations inlarged by the author. London: printed by William Bentley, for William Shears at the Bible near the little north-door of S. Pauls Church London*, 1650.

As this is not a diplomatic edition, we have not attempted to collate all copies of 1627, relying instead on the British Library copy that is also available on *Early English Books Online*.[1] We are, however, indebted for our transcription of the dedication to book three (sig. D5^r), mutilated in most copies, to a copy in the Folger Shakespeare Library.[2] We note major variations with later editions in our Textual Notes: some of these clearly represent some kind of editorial intervention, probably May's. Very occasionally we prefer readings of those

---

[1] Shelfmark 1068.i.6.
[2] STC 16887, copy 3 <https://luna.folger.edu/luna/servlet/s/ge9vm6> [accessed 14 October 2019].

editions to those of *1627*, but only when we are certain that the latter is simply a mistake or misprint. We have not collated the editions of 1657, 1659 or 1679, which were printed after May's death and have no textual authority. Our Textual Notes do not notice accidentals, and usually pass over the clarifications of spelling and prosody which took place in later editions.

We have taken as many steps as possible to render May's an accessible text. Besides modernizing spelling and capitalization, we have interfered systematically with May's original punctuation, which is extremely loose and often makes the overall grammar or sense of a passage difficult to follow. Among the changes has been the addition of quotation marks to characters' speeches, and the corresponding deletion of May's brackets around 'quoth he'. Even after such interventions, May's syntax can sometimes be obscure, particularly where Lucan's Latin is also problematic or compressed. Some passages remain stubbornly ungrammatical. We have also de-italicised proper names. Diacritics have not been included; ligatures such as æ and œ have become *ae* and *oe*; ∫ has been replaced by *s*, and *ij* by *ii*.

May's prosody, while fairly regular, has some distinctive features that a modern reader may find challenging; it also, occasionally, seems to aim at irregular effects. To help the reader, we have inserted grave accents to highlight syllables that would be elided in modern English but that are sounded here (e.g. 'deservèd'), and also commented on unusual or unexpected features of his practice in our notes. Otherwise, we have preserved the text as printed in *1627*, or occasionally later editions when May appears to have clarified his prosodic intention. We therefore reproduce that text's contractions, even though they by no means cover all the actual elisions or contractions demanded by the meter. The following features of the translation's prosody occur very frequently, meriting only the occasional reminder in our commentary: we list them here by way of guidance. a) The monosyllabic pronunciation of words such as *heaven, given, even, tower, power*, or the pronunciation of longer words compounded from these. b) Words ending in *-ious, -uous, -ian, -ion, -eous*, and so forth, which are typically monosyllabic, the 'i', 'e' or 'u' being treated as a 'y' in modern English. This usage extends also to classical names: *Curii, Circius* or *Pentheus*, for example, have only two syllables (1. 186, 1. 436, 6. 404). However, this rule does not apply in line-endings, or very occasionally elsewhere: for example, when ending a line, *Curio, ocean* or *motion* typically have three syllables and rhyme with 'no', 'can' and done', respectively. c) The unanglicized treatment of classical plurals: *Turones*, for example, is pronounced so as to rhyme with 'phoneys', not 'Toblerones' (1. 467). Yet here too there are some exceptions, in particular *Gades* (modern Cádiz), which May appears to pronounce monosyllabically (e.g. 3. 303). Finally, the almost invariable elision of middle syllables ending in 'r', and many also in 'n'. Thus, for example, *barbarous* is pronounced 'barb'rous', *temperately* 'temp'rately', *neighbouring* 'neighb'ring' and *every* 'ev'ry'; *evening* 'ev'ning' and *darkening* 'dark'ning'.

Throughout this edition we refer to May's text using Arabic numerals for each book (e.g. 1. 201, 8. 405) and to Lucan's original Latin text using Roman numerals (e.g. I. 201, VIII. 405). References to Lucan's text are to Farnaby's 1618 edition, slightly modernized; we note differences from modern editions when appropriate. Readers interested in chasing up later editors' readings or conjectures (for example those of Richard Bentley or A. E. Housman), sometimes mentioned in our notes, will find them in Lucan, *Bellum Ciuile*, ed. by D. R. Shackleton-Bailey (Stuttgart: Teubner, 1997). We typically refer to May as 'M.', Lucan as 'L.' and Farnaby as 'F.'. All translations of Lucan are our own unless indicated.

[FRONTISPIECE VERSES]

This dying figure that rare Lucan shows
Whose lofty genius great Apollo chose
When Roman liberty oppressed should die,
To sing her sad and solemn obsequy   *funeral dirge*
In stately numbers, high as Rome was great;[1]
And not so much to years indebted yet
As thou, famed Maro, when thy infant verse
The gnat's low funeral did first rehearse.[2]
Thy favoured Muse did find a different fate:
Thou got'st Augustus' love, he Nero's hate;
But 'twas an act more great and high, to move
A prince's envy than a prince's love.

---

[1] This dying figure] i.e. the engraving of Lucan committing suicide on the title page. high] lofty, sublime; cf. line 11.

[2] Maro] Virgil; *Culex* ('Gnat') was thought to be one of his early works by Renaissance readers, though modern editors regard it as spurious; Spenser translated it in 1591. The point that L. wrote the *Bellum Ciuile* at an even younger age is made in Publius Papinius Statius, *Silvae*, ed. and trans. by D. R. Shackleton Bailey, revised by Christopher A. Parrott (Cambridge, MA: Harvard University Press, 2015), II. 7. 73–74 (the muse Calliope speaking to the infant Lucan), which M. imitated in introductory poems to his *Continuation* (1630) and *Supplementum Lucani* (1640). It is also recorded as one of L.'s own boasts in the ancient biography now attributed to Suetonius, which M. drew on for his own 'Life of Marcus Annaeus Lucanus'.

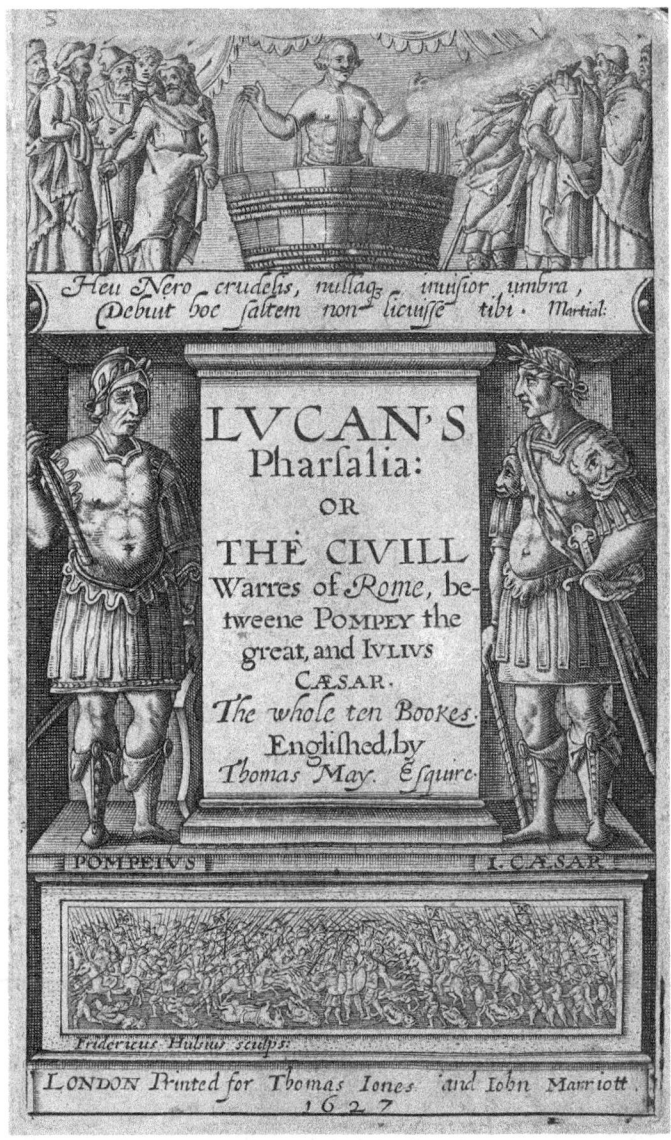

The title page of 1627, showing Lucan's suicide at the top, the battle of Pharsalus at the bottom, and in the middle Pompey (left) and Caesar (right): © The British Library Board (shelfmark 1068.i.6). The Latin beneath Lucan's death means 'Alas, cruel Nero, than whom no ghost is more detested: this at least [i.e. causing Lucan's death] ought not to have been permitted you': see Martial, *Epigrammata*, ed. by W. M. Lindsay, 2nd ed. (Oxford: Clarendon Press, 1902), VII. 21. 3–4 (a poem on Lucan's birthday). The engraver, 'Fridericus Hulsius' i.e. Friedrich von Hulsen (1580–1655), was active in England in 1627.

To the True Lover of All Good Learning and Just Honour of his Own Rank, William, Earl of Devonshire, &c.[1]

MY LORD,

The great subject of this stately poem, together with the worth of the noble author,[2] have emboldened me to present the translation (how meanly soever I have performed it) to your honourable hand. I cannot but presume that the high and rich conceits of Lucan from your deep judgement shall find their proper and due approbation; and my defects, from your noble candour, an easy and gentle censure. The matter of this work is a true history adorned and heightened with poetical raptures, which do not adulterate nor corrupt the truth, but give it a more sweet and pleasant relish.[3] The history of it is the greatest of histories, the affairs of Rome, whose transcendent greatness will admit no comparison with other states either before or after it. Rome was then at that great height, in which St Augustine wished to have seen it,[4] which after ages almost with adoration have admired, and do rather conjecture than fully comprehend.[5] The blood of her valiant citizens, and the conquests and triumphs of so many ages, had raised her now to that unhappy height, in which she could neither retain her freedom without great troubles, nor fall into a monarchy but most heavy and distasteful.[6] In one, the greatness of private citizens excluded moderation; in the other, the vast strength and forces of the prince gave him too absolute and undetermined a power. The vices of Rome did at this time (saith learned Heinsius)[7] not only grow up to their power, but overthrow it. Luxury and Pride, the wicked daughters of so noble a mother as the Roman Virtue, began to consume that which brought them forth. These were the seeds of that faction which rent the state and brought in violently a change of government. The two heads of this great division (if we may term Pompey the head of a faction, and

---

[1] William Cavendish, second Earl of Devonshire, 1590–1628 (d. 20 June). As a boy he was a tutee of Thomas Hobbes, who dedicated his translation of Thucydides to him in 1628. He became the second earl of Devonshire in early 1626. May also dedicated book six to him (see below). His son, also called William (1617–1684), inherited the title after his death.

[2] noble author] Implying a parallel between L. and Devonshire. L.'s aristocratic lineage is stressed in M.'s 'The Life of Marcus Annaeus Lucanus'.

[3] The matter ... relish] Agreeing with both sides in the controversy over whether poetry was superior to history and whether Lucan was poet or historian.

[4] St Augustine ... it] A reference to the story, popular in the seventeenth century, that St Augustine (354–430 AD) had three wishes — to have seen Christ alive, to have heard St Paul preach and to have witnessed Rome at its peak.

[5] conjecture] Estimate, guess at.

[6] monarchy ... distasteful] See 1. 5n.

[7] Daniel Heinsius (1580–1655), a Dutch classical scholar, acquainted with Ben Jonson and Thomas Farnaby. He was to meet M. in the Netherlands in 1640 (Paleit, *War, Liberty, and Caesar*, p. 286). The allusion is untraceable and disappeared from editions after 1627.

not rather the true servant of the public state) were Pompey the Great and Julius Caesar, men of greater eminence than the former ages had seen any, whose prosperous achievements in foreign wars had too far enabled them to ruin that state which before they served. The author of it was a noble Roman, rich in his mind as his large fortunes, of whose happy conceits and high raptures I forbear to dispute, or any way anticipate your Lordship's judgment. To whose noble censure I refer both the author and my poor endeavours, and shall ever rest

Your Lordship's to command

THO: MAY.

THE LIFE OF
MARCUS ANNAEUS LUCANUS

Marcus Annaeus Lucanus[1] was by nation a Spaniard and born at Cordoba.[2] His father's name was Marcus Annaeus Mela, son to Lucius Annaeus Seneca the orator, and brother to Julius Gallio and Lucius Seneca the philosopher, Nero's tutor. The two elder brothers, employed at Rome in state affairs (especially Seneca), arrived at the height both of dignity and renown. They were both senators, and by their worthy endeavours deserved not only to be powerful in their own times but famous to all posterity. Marcus Mela, the youngest brother, content with that title which his birth gave him, a Roman knight, and preferring the sweetness of a country life before the glorious trouble of a court employment, lived at home at his native Cordoba.[3] He married Caia Acilia, the daughter of Acilius Lucanus the orator, on whom he begat Marcus Annaeus Lucanus, surnamed of his grandfather by the mother's side. Annaeus Mela, though but a Roman knight, was (saith Tacitus) a great man, and he begat Lucan, no small addition to his greatness; a great testimony of Lucan's worth from so judicious an author as Cornelius Tacitus.[4] He was born at Cordoba the third of the Nones of November, in the second consulship of Caius Caesar Germanicus with Lucius Caesianus. When he was eight months old, his father brought him to Rome to season his infancy (so soon as it might be capable) with the choicest education in learning and manners. At which time (if we

---

[1] M.'s biography selects from and occasionally expands several sources, chiefly Tacitus, *Annales*, XV–XVI, the life in Pietro Crinito's *De Poetis Latinis* (1st ed. 1505, but often republished), and the various ancient and more recent biographies, one now attributed to Suetonius, found in many early modern editions of L.'s text. This included the collated biography of Giovanni Sulpizio, first printed in 1493, which was reprinted in F.'s 1618 edition. Such accounts contained both positive and less positive material on L.; M.'s version is overwhelmingly favourable, stressing L.'s virtuous parentage, eloquence, learning and 'wit', and finally his confrontation with Nero and heroic suicide.
[2] Marcus ... Cordoba] A verbatim rendering of the first line of Crinito's biography.
[3] Marcus Mela ... native Cordoba] M.'s wording and anti-courtly emphasis, although Mela's relatively retired existence is mentioned in the Suetonian life: 'Lucan' in *Suetonius*, trans. by J.C. Rolfe, 2 vols, Loeb Classical Texts (Cambridge, MA: Harvard University Press, 1914) pp. 482–83.
[4] Annaeus Mela ... Tacitus] Selectively paraphrasing Tacitus, *Annales*, XVI. 17: see Cornelius Tacitus, *Annalium Ab Excessu Divi Augusti Libri*, ed. by C. D. Fisher (Oxford: Clarendon Press, 1906). One phrase ('and he begat Lucan, no small addition to his greatness') is appropriated entirely, but otherwise M. selects so as to exaggerate the favourable aspects: Tacitus criticizes Mela for his 'back-to-front ambition' (*praeposteram ambitionem*) in attempting to match consular power while only an *eques* (knight), highlights his financial greed and does not say that he was 'a great man'.

may credit fame, and as was before reported of Plato) bees swarmed about the child's cradle and pressed in clusters toward his mouth.[5] A happy presage (as the learned interpreted it) of his future wit and admired eloquence. His tutors and schoolmasters were the most eminent and famous men of those times, Rhemnius Palaemon the grammarian and Flavius Virginius the rhetorician. By whose careful instructions, as by his own diligence and admirable facility of natural wit, he arrived in a short time to an high perfection as well in the Greek as Roman language. Of all his school fellows, he most used the friendship of Saleius Bassus and Aulus Persius the satirist. He married Polla Argentaria, the daughter of Pollius Argentarius, a noble, rich, and learned lady. Brought to the court by his uncle Seneca, he grew suddenly into great favour with Nero the emperor. He was made quaestor before the usual time and admitted into the College of Augurs. But what virtue could long be safe in such a court, the jealous tyrant being not able to brook another man's praises? Who, amongst all his other cruelties, was most severe in depressing the fame of deserving men. Nero therefore, envying the wit and excellent poetry of Lucan, suppressed his works, and forbade him any more to recite verses. Which indignity, of all other most hard to be endured (as witty Martial: *qui velit ingenio cedere rarus erit*),[6] discontenting Lucan, drew him into Piso's conspiracy. The conspiracy detected, Lucan by Nero was commanded to die, but liberty given him to choose his death. Who after a full feast, bade the physicians cut his veins, and when he perceived, through loss of blood, his hands and feet to wax cold, and the vital spirits forsaking the outward parts of his body, with a mind and look undaunted[7] he recited these verses of his own, in the third book of his *Pharsalia*.

> *Scinditur avulsus, nec sicut vulnere sanguis*
> *Emicuit lentus, ruptis cadit undique venis;*
> *Discursusque animae diversa in membra meantis*
> *Interceptus aquis; nullius vita perempti*
> *Est tanta dimissa via.*[8]

But others say he did not repeat these verses, but those in the ninth book, which is more likely:

> *Sanguis erant lachrymae: quaecunque foramina novit*

---

[5] The legend of the bees is reported in the Lucanic biography 'from a very ancient commentary', often reprinted in the Renaissance. It was a myth often told about men of letters or great wisdom: the application to Plato is first mentioned in Cicero, *De Divinatione*, I. 36. 78–79 (in *De Senectute, De Amicitia, De Divinatione*, trans. by W. A. Falconer, Loeb Classical Texts (Cambridge, MA: Harvard University Press, 1923)).

[6] *Qui velit ... erit*] 'Rare is the man willing to come second in wit'. Martial, *Epigrammata*, IX. 8. 10.

[7] with a mind and look undaunted] L.'s suicide is found in all biographical sources, but this heroic emphasis is M.'s.

[8] III. 638–42 (3. 687–93); the death of Lycidas. Printed as in 1627.

> *Humor, ab his largus manat cruor: ora redundant,*
> *Et patulae nares: sudor rubet: omnia plenis*
> *Membra fluunt venis: totum est pro vulnere corpus.*[9]

These were his last words. He died the day before the Kalends of May, in the seven and twentieth year of his age, Nerva Sullanus and Vestinius Atticus being consuls.[10] He was buried at Rome in his own most fair and sumptuous gardens.

---

[9] IX. 811–14 (9. 921–26); the death of Tullus. Printed as in *1627*.
[10] Nerva ... Atticus] More correctly, Silius Nerva and Vestinus Atticus (Tacitus, *Annales*, xv. 48. 1, here followed by Crinito). But the 'life from a very ancient commentary' often printed in Renaissance editions, has 'Nerva Syllanus', as does Giovanni Sulpizio's biography, reprinted in F. (sig. A5ʳ), which also spells 'Vestinus' as 'Vestinius'.

To my Chosen Friend, the Learned Translator of Lucan, Thomas May, Esquire.

    When, Rome, I read thee in thy mighty pair,
    And see both climbing up the slippery stair
    Of Fortune's wheel by Lucan driv'n about,
    And the world in it, I begin to doubt
5   At every line some pin thereof should slack,
    At least, if not the general engine crack.[1]
    But when again I view the parts so peized,[2]   *arranged*
    And those in number so, and measure raised,
    As neither Pompey's popularity,
10 Caesar's ambition, Cato's liberty,
    Calm Brutus' tenor start, but all along
    Keep due proportion in the ample song,
    It makes me, ravished with just wonder, cry
    'What Muse, or rather god of harmony
15 Taught Lucan these true moods?' Replies my sense,
    'What gods but those of arts and eloquence,
    Phoebus, and Hermes? They whose tongue or pen
    Are still th'interpreters 'twixt gods and men!'
    But who hath them interpreted, and brought
20 Lucan's whole frame unto us, and so wrought
    As not the smallest joint or gentlest word
    In the great mass or machine there is stirred?
    'The self-same Genius!' — so the work will say,
    'The Sun translated, or the Son of May.'[3]

Your true friend in Judgement and Choice,
BEN. JONSON.

---

[1] general engine crack] Alluding to Lucan's image of the 'engine of the world [*machina mundi*]' breaking apart in civil war (1. 79-80); translated by M. as 'the falling world's now jarring frame' (1. 87). See Andrew Shifflett, '"By Lucan Driv'n About": A Jonsonian Marvell's Lucanic Milton', *Renaissance Quarterly*, 49 (1996), 803-23.

[2] parts so peized] William Drummond of Hawthornden recorded Jonson in 1619 as saying 'that Lucan, taken in parts, was good divided: read altogether, merited not the name of a poet' (Jonson, *Works*, v, p. 363).

[3] The Sun ... of May] i.e. Apollo, god of the sun, and Mercury, son of the goddess Maia; cf. line 17. Apollo is also god of poetry, thus *Lucan's Pharsalia* is also 'Phoebus' (i.e. poetry) translated, and Thomas May's 'son'.

To his All-Deserving and Learned Friend, the Translator of *Lucan*: Thomas May Esquire.

Pompey and Caesar, worthies more than men,
Are more than worthy of a lasting story,
And worthy more than of a vulgar pen
To raise the trophies of deservèd glory.
Who now is fit but May, as Lucan then?
Change but the language and the sooth to say,
May is their Lucan, and their Lucan, May.
Forward sweet friend, led by rich Lucan's vein:
Nor is thy praise the less, but more thy pain.
    H. V.[4]

---

[4] Identity unknown; conceivably a relative of John Vaughan, the author of the next poem.

Upon this Unequalled Work, and the Author.

Rome had been still my wonder; I had known
Lucan in no expression but his own;
And had as yet conjectured it a wrong,
To have praised Caesar in another tongue.
5 To bring forth one that could but understand,
I thought a pride too great for any land,
Yea, for Rome's self. Who would be posed to tell
How great she was, when she could write so well,
'Til truth was nearer brought by thee; 'til I
10 Found Lucan languaged like my infancy;   *able to speak*
'Til Rome was met in England in that state
That was, at once, her greatness and her fate;
So all to us discovered, that nought's hid
Which either she could speak, or Caesar did.
15 Beyond which, nothing can be done by thee,
Though thou hadst more of Lucan than we see
Revealed in this, wherein there is so much
Of miracle, that I durst doubt him, such   *dared*
As thou hast rendered him. But that I know
20 'Tis cross to be thy friend and Lucan's foe,   *contradictory*
Whom thou hast made so much thy self that we
May almost strive about his pedigree,
Since Rome hath nothing left to prove him hers
But the foul instance of his murderers.
25 So neatly hadst thou robbed her of his name,
That she can only rescue't with a shame,
Which may she do whilst nations reckon thee
Lucan in all except Rome's infamy.[5]

J. VAUGHAN.[6]

---

[5] Lucan ... infamy] i.e. M. resembles L. in everything except his cruel death.
[6] Almost certainly John Vaughan (1603–1674), the lawyer who was part of M.'s and Ben Jonson's circle during the late 1620s: Hyde, *The Life*, I, pp. 34, 37. An MP both before and after the Civil War, he became chief justice of the common pleas in 1668. During 1627, Jonson and he also contributed dedicatory poems to Michael Drayton's *The Battle of Agincourt*.

LUCAN'S
Pharsalia

The First Book.

The Argument of the First Book.[1]

The fatal causes of this war are shown,
Enragèd Caesar passes Rubicon,
Invades Arim'num, where to him from Rome   *Ariminum*
Curio, and both the banished tribunes come
5   With new incitements to these civil wars.
Caesar's oration to his soldiers,
Bold Laelius' protestation, which by all
The rest confirmèd makes the general
Draw out from every part of France at once
10 His now dispersed and wint'ring legions,
Rome's fear; great Pompey with the Senate flies;
Heaven, air and earth are filled with prodigies.
The prophets thence and learnèd augurs show
The wrath of Heaven and Rome's ensuing woe.

Wars more than civil on Emathian plains   [I. 1]
We sing;[2] rage licensed; where great Rome distains[3]
In her own bowels her victorious swords;
Where kindred hosts encounter, all accords

---

[1] The Argument] M.'s arguments to each book follow and occasionally expand the Latin *argumenta* of Giovanni Sulpizio, first printed in 1493 and much re-used by later editors and publishers. They offer a 'table of contents' but also inject some personal emphasis or interest. Significant additions or emphases are highlighted in the notes below.

[2] Emathian] Thessalian. Pharsalus, the climactic battle between Pompey and Caesar, was fought in Thessaly in 48 BC (see book seven), as was the battle of Philippi, fought between Octavian (later Augustus) and Brutus, in 42 BC. The ending '-ian' is usually monosyllabic in M.'s translation, as are '-ield', '-ious' and similar formulations (cf. 'impious', 1. 5).

[3] great Rome distains] *populum potentem*, 'a powerful people' (1. 2). 'Distains' means 'discolours' and even 'defiles' (*OED*, s.v. 1, 2); L.'s term, *conversum*, implies simply 'turned inwards' (1. 3).

5 Of empire broke;[1] where armed to impious war[2]
   The strength of all the shaken world from far
   Is met; known ensigns ensigns do defy,
   Piles against piles,[(a)][3] 'gainst eagles eagles fly.
       What fury, countrymen, what madness could[4]   [1. 8]
10 Move you to feast your foes with Roman blood?
   And choose such wars as could no triumphs yield,[5]
   Whilst yet proud Babylon unconquered held
   The boasting trophies of a Roman host,
   And unrevengèd wandered Crassus'[(b)] ghost?[6]
15 Alas, what seas, what lands might you have ta'en   *taken*
   With what blood's loss, which civil hands had drawn?[7]
   Yours had been Titan's rising, yours his set,   *the sun*
   The kingdoms scorchèd in meridian heat
   And those where winter which no spring can ease
20 With lasting cold doth glaze the Scythian seas;   *turn to glass*
   The Seres yours, the wild Araxis too,
   And those that see Nile's spring, if any do;
   Then 'gainst thy self, if war so wicked, Rome,
   Thou love, when all the world is overcome,[8]
25 Turn back thy hand: thou didst not want a foe.
       But now that walls of half-fall'n houses so   [1. 24]
   Hang in Italian towns, vast stones we see
   Of ruined walls, whole houses empty be,
   And ancient towns are not inhabited;

---

[1] accords of empire] *foedera regni*, 'leagues of monarchy' (1. 4), meaning the triumvirate of Caesar, Crassus and Pompey (60–53 BC). 'Monarchy' (*regnum*) is L.'s term for Caesar and Pompey's dominance of Roman politics (see e.g. 1. 94–95, 118, 310–12), but is also deployed tendentiously by his major characters (e.g. 1. 338). Whereas L. uses *regnum* as an umbrella term for various kinds of legitimate and illegitimate power, M. attempts to distinguish between monarchy and tyranny, though not entirely consistently — see 5. 239 and 5. 295–96.

[2] impious war] *commune nefas*, 'collective crime' (1. 6).

[3] Piles against piles] M., like Arthur Gorges, uses the neologism 'piles' (for *pila, pilis*) for the iconic Roman weapon: see M.'s historical footnote (a). Marlowe used 'darts'.

[4] madness] *tanta licentia ferri*, 'so great free-dealing in the sword' (1. 8).

[5] no triumphs yield] Roman victories over external enemies were celebrated in triumphal processions through Rome; but this is a civil war.

[6] The boasting trophies ... Crassus' ghost] Lit. 'enemy spoils' (*tropaeis*, 1. 10); L. means the standards of Marcus Crassus the triumvir, which were lost at the battle of Carrhae in 53 BC, in a catastrophic defeat inflicted by the Parthians.

[7] drawn] *hauserunt*, 'drank' (1. 14); for M.'s use of 'draw' in this sense, see *OED*, s.v. 2.23b. See Textual Notes.

[8] is overcome] *sub Latias leges ... miseris*, 'subjugated to Latin laws' (1. 22). L. here entreats Rome directly.

30 That untilled Italy's with weeds o'erspread
    And the neglected ploughs want labouring hands:
    Not thou, fierce Pyrrhus, nor the Punic bands
    This waste have made;[1] no sword could reach so far.
    Deep pierce the wounds received in civil war.
35   But if no other way to Nero's reign   [1. 33][2]
    The Fates could find, if gods their crowns obtain
    At such dear rates, and heaven could not obey
    Her Jove, but after the stern giants' fray,
    Now we complain not, gods: mischief and war
40 Pleasing to us, since so rewarded, are.[3]
    Let dire Pharsalia groan with armèd hosts
    And glut with blood the Carthaginian ghosts;[4]
    With these let Munda's(c) fatal battle go,[5]
    Mutina's(d) siege, Perusia's(e) famine too;
45 To these add Actium's(f) bloody naval fight,[6]
    And near Sicilia(g) Sextus' slavish fleet.[7]
    Yet much owes Rome to civil enmity
    For making thee our prince:[8] when thou the sky,
    Though late, shall climb, and change thine earthly reign,
50 Heaven, as much graced, with joy shall entertain
    And welcome thee; whether thou wouldst put on
    Jove's crown, or ride in Phoebus' burning throne[9]

---

[1] fierce Pyrrhus ... Punic bands] King Pyrrhus of Epirus and Carthage, historic enemies of Rome. L.'s *Poenus*, 'the Carthaginian' (1. 31), suggests Carthage's Hannibal; M.'s plural may derive from F., who glosses the term as meaning the Carthaginian people as well as Hannibal.

[2] 35–72] In place of the normal epic muse, L. encomiastically invokes the emperor Nero. Many early modern commentators, including F., read this passage as ironic.

[3] heaven could not obey ... rewarded, are] In Greco-Roman myth, Jupiter became king of the gods only after defeating the giants' rebellion.   mischief and war] *scelera ipsa, nefasque*, 'those crimes and abomination' (1. 37).

[4] And glut with blood...] i.e. who still thirst for vengeance on Rome, their ancient enemy. 'Glut with blood', together with 'groan' in l. 41 for *Impleat*, 'fill' (1. 39), may echo Marlowe's 'Pharsalia groan with slaughter, | And Carthage souls be glutted with our bloods' (*LFB*, lines 38–39).

[5] Munda's ... fleet] A list of decisive battles in the Roman civil wars, now deemed a price worth paying for Nero's rule.

[6] bloody naval fight] M.'s idiom; *quas premit aspera, classes, | Leucas*, 'the fleets overwhelmed by rough Leucas [i.e. Actium]' (1. 43–44).

[7] near Sicilia] *ardenti ... sub Aetna*, 'underneath burning Etna' (1. 43).

[8] For making thee our prince] *Quod tibi res acta est*, 'that this matter was performed for you' (1. 45).

[9] burning throne] *flammigeros currus*, 'flame-wielding chariots' (1. 48). M. possibly echoes Old Testament imagery (e.g. Daniel 7. 9, *KJV*, 'his throne was like the fyrie flame, & his wheels as burning fyre'; Ezekiel 1. 26–27).

(Earth will not fear the change).¹ Thence may'st thou shine
Down on thy world: to thee all powers divine
55 Will yield, and nature to thy choice will give
What god to be, or where in heaven to live.²
But near the Northern Bear O do not reign,   *Ursa Major*
Nor cross the point of the meridian,³
From whence obliquely thou shouldst Rome behold.
60 If all thy weight one part of heaven should hold,
The honoured load would bow heaven's axle-tree;⁴   *axle*
Hold thou the middle of the poisèd sky:
Let all the air between transparent be,
And no dark cloud 'twixt us and Caesar fly.⁵
65 Then let mankind forget all war and strife,
And every nation love a peaceful life.⁶
Let peace through all the world in this blessed state
Once more shut warlike Janus' iron gate.⁷
O be my god: if thou this breast inspire,
70 Not Phoebus I'll from Cirrha's shades desire
Nor Nysa's Bacchus:⁸ Caesar can infuse
Virtue enough into a Roman muse.⁹

    The cause of these great actions I'll declare,   [1. 67]¹⁰
And ope a mighty work, what drew to war   *open*
75 Our furious people and the world beside:
Fate's envious course, continuance still denied
To mighty states, who greatest falls still fear,

---

¹ will not fear the change] i.e. of an altered sun, as L. makes clear (*mutato sole*, 1. 49). The contrast is with the destruction when Phaethon, son of the sun god, drove his father's chariot off its wonted route, scorching the whole earth and killing himself.

² or where in heaven to live] *ubi regnum ponere mundi*, 'where to place the monarchy of the universe' (1. 52).

³ Nor cross ... meridian] M.'s idiom; L. here mentions the hot southern hemisphere.

⁴ If all ... axle-tree] *Aetheris immensi partem si presseris unam, | Sentiet axis onus*, 'were you to press down on part of the immense sky, the axle [i.e. of the heavenly sphere] would feel the burden' (1. 56–57). Early modern commentators often suspected a jab at Nero's obesity in these lines.

⁵ Caesar] i.e. Nero.

⁶ love a peaceful life] *Inque vicem gens omnis amet*, 'every race love each other' (1. 61).

⁷ Janus' iron gate] The Romans shut the Temple of Janus at the conclusion of war.

⁸ Not Phoebus ... Bacchus] L. rejects traditional sources of divine inspiration. 'Cirrha's shades' is Apollo's shrine at Delphi. Nysa is the birthplace of Bacchus. See Textual Notes.

⁹ Caesar ... muse] L. directly addresses Nero here. 'A Roman muse', M.'s idiom for *vires Romana in carmina*, 'strength for a Roman poem' (1. 66), emphasises the substitution of Nero for the normal epic muse: for virtue in the sense of 'force' or 'energy' see OED, s.v. †5a.

¹⁰ 73–198] The causes of the civil war (= 1. 67–182). L. gives several; M.'s singular 'cause' (for *causas*, 'causes') is misleading.

And Rome not able her own weight to bear.¹
So when the knot of nature is dissolved,²
80 And the world's ages in one hour involved
In their old Chaos, seas with skies shall join
And stars with stars confounded lose their shine;
The earth no longer shall extend her shore
To keep the ocean out; the moon no more
85 Follow the sun, but scorning her old way,
Cross him, and claim the guidance of the day.³
The falling world's now jarring frame no peace,
No league shall hold;⁴ great things themselves oppress.⁵
The gods this bound to growing states have set:
90 But to no foreign arms would Fortune yet
Lend her own envy o'er great Rome, that awes
Both land and sea;⁶ she's her own ruin's cause,
Subjected jointly to three lords.⁽ʰ⁾⁷ How ill
Prove sharèd rule's accords, and fatal, still?⁸
95 Ambition-blinded lords,⁹ what's th'happiness

---

¹ Fate's envious course] The first cause: the hostility of providence.   continuance … mighty states] *summisque negatum* | *Stare diu*, 'the denial of long-standing to what is preeminent' (1. 70–71).   fear] A twist not in L., who simply mentions 'heavy falls under excessive weight', *nimioque graves sub pondere lapsus* (1. 71).

² knot of nature is dissolved] M. adds 'of nature'; L.'s *compage* means 'structure, joint, fabric, frame' (1. 72). Stoics believed that the cosmos periodically was destroyed, falling back into a state of primeval chaos.

³ the moon … day] *fratri contraria Phoebe* | *Ibit, & obliquum bigas agitare per orbem* | *Indignata, diem poscet sibi*, 'Phoebe [the moon-goddess] will go against her brother and, not deigning to drive her chariot aslant across the sky, demands the day for herself' (1. 77–79). F. glosses 'the moon does not follow the sun'.

⁴ The falling world's now jarring frame] *totaque discors* | *Machina divulsi turbabit foedera mundi*, 'and the whole discordant machine will overturn all bonds of a world torn asunder' (1. 79–80). A famous image, used with reference to L. and M.'s translation in Ben Jonson's dedicatory poem (see above, p. 43).

⁵ great … oppress] *In se magna ruunt*, 'great things collapse onto themselves' (1. 81).

⁶ growing states … foreign arms] L. talks only of *laetis … rebus*, 'happy circumstances' (1. 81) and *gentibus ullis*, 'any peoples' (1. 82).

⁷ she's her own … three lords] L. here accuses *Roma*, 'mother Rome', directly (1. 84–85). The 'three lords' are the first triumvirate of Crassus, Caesar and Pompey. L. terms them 'masters' (*dominis*, 1. 85), a term elsewhere in L. indicating political enslavement.

⁸ How ill … still] L. also accuses (besides Rome) 'the bestial compacts of monarchy, never before distributed among a crowd' of bringing about civil war (*nec unquam* | *In turbam missi feralia foedera regni*, 1. 85–86). See 1. 5n.

⁹ Ambition-blinded lords] *nimiaque cupidine caeci*, 'blind with excess lust [of power]' (1. 87). 'Ambition' is a key index of character for M., often applied to Caesar (see e.g. 1. 132, 163, and also *Continuation*, sigs D2ᵛ, K1ᵛ) and to other tyrannical or morally compromised figures (see e.g. 3. 255, 7. 436, 10. 50, 171, 183; *Continuation*, sigs C1ᵛ–C2ʳ, D1ᵛ). The truly virtuous are, contrastingly, free of ambition: see 2. Ded. 10n.

>   To mix your powers, and jointly th'earth possess?
>   Whilst land the sea, and air the land shall bound,
>   Whilst labouring Titan runs his glorious round,
>   And through twelve heavenly signs night follows day,[1]
> 100   No faith keep those that kingdoms jointly sway;
>   Rule brooks no sharers. Do not this believe
>   In foreign states: Rome can examples give.[2]
>   A brother's blood did our first walls distain,
>   Nor was the spacious earth and wat'ry main
> 105   This mischief's price: a refuge for thieves fled,
>   A little house this brothers' hatred bred.[3]
>   This jarring concord lasted for a space   [1. 98]
>   Dissembled 'twixt the two,[4] for Crassus was
>   The war's sole let, like that small neck of land   *hindrance*
> 110   That in the midst of two great seas does stand,
>   And will not let them join; that ta'en away,
>   Straight the Ionian meets th'Aegean Sea.[5]
>   So when war-parting Crassus, sadly slain,
>   With Roman blood did Asian Charan stain,
> 115   That Parthian loss to home-bred rage gave reins.[6]
>   More than you think you did, fierce Parthians,
>   That day: our civil war your conquest wrought,
>   And now Rome's empire by the sword is sought.[7]
>   That state, that mistress o'er the world did reign,[8]
> 120   Ruled land and sea, yet could not two contain.
>   For Julia's[(i)] death, whom cruel Fates before

---

[1] heavenly] A disyllable ('heav'nly'): see Note on Editorial Practice.

[2] foreign states … give] *nec gentibus ullis | Credite, nec longe fatorum exempla petantur*, 'don't look to other races, nor conduct a long search for instances of fate' (1. 93–94).

[3] A brother's blood…] A reference to one of Rome's foundation myths. Romulus killed his brother Remus for leaping mockingly over the city's small walls. a refuge … bred] L. refers here to the *exiguum asylum*, 'little Asylum' (1. 97), a sanctuary for outlaws supposedly founded by Romulus to grow Rome's population. As L.'s early modern editors point out, the Asylum was a temple rather than a 'small house'; in Marlowe, 'one poore churche' (*LFB*, line 97).

[4] jarring concord … Dissembled] *concordia discors*, a famous oxymoron.   Dissembled] *non sponte*, 'involuntary' (1. 99). The idea of active deception may come from F., who describes it as 'not sincere', *non sincera*.

[5] 109–12] Crassus, the third triumvir, is compared to the isthmus of Corinth keeping apart the Aegean and Ionian seas, i.e. Caesar and Pompey.

[6] Asian Charan] *Assyrias … Carras*, 'Assyrian [i.e. Parthian] Carrhae' (1. 105); cf. 1. 11–14. 'Charan' (now Harran), the modern name, is supplied by F.

[7] Rome's … is sought] *Dividitur ferro regnum*, 'the monarchy [of the triumvirs] is divided by the sword' (1. 109). See 1. 5n, 1. 95n.

[8] That state … reign] *populique potentis … | Fortuna*, 'the fortune of a powerful people' (1. 109–11); 'did reign' is M.'s idiom for *possidet*, 'owned' (1. 110).

Had slain, the pledge of their alliance bore
Down to her grave.¹ If Fate had spared her life,
Her furious husband and stern father's strife
125 She had composed, and made their armèd hands
Let fall their swords, and join in friendship's bands,
As once the Sabine women, interposed,
Their sires' and husbands' bloody jars composed.²   *strife*
    Thy death, fair Julia, breaks off all accords   [1. 119]
130 And gives them leave again to draw their swords.³
On both sides powerful emulation bears
On their ambitious spirits:⁴ great Pompey fears
That his piratic laurel should give place
To conquered France, and Caesar's deeds deface
135 His ancient triumphs;⁵ Fortune's constant grace
Makes him impatient of a second place.
Nor now can Caesar a superior brook,   *tolerate*
Nor Pompey brook a peer.⁶ Who justlier took
Up arms, great judges differ:⁷ heaven approves
140 The conquering cause, the conquered Cato loves.⁸
Nor were they equal: one in years was grown
And, long accustomed to a peaceful gown,
Had now forgot the soldier: fame he bought
By bounty to the people, and much sought
145 For popular praise; his theatre's loud shout
Was his delight;⁹ new strength he sought not out,

---

¹ Julia's death … grave] Caesar's daughter was married to Pompey in 59 BC, cementing their pact: L. often refers to Caesar as 'the father-in-law' and Pompey as 'son-in-law'. cruel Fates] *Parcarum*, the personified sister-fates. On L.'s *fatum/fata* see Introduction, p. 8 and note.
² the Sabine women … composed] Abducted by Romulus' Romans to become brides, these women interceded in the war between their new husbands and their Sabine fathers, preventing bloodshed.
³ to draw their swords] *bellum movere*, 'wage war' (1. 119).
⁴ their ambitious spirits] Not in L.; see 1. 95n.
⁵ great Pompey … ancient triumphs] Caesar's campaigns in Gaul (M.'s 'France', 1. 134) threatened to overshadow Pompey's less recent achievements.   piratic laurel] Pompey cleared the Mediterranean of Cilician pirates; 'laurel' is a victory wreath. In the Latin, 1. 132–36 directly address Pompey.
⁶ a peer] *parem*, 'an equal' (1. 125); M. elsewhere uses 'peer' in the sense of 'nobleman'.
⁷ great judges differ] *scire nefas*, 'it is unlawful to know' (1. 127). L. alludes to the problem of directly criticising Caesar's cause during his descendants' rule.
⁸ heaven … loves] *Victrix causa deis placuit sed victa Catoni*, a celebrated aphorism (1. 128). L. implies Cato's moral judgment was better than that of the gods.
⁹ his theatre's loud shout] Merely *plausu*, 'clapping' (1. 133) in L. The theatre of Pompey, Rome's first stone theatre, was dedicated in 55 BC.

      Relying on his ancient fortune's fame,
      And stood the shadow of a glorious name.
      As an old lofty oak, that heretofore
150 Great conquerors' spoils and sacred trophies bore,[1]
      Stands firm by his own weight, his root now dead,
      And through the air his naked boughs does spread,
      And with his trunk, not leaves, a shadow makes,
      He, though each blast of eastern wind him shakes
155 And round about well-rooted trees do grow,
      Is only honoured. But in Caesar now
      Remains not only a great general's name,
      But restless valour, and in war a shame
      Not to be conqueror; fierce, not curbed at all,
160 Ready to fight where hope or anger call
      His forward sword; confident of success,
      And bold the favour of the gods to press:
      O'erthrowing all that his ambition stay[2]
      And loves that ruin should enforce his way.
165 As lightning by the wind forced from a cloud
      Breaks through the wounded air with thunder loud,
      Disturbs the day, the people terrifies,
      And by a light oblique dazzles our eyes,
      Not Jove's own temple spares it;[3] when no force,
170 No bar can hinder his prevailing course,
      Great waste, as forth it sallies and retires,
      It makes and gathers his dispersèd fires.
         These causes moved the chiefs, and such as are   [1. 158]
      In mighty states the common seeds of war.[4]
175 For since our chests the conquered world hath filled[5]
      Too full, and virtue did to riches yield;
      Since spoils and warlike rapine taught us riot,   *extravagance*
      Excess in plate, in buildings' reins, the diet   *curbs*

---

[1]   Great conquerors' spoils...] *Exuvias veteris populi sacrataque* ... | *Dona ducum*, 'the relics of an ancient people and the consecrated gifts of leaders' (1. 137–38).
[2]   ambition] *summa petenti*, 'seeking the utmost' (1. 149); see 1. 95n.
[3]   Jove's own temple] *sua templa*, 'its temples' i.e. the sky (1. 145). The thunderbolt is Jupiter's weapon.
[4]   In mighty ... war] *quae populos semper mersere potentes*, 'which have always destroyed [lit. 'sunk'] mighty peoples' (1. 159). L. now introduces a new cause: Rome's imperial success and its loss of virtue as moral reason for its decline.
[5]   our chests] *opes*, 'wealth' (1. 160).

Of former times we scorn;¹ that soft attire,
180 That women were ashamed of, men desire.
Strength-breeding poverty is fled and nought
But wealth from all the spoilèd world is sought,
The bane of states;² those lands increased they hold
In th'hands of unknown tenants, which of old
185 Camillus' ploughshare wounded and the hands
Of th'ancient Curii tilled.³ The state now stands
Not as of old, when men from avarice free
Could live in peace and wished but liberty.⁴
Hence quarrels grow; what poverty esteemed
190 A vilde offence, now's greatest honour deemed   *vile*
By sword our country's power in curb to hold.⁵
Might measures right,⁶ laws and decrees are sold,
Consuls' and tribunes' jars all right suppress,
Fasces are bought,⁷ the peoples' suffrages
195 Corruptly sought and given; hence bloody jars
Oft stain elections in the field of Mars.
So griping usury grows,⁸ so faith is lost,
And civil war, as gainful, sought by most.
    By this time Caesar the cold Alps o'erpassed,⁹   [1. 183]

---

¹ Since spoils...] In L., riot = *luxus*, 'extravagance' (1. 162). Both Latin and English terms suggest a wanton, dissolute lifestyle. John Rider's *Rider's Dictionary* (London: Adam Islip, 1606), sig. Tt iiii^v, defined *luxuria* and *luxus* as 'riot, all superfluitie in carnal pleasure, ranknesse'; cf. *OED*, s.v. 2. buildings' reins] *tectisve modus*, 'curbs on buildings', i.e. architectural moderation (1. 163); the phrase is in apposition with 'the diet of former times'. Early Roman law restricted extravagance in dress, belongings and buildings. 1627 has 'reigns' here, perhaps suggesting (against the Latin) the sense of 'excess ... reigns' rather than 'in buildings' reins ... we scorn'.
² Strength-breeding poverty...] *fecunda virorum | Paupertas*, 'poverty, fertile in men' (1. 164–65). The bane of states] *Quo gens quaeque perit*, 'by which every race perishes' (1. 167).
³ Camillus ... Curii tilled] Examples of republican virtue. 'Curii' is disyllabic, following M.'s typical elision of the 'i' in final syllables: see 1. 2 and note.
⁴ The state ... liberty] *Non erat is populus, quem pax tranquilla iuvaret, | Quem sua libertas immotis pasceret armis*, 'this people was not one whom tranquil peace could help, whom their own liberty could nourish, their weapons unmoved' (1. 171–72).
⁵ in curb to hold] To dominate through constraint. Lit. *Plus patria potuisse sua*, 'to have more control than one's country' (1. 175).
⁶ Might measures right] 'Force was the measurement of law' (*mensuraque iuris | Vis erat*, 1. 175–76).
⁷ Fasces are bought] The fasces, literally a bundle of twigs held together by a red strap with an axe protruding, were a symbol of consular authority.
⁸ So griping usury grows] M. omits the second half of the line, *avidumque in tempore foenus*, 'interest greedy for its time' (1. 181).
⁹ o'erpassed] Possibly echoing Marlowe's 'overpast' (*LFB*, line 187) for L.'s *superaverat*, 'had surmounted (1. 183).

200   In his great thoughts the future war had cast,¹
      And now to Rubicon's small current come,
      He dreams the image of affrighted Rome
      With countenance sad through dusky night appears.
      On her tower-bearing head her hoary hairs
205   Hung down all torn, her arms were nak'd, when she
      Thus sighing speaks:² 'O whither carry ye
      My ensigns, soldiers? If you come as friends,
      As Roman citizens, your march here ends.'⁽ᵏ⁾
      A sudden fear straight chills the general's veins:
210   His hair's with horror raised, faintness detains
      His steps upon the bank; then thus he prays.³
      'Thou, Jove, whose eye these city walls surveys
      From thy Tarpeian hill:⁴ you deities
      Of Troy,⁵ and Romulus-hid mysteries,⁶
215   Thou Latian Jove worshipped on th'Alban mount,⁷
      You Vestal fires,⁸ and Rome, whom I account
      My greatest god, bless this attempt. Not thee
      Do I invade:⁹ conqueror by land and sea
      Thy Caesar comes, thy soldier still: be he,

---

¹ In his great thoughts ... cast] *Ingentesque animo motus, bellumque futurum | Ceperat*, 'he had conceived in his mind great rebellions and war to come' (1. 184–85). While modern commentary reads *motus* (lit. 'movements') in its political sense as 'rebellion', many early modern commentators thought it referred to motions in Caesar's mind. Cf. Marlowe: 'His mind was troubled, and he aimed at war' (*LFB*, line 188).

² her hoary hairs ... speaks] *canos effundens ... crines, | Caesarie lacera, nudisque adstare lacertis*, 'her white hair hung down in mangled locks and she stood there with naked limbs' (1. 188–89); cf. Marlowe's 'whose hoary hairs were torn | ... | and arms all naked' (*LFB*, lines 188, 191). Thus sighing speaks] *gemitu*, 'with a groan' (1. 190); cf. Marlowe's 'broken sighs' (*LFB*, line 191).

³ thus he prays] *mox ait*, 'forthwith he spoke' (1. 195).

⁴ Thou, Jove ... hill] The temple of Jupiter Optimus Maximus was built on the Tarpeian rock. M.'s '*these* city walls', not in L., gives the impression that Caesar, on the Gallic frontier, could see the walls of Rome.

⁵ deities | Of Troy] Simplifying L.'s *Phrygiique penates | Gentis Iuleae*, 'and Phrygian [i.e. Trojan] household deities of the clan of Iulus' (1. 196): Caesar's clan, the Julii, claimed descent from Iulus, son of Aeneas of Troy.

⁶ Romulus-hid mysteries] *rapti secreta Quirini*, 'mysteries of Quirinus, snatched away' (1. 197): in Roman legend Romulus vanished in a heavenly cloud and was worshipped as the god Quirinus.

⁷ Thou ... mount] Mount Alba is the location of the sanctuary of Jupiter Latiaris, the god of the league of Latin cities.

⁸ Vestal fires] Vesta was protector of the state fire: her hearth's extinction portended doom to Rome.

⁹ invade] *furialibus armis | Persequor*, 'pursue with frenzied arms' (1. 200–01).

220	He in the fault, that caused this enmity.'¹	
	Then brooking no delay, the stream shower-swelled	
	He marches o'er. So in a Libyan field	
	A lion viewing his stern foe at hand,	
	'Til he collect his ire doth doubtful stand,	*rage*
225	But straight when his tail's swinge has made him hot,	*lashing*
	And raised his shaggy mane, from his wide throat	
	He roars; then if a Mauretanian spear	
	Or shaft have pierced his side, void of all fear,	
	Regardless of that wound he rushes on.²	
230	Gently along flows ruddy Rubicon	[I. 213]
	From a small spring, when summer's in her pride,³	
	And gliding through the valley does divide	
	Gallia from Italy: now winter lent	
	Him strength, and Cynthia her full horns had spent⁴	*the moon*
235	In showers to raise his flood, and melted snow	
	The moist east wind made down the Alps to flow.	
	The horsemen first pass o'er the violent stream,	
	And take the water's fury; after them,	
	The current's violence being broke before,	
240	The footmen find the earlier passage o'er.⁵	
	But now when Caesar has o'ercome the flood,	
	And Italy's forbidden ground had trod,	

---

¹ be he ... emnity] Replicating L.'s anaphora but depersonalizing: *Ille erit ille nocens, qui me tibi fecerit hostem*, 'He, he will be the guilty one, who made me your enemy' (I. 203).
² So in a Libyan field...] *squalentibus arvis | Aestiferae Libyes*, 'in the untilled fields of scorching Libya' (I. 205–06). Mauretanian spear] *levis ... lancea Mauri*, 'the Moor's nimble lance' (I. 210). Void of all fear] Added by M. he rushes on] In L. the lion rushes 'through' or 'along' the blade or point of the spear, *per ferrum* (I. 212).
³ when summer's in her pride] *cum fervida canduit aestas*, 'when scorching summer burns' (I. 214). M. uses English poetic idiom: see e.g. Spenser, *Faerie Queene* (London: William Ponsonbie, 1590), I. i. 7. 4; Shakespeare, Sonnet 104, line 4; *Romeo and Juliet*, I. 3. 10. References to Shakespeare are to William Shakespeare, *The Complete Works: Modern Critical Edition*, ed. by Gary Taylor, John Jowett, Terri Bourus, Gabriel Egan, et al., The New Oxford Shakespeare (Oxford: Oxford University Press, 2016).
⁴ Cynthia] M. omits *tertia* [*Cynthia*], 'the *third* moon' (I. 218), probably meaning the third day of a new moon.
⁵ The horsemen ... o'er] M. has Caesar's cavalry first fording the river, then the infantry, but L. states that the horse were first placed at an angle in the river (*in obliquum opponitur amnem*) to break the force of the water (*excepturus aquas*, I. 220–21), allowing the infantry to cross (I. 221–22). M.'s version agrees with Hortensius's commentary (Basle: Henricus Petrus, 1578, col. 53 A), 'violent stream' (237), not in L., seemingly echoing Hortensius's *violentia fluminis*. Marlowe also states that the horse 'to scape the violence of the stream first waded' i.e. crossed (*LFB*, line 223; the phrasing again suggests Hortensius). In later editions M. corrected this passage: see Textual Notes.

'Here peace, and broken laws I leave', quoth he,
'Farewell all leagues: Fortune, I'll follow thee.
245 No more we'll trust:[1] war shall determine all.'
This said, by night the active general
Swifter than Parthian back-shot shaft, or stone
From Balearic slinger, marches on
T'invade Ariminum,[2] when every star
250 Fled from th'approaching sun but Lucifer,   *the morning star*
And that day dawned, that first these broils should see.
Either the moist south winds, or heaven's decree
With pitchy clouds darkened the fatal day,
When now the soldiers by command made stay
255 I'th'market place. Shrill trumpets flourished round,
And the hoarse horns wicked alarums sound.[3]
With this sad noise the people's rest was broke:
The young men rose and from the temples took
Their arms, now such as a long peace had marred,[4]
260 And their old bucklers now of leather's bared,[5]   *shields; made bare*
Their blunted piles not of a long time used
And swords with th'eatings of black rust abused.
    The Roman colours and known eagles then   *[1. 244] standards*
And Caesar in the midst high-mounted seen,
265 The townsmen's trembling joints for horror faint,
And to themselves they make this sad complaint:
'O ill-built city, too too near the Gaul,
O sadly situated place. When all
The world have peace,[6] we are the spoil of war,
270 And first that are invaded: happier far
Might we have lived in farthest north or east,
Or wand'ring tents of Scythia, than possessed
The edge of Italy.[7] This town of ours

---

[1] No more we'll trust] Renaissance editions read 'we have placed our trust in the fates' (*Credidimus fatis*, 1. 237) — which M. reads as implying Caesar no longer does. Modern editions often follow Housman's conjecture, *credidimus satis his*, 'we have placed our trust long enough *in these* [referring to *foedera*, 'leagues']'.

[2] Ariminum] The first Italian town after leaving Cisalpine Gaul.

[3] wicked] *non pia*, 'impious' (1. 238) — because in civil war.

[4] marred] L., more neutrally, has *dabat*, 'given' (1. 241).

[5] of leather's bared] *nuda iam crate*, 'with framework now exposed' (1. 241), i.e. with leather worn away. Many early modern commentators knew that Roman shields were made of leather stretched over a wooden frame. The apostrophe is M.'s.

[6] peace] *pax alta ... | Et tranquilla quies*, 'deep peace and tranquil repose' (1. 249–50).

[7] happier far | Might we have lived...] L. has them wish that *Fortune* had placed them in these far-off locations (1. 251).   farthest north] *gelida sub Arcto*, 'beneath the frozen Bear' (1. 252).   Wand'ring tents of Scythia] *errantesque domos*, 'wandering homes' (1. 253).

First felt the furious Gauls and Cimbrian powers;[1]
275 Hither the Libyans first and Germans come;[2]
This is war's way, when Fortune threatens Rome.'[3]
Thus silently they mourn and durst not lend   *dare*
Their grief a word nor tears in public spend;
As birds by winter's raging cold are stilled[4]
280 And the mid-ocean does no murmur yield.
But when bright day dissolved the damps of night,
The Fates new firebrands bring and stir to fight
Caesar's yet doubting mind, leaving no pause
To shame, but fortune finds him out a cause
285 Of arms and labours to make just his war.
The factious tribunes by the Senate are
Against their sacred privilege exiled
And by the Gracchi's[(l)] factious names reviled.[5]
These now to Caesar came, and brought along
290 With them bold Curio's[(m)] mercenary tongue,
That tongue that, once the people's, boldly stood
'Gainst armèd great ones for the public good.[6]
He, when he saw the general musing, said,[7]

[1] furious Gauls...] *Senonum motus, Cimbrumque ruentem*, 'the invasion of the Senones and onrushing Cimbrians' (1. 254); cf. Marlowe's 'the *Gaules*, and furious *Cymbrians*' (*LFB*, lines 256–57).

[2] Libyans first and Germans] *Martem Libyae, cursumque furoris | Teutonici*, 'the Libyan war-god and the charge of Teutonic frenzy' (1. 255–56). The first reference is possibly to Hannibal's crossing the Alps (218 BC), although it was his brother Hasdrubal who invaded Italy via this route from Gaul in 208 BC. It is unclear what L.'s mention of Germanic fury refers to.

[3] war's way] 'way' here means 'route' (*iter*, 1. 257).

[4] winter's raging cold] *bruma* ('winter', 1. 259); cf. 'winter's rage' (Marlowe, *LFB*, line 261).

[5] The factious tribunes...] In 49 BC the Senate expelled the tribunes of the plebs, Q. Cassius Longinus and Marcus Antonius, exposing the class divisions in the civil war (cf. 1. 193): they immediately fled to Caesar. M.'s choices are noteworthy. He translates *discordes* ('turbulent', 1. 266) as 'factious', adding the same epithet (not in L.) to 'the Gracchi', the famous champions of Roman plebeian interests. He omits L.'s *minax*, 'threatening', of the Senate (1. 267), and the lack of resolve of the 'wavering city' (*ancipiti urbe*, 1. 266). M.'s 'violated their sacred privilege' translates F.'s gloss, 'the violation of the sacrosanct right of tribunician authority' (*violato Tribuniciae potestatis sacrosancto iure*), for L.'s *Victo iure*, 'overturned right' (1. 267).

[6] bold Curio's...] G. Scribonius Curio, tribune of the plebs in 50 BC, who later became a prominent Caesarian; cf. 4. 643 ff.   boldly stood ... public good] *libertatemque tueri | Ausus, & armatos plebi miscere potentes*, 'who dared to protect liberty and level the militarily powerful with the plebs' (1. 270–71).

[7] He ... said] There now follows in close succession three set-piece speeches, by Curio (1. 294–313), Caesar (1. 321–78) and the centurion Laelius (1. 387–415). Collectively these, and the imagined responses to them, set out L.'s view both of Caesar's cause and of his and his soldiers' motivations.

'While this my voice, Caesar, thy cause would aid,
295 We did prorogue, though 'gainst the Senate's will,
Thy government, while oratory's skill
Could turn the wav'ring people's hearts to thee.¹
But since by war's rough hand laws silenced be,²
We are exiled, and gladly it sustain³
300 To be endenized by thy sword again.   *made a citizen, enfranchised*
Whilst their yet strengthless side is only scared,⁴
Use no delay: delay hurts men prepared.
A greater price on equal danger here
Is set.⁵ In Gallia's war alone ten year
305 Thou hast consumed: but here, one field well fought,
Rome has the world to thy subjection brought.
Now thy return from France with victory
No pompous triumph waits; no bays for thee   *laurel wreath*
Shall deck the Capitol; base Envy's hands
310 Keep back thy due.⁶ Conquest of warlike lands
Is made a crime in thee, and Pompey's pride
Excludes thy rule.⁷ Nor can'st thou now divide
The world; the world thou may possess alone.'
This speech gave fire to Caesar, too too prone
315 Before to war;⁸ so peoples' shouts raise more
A fierce Olympic steed striving before

---

¹ We did prorogue...] *traximus imperium*, 'I extended your command' (1. 275), i.e. Caesar's authority as proconsular commander in Gaul, carrying the right to command legions. 'Prorogue' comes from F.'s *prorogaretur*.   wav'ring people's hearts] In L. *dubios Quirites*, 'uncertain citizens' (1. 276). M. also omits Curio's *tunc, cum mihi Rostra tenere | Ius erat*, 'while I had the right of occupying the Rostrum' (the place from which tribunes spoke in the Forum), 1. 275–76.
² rough hand] Added by M.
³ gladly it sustain] 'it' means exile, *Exilium* (1. 279).
⁴ scared] The modern pronunciation agrees more with 'prepared' in the next line, but the original spelling in 1627 is 'scarred', a variant found in other early modern texts (see *OED*, 'scare, v.', 1.a.β), and certainly pronounced to rhyme with 'hard' elsewhere in M.'s text: see e.g. 1. 715, 9. 831. It may be that M.'s intended pronunciation varies depending on context.
⁵ A greater price ... Is set] Caesar faces the same dangers as in his Gallic campaigns, but for far greater rewards (rule of Rome). 'Danger' translates *labor atque metus*, 'toil and fear' (1. 282).
⁶ base Envy's hands ... thy due] *Livor edax*, 'ravenous envy' (1. 288); 'due' translates *cuncta*, 'everything'.
⁷ Pompey's pride | Excludes thy rule] L.'s Curio, not mentioning pride, emphasises family impiety: *socerum depellere regno | Decretum genero est*, 'the son-in-law has determined to drive off the father-in-law from the monarchy' (1. 289–90). See 1. 5n.
⁸ gave fire to Caesar] *tantum tamen addidit irae*, 'yet it greatly enhanced his rage' (1. 292).

       To force the lists, and break th'opposing bars.¹
       Straight to the standard all his soldiers
       Caesar assembling, 'midst their murmuring noise
320 Commands a silence with his hand and voice.
          'Fellows in arms, that have endured with me   [1. 299]
       A thousand dangers, now the tenth year free,²
       Have our spent bloods in northern climes deserved   *climates*
       This, all our wounds, so many winters served
325 Under the Alps?³ Not more provision Rome
       Would make for war, if Hannibal had come
       Over the Alps:⁴ cohorts they reinforce,
       Forests are felled for shipping, all the force
       Of land and sea is armed 'gainst Caesar now.⁵
330 What more (had we been vanquished) would they do
       If the fierce Gauls our flying backs pursued,
       That dare now wrong us when our wars conclude
       Successfully, and friendly gods us call?⁶
       Let the long peace-enfeebled general
335 His gowns and new-raised soldiers bring along;⁷
       Vain names the Catos, and Marcellus' tongue.⁸

---

¹ A fierce Olympic steed ... bars] L.'s simile describes an *Eleus sonipes*, 'thunder-footed steed of Elis [a city near Olympia]', thrusting against the doors of its 'enclosed prison' (*carcere clauso*) and loosening its bars before a race (1. 294). M.'s translation, however, evokes a horse trying to enter the 'lists', the space marked out for a tournament or joust (*OED*, s.v. 3.9a.). M. reuses lines 315–16 in book two of *The Victorious Reign of Edward III* (London: John Beale for T. Walkley and B. Fisher, 1635), sig. D2ᵛ, describing the disaffected Robert of Artois inciting the English king to war, and going on to compare Artois explicitly to Curio.

² now the tenth year free] *decimo iam vincitis anno*, 'now you are victors in the tenth year' (1. 300), i.e. of Caesar's Gallic command. See Textual Notes.

³ Under the Alps?] M. omits Caesar's mention of *mortes*, 'deaths' (of soldiers during the campaign, 1. 302).

⁴ Not more provision...] *Non secus ingenti bellorum Roma tumultu | Concutitur*, 'Not otherwise is Rome shaken by the vast tumult of wars, [than if Hannibal...]', 1. 303–04; cf. 1. 32–33.

⁵ is armed 'gainst Caesar now] *Iussus Caesar agi*, 'Caesar is ordered to be routed' (1. 307).

⁶ friendly gods us call] Omitting *ad summa*, '[call] to the highest matters' (1. 310), i.e. (implicitly) dominance of Rome.

⁷ His gowns] *partesque ... togatae*, 'togaed faction' (1. 312), an allusion to the Senate's support for Pompey. The Roman toga, habitually translated by M. as 'gown', symbolises senatorial government but also the arts of peace (hence in this line paired with 'new-raised soldiers'); cf. 1. 142.

⁸ Vain names...] A line governed by the verb in lines 334–35, 'let him ... bring along'. An awkward translation of *Marcellusque loquax, & nomina vana Catones*, 'babbling Marcellus and those empty names, the Catos' (1. 313) — probably meaning the consul of 49 BC, C. Claudius Marcellus, and the reputation of both Cato and his ancestor, Cato the Elder, for stern republican virtue.

>   Must he with foreign and bought clients be
>   Glutted with still-continuing sovereignty?¹
>   Can he triumphant chariots mount before
> 340 The years appointed,⁽ⁿ⁾ and let go no more
>   Honours usurped?⁽ᵒ⁾ Why should I now complain
>   Of the law's breach,² and famine⁽ᵖ⁾ made for gain?
>   Th'affrighted forum⁽ᵠ⁾ with armed men beset,
>   Drawn swords environing the judgement seat,
> 345 When 'gainst all law Milo, for murder tried,
>   Pompey's proud colours closed on every side?³   *standards*
>   Now lest his age, though tired, a private state
>   Should end, by impious civil war his hate
>   He seeks to glut, scorning but to excel
> 350 His master Sulla's guilt.⁴ As tigers fell   *savage*
>   Whom their fierce dam with slaughtered cattle's blood
>   Was wont to nourish in th'Hyrcanian wood,
>   Ne'er lose their fury: so thou, Pompey, used
>   To lick the blood that Sulla's swords diffused,
> 355 Retain'st thy former thirst; never again
>   Grow those jaws pure, that blood did once distain.   *defile*
>   When wilt thou end thy too long tyranny,⁵
>   Where bound thy guilt?⁽ʳ⁾⁶ In this at least to thee
>   A pattern let thy master Sulla be,
> 360 To leave off such usurpèd sovereignty.⁷
>   After the pirates,⁸ and tired Pontic king
>   Whose war to end scarce poison's⁽ˢ⁾ help could bring,⁹

---

¹ sovereignty] *regno*, 'monarchy'; cf. 1.5n, 2. 340n, 5. 295–96n. 'Sovereignty' is almost always trisyllabic in M.'s translation.

² Of the law's breach] *iura ... totum suppressa per orbem*, 'laws suppressed throughout the whole world' (1. 318).

³ Milo, for murder tried...] Titus Annius Milo was tried for the murder of Clodius Pulcher in 52 BC: in response to unrest on the first day of the trial, Pompey illegally placed an armed guard in the forum, a tactic that prevented Cicero from delivering his speech in defence. L. does not mention Milo explicitly (M. relies on F.); cf. 2. 511.

⁴ by impious civil war... guilt] *Bella nefanda parat suetus civilibus armis*, 'accustomed to civil strife, he prepares impious wars' (1. 325). Pompey was the son-in-law and protégé of Sulla. L. frequently draws attention to their close relationship.

⁵ too long tyranny] *tam longa potentia*, 'power of such long duration' (1. 333).

⁶ thy guilt] *scelerum*, 'crimes' (1. 334).

⁷ Caesar 'reminds' Pompey that Sulla relinquished his role as Dictator, retiring in 80 BC to Puteoli to spend his last years as a private citizen. M. redeploys the charge of usurped sovereignty against Caesar before his own assassination in the *Continuation*, sig. K1ʳ.

⁸ the pirates] See 1. 135n.

⁹ king ... could bring] Mithridates VI of Pontus.

Must Caesar's fall Pompey's last triumph make
Because, commanded, I did not forsake
365 My conquering army?¹ But if I be barred
My labour's meed, let these have the reward   *recompense*
Of their long service; let these soldiers all
Triumph, though under any general.
Where shall their bloodless age after the war
370 Find rest? What lands shall my old soldiers share?
Where shall they plough? Where shall their city stand?
Are pirates,⁽ᵗ⁾ Pompey, worthier of land?²
March on victorious colours, march away:
The strength that we have made we must employ.
375 He gives the strongest all things, that denies
His due; nor want we aiding deities,
Nor spoil these arms do seek, nor sovereignty;
But to free Rome, though bent to slavery.'
 Thus spake he: the yet doubting soldiers   [1. 352]
380 Uncertain murmurs raise. Though fierce with war's
Long use, their household gods their minds 'gan move,   *began to*
And piety; but straight the sword's dire love
And fear of Caesar turned them back again.
Laelius the first file's leading did obtain,³
385 For saving of a Roman soldier
Oak-crowned, and freed from duties of the war.⁴
'If I may speak, Rome's greatest general,
Thy soldiers' thoughts', quoth he, 'it grieves us all
That such long patience kept thee from so just
390 A war:⁵ or didst thou not thine army trust?
While life-blood keeps this breathing body warm,

---

¹ Must Caesar's fall...] *Vltima Pompeio dabitur provincia Caesar*, 'must Caesar be given to Pompey as his last province?' (1. 338). Provincial governorships were typically given to Roman politicians after holding the consulship, although this practice had been overturned during the triumvirate.   forsake ... army] Lit. *victrices aquilas deponere*, 'lay aside my conquering eagles' (1. 349).

² pirates ... land?] See 1. 135n.

³ the first file's leading] i.e. Laelius is the leading centurion of a legion, holding 'the offices of the *Primipilus*' (*summi ... munera pili*, 1. 356): he seems to be L.'s invention.

⁴ For saving ... war] M. (mis)reads *emeritique gerens insignia doni*, 'bearing the badge of a thoroughly deserved award' (1. 257) as referring to the *stipendium emeritum* received by legionaries discharged honourably from service, probably by looking up *emeritus* in a standard Latin lexicon. In fact L. means the 'civic crown', made of oak leaves, which soldiers like Laelius received for saving a citizen's life in battle (*Servati civis*, 1. 358). F. has the correct interpretation.

⁵ kept thee from so just | A war] *tuas tenuit ... vires*, 'restrained your strength' (1. 361).

64 THOMAS MAY

While brandished darts fly from this agile arm,[1]
Wilt thou weak gowns and Senate's reign endure?[2]
In civil war is conquest so impure?
395 Lead us through Libya's gulfs, cold Scythian land,
Lead us o'er thirsty Afric's scorchèd sand. *Africa's*
This arm the conquered world behind to leave[3]
Has ploughed the British ocean's curlèd wave[4]
And broke the Rhine's swift current; thy command
400 To do, my will's as steady as my hand.[5]
He's not my friend,[6] 'gainst whom thy trumpets sound.
By these thy colours, which ten camps have found[7]
Ever victorious, Caesar, here I swear,
And by thy triumphs o'er what foe soe'er:
405 If thou command me spill my brother's life,
Kill my old father, or my pregnant wife,[8]
I'll do't, though with a most unwilling hand;
Fire temples, rob the gods at thy command,
Great Juno's temple in our flames shall sink;[9]
410 If to encamp on Tuscan Tiber's brink,
I'll boldly pitch in Italy thy tent.
If to dismantle towns be thy intent,
These arms of mine the battering ram shall place,[10]
Although the city thou wouldst quite deface
415 Were Rome itself.' The soldiers all agree,

---

[1] darts] *pila*: see 1. 7n.
[2] weak gowns and Senate's reign] 'The degenerate toga' (*Degenerem ... togam*, 1. 365). Laelius could mean Caesar surrendering his military command and becoming a civilian, but M. follows commentators like F. in supposing he refers derisively to Caesar's senatorial opponents; cf. 1. 335n. reign] *regnum*, 'kingdom, monarchy'; cf. 1. 5n.
[3] to leave] i.e. to leave the world conquered behind them.
[4] the British ocean's curlèd wave] 'the ocean's swelling wave' (*Oceani tumidas ... undas*, 1. 370); M. echoes F. in identifying a reference to Caesar's British campaign of 54 BC.
[5] thy command | To do...] *Iussa sequi tam posse mihi, quam velle necesse est*, 'I must be able as much as want to follow your orders' (1. 372).
[6] my friend] 'my fellow citizen' (*civis meus*, 1. 373).
[7] ten camps] One for each of Caesar's ten years of Gallic campaigning.
[8] If thou command me ...] Lit. 'if you order me to plunge my sword [*gladius*, the short sword of a legionary] into my brother's chest, my father's throat or wife's pregnant stomach' (*Pectore si fratris gladium, iugulo parentis | Condere me iubeas, plenaeque in viscera partu | Coniugis...*, 1. 377-79).
[9] Great Juno's temple] M. reads L.'s *numina ... Monetae* (1. 381) as referring to the temple of Juno Moneta on the Capitol, the home of the Roman state mint.
[10] If to dismantle towns...] 'to overthrow and level whatever walls you please' (*quoscumque voles in planum effundere muros*, 1. 384).   shall place] 'scatter the stones asunder' (*disperget saxa*, 1. 384).

	And promise him their lifted hands on high	
	To any war. Their shout not that can pass,	
	Which the loud blast of Thracian Boreas	*north wind*
	On piny Ossa makes, and bows amain	*vehemently*
420	The rattling wood, or lets it rise again.¹	
	Caesar, perceiving that the Fates gave way	[1. 392]²
	To war, and his men prone, fearing delay,³	
	His troops through France dispersed straight calling home,	
	With flying colours marches on to Rome.	
425	They leave their tents pitched by Lemanus' lake,⁽ᵛ⁾	
	And those on Vogesus' high rocks forsake,⁴	
	Which awed the painted Lingones so strong.	
	Isara's fords they leave that run so long	
	Alone, but in a river of more fame	
430	Falling to the ocean bears another name.⁵	
	The yellow Ruthens eased of their long fear,	*are eased*
	Mild Atax joys no Roman ships to bear,	
	And Varus, Italy's increasèd bound.⁶	
	That haven, Alcides' consecrated ground,	
435	With cliffs o'erlooks the sea; no north-west wind	
	Nor west blow there; Circius their proper wind	*north-north-west wind*
	Reigns there, where safe Alcides' fort does stand.⁷	*Hercules'*
	And that still doubtful coast, that sea and land	

---

¹ Their shout...] i.e. their shout is as loud as that sound made by the north wind. and bows ... again] 'a sound arises from the forest being pushed down, the trunks bending, or from when it [the forest] springs back into the air' (*curvato robore pressae | Fit sonus, aut rursus redeuntis in aethera sylvae*, I. 391–92).

² l. 421–96] A catalogue of the tribes and regions abandoned by the troops following Caesar to war.

³ his men prone] i.e. were eager for war, a literal translation of *tam prono milite* (I. 393). fearing delay] 'lest he should delay Fortune through any slackness' (*ne quo languore moretur | Fortunam*, I. 393–94).

⁴ rocks] Reading *rupem*, 'crag': modern editions print *ripam*, 'shore' (I. 397).

⁵ Isara's fords...] M.'s verbs are confusing here: 'run' (l. 428) refers to the river Isara's 'fords' (lit. *vada*, 'shallows'), 'bears' (l. 430) to the river Isara. The river 'of more fame' (l. 429) is the Rhône. There is one extra syllable in this line; although M. does not signal it, 'the ocean' is probably elided.

⁶ The yellow Ruthens ... increasèd bound] The Ruteni (M.'s 'Ruthens') were a Gallic tribe in the south of the Massif Central; M.'s 'long fear' paraphrases *longa statione*, the 'long-standing garrison' of the Romans (I. 402). 'Yellow' here refers to hair-colour. The Atax and the Varus (which divided Italy from Gaul) are rivers.

⁷ That haven ... does stand] Herculis Monoeci Portus (modern Monaco) on the Gallic coast, a city supposedly founded by Hercules; 'haven' is monosyllabic. l. 435–36 paraphrase *solus sua litora turbat | Circius, & tuta prohibet statione Monoeci*, 'Circius [the local wind] alone disorders its shores and keeps the garrison of Monoecus safe' (I. 407–08).

  Challenge by turns: firm land it is when low
440 The ocean ebbs, but sea at every flow.¹
  Whether the wind strong blowing from the Pole²
  And then retiring, to and fro do roll
  The sea, or that the moon his course do guide,³
  Or burning Titan moist food to provide,   *sun*
445 Attracting lift the ocean to the sky,
  Seek you that labour for such a skill:⁴ for me,
  Whate'er thou be that cause this ebb and flow,
  Be still concealed, since heaven will have it so.⁵
  They march away that Nemasus did hold,⁶
450 And Adour's banks, where Tarbe does enfold
  In her crook'd shore the sea that gently flows.⁷
  The Santoni rejoice now freed from foes:
  The Leuci and Rhemi, archers good; with these
  Th'Bituriges, and spear-armed Suessones,
455 The dwellers near Sequana, skilful riders;⁸
  The Belgae, hook-armed chariots' expert guiders;⁹
  Sprung from the Trojan blood the Hedui
  That durst claim brotherhood of Italy,¹⁰   *dare to*
  Rebellious Nervians⁽ˣ⁾ stained with Cotta's fate,¹¹
460 And they that in loose mantles imitate
  Sarmatia, fierce Batavians whom to war

---

¹ at every flow] i.e. at high tide; L. goes on to discuss the origins of tides.
² from the Pole] *ab extremo … axe*, 'from the farthest axis' (1. 412); M. assumes, with F., the Pole star (Polaris).
³ his course] The sea's.
⁴ that labour … skill] *quos agitat mundi labor*, 'who are stirred up by the universe's toil' (1. 417): i.e. natural philosophers.
⁵ heaven] 'the gods' (*superi*, 1. 419).
⁶ Nemasus] See Textual Notes.
⁷ Adour's … flows] M. uses the modern French name, following F. in identifying L.'s *Aturi* with the river Adour (in Aquitaine), and *Tarbellicus* with 'Tarbe', a nearby town in the Pyrenees. L. now catalogues various tribes: see Glossary, s.v. 'Gaul'.
⁸ skilful riders] L. describes an ability to turn horses *in gyrum*, 'in a tight circle' (1. 425).
⁹ hook-armed chariots] Reading *rostrati … covinni* (1. 426, F.'s choice, following Grotius). Many early modern texts also had the now preferred *monstrati … covinni*, 'chariot … demonstrated [to the Belgae]', i.e. the Belgae had acquired the skill from someone else such as the Britons, as in Marlowe's 'The *Belgians* apt to govern *British* cars' (*LFB*, line 427).
¹⁰ Sprung from … Italy] 'Arvernian tribes who dared to feign themselves brothers of Rome by blood-descent from Troy' (*Arvernique ausi Latio se fingere fratres, | Sanguine ab Iliaco populi*, 1. 427–28). Early modern commentators pointed out that it was the Hedui, a neighbouring tribe, who made this claim: M. 'corrects' L. 'Hedui' is disyllabic.
¹¹ stained with Cotta's fate] The Nervii took part in the 54 BC uprising led by Ambiorix, during which Caesar's general Aurunculeius Cotta was ambushed and killed.

Crook'd trumpets call, those that near Cinga are,[1]
Where Araris, with Rhodanus now met,   *Rhône*
Runs joined into the sea, the men whose seat
465 Is on Gebenna mount covered with snow.
The Pictones now free their fields can plough,
The fickle Turones are not restrained
By garrison, the Andian now disdained
To pine in Medua's thick fogs, but goes
470 For pleasure where delightful Liger flows.
Fair Genabos is freed from garrison,[2]
Trever is glad the war from thence is gone,
The Ligures, now shorn, once like the rest
Long-haired, of all the unshorn Gauls the best;[3]
475 And where with off'rings stained of human blood
Hermes and Mars their cruel altars stood,
And Jove's, that vile as Scythian Dian's are.[4]
Then you, that valiant souls and slain in war[5]
Do celebrate with praise that never dies,
480 The Bards, securely sung your elegies.[6]
You Druids, now freed from war, maintain
Your barbarous rites and sacrifice again:[7]
You what heaven is, and gods, alone can tell,
Or else alone are ignorant; you dwell
485 In vast and desert woods,[8] you teach no spirit
Pluto's pale kingdom can by death inherit;[9]

---

[1] near Cinga are] In L. this clause and the next refer to different places, something M.'s syntax obscures.
[2] 467-71] These lines (1. 436-40) are now considered spurious. Although known to certain scholars, they did not appear in most sixteenth-century editions; but Grotius, followed by F., believed them genuine: see *M. Annei Lucani Pharsalia ... ex emendatione H. Grotii, cum eiusdem ad loca insigniora notis* (Leiden: ex officina Plantiniana Raphelengii, 1614), ad loc.
[3] now shorn ... unshorn] L. puns on hairstyle, in a play on Romanized Gaul (*Gallia Togata* — Cisalpine Gaul) and 'Long-haired' (i.e. unconquered) Gaul, *Gallia Comata*.
[4] Hermes ... Dian's are] M., like Marlowe and Gorges, follows a common gloss, translating L.'s *Teutates*, *Hesus* and *Taranis* (Gallic deities) with the names of the Roman gods Mercury, Mars and Jupiter. Scythian Diana was worshipped with human sacrifice, hence M.'s 'vile' (*non mitior*, 'not more gentle [than Diana's altars]', 1. 446); cf. 3. 91–92, 6. 81–82.
[5] valiant souls and slain in war] Cf. Marlowe's 'valiant souls slain in your wars' (*LFB*, line 444, for *fortes animas, belloque peremptas*, 1. 447).
[6] elegies] Merely *carmina*, 'poems, songs' in L., 1. 449.
[7] barbarous] The pronunciation of 'barbarous' is probably disyllabic, eliding the middle 'a', and so throughout.
[8] desert woods] 'deep woods, in groves far from the light of day' (*nemora alta, |... remotis lucis*, 1. 452–53).
[9] Pluto's ... inherit] Omitting *tacitas Erebi sedes*, 'the silent seat of Erebus [the underworld]'; 'inherit' is M.'s idiom for *petunt*, 'seek' (1. 456).

68   Thomas May

They in another world inform again.   *take form*
Death long life's middle is (if you maintain
The truth): the Northern people happy are[1]
490   In this their error, whom fear greatest far
Of all fears injures not, the fear of death.
Thence are they prone to war, nor loss of breath
Esteem,[2] nor spare a life that comes again.
They that the hairèd Cayci did contain
495   In their obedience,[3] marching now to Rome
From Rhine's rude banks and new-found country come.[4]
    When Caesar's now collected strength had bred   [1. 466][5]
More lofty hopes, through Italy he spread
His troops, and all the neighbouring cities seized.[6]
500   Then idle rumours their true fears increased,
And pierced the people's hearts; swift fame 'gan show   *began to*
The war's approach and their ensuing woe.
Then every tongue a false alarum yields:
Some dare report that on the pasture fields
505   Of fair Mevania is the war begun,
And bloody Caesar's barbarous cohorts run[7]
Where Umbrian Nar does into Tiber flow;
That all his eagles and joined standards now
With a vast strength make furious approach.[8]
510   Nor do they now suppose him to be such,
As once they saw him; fiercer far than so
They think, and savage as his conquered foe;
That all the inhabitants 'twixt th'Alps and Rhine,
Drawn from their countries and cold northern clime,

---

[1] happy are] See Textual Notes.
[2] nor ... Esteem] M.'s idiom for *animaeque capaces | Mortis* ('minds ready for death', I. 461–62).
[3] contain | In their obedience] Reading *bellis arcere* (1. 463), 'to keep from war'; modern editions accept Bentley's emendation *Belgis arcere*, 'to keep from the Belgae'.
[4] and new-found country come] Blunting L.'s charge of betraying Rome's imperial mission: *Deseritis ... apertum gentibus orbem*, 'you abandon a world [now] open to all peoples' (1. 465).
[5] 497–740] Caesar's invasion of Italy and the panic, prodigies and doom-laden prophecies that result.
[6] neighbouring] Probably pronounced disyllabically.
[7] bloody ... cohorts] In L. Caesar is 'savage, cruel' (*saevi*), and the 'cohorts' are divisions of cavalry (*alas*, 1. 476).
[8] With a vast ... approach] *Agmine non uno, densisque incedere castris*, 'he was coming with no single column, and with densely packed encampments' (1. 478). 'Furious' is, unusually, trisyllabic.

515 Follow, and Rome (a Roman looking on)
By barbarous hands shall fall. Thus every one
By fear gives strength to fame; no author known,
They fear what they suppose.¹ But not alone
The people does this vain surmise deceive.
520 The Senate shakes; the affrighted Fathers leave
Their seats, and flying to the consuls give
Directions for the war;² where safe to live,
What place t'avoid, they know not; whither ere   *sooner*
Their sudden wits directs their steps, they bear
525 Th'amazèd people forth in troops, whom nought
So long had stirred.³ A man would then have thought
The city fired,⁴ or th'houses' sudden fall
By earthquake threatened; the mad people all
With hasty steps so unadvisèd run,
530 As if no way at all were left to shun
Their imminent and feared destruction
But to forsake their habitation.⁵
As when rough seas, by stormy Auster blown   *south wind*
From Libya's sands, have broke the main-mast down,⁶
535 Master and mariners their ship forsake
Not torn as yet, leap into th'sea, and make
Themselves a shipwreck: so from th'city they
Fly into war.⁷ No sire his son can stay,⁸
No weeping wife her husband can persuade,
540 No nor their household gods, 'til they have made

---

¹   no author known ... suppose] L., more clearly, has *nulloque auctore malorum | Quae finxere, timent*, 'with no author of these evils, they fear what they have fabricated' (1. 485-86).

²   affrighted Fathers...] Roman senators were called 'conscript Fathers', *patres conscripti*. L. has them fleeing the *curia*, 'Senate-house', as well as their seats (1. 487).   Directions for the war] *invisaque ... decreta*, 'hated decrees' (1. 488-89); i.e. the *senatus consultum ultimum*, the declaration of a state of emergency.

³   whither ... had stirred] 'the momentum of their flight [propels them]' (*fugae ... impetus*, 1. 491) '[...] and the columns, clinging together in a long line, burst forth [from the city]' (*serieque haerentia longa | Agmina prorumpunt*, 1. 492-93).

⁴   The city fired] *credas tecta nefandas | Corripuisse faces*, 'you would think that execrable torches had seized hold of the houses' (1. 493-94).

⁵   As if ... habitation] *velut, unica rebus | Spes foret afflictis patrios excedere muros*, 'as if the only hope in such affliction were to abandon their ancestral walls' (1. 496-97).

⁶   have broke ... down] Paraphrasing *Fractaque veliferi sonuerunt pondera mali*, 'and the broken weight of the sail-bearing mast has groaned' (1. 500).

⁷   they | Fly into war] i.e. 'they *flee* into war' (*In bellum fugitur*, 1. 504).

⁸   sire] *languidus aevo | ... parens*, 'father faint with age' (1. 504-05).

Vows for their safety; none an eye dares cast
Back on loved Rome, although perhaps his last.[1]
Irrevocably do the people fly.[2]
   You gods that easily give prosperity, [1. 510]
545 But not maintain it:[3] that great city, filled
With native souls and conquered, that would yield
Mankind a dwelling, is abandoned now
An easy prey to Caesar.[4] When a foe
Begirts our soldiers in a foreign land,
550 The little trench night's danger can withstand,
And sudden work raised out of earth endures
The foe's assault, the encampèd's sleep secures.[5]
Thou Rome, a war but noised, art left by all,
Not one night's safety trusted to thy wall.
555 But pardon their amaze: when Pompey flies
'Tis time to fear. Then lest their hearts should rise
With hope of future good,[6] sad augury bodes
A worse ensuing fate: the threat'ning gods
Fill heaven and earth and sea with prodigies.
560 Unheard-of stars by night adorn the skies, [1. 526][7]
Heaven seems to flame, and through the welkin fire   sky
Obliquely flies;[8] state-changing comets dire
Display to us their blood-portending hair,[9]
Deceitful lightnings flash in clearest air.
565 Strange formèd meteors the thick air had bred

---

[1] none an eye ... his last] Omitting *nec limine quisquam | Haesit*, 'nor did anyone pause on their threshold' (1. 507–08).

[2] the people] *vulgus*, 'the mob' (1. 509).

[3] You gods ...] M. was fond of this aphorism about the mutability of providential favour; cf. *Continuation*, sig. J6ᵛ, and (with a slightly different translation) *The History of the Parliament*, p. 4, describing the happy state of England at James I's accession. M.'s 'maintain', rendering L.'s *tueri*, 'preserve, keep safe' (1. 510), may owe something to the Machiavellian idea of *mantenere lo stato*.

[4] is abandoned now...] M. omits *Ignavae ... manus*, 'cowardly bands [abandon Rome]' (1. 514).

[5] the encampèd's sleep] i.e. the sleep of those who are encamped.

[6] hearts] *trepidas mentes*, 'fearful minds' (1. 523).

[7] 516–89 A catalogue of prodigies foretelling the disaster of civil war — and (from L.'s perspective) of Caesar's victory.

[8] fire | Obliquely flies] Probably meteors, a meaning somewhat blurred by M.'s singular 'fire' for L.'s *faces*, 'firebrands' (1. 528).

[9] state-changing comets...] *terris mutantem regna cometen*, 'the comet that brings change to earthly monarchies' (1. 529). blood-portending hair] *crinemque timendi sideris*, 'hair of a star to be feared' (1. 529); M. and L. play on Greek *komētēs*, 'long-haired'. 'To us' is not in L.

	And promise him their lifted hands on high	
	To any war. Their shout not that can pass,	
	Which the loud blast of Thracian Boreas	*north wind*
	On piny Ossa makes, and bows amain	*vehemently*
420	The rattling wood, or lets it rise again.[1]	
	Caesar, perceiving that the Fates gave way	[1. 392][2]
	To war, and his men prone, fearing delay,[3]	
	His troops through France dispersed straight calling home,	
	With flying colours marches on to Rome.	
425	They leave their tents pitched by Lemanus' lake,(v)	
	And those on Vogesus' high rocks forsake,[4]	
	Which awed the painted Lingones so strong.	
	Isara's fords they leave that run so long	
	Alone, but in a river of more fame	
430	Falling to the ocean bears another name.[5]	
	The yellow Ruthens eased of their long fear,	*are eased*
	Mild Atax joys no Roman ships to bear,	
	And Varus, Italy's increasèd bound.[6]	
	That haven, Alcides' consecrated ground,	
435	With cliffs o'erlooks the sea; no north-west wind	
	Nor west blow there; Circius their proper wind	*north-north-west wind*
	Reigns there, where safe Alcides' fort does stand.[7]	*Hercules'*
	And that still doubtful coast, that sea and land	

---

[1] Their shout...] i.e. their shout is as loud as that sound made by the north wind. and bows ... again] 'a sound arises from the forest being pushed down, the trunks bending, or from when it [the forest] springs back into the air' (*curvato robore pressae | Fit sonus, aut rursus redeuntis in aethera sylvae*, 1. 391–92).

[2] l. 421–96] A catalogue of the tribes and regions abandoned by the troops following Caesar to war.

[3] his men prone] i.e. were eager for war, a literal translation of *tam prono milite* (1. 393). fearing delay] 'lest he should delay Fortune through any slackness' (*ne quo languore moretur | Fortunam*, 1. 393–94).

[4] rocks] Reading *rupem*, 'crag': modern editions print *ripam*, 'shore' (1. 397).

[5] Isara's fords...] M.'s verbs are confusing here: 'run' (l. 428) refers to the river Isara's 'fords' (lit. *vada*, 'shallows'), 'bears' (l. 430) to the river Isara. The river 'of more fame' (l. 429) is the Rhône. There is one extra syllable in this line; although M. does not signal it, 'the ocean' is probably elided.

[6] The yellow Ruthens ... increasèd bound] The Ruteni (M.'s 'Ruthens') were a Gallic tribe in the south of the Massif Central; M.'s 'long fear' paraphrases *longa statione*, the 'long-standing garrison' of the Romans (1. 402). 'Yellow' here refers to hair-colour. The Atax and the Varus (which divided Italy from Gaul) are rivers.

[7] That haven ... does stand] Herculis Monoeci Portus (modern Monaco) on the Gallic coast, a city supposedly founded by Hercules; 'haven' is monosyllabic. 1. 435–36 paraphrase *solus sua litora turbat | Circius, & tuta prohibet statione Monoeci*, 'Circius [the local wind] alone disorders its shores and keeps the garrison of Monoecus safe' (1. 407–08).

       Challenge by turns: firm land it is when low
440 The ocean ebbs, but sea at every flow.¹
       Whether the wind strong blowing from the Pole²
       And then retiring, to and fro do roll
       The sea, or that the moon his course do guide,³
       Or burning Titan moist food to provide,   *sun*
445 Attracting lift the ocean to the sky,
       Seek you that labour for such a skill:⁴ for me,
       Whate'er thou be that cause this ebb and flow,
       Be still concealed, since heaven will have it so.⁵
       They march away that Nemasus did hold,⁶
450 And Adour's banks, where Tarbe does enfold
       In her crook'd shore the sea that gently flows.⁷
       The Santoni rejoice now freed from foes:
       The Leuci and Rhemi, archers good; with these
       Th'Bituriges, and spear-armed Suessones,
455 The dwellers near Sequana, skilful riders;⁸
       The Belgae, hook-armed chariots' expert guiders;⁹
       Sprung from the Trojan blood the Hedui
       That durst claim brotherhood of Italy,¹⁰   *dare to*
       Rebellious Nervians⁽ˣ⁾ stained with Cotta's fate,¹¹
460 And they that in loose mantles imitate
       Sarmatia, fierce Batavians whom to war

---

¹ at every flow] i.e. at high tide; L. goes on to discuss the origins of tides.
² from the Pole] *ab extremo ... axe*, 'from the farthest axis' (1. 412); M. assumes, with F., the Pole star (Polaris).
³ his course] The sea's.
⁴ that labour ... skill] *quos agitat mundi labor*, 'who are stirred up by the universe's toil' (1. 417): i.e. natural philosophers.
⁵ heaven] 'the gods' (*superi*, 1. 419).
⁶ Nemasus] See Textual Notes.
⁷ Adour's ... flows] M. uses the modern French name, following F. in identifying L.'s *Aturi* with the river Adour (in Aquitaine), and *Tarbellicus* with 'Tarbe', a nearby town in the Pyrenees. L. now catalogues various tribes: see Glossary, s.v. 'Gaul'.
⁸ skilful riders] L. describes an ability to turn horses *in gyrum*, 'in a tight circle' (1. 425).
⁹ hook-armed chariots] Reading *rostrati ... covinni* (1. 426, F.'s choice, following Grotius). Many early modern texts also had the now preferred *monstrati ... covinni*, 'chariot ... demonstrated [to the Belgae]', i.e. the Belgae had acquired the skill from someone else such as the Britons, as in Marlowe's 'The *Belgians* apt to govern *British* cars' (*LFB*, line 427).
¹⁰ Sprung from ... Italy] 'Arvernian tribes who dared to feign themselves brothers of Rome by blood-descent from Troy' (*Arvernique ausi Latio se fingere fratres, | Sanguine ab Iliaco populi*, 1. 427–28). Early modern commentators pointed out that it was the Hedui, a neighbouring tribe, who made this claim: M. 'corrects' L. 'Hedui' is disyllabic.
¹¹ stained with Cotta's fate] The Nervii took part in the 54 BC uprising led by Ambiorix, during which Caesar's general Aurunculeius Cotta was ambushed and killed.

　　　　Crook'd trumpets call, those that near Cinga are,[1]
　　　　Where Araris, with Rhodanus now met,　　　　　　　　　Rhône
　　　　Runs joined into the sea, the men whose seat
465　　Is on Gebenna mount covered with snow.
　　　　The Pictones now free their fields can plough,
　　　　The fickle Turones are not restrained
　　　　By garrison, the Andian now disdained
　　　　To pine in Medua's thick fogs, but goes
470　　For pleasure where delightful Liger flows.
　　　　Fair Genabos is freed from garrison,[2]
　　　　Trever is glad the war from thence is gone,
　　　　The Ligures, now shorn, once like the rest
　　　　Long-haired, of all the unshorn Gauls the best;[3]
475　　And where with off'rings stained of human blood
　　　　Hermes and Mars their cruel altars stood,
　　　　And Jove's, that vile as Scythian Dian's are.[4]
　　　　Then you, that valiant souls and slain in war[5]
　　　　Do celebrate with praise that never dies,
480　　The Bards, securely sung your elegies.[6]
　　　　You Druids, now freed from war, maintain
　　　　Your barbarous rites and sacrifice again:[7]
　　　　You what heaven is, and gods, alone can tell,
　　　　Or else alone are ignorant; you dwell
485　　In vast and desert woods,[8] you teach no spirit
　　　　Pluto's pale kingdom can by death inherit;[9]

---

[1]　near Cinga are] In L. this clause and the next refer to different places, something M.'s syntax obscures.

[2]　467–71] These lines (1. 436–40) are now considered spurious. Although known to certain scholars, they did not appear in most sixteenth-century editions; but Grotius, followed by F., believed them genuine: see *M. Annei Lucani Pharsalia ... ex emendatione H. Grotii, cum eiusdem ad loca insigniora notis* (Leiden: ex officina Plantiniana Raphelengii, 1614), *ad loc.*

[3]　now shorn ... unshorn] L. puns on hairstyle, in a play on Romanized Gaul (*Gallia Togata* — Cisalpine Gaul) and 'Long-haired' (i.e. unconquered) Gaul, *Gallia Comata*.

[4]　Hermes ... Dian's are] M., like Marlowe and Gorges, follows a common gloss, translating L.'s *Teutates*, *Hesus* and *Taranis* (Gallic deities) with the names of the Roman gods Mercury, Mars and Jupiter. Scythian Diana was worshipped with human sacrifice, hence M.'s 'vile' (*non mitior*, 'not more gentle [than Diana's altars]', 1. 446); cf. 3. 91–92, 6. 81–82.

[5]　valiant souls and slain in war] Cf. Marlowe's 'valiant souls slain in your wars' (*LFB*, line 444, for *fortes animas, belloque peremptas*, 1. 447).

[6]　elegies] Merely *carmina*, 'poems, songs' in L., 1. 449.

[7]　barbarous] The pronunciation of 'barbarous' is probably disyllabic, eliding the middle 'a', and so throughout.

[8]　desert woods] 'deep woods, in groves far from the light of day' (*nemora alta, |... remotis lucis*, 1. 452–53).

[9]　Pluto's ... inherit] Omitting *tacitas Erebi sedes*, 'the silent seat of Erebus [the underworld]'; 'inherit' is M.'s idiom for *petunt*, 'seek' (1. 456).

They in another world inform again.   *take form*
Death long life's middle is (if you maintain
The truth): the Northern people happy are[1]
490   In this their error, whom fear greatest far
Of all fears injures not, the fear of death.
Thence are they prone to war, nor loss of breath
Esteem,[2] nor spare a life that comes again.
They that the hairèd Cayci did contain
495   In their obedience,[3] marching now to Rome
From Rhine's rude banks and new-found country come.[4]
    When Caesar's now collected strength had bred   [I. 466][5]
More lofty hopes, through Italy he spread
His troops, and all the neighbouring cities seized.[6]
500   Then idle rumours their true fears increased,
And pierced the people's hearts; swift fame 'gan show   *began to*
The war's approach and their ensuing woe.
Then every tongue a false alarum yields:
Some dare report that on the pasture fields
505   Of fair Mevania is the war begun,
And bloody Caesar's barbarous cohorts run[7]
Where Umbrian Nar does into Tiber flow;
That all his eagles and joined standards now
With a vast strength make furious approach.[8]
510   Nor do they now suppose him to be such,
As once they saw him; fiercer far than so
They think, and savage as his conquered foe;
That all the inhabitants 'twixt th'Alps and Rhine,
Drawn from their countries and cold northern clime,

---

[1] happy are] See Textual Notes.

[2] nor ... Esteem] M.'s idiom for *animaeque capaces | Mortis* ('minds ready for death', I. 461–62).

[3] contain | In their obedience] Reading *bellis arcere* (I. 463), 'to keep from war'; modern editions accept Bentley's emendation *Belgis arcere*, 'to keep from the Belgae'.

[4] and new-found country come] Blunting L.'s charge of betraying Rome's imperial mission: *Deseritis ... apertum gentibus orbem*, 'you abandon a world [now] open to all peoples' (I. 465).

[5] 497–740] Caesar's invasion of Italy and the panic, prodigies and doom-laden prophecies that result.

[6] neighbouring] Probably pronounced disyllabically.

[7] bloody ... cohorts] In L. Caesar is 'savage, cruel' (*saevi*), and the 'cohorts' are divisions of cavalry (*alas*, I. 476).

[8] With a vast ... approach] *Agmine non uno, densisque incedere castris*, 'he was coming with no single column, and with densely packed encampments' (I. 478). 'Furious' is, unusually, trisyllabic.

515 Follow, and Rome (a Roman looking on)
By barbarous hands shall fall. Thus every one
By fear gives strength to fame; no author known,
They fear what they suppose.¹ But not alone
The people does this vain surmise deceive.
520 The Senate shakes; the affrighted Fathers leave
Their seats, and flying to the consuls give
Directions for the war;² where safe to live,
What place t'avoid, they know not; whither ere   *sooner*
Their sudden wits directs their steps, they bear
525 Th'amazèd people forth in troops, whom nought
So long had stirred.³ A man would then have thought
The city fired,⁴ or th'houses' sudden fall
By earthquake threatened; the mad people all
With hasty steps so unadvisèd run,
530 As if no way at all were left to shun
Their imminent and feared destruction
But to forsake their habitation.⁵
As when rough seas, by stormy Auster blown   *south wind*
From Libya's sands, have broke the main-mast down,⁶
535 Master and mariners their ship forsake
Not torn as yet, leap into th'sea, and make
Themselves a shipwreck: so from th'city they
Fly into war.⁷ No sire his son can stay,⁸
No weeping wife her husband can persuade,
540 No nor their household gods, 'til they have made

---

¹ no author known ... suppose] L., more clearly, has *nulloque auctore malorum | Quae finxere, timent*, 'with no author of these evils, they fear what they have fabricated' (1. 485-86).

² affrighted Fathers...] Roman senators were called 'conscript Fathers', *patres conscripti*. L. has them fleeing the *curia*, 'Senate-house', as well as their seats (1. 487).   Directions for the war] *invisaque ... decreta*, 'hated decrees' (1. 488-89); i.e. the *senatus consultum ultimum*, the declaration of a state of emergency.

³ whither ... had stirred] 'the momentum of their flight [propels them]' (*fugae ... impetus*, 1. 491) '[...] and the columns, clinging together in a long line, burst forth [from the city]' (*serieque haerentia longa | Agmina prorumpunt*, 1. 492-93).

⁴ The city fired] *credas tecta nefandas | Corripuisse faces*, 'you would think that execrable torches had seized hold of the houses' (1. 493-94).

⁵ As if ... habitation] *velut, unica rebus | Spes foret afflictis patrios excedere muros*, 'as if the only hope in such affliction were to abandon their ancestral walls' (1. 496-97).

⁶ have broke ... down] Paraphrasing *Fractaque veliferi sonuerunt pondera mali*, 'and the broken weight of the sail-bearing mast has groaned' (1. 500).

⁷ they | Fly into war] i.e. 'they *flee* into war' (*In bellum fugitur*, 1. 504).

⁸ sire] *languidus aevo | ... parens*, 'father faint with age' (1. 504-05).

Vows for their safety; none an eye dares cast
Back on loved Rome, although perhaps his last.[1]
Irrevocably do the people fly.[2]
    You gods that easily give prosperity,   [1. 510]
545 But not maintain it:[3] that great city, filled
With native souls and conquered, that would yield
Mankind a dwelling, is abandoned now
An easy prey to Caesar.[4] When a foe
Begirts our soldiers in a foreign land,
550 The little trench night's danger can withstand,
And sudden work raised out of earth endures
The foe's assault, the encampèd's sleep secures.[5]
Thou Rome, a war but noised, art left by all,
Not one night's safety trusted to thy wall.
555 But pardon their amaze: when Pompey flies
'Tis time to fear. Then lest their hearts should rise
With hope of future good,[6] sad augury bodes
A worse ensuing fate: the threat'ning gods
Fill heaven and earth and sea with prodigies.
560 Unheard-of stars by night adorn the skies,   [1. 526][7]
Heaven seems to flame, and through the welkin fire   *sky*
Obliquely flies;[8] state-changing comets dire
Display to us their blood-portending hair,[9]
Deceitful lightnings flash in clearest air.
565 Strange formèd meteors the thick air had bred

---

[1] none an eye ... his last] Omitting *nec limine quisquam | Haesit*, 'nor did anyone pause on their threshold' (1. 507–08).

[2] the people] *vulgus*, 'the mob' (1. 509).

[3] You gods ...] M. was fond of this aphorism about the mutability of providential favour; cf. *Continuation*, sig. J6ᵛ, and (with a slightly different translation) *The History of the Parliament*, p. 4, describing the happy state of England at James I's accession. M.'s 'maintain', rendering L.'s *tueri*, 'preserve, keep safe' (1. 510), may owe something to the Machiavellian idea of *mantenere lo stato*.

[4] is abandoned now...] M. omits *Ignavae ... manus*, 'cowardly bands [abandon Rome]' (1. 514).

[5] the encampèd's sleep] i.e. the sleep of those who are encamped.

[6] hearts] *trepidas mentes*, 'fearful minds' (1. 523).

[7] 516–89 A catalogue of prodigies foretelling the disaster of civil war — and (from L.'s perspective) of Caesar's victory.

[8] fire | Obliquely flies] Probably meteors, a meaning somewhat blurred by M.'s singular 'fire' for L.'s *faces*, 'firebrands' (1. 528).

[9] state-changing comets...] *terris mutantem regna cometen*, 'the comet that brings change to earthly monarchies' (1. 529). blood-portending hair] *crinemque timendi sideris*, 'hair of a star to be feared' (1. 529); M. and L. play on Greek *kometēs*, 'long-haired'. 'To us' is not in L.

>   Like javelins long, like lamps more broadly spread.¹
>   Lightning without one crack of thunder brings
>   From the cold north his wingèd fires, and flings
>   Them 'gainst our Capitol;² small stars, that use
> 570   Only by night their lustre to diffuse,
>   Now shine in midst of day; Cynthia bright   *the moon*
>   In her full orb, like Phoebus, at the sight
>   Of earth's black shades eclipses;³ Titan hides,   *the sun*
>   When mounted in the midst of heaven he rides,
> 575   In clouds his burning chariot, to enfold
>   The world in darkness quite. Day to behold
>   No nation hopes,⁴ as once back to the east
>   He fled at sight of sad Thyestes' feast.⁵
>   Fierce Vulcan opes Sicilian Etna's throat,
> 580   But to the sky her flames she belches not,⁶
>   But on th'Italian shore obliquely flings.
>   Blood from her bottom black Charybdis brings;
>   Sadlier bark Scylla's dogs than they were wont.⁷
>   The Vestal fire goes out: on th'Alban mount
> 585   Jove's sacrificing fire itself divides
>   Into two parts, and rises on two sides,
>   Like the two Theban princes' funeral fires.⁸

---

¹ Like ... like] Omitting L.'s *nunc ... nunc* ('*now* like ... *now* like', 1. 532). L gives these varied shapes of lightning their own verb, *emicuit* ('shone out'); M. attaches them to the previous line. 'Javelins' is always disyllabic in M.

² Capitol] 'the head of Latium', *Latiare caput*, 1. 534. As F. explains, L. could also mean Rome or Alba Longa the ancient capital of Latium.

³ Cynthia ... eclipses] A valiant attempt at L.'s obscure *cornuque coacto | Iam Phoebe toto fratrem cum redderet orbe, | Terrarum subita percussa expalluit umbra*, 'The moon, when, her horns compelled, she was reflecting her brother [i.e. the sun] with her full disc, was struck by the earth's sudden shadow and went pale' (1. 538–39).

⁴ Day ... hopes] L. makes this a direct result of the sun's action in the previous lines.

⁵ Thyestes' feast] The sun disappeared at midday at the hideous crime of Atreus, who fed the unwitting Thyestes his own children; cf. 7. 512–13.

⁶ belches not] 'belches' is M.'s idiom for *tulit*, 'brought [into the air]', 1. 546.

⁷ Sadlier bark ... wont] *flebile saevi | Latravere canes*, 'wild dogs barked weepily' (1. 548–49): commentators took this to mean Scylla, the legendary sea-monster found opposite the whirlpool Charybdis in the straits of Messina, mentioned in 1. 582. According to Ovid, *Metamorphoses*, XIII. 730–34, Scylla's belly was begirt with ravening dogs (see *Metamorphoses*, ed. by W. S. Anderson (Stuttgart & Leipzig: Teubner, 1991)). See also 6. 72.

⁸ The Vestal fire ... funeral fires] M. follows commentators in understanding *ostendens confectas flamma Latinas*, 'the fire displaying the completion of the Latin [festivals, the Feriae Latinae]' (1. 550), to be the flame in Jupiter's temple on Mount Alba; cf. 1. 215, 7. 445–47. The Theban princes are Eteocles and Polynices, who warred for kingship; cremated together, the flame of their funeral pyre split in two.

	Earth opes her threat'ning jaws,¹ th'Alps' nodding spires	
	Shake off their snow, Thetis does higher now²	*the sea*
590	'Twixt Libyan Atlas, and Spain's Calpe flow.	
	The native gods did weep, Rome's certain thrall	*enslavement*
	The Lares' sweating showed, the off'rings fall	
	Down in the temples,³ and (as we have heard)	
	Night's fatal birds in midst of day appeared.	
595	Wild beasts at midnight from the deserts come,⁴	
	And take bold lodging in the streets of Rome.	
	Beasts make with men's articulate voice their moan;	
	Births monstrous both in limbs' proportion,	
	And number;⁵ mothers their own infants feared;	
600	Sybilla's fatal lines were sung and heard	
	Among the people.⁶ And with bloody arms	
	Cybel's head-shaking priests pronounced their charms,	
	I'th'people's ears howling a baleful moan,⁷	
	And ghosts from out their quiet urns did groan.	
605	Clashing of armour and loud shouts they hear	
	In desert groves, and threat'ning ghosts appear.	
	The dwellers near without the city wall	
	Fled: fierce Erinys had encompassed all	
	The town, her snaky hairs and burning brand	
610	Shaking, as when she ruled Agave's hand,	
	Or the self-maimed Lycurgus; such was she	
	Who once, when sent by Juno's cruelty,	
	Great Hercules (new come from Hell) did fright.⁸	

---

¹ Earth opes her threat'ning jaws] Lit. *Tum cardine tellus | Subsedit*, 'the earth sank on its axis' (1. 552–53): M. is following F.'s gloss (*Diducta in hiatum subsedit*, 'drawn into a gaping hole, it sank').

² Thetis] Always Tethys in Renaissance editions (1. 554); both are a metonym for the sea.

³ The Lares' ... in the temples] The Lares were personal household gods; L. may mean the *Lares praestites*, guardians of the state. Votive offerings were often suspended from temple walls.

⁴ from the deserts] 'leaving their woods' (*silvisque ... relictis*, 1. 559).

⁵ Births monstrous ... And number] Omitting a verb (probably 'appeared, were seen').

⁶ Sybilla's fatal lines...] A reference to the *Sybillini libri*, secret books of prophetic verse housed in the temple of Capitoline Jupiter and tended by a priestly college.

⁷ Cybel's ... moan] L. refers to two separate cults, those of Cybele and Bellona: lit. *quos sectis Bellona lacertis | Saeva movet, cecinere deos: crinemque rotantes | Sanguinei populis ululantur tristia Galli*, 'then those with cut arms, whom savage Bellona moved, sang of the gods; and the bloody Galli, whirling their locks, wailed tragedy at the nations' (1. 565–67).

⁸ fierce Erinys ... Hercules] A Fury, instrument of divine vengeance (M. simplifies L., who names three Fury-figures in the following lines: Erinys, Eumenis, Megaera (1. 572–77)). Agave, Lyurgus and Hercules were victims of Fury-inspired madness in Greco-Roman

Shrill trumpets sounded; dismal airs of night[1]
615 That horrid noise, that meeting armies yield,
Did then present. In midst of Mars his field
Rose Sulla's ghost, and woes ensuing told;[2]
Ploughmen near Anien's streams Marius behold
Rise from his sepulchre, and fly appalled.[3]
620 For these things were the Tuscan prophets called,   *summoned*
As custom was: the sagest of them all
Dwelt in Etrurian Luna's desert wall,[4]   *deserted*
Arruns, that lightnings' motion understands,
Birds' flight, and entrails oped.[5] He first commands
625 Those monstrous births, that from no seed did come[6]
But horrid issues of a barren womb,
To be consumed in fire, then all the town
To be encompassed in procession;[7]
Th'high priests (whose charge it is) he next doth urge,
630 The city walls with hallowed rites to purge
Through their whole circuit;[8] following after these,
Th'inferior priests, attired Gabinian-wise.[9]
The Vestal Maids with their veiled sister come
That only may see Troy's Palladium,[10]

myth. Agave murdered her son Pentheus. Lycurgus was punished for attacking Dionysus: M.'s 'self-maimed' (lit. *saevi*, 'savage', 1. 575) comes from F., who records that while Lycurgus thought he was cutting vines, he was cutting his own limbs. Juno used a Fury to inspire madness in Hercules: after returning from the Underworld, he killed his wife and children.

[1] dismal airs of night] 'Black night' (*nox atra*, 1. 579); M. possibly puns on 'airs' which can also mean 'tunes'.

[2] Sulla's ghost] Cf. 1. 359.

[3] Ploughmen ... appalled] In L., *agricolae*, 'farmers' are witnesses. 'Anien' seems to anglicize L.'s *Aniens*, 'of the river Anio', although it could be a shortened version of the river's modern Italian name, the Aniene. In L. Marius's tomb is 'broken', *fracto*, and the river waters are 'icy', *gelidas* (1. 582–83). On Marius cf. 2. 72–74n.

[4] Etrurian Luna] *Luna* in Grotius's and Farnaby's texts, but earlier editions mention the now preferred variant *Luca*.

[5] Arruns] A fictional soothsayer.

[6] monstrous births ... come] *Monstra ... quae nullo semine discors | Protulerat natura*, 'Prodigies which a disordered nature had produced, without seed' (1. 589–90). 'Monstrous births' may recall Iago in Shakespeare's *Othello*, 1. 3. 375.

[7] procession] Elaborating on L.'s *ambiri*, 'encircled' (1. 593); as F. notes, L. here describes a Roman purgation rite. M. omits *pavidis a civibus*, '[encircled by] the terrified citizens' (1. 592). 'Procession' has four syllables.

[8] circuit] In L. the *pomerium*, the legal-religious boundary of the city.

[9] Gabinian-wise] i.e. the toga worn in such a way as to leave the arms free.

[10] veiled sister ... Palladium] 'veiled sister' translates *vitata sacerdos*, 'be-ribboned priest' (1. 597); M.'s word hints at the frequent early modern comparison of the Vestal Virgins (who were pledged to chastity, and tended the shrine of Vesta) to nuns. The Palladium was a

635	Then those that Sibyl's secret verses keep	
	And Cybel yearly in still Almon steep;[1]	
	Septemviri that govern sacred feasts,	
	The learnèd augurs and Apollo's priests;	
	The noble Flamen Salius, that bears	
640	On his glad neck the target of great Mars.[2]	shield
	Whilst they the town compass in winding tracts,	
	Arruns the lightning's dispersèd fire collects	
	And into th'earth with a sad murmur flings,	
	Then names the places,[3] and to th'altar brings	
645	A chosen bull. Then wine betwixt his horns	
	He pours, and sprinkles o'er with salt and corn	
	His knife; the bull, impatient, long denies	
	Himself to so abhorred a sacrifice,	
	But by the girded sacrificer's strength	
650	Hanging upon his horns, o'ercome at length,	
	Bending his knees, holds forth his conquered neck.	
	Nor did pure blood come out,[4] but poison black,	
	Instead of blood, from the wound opened flies.	
	Arruns grew pale at this sad sacrifice,	
655	And the gods' wrath he in the entrails seeks,	
	Whose colour scared him: pale they were with streaks	
	Of black, th'infected blood congealèd shows	
	(Sprinkled with different paleness) various.	
	The liver putrified, on th'hostile side	
660	Were threat'ning veins;[5] the lungs their fillets hide;	
	A narrow line divides the vital parts;	
	The heart lies still, and corrupt matter starts	

figurine of Athene, supposedly guaranteeing its city's invulnerability, and believed to have been carried to Rome from Troy by Aeneas.

[1] those that Sibyl's secret ... steep] M.'s 'Almon' anglicizes L.'s *Almone*, 'the Almo' (1. 600); priests of Cybele bathed her cult statue in this river yearly. See Textual Notes.

[2] Septemviri ... Mars] Various Roman priesthoods. 'Apollo's priests' are lit. *Titii sodales*, 'the Titian Brethren' (1. 602); M. uses F.'s gloss. M. omits some of 1. 604 and as a result fails to distinguish the *flamines* (priests recruited from patrician families, devoted to individual deities) from the 'Salian Brethren', who looked after the shields of Mars (*ancilia*).

[3] Then names the places] Literally rendering *datque locis nomen* (1. 608). Early modern commentators explain this as naming a sacred spot, the Bidental, for animal sacrifice. That M. doesn't elaborate here, together with his clumsy anglicisation of Roman river names and the confusion above (see 1. 618, 636, 640n), suggests that he translated much of this section without close use of a commentary.

[4] pure blood] *cruor ... solitus*, 'the customary gore' (1. 614).

[5] th'hostile side] Ancient soothsayers divided the liver into different sides, the familiar and hostile.

Through gaping clefts; no part o'th'caul is hid;   *membrane*
And that which never without danger did
665 Appear, on th'entrails was a double head.
One head was sick, feeble, and languishèd:
The other quick his pulses nimbly beats.¹
By this when he perceived what woe the fates
Prepared,² he cried aloud, 'All that you do,
670 O gods, I must not to the people show:³
Nor with this hapless sacrifice can I,
Great Jupiter, thy anger pacify.⁴
The black infernal deities appear
In th'entrails; woes unspeakable we fear,
675 But greater will ensue. You gods lend aid,
And let no credit to our art be had,
And counted Tages' fiction.'⁵ Thus, with long
Ambages, darkly the old Tuscan sung.⁶   *ambiguity, equivocations*
But Figulus,⁷ whose care it was aright   [1. 634] *correctly*
680 To know the gods and heavens, to whom foresight
Of planets and the motion of each star,⁸
Not great Egyptian Memphis might compare,
'Either no laws direct the world',⁹ quoth he,
'And all the stars do move uncertainly,
685 Or, if Fates rule, a swift destruction
Threatens mankind and th'earth. Shall cities down
By earthquakes swallowed be? Intemperately

¹ The other ... beats] Omitting *improba*, 'perversely' (1. 629).
² what woe the fates | Prepared] *magnorum fata malorum*, 'a destiny of massive evil' (1. 630).
³ All that you do ... show] In L., Arruns says it is *vix fas*, 'scarcely permissible' (1. 631), to reveal divine intention. M.'s 'do' (1. 669) indicates that he read *movetis* (lit. 'you move', 1. 631), rather than the variant *monetis* ('you warn'), preferred by F. following Grotius.
⁴ Nor ... pacify] M. adds 'hapless' and 'anger' here, suggesting he is now following the commentaries again, many of which interpolate these terms in their paraphrases.
⁵ And let no credit ...] *Et fibris sit nulla fides*, 'and let the entrails not be credited' (1. 636); M. follows a commentary, e.g. F.'s *et fallat aruspicina ars*, 'and let the art of reading entrails be false'. In legend Tages was the founder of the art of Etruscan divination.
⁶ the old Tuscan] M. adds 'old'.
⁷ Figulus] Publius Nigidius Figulus (c. 100-45 BC), a writer on astrology and natural history. His speech (1. 683-715) largely concerns astrological portents, turning at the very end to political concerns (1. 708-15).
⁸ to whom foresight] i.e. 'to *whose* foresight'.   Of planets ... each star] Translating *stellarum* as 'planets' and *astra* as 'stars' (1. 640-01); both mean 'stars' in first-century AD Latin.
⁹ Either no laws direct the world] *Aut hic errat ... nulla cum lege per aevum | Mundus*, 'either this universe wanders lawlessly through the tract of time...' (1. 642-43).

           Shall air grow hot?¹ False earth her seeds deny?²
           Or shall the waters poisoned be? What kind
690   Of ruin is it, gods, what mischiefs find
           Your cruelties?³ Many dire aspects meet;⁴
           If Saturn cold in midst of heaven should sit,
           Aquarius would Deucalion's flood have bred
           And all the earth with waters overspread.⁵
695   If Sol should mount the Nemean Lion's back,
           In flames would all the world's whole fabric crack
           And all the sky with Sol's burnt chariot blaze.⁶
           These aspects cease:⁷ but thou, that burn'st the claws   *remain at rest*
           And fir'st the tail of threat'ning Scorpion,   *set fire to*
700   What great thing breed'st thou, Mars? Mild Jove goes down
           Oppressèd in his fall, and in the skies
           The wholesome star of Venus dullèd is;
           Mercury loses his swift motion,
           And fiery Mars rules in the sky alone.⁸
705   Why do the stars, their course forsaking, glide
           Obscurely through the air? Why does the side
           Of sword-bearing Orion shine too bright?
           War's rage is threatened; the sword's power all right

---

¹ Intemperately ... hot?] A literal translation of *an tollet feruidus aër | Temperiem?* (1. 646–47). Most commentators understood a reference to plague here (believed to be transported through hot air).
² False earth ... deny?] *segetes tellus infida negabit?*, 'will the faithless earth deny crops?' (1. 647).
³ mischiefs ... your cruelties] 'mischiefs' translates *peste*, 'pestilence', 1. 649.
⁴ Many dire aspects meet] Lit. *extremi multorum tempus in unum | Convenere dies*, 'the end times for many have converged on one moment in time' (1. 650–51). M.'s 'aspects', probably drawn from the commentaries (e.g. F.'s *exitiales ... aspectus*, 'lethal aspects'), is a technical astrological term meaning the angles planets make with each other and with different parts of the sky.
⁵ If Saturn ... overspread] M. compresses L.'s *Stella nocens nigros Saturni accenderet ignes*, 'Saturn's harmful star, burning its black fires' (1. 652); i.e. if Saturn were to govern the height of heaven, it would induce Aquarius to bring on a cataclysm (in Greco-Roman myth, Deucalion was the sole survivor of a world-destroying flood).
⁶ If Sol ... blaze] i.e. the Sun, by encroaching on the sign of Leo (the Nemean Lion) would bring about the end of the world.   flames ... fabric crack] *toto fluerent incendia mundo*, 'conflagrations would flow through the whole world' (1. 656). For M.'s different idiom of cracking fabrics, see 1. 87n.
⁷ aspects] Translating *ignes*, 'fires'.
⁸ Mild Jove ... sky alone] i.e. Mars (whose adjective 'fiery' is added by M.) is on the move into Scorpio, and dominates the beneficent planets Jupiter, Venus and Mercury: this, accompanied by the over-bright appearance of Orion, portends war.

	Confounds by force;[1] impiety shall bear	
710	The name of virtue,[2] and for many a year	
	This fury lasts.[3] It boots us not to crave	
	A peace: with peace a master we shall have.[4]	
	Draw out the series of thy misery,	
	O Rome, to longer years, now only free	
715	From civil war.'[5] These prodigies did scare	
	The multitude enough: but greater far	
	Ensue. As on the top of Pindus' mount	
	The Thracian women full of Bacchus wont	
	To rave, so now a matron ran, possessed	
720	By Phoebus urging her inspirèd breast.[6]	
	'Where am I carried now? Where leav'st thou me,	[1. 678][7]
	Paean, already rapt above the sky?	*Apollo; taken, seized*
	Pangaea's snowy top, Philippi plains	
	I see.[8] Speak, Phoebus, what this fury means:	
725	What swords, what hands shall in Rome's battles meet,	
	What wars without a foe? O whither yet	
	Am I distracted?[9] To that eastern land,	
	Where Nile discolours the blue ocean:	
	There, there alas I know what man it is,	
730	That on Nile's bank a trunk deformèd lies.[10]	

[1] the sword's power ... force] L.'s *potestas* here means authorized power, not mere strength (1. 664); cf. 1. 357n.

[2] impiety ... virtue] *scelerique nefando nomen erit virtus* ('virtue will be the name given to unspeakable wickedness', 1. 667).

[3] lasts] i.e. will last.

[4] with peace a master we shall have] *Cum domino pax ista venit*, 'that peace comes with a master' (1. 670); L. stresses the conclusion to the civil war as enslavement, not peace as such.

[5] now only free | From civil war] *civili tantum iam libera bello* (1. 672). Modern commentators generally take *civili bello* as an ablative of duration, meaning 'only free *during* civil war' (i.e. its ending will extinguish liberty), but M.'s Figulus seemingly highlights the moment before hostilities start.

[6] As on the top of Pindus'... breast] The reference is to the cult of Bacchus and its reputedly crazed female acolytes. 'Full of Bacchus' translates *plena ... Lyaeo* (1. 675; Lyaeus was one of Bacchus' names), suggesting prophetic and sexual possession as well as drunkenness. wont | To rave] i.e. *are* wont. ran] Omitting *attonitam ... per urbem*, 'through the astonished city' (1. 677); some Renaissance editors read *attonita* [*matrona*], i.e. 'the astonished matron'.

[7] 721-40] The speech of L.'s invented matron, foretelling via the conceit of a ride through the air the various theatres and battles of the forthcoming war.

[8] Pangaea's snowy top ... plains] M. omits L.'s third location, 'beneath mount Haemus' (*Aemi sub rupe*, 1. 680).

[9] distracted?] *Quo diversa feror*, 'what different places am I carried away to?' (1. 683). M.'s 'distracted' is physical ('drawn in different directions') but also psychological (*OED*, s.v. 2).

[10] There, there alas ... lies] M. adds the repetition and 'alas': a reference to Pompey. See 8. 716-809. M.'s 'on *Nile's* bank' develops L.'s *arena*, 'on the sand' (1. 685).

O'er Syrtes' sands, o'er scorchèd Libya
Whither the relics of Pharsalia   *remnants*
Erinys carried, o'er th'Alps' cloudy hill,
And high Pyrene am I carried still;[1]
735 Then back again to Rome, where impious
And fatal war defiles the Senate-house.[2]
The factions rise again; again I go
O'er all the world. Show me new kingdoms now,
New seas;[3] Philippi I have seen.' This spoke,
740 The furious fit her wearied breast forsook.[4]

FINIS *Libri Primi*[5]

---

[1] O'er ... carried] i.e. the matron is transported by Erinys (see l. 608) over Africa and Spain, future theatres of civil war (Thapsus, 46 BC, after which Cato the Younger committed suicide at nearby Utica; the battle of Munda, 45 BC, the final battle of the civil war). Modern editions print *Enyo* for *Erinys*. M. omits L.'s *dubiam* [*Syrtim*], 'the doubtful Syrtes' (1. 686). M.'s 'relics', translating L.'s *acies*, 'battle lines' (1. 688), emphasises that these are the survivors of Pharsalia.

[2] impious ... Senate-house] An allusion to Caesar's assassination in March 44 BC. For M.'s use of the term 'fatal', see Introduction, p. 8.

[3] new kingdoms...] *nova ... litora ponti,* | *Telluremque novam,* 'new seashores, new lands' (1. 693–94).

[4] The furious fit ... forsook] *& lasso iacuit defecta furore,* 'and collapsed, enfeebled by her exhausted frenzy' (1. 695).

[5] 'The end of the First Book'.

Annotations on the First Book

(a) Roman darts or javelins, which their footmen used, about five foot long. If any man quarrel at the word pile, as thinking it scarce English, I desire them to give a better word. For dart or javelin is a word too general, and cannot intimate a civil war; for darts had fought against darts, though[1] a Roman army had fought against barbarous and foreign nations. But *pilum* was a peculiar name to the Roman darts, and so meant by Lucan: which if any deny, let him read these verses in the seventh book of our author:

> *sceleris sed crimine nullo*
> *Externam maculant Chalybem, stetit omne coactum*
> *Circa pila nefas.*[2]

(b) Marcus Crassus, a great, and rich Roman, ruling the province of Syria, went with a consular army to the Parthian war, and was there defeated and slain, together with his son and his whole army, by Surena the king's general.[3]

(c)[4] Near Munda a city in Spain, the two sons of Pompey were overcome by Julius Caesar. Gnaeus was slain, and Sextus fled, thirty thousand Pompeians were there slain; insomuch that Caesar to besiege the conquered, made a countermure[5] of dead carcasses.

(d) Antonius besieged D. Brutus in Mutina a city of Gallia Cisalpina: in raising which siege, both the consuls, Hircius and Pansa were slain; but Augustus afterward raised it.

(e) Perusia a city in Thuscia, whither Lucius Antonius had fled, was by Augustus forced to yield through famine.

(f) Where Augustus in a sea-fight vanquished Antonius and Cleopatra.

(g) A fight on the Sicilian sea, where Sextus Pompeius had armed slaves and bondsmen against Augustus, by whom he was there defeated.

(h)[6] These three were Crassus, Caesar, and Pompey; who all excelling in wealth, dignity, fame, and ambition, reconciled to each other, and linked together in affinity, entered into such a league, that nothing should be done in the Commonwealth, that displeased themselves, dividing among themselves,

---

[1] though] i.e. 'even if'.
[2] *sceleris sed ... nefas*] VII. 517–19. M.'s translation (7. 587–88) is 'But no dire crime could stain the foreign steel: | Nought could work mischief, but the Roman pile'.
[3] M.'s synopsis of Crassus's career agrees closest with Appian, *The Civil Wars*, II. 18 (Appian, *Roman History*, trans. by Horace White, 4 vols, Loeb Classical Texts (Cambridge, MA: Harvard University Press, 1913), III, p. 261).
[4] Notes (c)–(g) translate notes in F. (on I. 41–43).
[5] countermure] A second or supplementary defensive wall.
[6] Note (h) translates a note in F. (on I. 84).

provinces, and armies. Pompey by his lieutenants governed Spain and Africa, Caesar had his government over all Gallia prorogued for another five years; Crassus governed all Syria.

(i) Julia, a virtuous Roman lady, daughter to Caesar and wife to Pompey the Great; who died untimely for the Commonwealth,[1] since her life might have preserved peace between her husband and her father.

(k) Beside Rubicon was a pillar raised up, and upon it a decree of the Senate engraven, that it should not be lawful for any to come armed homeward beyond that place.[2]

(l)[3] Quintus Cassius and Marcus Antonius, tribunes of the people, for speaking boldly in the behalf of Caesar were condemned out of the court by the two consuls Marcellus and Lentulus, who upbraided them with the sedition of the Gracchi, and threatened the same end to them unless they departed. The tribunes, escaping out of the city by night in poor and base attire, fled to Caesar, and with them Curio.

(m) This Curio had lately been tribune of the people, and a great enemy to Caesar. He was beloved by the vulgar[4] and an excellent speaker, but being much in debt, Caesar relieved him and made him of his faction.

(n)[5] The lawful age to triumph in was thirty years old; but Pompey the Great had triumphed over Iarbas king of Numidia when he was but four and twenty years old.

(o) The praetorship Pompey without voices[6] took to himself, being twenty-three years old. He was consul alone, and had held other honours[7] contrary to custom.

(p) Pompey the Great, that he might be chosen at Rome overseer for corn, took a course that none should be brought in from other parts, insomuch as that the city endured famine; upon which Clodius could say, 'the law was not made for the famine, but a famine was brought in of purpose, that such a law might be made'.

(q) When Milo was arraigned for Clodius's death, Pompey, to suppress the tumult of the people, environed the judgement place with armed men, a thing unlawful to do.[8]

---

[1] untimely for the Commonwealth] Translating F.'s *immatura propter Remp[ublicam] morte* (on 1. 111). The rest of this note is M.'s own synopsis.
[2] Note (k) translates a note in F. (on 1. 189).
[3] Notes (l) and (m) translate notes in F. (on 1. 267, 269).
[4] beloved by the vulgar] In F. *populo acceptus*, 'well-received by the people' (on 1. 269).
[5] Notes (n)–(s) are taken from, and mostly translate, notes in F. (on 1. 316–19).
[6] without voices] In F. *nullis suffragiis*, i.e. unelected (on 1. 317).
[7] other honours] F. (on 1. 317) is more specific, mentioning the extraordinary prefectural appointments and extended provincial commands Pompey enjoyed.
[8] a thing unlawful to do] M.'s comment; F. (on 1. 319) quotes from Cicero's *pro Milone* to similar effect.

(r) Sulla, 60 years old, gave over his dictatorship and lived privately at Puteoli.

(s) Mithradates king of Pontus warred with the Romans forty years. He was weakened and received overthrows from Sulla and Lucullus and conquered[1] by Pompey. Being besieged in a town by his son Pharnaces, he could not poison himself, having much used antidotes, but fell upon his sword and died.

(t) Pompey the Great had made a colony of Cicilian pirates, whom he had vanquished.[2]

(v) Lac de Lorange.[3] These several towns and countries of France, where Caesar's army lay in garrison, and from whence they were now drawn, are here set down by their old names; and this little volume will not afford room so far to enlarge my annotations, as to set down the names as they are now called, being all changed.

(x) The most fierce people of the Belgians, where Teturius Sabinus and Arunculus Cotta, two of Caesar's lieutenants, with five cohorts were entrapped and slain by fraud of Ambiorix.[4]

---

[1] and conquered] i.e. 'and *was* conquered'.
[2] Note (t) is taken from two cross-referenced notes in F. (on I. 336 and II. 576). The pirates in question are Cilician, not Cicilian — a mistake from 1626 on, never corrected.
[3] A curious misprint for Lake Geneva, known in French in M.'s time either as *Lac de Lausanne* or *Lac Leman*. F., however, had spelt the former as 'Lac de Lozanne' in his commentary (on I. 397); is there a confusion with the French name for a lozenge here, 'lozange' or 'lorange'?
[4] A slightly garbled reprise of notes in F. (on I. 429). F. describes the Nervians as 'a most ferocious Gallic-Belgian people' (*Galliae Belgicae pop. ferocissimus*), but indicates that the Roman disasters referred to in M.'s note involved two different tribes, the Eburones and Carnutes.

To the Right Honourable William Earl of Pembroke,[1] Lord High Steward of His Majesty's Household, and Knight of the Most Noble Order.[2]

To you, right noble lord, I here present
This second book, the deathless monument
Of Brutus' worth, and sacred Cato's praise,[3]
As high, as rich as Fame herself could raise
5   A monument.[4] These favoured neither side,
Nor fought for Caesar's reign, nor Pompey's pride,
Nor came engagèd by a private cause.
For Rome, her state, her freedom, and her laws
Their loyal virtue stood. If such an one,
10 Free from ambition, free from faction,[5]
An honest lord, a noble patriot,[6]
Our age do seek (my lord I flatter not),
Think, with mine, the voice of public fame
Would Pembroke name as soon as any name.[7]

---

[1] To the Right Honourable] This poem is the first of eight dedicatory epigrams to English aristocrats that appeared in front of books two to nine in several variants of 1627, but no other editions, and which suggest links between Lucan's narrative and contemporary politics: see Introduction, pp. 24–25. William Herbert, third Earl of Pembroke (1580–1630), son of Mary Sidney the translator and nephew of Sir Philip Sidney, was a senior Privy Councillor, courtier and literary patron under James I and Charles I. Possessing, like most of the Herbert-Sidney clan, strongly Protestant, anti-Spanish tendencies, he was a rival and opponent of the Duke of Buckingham, although the two men enjoyed a fragile peace in the early years of Charles I's reign. M. nods to this orientation in the term 'patriot' (line 11), and in opposing Pembroke to 'ambition' and 'faction', vices increasingly associated with Buckingham during the late 1620s. M.'s model is Jonson, *Epigrams*, 102, first published in 1616 and also on Pembroke (Jonson, *Works*, v, p. 169); see Paleit, *War, Liberty, and Caesar*, pp. 215–24.

[2] Lord High Steward] A major office in the royal household, granted to Pembroke as part of the attempt to reconcile him with Buckingham. Although rumoured from the beginning of Charles I's reign, the role was only officially conferred on 18 August 1626. of the Most Noble Order] i.e. of the Garter. Pembroke acquired this honour on 9 July 1603.

[3] Brutus' worth, and sacred Cato's praise] M. here compares Pembroke to Brutus and Cato: see below, 2. 247–414 and esp. 402–14 for L.'s praise of Cato in similar terms. For a strong parallel in political-ethical sensibility, also treating Cato and Brutus as isolated examples of virtue, cf. Jonson, *Sejanus*, I. 1. 89–90, 95 (*Works*, II, p. 241), 'Where is now the soul | Of god-like *Cato*? ... Or where the constant *Brutus*...?'.

[4] To you ... A monument] For this opening conceit see Horace, *Odes*, III. 30: 'A monument by me is brought to pass | Outliving Pyramids ... bright Fame shall raise my memory, | Renewed with future praise' (trans. by Sir Thomas Hawkins (London: Augustine Mathews for William Lee,1625), lines 1–2, 7–8).

[5] Free from ambition, free from faction] cf. Jonson, *Epigrams*, 102. 14–15: Pembroke has 'one true posture, though besieged with ill | Of what ambition, faction, pride, can raise'.

[6] a noble patriot] cf. Jonson, *Epigrams*, 102. 13: 'But thou, whose noblesse keeps one posture still'.

[7] Pembroke name as soon as any name] cf. Jonson, *Epigrams*, 102. 1–2: 'I do but name thee Pembroke, and I find | It is an epigram on all mankind'.

LUCAN'S
Pharsalia

The Second Book.

The Argument of the Second Book.[1]

Th'author complains that future fates are known,
The sorrow of affrighted Rome is shown.
An old man calls to mind the civil crimes
Of Marius' and Sulla's bloody times.
5   Brutus with Cato does confer; to whom
Chaste Marcia, come from dead Hortensius' tomb,
Again is married in a funeral dress.
Pompey to Capua flies. What fortresses
By Caesar are surprised, who without fight
10 Puts Sulla, Scipio, Lentulus to flight,
And takes Domitius at Corfinium.
Pompey's oration. From Brundisium
He sends his eldest son to bring from far
The eastern monarchs to this civil war.[2]
15 But, there besieged by Caesar, scarce can he
'Scape safe away by night's obscurity.

Now the gods' wrath was seen; plain signs of war   [II. 1]
The world had given; forespeaking Nature, far
From her true course, tumultuous monsters made,
Proclaiming woe. O Jove,[3] why dost thou add
5   This care to wretched men, to let them see
By dire portents their following misery?
Whether the world's Creator, when he did
From the dark formless Chaos light divide,
'Stablished eternal laws to which he tied
10 The creatures and himself, and did divide
The world's set ages by unchangèd fate;[4]

---

[1]   The Argument] See Argument to book one and note.
[2]   his eldest son] Gnaeus Pompeius.
[3]   Jove] *rector Olympi*, 'ruler of Olympus' (II. 4).
[4]   Whether ... unchangèd fate] As F. clarifies, this is the doctrine of providential determinism, derived from the Stoics.

Or whether, nothing preordained, the state
Of mortal things chance rules;[1] yet let that be
Secret that thou intend'st — let no eye see[2]
His future fate, but hope as well as fear.
    When the sad city had conceived how dear   [II. 16]
Heaven's truth would cost the world,[3] her general woe
Proclaimed a fast.[4] The mourning Senate go
Like the plebeians clad; the consuls ware   *wore*
No purple robes, no words their grief declare,
Mute is their sorrow. Such a silent woe
A dying man's amazèd household show,
Before his funeral conclamation,
Before the mother's lamentation
Call on the servants weeping; but when she
Feels his stiff limbs, dead looks and standing eye,[5]
Then 'tis no fear but grief: down she doth fall,
Howling upon him. So Rome's matrons all
Leave off their habits and attires of grace
And in sad troops the altars do embrace.
One weeps before the gods, one her torn locks
Throws in the sacred porch, another knocks
Her breast against the ground; the god, whose ears
Were used to prayers, now only howling hears.
Nor to Jove's temple did they all repair:
They part the gods, no altar wants his share
Of envy-making mothers. But one there
Her plaint-bruised arms and moistened cheeks did tear:
'Now, now,' quoth she, 'O mothers, tear your hair,
Now beat your breasts, do not this grief defer

---

[1] Or whether ... chance rules] The Epicurean view (again, as pointed out by F.). M. compresses here, omitting *sed fors incerta vagatur*, 'but chance wanders uncertainly' (II. 12).

[2] let no eye] *mens*, 'mind' (II. 15).

[3] world] M. reads *orbi* here, now the preferred reading, but for F. and other early modern editors, a variant reading for *urbi*, 'the city'.

[4] Proclaimed a fast] M.'s invention. L.'s *ferale* ... | *Iustitium* (II. 17–18) is an edict suspending legal business in time of emergency. Hortensius (col. 155 B) is the only commentator to imply it also included the shutting of *tabernae* (shops or bars). M. may also have been thinking of fasts in the Bible, e.g. 'So the people of Nineveh believed God, and proclaimed a fast, and put on sackcloth, from the greatest of them even to the least of them' (Jonah 3. 5, KJV).

[5] standing eye] A notorious textual crux. Early modern editions read *oculos minaces*, 'threatening eyes' or, like F., *iacentes*, 'lying down [closed?] eyes' (II. 26). Bentley's conjecture, *oculos natantes*, 'swimming eyes', is now preferred. M. may echo Shakespeare, who uses 'standing eye' of rage ('deadly-standing eye', *Titus Andronicus*, 3. 32) or grief ('water-standing eye', *Henry VI Part 3*, 28. 40).

40	'Til the last ills: while the chiefs doubtful are,	
	We may lament; when one is conqueror,	
	We must rejoice.' Thus grief itself did move.[1]	
	Such just complaints against the powers above	[II. 43]
	The soldiers make, that to each army turn:	
45	'O miserable men, that were not born	
	When Carthage warred at Trebia's overthrow	
	Or Cannae's mortal field![2] Nor beg we now	
	For peace, O gods: stir each fierce nation,	
	Raise mighty cities, let the world in one	
50	Conspire: let Median powers from Susa come,[3]	
	Nor let cold Ister hold his Scythians from	
	This war; the Suevians from the northern clime	
	Let Albis send, and the rude head of Rhine;	
	Make us all peoples' foes, so not our own.	
55	Here let the Daci, there the Getes come on:[4]	
	Let one his forces against Spain employ,	
	'Gainst th'eastern bows let t'other's eagles fly;	
	Let Rome have war with all, or if our names	
	You gods would ruin, let the sky to flames	
60	Dissolved fall down and quite consume our coasts,	
	Or thunder strike both captains with their hosts	
	While they be guiltless, Jove. Seek they to try	
	With so much mischief who Rome's lord shall be?[5]	
	'Twere scarce worth civil war that none should reign.'	
65	Thus then did bootless piety complain.	
	But the old men, moved with particular grief,	[II. 63][6]
	Curse their old age and ill-prolongèd life,	
	Their years reserved again to civil war.	
	(a)One, seeking precedents for their great fear,	

[1] did move] *his se stimulis dolor ipse lacessit*, 'grief wounds itself with its own incitements' (II. 42).

[2] When Carthage ... mortal field] The battles of Trebia (218 BC) and Cannae (216 BC) were infamous defeats inflicted on Rome by Hannibal. 'Miserable' (II. 46) is untypically four syllables, emphasizing the tone of complaint. 'Trebia's' (II. 47) has three syllables.

[3] Susa] Capital of the Persian and then Parthian empires. F. (on II. 49) points out the confusion of implicitly calling Parthians 'Medes' or Persians (the people they supplanted). 'Nation' (2. 49), towards the beginning of the sentence, is trisyllabic.

[4] Getes] Untypically anglicized, and pronounced so as to rhyme with 'feats'.

[5] Rome's lord] M. follows F. and other editors in reading *Vrbi*, 'the city's' (II. 61), here, but gives *orbi*, 'the world's [lord]' as an alternative, which modern scholars sometimes prefer.

[6] 2. 67–246 (= II. 63–233)] A long recollection of the earlier civil conflict at Rome between Marius and Sulla, which took place largely in the 80s BC.

	'Such woes', quoth he, 'the gods intended us:	
70	When after^(b) both his triumphs, Marius	
	His flying head among the reeds and sedge	
	Once hid, the fens then covered Fortune's pledge.¹	
	But, taken, he endured a prison's stinch,	*stink*
75	And his old limbs did iron shackles pinch.²	
	To die a consul, happy and in Rome,	
	Beforehand^(c) suffered he for guilt to come.	
	Death fled him oft, and power to shed his blood	
	In vain a Cimbrian^(d) had, who trembling stood:	
80	Off'ring a stroke, his falt'ring hand the sword	
	Let fall. His dungeon did strange light afford:	
	Th'affrighted Cimbrian Furies seemed to see,	
	And heard what Marius afterward should be:	
	"Thou can'st not touch this life: to Fate he owes	
85	Thousands of lives ere he his own can lose.	
	Cease thy vain fury: if you Cimbrians would	
	Revenge on Rome your slaughtered nation's blood,	
	Save this old man, whom their stern will to serve	
	Not the gods' love but anger did preserve."	
90	A cruel and fit man, when Fate contrived	
	Rome's ruin: he, on Libyan coasts arrived,	
	Wandered through empty cottages upon	
	Triumphèd Jugurth's spoiled dominion,	
	And Punic ashes trod. Each other's state	
95	Carthage^(e) and Marius there commiserate,³	
	And both cast down, both now the gods excused.	
	But into Marius' mind that air infused	
	A Libyan rage: when Fortune turned again,	
	Slaves from^(f) their lords, and prisoners from the chain	
100	He freed and armed; no man his ensigns bore,	
	But who the badge of some known mischief wore,	

---

¹ Marius ... pledge] Gaius Marius ('Marius' here pronounced trisyllabically, 2. 72, although disyllabic at 2. 84 and 98), held the consulship seven times and celebrated two triumphs. He tried to hide in marshland at the mouth of the Liris after being forced to flee Rome in 86 BC, and confronted a Cimbrian sent to execute him after his capture and imprisonment at Minturnae.

² prison's stinch ... shackles pinch] M. imitates these lines, with reference to Marius, in *The Victorious Reign of Edward III*, sig. N4ᵛ: 'The prison's stinch, the shackles that he bore, | The bread he begged on wasted Affrick's shore, | Which he himself before had overcome, | Made his return so sad to wretched Rome.'

³ commiserate] Lacking the usual contraction in the third syllable.

And brought guilt to the camp.¹ O Fates, how sad
A day was that,² when conquering Marius had
105 Surprised the walls? How swift flew cruel death?
Senators with plebeians lost their breath.
The sword raged uncontrolled, no breast was free;
The temples stained with blood, and slippery
Were the red stones with slaughter; no age then
110 Was free, the near-spent time of agèd men
They hastened on, nor shamed with bloody knife
To cut the infant's new-spun thread of life.³
What crime had infants done to merit death?
But 'twas enough that they could lose their breath.⁴
115 Fury directs them: guilty lives to take
Alone, seemed too remiss; for number-sake   *number's sake*
Some fall; one cuts off heads he does not know,
Whilst empty-handed he's ashamed to go;
No hope to 'scape, but kiss the blood-stained⁽ᵍ⁾ hand
120 Of Marius; though a thousand swords did stand
Ready, base People, did you not disdain
At such a price a life though long to gain,
Much less a time so short, so troublesome,
And breath but respited 'til Sulla come?
125 Who now has time to wail plebeian fates?
Scarce can we thine, brave Baebius,⁽ʰ⁾ whom the hates
Of the fierce multitude in pieces tore,⁵

---

¹ no man ... the camp] M. quoted the Latin lines (II. 96–98) in his *Historiae Angliae Parliamenti Breviarium* (London: Charles Sumptner for Thomas Bruster, 1650), sig. G2ʳ, when describing Charles I's attempts to gain assistance from the notorious army of the Duke of Lorraine. He did the same, adding the English wording of ll. 101–03, in his subsequent English version, *History of the Parliament*, sig. H3ʳ. Perhaps as a result, 2. 101–02 are (mis)quoted under 'Rebellion' in Joshua Poole's *The English Parnassus* (London: for Thomas Johnson, 1657), p. 464.

² how sad] Reflecting the redoubling in L: *quis ille,* | *Quis fuit ille dies,* 'what a day, what a day that was' (II. 98–99).

³ Senators ... thread of life] Together with the Latin (II. 101–07), this passage is printed (and described as 'exquisitely translated') in John Weever, *Ancient Funerall Monuments* (London: Thomas Harper, 1631), p. 460, when describing 'the cruelty of the Scots' who invaded northern England, despoiling churches and slaughtering inhabitants, during the reign of Edward I. with bloody knife] M.'s vivid addition (albeit demanded by the rhyme).

⁴ But 'twas enough ... breath] To create a rhyme M. lessens the brevity of L.'s *Sed satis est iam posse mori,* 'but now it is enough to be able to die' (II. 109).

⁵ fierce multitude ... tore] M. follows F.'s *multitudinis* rather than L.'s *corona,* 'ring' (of people surrounding Baebius; II. 120). M.'s 'dismemberment' suggests the reading *discerpsisse,* 'rend, tear', which is noted as a variant by F. and other editors who print *discessisse,* 'to separate'.

Nor thine, Antonius,⁽ⁱ⁾ that thy death before
Couldst prophesy, whose gray head bleeding yet
130　On Marius' table the rude soldier set.
Torn are the headless Crassi:^(k) impious wood
Is stained with sacred tribunicial^(l) blood.
Thou, Scaevola,^(m) that didst a kiss disdain
Of Marius' hand, at Vesta's altar slain
135　And never quenchèd fires:[1] but age's drought
Left thee not so much blood, as would put out
The flame. His seventh⁽ⁿ⁾ consulship now come,
Old Marius dies, a man that had o'ercome
Fortune's worst hate, and her best love enjoyed,
140　And tasted all that Fates for man provide.
　　How many near the Colline port were killed, [II. 134]
How many carcasses on heaps were piled
At Sacriportum?^(o) Where almost her seat
Had the world's empire changed, and Samnis yet
145　Hoped deeper far to wound the Roman name,
Than at the Caudine^(p) Forks.[2] Then Sulla came
With a revenge more bloody;[3] his sword reft
Rome of that little blood before was left.[4]
Whilst cutting off (cruel chirurgian)[5]　　　　　　　　　　*surgeon*
150　Th'affected parts, too far his lancing hand
Follows the sore: now guilty men are slain
So long, 'til none but guilty men remain;
Anger not curbed by law breaks forth; they wreak
Their private hatreds now, for Sulla's sake
155　All is not done, for everyone fulfils
Their own bloodthirsty and revengeful wills,
Pretending his command.[6] With impious steel
Servants their masters, sons their fathers kill;

---

[1]　Baebius ... Antonius ... Scaevola] Together with the Crassi (father and son) L. names three victims of Marius.

[2]　Colline port ... Sacriportum ... Caudine Forks] The first two were battle-grounds between Sulla and Marius: L. compares their slaughter with that of the Caudine Forks (321 BC), when the Samnites (M.'s 'Samnis') inflicted a major defeat on Rome.

[3]　a revenge more bloody] *immensis ... cladibus*, 'with immense destruction' (II. 139).

[4]　his sword ... was left] In L., Sulla drinks Rome's last blood *(Ille | Hausit,* II. 140 41).

[5]　cruel chirurgian] Not in L.; translates F.'s *acrior chirurgus*.

[6]　Their own ... his command] Interpretation and expansion of L.'s *non uni cuncta dabantur, | Sed fecit sibi quisque nefas. Semel omnia victor | Iusserat*, 'All this was not being done for one man (Sulla): each committed his own sacrilege. The victor had ordered everything when he ordered once' (II. 146–47).

	Which son shall be the parricide, by strife	
160	They seek; a brother sells a brother's life.	
	Some hide themselves in tombs, live men remain	
	Among the dead, beasts' dens can scarce contain	
	The flying multitude: one strangled dies	
	By his own hand; one from a precipice	
165	Dies broken with the fall, preventing so	
	The tyranny of his insulting foe.	
	His funeral pile one making, ere he dies	
	Leaps in, and whilst he may, those rites enjoys.	
	Great captains' heads borne through the streets on spears	
170	Are piled up in the Market; there appears	*the Forum*
	Each secret murder; not so many heads	
	In stables of the tyrant Diomed's	
	Thrace saw, nor Libya on Antaeus' wall,	
	Nor mourning Greece in Oenomaus' hall.¹	
175	Limbs putrefied, which all known marks had left	
	Worn out by eating time, by fearful theft	
	The wretched parents take, and bear away;	
	Myself (I still remember that sad day),²	
	Desirous those forbidden rites to do	
180	To my slain brother's head, searched to and fro	
	The carcasses of Sulla's peace, to see	
	What trunk 'mongst all would with that head agree.	
	What need I tell how Catulus was paid	
	With blood, and Marius a sad off'ring made?³	
185	Who, mangled, sacrificed before the tomb	
	Of his perchance unwilling foe did come.	
	His⁽ᑫ⁾ mangled joints, as many wounds as limbs	
	We saw, yet no wound deadly given him	
	Through his spoiled body: an example rare	*throughout*
190	Of cruelty, a dying life to spare.⁴	

---

¹ tyrant Diomed's ... Oenomaus' hall] Examples of mythological cruelty. Diomedes, king of Thrace (*Bistonii ... tyranni*, 'the Bistonian tyrant', II. 163), fed his horses on human flesh, Antaeus nailed his guests to a wall, and Oenomaus, king of Elis (whom L. does not explicitly name), slaughtered his daughter's suitors 'in the Pisan palace' (*Pisaea ... aula*, II. 164, a reference to Elis' capital city).

² Myself] It is still an old man speaking. The phrase in parenthesis is mostly M.'s; L. simply says *Meque ipsum memini*, 'I remember that I myself...' (II. 179).

³ Catulus was paid ... Marius a sad off'ring] Quintus Lutatius Catulus, the Elder. In L., the spirit of Catulus has been 'placated' with enemy-blood, *manes* | *Placatos* (II. 173–74). Marius Gratidianus, whose slow death by torture is here portrayed, was Marius's nephew.

⁴ His mangled joints ... to spare] This grisly description is quoted, alongside some of L.'s

His hands chopped off, his tongue cut out as yet
Wagged, and the air did with dumb motions beat;
One slits his nostrils, one cuts off his ears;
His eyes out last of all another tears,
195 Left in 'til then his mangled limbs to see;
A thing past credit, one poor man should be   *beyond belief*
The subject of so many cruelties.
A lump deformed, his mangled body lies
So strangely slaughtered;[1] not disfigured more
200 Floats a torn shipwrecked carcass to the shore
From the mid-sea. The fruit of all your toil
Why do you lose, and Marius' face so spoil
That none can now discern him? 'Twere more need
Sulla should know him, to applaud the deed.
205 ^(r)Praeneste's fortune saw her men all die[2]
In one death's space: the flower of ^(s) Italy,
The only youth of Latium sadly slain,
Did wretched Rome's Ovilia distain.[3]
So many men to cruel death at once
210 Oft earthquakes, shipwrecks or infections
Of air or earth, famine or war hath sent;
Never before a doom of punishment.[4]   *sentence*
The soldiers thronged could scarcely wield at all
Their killing hands, the slain could hardly fall
215 Supported so; but number did oppress
The dying people and dead carcasses
Increased the slaughter, falling heavily
On living bodies. His strange cruelty,[5]
Secure and fearless, Sulla from above

Latin (ll. 177–79), to illustrate the cruelty of the 'Service-book savages' in the Puritan tract by 'Dwalphintramis', *The Anatomie Of The Service Book* (location and printer unknown, 1641), sig. F4^v.

[1] A lump ... slaughtered] *Sic mole ruinae | Fracta sub ingenti miscentur pondere membra*, 'thus his broken limbs, in a mass of ruin, are mixed together beneath a huge weight' (ll. 187–88).

[2] die] *ense recisos*, 'sliced by the sword' (l. 194).

[3] Praeneste's fortune ... Ovilia] Sulla sacked Praeneste in 83 BC, slaughtering five thousand Roman prisoners. The *Ovilia* were sheepcot-like enclosures, used to divide people into voting units during elections.

[4] doom of punishment] Simply *poena*, 'punishment', in L. (l. 201).

[5] strange cruelty] *tanti ... sceleris*, 'so great a crime' (ll. 207–08). M.'s is fairly common literary idiom — see e.g. 'thy strange apparent cruelty', Shakespeare, *Merchant of Venice*, IV. 1. 20.

	Beheld, nor could so many thousands move	
220	His heart,¹ by him commanded all to die.	
	I'th'Tyrrhene gulf their piled-up bodies lie.	
	The first thrown in under the water lay,	
	The last on bodies; strongest ships they stay,	
225	And Tiber, parted by that fatal bay,²	*dam, embankment*
	Sends one part to the sea, carcasses stay	
	The other, 'til the violent stream of blood	
	Enforced the waters' course to Tiber's flood.³	
	Nor can the banks the river now contain,	
230	But o'er the fields the bodies float again,	
	Rolling at last into the Tyrrhene main;	
	On the blue waves it sets a purple stain.	
	For this did Sulla merit to be styled	
	'Happy' and ⁽ᵗ⁾'Saviour', and in Mars his field	
235	To be interred?⁴ But these black mischiefs are	
	To be endured again:⁵ this cruel war	
	Will the same order and conclusion take,	
	But fears more horrid suppositions make,	
	And in this war mankind shall suffer more.	
240	The exiled Marii sought but to restore	
	Themselves again, and Sulla's victories	
	Sought but the ruin of his enemies.	
	Their aims are higher:⁶ both, long powerful, take	
	Up arms, and neither civil war would make	
245	To do as Sulla did.' Thus wails old age,	
	Rememb'ring past, and fearing future rage.	
	This terror struck not noble Brutus' heart,⁷	[II. 234]

¹ nor could ... move | His heart] F. prints *Non piguit*, 'he wasn't ashamed'; modern editions prefer *non timuit*, 'he didn't fear to' (II. 209).
² bay] *strage cruenta*, 'bloody heap' (II. 212).
³ 'til the violent stream ... flood] i.e. the force of the blood-deluge, joined with the river waters, helped to burst a path through the piles of corpses to the sea (II. 214–17).
⁴ 'Happy' and 'Saviour'] Sulla's epithet was 'happy' (*Felix*) and on his return to Rome he was hailed as 'Saviour' (*Salus*).
⁵ black mischiefs] Intensification of L.'s *Haec ... patienda*, 'these things to be endured again' (II. 223).
⁶ Their aims are higher] *alio*, 'for a different purpose' (II. 230–31), i.e. monarchical rule by winning a civil war. Possibly suggesting the high-aspiring villains of Renaissance tragedy: see 2. 418n.
⁷ noble Brutus] Marcus Junius Brutus, Caesar's future assassin (cf. 7. 667, 9. 20). L.'s epithet is *magnanimus*, 'great-hearted' (II. 234); L.'s 'noble' was often applied to Brutus in early modern England (e.g. the 'seid chiuallerous noble Brutus' in Caxton's 1481 translation of Cicero's *De Senuctute*, sig. g8ʳ).

Nor in this frightful stir was he a part
Of the lamenters, but at midnight he
250 (When now her wain Parrhasian Helice
Turned)¹ at his uncle Cato's no large house
Knocks.² Him he finds waking and anxious,
For Rome and the whole state a fearful man,
Not for himself;³ when Brutus thus began.
255 'Banished and flying virtue's only hold
And refuge, which no storm of fortune could
E'er reave thee of, guide thou this wavering heart,   *deprive*
And to my thoughts a certain strength impart.
At Caesar's side or Pompey's others stand:
260 O'er Brutus none but Cato shall command.
Wilt thou keep peace, and in this doubtful age
Unshaken stand? Or mingling with the rage
Of the mad rout, this civil war approve?
Others to this sad war bad causes move:
265 One his stained house in peace and fear of laws,⁴
Another fights for want, mingling that cause
With the world's wreck. Blind fury leads on none,
All drawn with gainful hopes, but thee alone
The war itself affects.⁵ What boots it thee
270 T'have been so long from the times' vices free?
This only meed of thy long virtue take:⁶   *reward, recompense*
The wars find others guilty, thee they make.
But let not wicked war have power t'employ
These hands, O gods; let not thy javelin fly⁷

---

¹ Parrhasian Helice | Turned] i.e. at midnight.
² Cato's no large house | Knocks.] Marcus Porcius Cato, later 'Cato Uticensis' or 'Cato the Younger', brother of Brutus's mother Servilia. Famed for his frugality and strictness, Cato was an exemplary figure in early modern England — see Introduction, p. 21n. In M.'s *Continuation* he is termed the 'soule of Roman libertie' and his suicide in 46 BC is portrayed in detail (sigs D3v, F3r–F7r). For Jonson's possible influence on M.'s portrait, see 2. Arg. (and notes), 2. 358n.
³ For Rome ... Not for himself] Characteristically 'patriotic'; cf. 2. Ded. 7–12. 'Not for himself' is language commonly used of Christ, saints or martyrs in early modern England.
⁴ One ... laws] *Hos polluta domus, legesque in pace timendae*, 'These men [are driven to war] because of a disgraced house, and laws to be feared in peace-time' (II. 252) — i.e. to escape legal punishment for domestic crimes.
⁵ thee alone | The war itself affects] *tibi uni | Per se bella placent?*, 'To you alone, Cato, is [civil] war pleasing for itself?' (II. 255–56).
⁶ meed ... virtue take] In F. and many other early modern editions a question: *Hoc solum longae pretium virtutis habebis?*, 'Will you have this meed alone of thy long virtue?' (II. 258).
⁷ let not ... fly] *ferantur* (II. 262); modern editions print *ferentur* ('will not fly'). The first

275 'Mongst others in a thick, sky-dark'ning cloud;
Let not such virtue be in vain bestowed.
The war's whole chance will cast itself on thee.
Who would not die upon that sword and be
Cato's offence, though slain by another hand?
280 Thou mightst alone and quiet better stand,
As stars in heaven still unshaken are[1]
When lightnings, storms and tempest rend the air
Nearer to earth. Wind's rage and thunder's spite
Plain grounds must suffer, when Olympus' height,
285 Placed by the gods above the clouds, is free:[2]
Small things jars vex, the great ones quiet be.[3]
'Twill glad proud Caesar in this war to hear
So great a citizen has deigned t'appear:
Nor will it grieve him that great Pompey's side
290 Is chose, not his: 'twill be enough his pride
That Cato has approved of civil war.[4]
Rome's Senate and both consuls armèd are
Under a private man,[5] and many more
Of note and worth; to these add Cato too
295 Under command of Pompey: none lives free
In all the world but Caesar.[6] But if we
Do for our country's laws and freedom go
To war, then Brutus is not Caesar's foe
Nor Pompey's, but the conqueror's, whoe'er.'[7]
300   Thus Brutus spake, when from an inside clear   [II. 284]
These sacred words drew Cato: 'We confess,

---

two syllables of 'javelin' are elided.
[1] heaven] Disyllabic, uncharacteristically: see Note on Editorial Practice.
[2] Olympus' height, | Placed by the gods] *nubes excedit Olympus | Lege deum*, 'by the law of the gods, Olympus towers over the clouds' (II. 271–72); modern editions place a full stop after Olympus.
[3] Small things … quiet be] i.e. great things remain untroubled by things which disturb smaller entities.
[4] 'twill be enough his pride … civil war] i.e. to his pride. 'Pride', like 'proud' (2. 287), is M.'s interpolation: in L. Caesar is *laetus*, 'happy', and 'pleased' (*placet*) that Cato will take part (II. 273–76).
[5] private man] The Senate had offered Pompey command of the war despite him holding no public office.
[6] none lives free … but Caesar] L.'s Brutus offers a more explicit image of servility: Cato is *sub iuga*, 'beneath [Pompey's] yoke' (II. 280), given that to be commanded by a *privatus* is a form of slavery.
[7] But if we … conqueror's, whoe'er] i.e. the patriotic action is not to fight in this civil war, but to fight the victor of that civil war after it is concluded.

Brutus, that civil war's great wickedness:
But where the Fates will lead, virtue shall go
Securely on.¹ To make me guilty now
Shall be the gods' own crime. Who would endure   305
To see the world dissolve, himself secure?
Who could look on when heaven should fall, earth fail
And the confused world perish, and not wail?
Shall unknown nations in our Roman war
Engage themselves, and foreign kings from far   310
Crossing the seas? And shall I rest alone?
Far be it, gods, the Daci and Getes should moan²
Their losses in Rome's fall and Cato lie
Secure. As parents when their children die
In person mourn, build up with their own hands   315
The funeral pile and light the fatal brands,
I will not leave thee, Rome, 'til I embrace
Thy hearse and, Liberty, thy dying face,
And fleeting ghost with honour do attend.
So let it go: let th'angry gods intend   320
A complete Roman sacrifice; no bloods
Will we defraud the war of. Would the gods
Of heaven and Erebus would now strike dead
For all our crimes this one condemnèd head.
Devoted Decius by his foes could fall:³   325
Me let both Roman hosts assault, and all
Rhine's barbarous troops; let me i'th'midst receive
All darts, all wounds, that this sad war can give.
Let me redeem the people;⁴ let my fate,
Whate'er Rome's manners merit, expiate.   330
Why should the easily conquered people die,
That can endure a lord?⁵ Strike only me,

---

¹ where the Fates will lead] An echo of the famous dictum of the Stoic Cleanthes, translated by Seneca as *Ducunt volentem fata, nolentem trahunt*, 'Fates lead the willing man, drag the unwilling': *Epistles*, trans. by Richard M. Gummere, Loeb Classical Texts (Cambridge, MA: Harvard University Press, 1917), 107. 11. For M.'s neo-Stoic use of 'secure', see Introduction, p. 21.
² Getes] Pronounced to rhyme with 'meets' or 'fates'; however, even with this pronunciation, the line is a syllable too long.
³ Devoted Decius] A pun on the Roman ritual of *devotio*, a rite of self-sacrifice in battle associated with the Decii Mures family.
⁴ redeem] *redimat* ('atone', II. 312), but also recalling Christ's role as redeemer.
⁵ Why ... lord?] L.'s Cato is more critical: *Ad iuga cur faciles populi, cur saeva volentes | Regna pati pereunt?*, 'Why are the people easily yoked, why do they perish desiring to

	Me with all swords and piles, that all in vain	
	Our wrongèd laws and liberties maintain:	
335	This throat shall peace to Italy obtain.	
	After my death he that desires to reign	
	Need not make war, but now let's follow all	
	The common ensigns,[1] Pompey general.	
	Though he o'ercome, 'tis not yet known that he	
340	Means to himself the world's sole monarchy.[2]	
	I'll help him conquer, lest he should suppose	
	He conquers for himself.' From this arose	
	Young Brutus' courage;[3] this grave speech too far	
	Made the young man in love with civil war.	
345	Now Phoebus driving the cold dark away,	[II. 326][4]
	They heard a noise at door:(v) chaste Marcia,	
	Come from Hortensius' tomb, stood knocking there,	
	Once given a maid in marriage happier,	
	But when the fruit and price of wedlock she	
350	Three births had paid, another family	
	To fill, was fruitful Marcia lent a bride,	
	To join two houses by the mother's side.	
	Now when Hortensius' ashes urnèd rest,[5]	
	She in her funeral robes, beating her breast	
355	With often strokes and tearing her loose hair,	
	Sprinkled with ashes from the sepulchre,	
	To please sour Cato with a gesture sad[6]	
	Thus speaks: 'Whilst blood and childing strength I had,	*childbearing*
	Cato, I did thy will, two husbands took:	
360	Now worn away, and with oft travel broke	*travail, labour*
	I come, no more to part: grant now our old	

endure savage monarchy?' (II. 314-15). 'Easily' (2. 331) is probably contracted to 'eas'ly' in pronunciation.

[1] common ensigns] *publica signa*, i.e. the official standards of the Roman state (II. 319).

[2] 'tis not yet known ... the world's sole monarchy] 'the right/law [i.e. rule] of the whole world' (*totius ... ius ... mundi*, II. 321). M.'s 'not yet known' captures the uncertainty in *non bene compertum*, 'not ascertained' or 'not verified'; cf. 1. 338n.

[3] courage] *acres | Irarum ... stimulos*, 'the bitter spurs of anger' (II. 323-24), a problematic outcome given the Stoic disapproval of anger. M.'s 'courage', followed by 'this grave speech' (2. 343, for *sic fatur*, 'so he spoke', II. 323), appears to render the ending of this scene less ambivalent than in L.

[4] 2. 345-414] Cato marries Marcia (again). Marcia was married twice: first as the (second) wife of Cato, and then in 56 BC to Quintus Hortensius Hortalus (consul 69 BC), in order to bear him an heir.

[5] urnèd] Placed in an urn; M.'s coinage.

[6] sour Cato] M.'s epithet, not in L.; cf. 2. 402. See Introduction, p. 21-22.

Wedlock's untasted rites, grant me to hold
The empty name of wife, and on my tomb
Write 'Cato's Marcia', lest in time to come
365 It may be asked whether I left the bed
Of my first lord bestowed or banishèd.
Nor come I now prosperity to share,
But to partake thy labours and sad care.
Let me attend the camp: leave me not here
370 In peace, Cornelia to the war so near."[1]
These speeches moved the man, though these times are   [II. 350]
Unfit for Hymen, when Fate calls to war;
Without vain pomp to tie a nuptial knot
In the gods' presence he refuses not.
375 No garlands on the marriage doors were worn,
Nor linen fillets did the posts adorn,
No bridal tapers shone, no bed on high   *candles*
With ivory steps and gold embroidery,
No matron in a towered crown, that led
380 The bride, forbid her on the threshold tread;
No yellow veil covered her face, to hide
The fearful blushes of a modest bride;
No precious girdle girded her loose gown,
No chain adorned her neck, nor linen down
385 From off her shoulders her nak'd arms o'erspread:
So as she was, funeral habited,
Even like her sons, her husband she embraced,
A funeral robe above her purple placed.[2]
The usual jests were spared; the husband wants,   *lacks*
390 After the Sabine use, his marriage tants.   *taunts*
None of their kindred met; the knot they tie
Silent, content with Brutus' auspicy.[3]
His o'ergrown hair he from that sacred face
Shaves not, nor will in his sad looks embrace[4]
395 One joy (since first that wicked war begun
He lets his unshorn hoary locks fall down

---

[1] Cornelia] Pompey's wife. See 3. 23n.
[2] So as ... placed] A useful example of M.'s variable attitude to metrification: the first 'funeral' (2. 386) is trisyllabic, but the second (2. 388) elides the second syllable.
[3] 2. 375–92] This lacks all the main features of a Roman wedding, including the Sabine custom of abusive ribaldry directed at the groom. Brutus does, however, act as *auspex*, a kind of 'best man' (II. 371).
[4] sad looks] *duro ... vultu*, 'hard expression' (II. 373).

O'er his rough front, and a sad beard to hide
His cheeks: for he alone from factions freed
Or hate, had leisure for mankind to weep),[1]
400 Nor in his bridal bed would Cato sleep:
Even lawful love could continence reject.[2]
These were his manners, this sour Cato's sect,
To keep a mean, hold fast the end, and make   *moderation*
Nature his guide, die for his country's sake.
405 For all the world, not him, his life was lent
He thinks; his feasts but hunger's banishment,
His choicest buildings were but fence for cold,
His best attire rough gowns, such as of old
Was Roman wear, and nothing but desire
410 Of progeny in him warmed Venus' fire;
Father and husband both to Rome was he,
Servant to justice and strict honesty
For th'public good; in none of Cato's acts
Creeps self-born pleasure, or her share exacts.
415   Now with his fearful troops Pompey the Great   [II. 392]
To Trojan Capua fled,[3] meant there to seat
The war, his scattered strength there to unite,
And his aspiring foe's assaults to meet[4]
Where Apennine, raised somewhat higher, fills
420 The midst of Italy with shady hills,
Than which no part of earth does swell more high
In any place, nor nearer meets the sky.
    The mountain 'twixt two seas extended stands   [II. 399]
(Th'upper and lower sea):[5] on the right hand

---

[1] factions freed | Or hate] *studiis odiisque*, 'enthusiasms and hatreds' (II. 377). 'Faction'/'factious' was a freighted political term in early Stuart England, and also in M.'s vocabulary: see Introduction, p. 24, pp. 25–6n. Here it relies on F.'s paraphrase *partium studiis*, 'partisan enthusiasms'.

[2] continence] *robur*, 'toughness' (II. 379), usually connected with mental constancy in Stoic discourse. Other early modern commentators (not F.) paraphrase as *continentia*, here meaning sexual abstinence.

[3] Trojan Capua fled] *Moenia Dardanii ... Campana coloni*, 'the Campanian walls of a Trojan colonist' (II. 392). M. derives 'Capua' from F.'s note.

[4] meant there ... assaults to meet] *hinc summa moventis | Hostis in occursum sparsas extendere partes*, 'thence to stretch out his scattered forces against the onslaught of an enemy exerting the utmost' (II. 393–94). M.'s 'aspiring', though implicit in L.'s *summa moventis* or F.'s paraphrase *summa molienti*, 'endeavouring the utmost', has overtones of English tragic over-reachers, e.g. the Caesar 'of high aspiring thoughtes' in the anonymous *The Tragedie of Caesar and Pompey* (London: George Eld for John Wright, 1607), sig. D3ᵛ.

[5] The mountain ... sea] i.e. the Apennine range. As F. explains, for Romans the 'upper sea'

425 Is Pisa, seated on the Tyrrhene shore;
     Ancona on the left, vexed evermore
     With storms and winds that from Dalmatia blow.¹
     Here from vast fountains do great rivers flow,
     And into th'double seas' divorce do slide
430 In several channels: down on the left side
     Metaurus swift and strong Crustumium flow;
     Isapis joined t'Isaurus, Sonna too
     And Aufidus the Adriatic beats;
     Eridanus, than which no river gets
435 More ground, whole forests rolls into the sea
     O'erturned, and robs of rivers Italy.
     They say that poplars on this river's side
     First grew, when Phaethon amiss did guide
     The day;² his wand'ring chariot burnt the sky
440 And scorched the earth; all rivers then were dry
     But this,³ whose streams did Phoebus' fires withstand.
     Not less than Nile, if on plain Libyan sand
     It flowed like Nile; not less than Ister 'twere,
     Unless that Ister, running everywhere,
445 The streams that fall into all seas does meet
     And not alone the Scythian Ocean greet.⁴
     From springs that down the hill's right side do flow
     Rutuba, Tiber, swift Vulturnus grow;
     Night-air infecting Sarnus, Liris too
450 Runs, strengthened by the Vestine rivers, through
     Maricae's woody lands; Siler, that glides
     Through Salerne's fields;⁵ Macra, whose ford abides
     No ships, into the sea near Luna fall.
     The hill (where he in length extended all,
455 Meeting the bending Alps, France oversees)
     To th'Umbrians, Marsians and Sabellians is
     Fertile, and does with woody arms embrace

is the Adriatic and the 'lower sea' the Tyrrhenian, off Italy's west coast.
¹ right hand ... Dalmatia] The perspective is of someone looking south along the Apennine range. Thus the lands, rivers and sea to the east are on the left (2. 430 ff.), and the western ones on the right (2. 447 ff.).
² Phaethon] cf. 1. 53n. Phaethon's grieving sisters were turned into poplar trees (afterwards associated with mourning).
³ But this...] The river Eridanus.
⁴ Ister ... Scythian Ocean] L. means that via distributaries the Ister falls into other seas too.
⁵ Salerne's] Anglicized in pronunciation, to rhyme with 'ferns'.

The people of the ancient Latin race.
Nor leaves he Italy, before he end
460 In the Scyllaean caverns, and extend
Unto Lacinian Juno's house his hill.[1]
Longer he was than Italy, until
The sea divided him, and water forced
The land; then, when two meeting seas divorced
465 What was conjoined, part of the hill the sea
Gave to Pelorus in Sicilia.[2]
    Caesar, now mad of war, loves not to find   [II. 439][3]
But make his way by blood, nor is his mind
Joyed that in Italy he sees no foes,
470 No countries guarded from him, meets no blows,
But counts his journey lost; desires to break
Not open gates, and loves his march to make
By fire and sword, not sufferance; thinks it shame
To tread permitted paths and bear the name
475 Of citizen. The Italian cities are[4]
Doubtful which way to lean, and though when war
Makes her first feared approach, all easily
Will yield, with bulwarks yet they fortify
Their walls, dig trenches round about below;
480 Vast stones and weapons from above to throw
They get, and engines on their walls provide.
The people most incline to Pompey's side,
But faith with terror fights: so when we see   *loyalty*
The south wind's horrid blasts possess the sea,
485 The waves all follow him, 'til by the stroke
Of Aeolus his spear, the opened rock
To the rough seas lets out the eastern wind;[5]
They still retain, though new assaults they find,

---

[1] Nor leaves he...] i.e. the Apennine mountain range. For the meaning of 'Scyllaean caverns' see 1. 583n. L. only refers to *templa Lacinia*, 'Lacinian temples' (II. 434); M.'s specification of Juno's temple derives from F. or another commentary.
[2] Pelorus in Sicilia] i.e. Mount Pelorus in Sicily had been part of the Apennine mountain range until divided by the straits separating Sicily from the mainland.
[3] 2. 467–508] The Italian peoples consider whom to support in the war. L. suggests in the following passage that they only succumbed to a bloodthirsty Caesar out of fear. A different interpretation, that actually many cities were supporters of Caesar, is pointed out by F. and implicit in some of M.'s historical notes.
[4] The Italian cities] Probably eliding 'the'.
[5] Aeolus his spear] Aeolus is the god of winds. In this extended simile, Caesar is the east wind, Pompey (or the Roman state) the south.

The old, though th'east wind th'air with dark storms fill;
490 The ocean does the south wind challenge still.
But people's minds fear changes easily,
And Fortune sways their wavering loyalty.
By Libo's flight Etruria's naked left,[1]
And Umbria, Thermus[y] gone, of freedom reft;
495 Sulla, far differing from his father's fame
In civil war, flies hearing Caesar's name;
Varus[z] before the first assault forsakes
Auximum's walls, and flight disordered takes
O'er rocks and deserts; Lentulus[a] is beat
500 From Asculum; the foes pursuing get
His men, that now alone the captain flies   *so that*
With empty standards, reft of companies.
Thou, Scipio,[b] leav'st the trust committed thee,
Luceria's fort, though in thy camp there be
505 The valiant'st youth, whom fear of Parthian war
From Caesar took; whom Pompey, to repair
His French loss, lent him and, while he thought good,
Bestowed on Caesar th'use of Roman blood.[2]
But fair Corfinium's well-fenced walls contain   [II. 478][3]
510 Thee, stout Domitius:[c] in thy camp remain
Those that arraignèd Milo did enclose.[4]
He, when a cloud of dust from far arose,
And on bright arms the sun reflecting shone,
And glittering swords, cries, 'Run, my soldiers, run
515 Down to the river, drown the bridge; and thou,
Increased from all thy emptied fountains now,
Rise, swelling stream: break down and bear away
This scattered bridge! There let the war now stay,
Let thy banks make our furious enemy
520 Linger a while: we'll count it victory

---

[1] By Libo's flight ...] In lines 493–508 L. attacks the cowardice of Rome's commanders, targeting i) L. Scribonius Libo, who had been deployed to take command of Etruria, but fled at the approach of Caesar; ii) the praetor Quintus Minucius Thermus, who had been fortifying Iguvium in Umbria; iii) Faustus Sulla, son of the dictator; iv) Attius Varus, who abandoned Auximum; v) Lentulus Spinther, who was driven from Asculum; vi) Q. Caecilius Metellus Pio Scipio.

[2] The valiant'st youth ... blood] Scipio was assigned two legions to defend Syria after Parthian incursions in 51 BC, one from Pompey, one from Caesar; Pompey's had already been loaned to Caesar to compensate for military losses in 53 BC.

[3] 2. 509–60] The attempted defence of Corfinium by Domitius Ahenobarbus.

[4] arraignèd Milo] *polluto*, 'stained with blood-guilt' (II. 480). For Milo, see 1. 346n.

That Caesar first stays here.' This said, in vain
He sends swift cohorts from the town amain.   *with full force*
    For Caesar first, when from the fields he spied   [II. 492]
His passage lost by bridge, enragèd cried,
525 'Cannot your walls, base cowards, shelter you
Enough, but that the fields and rivers too
Must help? I'll pass, though Ganges in my way
Rolled all his strength; no stream shall Caesar stay
Since Rubicon is past. Go, wingèd horse:[1]
530 Second, bold foot; the bridge now falling force.'
Thus spake he: forth the wingèd horsemen ride,
And, like a storm of hail, on t'other side
The water their well-brandished javelins light.
Caesar then takes the river, puts to flight
535 The soldiers all that were in station
To guard the bank, and safe before the town
Is come: when straight up lofty works are thrown
And engines raised, the walls to batter down.
    When lo (O shame of war!), opening the gate,   [II. 508]
540 The soldiers brought their captain bound and at
The feet of his proud foe present. But he,
With looks not shaming high nobility,
Offers his throat undaunted. Caesar sees
Death's sought and mercy feared, then thus replies:
545 'Live, though thou wouldst not, by our bounty live,
Enjoy this light, and to the conquered give
Good hope. Th'example of our clemency
Be thou, or else again war's fortunes try;
Nought for this pardon Caesar from thy hands
550 Expects, if thou o'ercome.' With that, commands
T'unbind him. Had his death the conqueror pleased,
How much a Roman's blush had fortune eased![2]
For following Rome's, the Senate's, Pompey's arms,
Pardon t'a Roman was the worst of harms.
555 He, yet unfeared, his anger doth retain,

---

[1] wingèd horse] *equitum ... catervae*, 'cavalry-troops' (II. 498). M. means 'swift': see e.g. Shakespeare, Sonnet 51, lines 7–9: 'though mounted on the wind, | In winged speed no motion shall I know. | Then can no horse with my desire keep pace'.

[2] Had his death ... fortune eased!] *Heu quanto melius vel caede peracta | Parcere Romano potuit fortuna pudori!*, 'Alas, how much better if fortune could have spared Roman shame, even at the cost of his killing!' (II. 517–18). M. interjects Caesar's own pleasure here, reinforcing a parallel with his later pardoning of Afranius (4. 371–76).

>
> Speaks thus t'himself: 'Wilt thou, base man, again
> See Rome, or seek peaceful retirements? No,
> Rather into war's fury dying go,
> Rush boldly through the midst, sure end to make
> 560 Of this loathed life, and Caesar's gift forsake.'
> Pompey, not knowing he was ta'en, provides [II. 526]¹
> Forces to strengthen with joined power his side,
> Meaning his camp next morning to remove.
> The soldiers' spirits before their march to prove,
> 565 He thus with a majestic voice bespake
> His silent troops:² 'Guilt-punishers, that take
> The better side, you truly Roman band,
> Armed by the state,³ no private man's command,
> Fear not to fight:⁴ Italy's wasted all
> 570 By barbarous troops, through the cold Alps the Gaul
> Is broken loose;⁵ blood has already dyed
> Caesar's polluted swords. The gods provide
> Well, that the mischief there begins and we
> First suffer wrong.⁶ O now let Rome by me
> 575 Take punishment, nor can you call it here
> True war, but our revenging country's ire:
> Nor is this more a war, than that wherein
> Nak'd-armed Cethegus, and fierce Catiline
> Meant to fire Rome, Lentulus and their mates.⁷
> 580 O madness to be pitied: when the Fates
> Would with Camillus and Metellus join
> Thee, Caesar, thou to Marius shouldst incline,

---

¹ 2. 561–635] Pompey addresses his troops.
² The soldiers' spirits...] *iras*, 'wrath' (II. 521); probably pronounced monosyllabically. with a majestic voice] *veneranda voce*, 'a voice to be revered' (II. 530). The term 'majestic' is used particularly of Pompey by M.: see Introduction, p. 17.
³ Armed by the state] *senatus*, 'the Senate' (II. 532). The distinction is constitutionally meaningful: Caesar claimed the Senate was manipulated by Pompey and in its rush to war had suppressed other institutions like the Tribunate.
⁴ Fear not to fight] In L. *votis deposcite pugnam*, 'demand wars with your prayers!' (II. 533).
⁵ the Gaul] *Gallica rabies*, 'Gallic frenzy' (II. 535).
⁶ The gods ... suffer wrong] i.e. thanks to the gods, Pompey's men have not incurred the guilt of starting a civil war.
⁷ Nak'd-armed Cethegus ... mates] 'Lentulus and their mates' are co-subjects of the sentence with Cethegus and Catiline. This refers to the attempted coup of 63 BC led by L. Sergius Catilina (Catiline). M.'s epithet 'fierce', applied elsewhere to Catiline (6. 904, 7. 71) is not in L. 'Nak'd-arm'd', translating *exertique* (II. 543), refers to the garments worn by the Roman clan of the Cethegi (cf. 6. 905). See Textual Notes.

And Cinna;[1] fall thou shalt, as Lepidus
Fell under Catulus;[2] Carbo by us
585 Beheaded, buried in Sicilia lies,
And he that made the Spaniards fierce to rise,
Banished Sertorius;[3] though I grudge with those
Thou, Caesar, should be placed, and Rome oppose
My arms 'gainst thee. Would from the Parthian war
590 Crassus had safe returned and conqueror,
That thou in such a cause as Spartacus
Mightst fall;[4] but, if the gods intend, to us
Thou shalt one title add. This arm a dart
Can ably brandish yet, about this heart
595 The blood is hot: know then, not all that love
To live in peace, in war will cowards prove.[5]
Nor let my age affright you, though he call
Me worn and weak: let an old general
Be in this camp, in that old soldiers be.
600 I have attained whate'er a people free
Can give, and nothing but a monarchy
Above me left: he that in Rome would be
Greater than I, no private state demands.
Here both Rome's consuls, here her Senate stands:[6]
605 Shall Caesar then subdue the Senate? Sure
Th'art not quite shameless, Fortune, to endure
Things should so blindly turn. Does rebel France,
So long a-taming, and those wars advance
His thoughts so high? Because from Germany
610 He fled and, calling a small stream a sea,
On the sought Britons turned his flying back?[7]

---

[1] And Cinna] i.e. Caesar could have been ranked with saviours of Rome, but chose to become another agent of internal Roman strife and plebeian insurrection, like Marius and Cinna (who instituted a reign of terror after Marius' death). Caesar was Marius's nephew.
[2] Lepidus ... Catulus] A reference to Catulus' suppression of Lepidus' uprising in 77 BC; cf. 8. 943.
[3] Carbo ... Sertorius] Carbo was an ally of Marius and Cinna against Sulla; Sertorius, also a pro-Marian, ruled a large part of Spain until Pompey was put in charge of the campaign against him.
[4] Would ... fall] See 1. 14n.
[5] To live in peace] Translating F.'s *in pace vivere*. L.'s Pompey is more contemptuous: *Qui pacem potuere pati*, 'who could suffer peace' (II. 559).
[6] both Rome's consuls] i.e. Lucius Lentulus and Caius Marcellus, consuls in 49 BC.
[7] Does rebel France ... flying back] Pompey belittles Caesar's achievements: the conquest of Gaul, and expeditions across the Rhine and to Britain.

Or swells he 'cause all Rome, though armed, forsake
The city, hearing his fierce troops are nigh?
Ah, fool, they fly not thee: all follow me.
615 My glorious ensigns on the ocean borne,
Ere Cynthia twice had filled her wanèd horns,
All pirates fled the seas, and at my hand
Humbly craved dwellings in a narrow land.[1]
I that stout king, that stayed Rome's growth, did force,
620 Flying along the Scythian seas' divorce,[2]
(Which Sulla ne'er could bring to pass) to die
By his own hand.[3] No land from me is free;
My trophies all that Titan sees possess.[4]
Going from thence Phasis' cold river sees
625 Me conqueror in the north; in the hot zone
Known Egypt and Syene, that at noon
No shadow spreads; my laws the west obeys;
Baetis, that meets the farthest western seas;
Me tamed Arabia knows, th'Aeniochs bold,
630 And Colchis famed for her stol'n fleece of gold;
The Cappadocians from my colours fly,
And Jews that serve an unknown deity;
Me soft Sophene fears, th'Armenians,
Taurus, and the subdued Cilicians:
635 What wars for him but civil do I leave?'
  These words his soldiers with no shout receive, [II. 596][5]
Nor are they eager of the fight; their fears
Great Pompey sees, and back his standard bears,
Loath in so great a war to venture men
640 O'ercome with fame of Caesar yet not seen.
As a bull beat in the first fight he tries,

---

[1] Ere Cynthia ... narrow land] Pompey recalls his triumph over Mediterranean pirates in 67 BC, which apparently took less than two months; he settled some of the defeated in Soloi (Southern Turkey), renaming it Pompeiopolis.
[2] Flying along ... divorce] '[I drove him into] exile through the separating forks of the Scythian sea', *per Scythici profugum divortia Ponti* (II. 580). Modern readers assume this is the Isthmus of the Crimea; F. believes it references the by-ways and criss-cross paths leading to Armenia.
[3] stout king ... own hand] i.e. Pompey's defeat of Mithridates, which resulted in the Pontic king's suicide. M. misses the irony of L.'s *Sylla felicior*, 'I, more happy/lucky/blessed than Sulla', a pun on Sulla's sobriquet 'Felix' (II. 582).
[4] No land...] A catalogue of territories and peoples conquered by Pompey, incorporating references to victories over Mithridates, in Jerusalem, Armenia and Cilicia.
[5] 2. 636–93] Pompey flees to Brundisium.

Through th'empty fields and desert forests flies
Exiled, and tries 'gainst ev'ry tree his horns,
Nor 'til his strength be perfited returns   *perfected*
645   To pasture; then, recovering his command,
Maugre the herdsman, leads them to what land   *despite*
He list:¹ so now, as weakest, Italy   *pleases him*
Does Pompey leave and through Apulia fly,
Himself immuring in Brundisium's hold,   *walling within*
650   A town by Cretan colonies of old
Possessed, that in th'Athenian navy fled
When lying sails reported Theseus dead.²
Hence Italy's now straightened coast extends
Herself in form of a thin tongue, and bends
655   Her horns t'inclose the Adriatic Sea,
Nor yet could these straight shut-up waters be
A haven, if high cliffs winds' violence
Did not restrain, and the tired waters fence.³
On both sides nature, the winds' tyranny
660   To stop, high cliffs opposes to the sea,
That ships by trembling cables held may stand.
Hence all the main lies ope, if to thy land   *the sea; open*
We sail, Corcyra, or our courses bend
On the left hand, where Epidamnus tends
665   To the Ionian.⁴ Thither sailors fly
When th'Adrian's rough, and clouds obscure the high   *Adriatic*
Ceraunian mountains, and with violent dash
The foaming seas Calabrian Sason wash.
  When of forsaken Italy there was   [11. 628]

---

¹ As a bull ... list] An extended simile, modelled partly on Virgil, *Georgics*, III. 224–36: see *Opera*, ed. by R. A. B. Mynors (Oxford: Clarendon Press, 1969). M.'s verbal choices — 'perfited', 'maugre' and 'list' — impart a consciously archaic tone, perhaps recalling numerous bull similes in Spenser's *Faerie Queene* (e.g. VI. 5. 19).

² Brundisium ... Theseus dead] According to legend Brundisium's origins lay in the Cretan settlers who came with the Athenian Theseus after his expedition to Crete to defeat the Minotaur. Though successful in destroying the monster, Theseus forgot to put up the white sails that would forewarn his father Aegeus that he was alive: seeing the 'lying [black] sails', Aegeus committed suicide.

³ Hence ... fence] As F. explains, the harbour of Brundisium (from the Greek *Brentesion*, 'deer's head') consisted of a round inner harbour, and an outer harbour running between two promontories with sinuous inner coastlines, thus resembling the head of a deer. 'Violence' (2. 657) is trisyllabic, although M. typically treats 'vio-' as one syllable (as at 2. 667, below).

⁴ Corcyra ... Ionian] i.e. one could sail to Corfu or, bearing north-east and crossing the Ionian Sea, to Epidamnus (= Dyrrachium).

670	No hope at all, nor that the war could pass	
	Into the Spanish coast,¹ for 'twixt that land	
	The lofty Alps did interposèd stand,²	
	Thus th'eldest of his noble progeny	
	Pompey bespake.³ 'The world's far regions try,	
675	Nile and Euphrates, wheresoe'er my name	
	Is spread, and all the cities where Rome's fame	
	I have advanced.⁴ Bring back unto the seas	
	The now dispersed Cilician colonies.⁵	
	The strength Pharnaces holds I charge thee bring;	
680	Arm my Tigranes, and th'Egyptian king,⁶	
	Those that inhabit both Armenias o'er,⁷	
	And the fierce nation by the Euxine shore,	
	Riphaean bands, and those where Scythian cars	
	On his slow back congealed Maeotis bears.	
685	Why speak I more? Through all the east, my son,	
	Carry this war, through every conquered town	
	I'th'world, to us all triumphed regions join.	
	But you, whose names the Latian feasts do sign,⁸	
	To Epire sail with the first north-east wind,⁹	*Epirus*
690	Through Greece and Macedon new strength to find	
	While winter gives us respite from the war.'	
	To his commands they all obedient are,	
	And from th'Italian shore their anchors weigh.	
	Caesar, impatient of war's long delay	[II. 650]¹⁰
695	Or rest,¹¹ lest changing fates might aught withstand,	

---

¹ the war ... | Into the Spanish coast] 'nor could war be turned to the hardy Spanish' (*ad duros ... Iberos*, II. 629), an approving description a seventeenth-century Englishman might want to avoid.
² 'twixt that land] i.e. between Italy and Spain.
³ th' eldest] Gnaeus Pompeius.
⁴ The world's far regions try...] Pompey calls on Gnaeus to summon all the forces of the east he had previously subdued (Pontus, Armenia, Egypt, as far east as the Sea of Azov).
⁵ Cilician colonies] See 2. 634n.
⁶ th'Egpytian king] *Pharios ... reges*, 'the Pharian monarchs', referring to the joint rule of Ptolemy and Cleopatra (II. 636); cf. 8. 515 ff.
⁷ those that ... both Armenias o'er] *populos utraque vagantes | Armenia*, 'peoples wandering through both [Greater and Lesser] Armenias' (II. 637-38).
⁸ But you...] The consuls, whose names were inscribed in the calendar (*Fasti*) to mark each year.
⁹ north-east wind] *Boreas*, 'north wind' (II. 646); in fact a south-west wind is necessary to make this voyage.
¹⁰ 2. 694-786] Caesar besieges Brundisium; Pompey escapes by sea.
¹¹ rest] *pacis*, 'of peace' (II. 650).

His flying son-in-law pursues at hand.
So many towns at first assault surprised
And forts disarmèd, others had sufficed;
Rome, the world's head, war's greatest booty, left
700 A prey; but Caesar, in all actions swift,
Thinking nought done whilst aught undone remained,
Fiercely pursues, and though he have obtained
All Italy, and that great Pompey lives
In th'utmost edge, that both are there, he grieves.[1]
705 Nor would he let his foes pass forth again
By sea, but seeks to stop the wat'ry main
And with vast hills dam up the ocean.
But this great labour is bestowed in vain:
The sea those mountains swallows, mixing all
710 With sands below. So if high Eryx fall
Into the midst of the Aegean Sea,[2]
No land above the water seen can be:
Or if the lofty Gaurus, quite torn down,
Were to the bottom of Avernus thrown.
715 But when no earth thrown in would firmly stand,
Then with a bridge of fastened ships the land
He joins; each galley do four anchors stay.[3]
Once o'er the sea proud Xerxes such a way
Made, by report, when joined by bridge he saw
720 Sestos t'Abydos, Europe t'Asia,
And fearing not th'east wind nor west's affront,
Walked o'er the curlèd back of Hellespont.[4]
When ships their sails round about Athos spread,
So now this haven's mouth ships straitenèd,[5]   *narrowed*

---

[1] that both are there] Caesar grieves that he and Pompey still 'share' Italy (*communem esse*, II. 660).

[2] Aegean Sea] Modern editions read *Aeolii*, 'Aeolian' (the sea to the north of Sicily), instead of *Aegaei*, 'Aegean' (2. 711; II. 665), following Bentley's conjecture.

[3] But when ... anchors stay] *Tunc placuit caesis innectere vincula silvis, | Roboraque immensis late religare catenis*, 'then [Caesar] chose to tie bonds to felled forests, and bind the trunks with immense chains' (II. 670-71). M.'s mention of ships and four anchors derives from F. who is following Caesar, *Commentarii de Bello Ciuili*, 1. 25. 6-7 (see the edition ed. by Renatus du Pontet (Oxford: Clarendon Press, 1908)).

[4] proud Xerxes ... Hellespont] M.'s Xerxes is the common early modern reading: on metrical grounds modern editors prefer *Persem*, 'the Persian' (II. 672). In 480 BC the Persian emperor, Xerxes, as part of an attempted invasion of Greece, joined Sestos and Abydos (towns on either side of the Hellespont, the sea dividing Europe and Asia) with a bridge of ships.

[5] So now ... straitenèd] *sic ora profundi | Arctantur casu nemorum*, 'thus the mouth of

725	On which their bulwarks up apace they raise,[1]	
	And lofty towers stand trembling on the seas.	
	When Pompey saw that a new land o'erspread	
	The ocean's face, care in his breast is bred	
	To ope the sea, and carry forth the war.[2]	
730	Filled sails and stretching shrouds the ships oft bare	ropes; bore
	Against these works; breaking them down made room	
	Into the sea for other ships to come;	
	Oft well-driven engines lightened the dark night[3]	
	With flying fires. When time for their stol'n flight	
735	Was come, he warns his men no sailor's noise	
	Might on the shore be heard, nor trumpet's voice	
	Divide the hours, nor cornet's sound at all	
	The mariners should to their charges call.	
	Now near her end Virgo began to be,	
740	And Libra follows, his first day to see.[4]	
	The silent fleet departs: the anchors made	
	No noise, when from thick sands their hooks are weighed;	
	Silent, while they the sail-yard bow, and rear	
	The main-mast up, the fearful masters are;[5]	
745	The sailors softly spread their sails, nor dare	
	Shake their strong shrouds within the whizzing air.[6]	
	The general makes his prayer, Fortune, to thee,	
	To give him leave t'abandon Italy	
	Since thou'lt not let him keep it; but, alas,[7]	
750	The Fates will scarce grant that. The waters flash,	

the sea was enclosed by the cutting down of groves' (II. 677–78); M.'s 'ships' derives from F.'s *ratibus* (probably meaning 'rafts' in this context), again following Caesar, *Commentarii*, I. 25. 8.

[1] bulwarks ... raise] *multo aggere*, 'a great mound' (II. 678–79). M.'s 'bulwarks' comes from F.'s detail of 'beams covered with earth [*trabibus terra constratis*]', again taken from Caesar, *Commentarii*, I. 25. 9.

[2] carry forth the war] *spargatque per aequora bellum*, 'and scatter war through the seas' (II. 682).

[3] well-driven engines] 'the ballista, wielded by strong limbs' ('*tortaque ... validis ballista lacertis,*' II. 686): a ballista was a siege weapon, shaped like a cross-bow, which threw large bolts.

[4] Virgo ... Libra] Virgo gives way to Libra at the autumnal equinox: hence, L. has Pompey leaving Italy in mid-September 49 BC.

[5] Silent ... masters are] i.e. the masters are silent while they rear up the bow and mainmast.

[6] whizzing air] *ne sibilet aura*, 'lest a breath of wind should make a whisper' (II. 698). In early modern English, normally objects 'whizz' in the air: see e.g. 6. 199 or Shakespeare, *Julius Caesar*, II. 1. 44, 'The exhalations whizzing in the air'.

[7] alas] M's addition.

      And furrowed with so many keels at once
      The stem-beat sea with a vast murmur groans.[1]
        The foes let in by gates and up the wall
      (Which faith, by Fortune turned, had opened all)[2]
755 Along the haven's stag-like horns they run
      Swiftly to shore, grieved that the fleet was gone.
      Is Pompey's flight so small a victory?[3]
      A straiter passage let him out to sea,   *narrower*
      Than where th'Euboean channel Chalcis beats.
760 Here stuck two ships, which fast the engine gets
      In sight, and near the shore the skirmish tried:[4]
      Here first the sea with civil blood was dyed.
      The fleet escaped, of those two ships bereft:
      So when Thessalia Jason's Argo left
765 For Colchis bound, Cyanaean Isles at sea
      Shot forth; the tail-maimed ship escaped away
      Amidst the rocks; in vain the islands beat
      The empty sea; she comes a sailer yet.[5]
        Now that the sun was near, the eastern sky   [11. 719]
770 Declared, pale-faced before his rosy dye;
      The Pleiades grow dim; each nearer star
      Loses his light, Boötes' lazy car   *ox-driver constellation; cart*
      Turns to the plain complexion of the skies,
      And Lucifer, the great stars darkened, flies
775 From the hot day. And now wert thou at sea,
      Pompey, not with such fate as when from thee
      The fearful pirates through all seas retired:
      Fortune revolts, with thy oft triumphs tired.
      Now, with thy country, household gods, thy son

---

[1] The waters flash ... groans] Modern editors suspect a missing line in this sentence (between 11. 702 and 11. 703), but early modern texts, punctuated differently, do not.

[2] faith, by Fortune turned] *fato conversa fides*, 'loyalty shifted by fate' (11. 705).

[3] Is Pompey's flight...] In L. not a question but a complaint: *Heu pudor, exigua est fugiens victoria Magnus*, 'Alas, for shame: a fleeing Pompey is scant victory' (11. 708).

[4] which fast ... gets in sight] *classique paratas | Excepere manus*, 'and were grabbed by hands ready for the fleet' (11. 711–12). M.'s 'engine', meaning here 'military contraption' (*OED*, 2.4.a), probably derives from F.'s mention of iron hooks designed to hold fast the escaping ships.

[5] a sailer yet] Allusion to the voyage of Argo, led by Jason, to obtain the Golden Fleece in Colchis. The voyage famously entailed passage through the Clashing Rocks (Cyanean Isles): but though the rear of the ship was caught by the meeting of the Rocks and her rudder was lost, Argo was able to sail on.

780 And wife, art thou a mighty exile gone.[1]
A place for thy sad death is sought afar:
Not that the gods envy thee sepulchre
At home, but damned is Egypt to that crime
And Latium spared, that Fates in foreign clime[2]
785 May hide this mischief, and the Roman land
Clear from the blood of her dear Pompey stand.[3]

FINIS Libri Secundi.[4]

---

[1] country] While L. includes wife, son and household gods (II. 728–29), 'country' is M.'s addition, probably influenced by his recognition that here L. reworks Aeneas' departure from Troy (*feror exsul in altum | Cum sociis natoque penatibus et magnis dis*, 'I am carried in exile onto the sea, with my companions, son, household gods and gods of my country', *Aeneid*, III. 11–12, in *Opera*, ed. by Mynors).
[2] Fates] In L. *Fortuna* (II. 735).
[3] A place for thy sad death…] Foreshadowing Pompey's later death in Egypt (8. 777 ff.).
[4] 'End of the second book'.

Annotations on the Second Book

(a) An old man, to express the present calamity, repeats the whole course of the civil war between Marius and Sulla, as it follows in this discourse.[1]

(b) Marius had twice triumphed, once over Jugurtha King of Numidia, and afterward over the Cimbrians and Teutones. But afterwards, envying the honour of Sulla, to whose hands Bocchas King of Mauritania had delivered Jugurtha, and endeavouring by the aid of Sulpitius, Tribune of the people, to hinder Sulla from his expedition against Mithradates King of Pontus, had incensed Sulla (being then warring in Campania) so far, that Sulla brought his army to Rome, and entering the City, subduing his adversaries, got them to be judged enemies by the Senate's decree and banished the city. Marius, escaping by flight, hid himself in the fens near Minturnae, but being there taken, he was put in a dungeon at Minturnae.[2]

(c) Marius suffered beforehand at Minturnae for those cruelties which he afterwards acted at Rome, when he returned and was consul the seventh time.[3]

(d) The executioner of Minturnae being a Cimbrian, entering the dark dungeon to kill Marius, saw fire sparkling out of Marius his eyes, and heard a voice saying, 'Darest thou kill Caius Marius?' At which the Cimbrian, affrighted, fled away, and the men of Minturnae, moved with pity and reverence of the man that once had saved Italy, released C. Marius, and let him go.[4]

(e) Marius escaped from Minturnae, took flight by obscure passages toward the sea, and getting into a ship, a tempest arising, was cast upon the islands called Meninges, where he received some companions, and heard that his son with Cethegus were gotten safe into Afric to Hiempsal. He then sailed to the coast of Carthage, but being forbidden by the Lictor of Sextilius the Praetor to set foot in Afric, 'Go tell thy Praetor', quoth he, 'that thou hast seen Caius Marius sitting in the ruins of Carthage', not unfitly comparing the ruined estate of that great city to his own now decayed fortunes.[5]

(f) When Caius Cinna the consul appealed to the people for restoring those banished men whom the Senate at request of Sulla had judged enemies, a

---

[1] Translation of F. on II. 64.
[2] Translation of F. on II. 69.
[3] Paraphrase of F. on II. 74 and II. 75.
[4] Translation of F. on II. 75, which also clarifies the Cimbrian identity of Marius's assassin (not specified initially by L.).
[5] M.'s note translates F. on II. 88 ff. (itself condensed from Plutarch, *Life of Marius*, 40. 1–4, in *Lives*, trans. by Bernadotte Perrin, 11 vols, Loeb Classical Texts (London: W. Heinemann, 1914–23), IX. p. 575), but with a number of differences: in F. and Plutarch, Marius is released by Minturnae's inhabitants rather than escaping; in F. he then boards a *scapha* (a light boat), although Plutarch calls it a ship; and is then cast on an island, Meninx, not several.

great contention arising, Cinna was expelled the city by his colleague Gnaeus Octavius and, flying, solicited the cities of Italy to war. He armed slaves and prisoners, and joining himself to Marius returning, they entered Rome in a fourfold army — Cinna, Marius, Carbo, Sertorius — and tyrannized over their adversaries.[1]

(g) Marius had given this token to his soldiers, that they should kill all whom he did not resalute, and offer his hand to kiss.[2]

(h) Baebius was torn in pieces by the soldiers.[3]

(i) Marcus Antonius, an excellent orator, that by his eloquence made the murderers relent. At last, his head being cut off, Anius the tribune brought it to Marius, as he was at supper, who, handling it a while and scoffing at it, commanded it to be nailed to the Rostra.[4]

(k) Fimbria, a cruel soldier of Marius, killed the two Crassi, father and son, in each other's sight.[5]

(l) That place of the prison, from whence offenders used to be cast down headlong, was stained with the blood of Licinius the Tribune, whose office was sacred.[6]

(m) Mucius Scaevola, the high priest, an old man, embracing the altar of Vesta, was there slain.[7]

(n) C. Marius, entering his seventh consulship, within thirteen days after died mad of a disease in his side, being 70 years old, having tasted the extremities of prosperity and adversity.[8]

(o) At Sacriportum, not far from Praeneste, Sulla overcame Caius Marius the son of old C. Marius, who fled to Praeneste. Sulla sent Lucretius Ofella to besiege him there, but Marius, offering to escape through a mine underground and being discovered there, killed himself. Sulla then, not ten furlongs from Porta Collina, overthrew Lamponius and Telesinus, two captains of the Samnites who came to raise Ofella's siege. At these two places Sulla slew above seventy thousand men.[9]

(p) Marius had promised the Samnites, who had been of his party, that he would

---

[1] Slightly condensed from F. on II. 94-95.
[2] Translation of F. on II. 113.
[3] Abridged translation of F. on II. 119.
[4] Translation of F. on II. 122 but omitting F.'s references to Valerius Maximus and Cicero's *De Oratore*.
[5] Abridged translation of F. on II. 124 with the addition of Fimbria's name from L.
[6] Abridged translation of F. on II. 125: F. adds that some commentators believe L. refers to the *rostra*, from which the tribunes gave speeches.
[7] Translation of F. on II. 126.
[8] Translating of F. on II. 130 and II. 131.
[9] Translation of F. on II. 134.

translate the seat of the empire from Rome to them, who now conceived a hope of subjecting the Romans more than once they did at Furcas Caudinas, where the Romans under the conduct of Titus Veturius and Spurius Posthumius received a disgraceful overthrow.[1]

(q) Quintus Luctatius Catulus, which had been colleague with C. Marius and triumphed with him over the Cimbrians, hearing that Marius was determined to put him to death, entering his chamber, voluntarily choked himself. In revenge of which, his brother Catulus obtained of Sulla that Marius the brother of C. Marius might be delivered into his hands, who sacrificed him at his brother's tomb and, wounding his arms, thighs and legs, he cut off his nose and ears, cut out his tongue, and digged out his eyes, letting him so live awhile that he might die in pain of every limb.[2]

(r) Lucretius Ofella, by Sulla's command having taken Praeneste, had killed or cast in prison all the senators that he found there of Marius' faction: but Sulla coming thither, commanded five thousand men of Praeneste, who in hope of mercy had cast away their arms and prostrated themselves upon the ground, to be all slain.[3]

(s) Sulla commanded four whole legions which had been of his enemies' side, among whom were many Samnites, to be all killed at one time in the field of Mars.[4]

(t) Sulla called himself Felix; he named his son Faustus, and his daughter Fausta. Leaving his Dictatorship, he lived privately at Puteoli, where he died eaten with lice. His funerals were kept with great honour in the field of Mars.[5]

(v) Marcia being a virgin was married to Cato, by whom she had three children; and then his friend Hortensius desiring to have her and wanting children, Cato bestowed her upon him, being then great with child; after Hortensius his death she returned thus to Cato.[6]

(x) Cornelia the daughter of Lucius Scipio, and widow of Publius Crassus, was married to Pompey after Julia's death.[7]

---

[1] Translation of F. on II. 136.
[2] Translation of F. on II. 173. Modern editions name the consul Lutatius.
[3] Adaptation of F. on II. 194, omitting that Cethegus had given the citizens of Praeneste hope of pardon, and that Sulla afterwards scattered the bodies over the fields.
[4] Adaptation of F. on II. 196, omitting that the enemies were adherents of Cinna and Marius and were killed in a public residence in the field of Mars.
[5] Adaptation of F. on II. 221–22. In Latin 'Felix' means 'happy' and 'Faustus/Fausta' means 'fortunate'.
[6] Largely following F. on II. 327, but drawing the detail of three children from L.'s own narrative and omitting F.'s additional report of Caesar's jest that Cato sent her away poor and remarried her rich (Hortensius was very wealthy).
[7] Abridged translation of F. on II. 349. While all editions have this note, in the text itself (x) is absent (it should direct the reader at 2. 371).

(y) At the fame of Caesar's approach, the governors through Italy all fled, not daring to withstand him or maintain any forts against him. Many of those are here named: first Scribonius Libo leaves his charge at Etruria, and Thermus forsakes Umbria; Faustus Sulla, son to Sulla the Dictator, wanting his father's spirit and fortune in civil war, fled at the name of Caesar.[1]

(z) Atius Varus, when he perceived that the chief citizens of Auximum favoured Caesar, took his garrison from thence and fled.[2]

(a) Lentulus Spinther, with ten cohorts, kept the town of Asculum. Who, hearing of Caesar's coming, fled away, thinking to carry with him his cohorts, but was forsaken by most of his soldiers.[3]

(b) Lu. Scipio, father-in-law to Pompey the Great, fled from Luceria, although he had two strong legions. Marcellus, to diminish the strength of Caesar, counselled the Senate to make a decree that Caesar should deliver one legion, and Pompey another, to Bibulus, whom they pretended to send to the Parthian war. Caesar, according to the Senate's decree, delivered to him one legion for himself, and another legion which he had borrowed of Pompey for a present supply, after the great loss received by his two praetors Teturius and Cotta. Both these legions Caesar delivered, and they were now in Scipio's camp.[4]

(c) Lu. Domitius Ahenobarbus, with twenty cohorts, was in Corfinium; he had with him those soldiers of Pompey's who had enclosed the forum, when Milo was arraigned for Clodius' death. He sent five cohorts to break down the bridge of the river, which was three miles from the town; but those cohorts, meeting the forerunners of Caesar's army, were beaten back again.[5]

(d) Spartacus, a Thracian fencer, fled with 70 companions of his, from Lentulus his games at Capua, and gathering slaves to his party, and arming them, made up an army of 70,000. He overcame many Roman praetors, and consuls: at last he was vanquished, and slain by Marcus Crassus.[6]

(e) Caesar, having wasted Germany with fire and sword, after eighteen days returned into France, cutting down the bridge behind him, that it should not be useful to the Germans: which Pompey detractingly calls a flight.[7]

---

[1] Only the phrase 'Faustus Sulla ... fortune' is from F. (on II. 464): the other details are possibly condensed from Caesar's *Commentarii*, or from L.'s own narrative.
[2] Translation of F. on II. 466.
[3] Translation of F. on II. 468.
[4] Translation of F. on II. 474–75.
[5] Drawn from F. on II. 478–82.
[6] Translation of F. on II. 554. Though all editions include this note none mark it at 2. 591 in the text.
[7] Translation of F. on II. 570. Though all editions include this note none mark it at 2. 610 in the text.

To the Right Honourable Edward, Earl of Mowbray, Knight of the Most Noble Order.[1]

On whom, renownèd Sheffield, if not you
Can Lucan fitly his third book bestow?
A theme on which no other poet light,   *settles*
The brave description of a naval fight.[2]
5   Vouchsafe to read it, noble lord, and cast
A pleasing eye back on your actions past,
When your famed valour on the wat'ry main
In blessed Eliza's ne'er forgotten reign
So oft was shown, so often quelled the pride
10 Of boasting Spain, and with their slaughter dyed
Blue Neptune's face.[3] O that a muse as high
As Lucan's was, might to posterity
Blazon your worth:[4] but since such happy bays   *laurels*
Grow not in every age nor clime, where praise
15 Is merited,[5] accept this mention now
From one, though mean, yet one that honours you.

---

[1] Edmund [not Edward] second baron Sheffield, first Earl of Mulgrave [not Mowbray] (1565–1646). A veteran of the Elizabethan wars against Spain, Sheffield represents a now neglected spirit of militant Protestant nationalism, implicitly equated (as in other dedications) with true nobility. For M.'s misnamings, see Intro, p. 25.   Knight of the Most Noble Order] The Order of the Garter, bestowed on Sheffield in 1593.

[2] a naval fight] The subject only of the last part of book three: see 3. 551 ff., below.

[3] your actions past ...] Sheffield commanded three ships in the campaign of 1588 in which the Spanish Armada was destroyed. He was also a vigorous persecutor of Catholics in the 1590s and early 1600s.

[4] O that a muse ... worth] 'High' is M.'s typical epithet for Lucan, here suggesting lofty martial heroism. 'Blazon', lit. 'describe in proper heraldic language', but also suggesting 'blaze', recalls Shakespeare, *Henry V*, Prologue. 1 ff., 'O for a muse of fire', where national military success is again the topic.

[5] but since ... merited] i.e. since such heroic feats are not always acknowledged or rewarded as they should be.   happy bays] The good fortune to be publicly decorated for one's deeds.

LUCAN'S
Pharsalia

The Third Book.

The Argument of the Third Book.[1]

Fair Julia's ghost a dream to Pompey shows.
Curio for corn into Sicilia goes.[2]
To Rome comes Caesar with unarmèd bands,[3]
Where though Metellus all in vain withstands,
5 He robs the Treasury. Each nation's name
That to the war in aid of Pompey came.
Caesar thence hastes to Spain, and by the way
Lays cruel siege to true Massilia,[4]
But stays not there himself: Brutus maintains
10 The siege, and Caesar's first sea-conquest gains.[5]

Now had the wind-stuffed sails brought out the fleet, [III. 1][6]
And all the navy on the ocean set;
The sailors all looked to the Ionian Sea.
Only great Pompey never turned his eye
5 From the Italian coast, his country's shore,
And ports that he shall never visit more.
All the high cliffs no more for clouds he sees,
And the hills, lessening, vanish from his eyes.
Sweet sleep did then his weary limbs compose,
10 When Julia's ghost through the cleft ground arose
In woeful wise, and with a funeral brand
Seemed Fury-like before his face to stand.[7]

---

[1] The Argument] See note on Argument to book one.
[2] Fair Julia's] When compared with his model, Giovanni Sulpizio's *argumentum*, M. highlights Julia and downplays Pompey's abandonment of Italy.
[3] with unarmèd bands] M.'s addition, based on 3. 76.
[4] Lays cruel siege] In Sulpizio merely *vexat*, 'he troubles'.
[5] Brutus maintains...] Unlike Sulpizio, stressing Caesar's victory at sea. 'Brutus' is Decimus Junius Brutus Albinus, a follower of Caesar, not the Brutus of book two.
[6] 1–48] Julia, Pompey's dead ex-wife, appears to Pompey in a dream. 3. 1–7 were changed in later editions: see Textual Notes.
[7] When Julia's ghost ... stand] L. refers to the *dira ... plena horroris imago*, 'terrible likeness, full of horror' raising her *caput moestum*, 'gloomy head' (III. 9–10). M. adds 'with

'From the blessed souls' abode, th'Elysian field,
To Stygian darkness and damned ghosts exiled
15 Since this sad war,[1] I saw the Furies fire
Their brands', quoth she, 'to move your wicked ire.[2]
Charon prepares more boats for souls to come,
And hell's enlargèd for tormenting room.[3]
Three sisters' speedy hands cannot suffice,
20 For breaking threads has tired the Destinies.[4]
Pompey, whilst mine, a life triumphant led;
Thy fortunes changèd with thy marriage bed.
Strumpet Cornelia, damned by destiny
To ruin her great lords, could marry thee,
25 My funeral fire scarce out.[5] Let her in flight
Attend thee now, and through this civil fight[6]
Follow thy standard, whilst I still have power
To break your rest at every sleepy hour.
No hour gives freedom to your love's delight:
30 The day holds Caesar, Julia holds the night.
Lethe's dull waters made not me forget
Thee, husband, and hell princes did permit
That I should follow thee; through both the hosts
I'll rush, while thou art fighting. Julia's ghost
35 Shall tell thee still whose son-in-law thou art:
Think not that war shall this alliance part;
This war shall make us meet again.'[7] This said,
She through her fearful lord's embraces fled.
He, though the gods by ghosts do threaten, still

a funeral brand', probably deriving the detail from F. (on III. 11).
[1] sad war] *bellum civile*, 'civil war' (III. 14).
[2] to move ... ire] Added by M., probably from F.'s paraphrase, *vestris furialibus armis incitandis*, 'to inflame your infuriate arms' (on III. 15).
[3] Charon] *Acherontis adusti | Portitor*, 'the ferryman of burnt Acheron' (III. 16–17). Charon, the Styx and Elysium are all standard features of the Roman Underworld, as is the river Lethe (pronounced disyllabically), whose water induces forgetfulness; cf. 3. 31 below.
[4] Destinies] Clotho, Lachesis and Atropos, the Fates (*Parcae*).
[5] Strumpet Cornelia] Cornelia, Pompey's present wife. 'Strumpet' translates L.'s *pellex* 'mistress, concubine' (III. 23). Gorges, *Lucan's Pharsalia: containing the ciuill warres betweene Caesar and Pompey* (London: Nicholas Okes for Edward Blount, 1614), p. 82, also uses 'strumpet'. F. notes that the charge is unfair, but for M. the term is significant; cf. 8. 119. Editions from 1631 included a historical note (a) here: see Textual Notes.
[6] through this civil fight] *per bella, per aequora*, 'through wars, through seas' (III. 24).
[7] Think not ... meet again] Rendering L.'s sharper *Abscidis frustra ferro tua pignora. bellum | Te faciet civile meum*, 'in vain you cut off your [marriage] pledges with the sword; civil war will make you mine' (III. 33–34).

	Madder of war,[1] with sure presage of ill,	
40	'Why are we scared', quoth he, 'with fancies vain?'[2]	
	Either no sense doth after death remain,	
	Or death is nothing.' Now the setting sun	
	To drown as much of his bright orb begun,	*began*
45	As the moon wants when after full she wanes,	
	Or grows near-full. Dyrrachium entertains	
	His navy now;[3] the sailors make to shore,	
	Pull down the sails,[4] and labour at the oar.	
	Caesar, perceiving all the ships were gone	[III. 46][5]
50	Past sight with prosperous winds, and he alone	
	Left lord in Italy, no joy received	
	In th'honour of great Pompey's flight, but grieved	
	His foes fled safe along the ocean.[6]	
	No fortune could suffice this eager man;[7]	
55	Deferring of the war to him seemed more	
	Than this small conquest.[8] But he now gives o'er	
	War's cares awhile, intent on peace again,	
	And knowing how the people's loves to gain,[9]	
	That corn most stirs their hate, most draws their loves,	
60	That only famine to rebellion moves	
	Cities, and fear is bought, where great men feed	
	The slothful commons; nought starved people dread.[10]	
	Curio is sent to the Sicilian towns,[11]	
	Where once the violent sea did either drown	

[1] Madder of war] *Maior in arma ruit*, 'greater hurtles into war' (III. 37), a play on Pompey 'the Great'.
[2] Why ... vain] L. stresses visual deception: *quid ... vani terremur imagine visus?* ('Why do empty visions terrify us by their appearance?', III. 38).
[3] Dyrrachium ... His navy] *obtulit hospita tellus | Puppibus accessus faciles*, 'an hospitable land proffered easy harbour for his ships' (III. 43-44).
[4] the sails] *malo*, 'the mast' (III. 45). There are signs later in this book of M. adapting his nautical descriptions to suit seventeenth-century practice: see 3. 551-824, esp. 553n and 632n.
[5] 3. 49-119] Caesar travels to Rome.
[6] ocean] Pronounced trisyllabically, as it also is as a proper noun at 3. 80 below.
[7] eager man] L.'s term, *praecipiti*, 'headlong, hasty' (III. 51) matches his term *praeceps* for Caesar at II. 656 (there in M. 'impatient', 2. 694).
[8] No fortune ... conquest] i.e. Pompey's flight did more to vex Caesar, by delaying battle, than delight him through victory.
[9] the people's loves] In L. *vanos populi ... amores*, 'empty loves of the people' (III. 54).
[10] That only famine ... dread] M.'s syntax implies this is Caesar's belief, but L.'s comment could equally be narratorial. M.'s 'to rebellion moves' translates *asserit*, 'keeps in a condition of freedom' (*L&S*, 'assero', II. A).
[11] Curio] Caesar takes control of the corn-trade by sending subordinates to Sardinia and Sicily: on Curio see 1. 292n.

65 Or cut the land and made itself a shore
In the mid-land: the waters ever roar
And struggle there lest the two hills should close.¹
Part of the war into Sardinia goes:
Both famous islands for rich fruitful fields,²
70 No land to Italy more harvest yields,
Nor with more corn the Roman garners fills;   *granaries*
Not Libya these as granaries excels,
When Boreas' blasts (the south winds ceasing) tear   *the north wind*
The show'ring clouds and make a fruitful year.
75   These things provided thus, with peaceful shows³   [III. 71]
And troops unarmed to Rome the conqueror goes.
O had he but come home with victory
Only of Britain, France and Germany,⁴
What long triumphant pomp, what honour then,
80 What stories had he brought?⁵ How th'ocean
And the Rhine both his conquests bridèlèd,⁶   *bridled*
The noble Gauls and yellow Britons led
Behind his lofty chariot.⁷ Winning more
He lost those triumphs were deserved before.⁸   *which were*
85 No flocks of people now his coming greet
With joy, all fear his looks;⁹ none stand to meet
His troops. Yet proud is he such fear to move,
And would not change it for the peoples' love.¹⁰

---

¹ Where once ... close] i.e. the straits of Messina. L.'s meaning, less clear in M., is that the sea made a shoreline through the middle of the land (III. 60–61), the water providing a barrier 'lest the cleft mountains should seek to border each other again' (*ne rupti repetant confinia montes*, III. 63).
² Both famous islands] i.e. Sicily and Sardinia.
³ peaceful shows] *pacis habentia vultum*, 'having the face of peace' (III. 72). M.'s 'shows' implies disguise.
⁴ Britain, France and Germany] L. only specifies 'the Gauls', *Gallorum*, alongside the vaguer *Arctoque subacta*, 'subjugated north' (III. 76). M.'s translation is strong evidence for his use of Hortensius's 1578 commentary here, which explicitly argues (col. 291 C) 'he means Germany and the Britons [*De Germania & Britannis loquitur*]'.
⁵ stories] *belli facies*, 'appearances of war', III. 76; early modern commentaries interpret this to mean pageants displaying military victories during a triumph.
⁶ bridèlèd] i.e. bounded, tamed; the odd spelling (here printed following 1627) points to the trisyllabic pronunciation.
⁷ yellow Britons] i.e. yellow-haired; cf. 1. 431.
⁸ Winning more ... before] *Perdidit o qualem vincendo plura triumphum!*, 'O what a triumph he lost by conquering more!' (III. 79).
⁹ all ... looks] *tacitae videre metu*, 'in silence they look on in fear' (III. 81); M.'s phrasing is probably influenced by the stereotype of the tyrant developed in subsequent lines.
¹⁰ Yet proud ... love] The conventional definition of a tyrant, recalling *oderint dum*

Now Anxur's steepest hills he had o'erpassed,[1] [III. 84]
90 Where a moist path o'er Pontine fens is placed,
Where the high wood does Scythian Dian show,
Where to long Alba's feasts the consuls go.[2]
From an high rock he views the town afar,[3]
Not seen before in all his northern war.
95 Then thus (admiring his Rome's walls) he spake:
'Could men not forced by any fight forsake
Thee, the gods' seat? What city will they dare
To fight for? Here the gods their loves declare,[4]
That not the furious eastern nations,
100 Pannonians, or swift Sarmatians,
Daci, or Getes invade thee; Fortune spares
Thee Rome in this, to send thee civil wars,
Having so faint a chief.'[5] Then fearful Rome
He enters with his troops; they think him come
105 To fire and sack the city, not to spare
The gods themselves. This measure had their fear:
They think he'll do whate'er he can. No songs,[6]
No shouts they counterfeit in joyful throngs;
They scarce have time to hate. The Fathers meet
110 In Phoebus' temple by no lawful right
Of convocation, from their houses set *sprung*
And lurking-holes.[7] The consuls' sacred seat

metuant, 'let them hate me as long as they fear me' (Accius, in E. H. Warmington, ed., *Remains of Old Latin*, 4 vols, Loeb Classical Texts (Cambridge, MA: Harvard University Press, 1936), II, fr. 168), quoted by Cicero of Marcus Antonius (see *Phillipics*, trans. by Walter C. A. Ker, Loeb Classical Texts (Cambridge, MA: Harvard University Press, 1926), I. 33). M.'s 'proud' translates L.'s *gaudet*, 'rejoices' (III. 82).

[1] o'erpassed] cf. 1. 199.
[2] Where a moist path ... consuls go] A description of the ritual *Feriae Latinae*, as remarked in most early modern commentaries including F.'s; cf. 1. 587n. 3. 92 translates *Quaque iter est Latiis ad summam fascibus Albam*, 'and where the route is, for Latin fasces, to Alba's peak' (III. 87).
[3] the town] Rome.
[4] their loves declare] M.'s extrapolation from L.'s elliptic *Di Melius*, 'better the gods' (III. 93), typically read in early modern commentaries along the lines of 'may the gods provide better'. F. explains that the gods have seen a better thing, since war has not been waged by a foreign enemy.
[5] faint] Cowardly, fearful; in L. *Tam pavidum*, 'so frightened' (III. 96).
[6] songs] *omina festa*, 'joyful omens' (III. 101). Some modern editions read *fausta*, 'auspicious', for *festa*.
[7] The Fathers ... lurking-holes] i.e. members of the Senate (cf. 1. 520); L.'s sarcastic phrase is *Turba Patrum*, 'a mob of senators' (III. 105). 'Convocation' is F.'s term, recalling that for Anglican ecclesiastical assemblies; L. says *nullo cogendi iure*, 'by no law of compulsion' (III. 104). M. adds 'from their houses set'.

	Was not supplied; next them no praetor fills	
	His room, but empty stand those honoured sells.¹	*seats of dignity*
115	Caesar was all: the Senate sit to bear	
	Witness of private power and grant whate'er	
	He please to ask; crowns, temples, their own blood	
	Or banishment.² Fortune in this was good:³	
	He blushed more to command, than Rome t'obey.	
120	But Liberty in this durst make assay	[III. 112]⁴ *sought to test*
	By one, if law could overmaster force.⁵	
	Metellus, seeing the vast massy doors	
	Of Saturn's temple ready to fly ope,	*open*
	Running enraged, breaking through Caesar's troop,	
125	Before the yet unopened door he stayed.⁶	
	(Only the love of gold is not afraid	
	Of death and threat'ning swords; the laws are gone	
	And broke without one conflict; wealth alone,	
	The worst of things, had power this jar to make.)⁷	
130	Staying the rapine thus the tribune spake	
	Aloud to Caesar. 'Through this breast of mine	
	The temple opes: no treasure shalt thou find,	
	Robber, but what thou buy'st with sacred blood;	
	This office wronged will find a vengeful god.⁸	
135	A tribune's curse, pursuing Crassus, made	

---

¹ next them no praetor...] *non proxima lege potestas | Praetor adest*, 'no praetor, the next in legal authority, is present' (III. 106-07). M.'s 'honoured sells' (translating *curules*, 'pertaining to a magistrate', III. 107) alludes to the *sella curialis*, the ivory chair symbolic of a magistrate's power.
² private power] Not in L., but taken from F.'s description of Caesar here as a 'private man' (at III. 108).   crowns] *regnum*, 'monarchy' (III. 110); cf. 1. 5n.
³ Fortune ... good] Expanding L.'s more scornful and abrupt *melius, quod* ('Better that...' III. 111).
⁴ 3. 120-86] Caesar plunders the state treasury in the temple of Saturn, and is vainly resisted by Metellus, tribune of the plebs in 49 BC.
⁵ But Liberty ... force] Compressing an already awkward passage: *tamen exit in iram | Viribus an possent obsistere iura per unum | Libertas experta virum*, 'yet Liberty, testing whether through one man laws could resist force, went out into anger' (III. 112-14). M. seems to have understood the opening Latin words, which some modern editors have tried to amend, as referring to Metellus ('running enraged', 3. 124), although F. and other commentaries thought it meant provoking Caesar's wrath.
⁶ Metellus] M. omits L.'s *pugnax*, 'combative' (III. 114).
⁷ this jar to make] i.e. were it not for the love of gold, law would have been lost without any struggle at all (*discrimine nullo*, III. 119). L.'s contempt is clearer than M.'s, accusing wealth (*opes*) of being *pars vilissima rerum*, 'the very vilest part of things' (III. 120-21).
⁸ a vengeful god] *Deos*, 'gods' (III. 126); F. introduces the idea of vengefulness. Metellus's 'sacred blood' is due to his office.

A fatal Parthian war.¹ But draw thy blade:
Let not the people's eyes scare thee from this
Thy wickedness; the town forsaken is.
No wicked soldier from our treasuries
140 Shall pay himself: find other enemies
To spoil and conquer, other towns to give.
No need can thee to this foul rapine drive;²
In me alone, Caesar, thou find'st a war.'³
These words incensed the angry conqueror:
145 'In vain, Metellus, hop'st thou to obtain
A noble death', quoth he: 'we scorn to stain
Our hand in such a throat. No dignity
Makes thee worth Caesar's ire: must liberty
Be saved by thee? The fates confound not so
150 All things but that the laws, rather than owe
To thee their preservation, would be broke
And ta'en away by Caesar.'⁴ Thus he spoke,
But when the temple doors the tribune stout
Left not, more angry grown, he looks about
155 On his keen swords; to play the gown-man now
He had forgot;⁵ when Cotta 'gan to woo   *began*
Metellus to give o'er his enterprise: *give up*
'The freedom of men subjugated dies
By freedom's self,'⁶ quoth he, 'whose shadow thou
160 Shalt keep, if all his proud commands thou do.
So many unjust things have conquered we   *we who've been conquered*
Already suffered, and this now must be
Th'excuse t'our shame and most degenerate fear,
That nought can be denied. Now let him bear

---

¹ A tribune's curse] In 55 BC the tribune Caius Ateius Capito had issued formal curses in an effort to prevent Crassus' Parthian expedition (cf. 1. 11–14).
² this foul rapine] *Pacis ... exhaustae spolium*, 'the spoils of exhausted peace' (III. 132); modern editions sometimes prefer *exutae*, 'cast off [peace]'.
³ In me ... war] *Bellum Caesar habes*, 'you have war, Caesar' (III. 133); M. adds the self-sacrificial 'in me alone'.
⁴ The fates ... Caesar] *non usque adeo permiscuit imis | Longus summa dies, ut, non si voce Metelli | Serventur leges, malint a Caesare tolli*, 'long passage of time has not so confounded high things with low that the laws, could they be saved by Metellus's veto, would not prefer to be abolished by Caesar' (III. 138–40).
⁵ to play the gown-man] *simulare togam*, 'to pretend the toga'.
⁶ The freedom ... self] *Libertas ... populi, quem regna coercent | Libertate perit*, 'a people's freedom, oppressed by monarchy, by freedom dies' (III. 145–46). The second, injurious freedom may be freedom of speech; F. thought it was the freedom of the oppressor. The speaker is Lucius Aurelius Cotta.

165	Away from hence these seeds of wicked war.	
	Loss hurts those people that in freedom are:[1]	
	Worst to the lord is serving poverty.'[2]	
	Metellus is removed and opened be	[III. 153]
	The temple doors; all the Tarpeian hill	
170	With horrid noise the broken hinges fill,	
	And from the bottom of the temple there	
	The Roman people's wealth, which many a year	
	Had not been touched, which Carthage wars to us	
	And the two kings, Philip and Perseus,	
175	Both conquered brought, is ransacked;[3] gold they reave	*steal*
	Which flying Pyrrhus to thee, Rome, did leave,	
	For which Fabricius would no traitor be.[4]	
	Whate'er the virtuous frugality	
	Of our forefathers had yet kept unspent,	
180	And Asia's wealthy tributaries sent;	*sent as tribute*
	Whate'er Metellus brought from conquered Crete	
	And o'er the seas from Cyprus Cato set;[5]	
	The spoils of all the east, and treasures proud	
	Of captive kings, which Pompey's triumphs showed;	
185	This temple's impious robbing brought to pass,	
	That Rome then first than Caesar poorer was.	
	Now had great Pompey's fortune drawn from all	[III. 171][6]
	The world strong nations with himself to fall.[7]	
	Aid to the war so near first Grecia lends,	
190	And Cirrha on the rock;[8] Amphissia sends	

---

[1] in freedom are] *quos sua iura tuentur*, 'those whom their own laws protect' (III. 152).

[2] Worst ... poverty] *Non sibi, sed domino gravis est, quae servit, egestas*, 'The want of the slave is painful to his master, not himself' (III. 153).

[3] Perseus] *Perses*, 'the Persian' i.e. the king of Persia or the Persians (III. 158).

[4] flying Pyrrhus ... traitor be] Pyrrhus of Epirus (c. 319–272 BC), an enemy of Rome, was unable to corrupt the consul Fabricius. Modern editions sometimes follow Housman in reading *Gallus*, 'the Gaul', for Pyrrhus (III. 159).

[5] Whate'er Metellus ... set] Quintius Caecilius Metellus Creticus (consul 69 BC) conquered Crete. Cato (introduced by L. in book two) was sent to bring the treasures of the new province, Cyprus, to Rome in 58 BC.

[6] 3. 187–283] A catalogue of Pompey's allies and their places of origin, balancing that of Caesar's forces (1. 421–96), and starting with the peoples of Greece, then moving to the near and far east, before finishing in Africa. Throughout, M. often adopts the definitions or paraphrase of the early modern commentaries.

[7] strong nations] *urbes*, 'cities' (III. 170).

[8] Cirrha on the rock] Translating F.'s gloss *ad rupem sita* not L.'s *scopulosa*, 'rocky' (III. 172); cf. 1. 70.

Her Phocian bands, Parnassus' learnèd hill[1]
From both her tops sends men, Boeotians fill
The camp, near whom th'oraculous waters flow
Of swift Cephisus; men from Pisa too,
195 And Theban Dirce, and where under sea
Alpheus sends his streams to Sicily.[2]
Th'Arcadians leave their Maenalus and from
Herculian Oeta the Trachinians come.[3]
The Thesprots came, and their now silent oak
200 Th'Epirots near Chaonia forsook.[4]
Athens, though wasted now with musters quite,
Yet levies men, and to this civil fight
Three Saliminian ships sends from her fleet
To Phoebus dedicated;[5] Jove-loved Crete
205 From Gnossos and Gortina sends t'th'field
Archers that need not to the Parthians yield;[6]
Soldiers from out Dardanian Oricum,
From Athamas and from Encheleae come,
Famed for transformèd Cadmus' funerals;[7]
210 From Colchos, where Absyrtus foaming falls
Into the Adrian; those where Peneus flows;   *Adriatic*
He that Iolchos in Thessalia ploughs —
Thence was the sea first tried, when Argo bore
Those that first sailèd to a foreign shore,
215 And first of all committed frail mankind
To mercy of the raging sea and wind:

---

[1] Parnassus' learnèd hill] M. adds 'learnèd'; Parnassus was the legendary home to Apollo and the Muses.
[2] Theban Dirce] L., more allusively, has 'Cadmean' (*Cadmea*, III. 175).
[3] Herculian Oeta...] Mt Oeta is the peak on which Hercules died and was apotheosized.
[4] Epirots] *Sellae* (III. 180), a people of Epirus; M. omits the Dryopes (III. 179).
[5] Saliminian ships ... to Phoebus dedicated] *Exhausit totas quamvis dilectus Athenas, | Exiguae Phoebea tenent navalia puppes, | Tresque petunt veram credi Salamina carinae* (III. 181–83), 'Although the levy drained all Athens, a small number of vessels hold the dockyards of Apollo and three ships seek to prove [the legend of] Salamis true'. M. seems to follow F. in assuming this line goes with together with the reference to Salamis in 3. 203; L. probably alludes to the naval victory at Salamis over Persia, achieved by Greek fleets led by Athens in 480 BC, although the meaning is obscure.
[6] Jove-loved Crete ... yield] Omitting *centenis ...| Vetus ... populis*, 'ancient [Crete] of a hundred peoples' (III. 184–85). M.'s 'Parthians' translates *Eois*, 'Easterners' (III. 186).
[7] Cadmus' funerals] In Greek myth Cadmus was transformed into a snake at the end of his life. 'Encheleae' (3. 208) is trisyllabic, the three concluding vowels being pronounced as one syllable.

That ship taught men a way unknown to die.¹
From Thracian Haemus, and from Pholoë
Belied with centaurs, and from Strymon too,   *counterfeited*
220 From whence the birds to Nile in winter go,
From barbarous Cone, where into the seas
Six-headed Ister does one channel ease²
At Peuce, soldiers come; the Mysian
And cold Caicus-washed Idalian,
225 Barren Arisbe helps, and Pitane:³
Celenae by Apollo's victory
Condemned, that cursed Minerva's fatal gift;⁴
Where into crook'd Maeander Marsyas swift
Falling, there mingled back again does flow;
230 The land that from gold-mines lets Hermus go
And rich Pactolus;⁵ those of Ilium
With Ilium's fate to falling Pompey come;⁶
The tale of Troy and Caesar's pedigree
Drawn from Iulus could no hindrance be.⁷
235 The Syrian people from Orontes go,
Windy Damascus, happy Minos too;⁸
Gaza, and Idumaea rich in palms;
Instable Tyre, Sidon whom purple fames: *unstable*
These ships bound to the war the Cynosure   *Ursa Minor*
240 Guides straight along the sea, to none more sure.⁹
Phoenicians, that (if fame we dare believe)

---

¹ Argo bore...] In Greco-Roman myth Argo was the first ship; cf. 2. 768n, 3. 213. That ship ... die] *fatisque per illam | Accesit mors una ratem*, 'through that ship one [more manner of] death was added to men's fates' (III. 196–97).
² Six-headed Ister] *Multifidi*, 'manifold' (III. 202); M. gets the idea of six mouths from commentaries. 'Cone' two lines above is disyllabic.
³ At Peuce ... Pitane] 'Peuce' and 'Pitane' have voiced final syllables.
⁴ Celenae ... fatal gift] Celenae's inhabitants 'curse' the flute, the invention of Minerva, because their satyr Marsyas challenged Apollo to a musical contest which ended in Marsyas' defeat and flaying. His name was then given to the river (as 3. 228 picks up).
⁵ The land ... rich Pactolus] *Passaque ab auriferis tellus exire metallis | Pactolon: qua culta secat non vilior Hermus*, 'the soil which suffers Pactolus to spring from gold-bearing ore, where Hermus, equally rich, cuts through the tilth' (III. 209–10).
⁶ of Ilium | With Ilium's fate] An example of M.'s flexible metrification: the first 'Ilium' (i.e. Troy) has three syllables here, but the second only two.
⁷ Drawn from Iulus ... be] *Phrygiique ferens se Caesar Iuli*, 'Caesar asserting descent by Trojan Iulus' (III. 213); see 1. 214n. 'Iulus' has three syllables.
⁸ Minos] Most modern and early modern editions print Ninos here. Probably a slip from M., never corrected.
⁹ to none more sure] i.e. offering clearer guidance to no other ships.

To human speech first characters did give:
The rivers yet had not with paper served
Egypt, but carved beasts, birds and stones preserved
245 Their magic language.¹ Taurus' lofty wood
Forsaken is; Tarsus, where Perseus stood;
From Coricus digged from an hollow rock,
Mallos and Aegae the Cilicians flock,
No pirates now but to a just war pressed.²   *conscripted*
250 Fame of this war had stirred the farthest east
Where Ganges is, that only cross does run
Of all earth's rivers to the rising sun,
And rolls his waves against the eastern wind:
Philip's great son, there stayed, was taught to find
255 The world more large than his ambitious mind
Conceived it;³ and where double-channelled Ind
Feels not Hydaspes' mixture; Indians,
That suck sweet liquor from their sugar canes;⁴
And those, whose hair with saffron is be-dyed,
260 Whose garments loose with coloured gems are tied,
Those that alive their funeral piles erect,
And leap into the flames, helping t'effect
Fate's work: what glory 'tis, content to live
No more, the remnant to the gods to give!⁵
265 Fierce Cappadocians, th'hardy nations
Near to Ammannus, the Armenians
Near strong Niphates,⁶ the Coastrae from
Their lofty woods, and the Arabians come
Into an unknown world, wond'ring to see
270 Shadows of woods on the right hand to be.
Farthest Olostrians come to Roman war;⁷

---

¹ The rivers yet ... language] *Nondum flumineas Memphis contexere biblos | Noverat*, 'Egypt didn't yet know how to weave together rivery books' (III. 222–23) i.e. papyrus.
² the Cilicians ... pressed] *Itque Cilix iusta iam non pirata carina*, 'and now no longer a pirate, the Cilician goes in a lawful ship' (III. 228).
³ Philip's great son ... Conceived it] *Pellaeus ... ductor*, 'the general of Pella' (III. 233), i.e. Alexander the Great, who 'stated himself beaten by the magnitude of the world', *magno vinci se fassus ab orbe est* (III. 234). For M.'s interest in ambition, see Introduction, p. 24, pp. 25–6n.
⁴ sugar canes] M. follows F.'s English gloss for L.'s *tenera ... ab arundine*, 'from a tender stalk' (III. 327).
⁵ what ... give] Omitting *Iniecisse manum fatis*, 'to have taken hold of one's fates' (III. 241–43).
⁶ strong Niphates] *volventem saxa*, 'rock-rolling' (III. 245).
⁷ Olostrians ... to Roman war] *furor ... movit Romanus*, 'Roman madness impels [them]'

Carmanian captains too, who southward far
See not the set of the whole Northern Bear: *Ursa Major*
By night but little shines Boötes there,   *ox-driver constellation*
275 The Ethiopian land not seen at all
By any of the signs Septentrional[1]   *northern*
But crooked Taurus' hoof. Those people too
Whence great Euphrates and swift Tigris flow:
From one spring Persis sends them; 'tis unknown
280 What name, should those two channels meet in one,
They'd bear. Euphrates, flowing on the fields
That profit there, that Nile in Egypt yields,[2]
But Tigris swallowed by the gaping earth
Long hides his course, but at his second birth
285 Denies not to the sea his new-born flood.
Betwixt both camps fierce Parthians neuters stood,   *declaring neutrality*
Content that they alone had caused this war.[3]
With poisoned arrows wand'ring Scythians far
Come to the camp, whom Bactros' icy flood
290 Encloses, and Hyrcania's desert wood;
The valiant Heniochian horsemen there[4]
Sprung from the Spartan race; Sarmatians near
To the fierce Moschi, where cold Phasis glides,
And Colchos' richest pasture fields divides;
295 Where Halys fatal to the Lydian king
Does flow;[5] where Tanaïs that draws his spring   *the Don*
From the Riphaean hills, and doth divide
Europe from Asia, giving to each side
The name of several worlds,[6] and (as he bends)
300 Now to this world, now that increase he lends;

(III. 249). 'Olostrians', a people of India, follows F.'s reading *Olostras* (III. 249), first suggested by Grotius, rather than the previously common (and now accepted) *Orestas* or *Oretas*, tribes nearer Rome.

[1] Septentrional] Pronounced with four syllables.
[2] there ... yields] i.e. in the same way the Nile floods its river-basin.
[3] had caused this war] *Contenti fecisse duos*, 'content that they had made two [opponents]' (III. 266): i.e. by killing the third triumvir, Crassus (cf. 1. 11–14).
[4] valiant Heniochian] The first word is disyllabic, following M.'s usual practice; 'Heniochian' has four syllables (two in the middle).
[5] the Lydian king] Croesus (L. names him, III. 272). The river Halys was 'fatal' because the Delphic oracle warned that by crossing the river he would destroy a great empire. He did, not realizing the empire was his own.
[6] giving ... worlds] *diversi nomina mundi | Imposuit ripis*, 'and has imposed the names of different worlds on either bank', meaning Europe and Asia (III. 273–74: L., unlike M., mentions these afterwards).

	Where slow Maeotis, driven into the seas,	*the Bosporus*
	Takes from the pillars of great Hercules	
	Their fame, denying that the Gades alone[1]	*Strait of Gibraltar*
	Admit the sea;[2] Scythonian nations,[3]	
305	The valiant Arians, Arimaspians	
	With gold-decked locks, and swift Gelonians;	
	The Massagetes, their thirst that satisfy[4]	
	With the same horses' bloods whereon they fly.	
	Not Cyrus leading th'eastern troops,[5] nor when	[III. 280]
310	Xerxes by darts numb'ring his armèd men	
	Came down, nor Agamemnon bound to set	
	His brother's ravished wife with that famed fleet,	
	So many kings brought under their commands,	
	So many nations drawn from several lands,	
315	Different in language and attire, nor ere	*before*
	Did Fortune bring so many men to bear	
	Part in a mighty ruin, making all	
	Sad obsequies at Pompey's funeral.	
	Marmaric troops the hornèd Ammon pressed,[6]	
320	And all scorched Afric from the farthest west	*Africa*
	To th'eastern shore send aid, as far as lie	
	The Syrtes' gulfs: lest Caesar severally	
	And oft be troubled, here all nations[7]	
	Pharsalia brings to be subdued at once.	
325	Caesar now leaving fearful Rome in haste	[III. 298][8]
	With his swift troops the cloudy Alps o'erpassed:[9]	
	But though his fame all people else affright,	
	Phocian Massilia[(f)] dares yet keep aright	
	Her faith, and far from Greekish levity[10]	

---

[1] Gades] Pronounced monosyllabically, to rhyme with 'shades'; cf. 4. 740, 9. 481, 10. 526.

[2] Where ... sea] L. juxtaposes the two entrances to the Mediterranean. L.'s *torrens* (III. 278) means 'burning, rushing', not 'slow', but M. clearly read in the commentaries that Maeotis was a marsh.

[3] Scythonian] *Sithoniae gentes* (III. 280). Modern editions print *Essedoniae*.

[4] their thirst that satisfy] i.e. who satisfy their thirst.

[5] th'eastern troops] *Memnoniis ... regnis* 'from Memnon's kingdoms' (III. 284).

[6] hornèd Ammon] The oracle of Jupiter Ammon in the oasis of Libya, which Cato and his soldiers visit later in the narrative: see 9. 586–676.

[7] all nations] *orbem*, 'the world' (III. 297); 'nations' is trisyllabic.

[8] 3. 325–824] Caesar's siege of Massilia and the subsequent sea battle.

[9] o'erpassed] Echoing 1. 199 and 3. 89, also of Caesar; L.'s word is *superevolat*, 'flies over' (III. 299).

[10] Greekish levity] Massilia was a Greek colony; L. here expresses Roman contempt for Greek military prowess.

330	The cause, the laws, not Fortune follows she:	
	But first of all they labour to assuage	
	With peaceful parley his uncurbèd rage	
	And stubborn mind, and to their foe now nigh	
	They send an olive-bearing embassy.[1]	
335	'As Latium's annals can true mention make,	[III. 307]
	Massilia still was ready to partake	*always*
	The fate of Rome in any foreign war,	
	And now if triumphs over nations far,	
	Caesar, thou seek, to such a conflict take	
340	These hands and lives of ours.[2] But if you make	
	Sad civil war,[3] then give us leave to bend	
	To neither side and nought but tears to spend.[4]	
	Let not our hands in wounds so sacred be;[5]	
	If th'heavenly gods had civil enmity,	
345	Or earth-born giants should assault the sky,	
	No aid to Jove durst human piety	
	By arms or prayers lend; their states above	
	We know not, but are bound to think that Jove	
	Has thunder still.[6] Besides, how many from	
350	All nations now do voluntaries come?[7]	*volunteers*
	The slothful world does not vice so abhor	
	That you should need forced swords to civil war.	
	Would every people would this cause refuse,	
	And this sad war no hands but Roman use.	
355	Some hands would falter at their fathers' sight,	
	And brothers faintly would 'gainst brothers fight.[8]	
	The war will soon have end, if foreign states	

[1] olive-bearing] *Cecropiae praelata fronde Minervae*, 'bearing the branch of Cecropian Minerva' (III. 306).
[2] Latium's annals...] i.e. Rome's history books can attest to the loyalty of the Massilians (allies of Rome since the second Punic war).
[3] But ... civil war] *At si funestas acies, si dira paratis | Proelia discordes*, 'but if you are readying for calamitous battle and dire conflict, bringing discord...' (III. 312–13).
[4] to bend ... side] *secretumque damus*, 'and provide a bolthole' (III. 314).
[5] in wounds ... be] i.e. be responsible for making them. 'Sacred', translating *sacra* (III. 315), here means 'to be abominated', i.e. as the commentaries suggest, by violating law and sacred oaths; cf. 3. 134.
[6] Has thunder still] *adhuc coelo solum regnare Tonantem*, '[Jove] the Thunderer yet reigns alone in heaven' (III. 320).
[7] voluntaries] M.'s idiom (*OED*, s.v. 'voluntary', 2. 9); L. has *gentes*, 'peoples' (III. 321).
[8] Some hands ... fight] A question in L.: *cui non ... languebit dextra ...?*, 'whose hand will not faint?' (III. 326).   faintly ... fight] *telaque prohibebunt spargere*, 'and hold back from hurling weapons' (III. 327).

You use not t'exercise their ancient hates.[1]
Our humble suit is, that within our wall   *entreaty*
360 Thou'ldst trust thyself, and leave behind thee all
Thy threat'ning eagles: let us this obtain,
To shut out war and Caesar entertain.
Let this place free from guilt safely receive
Thyself and Pompey, if fates please to give
365 Peace to unconquered Rome; here both may meet
Unarmed. But why, when danger did invite
Thy wars to Spain, turned'st thou to us aside?
We are of no avail to turn the tide
Of your great wars; our arms have provèd still   *invariably*
370 Unfortunate. When fortune did exile
Us from our first plantation, here we sat,   *colony*
And Phocis' sacked towers hither did translate: *transfer*
Here in a foreign coast and weak-walled town
Safe have we lived; our faith is our renown.[2]   *loyalty*
375 If thou intend siege to our walls to lay,
Or through our gates t'enforce a speedy way,
In the defence we are resolved to die,
And fury of the sword and fire to try.
If thou divert our waters' course, the ground
380 We'll dig and lick the puddle we have found.
If food should fail, flesh of our children slain
(Fearful to touch or see) our jaws should stain.[3]
For liberty to suffer we'll not fear
What once Saguntum, when besieged, could bear
385 In Carthage-war:[4] our babes in vain that strive
To suck their mothers' dried-up breasts, we'll give
Freely to th'fire; a wife shall sue for death
At her dear husband's hand; a brother's breath
A brother's hand shall stop; this civil war

---

[1] t'exercise their ancient hates] *si non committitis illis | Arma, quibus fas est*, 'if you don't put arms in the hands of those for whom it is legitimate' (III. 328–29), i.e. foreign nations.
[2] our faith is our renown] *Inlustrat quos sola fides*, 'The only thing which gives us glory is our fidelity' (III. 342).
[3] flesh of our children ... stain] *tunc horrida cerni, | Foedaque contingi maculato carpere morsu*, 'we are prepared with stained mouth to eat things horrible to see and disgusting to touch' (III. 347–48). A rare instance of M. being more macabre than L.
[4] Saguntum ... Carthage-war] The Spanish city of Saguntum, loyal to Rome, was besieged and eventually destroyed by the Carthaginians in 219 BC; its inhabitants committed mass suicide.

390 We'll choose o'th'two.'¹ So spoke th'ambassador.²
    But Caesar's troubled look his anger speaks   [III. 356]
Before his words: but this at last.³ 'These Greeks
Vain hope of our departure has possessed:
Though we were marching to the farthest west,
395 Yet have we time to sack Massilia.⁴
Soldiers, rejoice, fate meets us in the way
With war. As winds in th'empty air do lose
Their force unless some strong grown oak oppose;
As mighty fires for want of fuel die,
400 So want of foes breeds our calamity.⁵
Our strength were lost unless some durst stand out
To be subdued.⁶ But if I come without
My arms, they will receive me;⁷ they desire
Not to exclude but take me prisoner.
405 But they (forsooth) would fain that guilt eschew
That follows civil war;⁸ I'll make them rue
Their asking peace, and know that nought can be
Safer than war to those under me.'⁹
Then on he marches; the town fearless shut
410 Their gates, and soldiers on the rampiers put.¹⁰   *ramparts*
    Not far off from the walls a hill there stood,   [III. 375]
Whose top was like a field, level and broad;
Which Caesar in surveying judged to be
Safe for a camp and fit to fortify.¹¹

---

¹ o'th'two] *bellumque coacti | Hoc potius civile gerent*, 'if forced to war, they will prefer to fight this civil sort' (III. 354–55).
² th'ambassador] *Graia iuventus*, 'the Greek youth' (III. 355).
³ but this at last] *tandem testata est voce dolorem*, 'finally he expressed his grievance in words' (III. 357).
⁴ Massilia] Given four syllables here, although elsewhere (e.g. 3. 328) the last two vowels are elided into one, following M.'s usual practice.
⁵ our calamity] *mihi nocet*, 'is harmful to me' (III. 365).
⁶ Our strength ... subdued] *damnum putamus | Armorum, nisi qui vinci potuere, rebellent*, 'we think it a condemnation of our arms, if they, who could have been conquered, do not rebel' (III. 365–66).
⁷ receive me] M. omits Caesar's self-characterisation as *degener*, 'base' (III. 367), i.e. for not fighting.
⁸ But they ... war] M.'s 'forsooth' captures the mockery: *at enim contagia belli | Dira fugant*, 'But they put to flight the deadly contagion of war, indeed!' (III. 369–70).
⁹ I'll make them ... me] L.'s Caesar addresses these remarks directly to the Greeks.
¹⁰ on the rampiers put] *& densa iuvenum vallata corona*, '[the walls] fenced round by a dense circle of youths' (III. 373–74).
¹¹ in surveying] M.'s added technicality: in L. 'it seemed [safe and fit] to the general' (*Visa duci...*, III. 378).

415	The town's near'st part did an high castle raise	
	Equal to th'hill; in midst a valley was.	
	Caesar resolves on a laborious thing,	
	To fill the valley and together bring	
	Both hills; but first to shut up quite the town	
420	By land, from both sides his high camp brings down	*of his high camp*
	A long work to the sea, a bulwark raised	
	Of turfs with rampiers on top, and placed	
	In length to cut all conveys from the town.[1]	*conveyance*
	This was a thing forever to renown	[III. 388]
425	This Greekish town, to stay the violent course	
	Of this hot war, not ta'en by sudden force	
	Or fear: when Caesar all the rest o'errun,	
	This city's conquest asked him time alone.	
	'Twas much to stay his fates:[2] Fortune, in haste	
430	To make him lord of all the world,[3] did waste	
	Time at this siege. Now round about the town	
	The lofty woods are felled, large oaks hewn down[4]	
	To fortify with posts the bulwark's side,	
	Lest earth too brittle of itself should slide	
435	Away, not able the towers' weight to bear.	
	A wood untouched of old was growing there	[III. 399][5]
	Of thick-set trees, whose boughs spreading and fair,	
	Meeting obscurèd the enclosèd air,	
	And made dark shades exiling Phoebus' rays;[6]	
440	There no rude fawn nor wanton silvan plays,	*wood-dweller*
	No nymph disports,[7] but cruel deities	
	Claim barbarous rites and bloody sacrifice:[8]	

[1] to cut ... town] L. only says Caesar 'encloses the waters and floods of the field with a ditch', *fontesque & pabula campi | Amplexus fossa* (III. 385–86); the strategic intention is outlined by F.

[2] his fates] Merely *fata*, 'the fates', in L. (III. 392), which also expresses this thought as a rhetorical question.

[3] Fortune, in haste ... the world] *virum toti properans imponere mundo*, 'hurrying to impose one man on the whole world' (III. 393).

[4] The lofty ... hewn down] *Procumbunt nemora, & spoliantur robore sylvae*, 'groves are felled, and woods spoiled of their timber' (III. 394).

[5] 3. 436–492] Caesar fells a sacred grove. John Evelyn quotes 3. 436–77 in his *Sylva, or a Discourse of Forest Trees*, 2nd ed. (London: John Martyn and James Allestree, 1670), p. 243.

[6] dark shades] *gelidas ... umbras*, 'icy shades' (III. 401).

[7] no rude fawn ... disports] *ruricolae Panes, nemorumque potentes | Sylvani, Nymphaeque*, 'countryside Pans, grove-ruling Silvans and Nymphs' (III. 402–03). M.'s erotic touches: amorous silvans and wanton nymphs are clichés of early modern literature.

[8] bloody sacrifice] *structae sacris feralibus arae*, 'altars built for wild rituals' (III. 404).

Each tree's defiled with human blood. If we
Believe traditions of antiquity,
445 No bird dares light upon those hallowed boughs,
No beasts make there their dens, no wind there blows,
Nor lightning falls; a sad religious awe   *grave*
The quiet trees, unstirred by wind, do draw.[1]
Black water-currents from dark fountains flow;
450 The gods' unpolished images do know
No art, but plain and formless trunks they are.[2]
Their moss and mouldiness procures a fear;[3]   *brings about, induces*
The common figures of known deities
Are not so feared; not knowing what god 'tis
455 Makes him more awful. By relation[4]   *report*
The shaken earth's dark caverns oft did groan,
Fall'n yew trees often of themselves would rise,
With seeming fire oft flamed th'unburnèd trees,
And winding dragons the cold oaks embrace.[5]   *snakes*
460 None give near worship to that baleful place;
The people leave it to the gods alone.
When black night reigns, or Phoebus gilds the noon,[6]   *the sun*
The priest himself trembles, afraid to spy
Or find this wood's tutelar deity.[7]   *guardian*
465   This wood he bids them fell, not standing far   [III. 426]
From off their work. Untouched in former war,
Among the other barèd hills it stands,
Of a thick growth. The soldiers' valiant hands
Trembled to strike, moved with the majesty,
470 And think the axe from off the sacred tree
Rebounding back would their own bodies wound.

---

[1] sad religious ... draw] *non ullis frondem praebentibus auris, | Arboribus suus horror inest*, 'with no breezes supplying the leaf, their own shuddering is inside the trees' (III. 410–11).

[2] but plain ... are] *caesisque extant informia truncis*, 'and stand out shapeless from carved trunks' (III. 412–13).

[3] Their moss ... a fear] *Ipse situs, putrique facit iam robore pallor | Attonitos*, 'the site itself and the pallor of the rotten wood astounds men' (III. 414–15); M. derives 'moss' from F.

[4] By relation] 'relation' has four syllables, as often but not always when concluding one of M.'s lines with '-ion'.

[5] cold oaks] M.'s adjective.

[6] gilds] M.'s expression.

[7] tutelar deity] *dominumque ... luci*, 'master of the grove' (III. 425); F. uses the paraphrase *tutelarem*, 'safeguarding'.

	Th'amazement of his men when Caesar found,[1]	*mental stupefaction*
	In his bold hand himself an hatchet took,	
	And first of all assaults a lofty oak,	
475	And having wounded the religious tree,	
	'Let no man fear to fell this wood,' quoth he,	
	'The guilt of this offence let Caesar bear.'[2]	
	The soldiers all obey, not void of fear,	
	But balancing the gods' and Caesar's frown.[3]	
480	The knotty holms, the tall wild ashes down,	*holm-oaks*
	Jove's sacred oak, ship-building alder falls,	
	And cypress worn at great men's funerals,[4]	
	Losing their leaves are forced t'admit the day;	
	The falling trees so thick each other stay.	
485	The Gauls lament to see the wood destroyed,	
	But the besiegèd townsmen, all o'erjoyed,	
	Hope that the wrongèd gods will vengeance take.[5]	
	But gods oft spare the guiltiest men, and make	
	Poor wretches only feel their vengeful hand.[6]	
490	When wood enough was felled, wains they command	*carts*
	From every part; ploughmen their seasons lose,[7]	
	Whilst in this work soldiers their teams dispose.	
	But weary in this(g) ling'ring war to stay	[III. 453][8]
	Before the walls, Caesar goes far away[9]	

---

[1] Th'amazement] *magno ... terrore*, 'huge terror' (III. 432); modern editions print *torpore*, 'numbness'.

[2] The guilt ... bear] *Credite me fecisse nefas*: 'believe that I have committed the sacrilege' (III. 437).

[3] balancing ... frown] i.e. fearing Caesar's wrath over the gods'.

[4] great men's funerals] *non plebeios luctus*, 'non-plebeian mourning' (III. 442); on 'great men' as a term for ambitious aristocrats cf. 5. 392, 8. Ded. 9. 'Sacred oak' translates *Dodones* (III. 441): oaks of Dodona in Epirus were sacred to Zeus/Jupiter.

[5] the besiegèd townsmen ... vengeance take] M. uses the prosaic 'townsmen' for L.'s epic *iuventus* ('the youth', III. 446) several times in this episode. See also 3. 500, 527; cf. 1. 265. M. translates F.'s paraphrase here, *deos sperans violati luci ultores*, 'hoping the gods would avenge the grove's violation'; the Latin, *quis enim laesos impune putaret | Esse deos?*, 'for who would think that the gods could be wounded without punishment?' (III. 447–48), sceptically implies there may be no such gods.

[6] But gods ... hand] *servat multos Fortuna nocentes: | Et tantum miseris irasci numina possunt*, 'Fortune protects many guilty men, and divine forces can be enraged only at the wretched' (III. 448–49).

[7] ploughmen ... lose] *Agricolae raptis annum flevere iuvencis*, 'The farmers wept at the [lost] year, their teams of oxen snatched away' (III. 452).

[8] 3. 493–550] The siege is renewed in Caesar's absence but fails completely.

[9] far away] *extremaque mundi*, 'to the end of world' (III. 454). In L. Caesar is not 'weary' but *impatiens*, 'impatient' (III. 453).

495	To meet his troops in Spain. His army stays
	Before the town; there lofty forts they raise,
	And bulwarks equalling the height o'th'town,
	Which had in earth no fixed foundation,
	But rollèd to and fro, the cause unknown.[1]
500	The townsmen viewing this strange motion,[2]
	Thought it some earthquake, where the struggling wind
	From the earth's caverns could no passage find,
	But much they wonder their own walls stand fast.
	From thence against the town their piles they cast,[3]
505	But the Greeks' missile-weapons did more harm
	To Caesar's men, sent from no feeble arm
	But mighty engines with a whirlwind's might;
	These not content one breast alone to split,
	Through many bodies, bones and armours cleave,
510	Not losing in one wound their strength, and leave
	Behind them many deaths. But when they throw
	Great massy stones, the mortal force is so
	As from a mountain's top a falling rock,
	Which the wind's force and ruining time has broke,[4]
515	Not only kills what man soe'er it dash,
	But every limb does into pieces pash. *hurl violently*
	But when with fence of shields conjoinèd all
	The sheltered soldiers could approach the wall,
	Their heads all covered like a fish's shell,[5]
520	Those darts and stones fly over them, which fell
	With danger on their heads before. But now
	The Greeks at such small distance could not throw,
	Nor th'engine change;[6] content with weight alone

---

[1] there lofty forts they raise … the cause unknown] *stellatis axibus agger | Erigitur, geminasque aequantes moenia turres | Accipit, hae nullo fixerunt robore terram, | Sed per iter longum causa repsere latent*, 'a mound is raised lattice-wise, and receives twin towers equalling the walls; these are fixed by no timber to the ground but crept forward on their long journey by a hidden cause [probably wheels]' (III. 455–58).

[2] strange motion] The construction's vibration: *cum nutaret … onus*, 'when the weight shook' (III. 459).

[3] their piles they cast] i.e. the Roman besiegers.

[4] ruining time] 'ruining' is disyllabic; contrast the disyllabic 'ruins' (3. 550, below).

[5] like a fish's shell] Not in L.; M. follows F.'s observation that a Roman shield-roof 'resembles fish-scales', *in morem squammarum*.

[6] now … change] *nec Grais flectere iactum, | Aut facilis labor est longinqua ad tela parati | Tormenti mutare modum*, 'nor was it an easy task for the Greeks to bend the trajectory or change the fashion of a siege-engine designed for aiming at weapons far away' (III. 478–80).

On their foes' heads they roll down heavy stone.
525 But while the fence did last, hurtless did all[1]
Their stones and darts, like hail on houses, fall;
Until the townsmen's teasèd valour broke[2]   *irritated*
(When Caesar's men were tired with often strokes)
The fence and did their joinèd shields divide.
530 Then did a thin earth-covered work proceed;[3]
Under whose covert those that lay did fall[4]   *shelter*
To work in undermining of the wall.
Sometimes the back-forced ram did strongly drive
Forward, the well-compacted wall to rive.[5]   *tear apart*
535 But from above with fires, with often strokes
Of broken bars, stakes and fire-hardened oaks
They force the fence: the work broke down and vain,[6]
The soldiers, tired, fly to their camp again.
The Greeks then sally forth, not satisfied
540 That their walls safely stand, and fireworks hide
Under their arms;[7] no mortal bow nor spear   *deadly*
Arms the bold youth, but flaming fire they bear,
Which with swift wings into the Roman trench
The strong winds carry; nought has power to quench
545 Or slacken it, the wood though green dissolves,
And in black clouds of smoke the air involves.   *coils*
But fire all pieces of the buildings take;
Not only wood but stones and rocks do crack
And moulder into ashes: greater now
550 The falling bulwarks in their ruins show.
   The conquered now losing all hope by land   [III. 509][8]
Resolve the hazard of sea-fight to stand.
Their ships' fore-deck no gilded names adorn;[9]

---

[1] the fence] i.e. the shield-roof; L.'s term is *armorum series*, 'serried rank of weapons' (III. 482).

[2] teasèd valour] *virtus incensa*, 'inflamed virtue' (III. 484). Modern editions read the MS variant *virtus incerta*, 'uncertain virtue', and attribute it to Caesar's soldiers, not the Massilians.

[3] earth-covered work] *vinea*, 'a moveable shed' (III. 487).

[4] covert] *pluteis, & tecta fronte*, 'boards and covered front' (III. 488).

[5] the well-compacted wall to rive] Omitting *& impositis unum subducere saxis*, 'and knock out one of the inserted stones' (III. 492).

[6] and vain] i.e. the work is in vain (*frustraque labore*, III. 495).

[7] fireworks hide] *coruscas ... faces*, 'wavering torches' (III. 498–99).

[8] 3. 551–823] The sea-battle for Massilia, 49 BC.

[9] no gilded names adorn] *non robore picto | Ornatas decuit fulgens tutela carinas*, 'no

But timber plain, such as the woods had borne
555 Growing,¹ make stations firm for naval fight.
Now down the stream of Rhodanus the fleet   *Rhône*
From Staechas comes to sea, and there attends
Brutus' praetorian ship:² Massilia sends
Her utmost strength to trial of the war;
560 Old men and beardless boys all armèd are.
The fleet then ready on the ocean
Was rigged, and old worn ships repaired again.³
Now when the sky is clear, and his bright rays
On the calm sea the rising sun displays,
565 The north and southern winds their fury spare
And leave the calmèd ocean fit for war,
Both nations rowing from their stations meet,
Here the Caesarian, there the Grecian fleet.
With oft and lusty strokes of rowers from
570 The havens trembling the great galleys come.
The horns of Caesar's fleet-galleys that bore
Three oars aside, and some that went with four
Or more did make, themselves opposing so
In front, behind them smaller vessels go,
575 Liburnian galleys with two oars content.⁴
Conjoined in form of an half moon they went.
Brutus' praetorian galley swept the sea:
Like a vast house, than th'rest more high was she,

glittering figure-head, with painted woodwork, graced decorated ships' (III. 510-11). M.'s 'names' may misread F.'s *numen*, 'divinity' (referring to how ships in antiquity often carried painted images of deities) as *nomen*. It may also substitute seventeenth-century naval detail: the names of early modern vessels were often painted in gold along the prow.

¹ such as ... Growing] *qualis procumbit montibus arbor*, 'a tree of the sort that falls from the mountains' (III. 512).

² Brutus' praetorian ship] *turrigeram ...carinam*, 'tower-bearing vessel' (III. 514). The flagship of a Roman fleet was termed 'the praetorian ship', *praetoria navis*, the term L. later uses (and M. translates at 3. 577): it was commanded by Decimus Brutus (not to be confused with Marcus Junius Brutus, the future tyrannicide).

³ The fleet ... again] L. makes clear that not only were the floating vessels manned (*accepit viros*) but ships out of service sought in the shipyards (*navalibus*, III. 519-20). 'Ocean' (3. 561) is given three syllables here, but probably two mid-line at 3. 566.

⁴ fleet-galleys...] M. simplifies and clarifies: 'fleet-galleys that bore | Three oars aside' in L. is simply *triremes* (III. 529); 'four | Or more did make' condenses L.'s more elaborate description of rising banks of rowers and pine-trunks (i.e. oars) plunging into the sea (III. 530-32); and 'opposing so | In front' omits L.'s *aperto ... pelago*, 'on the open sea' (III. 532-33), probably taking 'in front' from the Renaissance reading *lunata fronte*, 'horn-shaped vanguard' (III. 533; modern editions print *lunata classe*, 'two-horned fleet'), although their position could be inferred from the general description.

	And rowed with six strong oars on a side.[1]	
580	But when so little sea room did divide	[III. 538]
	Both fleets, as that one stroke would make them meet,	
	Numberless voices the vast air did greet;	
	Ploughing the seas, soldiers' loud shouts quite drowned[2]	
	The noise of rowing and shrill trumpets' sound.	
585	Then sweep they the blue waves; the rowers seat	
	Themselves, and 'gainst their breasts strong strokes they set:	
	Ships against ships, beaks meeting beaks resound,	
	And run astern;[3] the air is darkened round	
	With flying darts,[4] which falling th'ocean hide.	
590	Then turning their forecastles far more wide	
	They make their horns t'engirt the adverse fleet.[5]	*encircle*
	As when strong winds with tides repugnant meet,[6]	*offering opposition*
	One way the sea, the waves another go,	
	These ships upon the furrowed ocean so	
595	Make different tracts, and waves upon the main	*sea*
	Which oars raised, the sea beats down again.[7]	
	But the Greek vessels were more nimble far	
	Either to fly, or turn about the war.[8]	
	They could without long tedious turning wield	
600	Themselves, and quickly to the stern could yield;	
	The Roman ships slow-keeled would firmly stand	
	And lend sure footing, like a fight by land.	
	The master then of his praetorian ship	*helmsman*
	Brutus bespake: 'Why dost thou let them slip?	
605	Leave thy sea-tricks and join the battles close;	

---

[1] rowed ... side] Condensing *Verberibus senis agitur, molemque profundo | Invehit, & summis longe petit aequora remis*, 'it was driven forward by six blows [i.e. of banks of oars] and hauls its huge mass through the deep, and seeks the ocean with its highest oars from a great distance' (III. 536–37). M.'s meter is irregular at 3. 579, but probably deliberately: 'rowed' is spelt 'row'd' in the original texts.

[2] drowned] M.'s pun; *premitur*, 'suppressed' (III. 541).

[3] run astern] *In puppim rediere rates* (III. 545): M. quotes F.'s gloss (which is, unusually, in English).

[4] darkened] *texerunt*, 'covered, filled' (III. 546).

[5] horns] i.e. of a two-pronged attack.

[6] strong winds] *Vt, quoties aestus Zephyris, Eurisque repugnat*, 'As so often the tide resists the North and East Winds' (III. 549).

[7] Ships against ships ... down again] 3. 587–96 are quoted in Poole's *The English Parnassus*, sig. Aa2ᵛ, s.v. 'sea-fight'. Again, the meter is irregular at 3. 596, with the spelling 'rais'd' in the original texts preventing an expansion to 'raisèd'.

[8] turn about the war] *pugnamque lacessere*, 'provoke battle' (III. 553).

	'Gainst the Phocaic stems our ships oppose.'¹	*Massilian prows*
	He straight obeys, and turns his own broad side	
	Against their stems; what ship soe'er they tried	*the Massilians*
	To encounter her, with her own stroke o'ercome	
610	Sticks fast and is surprised. They hook in some,	*the Romans*
	With oars some, some they with chains hold fast;	
	On the sea's covered face the war is placed.²	*surface*
	No brandished javelins manage now the war,	
	No darted steel bestowing wounds from far:	
615	Hands join with hands, and in this naval fight	
	The sword acts all.³ In their own ships upright	
	They face their foes' prone strokes; some fall down slain⁴	
	In their own ships; dyed is the ocean,⁵	
	And the waves stiffened with congealèd blood.	
620	Ships hooked together could not meet, withstood	
	By falling carcasses; some half-dead sink	
	And their own blood mixed with salt-water drink;	
	Some that desire their struggling lives to keep	
	Fall in the ruins of their broken ship.⁶	
625	Javelins that missed the aim they did intend,	
	Fall in the sea and finish there their end,	
	Finding there bodies to receive a wound.	
	A Roman ship by Greeks environed round	[III. 583]
	Fights stiffly still,⁷ on left hand and on right	
630	Maintaining long 'gainst all a doubtful fight,	
	Upon whose lofty deck whilst Tagus bold	
	Strived a seizèd Grecian flag to hold,⁸	

---

[1] Why dost thou ... oppose] *paterisne acies errare profundo? | Artibus et certas pelagi? iam consere bellum: | Phocaicis medias rostris oppone carinas*, 'Why do you allow their battle lines to wander, and compete in sea-manoeuvres? Put the middle of our ships in the path of the Massilian prows' (III. 559-61).

[2] On the sea's ... placed] *tecto stetit aequore bellum*, 'the sea was covered over, the war stood still' (III. 566).

[3] The sword acts... all] *plurima ... | Ensis agit*, 'the sword does most of the work' (III. 569-70).

[4] some fall down] *multi*, 'many' (III. 571). Modern editions, more logically, print *nulli*, 'none'.

[5] dyed is the ocean] *cruor altus in unda | Spumat*, 'gore foams deep in the wave' (III. 572-73).

[6] Some that desire ... broken ship] Underplaying L.'s ironic contrast between souls struggling *lenta cum morte*, 'against slow death', and the *subita ruina* ('sudden ruin') of their vessel (III. 578-79).

[7] Fights stiffly still] Detail from F.'s gloss (on III. 583-4), not in L.

[8] Tagus bold] The common early modern reading; modern editions prefer *Catus* (III. 586). flag] L.'s *aplustre* means a decorated stern, often including banners, as indicated

Two darts together sent together split
His breast and back, and in the middle meet;
635 The blood not knowing yet which way to run
Makes stand, but out at last both darts are thrown;
He in two wounds his dying soul divides.[1]
Hither his ship whilst hapless Telo guides —
Than whom no better on a boist'rous sea
640 Could guide a ship; none better knew than he
Tomorrow's weather, if the sun he spied
Or moon, and could for future storms provide[2] —
He with his stem a Roman ship had broke,   *prow*
But through his heart a trembling javelin stroke;   *struck*
645 His ship turns off following his dying hand.
Gyareus, leaping to his friend's command[3]
Straight with a Roman javelin strongly flung
Was slain, and to the ship fast nailèd hung.
 Two twins stand up, their fruitful mother's fame,   [III. 603]
650 That from one womb with fates far different came
(Death parts them:[4] their sad parents, reft of one,   *bereft*
Without mistaking know their living son,
Whose looks the cause of lasting sorrow keep,
And make his friends for his slain brother weep).[5]
655 One of those twins from his Greek ship was bold
Upon a Roman keel to lay strong hold,[6]
But from above a stroke cuts off his hand,
Which in the place did still fast bended stand,
And kept the hold; the nerves more stiff became
660 By death. His courage by this noble maim

in early modern commentaries (III. 586); M.'s 'flag' is probably a deliberate simplification or transposition from early modern naval practice; cf. 3. 726. 'Grecian' is untypically trisyllabic.

[1] but out ... divides] *largus cruor expulit hastas, | Divisitque animam, sparsitque in vulnera letum*, 'massed gore expelled the spears, and split his life in two and distributed his death into the wounds' (III. 589–90).

[2] for future storms provide] *Semper venturis componere carbasa ventis*, 'could always trim the sails for future winds' (III. 596).

[3] to his friend's command] *in sociam erumpere puppim*, 'to sally forth to the allied stern' (III. 600). Modern editions read *erepere*, 'climb up'. M. may follow F. who says that Gyareus (another Massilian) was 'about to take over Telo's office', *occupaturus munus Telonis*.

[4] Death] *mors saeva*, 'cruel death' (III. 605).

[5] And make his friends ... weep] *et amissum fratrem lugentibus offert*, 'he [the surviving brother] presents his lost brother to those who mourn him' (III. 608). M.'s description of the sea-battle emphasises friendship more consistently than L.

[6] One ... hold] Omitting *mistis obliquo pectine remis*, 'when the oars were entangled in a slanting comb-pattern' (III. 609).

Was raised, and greater by this accident[1]
His valiant left hand 'gainst his foes he bent,
And rushes on his lost right hand to reach,
But that (alas) another sword did fetch
665 Off by the shoulder: now both hands were gone, *shield*
Nor sword, nor target could he wield; yet down
He did not sink, but naked-breasted stood,
Foremost to save his armèd brother's blood,
And there all darts, all wounds that were ordained
670 For many deaths, one dying breast contained.[2]
And then his soul fleeting so many ways *dispersing*
He recollects, and in his tired limbs stays
That little strength and blood was left, to skip *that was left*
Before his death into the Roman ship,
675 His enemies by weight alone t'oppress.
For now the ship, laden with carcasses
And full of blood, bored through the side had been,
And through her leaks drinking the water in,
Was filled up to the hatches; sinking then
680 It turned the face of the near ocean.[3]
The waters to the sinking ship gave way,
And in her room closed up again. That day
Miraculous fates the ocean did behold.[4]
An iron hook thrown to lay violent hold [III. 635]
685 Upon a ship, on Lycidas did light:[5]
Drowned had he been, but his friends hindered it,
And on his lower parts caught hold. In two
The man was plucked: nor did his blood spin slow
As from a wound,[6] but gushing in one spout,
690 From all his broken veins at once let out;
Into the sea falls his life-carrying blood.
Never so great a passage open stood

---

[1] His courage ... accident] *Crevit in adversis virtus: plus nobilis irae | Truncus habet*, 'his virtue grew in misfortune; the noble torso was more enraged' (III. 614–15).
[2] one ... contained] Omitting L.'s *Emerita iam morte*, 'having already earned death' (III. 622).
[3] It turned ... ocean] *Vicinum involvens contorto vertice pontum*, 'sucking in the neighbouring water with whirling eddy' (III. 631); 'ocean' is trisyllabic.
[4] Miraculous fates] *varii miracula fati*, 'various wondrous deaths' (III. 634). The line is irregular, suggesting a contraction to 'Mirac'lous', or an elision to 'th'ocean', but neither are signalled in the original texts.
[5] Lycidas] A Massilian sailor.
[6] blood spin slow] On blood 'spinning' (i.e. spurting), see *OED*, s.v. 2.6a.

	To let out any soul.¹ Life straight forsakes	
	His lower half, since vital parts it lacks:	
695	But in his upper half (since in that part	
	Lay the soft lungs and life-sustaining heart),²	
	Death stays a while, and finds repugnancy,	*aversion, resistance*
	Nor at one time could all his members die.	
	The men that manned one ship, eager of fight,	[III. 647]
700	All pressing to one side leave empty quite	
	The other side,³ whose weight o'erturned the ship,	
	Which topsy-turvy sinking down did keep	
	The sailors under water:⁴ all of them	
	Were drowned, nor could their arms have room to swim.	
705	One horrid kind of death that day was seen:	
	A young man swimming was, whose breast between	
	Two meeting ships' sharp stems was borèd through:	
	The brazen stems through bones and flesh did go,	
	And made a noise;⁵ his squeezèd belly sent	
710	Up through his mouth blood mixed with excrement.	
	But when the ships divide themselves again,⁶	
	The body thrown into the ocean,	
	The water through his borèd bosom came.	
	Now in the sea shipwrecked Massilians swam	
715	Towards their fellows' ship to save their lives,⁷	
	But that, already overburdened, strives	
	To keep her friends (though thus distressèd) out,⁸	
	And from above with swords the soldiers cut	

---

¹ In two ... soul] These lines were often thought to have been recited by Lucan when committing suicide: see pp. 9n., 41.

² soft lungs and life-sustaining heart] *At tumidus qua pulmo iacet, qua viscera fervent*, 'where the swollen lung resides, where the innards are hot' (III. 644).

³ The other side] Omitting *Qua caret hoste*, 'which lacks an enemy' (III. 649).

⁴ under water] By trapping the men beneath the 'hollow vessel', *cava ... carina* (III. 650).

⁵ The brazen stems ... noise] *Nec prohibere valent obtritis ossibus artus, | Quo minus aera sonent*, 'nor were his limbs, their bones crushed, able to prevent the bronze [prows] clashing' (III. 656–57). The prows of Roman warships were typically made of bronze to ram opponents.

⁶ when ... again] *Postquam inhibent remis puppes, ac rostra reducunt*, 'after the sterns are restrained by oars and the prows moved back' (III. 659).

⁷ swam ... to save their lives] Translating F.'s note, *conati vitae suae consulere ... natando*, rather than L.'s *iactatis morti obluctata lacertis*, 'struggling against death by hurling their limbs about' (III. 662).

⁸ But that ... out] *at illi | Robora cum vetitis prensarent altius ulnis, | Nutaretque ratis populo peritura receptor*, 'but when they pressed higher up on the wood with forbidden elbows, and the tottering ship was about to sink under the accumulation of people' (III. 664–65).

Their arms when hold upon the ship they lay,
720 Then down again into the sea fall they,
Leaving their hands behind;[1] the ocean
Can now no longer their maimed trunks sustain.
But now when all the soldiers' darts were gone,
Fury finds weapons: oars by some are thrown
725 Against their foes with a strong arm; the mast
Do some tear down, and in their fury cast;[2]
Some tear the sailors' seats; boards from the deck
Some throw;[3] for weapons they their ships do break.
Some wanting swords their friends' dead bodies spoil;[4]
730 From his own breast one draws the mortal pile,
With the left hand holding the wound, so long
To keep in blood and strength, 'til he had flung
The javelin at his foe, then lets it run.[5]
But nothing wrought so much destruction   [III. 680]
735 At sea as sea's opposèd element,
The fire, which wrapped in unctuous stuff was sent,
And sulphur balls.[6] The ships apt fuel were,
Their pitch and melting wax took easily fire,[7]
Nor now could water quench th'unruly flame:
740 Fragments of broken ships still burning swam.
Into the sea to quench his fire one skips,
For fear of drowning to the burning ships
Another cleaves: that death, that was most near
Among a thousand deaths, they most did fear.[8]

---

[1] the soldiers] *Impia turba*, 'the impious mob' (III. 666). M.'s translation of this section allows for more valiant fellowship than L.'s account.   their hands behind] L. also portrays 'their arms, hanging from the Greek ship', *Brachia linquentes Graia pendentia puppe* (III. 667).

[2] the mast] Translating *aplustre* (cf. 3. 632), the curved stern of a ship. M. reads 'cast' (*tortum*, III. 672): modern editions read *totum*, the 'whole [stern]'.

[3] boards ... throw] *expulso remige*, 'hurling away the oars', III. 673.

[4] wanting swords ... spoil] M. transposes 'wanting swords' from its position in Renaissance editions, where it is attached to the action in the following line.

[5] lets it run] i.e. the blood from the wound. 'Destruction', in the next line, is given four syllables to rhyme with 'run'.

[6] which ... balls] *nam pinguibus ignis | Affixus tedis, & tecto sulfure vivax | Spargitur*, 'for living fire, fixed to fattened torches and concealed sulphur, spreads' (III. 681-83): i.e. wildfire, Greek fire. M.'s notion of 'sulphur balls' derives from contemporary military usage: see e.g. the comprehensive instructions about using balls of wildfire in land or sea battle in Thomas Smith, *Certain Additions to the book of Gunnery, with a Supply of Fireworks* (London: Humphrey Lownes for W. Ponsonby, 1627), pp. 29-56.

[7] easily] Probably contracted in pronunciation to 'eas'ly'.

[8] that death ... fear] *Mille modos inter leti mors, una timori est, | Qua coepere mori,*

745	Nor did their shipwrecked valour idly live:	
	Darts floating on the waves they take and give	
	Their fellows in the ship, or on the seas	
	Themselves those darts (though feebly) exercise.	
	When weapons want, the seas their weapons be:	
750	Foes grasping foes together gladly die.[1]	
	But in that fight one Phocian did excel:	
	To search the seas he under water well	
	Could keep his breath, dive to the lowest sands,	
	And loosen fastened anchors with his hands.[2]	
755	He, grappling with a foe down in the main,	sea
	Had sunk and drowned him, and himself again	
	Safe and a conqueror rose, but rising found	
	Ships in his way, and so at last was drowned.	
	Some with their arms on their foes' oars lay hold	
760	To stay their flight; dear as they could they sold	
	Their lives:[3] some wounded, to keep off the blows	
	From their friends' ships, their bodies interpose.[4]	
	Tyrrhenus standing on the deck aloft,	[III. 709]
	Lygdamus with a Balearic shaft[5]	
765	Wounded: the ponderous lead his temples broke,	
	His falling eyes their hollow seat forsook,	
	The optic nerves and ligaments were broke;[6]	
	He now stark-blind, amazèd at the stroke,	
	Thinks this to be death's darkness. Finding then	
770	That all his limbs their perfect strength retain,	
	'Fellows,' quoth he, 'place me where I may throw	
	A pile and plant me as you use to do	
	Engines of war. This little life that now	
	Remains, Tyrrhenus, on all hazards throw;	
775	This body, though in part already dead,	
	Will serve for warlike uses, and instead	

'amongst a thousand ways to die, one death only prompted fear, the one by which they have begun to die' (III. 689-90).

[1] Foes ... gladly die] Compressing *& implicitis gaudent subsidere membris, | Mergentesque mori*, 'winding their limbs together, they rejoice to sink and drowning, to die' (III. 695-96).

[2] And loosen ... hands] Compressing into 'fastened' *Adductum quotiens non senserat ancora funem*, 'whenever the anchor had not responded to a pull on the rope' (III. 700).

[3] dear ... Their lives] *Non perdere letum | Maxima cura fuit*, 'their greatest concern was not to waste their death' (III. 706-07).

[4] their bodies interpose] *multus sua vulnera puppi | Affixit*, 'Many fixed their own wounds to the stern [i.e. to absorb the impact of blows from enemy ships]' (III. 707-08).

[5] Balearic shaft] A sling shot, not strictly 'shaft'.

[6] The optic nerves ... broke] M. adds 'optic nerves'.

	Of men alive take wounds.' Thus having spoke	
	In his blind aimless hand a pile he shook,	
	And threw it not in vain, which as it lit	*fell*
780	Below his belly noble Argus hit,	
	Whose weight now falling made it further glide.	
	Argus' unhappy sire on t'other side	[III. 726] *side of*
	The beaten ship then stood (to none would he,	
	When he was young, in feats of chivalry	
785	Give place;[1] his strength is now by age decayed,	
	And he no soldier but a pattern made).	*example*
	He, seeing his son fall, with trembling step	
	Stumbling along came to that side the ship,[2]	*side of*
	And finding there the body panting yet,	
790	No tears fell from his cheeks, nor did he beat	
	His woeful breast;[3] his hands now stiff were grown,	
	And all his joints cold numbness seizes on;	
	A sudden darkness closes up his eyes,	
	That he discerns not Argus whom he sees.	
795	Argus his dying head began to rear	
	And feeble neck, seeing his father there,	
	Speechless, yet seemed in silence to demand	
	A kiss, and to invite his father's hand	
	To close his dying eyes. But the old man	
800	Free from amaze,[4] when bloody grief began	*astonishment*
	To recollect his strength, 'I will not lose	
	That time', quoth he, 'that angry Fate bestows.[5]	
	Pardon thy wretched father, that from thee,	
	Argus, and from thy last embrace I flee:	
805	Thy wound's warm blood yet signs of life do give,	
	Th'art but half dead, and yet a while may'st live;	
	I'll go before thee, son.'[6] These words expressed,	
	And with a bloody sword piercing his breast,	
	He leapt into the sea, hasting to death	
810	Before his dearest son:[7] his flitting breath	
	Unto one single kind of destiny	

---

[1] feats of chivalry] *Phocaicis ... in armis*, 'in Massilia's wars' (III. 728). See Textual Notes.
[2] with trembling step | Stumbling along] *saepe cadens*, 'often falling' (III. 731).
[3] woeful breast] M.'s adjective.
[4] amaze] *torpore*, 'debility' (III. 741).
[5] angry Fate bestows] *A saevis permissa Deis*, 'permitted by the cruel gods'. M. omits the next clause, *iugulumque senilem | Confodiam*, 'and I will slit my aged throat' (III. 743-44).
[6] I'll ... son] *& adhuc potes esse superstes*, 'and you indeed can still outlive me' (III. 747).
[7] And with a bloody sword...] L. makes his sword-wound contrast with his decision to jump (III. 748-49).

He durst not trust.¹ Now great commanders die;²   *dared*
And now no longer doubtful is the fight.
Some of the Greeks are sunk,³ by hasty flight
815 Some get into the haven; others bear
(Changing their load) the Roman conqueror.⁴
But now sad parents' mournings fill the town;
The shore with mothers' lamentation
Did ring.⁵ Instead of her dear husband's face
820 A weeping wife mistaken did embrace
A Roman; fathers, funeral rites to give,
About their sons' deformèd bodies strive.⁶
But Brutus, conqueror on the ocean⁷
To Caesar's side first naval honour won.   *for*

FINIS *Libri Tertii*⁸

Annotations on the Third Book⁹

(a) Caesar had sent Caius Fabius his Lieutenant with three legions into Spain, to dislodge Afranius a Lieutenant of Pompey's in the Pyrenaean straits: and now himself leaving Caius Trebonius to besiege Massilia by land, and Decius Brutus to besiege it by sea, goes with nine hundred horsemen into Spain to Fabius his camp.¹⁰

---

¹ his flitting ... trust] *Festinantem animam morti non credidit uni*, 'he did not entrust his hurrying soul to one death alone' (III. 751).
² Now ... die] *inclinant iam fata ducum*, 'the fates of the commanders alter' (III. 752); *inclino* can mean 'alter for the worse, sink', so M. infers the deaths of the Massilian leaders, some of whom did die in the historical battle.
³ Some ... sunk] *pars maxima*, 'the greatest part' (III. 753). M.'s apparent contradiction of L. possibly reflects other historical sources, e.g. Caesar (*Commentarii*, I. 58. 10), cited by F., which only mentions nine Massilian ships captured or sunk. M. could be unsettled by L.'s alterations to the historical record: see his note (h), after this book, and Introduction, p. 21.
⁴ conqueror] *Victores ... suos*, 'their victors' (III. 755).
⁵ But now ... ring] Rhetorical questions/exclamations in L. (III. 756–57). M.'s final '-ion' is disyllabic.
⁶ deformèd bodies] L., more clearly, has 'about a headless body', *de corpore trunco* (III. 760).
⁷ ocean] Probably disyllabic here, against M.'s usual practice (cf. 3. 680n), although 'conqueror' could be disyllabic instead.
⁸ 'The end of the third book'.
⁹ Several extra notes were added from 1631 onwards; see Textual Notes.
¹⁰ A slightly condensed translation of F.'s note to III. 453. The 'straits' means mountain passes.

To the Right Honourable Robert, Earl of Essex and Ew, etc.[1]

What name can fitter patronage afford   *more suitable*
To this fourth book, which keeps th'admired record
Of truth and faithful love, shown past belief
By valiant soldiers to a valiant chief,[2]
Than you, most lovèd lord? Here read and see
How, to th'amaze of all posterity,   *astonishment*
With his whole cohort bold Vulteius dies,[3]
Scorning to yield to Caesar's enemies,
Or live a vanquished man, a thing unknown
In Caesar's troops; how Curio,[4] overthrown,
Disdains both flight, and life, and strikes the foe
Into astonishment that soldiers so
Should prize a general.[5] If love of men
Be happiness, be happy, Essex, then,
As now you are, in love and public fame,
And be in England still an honoured name.[6]

---

[1] To the Right Honourable] Robert Devereux, second Earl of Essex (1591–1646), a staunch Calvinist and defender of parliamentary privilege. He recruited and commanded Protestant forces abroad during the Thirty Years War. He was not entirely trusted by James I or Charles I and became a Parliamentary general in the first English Civil War (1642–1646). In the 1626 and 1628 parliaments Essex spoke against the Duke of Buckingham and extra-Parliamentary government, notably the Forced Loan, of which he was publicly a refuser, as were many others of M.'s 1627 dedicatees. M.'s choice of Essex therefore has political implications; although avoiding reference to domestic politics, there are subtexts to his emphasis on Essex's military virtues, and also (more complexly) to the comparison to Vulteius and Curio. See Introduction, pp. 24–25.
[2] By valiant soldiers to a valiant chief] From 1620 (when he served under Horatio Vere, the dedicatee of 1627's book six) to 1625, Essex annually recruited and commanded English forces fighting on the Protestant side in the wars of the Palatinate. Although unblessed by victories, he was extremely popular with his soldiers, as also indicated here. This reputation acquired edge after the disastrous 1626 naval expedition against Spain, led by the militarily inexperienced Duke of Buckingham and other royal favourites; in the debates surrounding Buckingham's attempted impeachment in the 1626 Parliament, Essex was fiercely critical of the expedition's leadership and mismanagement. See John Morrill, 'Devereux, Robert Third Earl of Essex (1591–1646)', *ODNB*.
[3] Vulteius] A Caesarian officer who gets his men to commit suicide rather than surrender: see 4. 513–642 below.
[4] Curio] Pronounced as two syllables.
[5] that soldiers so | Should prize a general] In fact L. doesn't record the enemy's reaction to Curio's death and denounces him for proving a turncoat to Roman liberty (see 1. 290–92, 879–906 and notes). M.'s praise may derive instead from Florus, *Epitome of Roman History*, II. xiii. 33–34, who treats Vulteius and Curio's deaths successively as examples of *virtus* in calamity, although Florus also doesn't discuss enemy reaction (see the edition and trans. by Edward S. Forester (Cambridge, MA: Harvard University Press, 1984)).
[6] And be in England still an honoured name] The emphasis on aristocratic honour is

LUCAN'S
Pharsalia

The Fourth Book.

The Argument of the Fourth Book.[1]

Caesar in Spain near high Ilerda's walls
Encamps 'gainst two Pompeian generals.[2]
By sudden floods his camp endangered is.
Caesar divides the stream of Sicoris,
5 O'ertakes Petreius' flight, who bloodily
Breaks off his soldiers' new-made amity;
But by extremity of thirst compelled,
Afranius and himself to Caesar yield.
Famished Antonius yields t'his enemy.
10 Vulteius and his valiant cohort die
By their own swords.[3] Curio on Libyan sands
Is slain by Juba's Mauritanian bands.[4]

But now stern Caesar in Spain's farthest coast   [IV. 1][5]
Makes war:[6] on which, though little blood it(a) cost,
The fortunes of both generals much did stand.[7]
Afranius(b) and Petreius did command
5 Those camps with equal power, but concord made
Their government more firm: their men obeyed

---

typical of M.'s 1627 dedications. Here he may allude to a recent royal slight against Essex: in early 1627 he had been passed over for command of an expedition to aid the King of Denmark in favour of less experienced noblemen, and promptly resigned his commission (Morrill, 'Devereux, Robert'). The emphasis on 'public fame' (line 15) thus possibly invites a reader to consider how Essex has been treated privately.

[1]   The Argument] See note on Argument to book one.
[2]   two Pompeian generals] Petreius and Afranius. On their future actions and the death of Petreius see May's *Continuation*, sigs F1^r–F2^v, H1^v.
[3]   Famished Antonius ... Vulteius] For these episodes see 4. 440–512, 513–642 below.
[4]   Curio ... bands] See 4. 643–906 (cf. also 1. 292n on Curio). Juba was King of Numidia and a Pompeian ally.
[5]   4. 1–439] Petreius and Afranius are defeated by Caesar at the battle of Ilerda.
[6]   stern Caesar ... war] L.'s epithet for Caesar is *saevus*, 'savage/wild' (IV. 2): contrast 1. 506, where *saevus* is translated as 'bloody'. M. adds 'Spain's'.
[7]   The fortunes] *fati*, 'fate' (IV. 3).

Alternally both generals' commands.¹ *alternately*
Here, besides Romans, bold Asturian bands,
Light Vectones and Celtae⁽ᶜ⁾ were, that came
From France and with th'Iberi mixed their name.
    A little hill, not steep, of fertile lands   [IV. 11]
Swells up, on which the old Ilerda stands.
Before the town flows Sicoris' soft stream,
Among Spain's rivers of no small esteem,
On which a bridge of stone high archèd stood
T'endure the violence of a winter's flood.
The next hill the Pompeians' camp did bear,²
Equal to which Caesar his tents did rear.
The river in the midst both camps divides,
From whence the champion fields upon both sides   *champaign, floodplain*
Extend themselves beyond the ken of man.
Swift Cinga bounds them, that to th'ocean
Carries no name:⁽ᵈ⁾ Iber, where you two join,
That gives the land her name, takes from thee thine.³
    The first day they encamped from fight was free:⁴   [IV. 24]
The captains stood each other's strength to see,
Numb'ring the eagles. Shame did then begin
To damn their rage and hold their fury in;⁵   *condemn*
One poor day's respite to their country they
And broke laws gave; but Caesar, when the day
Declined, did with a sudden trench enclose
His camp about, and to deceive the foes⁶
His army in the front kept station
To hide the work; and when the morn drew on,
He sends swift troops the next hill to surprise,
That 'twixt the foes' camp and Ilerda lies.
Thither the foes with shame and terror make,
And by a nearer way the hill they take.⁷

---

¹ their men … commands] *tutelaque valli* | *Pervigil alterna paret custodia signo*, 'the ever-vigilant watches guarding the palisade obeyed alternating standards' (IV. 5–7).
² the Pompeians] Not a Lucanic term; L. refers to *signa … Magni*, 'the standards of Pompey' (IV. 17).
³ Swift Cinga … thee thine] i.e. the rivers Iber and Cinga join together to form one river, the Iber, from which the name 'Iberia' derives. 'Thee' and 'thine' address Cinga.
⁴ from fight was free] Lit. was free of 'bloody war' (*Marte cruento*, IV. 25).
⁵ To damn their rage] A pun on 'dam' i.e. to block off or impede; L. talks only of shame restraining wickedness and blood-frenzy (IV. 26–27).
⁶ and to deceive the foes] In L. he *did* deceive them: *fefellit* (IV. 30).
⁷ Thither the foes … take] The Pompeians, 'foes' from Caesar's perspective, occupy a hill.

       The fight grows there: on sword and valour one
40   Relies, the other on possession.¹
       Laden with arms march Caesar's soldiers up
       'Gainst the steep hill; their following fellows prop
       Their backs with targets up, to keep them so
       From falling back; their piles against the foe
45   They could not use. Piles guide their falt'ring steps;
       Hold, as they climb, they catch on shrubs and slips;²   *twigs*
       Their swords serve not to fight, but cut their way.
       This danger Caesar saw and sent away
       His horse to wheel, charging in flank the foe,
50   And all his foot retreat in safety so.
       The skirmish ended thus and neither side
       Obtained the conquest. Thus far fighting tried:³
       What other fates were added to this war
       Grew from th'unconstant motions of the air.
55   For by cold winter's dry north winds, the rain
       The clouds' congealèd bowels did contain.⁴
       Snows on the hills and tops of mountains lie,
       And frosts that at the sun's appearance fly.
       All lands within those western climates are
60   Hardened by winter's dry congealing air.
       But when the sun, now wexèd, warmer came   *waxed; grown in strength*
       To take possession of the heavenly Ram,⁵
       Making the equinoctial again;
       When day t'exceed the night in length began;⁶
65   When Cynthia, from the sun's conjunction   *the moon*
       But newly come, could hardly yet be known,

---

¹ possession] As often in line-endings, though rarely elsewhere, '-ion' is disyllabic; cf. 'station', 4. 33, but contrast 'exhalation', 4. 72.

² Hold ... slips] Sharply inverted word-order. In L. it is clear that the soldiers grip the shrubs and twigs, but steady their footsteps by planting their spears (IV. 41-43).

³ Thus far fighting tried] *Hactenus armorum discrimina*, 'Thus far the crises of arms' (IV. 48); as L. now goes on to explain, spring floods, bringing famine, posed far greater challenges. The following passage (4. 53-132) is dense in astronomical and scientific detail, some of it obscure or mistaken. M., though aided by F., frequently struggles to follow L.'s sense.

⁴ the rain | The clouds] Inverted syntax: M. means the clouds contained the rain.

⁵ heavenly Ram ... equinoctial again] The constellation Aries; M. simplifies L.'s *delapsae portitor Helles*, 'carrier of fallen Helle' (IV. 57), i.e. the legendary golden ram that bore Helle and her brother Phrixus away from their murderous stepmother Ino. Helle fell from the ram into the sea, which was then named 'Hellespont'; cf. 9. 1088.

⁶ When day...] In the northern hemisphere the sun enters Aries around the spring equinox, i.e. on or near 21 March. M. omits L.'s mention of the constellation Libra (IV. 58-59).

	Boreas sh'excludes, and fire from Eurus takes:¹	*north wind; east wind*
	He all the clouds that his whole quarter makes	
	Throws to the west with Nabathaean blasts;²	
70	The fogs that India, that Arabia casts,	
	Exhaled and grown under the rising sun;	
	Sky-darkening Corus' exhalation,	*north-west wind*
	Which cools the Indian air, now blown away,	
	From thence make hot the eastern country's day.	
75	Nor could the loads of those thick clouds fall down	
	On the mid-world:³ strong tempests drive them on	
	From north and south; alone does Calpe's ground	
	Drink the moist air — the furthest western bound	
	Where heaven's bowed hinge does with the ocean meet.	
80	The clouds driven thither could no further get:	
	Their vastness hardly could involvèd be	
	In such strait room as 'twixt that earth and sky.⁴	
	Those clouds then crushed together by the pole	
	Contract in th'air, and down amain they roll	*with full force*
85	In gushing showers; lightnings, though thick, retain	
	No flashing fire, extinguished by the rain.	
	Iris no colours can distinctly show,	
	Circling the air with an imperfect bow:⁵	
	She drinks the sea, and to the ocean⁶	
90	The ponderous waves fall from the sky again.	
	The Pyrenean snows, which Titan yet	*the sun*
	Could never melt, flow down; the rocks are wet	
	With broken ice; rivers their wonted way	
	Forsake; as channels the whole fields display	
95	Themselves; and now as shipwrecked on the seas	

---

¹ Boreas ... takes] i.e. the new moon has excluded the north wind and invites dry heat from the east wind. Early modern texts read *ab Euro* ('from the east wind', IV. 61); modern editions read *in Euro* ('while the east wind blew'). Unlike M.'s, L.'s verbs are in the past tense here, suggesting (as F. argues) that he is talking about winter weather before the equinox, or of weather in the east only.

² He] i.e. the sun. This sentence (4. 68–74) closely follows the Latin syntax (IV. 64–70): the meaning is that clouds and rains migrate westwards, leaving the east hot and dry. Nabathaean blasts] Gusts from the east: the Nabataei were a people of southern Arabia.

³ mid-world] In ancient geography the region between furthest east (India and Arabia) and extreme west (Spain).

⁴ strait room] i.e. narrow space. The sense is that even the space dividing earth from heaven can hardly contain these clouds.

⁵ Iris ... bow] Iris was the handmaiden of the gods; meteorologically, a rainbow.

⁶ ocean] For the trisyllabic pronunciation, cf. 3. 680.

Float Caesar's tents and drenchèd companies.
The stream breaks down his camp: rivers o'erflow
His trench and works, nor can the soldiers go
To forage; the drowned fields no vittle leave.   *provision*
100 The ways, by water covered, all deceive
The fetchers of provision. Then came on
A famine, still the sad companion   *always*
Of other woes; the soldiers, by no foes
Besieged, are pined; one his whole wealth bestows   *starving*
105 Upon a crust of bread not dearly sold.
(O meagre thirst of gain!) For ready gold
An hungry seller is not wanting there.
The waters now have all, no hills appear,
The joined rivers like o'erspreading fens
110 Cover high rocks; transported are the dens
Of beasts, the stream carries the struggling horse,
Not touching ground, and, as of greater force
Than th'ocean, repels the ocean's tide.[1]
The darkened pole does Phoebus' lustre hide,
115 And the black skies all colours do confound.
So lies the farthest part of the world's ground,   *the Arctic wastes*
Which the cold zone and frosts perpetual
Cover; those countries see no stars at all,
Their barren ice breeds nothing, good alone
120 To temper with their cold the torrid zone.
So let it be, great Jove; so let it be,
Neptune, whose three-forked sceptre rules the sea:
Thou, Jove, with storms perpetual fill the air;[2]
Thou, Neptune, let no rivers home repair,
125 Let no streams find prone passage to the main,   *downward*; *sea*
But with the ocean's tide turn back again.
Make the struck earth to deluge pervious,   *accessible*
These fields let Rhine o'erflow, and Rhodanus.   *Rhône*
Hither their course let all great rivers bend,
130 Hither Riphaean snows, lakes, fountains, send;
Hither all standing pools from far command,
And save from civil war this wretched land.
    But Caesar's fortune, with this little fear   [IV. 122]

---

[1] Than … tide] This line, printed as in *1627*, exemplifies M.'s flexible prosody: the first 'ocean' is probably trisyllabic as it finishes a clause, but the second only disyllabic.
[2] perpetual] Probably trisyllabic; contrast 4. 117.

	Of his content, returns greater than e'er;	
135	The gods 'gan favour, and deserved t'obtain	*began to*
	Pardon;[1] the clouded air cleared up again,	
	The mastered waters Sol in fleeces spread;	
	The night, presaging a fair morn, looked red.	
	Things keep their place, moisture the sky forsakes;	
140	Water (late high) her own low centre takes;	*finds a low level*
	Trees and emergent hills t'appear began,	
	The fields at sight of day grow dry again.	
	When Sicoris, to his own banks restored,	[IV. 130]
	Had left the field, of twigs and willow board	
145	They made small boats, covered with bullock's hide,	
	In which they reached the river's further side.[2]	
	So sail the Veneti if Padus flow;	*Po*
	The Britons sail on their calm ocean so;	
	So the Egyptians sail, with woven boats	
150	Of papery rushes in their Nilus floats.	*Nile*
	The army, in these boats transported now,	
	Build up a bridge, and fearing the overflow	
	Of the fierce stream, their work they do not end	
	Upon the bank, but o'er the fields extend.	
155	And lest again Sicoris should o'erflow,	
	In several channels cut, he suffers now	
	For his first crime. But when Petreius spied	
	That Caesar's fortune did all actions guide,	
	Ilerda he forsakes, trusting no more	
160	The strength of that known world, but seeking for	
	Untamèd nations, fierce with war's dire love,	
	(e)To that world's end the battle to remove.	
	When Caesar saw the hills and camp forsook,	[IV. 143]
	He bids his men take arms, and never look	
165	For bridge or ford, but with their hardy arms	
	Swim o'er the stream. The soldiers his alarms	*trumpet signals*
	Obey with speed, and rushing on to fight,	
	Venture those ways that they would fear in flight,	
	Then, taking arms, cherish their bodies wet,	*warm*
170	And their benumbèd joints with running heat,[3]	

---

[1] Pardon] i.e. the gods merit Caesar's 'forgiveness' for favouring him now more than ever. See Introduction, p. 8 and note.
[2] They] Caesar's forces.
[3] heat] A verb — they heat their water-chilled bones by running after the enemy.

'Til noon made shadows short: the horsemen then
O'ertake the hindmost of Petreius' men,
Who doubtful are whether to fight or fly.
    Two rocky hills lift their proud tops on high, [IV. 157]
175 Making a vale beneath: above, the ground
Is joined; below, safe passages are found
Through windings dark, which straits if once the foe[1]
Had in possession, Caesar well did know
He might from thence carry the war as far
180 As Spain's remote and barbarous nations are.[2]
'Run without rank,' quoth he, 'pursue your foes,
Turn back the war that by their flight you lose,
Make them turn face to face: though they would fly,
Give not the cowards leave basely to die,
185 But on their breasts let them receive our blows.'
This said, with swiftness they prevent their foes'
Flight to the hills, encamping close beside.
A narrow trench did both the camps divide,
And of so little distance was the place,
190 They might distinctly know each other's face.
There finding fathers, brothers, sons, they see
The wickedness of civil enmity.
And first, for fear standing a little mute,
With nods and swords lift up, friends friends salute;   *lifted up*
195 But when dear love conquered the law of wars,
Over the trenches leap the soldiers[3]
T'embrace each other: some their old hosts meet,
Some their schoolfellows,[4] some their kinsmen greet.
He was no Roman, that no enemy knew:
200 Sighs break their kisses, tears their arms bedew,
And though no act of blood were yet begun,
They fear the mischief that they might have done.
Why mourn'st thou, fool? Why dost thou beat thy breast
And weep in vain? Why hast thou now confessed[5]

---

[1] the foe] Petreius's troops, 'the foe' from Caesar's point of view.
[2] as far … barbarous nations are] *in terrarum devia inque feras gentes*, 'into pathless lands and wild peoples' (IV. 161–62); M. may be echoing F.'s paraphrase.
[3] Over … soldiers] Prosodically irregular, possibly demanding an expansion of 'soldiers' into three syllables, although the effect may be intended, as it surely is at 4. 199.
[4] schoolfellows] *studiis consors puerilibus aetas*, 'shared age of boyhood pursuits' (IV. 178).
[5] now confessed] Possibly M.'s or a printer's error for '*not* confessed', following the Latin (*nec te … fateris?*, IV. 184).

205 Thou 'gainst thy will to wicked war dost go?[1]
Stand'st thou in such great fear of him, whom thou
Thyself mak'st dreadful? Let his trumpets sound,
Neglect the cruel noise, let none be found
To bear his eagles, and the war there ends;
210 Caesar and Pompey, private men, are friends.[2]
Now Concord come, that all things dost enfold
In thy white arms,[3] and the world's safety hold,
The earth's blessed love: future impieties
Our age may fear;[4] the ignorance here dies
215 Of their misdeeds, and from excuse does bar
Their guilt — they know their foes their kinsmen are.
Sinister fates, that will by this short peace
Their future woes and wickedness increase!
'Twas peace and, in both camps mixed, soldiers strayed   [IV. 196]
220 And on the grass their friendly banquets made:
By the same fire together Bacchus' rites
They celebrate, and spend the watchful nights
In stories of the war, as lovingly
Together they in joining lodgings lie[5] —
225 Where first they did encamp, from what hand fled
Each pile — and boast of every valiant deed.   *spear*
Denying much they grant the wish of Fate,
And love the wretched soldiers renovate.[6]
This love their future wickedness increased,
230 For when Petreius saw their friendly feast,[7]
Thinking himself and camp to sale betrayed,

---

[1]   wicked war] A favourite collocation of M. (it occurs nine times in the translation); L. has simply *sceleri*, 'wickedness' (IV. 184).

[2]   private men, are friends] In L. only Caesar is termed *privatus* (IV. 188).

[3]   white arms] M.'s addition, perhaps based on Lucian's 'white-armed Harmonia' ('In Praise of Demosthenes', in *Complete Works,* ed. by A. M. Harmon, K. Kilburn, M. D. Macleod and H. C. Hofheimer (Cambridge, MA: Harvard University Press, 2000), p. 19); 'white-armed' is also a common Homeric epithet for women.

[4]   future impieties ... fear] *magnum nunc secula nostra | Venturi discrimen habent*, 'now our age possesses the great turning point of things to come' (IV. 191–92).

[5]   Bacchus' rites...] i.e. they make libations of wine (*libamina,* IV. 198), pouring it onto the turf.   stories of the war] *bellorum fabula*, 'tale of wars' [not necessarily the civil wars] (IV. 200).   in joining lodgings lie] *iunctoque cubili*, 'on the same bed' (IV. 224). M. adds 'lovingly'.

[6]   Denying much...] *Et dum multa negant; quod solum fata petebant, | Est miseris renovata fides*, 'and while they disagree about many things, their trust was renewed, poor things, which was all that fate was seeking' (IV. 202–04).

[7]   friendly feast] *foedera pacis*, 'peace-treaty' (IV. 205).

	He arms his household servants to invade	*enter hurriedly into*
	Dire war,¹ and, guarded with a troop of those,	
	Out of his camp th'unarmed Caesarians throws.	
235	The sword, as in embraces joined they stood,	
	Divides them and disturbs the peace with blood.	
	Then wrath these war-provoking speeches gave:	
	'Soldiers unmindful of the cause you have,²	
	Though Caesar's conquest you cannot bestow	
240	Upon the Senate's cause, this you can do,	
	Fight 'til you are o'ercome: whilst you have hands	
	And blood,³ and whilst the war yet doubtful stands,	
	Will you go serve and trait'rous eagles take?⁴	*standards*
	And beg of Caesar he no odds would make	
245	Between his slaves, and at his hands desire	
	Your captains' lives? Our safeties treason's hire	*wages, payment*
	Shall never be, nor make we civil war	
	To live: by name of peace betrayed we are.⁵	
	People for veins of brass, which deep-hid lie,	
250	Would never seek, nor towns would fortify,	
	No stately horses to the war should pace,	
	No tower-like ships o'erspread the ocean's face,	
	If liberty for peace were e'er well sold.	
	Shall Caesar's soldiers damned obedience hold,	
255	Bound by a wicked oath, and you make light	
	Your faith because in a good cause you fight?	
	But pardon's hoped: O shame's dire funeral!	
	Not knowing this, great Pompey, thou o'er all	
	The world art must'ring and each farthest king	
260	Bringing to fight, whilst we are articling	*negotiating*
	Basely about thy safety.' This fierce speech	
	Turned back their minds and stirred war's wicked itch,⁶	

---

¹ Dire war] 'Dire' (here for *scelerata*, 'wicked', IV. 207), is one of M.'s favourite epithets, found forty-nine times in the translation and twenty-three times in the *Continuation*.

² unmindful of the cause you have] *Immemor o patriae, signorum oblite tuorum*, 'Unregarding of your country, forgetting whose standards you follow' (IV. 212).

³ whilst ... blood] Condensing F.'s paraphrase, rather than L.'s *quique fluat non multo deerit vulnere sanguis*, 'and blood will not be wanting to flow from many a wound' (IV. 216).

⁴ go serve and trait'rous eagles take] *ibitis in dominum?*, 'will you go over to a master/tyrant?' (IV. 217).

⁵ by name ... we are] *trahimur sub nomine pacis*, 'We are being drawn [into servitude] under the name of peace' (IV. 222): 'betrayed' probably comes from F.'s *prodimur*.

⁶ This fierce speech ... war's wicked itch] *Sic fatur & omneis | Concussit mentes, scelerumque reduxit amorem*, 'thus he spoke and shook every mind, and drew back their

>   As when wild beasts, weaned from the woods and shut
>   Up close to tame,¹ have off their wildness put
> 265 And learned t'endure a man: if blood once stain
>   Their jaws, their wildness straight returns again,
>   Their jaws grow hot, and their new boiling rage
>   The trembling keeper hardly can assuage.
>   They run on wickedness,² and what might seem
> 270 In a blind war the gods' or fortune's crime,
>   Deceivèd trust makes ours.³ At board and bed   *murdered*
>   The late-embracèd breasts are murtherèd,
>   And though unwillingly at first they draw,
>   Yet when their wicked swords drawn out they saw,
> 275 And striking were, their friends they truly hate
>   And with the stroke themselves they animate.⁴
>   Petreius' camp is with strange tumult filled
>   And horrid murther: sons their fathers killed,⁵   *murder*
>   And as if hidden mischief lost should be,
> 280 They boast their guilt, and let their captains see.⁶
>   Caesar, though robbèd of thy men, yet see   [IV. 254]
>   The gods' high favour: not so much for thee
>   On Egypt or Massilia's seas is done,
>   Nor so much honour in Pharsalia won.
> 285 ⁽ᶠ⁾For this sole crime of civil war does make

love of crimes' (IV. 235–36). 'Itch' means 'strong desire' (*OED*, s.v. 2), and has negative overtones; cf. e.g. Thomas Heywood, 'The Conspiracy of Cateline' in [G. Sallustius Crispus,] *The Two Most Worthy and Notable Histories which Remain Unmained to Posterity* (London: W. Jaggard for J. Jaggard, 1609), p. 14: '[Catiline's followers] did itch after a seconde ciuill Warre' (a translation of *Bellum Catilinae*, XVI. 4).

¹   to tame] Omitting *& vultus posuere minaces*, 'and have set aside their menacing expressions' (IV. 238).

²   They run on wickedness] *Itur in omne nefas*, 'They embark upon every kind of unspeakable crime' (IV. 243). 'To run on in [one's] wickedness' is frequent in early modern sermons and homilies: see e.g. William Perkins, *A Golden Chain* (Cambridge: John Leggat, 1600), p. 222, 'for if thou runne on in thy wickednesse, and still rebell against God, it is a thousand to one at length he will destroy thee'.

³   Deceivèd trust makes ours] Following Hugo Grotius's emendation to IV. 245, *Fecit nostra fides*, 'trust has made our own'; earlier and modern texts read *Fecit monstra fides*, 'monstrous trust has made'. F. follows Grotius but defends the original reading in his commentary.

⁴   themselves they animate] *animosque labantes | Confirmant*, 'confirm their faltering purpose' (IV. 249–50).

⁵   And ... killed] Translating *Et scelerum turba; rapiuntur colla parentum* (IV. 251), a line often omitted from modern editions.

⁶   They boast their guilt] *iuvat esse nocentes*, 'it pleases them to be guilty' (IV. 253): M.'s wording permits a contrast with 4. 226.

That thou at length the better cause shalt take.¹
The generals now their blood-stained soldier²
No more dare trust within the camp so near,
But by swift flight toward Ilerda make,
From whom all passage Caesar's horsemen take,
And there in those dry hills shut up their foes,
Whom Caesar strives with a deep trench t'enclose.
Cutting all water off, he lets them take
No springs, nor tents near to the river make.
They, seeing the way of death, convert their fear
To rage: their horses, that unuseful were
To men besieged, they kill, and since in flight
'Twere vain to hope, address themselves to fight.
Caesar perceives them coming and well knows
That death is sought by his devoted foes.
'Contain your piles and swords, soldiers,' quoth he: *restrain*
'I'll lose no blood to get this victory.
That foe that meets the sword ne'er gratis dies;³ *for free*
Hating their lives and cheap in their own eyes,
They come to mix our losses with their death;
They'll feel no wounds, but joy in loss of breath.
But let this heat forsake 'um, this mad fit — *them*
They'll lose their wish of death.' Caesar the fight
Forbids, and lets their choler spend in vain,
'Til Sol descended to the ocean, *the sun*
And stars appeared; then, when no hope's at all
Of fight, their fierceness does by little fall,
Their minds grow cold. So is most courage found
In late-hurt men, whilst freshness of the wound
And the blood hot gives nimble motion
To every nerve and muscles guide the bone;

---

¹ the better cause shalt take] *Dux causae melioris eris*, 'will be the leader of the better cause' (IV. 259), as the Pompeians' massacre contravened a truce. The sentiment is sarcastic. M. imitates the phrase 'better cause' in his *Continuation*, sig. C4ᵛ, as the Latin terminology of *meliori causae* makes clear in his *Supplementum Lucani* (Leiden: Willem Christiaens van der Boxe, 1640), II. 14–15.

² blood-stained soldier] *polluta nefanda | Agmina caede*, 'Battle-lines, polluted with unspeakable bloodshed' (IV. 259–60): the stain is moral as well as physical.

³ gratis dies] *Vincitur haud gratis, iugulo qui provocat hostem*, 'He who challenges the foe with his throat is not conquered for nothing' (IV. 275). Charles Cotton borrowed M.'s rendering for his translation of Montaigne's *Essays: The Essays of Michael seigneur de Montaigne* (London: for T. Basset, M. Gilliflower and W. Hensman, 1685), sig. Nn3ʳ (Ess., I. 47).

	If the wound-giver hold his hand and stay,	
	Then a cold numbness (strength being ta'en away)	
	Seizes the mind, and the stiff members ties,	
320	The wound grown cold (the blood congealing) dries.	
	The soldiers, wanting water, through each creek	[IV. 292]
	Of the digged earth for hidden fountains seek.	
	Not only now the mattock and the spade,	
	But swords earth-digging instruments are made.	
325	Down from the tops of mountains as profound	*deep*
	They go, as lies the lowest marish ground.	*marsh, marshy*
	Farther from day, and deeper in earth's mould	
	Drives not the searcher for Assyrian gold.¹	
	But no sought river's hidden course is shown,	
330	No springs appeared, opening the pumice stone,	
	No bubbling brook rolls little pibble stones,	*pebble*
	Nor sweating cave makes distillations.²	
	Weary with digging then, the sweating men	
	Are from those rocky pits drawn out again,	
335	And this vain search of water the dry air	
	Makes them less able to endure; nor dare	
	They feed their weary bodies, eating nought;	
	As medicine 'gainst thirst is hunger sought.	
	If the soft earth do moisture yield, they bring	
340	The clods and o'er their mouths with both hands wring.	
	The black unstirrèd mud, that every sink	*pool*
	Affords, by strife the greedy soldiers drink,	
	And what to save their lives they would have stuck	*hesitated*
	To take, now dying drink. Like beasts some suck	
345	Beasts' dugs, and when milk fails, with greedy jaw	
	Mere blood from their exhausted udders draw.	
	Herbs and green leaves they wring; bedewèd twigs	
	They lick, and juice of bleeding vines; small sprigs	
	Of trees they for their tender sap do squeeze.	
350	O happy men, whom barbarous enemies	[IV. 319]
	Flying, by⁽ᵍ⁾ poisoning all the rivers killed!	
	But, Caesar, though these rivers should be filled	
	With poisons, carrions and pale aconite	
	Growing on Cretan rocks, yet knowing it	

---

¹ Assyrian gold] Modern editions, following a conjecture by Housman, print *Astyrici*, from Asturias (gold from this area in northern Spain was famed). See also Textual Notes.
² 4. 229–32] See Textual Notes.

355 These Romans then would drink.[1] Their bowels now
Are scorched, their mouths and tongues dried rougher grow,
Their veins shrink up; their lungs in this distress,
Not moist, contract the breathing passages.
Breathings hard-drawn their ulcered palates tear,
360 They ope their thirsty mouths to drink night's air,   *open*
And wish such showers as all did lately drown,
And the dry clouds their looks are fixed upon.
But that which most increased their misery,
They were encamped not on dry Meroë,
365 Nor where the naked Garamantes plough
Hot Cancer's tropic, but between the flow
Of swift Iberus and full Sicoris:
The thirsty camp two neighbouring rivers sees.[2]
   Now both the generals yield: Afranius lays   [IV. 337]
370 Down arms and peace (become a suppliant) prays.[3]
Into the enemy's camp his starvèd bands
Drawing, before the conqueror's feet he stands,
Then begging pardon with a careless breast[4]
He lost no majesty,[5] but 'twixt his last
375 And former state, he bears himself in all
A conquered man, but yet a general.
   'Had I fall'n under a base enemy,   [IV. 344]
I had not lacked an hand my self to free:[6]
Know then the cause that now I beg to live;
380 I think thee, Caesar, worthy life to give.
For no side's favour, nor as foes to thee
Did we take arms; both generals were we
Before this civil war, and have maintained

---

[1] But, Caesar ... Romans then would drink] i.e. these Romans would knowingly drink deliberately poisoned water. M. copies L.'s apostrophe to Caesar but omits the idea he might 'pour' poison into the rivers himself (*infunda*s, IV. 323).

[2] Meroë ... rivers sees] *Non super arentem Meroen, Cancrique sub axe,* | *Qua nudi Garamantes arant, sedere,* 'They were not encamped on dry Meroë and beneath the region of Cancer, where the Garamantes plough' (IV. 333–34).

[3] peace ... prays] i.e. prays for peace. The parenthetical 'become a suppliant' refers to Afranius; 'suppliant' is disyllabic.

[4] careless breast] 'careless' translates *securo*, 'without care' (IV. 343); cf. 4. 387, 418 below.

[5] majesty] *maiestas* (IV. 341), the dignity of his rank.

[6] Had I fall'n ... to free] 'If fate had laid me low beneath a base enemy, a strong hand was not lacking to me for seizing death' (*Si me degeneri stravissent fata sub hoste,* | *Non derat fortis rapiendo dextera leto*, IV. 344–45). M. omits the agency of fortune and inserts the notion of death as freedom.

	The former cause; now we'll not fate withstand.	
385	Spain we deliver up, and ope the east;	*open*
	Of all the world behind thou now may'st rest	
	Secure, nor has much blood's effusion,	
	Sharp swords or wearied arms this conquest won.	
	Only thy foes that thou hast conquerèd	
390	Forgive. Nor beg we much: grant us to lead	
	Unarmed those lives that thou hast now bestowed;	
	Suppose that all our slaughtered troops lay strowed	*strewed*
	Over the fields. To mix unfortunate	
	With happy arms, and we participate	*participate in*
395	Thy triumphs, were unfit; our fates we know.	
	(h)Compel us not with thee to conquer now.'[1]	
	But Caesar gently, and with smiling cheer,	[IV. 363]
	Both pardons and dismisses them from war.	
	But when the league was firmly agreed upon,	
400	The soldiers to th'unguarded rivers run,	
	Fall on the banks, troubling the granted stream.	
	But long continued draughts in many of them,	
	Not suffering air through th'empty veins to fly,	
	Shut up their lives; nor could they easily	
405	Cease this dry plague, but though their guts they fill,	
	The covetous disease is craving still.	
	At last their nerves and strength again it brings.	
	O luxury, too prodigal of things,	
	Content with no provision easily brought,[2]	
410	Ambitious hunger for things dearly sought	
	O'er land and sea, pride of a sumptuous table:	
	See what small store to cherish life is able,	
	And nature please! These soldiers' fainting souls	
	No unknown consul's noble wine in bowls	
415	Of myrrh and gold restores; from fountains pure	
	Water and bread their fleeting lives assure.	
	Wretches that follow wars! These soldiers	
	Being now disarmed are made secure, from cares	
	Exempt, and innocent return again	
420	To their own towns. When peace they did obtain,	

---

[1] 4. 390–96] M. compresses the latter part of Afranius's speech, omitting his pleas to 'give respite/leisure to the weary' (*otia des fessis*, IV. 357), and that his army not take part in Caesar's triumph as captives (*partemque triumphi | Captos ferre tui*, IV. 361).

[2] easily] Probably contracted to 'eas'ly' in pronunciation: contrast 4. 404.

How much they grieved that ever they had cast
One pile, or suffered thirst, or ever asked
The gods in vain to grant them prosperous wars!
For to the happier fighting soldiers
425 What toils through all the world, what doubtful fields
Remain to fight? Though fortune always yields
Happy success, yet must they oftentimes
Conquer, spill blood throughout all lands and climes,
And follow Caesar through all fates of his.
430 When the world's ruin's near, he happy is
That knows his settled place.¹ Their weary arms
No war calls forth, their sleeps no loud alarms
Disturbs; their wives, children, and houses they,
And lands (though no deducted colony),
435 Enjoy;² by fortune from this burden freed,
No favour does their mind's disquiet breed:
One general saved their lives, t'other their own
Commander was. Thus happy they alone
Freed from desires the civil wars behold.
440 But through the world this fortune did not hold: [IV. 402]³
She durst act somewhat against Caesar's side. *dared to*
Where long ⁽ᶠ⁾Salonae's beaten with the tide
Of th'Adriatic Sea, where Zephyr blows *the west wind*
Upon the warm Jader's gentle flows,
445 Antonius, there trusting the warlike bands
Of his Curetes,⁴ whose environed lands
The Adriatic Sea encircles round,
Was straight beseigèd in the utmost bound,
Safe from war's reach, if famine, that alone
450 Conquers the strongest fortresses, were gone.

---

¹ 4. 430 ff.] Praise of the life of retirement in contrast with civil war, drawing on the model in Virgil's *Georgics* (II. 490–542). M.'s translation of this passage uses similar language: *Virgil's Georgicks Englished by Tho: May Esqr.* (London: Augustine Mathewes for Thomas Walkley, 1628), pp. 59–61.

² And lands ... Enjoy] Roman veterans granted gifts of land by their generals were classed as *coloni*, tenant-farmers who 'lead forth' or 'conduct' (*deducere*) a colony. Although literally translating L.'s *deductos ... colonos* (IV. 397), M.'s 'deducted' reflects his understanding of the technical nuance (see *OED*, s.v. †2).

³ 4. 440–642] The blockade of Caesarian forces led by Marcus Antonius, and the mass suicide of Vulteius and his men when their escape plan goes wrong.

⁴ Curetes] Reading *Curetum* over the preferred modern variant *Curictum*, 'inhabitants of Curicta [an island in the Adriatic]' (IV. 406), although F. associates the name with the same location in his commentary.

	The ground no pasture for their horses yields,	
	Nor yellow Ceres clothes the fallowed fields.	*corn*
	The men eat grass, and when the fields grow bare,	
	The grass from off their camp's dried turfs they tear.	
455	But when their friends on th'adverse shore they spied	*opposite*
	And Basilus the admiral,[1] they tried	
	New ways of flight by sea; for their stern-end	
	They did not hoist, nor did their keel extend	
	(As custom was), but with unusual sleight,	*method*
460	Firm timber boats to bear a mighty weight	
	They made. These empty boats on every side	
	Sustain the ship, whose double rank was tied	
	With chains across.[2] Nor were the oars disposed	*arranged*
	On the open front to the foes' darts exposed;	
465	Only that sea, that was enclosèd round	
	By those conjoinèd boats, their oars did wound.	
	A miracle of silent flight it showed;	
	She bore no sails, or sea discovered rowed.[3]	*open, uncovered*
	Now they observe the tides, 'til th'ebbing seas	
470	Leave the sands bare and make the shore increase:	
	Then from above into the ocean prone	
	The ship falls, by two galleys waited on:	
	O'er which a lofty threat'ning tower was reared,	
	Where spires and trembling pinnacles appeared.[4]	*turrets*
475	Octavius, keeper of th'Illyrian sea,[5]	
	Would not assault this ship too suddenly:	
	But his swift vessels thought it good to stay	
	'Til the easy passage might increase his prey,	

[1] Basilus the admiral] L. Minucius Basilus served under Caesar in Gaul 53–52 BC, then as a legate in the Adriatic in 49–48.

[2] These empty boats ... With chains across] A misleading translation of L.'s *Namque ratem vacuae sustentant undique cuppae | Quarum porrectis series constricta catenis | Ordinibus geminis obliquas excipit alnos*, 'Hollow barrels supported the raft entirely, a series of which, bound together by stretched out chains in double rows, supported the planks laid slanting across them' (IV. 420–22).

[3] Only that sea ... rowed] Again somewhat misleading: L. has the rowers plying their oars in the gaps between the 'beams' or planks (*trabibus*, IV. 423) of the raft, not M.'s 'conjoinèd boats'; the vessel's movement thus appears miraculous because of no visible oars or sail.

[4] O'er which ... pinnacles appeared] *Cunctas super ardua turris | Eminet, & tremulis tabulata minantia pinnis*, 'Over all a lofty tower looms, and decks threatening with their shuddering turrets' (IV. 431–32): a description of the temporary towers, shuddering in the swell, erected on Roman war-ships about to engage.

[5] Octavius] Marcus Octavius, commander of Pompey's Achaean fleet with Scribonius Libo: see 2. 493.

480	And farther onto sea by peace invites His rashly entered foes. Such are the sleights Of huntsmen, when their toils they have disposed And fearful deer in plumèd nets enclosed:[1] Their dogs of Crete and Sparta they contain,	*nets*
485	And their wide-mouthed Molossians restrain;[2] No dog is trusted in the wood, but he That can upon a full scent silent be And never open when he finds the game, Content alone to signify the same	*noisy*
490	By wagging of the string. Then presently The soldiers leave the isle and eagerly They come aboard the ship, when day's last light Gave place to the approach of dusky night. But the Cilicians of great Pompey's side,	*leash*
495	According to their old sea-craft,[3] had tied Chains through the midst o'th'sea, of which no show Appeared above, but loosely let them flow: The chain was fastened to th'Illyrian shore. The first and second ships, not stayed, got o'er;	
500	The third was caught, of burden much more vast, And to the rock by a drawn rope was cast. The rock hangs o'er the sea (a wonder 'tis) Hollow, and still (though falling) stands, with trees Making a shade: hither the sea by tides Oft drives, and in those darksome caverns hides	
505	Ships broke by Aquilon and drownèd men, Which hidden store the rock restores again, And when the caverns belch it up, in heat Sicilian Charybdis cannot get Pre-eminence.[4] Here did the great ship stand,	*north wind*

---

[1] when their toils … enclosed] *dum pavidos formidine cervos | Claudat odoratae metuentes aera pennae*, 'when [the huntsman] has corralled the deer, frightened by the *formido* and fearing the scents of the foul-smelling feather' (IV. 437–38); the *formido* or 'scare' was a lattice of multi-coloured feathers designed to prevent prey breaking through, as F. and other early modern commentaries explain.

[2] wide-mouthed Molossians] A breed of hunting-dog. 'Wide-mouthed', here translating *clamosa* (IV. 440), can mean 'noisy' (*OED*, s.v. 3).

[3] old sea-craft] This 'sea-craft' is a pirate stratagem (the Cilicians were pirates: see 1. 135n).

[4] in heat … Pre-eminence] i.e. a whirlpool more dangerous than the infamous Charybdis, to which L. gives the epithet *Tauromenitanam* after Tauromenium, a town in Sicily. 'Heat' translates *fervore*, 'boiling agitation' (IV. 461).

510	That was with valiant Opitergians manned:[1]	
	Her from all havens did all ships enclose,	*surround*
	Some from the rock, some from the shore oppose.	
	Vulteius found this under-water train	*snare, trap*
	(The master of the ship),[2] who all in vain	
515	Striving to cut the chains, did then desire	
	Without all hope to fight;[3] where to retire	
	Or how to conquer is not seen, but here	
	As much as snarèd valour could appear,	
	It did:[4] against so many thousand wights	*men*
520	That did enclose, scarce one full cohort fights,	*surround (them)*
	Not long indeed, for night in her black shade	
	Shut up the day, and peace the darkness made.	
	Then stout Vulteius thus 'gan animate	[IV. 474] *began to*
	The cohort fearing sad ensuing fate.[5]	
525	'Young men, that but for one short night are free,	
	Provide in time for fate's extremity:	
	There's no man's life is short, that does allow	
	Him time to seek his death, nor think it now	
	Less glorious that we meet a fate at hand.[6]	
530	The times of future life none understand.	
	'Tis equal praise of mind to give away	
	Our lives' last moment, and the hopèd stay	
	Of many years, so we the actors be;	
	No man can be compelled to wish to die.	
535	No way for flight is left: at every hand	
	Bent 'gainst our throats the stern Cilicians stand.[7]	
	Let fear be banished then: resolve to die,	

---

[1] Opitergians] Caesarian allies from Cisalpine Gaul.
[2] (The master of the ship)] See Textual Notes.
[3] Vulteius] On this character and early modern attitudes (including M.'s) to his suicide see Introduction, pp. 16–17, and below, 4. 557–58n.
[4] snarèd valour] *deprensa ... virtus* (IV. 469–70). The Latin *deprensus* is often used for cornered beasts (*TLL*, s.v. v/1. 70–71, 82 ff.). Both L. and M. continue the association with hunting begun at 4. 480–89.
[5] stout Vulteius ... animate] 'Vulteius, with great-spirited voice (*magnanima voce*), steadied (*Rexit*) his cohort' (IV. 475).
[6] there's no man's life is short, that] = 'no man's short life' (probably lengthened for metrical reasons); 'meet a fate at hand' translates *admoto occurrere fato*, 'run to reach a fate that has moved towards us' (IV. 480).
[7] stern Cilicians] M. follows the emendation *Intenti Cilices* (IV. 486) (on the basis of the surrounding enemies not being Roman) of Johann Rutgers, in his *Variarum Lectionum Libri Sex* (1616), as recorded by F. in his marginal note. Previous and modern editions read *intenti cives*, 'mindful citizens'.

And let your wishes meet necessity.
Nor shall we fall in a blind cloud of war,
540 As when two battles joined in darkness are:
When heaps of carcasses bestrew the field,
Valour lies buried, all are equal held.
But in a ship the gods have placèd us,
Both to our friends and foes conspicuous:
545 The isle, the continent, the seas allow
Witnesses to us, and two parties now
From diverse shores behold us; in our ends
What great and rare example Fate intends[1]
I know not. Whate'er chronicles afford
550 Of trust, of soldiers' faith maintained by sword,
We shall excel.[2] 'Tis a small thing to die
Upon our swords, Caesar, we know, for thee:
But greater pledges in this sad distress
We want, our great affections to express,[3]   *lack*
555 And envious fates us of much praises bar
That not our parents nor our children are
Here with us. Let our foes our valour find,
And fear our force and death-contemning mind:[4]   *death-despising*
Let them be glad that no more ships were caught.
560 Perchance they'll try by leagues what can be wrought,   *truces*
Proffering base life: would they would promise us
Pardon, to make our deaths more glorious,
Lest when we fall our killing swords upon,[5]
Our foes should call it desperation.
565 Much valour must deserve, that Caesar may
Account the loss of us a fatal day
Among so many thousand.[6] Should fate give
Egress from hence, I would not wish to live:

---

[1] Fate] *Fortuna*, 'Fortune', whom L.'s Vulteius addresses directly (IV. 497).
[2] Whate'er chronicles ... we shall excel] Modern editions translate differently (based on reading *transisset* for *transibit*, IV. 499).
[3] our great affections] *tanti ... amoris*, 'so great a love' for Caesar (IV. 502).
[4] Let our foes ... mind] A heroizing translation of *indomitos sciat esse viros timeatque furentes | Et morti faciles animos*, 'let them know we are men untamed, and fear our maddened spirits ready for death' (IV. 505–06).
[5] killing swords upon] i.e. fall upon our killing swords. M. retains L.'s hyperbaton but softens the vividness of *calido fodiemus viscera ferro*, 'we will dig into our flesh with the hot blade' (IV. 511).
[6] Much valour ... many thousand] i.e. despite the many thousands of men lost by Caesar, he will consider the loss of Vulteius's small group of men the true disaster.

	I have already cast away my breath,	
570	Drawn by the sweetness of approaching death.¹	
	A fury 'tis, which none but they can know	
	To whom near fates such knowledge do allow;	
	The gods death's sweetness do conceal, to make	
	Men live.'² A noble courage straight did take	[IV. 520]
575	The young men's minds,³ though all with weeping eyes	
	(Before the captain's speech) had viewed the skies	
	And feared to see the turn of Charles his wain:⁴	
	But now their valiant minds wish day again	
	After this speech, nor was day slow t'appear,	
580	Sol leaving Gemini and drawing near	*the sun*
	His height in Cancer, when the shortest night	
	Urged the Thessalian Archer.⁵ Day grown light	
	Discovered warlike Istrians on the land,	
	The fierce Liburnians, and Greek fleet that stand	
585	Covering the seas. They first, suspending fight,	
	Strive to o'ercome by covenants, and invite	
	The ship to yield by granting life; but they	
	Devoted, scorning life, stand in array,	*under a vow*
	Secure in sight, resolved what end to take;	
590	No storms their strong resolvèd minds could shake,	
	And though but few, by land and sea they fought	
	(Such confidence death's resolution brought)	
	Against innumerable hands. But when	
	War had drawn blood enough, their fury then	
595	Turned from their foes. The captain first of all,	

---

¹ Drawn by the sweetness of approaching death] *totusque futurae | Mortis agor stimulis*, 'I am completely carried away by the incitements of future death' (IV. 516–17); cf. below, 4. 573–74.

² The gods ... to make | Men live] *Victurosque Dei celant ut vivere durent, | Felix esse mori*, 'the gods hide from those who will live, so that they continue to live, that it is a happy thing to die' (IV. 519–20). M. follows F., who says that the gods, disliking that mortals should know 'how sweet and happy death is [*quam dulcis & felix mors sit*]', nonetheless permit those close to death to 'foretaste its sweetness [*dulcedinem eius praesentire*]'.

³ A noble courage ... minds] An enthusiastic rendition of *Sic cunctas sustulit ardor | Nobilium mentes iuvenum*, 'So a burning gripped the whole minds of the noble young men' (IV. 520–21). *Nobilium* is the reading until the eighteenth century; modern editions read *mobilium*, 'susceptible to being moved'.

⁴ Charles his wain] = Ursa Major (IV. 523), a traditional English name deriving from its association with Charlemagne.

⁵ Sol leaving ... Thessalian Archer] i.e. midsummer, when the sun is in Gemini and nearing Cancer. The Thessalian Archer is Sagittarius: this sign would be visible through the night at this time of year.

	Vulteius, off'ring his bare throat, 'gan call,	*began to*
	Seeking for death: 'Is there no soldier here	
	Worthy to shed my blood? Let him appear	
	And, killing me, show that himself dares bleed.'	
600	With that, of life his wounded breast was freed	
	By many swords: Vulteius thanks bestowed	
	On all but, dying, him to whom he owed	
	His first kind wound, he thankfully again	
	Requites with death. Thus meeting, all were slain,	
605	And on one side the war's whole mischief hung.	
	So the serpentine brood, by Cadmus sprung,	
	Fell by each other's hand, a dire presage	
	Of the ensuing Theban brothers' rage;	
	So those of th'waking dragon's teeth once framed	
610	In Colchos' fields, by magic spells inflamed,	
	With kindred blood the fields' ploughed furrows dyed,	
	Which mischief wrought by herbs, before untried,	
	Medea feared herself.[1] So fell these men	
	By bargained fate, and in the death of them	
615	To die was the least valour: they both fall	
	And kill at once; no right hand missed at all	
	Though at the point of death, nor to their blades	
	Owed they their wounds: a breast the sword invades,	
	Their throats invade their hands,[2] and if blind chance	
620	A brother's sword 'gainst brother did advance,	
	Or sons 'gainst father, with undaunted hand	
	And all their strength they strike. In this did stand	
	Their piety alone, that at one blow	
	They would dispatch them; on the hatches now,	
625	Half dead, they draw their bowels, and much blood	
	Streamed down into the sea; it did them good	
	To see the scornèd day, death to prefer,	
	And with proud looks despise the conqueror.	
	Now on the ship the heaps of bodies showed	

---

[1] 4. 606–13] Two famous fratricide myths. When founding Thebes, Cadmus sowed serpent-teeth: from these grew warrior-men who immediately turned on each other. Their descendants, the brothers Polyneices and Eteocles, killed each other (cf. 1. 587). In Colchis, as part of his quest for the Golden Fleece, Jason was commanded to yoke the fire-breathing bulls of Aeson and sow serpent-teeth, which also sprang forth as warriors: Medea's use of magical herbs, however, meant they fought against each other instead of killing Jason.

[2] Their throats ... hands] M. retains L.'s striking inversion, *iugulis pressere manum*, 'they pressed the hand with their throats' (IV. 562).

630 The slaughter made, on which the foes bestowed
Fit funerals, admiring much to see
To any captain such fidelity.[1]
Fame flying through the world did never raise
Any one ship with such resounding praise.
635 Yet will not coward nations, since such brave
Examples, learn to know that death to save
Their liberty is not a price so dear:[2]
But kingdoms armed with power of sword they fear.
Liberty can use arms,[3] and swords should be
640 (As men should know) to keep their liberty.
O would the Fates would let the fearful live,
That valour only death to men might give.
    Nor was that war that did in Libya grow   [IV. 581][4]
Less terrible than this: bold ^(k)Curio[5]
645 By a mild northern wind was wafted o'er
From Lilybaeum to that well-known shore,
Where Clupea seated is, and where he sees
Great Carthage's half-ruined edifice,
And pitching his first tents far from the main,   sea
650 Where Bagrada furrows the sandy plain,
Those hills and eaten rocks goes to behold,
Which were Antaeus' kingdom called of old.
Asking the cause of this old name, a clown   rustic
Thus tells the tale by long tradition known.
655   'For giants' births Earth yet not barren made   [IV. 593][6]

---

[1] admiring ... such fidelity] *ducibus mirantibus, ulli | Esse ducem tanti*, 'their leaders amazed that any leader should be of such importance to any man' (IV. 573). M. seems to suppose the *ducem* is Vulteius, although F. and other commentators assumed it means Caesar.

[2] not a price so dear] *quam sit non ardua virtus*, 'how it is not such an arduous virtue' (IV. 576).

[3] Liberty can use arms] Reading *saevis libertas utitur armis*, 'and liberty makes use of savage arms' (IV. 578), although all texts print *uritur armis* here, 'liberty is corroded by savage arms'. Almost certainly M.'s own mistake.

[4] 4. 643–906] Curio arrives in Africa via Sicily and sets up camp by the river Bagradas; Juba, king of Numidia, traps and kills Curio at Utica.

[5] bold Curio] Translating *audax*, which can mean 'courageous' (recalling M.'s praise of Curio, 4. Ded. 10–13), but also suggests transgressive audacity, referring to his corrupt going over to the Caesarian cause; cf. 1. 292n, 4. 879–906. In M.'s prosody, 'Curio' is typically given three syllables in line endings, to facilitate rhyme and rhythm, but two elsewhere (e.g. 4. 727), although the rule is not perfect: see e.g. 4. 795, where the pronunciation is trisyllabic.

[6] 4. 655–726] A mythical digression on Hercules's defeat of earth-born Antaeus. The passage, which may allegorize reason vs the body or Rome vs Africa, was well-known in

In Libyan caves a fearèd issue had,
Which to his mother brought as true a fame,
As Typhon, Tityus and Briareus' name.[1]
'Twas good for heaven Antaeus was not born
660 At Phlegra,[2] but this gift did more adorn
His mighty strength: into his limbs (though tired)
His mother's touch a vigour fresh inspired.
This cave his dwelling was, this mountain here
He lurked about, his food slain lions were:
665 His bed no leaves of trees, no skin of beasts;
His strength by sleeping on the ground increased.
By him th'inhabitants of Libya died,
And strangers all that to our coast applied.
His strength (not using a long time to fall)
670 Needed not Earth's rich gift: too strong for all
He was though standing up. At length, through fame
Of this dire plague, the great Alcides came,   *Hercules*
Whose hand both sea and land from monsters freed:
And for th'encounter each put off his weed,   *attire*
675 One's Nemean, t'other's Libyan lion's skin.[3]
Hercules oils his limbs ere he begin,   *before*
According to th'Olympic rites: but he[4]
Rubbed o'er his limbs with sand; it could not be
Enough to touch his mother with his feet.
680 They grapple then, and arms arms folded meet,
Striving each other's neck with heavy hand
To bend, yet both fixed and unbended stand.
Both wonder much to meet their match at length,
But Hercules used not his utmost strength
685 At the first bout, but wearied out his foe,
Which his oft blowing, and cold sweats did show:

early modern culture: it was rewritten by Julius Caesar Scaliger in his *Poetices*, VI, pp. 325–27, and may have inspired Milton's Antaeus simile: *Paradise Regained*, IV. 563–71, in John Milton, *Complete Shorter Poems*, ed. by John Carey (New York and London: Longmans, 1968).

[1] and Briareus' name] In Greek myth, Earth (Gaia) bred a race of giants including Typhon, Tityus and Briareus, who rebelled against the Olympian gods on the plains of Phlegra (referred to at 4. 660, below). The meter requires 'Tityus' to be disyllabic and 'Briareus' trisyllabic.

[2] 'Twas good ... Phlegra] i.e. as the gods might then have been defeated.

[3] Nemean ... lion's skin] Hercules defeated the Nemean lion in one of his labours, then wore its skin as a cloak. M.'s meter in this line is irregular.

[4] he] Antaeus. Hercules has prepared himself like a Greek athlete.

His shaking neck nor breast could firmly stand,
His bending hams yield to Alcides' hand. *thighs*
Alcides then about his short ribs cast
690 His conquering arms, and gripped his yielding waist;
Then, tripping up his legs, he fairly lays
His foe stretched out upon the sand. Earth stays
His sweat and fills with fresh blood every vein:
His arms grow brawny, his joints stiff again,
695 And his fresh limbs unclasp the other's hands.
Amazed at this new strength Alcides stands,
Nor feared he Hydra so in Lerna lakes,
Fruitful by loss of her reviving snakes,
Though then but young:[1] now both were equal grown,
700 One in Earth's strength, the other in his own.
Ne'er had stern Juno more encouragement
To hope:[2] she sees his limbs with sweating spent,
And his neck dried, as when he did sustain
The heavens,[3] but when he clasped his foe again,
705 Antaeus, staying not 'til he be thrown,
Falls of himself, and rises stronger grown:
His mother Earth to his tired members gives
What spirit she has, and labours when he strives.[4]
But when Alcides found Earth's touch to be
710 Strength'ning to him, "now thou shalt stand", quoth he,
"No more thou fall'st, nor will we trust again
The ground: this breast shall thy crushed limbs sustain.
Hither, Antaeus, shalt thou fall." This spoke,
Him striving to fall down aloft he took,
715 And grasped his middle fast: Earth could not lend
Strength to her dying son nor succour send.
But 'til his foe's breast stark and cold he found,
Alcides durst not trust him on the ground. *dared not*
From hence self-loved antiquity and fame,

---

[1] Hydra ... Though then but young] As one of his first labours (and so completed when he was young) Hercules slew the Lernaean Hydra, a nine-headed serpent who grew two new heads each time one was beheaded.
[2] stern Juno] Hercules was son of Jupiter and the mortal woman Alcmena: Juno despised him as a symbol of her husband's adultery and was partly responsible for devising his twelve labours, in the hope that he would be defeated and killed.
[3] sustain | The heavens] As part of his labour to retrieve the golden apples of the Hesperides, Hercules for a short time took on Atlas' task of holding the sky on his shoulders.
[4] spirit] Probably contracted to 'sp'rit' here, although the word is uncontracted elsewhere (e.g. 4. 772, below).

720 Old time's recorder, gave this place a name.
     But to these hills a nobler name gave he,
     That drew the Punic foe from Italy.   *Who*
     Scipio, arriving on our Libya, here
     Pitched his first camp: the ruins yet appear
725 Of that old trench; this place of all the rest
     Was first by Roman victory possessed.'[1]
         Curio, as if the place were fortunate   [IV. 661]
     And still retained those former captains' fate
     In war, rejoiced, and in this lucky place
730 Pitched his unlucky tents, which did deface
     The place's omen:[2] and provoked stern foes
     With strength unequal. Afric all that owes   *All of Africa which owes*
     Obedience to the Roman eagles then
     Was under Varus,[3] who (though strong in men
735 Of Italy) aid from the Libyan king
     Requires, to whom the world's far regions bring
     Their force with Juba. No one king alone
     Was master of such large dominion:
     In length, th'extent of his great kingdom's ground
740 Gades-neighbouring Atlas and Jove's Ammon bound   *Cádiz*
     Near Thera;[4] but in breadth the torrid zone
     Betwixt the sea and it, it coasts upon.
     So many people to his army press:
     Th'Autololes and wand'ring Nomadès,[5]
745 Gaetulians horsed without caparison,   *saddle*
     The Mauritanians, of complexion
     Like Indians, poor Nasamonians,[6]

---

[1] Scipio ... possessed] Scipio Africanus the Elder, whose campaigns in Africa forced the recall of Hannibal ('the Punic foe', 4. 722) from Italy to Carthage, leading to Scipio's final defeat of him at Zama in 202 BC.

[2] deface | The place's omen] *& collibus abstulit omen*, 'and he robbed the place of its good luck' (IV. 664).

[3] Varus] Attius Varus, a Pompeian (see 2. 497), whose later defeat off Carteia and death at Munda is treated at length in book six of M.'s *Continuation*.

[4] Gades-neighbouring ... Thera] Gades is pronounced to rhyme with 'shades' and 'neighbouring' is contracted to two syllables.   Thera] An island in the Aegean; however, all known texts read *Syrtibus*, 'the Syrtes' (IV. 675) in North Africa here, near where L. places the temple of Jupiter Ammon (see 9. 586–676).

[5] wand'ring Nomadès] Often spelt with three syllables in early modern culture, following the Greek and Latin *nomadēs*, 'herdsmen who wander for pasture'. L. has *Numidaeque vagi*, 'wandering Numidians' (IV. 677), but early modern commentaries, including F.'s, mention nomads.

[6] Indians, poor Nasamonians] The pronunciation of '-ians' is here untypically disyllabic;

                Scorched Garamantes, swift Marmaricans,
                Massylians that without saddles ride
750   And with a wand their bitless horses guide,
                Mazacian darts that Median shafts excel,
                Those that in empty cottages do dwell,¹
                African hunters that all darts refuse
                And their loose coats 'gainst angry lions use.²
755   Nor did the cause of civil war alone   [IV. 687]
                But private anger bring King Juba on.
                Curio, that year wherein he did defile
                Divine and human laws, strived to exile
                By tribunicial law from Libya's throne
760   This king and bar him his forefathers' crown,
                Whilst he would make thee, Rome, a monarchy.³
                He, mindful of the wrong, thinks this to be
                The greatest gift his sceptre could bestow.
                This Juba's fame affrighted Curio:
765   Besides, no soldiers firm to Caesar's side
                Were in his army, none that had been tried
                In Germany but, at Corfinium ta'en,
                False to new lords, did to their first remain
                Doubtful and thought both sides indifferent were.⁴   *the same, identical*
770   But when he saw all slack through slavish fear,
                That the night-guards their trenches did forsake,
                With a distracted spirit thus he spake.
                    'Daring conceals great fear: I'll first assay   [IV. 702] *attempt*
                The fight and put my soldiers in array⁵
775   While they are mine: doubt grows from rest alone.⁶

cf. also 'Massylians', 4. 749. M. reverts to contraction in 4. 751.
¹ *Those ... do dwell*] *Et solitus vacuis errare mapalibus Afer* | *Venator*, 'And the African huntsman, accustomed to wander among empty huts' (IV. 684). *Afer* is now a contested reading, but not in early modern editions.
² *And their ... use*] *Vestibus iratos laxis operire leones*, 'they smother angry lions with their loosened robes' (IV. 686).
³ *and bar him ... a monarchy*] *Libyamque auferre tyranno,* | *Dum regnum te Roma facit*, 'he strives to carry Libya away from a tyrant while he makes you a monarchy, Rome' (IV. 691–92). As popular tribune in 50 BC Curio had planned to dethrone Juba and annex Numidia.
⁴ *Besides ... indifferent were*] i.e. Curio couldn't rely on the battle-tested soldiers of Caesar's German campaigns (lit. *Rheni in undis*, 'in the waves of the Rhine', IV. 696) but only on those who had surrendered at Corfinium (see 2. 509 ff.).
⁵ *put my soldiers in array*] *campum miles descendat in aequum*, 'let the soldiers descend onto the level plain' (IV. 703).
⁶ *alone*] *semper*, 'always' (IV. 704).

> Fight shall prevent their consultation:
> When swords whet their dire wills and helmets hide
> Their blushes, who can then compare the side
> Or weigh the cause? They favour as they stand:¹
> 780 As no old hate does on the stage command
> Sword-players to meet; they hate by faction.'²   *gladiators*
> This said, in open field he leads them on,
> Whom the war's fortune, meaning to deceive
> After, at first does prosperously receive.
> 785 For Varus he defeated, following on
> Their flying backs in execution
> Even to the camp.³ When Juba first did know
> Of this sad field, and Varus' overthrow,
> Glad that the glory of the war did stay
> 790 For him, by stealth he leads his troops away,
> And without noise (commanding silence) goes,
> Fearing he should be fearèd of his foes.
> Sabura,⁴ next in honour to the king,
> With a small troop is sent before to bring
> 795 Curio on by provocation,
> As if the war were left to him alone;
> Himself with all his kingdom's strength below
> Keeps in the valley. The Ichneumon so,⁵
> Provoking by his tail's deceitful shade
> 800 Th'Egyptian asp, does at the last invade
> (Freed from the deadly venom's danger quite)
> The serpent's throat stretched out in vain to meet
> A flying shade; out the lost poison goes,

¹ They favour as they stand] *Qua stetit, inde favet*, 'a man inclines to the side he stands on' (IV. 708).
² As no old hate … they hate by faction] *veluti fatalis arenae | Muneribus non ira vetus concurrere cogit | Productos: odere pares*, 'just as no old anger forces those brought out in the games of the deadly gladiatorial arena to fight: they hate as opponents' (IV. 708–10). M. probably reads *pares* (IV. 710) as *partes* ('factions'), without known warrant. 'Sword-player' was used in early modern England for Roman gladiators (see *OED*). M.'s substitution of 'the stage' for the gladiatorial sand/arena was not unique: see e.g. *St. Augustine, of the City of God*, trans. by John Healey (London: George Eld, 1610), p. 124: 'But if two Fencers or sword-plaiers [lit. *gladiatores*] should come upon the stage [lit. *in harenam*, 'onto the sand']'. Theatrical motifs recur in M.'s *Continuation*. 'Faction' is trisyllabic, rhyming with 'on' in the next line.
³ flying backs] M. omits *foeda*, 'disgraceful [flight]' (IV. 713).
⁴ Sabura] Also spelt Saburra or (as in L.) Sabbura.
⁵ The Ichneumon so] Lit. *hostis*, 'enemy', of the asp (IV. 724). 'Ichneumon', the Egyptian mongoose, is taken from F.'s note, itself derived from Pliny's *Natural History*.

	And all about the asp's jaws vainly flows.	
805	Fortune assists this fraud: fierce Curio,	[IV. 730]
	Descrying not the strength of his hid foe,	*not seeing*
	Enjoins his horsemen all to issue out	
	By night, and range the unknown fields about:	
	And after them himself by break of day	
810	With all his eagles spread marches away,	
	Much (but in vain) entreated to suspect	
	Libyan deceit and frauds that still infect	
	The Punic wars.[1] But to his funeral	
	Fate gave him up, and civil war did call	
815	Her author on. O'er rocks and mountains high	
	They march, when on the hill from far they spy	
	The foe, who, cunning, seems to fly away	
	'Til he have set his battles in array	*battalions*
	Under the hill;[2] this Curio did not know	
820	But thought it flight, and like a conqueror now	
	Brings forth his troops into the open plain.	
	Then first discovered they this guileful train:	*trap*
	The seeming-fled Numidians they espied	
	On the hills' tops, enclosing every side.	
825	Curio and his lost troops astonished quite;[3]	*were astonished*
	The fearful could not fly, the valiant fight.	
	The horses now not fierce at trumpet's sound,	
	Chaw not their foaming bits, beat not the ground,	*champ*
	Spread not their manes, nor do their ears advance,	
830	Nor with their wonted spright curvet and prance:	*spirit*
	Their sweating shoulders fumed, their tired necks hung,	
	And their dried mouth thrust out their weary tongue,	
	Their breasts and throats hoarse with oft blowing grew,	
	Their heavy pulse far their spent bowels drew,	
835	The foamings dry and hot grew hard upon	
	The bloody bits; no strokes could force them on,	
	Nor often spurrings make them mend their speed.	
	Wounds make them go: to hasten on the steed	
	Boots not the rider, for the weary horse	*doesn't benefit*
840	In coming on wants courage, strength and force;	

[1] frauds that still infect | The Punic wars] *infectaque semper | Punica bella dolis*, 'Carthaginian warfare, always tainted with trickery' (IV. 736–37).
[2] O'er rocks … the hill] i.e. Juba's armies lure Curio's onto the plain by pretending to retreat.
[3] lost troops] *peritura*, 'doomed, about to perish' (IV. 748).

>   He only brings his rider to the foes,
>   And does his breast to all their spears expose.
>   But when the Libyan horse came coursing nigh,[1]
>   The ground did shake, and clouds of dust did fly
> 845 (As great as Thracian whirlwinds blow about)
>   O'er the sky's covered face, and darkness wrought.[2]
>   But when war's miserable fate did fall
>   Upon the foot, no doubtful field at all   *infantry*
>   Was fought: the battle in that time was done,
> 850 That men could die,[3] for forth they could not run
>   To make their flight, enclosed on every side.
>   From far by darts directly thrown they died,
>   Obliquely near:[4] not wounds alone they feel,
>   O'erwhelmed with storms of darts and weight of steel.
> 855 Pent up in a strait room the army's kept,   *narrow*
>   Those that for fear near'st to the middle crept,
>   Amongst their fellows' swords are not secure,
>   For the forefront, not able to endure   *vanguard*
>   The foe's assault, stepped back and straiter made   *narrower*
> 860 The globe; no room to wield their arms they had,   *compact body*
>   Their crowded limbs are pressed; one armèd breast
>   Against another driven to death is pressed.
>   The conquering Mauritanian could not have
>   So glad a spectacle as fortune gave,
> 865 He saw no bodies fall, no streams of blood:
>   Kept so by crowd upright the bodies stood.
>   Let Fortune this new parentation make   [IV. 788] *funeral rite*
>   For hated Carthage's dire spirits' sake:[5]
>   Let bloody Hannibal and Punic ghosts
> 870 Of this sad Roman expiation boast.
>   Let not in Libya, gods, a Roman fall
>   For Pompey or the Senate make at all:

---

[1] the Libyan horse came coursing nigh] *vagus Apher equos ut primum emisit in agmen*, 'when the nomadic African sent his horses against the first line of battle' (IV. 765).

[2] Thracian whirlwinds ... darkness wrought] *Bistonio ... turbine*, 'like a Bistonian whirlwind', IV. 767. F. notes that the Bistones are Thracian.

[3] the battle ... could die] *sed tempora pugnae | Mors tenuit*, 'but death occupied the duration of the warfare' (IV. 771–72).

[4] Obliquely near] i.e. at close range they were felled by slanting or oblique spear-thrusts, by straight ones from a distance.

[5] parentation make] M.'s 'parentation', a neologism for *Inferiis ... novis*, 'new funeral rites' (IV. 789), is probably inspired by F.'s reference to the Roman festival of Parentalia (a period of public mourning and commemoration of deceased family-members, held in February).

>   Us rather for herself let Africa
>   Conquer. His men o'erthrown when Curio saw,
> 875   And the dust laid with blood gave leave to see,
>   Scorning t'out-live such a calamity
>   Or hope in flight, he meets his death, to die
>   Forward and valiant by necessity.[1]
>   What now avails thy place and troubled bars[2]   [IV. 799]
> 880   From whence, a tribune, to seditious wars
>   Thou stirred'st the people and the Senate's right
>   Betrayed'st,[3] and couldst to civil war incite
>   The son and father-in-law? Thy death is wrought
>   Before these lords have in Pharsalia fought.
> 885   To see that field is not permitted thee.
>   This satisfaction in your bloods give, ye
>   Great ones, to wretched Rome, and pay for war.[4]
>   O happy Rome, and Romans happier far
>   Would but the gods above as careful be
> 890   To keep as to revenge our liberty!
>   Unburied Curio's noble flesh is food
>   For Libyan birds, but (since 'twill do no good
>   To conceal that which from time's injury
>   Fame still will vindicate) we'll give to thee
> 895   The praise that to thy life does appertain.
>   Rome never nurtured a more able man,
>   Nor one to whom (whilst good) the laws owed more:[5]
>   But vice then hurt our city, when the store
>   Of wealth, ambition, riot had declined[6]
> 900   To the worst part his yet unsettled mind,
>   And changèd Curio the state's fate controlled,[7]

---

[1] to die ... by necessity] *Impiger ad letum, & fortis virtute coacta*, 'energetic towards death, and brave by compelled virtue' (IV. 798)

[2] thy place and troubled bars] *rostra ... turbata, forumque*, 'troubled rostra and the forum' (IV. 799), where Roman politicians would address the people: M.'s 'bars' refers to English lawyers or accused pleading 'at the bar' (*OED*, s.v. 'bar' 23).

[3] to seditious wars ... people] *Arma dabas populis*, 'gave arms to the people' (IV. 801). M.'s 'seditious' may derive from F.'s hostile description of Rome's plebeian tribunes as 'firebrands of sedition [*seditionum faces*]'.

[4] and pay for war] i.e. price; L.'s idiom is *poenas*, 'punishment' (IV. 805).

[5] whilst good] *recta sequenti*, 'following the right path' (IV. 815).

[6] riot] See 1. 177n.

[7] the state's fate controlled] *momentum fuit ... rerum*, 'was the influential weight on the scale of things' (IV. 819).

Bribed by the spoils of France and Caesar's gold.¹
Though potent Sulla and fierce Marius,
Cinna, and Caesar's line got rule o'er us
905 By sword, to whom did such power ever fall?²
This man sold Rome, the other bought it all.³

FINIS *libri quarti*⁴

---

¹ the spoils of France and Caesar's gold] i.e. Caesar's victories in Gaul, 59–49 BC, gave him the spoils with which to bribe Curio.
² Sulla ... Marius ... Cinna] On these tyrannical examples see 2. 67–246, 2. 583n. M. omits the epithet *cruentus*, 'bloody' for Cinna (IV. 822) and softens the graphic *Ius licet in iugulos nostros sibi fecerit ense*, 'gained the right for themselves to hold the sword against our throats' (IV. 821).
³ the other] *emere omnes, hic vendidit Vrbem*, 'They all bought it, but this man sold Rome' (IV. 824). M.'s singular suggests Caesar or Caesar's house only.
⁴ 'End of the fourth book'.

Annotations on the Fourth Book[1]

(a) For this conquest much availed Caesar: having quieted Spain, he might securely prosecute the rest of the war, having debarred Pompey of those legions on which he most relied. This conquest cost little blood, for Afranius and Petreius, forced by famine, yielded to Caesar.[2]

(b) Afranius and Petreius, with equal power, with mutual love and care, governed five legions for Pompey in Spain, and chose Ilerda, by the appointment of Pompey, as a convenient seat for the war.[3]

(c) The Celtae, leaving France and passing the Pyrenaean mountains, seated themselves by the river Iberus, and were called Celtiberi.[4]

(d) Cinga falling into Iber loses his name to Iber, which also gives name to all Spain.[5]

(e) It was a policy [that] had often been used by barbarous enemies against the pursuing armies of the Romans, to poison all their rivers: it was done by Jugurtha, king of Numidia, Mithradates, king of Pontus, and Juba, king of Mauritania.[6]

(f) Fortune yet presumed to do somewhat against Caesar in his absence above about Illyrium, for Dolabella and Antonius, commanded by Caesar to possess the straits of the Adriatic Sea, encamped one on the Illyrian, the other on the Corcyraean shore. Pompey far and near was master of the seas, whose Lieutenants Octavius and Libo with great strength of shipping besieged Antonius, and by famine forced him to yield. Basilus from the other shore sent ships to aid Antonius, which were caught by the Pompeians in a strange snare, casting ropes across the sea under water not to be spied. Two of the ships escaped and got over the ropes; the third, which carried the men of Opitergium, was ensnared and held fast. The Opitergians in that place left an example memorable to all posterity, for being scarce a thousand men, they endured from morning to night the assaults of a great army round about them, and at last when valour could not possibly release them, rather than yield themselves into the enemy's hands, by the exhortation of their captain Vulteius all killed themselves.[7]

---

[1] Three additional notes were added in later editions. See Textual Notes.
[2] Paraphrase of F.'s notes on IV. 2 and IV. 3.
[3] Based on F.'s account of the way Pompey distributed responsibilities among his generals in his note to IV. 4: 'with equal power, with mutual love and care', translates F.'s *potestate aequali, fide & amore mutuo*.
[4] Translation of a clause from F.'s note to IV. 8.
[5] Translation of F.'s note to IV. 22.
[6] Slightly altering F.'s note to IV. 320.
[7] Translation of Florus, II. xiii. 30–33, most of which is quoted by F.

(g) In Africa also the side of Caesar, enduring the like calamity, showed the like valour. Curio, sent by Caesar to win Libya, having vanquished and put to flight Varus, was enclosed on the sudden by the unexpected horsemen and army of Juba, king of Mauritania. Curio might have fled when he saw the day lost but, much ashamed and scorning to return to Caesar after the loss of his legions, he died with all his men.[1]

---

[1] Translation of Florus, II. xiii. 34.

To the Right Honourable Robert, Earl of Lindsey, Lord Great Chamberlain of England.[1]

This book, brave lord, is yours, which best of all
Defines the virtues of a general,
And most of all the books sets Caesar forth,
His confidence, his wisdom and his worth;
His soldiers' mutiny,[2] which tried him more
Than all his dangers after, and before.
This searched great Caesar's depth, and made it known
The honours, which he wore, were all his own.
His confidence (if not too great) was shown
Crossing the stormy seas by might alone
In a small barque,[3] when his great spirit strove   *vessel*
With his good fortune, which should greatest prove.
Vouchsafe to read it, valiant lord, and find
Fit recreation for your active mind.

---

[1] To the Right Honourable] Robert Bertie (1582–1642), made Lord Great Chamberlain and Earl of Lindsey in 1626 (22 November). Like dedicatees of other books, he was militarily experienced in the wars against Catholic Spain. But M.'s comparison of him to Caesar in the dedication is probably satirical: in book five Caesar struggles with a mutiny and then makes a failed attempt to sail to Italy in a small boat, before heavy winter storms force him back to port (5. 271–437, 570–811). Bertie likewise had trouble with a mutinous English garrison at Bergen-ap-Zoom in 1624, and in late 1626 commanded a fleet which was forced to return home due to storms. The support of the Duke of Buckingham, however, ensured that he overcame these setbacks and received further military appointments before being made a member of the Privy Council in 1628. He died at Edgehill in 1642, a royalist commander.
[2] mutiny] See 5. 271–437.
[3] In a small barque] See 5. 570–811. 'Barque' is M.'s preferred term throughout the book for 'small boat'.

LUCAN'S
Pharsalia

The Fifth Book.

The Argument of the Fifth Book.[1]

Rome's flying Senate, met at Epire, chose	*Epirus*
Great Pompey general; faint Appius goes	
To Delphos' oracle to seek advice,	*Delphi's*
Which his own death obscurely signifies.	
5 Caesar, returned from Spain with victory,	
Quiets his soldiers' dangerous mutiny:	
Dictator then and consul both at Rome	
He makes himself, sails from Brundisium	
To Greece; but vexed with Antony's delays,	
10 In a small boat himself alone assays	
By night the stormy sea, and crosses o'er.	
His legions, all met on the Grecian shore,	
Address themselves for trial of the day.	
Pompey to Lesbos sends his wife away.	

Thus Fortune kept (mixing her good with ill)	[v. 1][2]
The two ^(a)war-wounded generals equal still	
For Macedonia. When with winter's snow	
The Pleiades did Haemus' top bestrow,[3]	*bestrew*
5 And when the time's new naming day drew near[4] —	
Old Janus' feast, beginner of the year[5] —	
Then both the consuls, at the utmost date	
Of their expiring honour, convocate	*summon together*

---

[1] See note on Argument to book one.
[2] 2 5. 1–77] The exiled Senate meet at Epirus and appoint Pompey commander of their forces.
[3] The Pleiades] The 'Seven Sisters' star-sign, found in the constellation of Taurus. In myth originally daughters of Atlas and Pleione, translated to the stars.
[4] the time's new naming day] *instabatque dies, qui dat nova nomina fastis*, 'the day approached which gives new names to the calendar' (v. 5). Romans identified each year by the names of its consuls.
[5] Old Janus' feast ... year] The first month of the Roman year was January, named after the god Janus.

	To Epire the fled Fathers, where a plain	*Epirus*
10	And foreign seat Rome's nobles did contain.¹	
	A borrowed court in foreign land heard all	
	The secrets of the state.² For who can call	
	That place a camp, where all Rome's fasces were	
	And axes borne?³ The reverend order there	
15	Taught all the people 'twas not Pompey's side,	
	But Pompey there a member did abide.⁴	
	Silence possessing the sad Senate then,	[v. 15]
	From an high seat thus Lentulus began:⁵	
	'If you retain a strength of mind as good	
20	As Roman spirits and your ancient blood	
	Befits, then think not in what land you are	
	As banishèd, from surprisèd Rome how far,	*unexpectedly attacked*
	But know the face of your own company.	
	Fathers that govern all, this first decree,	
25	Which yet all kingdoms and all people know:	
	We are the Senate. For if fortune now	
	Should carry us under the frozen wain	
	Of Ursa Major, or where days remain	
	Equal in length with nights, the torrid zone,⁶	
30	Thither the empire and dominion	
	Would follow us. When Rome by Gauls was fired,	
	And that to Veii Camillus was retired,⁷	
	There then was Rome: this order never lost	*senatorial order*
	Their right by changing place. Caesar can boast	
35	Only of mourning walls' possession,	
	And judgement seats by sad vacation	
	Shut up and silenced, empty mansions.	
	That court those fathers only sees, whom once,	
	When full, it banished; of that rank, whoe'er	
40	Is not a banished man, is sitting here.	

¹ nobles] *proceres*, 'leading men' (v. 10).
² A borrowed court in foreign land] *Hospes in externis ... curia tectis*, 'a visiting Senate-house amongst foreign buildings' (v. 11).
³ Rome's fasces ... axes borne] See 1. 194n.
⁴ side ... abide] *non Magni partes, sed Magnum in partibus esse*, '[that] this wasn't Pompey's faction but rather Pompey was member of a faction' (v. 13).
⁵ Lentulus began] Lucius Lentulus, the retiring consul of 49 BC.
⁶ or where days ... zone] *claususque vaporibus axis | Nec patitur noctes nec iniquos crescere soles*, 'the sky closed in mists allowed neither nights nor days to wax unequal' (v. 24–25). M.'s 'torrid zone' derives from a commentary (probably F.).
⁷ Veii] Monosyllabic.

We that long peaceful, free from guilt, have stood,
At war's first fury were dispersed abroad:
Now to his place each part returns again;
And for the loss of Italy and Spain,[1]
45 The gods the strength of all the world bestow.
Th'Illyrian sea has overwhelmed one foe,
And Libyan fields does slaughtered Curio,
No little part of Caesar's Senate, strow.[2]   *scatter*
Advance your eagles, follow fate, and grant
50 The gods your hope: do not that courage want
In this good fortune, which when first you fled,
Your cause stirred up. The year has finishèd
Our power:[3] you Fathers, whose authorities   *senators*
No time shall end, for th'public good advise:
55 Command great Pompey to be general.'
His name with joyful cries the Senate all
Receive, imposing upon Pompey straight
His country's and his own most wretched fate.[4]
Then faithful kings and nations had their praise.
60 Phoebus' sea-powerful Rhodes rewarded was,
And Spartans rough;[5] praised were th'Athenians;[6]
(b)Phocis made free with her Massilians.
Faithful (c)Deiotarus, young Sadalis,[7]
The valiant (d)Cotys, and (e)Rhasipolis
65 Of Macedon were praised; Juba, to thee
The Senate gives all Libya by decree;
And (O sad fate) ignoble Ptolemy,[8]
Worthy of treacherous subjects, unto thee,
The crime of all the gods and Fortune's shame,
70 Is granted the Pellaean diadem.[9]   *crown*

---

[1] Italy and Spain] *Hesperiam*, 'land of the West', usually meaning Italy (v. 38); F. comments on the loss of Spain as well.
[2] Th'Illyrian sea ... Curio] The fates of Vulteius and Curio (see 4. 513–906).
[3] Our power] i.e. of the legitimate consuls of 49 BC.
[4] most wretched] Added by M.
[5] Spartans rough] *gelidique inculta iuventus | Taygeti*, 'the unrefined youth of icy Taygetus' (v. 51–52).
[6] Athenians] *veteres ... Athenae*, 'ancient Athens' (v. 52); '-ians' here and at 5. 61 is disyllabic, as often in line-endings.
[7] young Sadalis] Inferred from commentaries noting that Sadalis was the son of Cotys.
[8] ignoble Ptolemy] M.'s epithet.
[9] Pellaean diadem] i.e. the Macedonian crown of Egypt (cf. note to 3. 256); the Ptolemaic dynasty was founded by the heirs of Alexander the Great.

A tyrant's sword over thy nation
Thou tak'st, proud boy: would 'twere o'er them alone.
O'er ^(f)Pompey's throat it is;¹ thy sister's crown
Thou tak'st and Caesar's impious action.²
75 The Senate now broke up, the troops all take
Their arms: the people and the captains make
For war's uncertain preparation.³
But ^(g)Appius fears war's doubtful chance, alone
Soliciting the gods th'events to hear,
80 And Phoebus' temple, that for many a year
Had been shut up at Delphos, opens he.⁴
    Parnassus with two tops reaching the sky   [v. 71]
'Twixt east and west equally distant lies,
To Bacchus'⁵ and Apollo's deities
85 Sacred, to whom in mixèd sacrifice
The Theban wives at Delphos solemnize   *conduct formally*
Their trieterics.⁶ This one hill alone
Appeared, when all the world was overflown   *flooded over*
And stood as middle 'twixt the sea and sky.
90 One top, Parnassus, then contented thee,⁷
For one alone did above water shew.   *show*
Young Phoebus there with shafts unusèd slew
The speckled Python, that in wait long lay
His banished mother, great with child, to slay:
95 Themis the kingdom then and Tripos held.⁸

¹   O'er Pompey's throat...] M. omits *donata est regia Lagi*, 'the kingdom of Lagus [Ptolemy's ancestor] was handed over' (v. 62).
²   Thy sister's ... action] *regnumque sorori | Ereptum est, soceroque nefas*, 'your sister has been despoiled of a kingdom and a father-in-law [Caesar] of an atrocity' (v. 64–65). Ptolemy, brother of Cleopatra, will have Pompey murdered to ingratiate himself with Caesar after his victory at Pharsalia (see 8. 563ff.).
³   uncertain preparation] *caeca sorte*, 'blind lottery [of war]' (v. 66).
⁴   5. 78–270] Appius consults the Delphic oracle over the outcome of the war and receives a deceptive answer.
⁵   Bacchus] Lit. *Bromio*, 'the Roarer' (v. 73), one of the cult-names of Bacchus.
⁶   trieterics] M.'s Latinate 'trieterics' is rare, used in English nearly always of the triennial festivals of Bacchus. M.'s 'wives' (5. 86) translates *Bacchae*, the female cult-followers of Bacchus (v. 75).
⁷   then contented thee] M.'s idiom; L. reports Parnassus 'scarcely' (*vix*) extruding one peak above the waters during the Great Flood (v. 77–78).
⁸   Young Phoebus ... Tripos held] Apollo, still yet to master archery ('shafts unusèd' = *adhuc rudibus ... sagittis*, 'with hitherto unskilled arrows', v. 80), slew the monstrous Python of Delphi for trying to harm his pregnant mother Leto, and then took over the oracle from its previous incumbent Themis, goddess of justice. M.'s Tripos is a confusing singular; L. has *tripodasque*, 'the tripods', meaning equipment used in Delphic ritual (v. 81).

But when ^(h)Apollo the cleft ground beheld
T'inspire oraculous truth, and further finds
The gaping earth exhale prophetic winds,[1]
Down in that sacred cave himself he hides,
100 And now turned prophet, there Apollo bides.
 Which of the gods lurks here? What deity   [v. 86]
Shot down from heaven vouchsafes to dignify
This cave? What heavenly god dwells here below,
That does the Fates' eternal courses know
105 And things to come?[2] And telling people sure,
Vouchsafes the touch of woman to endure?[3]
Whether this powerful god barely relate   *simply relates*
The fates, or his relation make them fate?[4]   *makes*
Perchance that spirit that all the world maintains,[5]
110 And the poised earth in empty air sustains,
Through these Cirrhaean caves does passage get,
Striving with his ethereal part to meet.[6]
This spirit once entered the virgin's breast,
Striking her human soul, sounds forth expressed
115 With hideous noise.[7] So urging flames come from
Sicilian Etna's overburdened womb;
Typhoeus so throws up his stones abroad
Pressed with Inarime's eternal load.[8]
 This god exposed to all, denied to none,   [v. 102]

---

[1] prophetic] *loquaces*, 'talkative' (v. 83). Line 5. 97 is metrically irregular.
[2] the Fates' eternal courses] Omitting *secreta*, 'the secrets [of eternal fate]' (v. 89).
[3] And telling ... endure] *ac populis sese proferre paratus, | Contactumque ferens hominis*, 'and prepared to proffer himself to the people, tolerating contact with a human' (v. 90–91). Early modern commentaries, including F., specifically mention the priestess.
[4] his relation makes them fate] *quod iubet ille canendo, | Fit fatum?*, 'Does what he commands by singing become fate?' (v. 92–93).
[5] that spirit] *pars magna Iovis*, 'the great part of Jupiter' (v. 95), which sustains the world and is exhaled from the Delphic caves. L. alludes here to the Stoic idea of the divinity of the universe. M.'s wording may derive from F., who cites as parallel Virgil's *spiritus intus alit*, 'the spirit nourishes within' (*Aeneid*, VI. 729), or from L.'s own *spiritus*, of the Delphic godhead (v. 165; cf. 5. 190).
[6] Striving ... meet] *et aetherio trahitur conexa Tonanti*, 'and, still wound together with aetherial Jove, is inhaled [by the priestess]' (v. 96). 'Ethereal' is trisyllabic.
[7] expressed ... noise] *oraque vatis | Solvit*, 'releases the prophet's tongue' (v. 98–99). Among early modern commentaries, Hortensius has her moaning (*emugit*, col. 547).
[8] So urging flames...] 5. 115–18 allude to Mt Etna and the volcanic island Inarime (four syllables), under which the giant Typhoeus was buried.   womb] M.'s idiom: lit. *ceu Siculus flammis urguentibus Aetnam | Vndat apex*, 'just as the Sicilian peak undulates, when the flames press on Mt. Etna' (v. 99–100).

120 Is freed from hearing human crimes alone.¹
To him no man whispers unlawful prayers,
For he things fixed unchangeable declares,
Forbidding men to wish, and graciously
Gives just men dwellings, though whole towns they be,
125 As once to Tyre.² He teaches us war's sleight,
As to th'Athenians in their naval fight
At Salamine;³ he clears, the causes shown,   *Salamis*
Earth's barrenness and air's infection.
Our age no gift of heaven wants more than this
130 Of Delphos' oracle, which silent is
Since kings, afraid to have their fates expressed,⁴
Forbid the gods to speak. Nor is the priest
Of Delphos for the god's long silence sad:
This oracle's cessation makes them glad.
135 For to that breast, where'er he do inspire,
Untimely death is punishment or hire   *reward*
Of his reception; the fit's vehemence
Too much o'ercomes the strength of human sense,⁵
And their frail souls the god's high motion shakes.
140 Appius, whilst too too near a search he makes
To know Rome's fate, to th'unstirred tripods
And silent caverns does his steps address.⁶
The priest, commanded t'ope that dreadful seat
And for the god a prophetess to get,
145 Finds young Phemonoë,⁷ as she careless roves
'Mongst the Castalian springs and silent groves,
And makes her break the temple doors. The maid   *break open*

---

¹ Is freed ... crimes alone] *ab humani solum se labe furoris | Vindicat*, '[this divine power] alone vindicates itself from the disgrace of human frenzy' (v. 102–03).
² Tyre] The Tyrians were commanded by the oracle to found colonies after an earthquake, and founded Sidon, Tyre and Gades [Cádiz]; cf. 3. 238.
³ He teaches us war's sleight] *dedit ille minas impellere belli*, 'he has granted the capacity to drive off threats of war' (v. 108), as in the advice given to Athens by the oracle in 480 BC before the battle of Salamis.
⁴ Since kings... expressed] *postquam reges timuere futura*, 'after kings feared things to come' (v. 113).
⁵ the strength of human sense] *Compages humana*, 'the human frame', v. 119.
⁶ too too near a search...] *Sic tempore longo | Immotos tripodas ...| Appius Hesperii scrutator ad ultima fati | Sollicitat*, 'So Appius, an investigator of the last moments of Italian fate, stirs up the tripods, which had been motionless for a long time' (v. 120–23).
⁷ a prophetess to get, | Finds] M. downplays L.'s violence: lit. 'the priest grabbed the trembling priestess (*pavidamque ... vatem*) and forced her [into the temple]', v. 124–27). M.'s pronunciation of 'Phemonoë' varies: here it is trisyllabic, rhyming with 'toe'.

	To stand in that most horrid place afraid,[1]	
	Thought by a vain deceit Appius to bring	
150	From his desire of knowing future things.	
	'Why hop'st thou, Roman, truth should here be shown?'[2]	
	The hill', quoth she, 'is mute, the god is gone:	
	Whether the spirit have left these caverns quite,	
	And to the world's far regions ta'en his flight;	
155	Or Pytho burnt by barbarous Brennus up	
	Did with the ashes fill this hole, and stop	
	Great Phoebus' way;[3] or that the gods' decree	
	Make Cirrha mute, thinking it prophecy	
	Enough that Sibyl's books among you live;[4]	
160	Or Phoebus, wont from out his temple drive	*to drive*
	All wicked persons, now no mouth have found	
	Worthy enough his oracles to sound.'[5]	
	The maid's deceit appeared; her fear implied	[v. 141]
	She falsely had the present gods denied.	
165	Then a white fillet ties her locks behind	*ribbon*
	With Delphian bays, and wreathèd garlands bind	
	Her hair before. The priest thrusts on the maid,	
	Who fearful still about the entrance stayed,	
	And durst no nearer to the god to come,[6]	
170	Nor to approach the temple's inmost room.	
	There, counterfeiting that she was possessed,	
	She utters from an undisturbèd breast	
	Feigned words with no confusèd murmur flowing,	
	Nor the least sign of divine fury showing.	
175	Her words so deeply could not Appius wound	
	As great Apollo's truth; no trembling sound	
	That broke her speech there was, no voice so shrill	
	As all the cave's capacious throat might fill;	
	Her laurel fell not from her frighted hair;	

---

[1] most horrid place] *Limine terrifico*, 'on that terrifying threshold' (v. 128).
[2] Why ... truth] *Quid spes ... improba veri | Te Romane trahit?*, 'What wicked hope for truth drags you here, Roman?' (v. 130-31).
[3] Pytho burnt by barbarous Brennus...] L. mentions only that Pytho (i.e. Delphi) burned because of 'a barbaric torch' (*barbarica lampade*, v. 134). The commentaries, including F., infer reference to the Gaul Brennus' torching of the sanctuary in 279 BC.
[4] Sibyl's books among you live] On the Sybilline books, see 1. 600-01n.
[5] All wicked persons...] The moral criticism is sharper in L.: abhorring 'the guilty' (*nocentes*), Apollo finds no-one 'in our age' (*nostro ... aevo*) worthy of his inspiration (v. 139-40).
[6] And ... come] M.'s addition.

	The temple and the wood unshaken were.	
180	These signs betrayed her fearful to receive	
	The god. When angry Appius did perceive	
	That 'twas no oracle, 'Thou wretch', quoth he,	
	'Both I and these abusèd gods will be	
185	Revenged for this, unless thou straight descend	
	And truly tell what all these stirs portend	
	To the affrighted world.'[1] With that the maid	
	Descends down to the oracle afraid,	
	And standing o'er the vault, the god possessed	
190	With a full spirit her unaccustomed breast.	
	The rock's so many years' unwasted spirit	[v. 161]
	He fills her with, and coming to inherit	
	A Delphian breast, ne'er filled he prophetess	
	Fuller: her former mind he banishes	
195	And bids all woman from her breast be gone.[2]	
	She raging bears in this distraction	
	Not her own neck; her hair upright throws down	
	The sacred ornaments and Phoebus' crown;	
	Her neck turns wildly round; and down she throws	
200	All tripods she meets with as she goes.	
	And with an inward fire she burns, which shows	
	Thee, Phoebus, wroth; nor dost thou only use	*angry*
	Thy pricks, thy flames and incitations now,	
	But bridles too:[3] the prophetess shall know	
205	More than she must reveal. All times are heaped	
	Up in one heap, and many ages crept	
	Into her wretched breast; things' orders too,	
	And all contend out into light to go.[4]	
	The Fates, desiring utterance, strive within:	
210	When the world ends and when it shall begin	
	The prophetess can tell, and understands	
	The ocean's depth and number of the sands.[5]	

[1] That 'twas no oracle...] Lit. *tripodas cessare*, 'that the tripods were silent' (v. 157). abusèd gods] *quos fingis*, 'whom you invent' (v. 158).
[2] all woman] *hominem*, 'humanity' (v. 168); cf. 5. 106n.
[3] nor dost thou ... bridles too] L. juxtaposes Apollo's 'whip and goads' (*Nec verbere solo | Vteris, et stimulis*) with the 'flames' (*flammas*) he ignites in her insides, adding that she 'received a bridle' (*Accipit & fraenos*), v. 174-76.
[4] things' orders ... to go] *Tanta patet rerum series, atque omne futurum | Nititur in lucem*, 'so mighty a sequence of things appears, and everything in the future struggles towards the light' (v. 179-80).
[5] ocean's depth] *modus* [*Oceani*], 'limit, boundary' (v. 181).

As the Cumaean Sibyl,¹ in a scorn
Her prophecies should serve all nations' turn,
215 From the vast heap of universal fate
With a proud hand culled out the Roman state,   *picked out*
So now the Phoebus-filled Phemonoë
Strives, obscure Appius, where to find out thee
'Mongst all the Delphian inspirations.²
220 Then first from her mad mouth the foaming runs,
And in the horrid cave were heard at once
Broke-winded murmurs, howlings and sad groans.
At last these words fall from the maid o'ercome:
'Great threats of war thou only freèd from,
225 Shalt in Euboea's pleasant valleys rest.'³
And there she stopped: Phoebus her speech suppressed.⁴
    Ye Tripodès, keepers of fate, that know   [v. 198]
All the world's secrets, and Apollo, thou
Skilled in all truth, from whom the gods conceal
230 No future times, why fear'st thou to reveal
That action that our empire's ruin brings,
Great captains' deaths and funerals of kings,
And all the people that with Rome shall bleed?
Have not the gods this mischief yet decreed?
235 Or stay those fates whilst planets are at strife
And doubt about condemning Pompey's life?⁵
Or hid'st thou, Fortune, to effect more sure
Our liberty's revenge and Brutus' cure
Of monarchy again?⁶ Then the maid's breast

---

¹ As … Sibyl] See 5. 159n. M. omits *in Euboico … recessu*, 'in her Euboean hole', v. 182.
² Strives … inspirations] Compressing *dum te consultor operti | Castalia tellure Dei vix invenit, Appi, | Inter fata diu quaerens tam magna latentem*, 'until she scarcely finds you, Appius, the consulter of the occluded god on Delphian land, [after] seeking you for a long time, hidden among such mighty destinies' (v. 187–89). Here '-ions' is disyllabic.
³ Euboea's pleasant valleys rest] *Euboici vasta lateris convalle*, 'in the vast vale of broad Euboea' (v. 196–97) — an ironic reference to the site of Appius's death. M. omits *tanti discriminis expers*, '[Appius] having no part in so great a crisis' (v. 194).
⁴ there … supressed] *caetera suppressit, faucesque Apollo obstruxit*, 'Apollo suppressed the rest and blocked her jaws' (v. 197).
⁵ stay those fates … Pompey's life] *& adhuc dubitantibus astris | Pompeii damnare caput, tot fata tenentur?*, 'Are the fates of so many held back, with the stars yet doubting to condemn Pompey to death?' (v. 204–05).
⁶ Or hid'st thou … monarchy again] *Vindicis an gladii facinus, poenasque furorum, | Regnaque ad ultores iterum redeuntia Brutos, | Vt peragat fortuna, taces?*, 'Or do you keep silent in order that fortune may carry out the deed of an avenging sword, and punishment for the madness [of civil war], and tyranny again meeting its downfall in an avenging

240	Shoved ope the temple doors, and out she pressed.	*open*
	Her mad fit holds, nor had she all explained:	
	Part of the god within her still remained,	
	And round about her wand'ring eyes he rolled.¹	
	Nor does her face one constant posture hold;	
245	But sometimes threat'ning, sometimes fearful 'tis,	
	Sometimes a fiery red her countenance dyes,²	
	Sometimes her pallid cheeks anger expressed,	
	Not fear;³ nor can her wearied heart find rest.	
	But as a while after the winds are ceased,	
250	The ocean murmurs;⁴ so oft sobbings eased	
	The maiden's breast. But 'twixt this inspired light	
	And her plain human understanding's sight	
	A darkness came;⁵ Phoebus oblivion sent;⁶	
	Then from her breasts the gods' high secrets went,	
255	And divinations to the Tripodès	
	Returned again.⁷ But when her fit 'gan cease	*began to*
	She falls. Nor didst thou, beguiled ⁽ⁱ⁾Appius, fear	
	From doubtful oracles thy death so near;	
	But in that tottering world with hopes most vain	
260	Thought quietly Euboea to retain.⁸	
	Ah, fool, what god but death could set thee free	
	Out of the world's general calamity	

Brutus?' (v. 206–08) — i.e. the assassination of Caesar, whose death at the hands of Brutus in 44 BC will recall the actions of his famous ancestor, the killer of Tarquinius Superbus in 509 BC.

¹ And round about...] *ille feroces | Torquet adhuc oculos*, '[Apollo] rolled her fierce eyes around' (v. 211–12); modern editions read the subject as *illa*, 'she rolled her eyes'. M. condenses L.'s next phrase, *totoque vagantia coelo | Lumina*, 'a gaze wandering over the whole sky' (v. 212–13).

² countenance] Possibly contracted to 'count'nance' in pronunciation.

³ Sometimes her pallid ... fear] *nec, qui solet esse timenti, | Terribilis sed pallor inest*, 'and a pallor there is in them, not as is usual with someone who is fearful, but rather terrible' (v. 215–16).

⁴ after the winds ... murmurs] *ut tumidus Boreae post flamina pontus | Rauca gemit*, 'as after the raucous blasts of the north wind, the swollen ocean groans' (v. 217–18).

⁵ But 'twixt ... came] *Dumque a luce sacra, qua vidit fata, refertur | Ad vulgare iubar*, 'and while she's returned from the sacred light in which she beheld Fate to the common brightness [of day]' (v. 219–20); M. follows F.'s paraphrase here.

⁶ oblivion] *Stygiam ... Lethen*, 'Stygian Lethe' (v. 221); cf. 3. 18n.

⁷ divinations] Combining L.'s *verum*, 'truth', which fled Phemonoë's breast, and *futura*, 'knowledge of things to come', which returned to the tripods (v. 222–23).

⁸ But in that tottering world...] *Iure ... incerto mundi* (v. 226) means either 'the uncertain law of the universe' or 'the [as yet] undecided command of the world'. quietly Euboea to retain] *subsidere*, 'settle in' (v. 226).

And war?¹ There shall thy hearse entombèd lie, *coffin*
And so possess Euboea quietly,²
265 Where th'sea by marble-famed Carystos is
Straitened,³ and pride-revenging Nemesis
Rhamnus adores;⁴ a straitened current strong
That channels holds, and Euripus along
Bears ships by violence, changing oft his tide,
270 From Chalcis to ill-harbouring Aulis' side.⁵
 By this time Caesar, come from conquered Spain [v. 237]⁶
With his victorious eagles, was again
Marching⁽ᵏ⁾ another way,⁷ when fate almost
The prosperous course of his whole war had crossed:⁸
275 For, conquered in no fight, the general
In his own camp 'gan fear the loss of all *began to*
His treason's fruit;⁹ those hands that faithful still
Had served his wars, now glutted with the fill
Of blood, began to quit their general.
280 Th'alarms' tragic sounds, not heard at all
Awhile, and cold sheathed swords their thirst of war
Had cooled;¹⁰ or else the greedy soldier,
Damning for gain both cause and general,

---

¹ Ah, fool...] *demens*, 'madman' (v. 228). Out of ... war?] *nullum belli sentire fragorem, | Tot mundi caruisse malis*, 'to feel no crash of war, and have avoided so many of the world's evils' (v. 228–29).
² There ... quietly] *secreta tenebis | Litoris Euboici memorando condite busto*, 'you will keep your secret knowledge, buried in a memorable tomb on the Euboean shore' (v. 230–01). M.'s language depends on Valerius Maximus, I. 8. 10, quoted by F., which he also uses for his historical note to 5. 257 (see Valerius Maximus, *Memorable Doings and Sayings*, ed. and trans. by D. R. Shackleton Bailey, 2 vols (Cambridge, MA: Harvard University Press, 2000)).
³ marble-famed Carystos] *saxosa*, 'rocky' (v. 232): F. glosses *marmore nobilis*.
⁴ pride-revenging ... adores] *tumida infesta colit qua numina Rhamnus*, 'where Rhamnus worships divinities hostile to the proud' (v. 233). F. alludes to the early modern commonplace of Nemesis as scourge of pride.
⁵ changing oft his tide ... Aulis' side] L.'s *cursum* means 'course, journey' (v. 236), but F.'s note argues that this refers to the erratic tides in the straits south of Euboea. 'Ill-harbouring' translates *iniquam classibus*, 'inimical to fleets' (v. 236), because of the treacherous tides.
⁶ 5. 271–437] Caesar suppresses a mutiny at Placentia.
⁷ With his ... another way] *alium laturus in orbem*, 'about to transfer [his eagles] to another world' (v. 237).
⁸ fate ... had crossed] M.'s idiom for *Avertere Dei*, 'the gods turned aside' (v. 238).
⁹ all | His treason's fruit] *successus scelerum*, 'the successes of crimes' (v. 242). 'Fruits of treason' is common English idiom: see e.g. Spenser, *Faerie Queene*, II. xiii. 31: 'But thou thy treason's fruit, I hope, shalt taste | Right sour'.
¹⁰ thirst of war] M.'s idiom for *belli furias*, 'furies of war' (v. 246). The rhyme requires 'soldier' (5. 282) to be disyllabic, a formula M. repeats at 5. 410–11.

	Would set his blood-stained sword at higher sale.	
285	Caesar not more in any danger tried	*tested*
	How tottering and unfirm a prop his pride	
	Had leaned upon,¹ and well might stagger, reft	*deprived*
	Of all those soldiers' hands,² and almost left	
	To his own sword. He that so many lands	
290	Had drawn to war, knows now the soldiers' hands,	
	Not his, must do the deed.³ Their plaints now be	
	Not dumb, nor timorous is their mutiny.	
	That cause that does suspicious minds restrain,	
	Whilst each one fears where he is feared again,	
295	And thinks that he himself distastes alone	*finds distasteful*
	His ruler's tyranny, in this was gone.⁴	
	Their number to secure their fear is able;⁵	
	Where all offend, the crime's unpunishable.	
	They pour out threats: 'Now, Caesar, let us cease	
300	From wicked war. Thou seek'st by land and seas	
	Swords for these throats, and upon any foe	
	Wouldst our too cheap-esteemèd lives bestow.	
	Some of us slain in war in Gallia lie,⁶	
	In Spain lie some, and some in Italy;	
305	O'er all the world thy army's slaughterèd	
	While thou o'ercom'st. What boots our blood that's shed	*does it benefit*
	'Gainst Gauls and Germans in the north so far?⁷	
	For all thou pay'st us with a civil war.	
	When Rome we took and made the Senate fly,	
310	What spoils from men or temples gathered we?	
	Guilty in swords and hands, all villainy	
	We go upon, virtuous in poverty	

¹ How tottering ... leaned upon] *Quam non e stabili, tremulo sed culmine cuncta | Despiceret*, 'how he looked down on everything not from a stable but trembling eminence' (v. 250–51). M.'s charge of 'pride' is not in L.
² reft ... hands] *Tot raptis truncus manibus*, 'mutilated, with so many hands snatched away' (v. 252).
³ knows now ... the deed] L. makes a more political point: *Scit non esse ducis strictos, sed militis, enses*, 'he realizes that drawn swords belong not to a general but his soldiers' (v. 254).
⁴ distastes alone | His ruler's tyranny] *regnorum iniusta gravari*, 'is weighed down by the injustice of monarchies' (v. 258). For the idiom of distasting monarchy, perhaps recalling this passage, see M.'s dedication to Devonshire.
⁵ to secure their fear] *metus exolverat*, 'had released their fears' (v. 259).
⁶ in Gallia lie] *Gallia ... | Eripuit*, 'Gaul has snatched away' (v. 264–65).
⁷ 'Gainst Gauls and Germans ... far] *Quid iuvat Arctois, Rhodano, Rhenoque subactis*, 'of what profit is it to have subdued the far north, the Rhône and the Rhine?' (v. 268). As F. points out, this means the Gauls and Germans.

Alone.¹ What end is there of war at all,
Or what can be enough, if Rome too small?
315 See our grey hairs, weak hands and bloodless arms:
Our use of life is gone, in war's alarms
Our age consumed. Send us now old at least
To choose our deaths.² This is our bad request:³
Our dying limbs on hard ground not to lay,
320 Nor strike steel helmets 'til our dying day;⁴
To seek some friends to close our eyes in death,
To get our proper piles, our last to breathe   *pyres*
In our wives' arms.⁵ Let sickness end our days;
Let's under Caesar find some other ways
325 Of death than sword. Why hoodwinked lead'st thou us
With a vain hope on acts portentuous,⁶   *prodigious*
As if in civil war we were not able
To know what treason is most profitable?⁷
Our wars have taught him nothing, if not this —
330 What we can do.⁸ Nor is this enterprise
Forbid by law: he was our general
In th'German wars, here we are fellows all;⁹
Whom treason soils, it makes of equal state.¹⁰
Besides in his unthankful estimate
335 Our valour's lost, and whatsoe'er we do
Is called his fortune. But let Caesar know
We are his fate. Though friended by the gods,

---

¹ virtuous in poverty | Alone] *Paupertate pii*, 'pious/dutiful in poverty' (v. 273).
² To choose our deaths] In L. simply *Ad mortem*, 'to our death' (v. 277).
³ bad request] *improba vota*, 'wicked prayers' (v. 277).
⁴ 'til our dying day] *anima ... fugiente*, 'as our life-force flees' (v. 279).
⁵ To seek some friends ... wives' arms] 'friends' is implied but not stated by L., who talks simply of seeking a hand, *dextram* (v. 280), and 'to fall amidst our wife's tears, and to know a pyre is prepared for one alone' (*Coniugis illabi lacrymis, unique paratum* | *Scire rogum*, v. 281–82). Soldiers' corpses were typically burned together.
⁶ Why ... portentuous] *Quid, velut ignaros ad quae portenta paremur,* | *Spe trahis?*, 'Why do you lead us on in hope, as if we're ignorant of the disasters for which we're being prepared?' (v. 284–85).
⁷ what treason is most profitable] *cuius sceleris sit maxima merces*, 'what crime has the highest price' (v. 286), i.e. the death of Caesar himself (*merces* has the specific sense of financial reward).
⁸ What we can do] *istas* | *Omnia posse manus*, 'that those hands can do everything' (v. 287–88).
⁹ fellows all] *Dux erat, hic socius*, 'He was my general, here he's my ally' (v. 290).
¹⁰ Whom ... state] *Facinus quos inquinat, aequat*, 'whom crime taints, it levels' (v. 290).

Caesar is nothing, if with us at odds.'[1]
This said, about his tent they muster all
340 With angry looks seeking their general.
    So let it go, ye gods, since piety[2]   [v. 297]
Forsakes us, and our hopes on vice rely:
Let discord make an end of civil war.
What general would not such a tumult scare?
345 But Caesar, that the fates still sudden tries,[3]
And loves through greatest dangers t'exercise
His fortunes, comes, nor 'til their rage abate
Stays he, but meets the fury of their hate.
Cities' and temples' spoils to them he ne'er
350 Denied, though Jove's Tarpeian house it were,
Senators' wives and daughters to deflower.[4]
All villainies would Caesar from his power
Have them ask freely, and war's guerdon love,   *reward*
And nothing fears but that his men should prove
355 Honest.[5] Ah, Caesar, art thou not ashamed
That civil war by thine own soldiers damned
Should be allowed by thee? Shall they first be
Weary of blood and hate impiety,[6]
Whilst thou run'st headlong on through wrong and right?
360 Give o'er, and learn to live out of a fight;
Give thy guilt leave to end. Why to these wars
Dost thou enforce unwilling soldiers?
The civil war flies from thee. On the top
Of a turf mount stands Caesar fearless up,
365 Deserving fear by his undaunted look,
And thus, as anger prompted him, he spoke.
    'Whom you with hands and looks did absent brave,   [v. 319]

---

[1] Though friended ... at odds] *licet omne Deorum | Obsequium speres; irato milite, Caesar, | Pax erit*, 'though you can hope for the utter compliance of the gods, Caesar, there will be peace if your soldiers are angered' (v. 293–95). In 'Caesar is nothing' M. is perhaps recalling 'Caesar was all' (3. 115).

[2] piety] *pietas, fidesque*, 'duty and loyalty' (v. 297).

[3] that ... tries] *Fata sed in praeceps solitus demittere*, 'But Caesar accustomed to cast down fate by headlong action' (v. 301).

[4] Jove's Tarpeian house] cf. 1. 213n.

[5] And nothing ... Honest] *Militis indomiti tantum mens sana timetur*, 'only the healthy mind of his unconquered army makes Caesar afraid' (v. 309).

[6] and hate impiety] *his ferri grave ius erit?*, 'Will the law of the sword be burdensome to them?' (v. 312–13).

Soldiers, unarmed and present now you have.¹
Here sheathe your swords, if you would end the wars.²
370 Sedition, that no act of valour dares,
Faint-hearted fools and flying spirits declares,   *fleeing; exposes*
Tir'd with their matchless captain's conquering state.³
But go, leave me to war with mine own fate;
These weapons will find hands when I cashier   *disband*
375 All you: as many men as swords are here,
Will fortune send me. Shall all Italy
In such a fleet with vanquished Pompey fly?
And shall my conquests not bring men to share
The wealthy spoils of this near-finished war,
380 Reaping the profit of your toil, and so
Unwounded with my laurelled chariot go?
You, an old, worn and bloodless company
(Then Rome's plebeians), shall my triumphs see.
Can Caesar's fortune feel the loss of you?⁴
385 If all the streams that into th'ocean flow
Should threaten to withdraw themselves, the seas
Would by the loss of them no more decrease
Than now they fill.⁵ Think you that such as ye
Can any moment to my fortunes be?   *decisive influence*
390 The gods' care never will so low descend,
That Fates your deaths or safeties should attend.
The Fates attend on great men's actions:⁶
Mankind lives for a few. And you, whom once
Spain feared and all the north, whilst under me,
395 If Pompey were your general, would fly.
Whilst Labienus did with Caesar stay,

---

¹ Whom you...] *Qui modo in absentem vultu, dextraque furebas, | Miles, habes nudum promptumque ad vulnera pectus*, 'You, soldiers, who just now were raging with look and hand at me in my absence, now have me present with a breast bare and ready for wounding' (v. 319–20).

² Here ... wars] Omitting *fuge*, 'and run away' (v. 321). Note that this line half-rhymes with the next couplet.

³ their matchless captain's conquering state] *ducis invicti rebus ... secundis*, 'the favourable circumstances of an unconquered leader' (v. 323). In the previous line, 'spirits' is probably contracted to 'sp'rits' in pronunciation.

⁴ Can Caesar's fortune ... you?] *Caesaris an cursus vestrae sentire putatis | Damnum posse fugae?*, 'Or do you think that Caesar's career could feel the loss of your desertion?' (v. 335–36).

⁵ Than now they fill] i.e. than now they grow by their addition.

⁶ The Fates attend ... actions] *Procerum motus haec cuncta sequuntur*, 'all these things follow the actions of leading men' (v. 342); cf. 3. 482n.

He was a man; now, a base runaway,
Flies with his chosen chief o'er sea and land.¹
Nor shall your faith in my opinion stand
400 Better, though me ye make nor enemy
Nor general. He that revolts from me,
And does not Pompey's faction straight maintain,
He never will my soldier be again.²
The gods themselves over my camp have care,
405 And would not venture me in such a war
Ere I have changed my men. A burden main   *mighty*
Has fortune from my weary shoulders ta'en;³
I may disarm those hands now lawfully,
Whose boundless hopes earth could not satisfy.⁴
410 Out of my camp! I'll for myself make wars:
Resign those eagles up to soldiers,
Base citizens. But those that authors were
Of this sedition,⁵ punishment shall here
Detain, not Caesar. Fall upon the ground,
415 Yield your disloyal heads and necks to wound;
And you, which now my camp's sole strength shall be,
Young soldiers, learn to strike, and learn to die
Viewing their deaths.' The foolish people then
'Gan tremble at his anger,⁶ and one man   *began to*
420 Made all them fear who had it in their hand
To ruin him,⁷ as if he could command
The swords themselves and without soldiers make
His wars.⁸ But in this punishment to lack

---

¹ Whilst Labienus ... land] Titus Labienus, a commander under Caesar until 50 BC, who crossed to Pompey's side in 49. A minor figure in L. (see 9. 630 ff.), M. awards him an heroic death in the *Continuation*, sig. I^v.
² He that revolts ... again] *quisquis mea signa relinquit, | Nec Pompeianis tradit sua partibus arma, | Hic nunquam vult esse meus*, 'Whoever leaves my standards and does not transfer his arms to the Pompeian side, never wishes to be my soldier' (v. 349–50). M. clearly had another edition besides F.'s here, which misprints *partibus* as *patribus*, 'fathers' (i.e. Pompeian senators).
³ A burden ... ta'en] L. gives Caesar an additional and sarcastic *heu!*, 'alas!', here (v. 354).
⁴ earth could not satisfy] *orbis*, 'the world' (v. 356).
⁵ that authors were ... sedition] *quibus haec rabies auctoribus arsit*, 'at whose instigation this madness took fire' (v. 359).
⁶ anger] *saeva sub voce*, 'his cruel voice' (v. 364).
⁷ in their hand | To ruin him] *Privatum factura*, 'could have made him a private man' (v. 366), in other words debarred from authorized military command.
⁸ without soldiers ... wars] *invito moturus milite ferrum*, 'able to move the steel even with the soldiery unwilling' (v. 366–67).

	Assisting swords he fears;¹ they, patiental,²	
425	Exceed the hope of their stern general.³	
	Not only swords but throats they offer; he	
	Fears nought but 'batement of their cruelty.⁴	*abatement*
	A ⁽ˡ⁾covenant dire this quarrel does decide,⁵	
	With punishment the army's pacified.	
430	In ten days' march to reach Brundisium⁶	
	He bids them straight, and call all shipping home,	
	That on crook'd Hydrus and old Taras then,	
	Leucas' close shores, and the Salapian fen	*hidden*
	Dispersèd were, and Sypus,⁷ o'er which stands	
435	Fruitful Garganus on Italian lands	
	Reaching the Adriatic, and there tastes⁸	
	Dalmatian north, Calabrian southern blasts.	
	Caesar without his troops goes safe alone	[v. 381]⁹
	To trembling Rome, now taught to serve a gown;¹⁰	
440	And (kind forsooth) yields at the people's prayer	
	to be dictator, ⁽ᵐ⁾honour's highest stair,	
	And joyful calendars, being consul, made.¹¹	
	For all those words ⁽ⁿ⁾then their beginning had,	
	With which e'er since our emperors we claw.¹²	*flatter*
445	But Caesar, that his power might want no law,	
	Falsely the name of magistrate purloins,	

---

¹ punishment] *scelus*, 'crime' in L. (v. 369).
² patiental] M.'s neologism for 'patient, suffering', directly translating L.'s noun *patientia* (v. 369). The meter suggests an awkward trisyllabic pronunciation.
³ stern general] *saevi*, 'cruel' (v. 369).
⁴ he ... their cruelty] *Nil magis, assuetas sceleri quam perdere mentes, | Atque perire timet*, 'He [Caesar] fears nothing more than that they lose their customary criminal intent and be ruined' (v. 371-72). Modern editions print *tenet*, changing the meaning to 'nothing sways minds accustomed to crime more than destroying and being destroyed'.
⁵ this quarrel does decide] *Parta quies*, 'Peace is produced' (v. 373). 'Covenant' is probably contracted in pronunciation to two syllables.
⁶ ten days' march] *decumis ... castris*, 'at the tenth camp' (v. 374); F. glosses *decem dierum itineribus*.
⁷ Sypus] Omitting *subdita ... | Montibus*, 'lying beneath the mountains' (v. 377-78).
⁸ there tastes] M.'s idiom; L.'s term *obnoxius* (v. 379) means 'exposed to' in this context.
⁹ 5. 438-63] Caesar pays a brief visit to Rome and continues his subversion of republican institutions.
¹⁰ serve a gown] *servire togae*, 'be enslaved to a toga [garment of peace]' (v. 382): i.e. Rome has given up without a fight; cf. 1. 335n.
¹¹ joyful ... made] *laetos fecit ... fastos*, 'made the calendars happy' (v. 384) by bearing Caesar's name as consul.
¹² our emperors we claw] *voces, per quas ... | Mentimur dominis*, 'those titles, by which we lie to our masters' (v. 385-86).

      And to his swords the Roman axes joins,
      Fasces t'his eagles,[1] and with fitting shame
      Signs the sad times.[2] For by what consul's name
450 Will the Pharsalian year be better known?
      A feigned assembly in the field is ^(o)shown;[3]
      The people give their suffrages compelled,
      Not lawfully admitted; th'urns are held,
      The tribes are cited, voices thrown in vain
455 Into the urn.[4] The augurs deaf remain,
      Though loud it thunder, and are forced to swear
      That birds auspicious, though sad owls, appear.[5]
      Thence that once-honoured power her dignity[6]
      First lost, but lest the times unnamed should be,
460 Our calendars do ^(p)monthly consuls fill.
      That god that dwells on Trojan Alba's hill
      Though not deserving (Latium conquered) sees
      The consuls' solemn nightly sacrifice.[7]
        Caesar departing thence runs forward right   [v. 403][8]
465 Swifter than whelp-robbed tiger or the flight[9]
      Of lightning o'er Apulia, where the field
      Unploughed no corn but slothful grass does yield,
      And, come to Cretan crook'd Brundisium, finds
      The sea unsailable for dangerous winds,
470 And the fleet fearful of cold winter's face.[10]

---

[1]   to his swords ... eagles] i.e. Caesar joins the symbols of civil authority (axes and fasces) to those of military power (cf. 1. 194n).

[2]   with fitting ... times] i.e. the year of Caesar's consulate and dictatorship will be marked by the trauma of Pharsalia and Pompey's death.

[3]   A feigned ... shown] *fingit sollemnia campus*, 'the field of Mars feigns ceremonies' (v. 392). M. translates F.'s note.

[4]   The tribes ... urn] *Decantatque tribus et vana versat in urna*, 'and reels off in order the names of the tribes and shakes [the pebbles, voting tokens] in an empty urn' (v. 394).

[5]   That birds ... appear] i.e. are claimed as well-omened, even though actually ill-omened ('sad') owls. M. omits *Nec caelum servare licet*, 'Nor is it licit to observe the sky' (v. 395).

[6]   dignity] *potestas*, 'authority' (v. 397).

[7]   That god ... sacrifice] The annual ceremonies conducted by the consuls on the Alban hill; cf. 1. 587n. The god is 'not deserving' (5. 462) of worship because complicit in Rome's fall.

[8]   5. 464–525] Caesar arrives at Brundisium and urges his fleet to make the crossing to Dyrrachium in Greece, but winter conditions make this impossible.

[9]   whelp-robbed tiger] *tigride faeta*, 'a mother tigress' (v. 405); F. suggests the loss of a cub.

[10] fearful of cold winter's face] *pavidas hyberno sidere classes*, 'a fleet fearful at the winter star [i.e. season]' (v. 408). 'Winter's face' is common English poetic idiom: e.g. 'cold winter's face' appears in Sidney's *Arcadia* [1593], ed. by Maurice Evans (London: Penguin, 1977), p. 286 (book II, ch. 11).

He thinks it shame thus to delay the pace
Of war and keep the haven, when the sea
Lies ope to men less fortunate than he,   *open*
And thus persuades his men to try the seas:[1]
475 'The northern winds more constantly possess
Both air and ocean, when they once begin,
Than those which the unconstant spring brings in.[2]
We have no turnings different shores upon;
Our way's forthright; the north wind serves alone.
480 Would he would stuff our sails, bending our masts,
And force us upon Greece with furious blasts,
Lest Pompey's galleys from Dyrrachium meet
With their swift oars our becalmèd fleet![3]
Then cut the cables that our fleet do stay:
485 We lose the storms, these clouds will pass away.'
    Now in the sea bright Sol had hid his head[4]   [v. 424] *the sun*
And stars appeared, the moon her shadows spread.
The fleet at once weighed anchor,[5] and drew out
The sails at length, which straight they turned about
490 To the ships' length, and spread the topsails too,[6]
To lose no gust of wind whatever blow.
When a soft gale had made the sails to swell
For a short space, down to the mast they fell
Again; that wind, that put them from the shore,
495 Was able now to follow them no more.
The sea's flat face now all becalmèd lies
Like standing pools; no waves, no billows rise.
So bridled is the Euxine sea,[7] whose course
Ister nor Thracian Bosporus can force:

---

[1] thus ... seas] *Expertes animos pelagi sic robore complet*, 'thus he fills with strength spirits unused to the sea' (v. 412).

[2] the unconstant spring] *Perfida nubiferi ... inconstantia veris*, 'the untrustworthy inconstancy of the cloud-bearing spring' (v. 415).

[3] becalmèd fleet] M. simplifies L.'s *languida ... carbasa*, 'slackened sails' (v. 421), probably following F.'s gloss. M.'s line is irregular.

[4] bright Sol had hid his head] Common early modern English idiom for L.'s *Phoebo labante sub undas*, 'Phoebus [the sun] sinking beneath the waves' (v. 424).

[5] weighed anchor] *pariter solvere rates*, 'together they loosed the ships [from their moorings]' (v. 426).

[6] and drew out ... topsails too] *et flexo navita cornu | Obliquat laevo pede carbasa*, 'and the sailor, with the yard arm bent, draws the sheets to the left-hand side' (v. 428-29). M. is misled here by F.'s *obliquato in longitudinem navis velo*, 'twisting the sail to the length of the ship'.

[7] Euxine sea] *Scythicas ... undas*, 'Scythian waters' (v. 436); M. follows F.'s *Pontus Euxinus*.

500	The frozen sea lets go those ships no more	
	That once it takes; the horses trample o'er	
	Safely where ships have sailed; the Bessians	
	Furrow Maeotis' frozen back with wains.	carts
	This cruel calm does the sad ocean make	
505	(As if the seas their nature did forsake)	
	Like standing pools. Th'ocean observes no more	
	His ancient course; he had forgot to roar.[1]	
	No tides flow to and fro, nor seems the sun	
	To dance upon the water's motion.[2]	
510	To many dangers this becalmèd fleet	
	Is subject: on one side they fear to meet	
	Pompey's swift galleys, on the other side	
	Detained at sea, a famine to abide.	
	From these new fears arose a new desire:	
515	They wish the ocean would collect his ire	
	And all the winds would wrestle, so it were	
	No calm;[3] but no such signs, no clouds appear:	
	The skies and seas conspired to take away	
	All hope of shipwreck. But th'ensuing day	
520	All clouded o'er did comfortable prove:[4]	
	Waves from th'sea's bottom rose, hills seemed to move.[5]	
	The ships were borne away, and as they swim,	
	The waves in crooked furrows follow them.	
	With prosperous winds and seas they reach the land,	
525	And anchor cast upon Paleste's sand.	
	The place, where first both generals(q) camps did pitch	[v. 461]
	Near to each other, was that region which	
	Swift Genusus and gentle Apsus round	
	Encompass; Apsus, because slow, profound	
530	And navigable is:[6] the other flows	

---

[1] forgot to roar] *non horrore tremit*, 'doesn't tremble with quivering [in the breeze]' (v. 446).

[2] To dance ... motion] M.'s idiom for *non Solis imagine vibrat*, 'nor glimmer with the reflection of the sun' (v. 446).

[3] the winds ... No calm] *nimiasque ... ventorum vires ... et sit mare*, '[they pray for] excessive power in the winds, so that the sea would be a sea' (v. 451–53).

[4] did comfortable prove] M.'s idiom, with no close correlation in the Latin.

[5] hills seemed to move] *movitque Ceraunia nautis*, '[the day] moved the Ceraunian [hills] to the sailors' (v. 457); M. follows F.'s gloss.

[6] Apsus ... navigable is] *Apso gestare carinas | Causa palus, leni quam fallens egerit unda*, 'the reason that Apsus bears ships is the marsh, which deceptively it drains with slow-moving water' (v. 463–64); M. translates F.'s gloss.

  (Increased by showers, and sun-dissolvèd snows)
  More swift. Both channels are but short; not far
  From sea the springs of both these rivers are.
  Here fortune first those two famed heroes brought
535 Together;[1] the vain-hoping world had thought[2]
  The generals, now no farther off removed,
  This wicked war would both have disapproved.
  Each other's face they saw, and well might hear
  Each other's voice: ah, Pompey, many a year
540 Not nearer did thy once loved father-in-law,
  Since that dear pledge, the death of Julia,
  And her young son, see thee, 'til stained with gore
  He saw thy face on Egypt's cursèd shore.[3]
  But part of Caesar's ^(r)forces left behind   [v. 476]
545 Made him protract the battle, though his mind
  Were fierce on fight; those bold ^(s)Antonius led,
  In civil wars now under Caesar bred
  For Leucas' fight.[4] Whom making long delay
  With threats and prayers thus Caesar calls away:
550 'Thou mischief of the world, why dost thou waste
  The gods' and fate's good will? My prosperous haste
  Has done all hitherto; Fortune from thee
  Requires the last hand to this speedily
  Successful war. Do Libya's quicksands lie
555 Or her devouring gulfs 'twixt thee and me?
  Have I committed thee to unknown seas,
  Or sent thee on untrièd casualties?[5]   *chances*
  Caesar commands thee not, coward, to go,
  But follow him; myself here, where the foe
560 Encampèd lies, am first arrivèd now.
  Fear'st thou my camp? We lose what fates bestow,
  And to the winds and seas I bootless plain.   *complain uselessly*
  My forward soldiers do not thou detain,

---

[1] two famed heroes] *tantae duo nomina famae*, 'two names of such fame' (v. 468).
[2] vain-hoping world] Omitting *miserique* 'wretched [world]' (v. 469).
[3] cursèd shore] Epithet added, foreshadowing Pompey's death at the mouth of the Nile: see 8. 713 ff. On Julia, see 1. 129 ff. 5. 540, above, is metrically irregular.
[4] bold Antonius ... fight] *Iam tum civili meditatus Leucada bello*, 'already now rehearsing Leucas in civil war' (v. 479). Marcus Antonius would be defeated at Actium (Leucas) in 31 BC.
[5] untrièd casualties?] If this is the pronunciation, 'casualties' is trisyllabic; alternatively, 'untried' has two syllables and the final word four.

	That would take any seas, if I judge right;	
565	They'd come through shipwreck under me to fight.	
	Now I must speak in grief, the world I see	
	Is not divided 'twixt us equally:	
	In Epire Caesar and th'whole Senate rest,	*Epirus*
	Thou art alone of Italy possessed.'	
570	But having often used such words as those,	
	They still delaying, Caesar 'gan suppose	*began to*
	The gods not wanting unto him, but he	
	To them,¹ and rashly did resolve to try	
	By night those seas, which they for fear forbore	
575	Although commanded, finding ever more	
	Bold actions thrive;² and hopes in a ⁽ᵗ⁾small boat	
	T'o'ercome those waves whole navies ventured not.	
	Now weary night war's toilsome cares did end.	[v. 504]³
	Poor men took rest, whose mean estates could lend⁴	
580	Their breasts sound sleep; the camp all silent proved,	
	When the third hour the second watch had moved.	
	With careful steps through this vast silence then	
	Caesar, what not the meanest of his men⁵	
	Would do, intends: leaves all, and goes alone	
585	With none but Fortune as his companion,⁶	
	And passing through the courts of guard,⁷ he finds	*guard-rooms*
	All fast asleep, complaining in his mind	
	That he could pass.⁸ But at the waterside	
	He found a boat with a small cable tied	
590	Fast to a rock. The man that owed and kept	*owned*
	This boat, not far from thence securely slept	
	In a small cottage of no timber trees	
	But woven reeds and barren bulrushes	
	Built up; a boat's turned bottom did suffice	

¹ The gods ... To them] *se deesse Deis, at non sibi numina*, '[he believed that] he was lacking to the gods, not that divine favour was lacking to him' (v. 499), i.e. he was failing to take up the opportunity the gods offered him.
² finding ... thrive] *temeraria prono | Expertus cessisse deo*, 'having tested that rash actions yield to a willing deity' (v. 501-02).
³ 5. 578–811] Caesar attempts to cross to Italy in the small boat of Amyclas, a poor fisherman, but is forced to turn back in the face of a storm.
⁴ mean estates] *fortuna minor*, 'lesser fortune' (v. 506).
⁵ the meanest of his men] *famulis*, 'domestic slaves' (v. 509).
⁶ companion] '-ion', untypically in a line-ending, is monosyllabic here.
⁷ courts of guard] *tentoria ... | ...vigilum*, 'the tents of the sentinels' (v. 510-11).
⁸ That he could pass] *quod fallere posset*, 'that he was able to deceive' (v. 512).

595   To fence his wall. There Caesar twice or thrice
      Knocked with his hand that all the cottage shaked:
      From his soft bed of sedge Amyclas waked.
      'What shipwrecked man', quoth he, 'knocks there, or whom
      Has fortune driven to my poor house to come
600   For shelter?' Speaking thus he from bed,
      And his fired match with better fuel fed,
      Secure from fear of war: such houses are
      (Full well he knows) no spoil for civil war.
      O safe blessed poor man's life,[1] O gift of all
605   The gods, not yet well known:[2] what city wall,
      What temple had not feared at Caesar's stroke?
      But when the door was ope, thus Caesar spoke: *open*
      'Enlarge thy hopes, poor man, expect to have
      More wealth from me than modesty can crave.[3]
610   Only transport me to th'Italian shore,
      This trade of living thou shalt need no more,
      No more shall labour thy poor age sustain.[4]
      Yield to thy fate; a god is come to rain
      Down showers of wealth thy little house upon.'[5]
615   Thus Caesar, though disguised, forgets the tone
      Of private men,[6] when poor Amyclas made
      This answer: 'Many things (alas) dissuade
      My mind from trusting of the seas tonight.
      The sun set pale, his beams dispersed, whose light
620   Partly to north and partly south inclined.[7]

---

[1]   O safe ... life] *O vitae tuta facultas | Pauperis, angustique lares!*, 'O safe ease of a poor man's life, and humble household gods!' (v. 527–28).
[2]   not yet well known] i.e. to be not yet well known.
[3]   More wealth] L.'s Caesar is vaguer, offering only *maiora*, 'greater things' (v. 532).
[4]   This trade ... sustain] *non ultra cuncta carinae | Debebis, manibusque inopem duxisse senectam*, 'you will no further owe everything to your vessel, and lead an impoverished old age in toil [lit. with your hands]' (v. 534–35). Modern editions follow Housman in assuming a lacuna between *manibusque* and *inopem*, placing them on different lines.
[5]   to rain ...upon] L.'s Caesar talks only of *opibus subitis*, 'sudden plenty' (v. 537) visiting the mariner's abode by a god's favour (possibly, but not explicitly, Caesar himself). Perhaps recalling Marlowe's *Tamburlaine*: 'see how he [Jupiter] rains down heaps of gold in showers' (1 *Tamburlaine*, I. 2. 182, in *The Complete Works*, ed. by Fredson Bowers, 2 vols, 2nd ed. (Cambridge: Cambridge University Press, 1981)).
[6]   Thus ... men] *quanquam plebeio tectus amictu | Indocilis privata loqui*, 'although clad in plebeian garment, untutored in speaking as a private man' (v. 537–38).
[7]   The sun set pale...] *non rutilas deduxit in aequora nubes*, 'did not lead reddened clouds down into the sea' (v. 541).   Partly ... inclined] L. here mentions the northern and southern winds (v. 542–43).

The middle of his orb but dimly shined,
And dazzled not the weak beholder's eyes:[1]
With dullèd horns did the pale moon arise,
Not free from clouds her middle part she had.
625 Her pointed ends no horn directly made;
First red betokening winds, then pale she was,[2]
And in dark clouds obscured her mourning face.
But the shore's noise, the murmur of the woods,
The dolphins playing up and down the floods
630 With course uncertain, I mislike;[3] no more
Like I the cormorants flocking to the shore:[4]
Nor that the hern, on her smooth wing relying   *heron*
Presumes to reach the skies with lofty flying;[5]
Nor that the crow waggling along the shore
635 Dives down,[6] and seems t'anticipate a shower.
But if affairs of weight require mine aid,
To use my skill I will not be afraid;
Either the winds and seas shall it deny,
Or I will reach the shore of Italy.'[7]
640   This said, loosing his vessel he puts on   [v. 560]
And spreads his sails, at whose first motion
Not only th'usual falling stars did make
In the dark[8] air a long and fiery track,
But even those stars which make their fixed abode[9]
645 In th'highest spheres[10] did seem to shake and nod.
The sea's black face a terror does diffuse;[11]

---

[1] And dazzled ... eyes] *Spectanteis oculos infirmo lumine passus*, 'suffering with its meagre light eyes to gaze on it' (v. 545).
[2] betokening] Probably contracted in pronunciation to 'betok'ning'.
[3] The dolphins ... mislike] *Nec placet incertus, qui provocat aequora, Delphin*, 'nor does the uncertain dolphin who challenges the sea please me' (v. 552); *incertus*, 'uncertain', refers to the dolphin's erratic course.
[4] the cormorants ... shore] *siccum quod mergus amat*, 'the dry land that the water-fowl loves' (v. 552).
[5] smooth wing] Probably following F.'s paraphrase, *leniter volanti*, 'soft-flying [plumage]', for L.'s *natanti*, 'swimming' (v. 554).
[6] Dives down] *caput spargens undis*, 'splashing sea-water on its head' (v. 555).
[7] of Italy] *litora ... | Iussa*, 'the shores commanded [by Caesar]' (v. 557-58).
[8] dark] M.'s addition.
[9] make their fixed abode] M.'s idiom; *fixa tenentur*, 'are held fixed', in L. (v. 563).
[10] th'highest spheres] *summis ... polis*, 'the highest heavens' (v. 563-64).
[11] The sea's black face ... diffuse] Transposing *niger*, 'black', from L.'s *horror* (which here probably means 'a shuddering' of the sea, not 'terror') to the sea; 'face' translates *terga*, lit. 'backs', i.e. the ridges of the waves (v. 564-65).

	The threat'ning waves in tracks voluminous	
	Boil up; the seas by blasts uncertain blown	
	Betoken many winds' conception.	
650	Then thus the master spake:¹ 'Behold how great	
	A danger the sea teems withal: as yet	
	Uncertain 'tis what wind — rough east or west —	
	Shall come. The barque's on every side distressed	
	With several waves:² the clouds and skies express	*different*
655	The south wind's rage, the murmur of the seas	
	The north-west wind. In such a storm to shore	
	Not safe nor shipwrecked can we e'er get o'er.³	
	No course but one of safety does remain,	
	Hopeless to steer our courses back again.	
660	Let's set our dangered barque a-land, before	
	We are too far gone from the Grecian shore.'	
	Caesar, presuming that all dangers great	[v. 577]
	Would yield to him, 'Contemn', quoth he, 'the threat	*despise*
	Of raging seas: spread sails,⁴ and if the sky	
665	Warrant thee not to go for Italy,	
	I'll warrant thee.⁵ The just cause why thou fear'st	
	Is this, because thou know'st not whom thou bear'st,	
	Him whom the gods never forsake; to whom	
	Fortune accounts it injury to come	
670	After his wish.⁶ Break through the waves;⁷ alone	
	Think thyself safe in my protection.	
	These are the troubles of the seas and skies,	
	Not of our barque: this barque, where Caesar is,	
	Her carriage shall protect.⁸ Nor long shall this	
675	Storm last, but happy for the ocean 'tis	
	This barque is here.⁹ O turn not back thy hand,	

---

¹ master] Of the vessel, i.e. Amyclas.
² several waves] *dubius ... pontus*, 'a treacherous sea' (v. 570).
³ In such a storm ... get o'er] *gurgite tanto | Nec ratis Hesperias tanget, nec naufragus oras*, 'in such a whirlpool [i.e. sea-storm] neither will the ship touch Italy, nor a shipwrecked mariner the shore' (v. 572-73).
⁴ spread sails] Omitting *ventoque furenti*, 'into the raging wind' (v. 578).
⁵ Warrant ... warrant] M.'s idiom for L.'s *coelo auctore ... | Me*, 'on the authority of the sky ... on my authority' (v. 579-80).
⁶ accounts it injury ... After his wish] *male ... meretur*, 'treat shabbily' (v. 582).
⁷ waves] *procellas*, 'gusts, storms' (v. 583).
⁸ this barque ... protect] *hanc Caesare pressam | A fluctu defendet onus*, 'the cargo will defend this vessel, laden with Caesar, from the swell' (v. 585-86).
⁹ but happy ... here] *proderit undis | Ista ratis*, 'this vessel will benefit the seas' (v. 587-88).

	Nor think upon Epire's adjoining land;[1]	Epirus'
	Think on Calabria's shore safe to arrive,[2]	
	Since no land else to me can safety give.	
680	Alas, thou knowest not why these terrors rise;[3]	
	In all these tumults of the seas and skies	
	Does Fortune strive to pleasure me.' No more	
	He spoke, when straight a furious whirlwind tore	
	From the rent barque her shrouds,[4] and down it flung	
685	The sails that on the trembling mainmast hung.	
	The joint-dissolvèd vessel sounds, when lo,[5]	
	Winds full of danger from all quarters blow:	
	First from th'Atlantic ocean Corus blows,	north-west wind
	Rolling the waves, and raisèd billows throws	
690	With violence against the rocks amain.[6]	with full force
	Him Boreas meets,[7] and turns them back again;	north wind
	The sea stands doubtful to what wind to yield,	
	But Scythian Boreas' fury wins the field.[8]	
	But though high waves he from the bottom rear,	
695	Yet to the shore those waves he cannot bear;	
	They meet with those that Corus brings, and break.	
	The seas thus raised (though now the winds were weak)	
	Would meet themselves. Nor must you now surmise[9]	
	Eurus is still, or shower-black Notus lies	south-east and south winds
700	Imprisoned close in Aeol's rocky cave.	Aeolus'
	They from their several quarters rush to save	
	With furious blasts their lands from being drowned,	
	And keep the sea within his proper bound.[10]	
	For oft (they say) small seas by violent wind	
705	Have been transported: so th'Aegean joined	

---

[1] Epire's adjoining land] M. adds the place-name, probably from F. or other commentaries.
[2] on Calabria's shore] *Calabro portu*, 'in Calabrian port' (v. 589).
[3] Alas ... rise] M. turns L.'s question, *quid tanta strage paretur | Ignoras?* ('Don't you know what is prepared with such destruction?', v. 591–92) into a lament.
[4] From ... shrouds] *laceros percussa puppe rudentes*, 'from the smitten vessel her tattered rigging' (v. 594).
[5] when lo] M.'s added interjection.
[6] First from ... amain] 5. 688–90 (v. 598–600) are addressed to Corus in L. 'Violence' is here trisyllabic, somewhat untypically.
[7] Boreas meets] Omitting L.'s epithet *gelidum*, 'icy' (v. 601).
[8] the field] M.'s added idiom; simply *vicit*, 'won' in L. (v. 603).
[9] Nor must you now surmise] Transforming L.'s *Non* [...] *Crediderim*, 'Nor would I believe' (v. 608–10).
[10] within his proper bound] *loco*, 'in place' (v. 612).

With the Tyrrhene, so with th'Ionian
The Adriatic met.[1] How oft in vain
That day the sea seemed mountains' tops t'o'erflow,
And yielding earth that deluge t'undergo.[2]
710 But such high waves on no shore raisèd be,
But from the world's far part and the main sea
They roll: the earth-embracing waters bring
Their monstrous waves.[3] So when the heaven's high king[4]
Helped his tir'd thunder with his brother's mace
715 To mankind's ruin, earth then added was
To Neptune's kingdom, when the sea confounded
All lands, and Tethys by no shore was bounded,   *the sea*
Contented with no limit but the skies.
Then also would those swelling seas arise
720 Up to the stars, had not great Jove kept down
Their waves with clouds. nor sprung that night alone
From natural causes:[5] the thick air was grown
Infected with the damps of Acheron,[6]
And clogged with foggy storms; waves from the main   *sea*
725 Fly to the clouds and fall like showers again.
The lightning's light is lost,[7] it shines not clear,
But shoots obscurely through night's stormy air.
The heavens then trembled; the high pole for fear
Resounded, when his hinges movèd were.
730 Nature then feared the old confusion:[8]

---

[1] so th'Aegean ... met] M.'s verbs 'joined and 'met' (lines 705–07) transform L.'s of crossing and sounding (*transit, sonat*, v. 613, 614) and may derive from commentaries.

[2] How oft in vain ... undergo] *Ah quoties frustra pulsatos aequore montes | Obruit illa dies! Quam celsa cacumina pessum | Tellus victa dedit!*, 'O how often that day were mountains struck in vain by the sea! What lofty pinnacles did the conquered earth yield to the bottom!' (v. 615–17).

[3] monstrous waves] *monstriferos ... sinus*, 'monster-bearing' waves (v. 620); Romans believed the earth was girdled by the ocean, 'the main sea' (v. 619).

[4] heaven's high king] *rector Olympi*, 'the ruler of Olympus', i.e. Jupiter (v. 620).

[5] From natural causes] *Non coeli nox illa fuit*, 'that night was not the sky's' (v. 627): commentaries took this to mean the darkness was not caused by the normal passage of the sun under the earth.

[6] the damps of Acheron] *infernae pallore domus*, 'with the paleness of the infernal abode' (v. 628). Possibly echoing Fulke Greville, *Alaham* (Prol., 8–10): 'Nor from the loathsome puddle Acheron, | ... Whose filthy dampes feed Lethe's sink', in *Certaine learned and elegant vvorkes of the Right Honorable Fulke Lord Brooke* (London: E[lizabeth] P[urslowe] for Henry Seyle, 1633).

[7] The lightning's light] Omitting *metuenda*, 'light to be feared' (v. 630).

[8] old confusion] *chaos* in L. (v. 634).

The elemental concord seemed undone,
And night, that mixed th'ethereal deities
With the infernal,[1] seemed again to rise.
Their hope of safety was that in this great
735 Wreck of the world they were not perished yet.
As far as you from Leucas' top may see
The quiet sea, so far could they descry   *catch sight of*
From waves' high tops the troubled ocean;[2]
But when the swelling billows fall again,
740 The mainmast-top scarce above water stands:
The topsails touch the clouds, the keel the sands.
For ground is seen from whence the seas arise
In hills; in waves the seas' whole water is.
Fear conquers art: the master does not know
745 Which wave to break, which wave to yield unto.
But the seas' discord only aids them now:
The barque one billow cannot overthrow,
Let by another's force which still sustains   *hindered*
The yielding side; the barque upright maintains
750 Her course, supported by all winds. No more
Low Sason's gulfs, Thessalia's crooked shore,
Or the Ambracian dangerous ports they feared,
But o'er the high Ceraunia to be reared
By billows. Caesar thinks it now to be
755 A danger worthy of his destiny:
'Are the gods troubled so to ruin me,[3]
Whom sitting here in a small barque', quoth he,
'They have assaulted with a storm so loud?[4]
If on the seas, not wars, they have bestowed
760 The glory of my death, fearless I come,
Ye gods, to any death that ye can doom:
Though this too hasty fate great acts break off,
I have already done things great enough.
The northern nations I have tamed, and quelled
765 My foes at home by arms:[5] Rome has beheld

---

[1] th'ethereal ... infernal] L., more simply, has *manes mistura Deis*, '[a night that would] mix ghosts with the gods' (v. 636).
[2] ocean] Here, as often in line-endings, trisyllabic.
[3] Are the gods ... me] *tantusne evertere ... | Me superis labor est?*, 'is it so great a task for the gods to overwhelm me?' (v. 654-55).
[4] with a storm so loud] *Tam magno ... mari*, 'in so vast a sea' (v. 656).
[5] and quelled ... arms] *inimica subegi | Arma metu*, 'I subdued my domestic enemies' forces by fear' (v. 661-62).

	Great Pompey my inferior; honours stayed	*withheld*
	From me in war, the people forced have paid.[1]	
	All Roman honours in my titles be.[2]	
	Let it be known, Fortune, to none but thee[3]	
770	(Though full of honour to the shades below	
	I both Rome's consul and dictator go)	
	I die a private death. O gods, I crave	
	No funeral:[4] let the sea's inmost wave	
	Keep my torn carcass; let me want a tomb	
775	And funeral pile, whilst looked-for still to come	*pyre*
	Into all lands I am, and ever feared.'	
	Thus having spoke (most strange) the tenth wave reared	
	His barque aloft, nor from the billow's top	
	Did she fall down, kept by the water up,	
780	'Til on the rocky shore she stood at last.	
	His fortune and so many kingdoms (cast	
	On shore) and towns again he did receive.	
	Caesar's return next morn could not deceive	[v. 678]
	His soldiers so, as his stol'n flight had done.	
785	About their general flock they every one,	
	Assaulting him with lamentations	
	And not ingrateful accusations:	
	'Whither did thy rash valour carry thee,	
	Too cruel Caesar?[5] To what destiny	
790	Did'st thou leave us, poor souls, venturing upon	
	Th'unwilling seas and storms thyself alone?	
	In thee to seek for death was cruelty,	
	When all the world esteems thy head so high,	
	And on thy life so many lives of ours[6]	
795	Depend. Did none of us deserve t'have power	
	Not to survive thee? Sleep did us detain	
	While thou wert tossed upon the wat'ry main.[7]	

[1] paid] M.'s idiom; L.'s Caesar refers to carrying the *fasces*, symbols of magistracy (v. 663); cf. 1. 194n.
[2] All ... be] M.'s 'honours' here translates *potestas*: L.'s Caesar says that his titles comprise all Roman political authority (v. 664), i.e. making him a de facto monarch.
[3] but thee] Omitting *quae sola meorum | Conscia votorum es*, 'you who are the only witness to my wishes' (v. 665–66).
[4] funeral] Trisyllabic; at 775 below, contracted.
[5] cruel] *dure*, 'hard, unfeeling' (v. 682).
[6] so many lives of ours] *tot ... populorum vita salusque*, 'the life and safety of so many peoples' (v. 685).
[7] thou ... main] M.'s idiom, 'the wat'ry main' possibly echoing Shakespeare, Sonnet 64. 7;

Was this the cause thou went'st to Italy?¹
(Alas it shames us) it was cruelty
800 To venture any man on such a sea;
For the last act of things such hazards be.²
Why dost thou tire the gods so much, to go
And venture the world's greatest captain so?³
From Fortune's work and favour thus t'have sent
805 Thee safe a-shore to us, be confident
Of the war's issue. This use dost thou make
Of the gods' favour — to escape a wreck
Rather than gain the world's sole sovereignty?'⁴
Thus while they talk, night past, the sun they see,
810 And a clear day; his waves the tirèd main
(By the winds' leave) composed and smoothed again.
    The captains also on th'Italian side,   [v. 703]⁵
When the tired ocean free from waves they spied,
By the pure north wind's rising thence conveyed
815 Their ships, which their skilled mariners had stayed
So long for fear, while winds auspicious failed.
Like a land army their joined navy sailed
On the broad sea, but the changed winds by night
Filled not their sails,⁶ but broke the order quite.
820 So cranes in winter Strymon's cold forsake
To drink warm Nile,⁷ and in their first flight make
(As chance directs) of letters various forms,⁸
When their spread wings are by the violent storms
Of strong south winds assailèd; by and by

L. has *cum te raperet mare*, 'while the sea was seizing you' (v. 689).
¹ Was this ... Italy] As F. explains, 'this' (*haec*, v. 691) probably means the intention of retrieving Caesar's remaining troops.
² For the last act ... be] *sors ultima rerum | In dubios casus, & prona pericula mortis | Praecipitare solet*, 'it is the ultimate risk/chance/destiny of events that tends to rush [men] into dubious chances and life-threatening dangers' (v. 692–93).
³ world's greatest captain] *mundi iam summa tenentem*, 'one holding the highest position in the world' (v. 694).
⁴ to escape ... sole sovereignty?] *non rector ut orbis, | Nec dominus rerum, sed felix naufragus esses?*, 'not to be ruler of the world or master of the state but a lucky ship-wreck survivor?' (v. 697–98).
⁵ 5. 812–31] Antony's fleet now joins with Caesar.
⁶ Filled not their sails] *velique tenorem | Eripuit nautis*, 'seized grip of the sails from the sailors' (v. 709–10).
⁷ warm Nile] M.'s epithet.
⁸ of letters various forms] Simply *varias... figuras*, 'various shapes', in L. (v. 713), but M. infers the detail from 5. 826.

825 In a confusèd globe all mingled fly;[1]
The letter's lost in their disrankèd wings. *thrown out of rank*
But the next morn, when rising Titan brings *the sun*
A stronger wind to drive the navy o'er,
They pass the vain-attempted Lissus shore
830 And to Nymphaeum come. South winds that blow
The haven on them (the north winds fled) bestow.
    When Caesar's legions all collected were, [v. 722–815][2]
And Pompey saw the war was drawn so near
To his own camp, he thinks best to provide
835 For his wife's safety, and in Lesbos hide
Thee, fair Cornelia, from the noise of war.
Alas in just and noble minds how far
Prevails true love?[3] True love alone had power
To make great Pompey fear war's doubtful hour.
840 His wife alone he wished free from that stroke
That all the world and Rome's whole fortune shook.[4]
But now a ready mind wants words in him:
He yields to sweet delays, from fate steals time.
But when th'approaching morn had banishèd rest,
845 And fair Cornelia, his care-wounded breast[5]
Clasping, from her averted husband seeks
A loving kiss, wond'ring to feel his cheeks
Moistened with tears, the hidden cause she fears,[6]
And dares not find great Pompey shedding tears.
850 He then thus mourning spake: 'O dearest wife,
Dearer to me than life[7] — not now, when life
I loathe — but in our best prosperity,

---

[1] In a confusèd globe] L.'s plural, *confusos ... orbes*, 'into confused spheres' (v. 715), is a little clearer.

[2] 5. 832–939] Pompey parts tearfully from his wife Cornelia, sending her to Lesbos for the duration of the conflict.

[3] how far ... true love] *quantum mentes dominatur in aequas | Iusta Venus!*, 'how much does rightful Love overmaster balanced minds!' (v. 727–28). L.'s language of 'balanced minds' draws on Stoic notions of imperturbability. M. creates his own balance with the 'true love' that follows (merely *amor*, 'love', in L. (v. 729)). L. addresses lines 838–41 (= v. 728–31) to Pompey.

[4] that stroke ... whole fortune] The stroke is Fortune's in L., *ictu | Fortunae* (v. 729–30); 'Rome's whole fortune' translates *Romanaque fata*, 'the fates/destiny of Rome' (v. 730).

[5] care-wounded breast] *gravidum ... curis | Pectus*, 'a breast weighed down [or pregnant] with cares' (v. 735–36).

[6] the hidden cause she fears] M.'s idiom; *percussaque caeco | Vulnere*, '[Cornelia], struck by a hidden wound' (v. 737–38).

[7] Dearer ... life] *dulcior*, 'sweeter' (v. 739).

LUCAN'S PHARSALIA

    That sad day's come which too too much have we,
    Yet not enough deferred. Caesar's addressed
855 For fight:[1] thou must not stay. Lesbos the best
    And safest place will be for thee to hide.
    Do not entreat me, sweet:[2] I have denied
    It to myself. Nor absent long shall we
    Remain,[3] for swift will this war's trial be:
860 Great things fall speedily.[4] To hear, not see
    Thy Pompey's danger is enough for thee.
    Thy love deceives me, if thou couldst endure
    To see this fight; for me to sleep secure
    With thee (this war begun) and from thine arms
865 To rise, were shame, when the war's loud alarms
    Shake all the world; and that thy Pompey came
    Sad with no loss to such a war were shame.[5]
    Nor shall thy husband's fortune altogether
    Oppress thee, far removed safer than either
870 People or king. And should the gods contrive
    My death,[6] let Pompey's better part survive,
    And a place be, whither I may desire,
    If fate and Caesar vanquish,[7] to retire.'
    Her weakness could not such great grief contain: [v. 759]
875 Her senses fled, she did amazed remain.[8]
    At length when sad complaints these words could frame,
    'My lord,' quoth she,[9] 'I have no cause to blame
    Our wedlock's fortune or the gods above:
    No death, no funeral divides our love.[10]

---

[1] Caesar's addressed | For fight] English military idiom, meaning arrayed in battle formation (*OED*, s.v. 'address', 14); *iam totus adest in proelia Caesar*, 'Caesar is wholly [i.e. with all his forces] present for battle' (v. 742).

[2] sweet] M.'s added endearment; cf. 5. 851n.

[3] Nor ... Remain] *non longos a me patiere recessus*, 'nor will you suffer long withdrawal from me' (v. 745).

[4] speedily] *properante ruina*, 'with sudden collapse' (v. 746).

[5] and that ... shame] *vereor civilibus armis | Pompeium nullo tristem committere damno*, 'I fear lest sad Pompey commit to civil war with no sacrifice' (v. 752–53).

[6] contrive | My death] *nostras impulerint acies*, 'overthrow our armies' (v. 756–57).

[7] Caesar] *victorque cruentus*, 'the bloody victor' (v. 758).

[8] she did amazed remain] M.'s wording; in L. the senses simply flee from her 'astonished breast', *attonito ... pectore* (v. 760).

[9] My lord] *Magne*, 'Magnus' (v. 767).

[10] no funeral ... love] Simplifying L.'s *Nec diri fax summa rogi*, 'nor the final torch [to light] the dread pyre' (v. 763–64).

880   We part the common and plebeian way:[1]
        For fear of war Cornelia must not stay.
        Let's be divorced to gratify the foe,
        Since he's at hand. Pompey, esteem'st thou so
        My faith, or think'st thou anything can be
885   Safer to me than thee? Depend not we
        Upon one chance? Can'st cruel thou command
        Thy absent wife this ruin's shock to stand?
        Or think'st thou it a happy state for me
        (While thy chance yet does doubtful stand) to die
890   For fear of future ill?[2] I will attend
        Thy death,[3] but 'til sad fame the news can send
        So far, I shall be forcèd to survive.
        Besides, thou wilt accustom me to grieve,
        And bear so great a sorrow, as I fear
895   (Pardon that I confess) I cannot bear.
        And if the good gods hear my prayers now,
        I last of all the happy news shall know.
        I on the rocks, when thou art conqueror,
        Shall careful sit, and even that ship shall fear
900   That brings the happy news. Nor will my fear
        Have end so soon as I thy conquest hear,
        So far removed from thee that Caesar may
        (Though flying) seize Cornelia as a prey.
        My banishment will Lesbos' shore renown,   *make famous*
905   And make the town of Mytilene known,
        Where Pompey's wife abides.[4] My last request
        Is this: if thou be conquered, and nought rest
        To save thy life but flight, to any bay
        Rather than that turn thy unhappy way.[5]
910   Upon my shore thou wilt be surely sought.'
        This said, from bed she leapt with grief distraught,   [v. 790]

---

[1] We … way] L.'s Cornelia is more critical: *sed sorte frequenti,* | *Plebeiaque nimis careo dimissa marito*, 'by too frequent and plebeian a lot, I lack a husband by being sent away' (v. 764–65).

[2] Or think'st thou … ill] *secura videtur* | *Sors tibi, cum facias etiamnunc vota, perisse* | *Vt nolim servire malis?*, 'Seems it to you an easy lot to have already perished, even while you pray for success, merely so that I shouldn't want to be enslaved to ills?' (v. 771–73). Modern editions mark a period after *perisse* and take *Vt nolim*… with the next sentence.

[3] I will attend | Thy death] *morte parata* | *Te sequar ad manes*, 'ready for death I will follow you to the shades' (v. 773–74).

[4] the town … abides] In L. *Mytileneas… latebras*, 'Mytilenean hide-out' (v. 786).

[5] unhappy way] *infaustam … carinam*, 'ill-omened vessel' (v. 789).

Her words with no delays to interlace,
Nor could she then her lord's sad breast embrace,[1]
Nor hang about his neck: the last fruit's gone
915 Of so long love, their griefs they hasten on,
And at the parting neither had the power
To say farewell. Never so sad an hour
In all their lives had they. Succeeding woes
Their minds by custom hardened could compose.[2]
920 She fainting falls,[3] and in her servants' hands
Lifted is borne to sea; but on the sands
She falls as if that shore she fain would keep.[4]   *gladly*
At last perforce she's carried to the ship.   *by force*
From her dear country's shore not so distressed
925 Fled she, when Caesar Italy possessed.[5]
With Pompey then she went: now all alone,
Wanting that guide, she from her lord is gone.[6]
Sleepless she spent in her now widowed bed
Cold and alone the night that followèd.[7]
930 That side that naked used not to be left,
Is of a husband's company bereft.
Oft would she, when her sleepy arms she spread,
With hands deceived embrace the empty bed:
Seeking her lord, her flight she would forget.
935 For, though love's flame fed on her marrow, yet
O'er all the bed she would not tumbling spread.[8]
Fearing to miss her lord, that part of bed
She kept, but fate did not so well ordain;[9]
The hour's at hand that brings her lord again.[10]

FINIS.

---

[1] embrace] 'clasp in a sweet embrace', *Sustinet amplexu dulci* (v. 793).
[2] minds by custom hardened] *Durata iam mente malis*, 'with mind now hardened by misfortunes' (v. 798).
[3] fainting falls] *Labitur infelix*, 'wretched, she swoons' (v. 799).
[4] as if ... keep] Added by M.; in L. she simply clings to the shore (v. 800).
[5] dear country's shore ... possessed] *patriam portusque ...| Hesperios, saevi premerent cum Caesaris arma*, 'while the forces of cruel Caesar oppressed the country and ports of Italy' (v. 803). In fact, Caesar's capture of Italy was relatively bloodless, possibly explaining M.'s rewording.
[6] from her lord is gone] *Pompeiumque fugit*, 'flees from Pompey' (v. 805); for M.'s use of 'lord' see 5. 877n.
[7] Sleepless ... followèd] In L., lines 5. 928–29 (= v. 805–06) address Cornelia.
[8] she would not] *Non iuvat*, 'it does not help her to' (v. 812).
[9] fate] *superi*, 'the gods above' (v. 814).
[10] her lord] 'Magnus' (*Magnum*, v. 815); cf. 5. 877n.

Annotations on the Fifth Book

(a) Pompey's losses, as we saw before in the second, third and fourth books, were these: all his garrisons beaten out of Italy, and himself driven from thence; Massilia sacked; all Spain lost, together with his army under the conduct of Afranius and Petreius. Caesar's losses: a cohort of Opitergians, which installed themselves on the Illyrian sea with their captain Vulteius, and Curio killed by king Juba.[1]

(b) Phocis was then made free as well as Massilia her colony, which Caesar besieged.

(c) Deiotarus king of Galatia brought to the army of Pompey six hundred horsemen.

(d) Cotys king of Thracia sent to the army five hundred horsemen under the conduct of his son Sadalis.

(e) Rhasipolis brought from Macedonia two hundred horsemen.[2]

(f) Ptolemy defrauded his sister Cleopatra of her share in the kingdom, and in killing Pompey saved Caesar the doing of that impious act.

(g) Appius the governor of Achaea, desirous to know the event of the civil war, compelled the chief priest of Delphos to descend to the oracle, which had not of a long time been used.[3]

(h) In the midst of the hill there was a deep hole into the earth, out of which came a cold spirit, as it were a wind, and filled the prophetesses with a fury so that they instantly prophesied of things to come.[4]

(i) Appius, thinking this oracle had warned him only to abstain from this war, retired himself into that country which lieth between Rhamnus, and Carystes, called Caela Euboea, where before the battle of Pharsalia he died of a disease, and was there buried, and so possessed quietly the place which the oracle had promised him.[5]

(k) Caesar was now returned to Placentia from Spain where he had conquered Afranius and Petreius two of Pompey's lieutenants, and was going from thence into Epire and Macedonia against Pompey; in the meantime this mutiny happened.[6]

(l) Caesar cashiered with ignominy all the ninth legion at Placentia; and with much ado after many prayers received them again, but not without taking

---

[1] Translating F.'s note (on v. 1), with expansions taken from L.'s own narrative.
[2] Notes (b) to (e) translate F.'s notes (on v. 53–55).
[3] Translating F.'s note (on v. 68), itself taken from Valerius Maximus (I. 8. 10). M. adds the detail of the oracle's falling out of use.
[4] Translating F.'s note (on v. 83).
[5] Translating F.'s note (on v. 224), itself taken from Valerius Maximus (I. 8. 10). M. adds 'quietly', to stress the irony.
[6] Loosely following F.'s notes (on v. 237–44).

punishment of the chief mutineers.¹

(m) Caesar made himself Dictator at Rome without a lawful election, that is neither named by the Senate nor consul; but eleven days after he left his dictatorship, having made himself and Publius Servilius consuls.²

(n) Then began all those names of flattery, which they afterward used to their emperor, as Divus, Ever Augustus, Father of his country, Founder of peace, Lord and the like.³

(o) After all government was in the hands of Caesar alone, all the ancient rites in creating of magistrates were quite taken away; an imaginary face of election was in the field of Mars; the tribes were cited, but were not admitted distinctly and in the true form to give their suffrages. The other orders were but vain; for the emperor commended him to the centuries whom he would have consul; or else designed him and chose him himself. There augury also was abused, and the augurers interpreted everything as they were compelled.⁴

(p) Under the emperors, consuls were oft chosen for half a year, for one, two or three months.⁵

(q) Pompey was then in Candavia; but when he heard that Caesar was come, and was possessed of Oricum, and Apollonia, he hasted to Dyrrachium. Caesar pitched his tents at one side of the river Apsus, and Pompey at the other.⁶

(r) Caesar, having landed his men the same night, sent back the ships to Brundisium for Antonius to transport the rest of his legions and his horsemen, whose slow coming made Caesar defer the fight.⁷

(s) This Marcus Antonius after the death of Julius Caesar had war with Augustus, by whom he was vanquished in a sea fight near Leucas.⁸

(t) When part of the army for want of ships stayed at Brundisium under Antonius, Gabinius and Calenus, Caesar impatient of delay resolved to go himself as a messenger to call them in a stormy night, and a little vessel, some say a boat that would bear twelve oars; but unknown to all his army he passed in a disguised habit through all the courts of guard, and went to sea.⁹

---

¹ Translating F.'s note (on v. 370), itself derived from Suetonius, *Divus Julius*, LXIX, in Suetonius, I, p. 120.
² Translating F.'s note (on v. 383).
³ Translating F.'s note (on v. 389) but adding 'of flattery' and omitting F.'s 'lest the right of oppression be lacking to the sword (*ne quod ferro saeviendi ius deesset*)'.
⁴ Closely following F.'s dense explication (on v. 392, 395); note especially the mention of 'the Emperor' (*Imperator*). But the idiom of 'all government' is M.'s, as is the vague 'other orders' instead of F.'s specific reference to the way names were cast in voting boxes (*cistas*) in Roman electoral procedure. M. also compresses a long note on the augurs into a simpler description of their coercion by the Caesars.
⁵ Following F.'s notes (on v. 398) but adding 'under the emperors'.
⁶ Translating F.'s note (on v. 461).
⁷ Translating F.'s note (on v. 476).
⁸ Translating F.'s note (on v. 479).
⁹ Compressing the notes of F. (on v. 503), which discuss how certain historians (Florus, Dio Cassius, Appian and Plutarch) differ about the type of vessel Caesar used.

To the Right Honourable William Earl of Devon: &c.[1]

To your most noble censure (honoured lord,   *evaluation*
Great in your virtues, as your fortunes, stored   *furnished*
With all things that first made nobility)[2]
Lucan appeals from the bold injury
5 Of cruel critics, who deny the name
Of poet to him, and presents this same
Sixth book to be his plea: this book, of all
His famed *Pharsalia*, most poetical.[3]
Here, if Erictho's horrid height, in spells
10 Blacker than night or her imagined hells,
Pass not the rites which Horace has bestowed
On dire Canidia, or Medea owed
To Ovid's wit; if this excel not all,
Under a noble judge let Lucan fall.[4]

---

[1] To the Right Honourable] William Cavendish, second Earl of Devonshire (1590–1628); also the dedicatee of the whole translation. Cavendish inherited the earldom in early 1626. He opposed Buckingham in the Lords during the 1626 Parliament and initially resisted paying the Forced Loan, though he ultimately subscribed in December 1627 (Christopher N. Warren, *Literature and the Law of Nations, 1580–1680* (Oxford: Oxford University Press, 2015), pp. 133–35). Cavendish's colonial interests brought him into conflict with Robert Rich, Earl of Warwick and the dedicatee of May's book nine: the privy council prevented them from duelling in 1623.

[2] honoured lord … nobility] M.'s stress on virtuous nobility echoes the language of many other dedicatory poems, and also his praise of Cavendish in his dedicatory epistle (p. 38) as having the 'deep judgment' of a learned aristocrat.

[3] Of cruel critics … most poetical] A riposte to early modern critics who thought Lucan more historian than poet (see Introduction, pp. 9–10), and again anticipated in M.'s dedicatory epistle to Cavendish.

[4] Erictho's horrid height … let Lucan fall] Praising L.'s witch Erictho, one of the great set pieces of the poem (see 6. 572–946). M.'s 'horrid height' recalls L.'s description of her *coma … horrida*, 'bristling hair' (VI. 656; not directly translated by M.), but also, more figuratively, her sublime fearsomeness — M. was later to use 'horrid height' to describe Revenge in his *Edward III*, sig. M1^v. 'Height' in both the terrifying and transporting sublime senses is a keynote of M.'s engagement with L., occurring frequently in his prefatory materials; here it is probably inspired by Ben Jonson's praise of Erictho in his notes to *The Masque of Queenes* (1609) as written with 'the most admirable height' and being the 'most horrid' of ancient literary witches (Jonson, *Works*, III, pp. 339, 343), including Ovid's Medea (*Metamorphoses*, VII. 1–403) and Horace's Canidia (*Epodi*, 3, 5 and 17; *Sermones*, I. 8. 24 ff., II. 1. 48 ff., II. 8. 95 ff., in *Opera*, ed. by Wickham and Garrod (Oxford: Clarendon Press, 1901)), to whom M. also compares her: see Jonson, *The Complete Masques*, pp. 533, 537.

LUCAN'S
Pharsalia

The Sixth Book.

The Argument of the Sixth Book.[1]

Caesar, enclosing Pompey with a fence
And trenches of a vast circumference,
Endures a famine, Pompey pestilence,
Who breaking through escapes a conqueror thence.[2]
5 Brave Scaeva's valour, and admirèd fight.[3]
Into Thessalia Caesar takes his flight;
Great Pompey follows: the description,
And poets' tales, that Thessaly renown.   *make famous*
To the dire witch Erictho Sextus goes,
10 This fatal war's sad issue to disclose:[4]   *outcome*
She quickens a dead carcass, which relates
To Sextus' ear his and his father's fates,
And craving then death's freedom to obtain,[5]
Is by a magic spell dissolved again.

When on near [(a)]hills both generals, fierce [(b)]of fight,[6]   [VI. 1][7] *neighbouring*
Had pitched their tents and drawn their troops in sight,
And the gods saw their match,[8] Caesar in Greece
Scorns to take towns or owe the destinies
5 For any conquest but his son-in-law's.   *Pompey's*

---

[1] The Argument] See Argument to book one.
[2] escapes a conqueror thence] i.e. 'escapes as a victor' not 'escapes the conqueror Caesar'.
[3] Scaeva's ... fight] Cassius Scaeva, a centurion of Caesar (see 6. 153–294).
[4] Sextus goes...] Sextus Pompey, Pompey's younger son. Lines 9–14 are quoted, together with whole passages of M.'s translation, during a discussion of grave-robbing in John Weever's *Ancient Funerall Monuments*, pp. 43–45.
[5] death's freedom to obtain] Not in M.'s model, the *argumentum* of Sulpizio, but expressing his frequent neo-Stoic emphasis on self-slaughter as freedom; cf. 2. 300 ff. (Cato) and 4. 523 ff. (Vulteius). See also Introduction, pp. 10–11.
[6] fierce of fight] *pugnae iam mente propinqui*, 'likeminded in wishing to fight' (VI. 1); modern editions read *propinquis ... iugis*, '[the generals drew up their troops] on neighbouring peaks'.
[7] 1–152] The siege of Dyrrachium.
[8] their match] *Parque suum* (VI. 3), 'their own pair', in the sense of gladiatorial opponents.

> The world's sad hour, that to a trial draws
> This war's main chance,[1] he wishes for alone,
> That cast of fortune that must ruin one.[2]
> Thrice on the hills his battle he arrayed,   *laid out*
> 10 And all his threat'ning eagles thrice displayed,
> Showing that he would never wanting be   *lacking*
> T'o'erthrow the Roman state.[3] But when he see   *sees that*
> No provocations could his son-in-law
> (Who close-entrenchèd lay) to battle draw,
> 15 From thence ^(c)he marched by woody passages
> And close, to take Dyrrachium's fortresses.[4]   *concealed*
> Thither a nearer way great Pompey takes   [VI. 15]
> Along the shore, and on high Petra makes
> His camp, to guard from thence Dyrrachium town,[5]
> 20 Safe (without men) by her own strength alone.[6]
> No human labour, no old structure made
> Her fence, which would (though ne'er so lofty) fade
> By force of war, or eating time o'ertaken.[7]
> A strength that by no engine can be shaken[8]
> 25 Her site and nature give; the sea profound
> And steep wave-breaking rocks enclose it round;
> But for one little hill an island 'twere;

---

[1] The world's sad hour, that to a trial draws] Translating *Funestam mundo ... horam*, 'the deadly hour for the world' and *In casum quae cuncta ferat*, 'which brings all to its outcome' (VI. 6-7).

[2] cast of fortune] *alea fati*, 'the die of fate' (VI. 7); both L. and M. recall Caesar's alleged *iacta alea est*, 'the die is cast', after crossing the Rubicon: see Suetonius, *Divus Julius*, XXII, in *Suetonius* I, pp. 76–77.

[3] To o'erthrow the Roman state] *Testatus nunquam Latiae se deesse ruinae*, 'bearing witness that he would never be absent from Latium's ruin' (VI. 10). M. follows F.'s *paratumque ad evertendum Rom. imperium*, 'and prepared to overthrow Roman government'.

[4] he marched ... fortresses] Omitting *praeceps*, 'rapidly/headlong' (VI. 14), a key attribute of L.'s Caesar.

[5] high Petra ... Dyrrachium town] Simplifying L.'s *quemque vocat collem Taulantius incola Petram*, 'and the hill which the native of Taulantii calls Petra' and *Ephyreaque moenia*, 'Ephyrean [i.e. Corinthian] fortifications' (VI. 16–17); Dyrrachium was supposedly a Corinthian colony.

[6] Safe ... alone] *tutam vel solis turribus*, 'safe purely by her towers alone' (VI. 18); the modern reading is *rupibus*, 'rocky terrain'. M. follows F.'s phrase *sine exercitu*, 'without an army'.

[7] eating time o'ertaken] *cuncta moventibus annis*, 'time moving all things' (VI. 21). The motif of eating time, originally from Ovid's *tempus edax rerum*, 'time devourer of all things' (*Metamorphoses*, X. 234), was common in early modern literature.

[8] engine] *nullo quassabile ferro*, 'shakable by no iron' (VI. 22), i.e. the sword or (figuratively) military force, but M. implies a siege engine.

	Ship-threat'ning rocks sustain the walls, and there	
	Th'Ionian Sea, raised by the south wind's blasts,	
30	Her temples shakes, and frothy foamings casts	
	O'er houses' tops. War-thirsty Caesar then[1]	[VI. 29]
	Conceived[(d)] a cruel hope, spreading his men[2]	
	Round on the hills, from every side t'enclose	
	With joinèd trenches his unwary foes:	
35	And all the ground surveying with his eye	
	Is not content alone to fortify	
	His works with brittle earth, but weighty stone	
	From quarries digs; vast rocks, houses torn down	
	And Greekish walls brought thither make a fence,	
40	Able the ram's assaulting violence	
	And all war's furious engines to withstand.	
	Hills levelled, valleys raised, make even land	
	In Caesar's works, with trenches wide enclosed	
	And towered castles on the hills disposed.	
45	With a vast circuit he takes in the ground,	
	About the pastures, woods and shelters round,	
	As 'twere for deer spreading a wide-stretched toil.[3]	*net*
	Pompey no room nor pasture wants, for while	*lacks*
	He thus enclosed by Caesar's trenches is,	
50	He removes camps (so many rivers rise,	
	And their whole course within this circuit run):	
	And Caesar, tired going to look upon	
	His works, makes often stays. Let ancient tales	[VI. 48] *stops often*
	To the gods' work ascribe the Trojan walls;	*attribute*
55	Let flying Parthians still admire alone	
	The brittle earth-built walls of Babylon.[4]	
	As far as Tigris and Orontes run,	
	As the Assyrian kings' dominion	
	Stretched in the east, a sudden work of war	
60	Encloses here. Lost those great labours are.[5]	

[1] War-thirsty Caesar] *avidam belli ... mentem*, 'mind eager for war' (VI. 29).
[2] spreading his men] Reading *diffusus*, Caesar 'spreading' his troops, rather than *diffusum ... hostem* (VI. 30), the 'spread-out enemy' he sought to encircle, which is the modern and often early modern reading. F. notes *diffusus* as a variant.
[3] deer] *feras*, 'wild beasts' (VI. 42).
[4] earth-built walls of Babylon] M. adds 'earth-built', perhaps to contrast with the god-built walls of Troy.
[5] Lost ... labours are] *tanti periere labores*, 'such great works perished there' (VI. 54). M. preserves L.'s obscurity — does this mean Caesar's gargantuan fortifications would swallow up Assyria, or that his efforts would be in vain when Pompey duly escaped?

So many hands would to Abydos put
Sestos, fill up the Hellespont, and cut
Corinth from Pelops' land, and from the seas   *the Peloponnese*
Take long Malea for the sailors' ease,
65 Or mend some part (though nature should deny)
Of the world's structure. Here war's quarters lie,
Here feeds that blood that in all lands must flow,[1]
The Libyan and Thessalian overthrow.
War's civil fury boils, kept straitly in.[2]   *narrowly*
70   The work's first structure Pompey had not seen,   [VI. 64]
As who in midst of Sicily safe dwell
When rough Pelorus barks, can never tell;[3]
As northern Britons cannot hear the roar
Of flowing seas against the Kentish shore.[4]
75 But when himself begirt so far he knew   *surrounded*
By a vast trench, he from safe Petra drew
His troops, and o'er the hills disposed them so
To keep the ranks of his besieging foe
More thin, and took of the enclosèd ground
80 As much in length, as is true distance found
'Twixt lofty Rome and th'Aricinian wood
Where Scythian Dian's adored image stood;[5]
As far as Tiber's stream from Rome's walls ends
By straight account, not as the river bends.[6]
85 No trumpets sound; piles uncommanded fly;
Mischief's oft done as they their javelins try.
Both chiefs are kept from fight by greater care:
Pompey, because his pasture fields are bare;
The ground he had by horse o'ertrampled was,

---

[1] Here feeds the blood] Reading *alitur*, 'is fed by' (VI. 61); some modern editions print *capitur*, 'is captured by'. The meaning is that all the republican blood spilt later in the civil war is contained in Caesar's siege.

[2] War's civil fury ... in] *Aestuat angusta rabies civilis arena*, 'the civil fury boils in a narrow arena' (VI. 63).

[3] When rough Pelorus barks] i.e. Sicily (Pelorus is a mountain of that island); 'barks' alludes to Scylla, the dog-girt monster in the straits of Messina (see 1. 583n).

[4] northern Britons ... Kentish shore] L. refers to *Rutupinaque litora*, 'the shores of Rutupinum' (VI. 67), which as F. says and M. probably knew is now Richborough in Kent, and *Caledonios Britannos*, 'the Caledonian Britons', i.e. Scots (VI. 68).

[5] As much in length ... image stood] See 3. 92 and note. L. has *Mycenaeae Dianae* (VI. 74), referring to the story (reported by F.) that Orestes, heir of the kingdom of Mycenae, transported an image of Scythian Diana to the Aricinian wood.

[6] As far as ... bends] i.e. the distance as the crow flies between Rome and the mouth of the Tiber at Ostia, approximately sixteen miles.

90	Whose horny hooves trod down the springing grass;	
	The war-like steed, wearied in those bared fields,	
	When the full rack provender far-brought yields,	
	Tasting his new-brought food, falls down and dies,	
	Treading the ring, failed by his trembling thighs.	*in a circle*
95	Their bodies waste by dire consumption:	
	The unstirred air draws moist contagion	
	Into a pestilential cloud; such breath	
	Nasis exhales from her dark caves beneath;	
	Such poisoned air, where buried Typhon lies,	
100	The ground sends forth; apace the army dies.[1]	
	The water from the air infection taking,	
	With costiveness torments the bowels aching,	*constipation*
	Dries their discoloured skin; their blood-swoll'n eyes	
	Do break, the fiery plague with botches flies	*tumours*
105	All o'er the face, their heavy heads fall down.	
	Now more and more sudden their death was grown,[2]	
	'Twixt life and death the sickness has no room,	
	But death does with the first faint symptoms come.[3]	
	By carcasses, which all unburied lie,	
110	Among the living grows mortality.	
	'Twas all the soldiers' burial to be cast[4]	
	Out of the tents. This plague was stayed at last	
	By blasts of strong air-stirring northern wind,	
	Ships fraught with corn, the shore and sea behind.	*stocked*
115	But Caesar,[5] free upon the spacious hills,	[VI. 106]
	No pestilence from air or water feels,	
	But (as if strait besieged) a famine strong	*narrowly*
	Is forced to suffer, corn as yet not sprong	*sprung*
	To the full height. His wretched men he sees	
120	Fall to beasts' food, eat grass, and rob the trees	
	Of leaves and tender twigs, and venturing more,	
	Death-threat'ning herbs from roots unknown they tore.	

---

[1] such breath | Nasis ... dies] Allusion to the poisonous fumes exhaled by volcanoes at Nisita and Etna, under which the giant Typhon was allegedly buried (cf. 4. 658, 6. 330). Most early modern editions read *Nesis*.

[2] Now ... grown] *Iam magis atque magis praeceps agit omnia fatum*, 'Now more and more headlong death (*fatum*) drives all' (VI. 98).

[3] But ... symptoms come] *Sed languor cum morte venit*, 'but languor comes with death' (VI. 100).

[4] soldiers'] *miseros ... cives*, 'wretched citizens' (VI. 102).

[5] Caesar] *hostis*, 'the enemy' (VI. 107).

Whatever they could bite, soften with heat,
Or through their wounded palates down could get,
125 And things, that human tables ne'er did know,
Content to eat, besieged^(e) their full-fed foe.
    When through the trenches Pompey pleased to make   [VI. 118]
His way, and freedom of all lands to take,
He seeks not th'obscure time of dusky night,
130 Scorning to steal a passage free from fight,
But rather force the trenches and break down
The forts,[1] and pass where ruin leads him on,
Through swords and slaughter to enforce his way.[2]
That part of the near trench most fitly lay,
135 Minutius' castle called:[3] trees thickly set,
Making a grove obscure, o'er-shadowed it.
Hither his cohorts, by no dust betrayed
He led, and suddenly the walls assayed.
So many Roman eagles glister round
140 The field at once, so many trumpets sound,
That now to swords the victory nought owes:
Fear had discomfited th'astonished foes.[4]
Yet (wherein valour only could be showed)
That ground where first they stood, they dying strowed.   *strewed*
145 But the Pompeians now want foes to slay:
Whole showers of piles in vain are thrown away.
Then fire rolled up in pitchy stuff they throw
Upon the works: the shaken turrets bow,
Threat'ning a fall, the battered bulwarks groan,
150 Beat by the ram's impetuous fury down,[5]
And o'er the trenches Pompey's eagles fly

---

[1] force the trenches ... The forts] *latis exire ruinis | Quaerit, & impulso turres confringere vallo*, 'He seeks to exit through the wide ruins, and to break down the turrets after upturning the rampart' (VI. 122–23).

[2] to enforce his way] Not a direct translation; cf. M.'s Caesar who 'loves that ruin should enforce his way' (1. 164).

[3] Minutius' castle called] M. (and F.) read *Minuti* (VI. 126): modern editions read *Minici*. F. notes that the name may derive from Appian (*The Civil Wars*, II. 60), who names its commander Minutius/Minucius.

[4] So many ... foes] 6. 141–42 (= VI. 130–31) are part of the same, cynical thought in L.: *ne quid victoria ferro | Deberet, pavor attonitos confecerat hostes*, 'in order that Pompey's victory should owe nothing to the sword, fear had struck the astonished foe'.

[5] ram's ... down] *Roboris impacti crebros gemit agger ad ictus*, 'the rampart groans at the frequent blows of concentrated force' (VI. 137). M.'s inference of a battering-ram echoes F.

To vindicate the Roman liberty.[1]
That place, which not a thousand companies [VI. 140][2]
Nor all the strength of Caesar could surprise,[3]
155 One man alone guards from the conquerors,
Denying Pompey's conquest whilst he wears
A sword, and lives. His name was Scaeva, once
A common soldier of those legions
That served in Gallia, then centurion[4]
160 By blood promoted, to all mischief prone,
And one that knew not in a civil war
How great a crime the soldiers' valours are.
He, when he saw his fellows leaving fight,
And seeking out safe places for their flight,
165 'Whither,' quoth he, 'base slaves and beasts, does fear [VI. 150]
(Unknown to all that arms for Caesar bear)
Drive you? Can you retire without one wound?[5]
Or are you not ashamed not to be found
Among the heap of men? Though faith were gone,[6] *faithfulness*
170 Anger (methinks) should make you fight alone.
We are the men of all through whom the foe
Has chose to break: let this day bloody go
On Pompey's side. I should far happier die
In Caesar's sight, but since the Fates deny[7]
175 Him for a witness, Pompey shall commend
My death. Your breasts and throats undaunted bend
Against their steel, and turn their weapons back.
The dust far off is seen, this ruin's crack
Has by this time entered our general's ears.
180 We conquer, fellows; Caesar straight appears

---

[1] To vindicate the Roman liberty] *iam mundi iura petebant*, 'now they sought the world's laws/rights' (VI. 138-39). The modern reading is *patebant*, 'the world's laws/rights lay open'. F. glosses *mundi iura* as '[eagles] about to set the world free from tyranny into liberty'.

[2] 6. 154-294] Caesar's centurion Scaeva wages a one-man war against the Pompeian forces.

[3] strength of Caesar] *Fortuna* (VI. 141), Caesar's frequent companion.

[4] centurion] *Latiam longo gerit ordine vitem*, 'he carried the Roman vine staff, in the long order [of centurions]' (VI. 146). The ending '-ion', as in the previous line, is disyllabic.

[5] Whither ... wound] Reading *O famuli turpes, servum pecus, absque cruore | Terga datis morti?* ('O shameful slaves, servile herd, do you turn your backs on death without bloodshed?', VI. 152-53); modern editions think the first line spurious, leaving *Terga datis mori*, 'do you turn your backs on death', as a solitary question. L.'s Scaeva also accuses his fellows of *pavor ... impius*, 'undutiful fear' (VI. 150-51).

[6] faith] *pietate*, 'duty/reverence' (VI. 155).

[7] the Fates] *Fortuna* (VI. 159).

	To challenge (though we die) this fort.' His voice	[VI. 165]
	More than th'alarum's first inciting noise	
	Their fury stirred: then, wond'ring at the man,	
	And eager to behold, the soldiers ran	
185	To see if valour, disadvantaged so,	
	Surprised by place and number, could bestow	
	Aught more than death. He, making good alone	
	The falling work, first throws dead bodies down	*fortification*
	From the full tower, to overwhelm the foes.	
190	The posts, the walls, slaughter itself bestows	
	Weapons on him, threat'ning himself to fall	
	Down on their heads, and thrusts off from the wall	
	The breasts of scaling foes with poles and stakes,	
	And with his sword cuts off his hand that takes	
195	Hold on the bulwark's top; and with vast stones	
	Pashes their heads in pieces, breaks their bones,	*smashes*
	And dashes out their weakly-fencèd brains.	
	Down on another's hair and face he rains	
	Pitch fired;[1] the fire whizzes in burning eyes.	*sizzles*
200	But when the piled-up carcasses 'gan rise	[VI. 180] *began to*
	To equal the wall's height, as nimbly then	
	Into the midst of Pompey's armèd men	
	Scaeva leaps down from thence, as libbards fierce	*leopards*
	Break thorough the besetting huntsmen's spears.	*through*
205	Then Scaeva, wedged in round, and by th'whole war	
	Enclosed, yet where he strikes is conqueror.[2]	
	His sword's point dull with blood congealèd grows	
	And blunt, nor does it pierce but bruise his foes.	
	His sword has lost the use, and without wound	
210	It breaks men's limbs. The foes encircling round	
	At him direct their weapons all,[3] and all	
	Their hands aim right, and javelins rightly fall:	
	There fortune a strange match beholds,[4] one man	
	'Gainst a whole war. His strong shield sounded then	
215	With often strokes; his broken helmet, beat	*frequent*

[1] Pitch fired] *flamma*, 'flame' (VI. 178): the technical detail derives from F.
[2] by th'whole war ... is conqueror] *et omni | Vallatus bello vincit, quem respicit, hostem*, 'walled in by the whole war he conquers the enemy whom he sees behind him' (VI. 184–85).
[3] The foes encircling round] Humanizing *Illum tota premit moles, illum omnia tela*, 'the whole mass, all the weapons press upon him' (VI. 189); F. glosses *moles* as 'the mass of the enemy'.
[4] strange match] *Parque novum*, 'a new gladiatorial combat' (VI. 191); cf. 6. 3n.

	Down to his temples, wrings with pain and heat,	*twists, is squeezed*
	And nothing else protects his vital parts	
	But th'outside of his flesh struck full of darts.¹	
	Why with light darts and arrows do you strive	[VI. 196]
220	(Vain fools) such wounds as cannot kill to give?²	
	Let the phalaric strong her wildfire throw,³	*javelin*
	Or massy walls of stone 'gainst such a foe:	
	Let batt'ring rams, and war's vast engines all	
	Remove him thence;⁴ he stands for Caesar's wall	
225	'Gainst Pompey's course. His breast no arms now hide:	
	Scorning to use a shield,⁵ lest his left side	
	Should want a wound and he be forced to live	
	By his own fault, what wounds the war can give	
	He takes alone; and bearing a thick wood	
230	Of darts upon his breast, now wearied stood	
	Choosing what foe to fall on. So at sea	
	Do whales and monstrous beasts of Libya;⁶	
	So a Gaetulian elephant, closed in	
	By hunters round, all shafts from his thick skin	
235	Beats back and breaks, or, moving it,⁷ shakes off	
	The sticking darts (his bowels safe enough)	
	And through those wounds no blood he loses; so	
	So many shafts and darts cannot bestow	
	One death. At last, a Cretan bow let fly	
240	A sure Gortynian shaft: in the left eye	
	Of Scaeva struck the shaft. He, void of fears,	
	The ligaments and optic sinews tears,	
	That th'arrow's forkèd iron head did stay,	

---

¹ th'outside of his flesh] *summis ossibus*, 'the surface of his bones' (VI. 195).
² such wounds as cannot kill] *haesuros nunquam vitalibus ictus*, 'blows that will never stick in the vital parts' (VI. 197).
³ Let the phalaric ... wildfire throw] *Hunc aut tortilibus vibrata phalarica nervis | Obruat*, 'let the phalarica launched from tightened bowstrings overthrow him' (VI. 197-98). The *phalarica* is a javelin wrapped in ignited pitch. M.'s coinage 'phalaric' is rare (see Introduction, p. 17); M.'s added 'wildfire' echoes F.'s English gloss to III. 680 (3. 736-37), which F. references in his commentary on this passage.
⁴ thence] *limine portae*, 'from the threshold of the gate' (VI. 200).
⁵ Scorning to] *veritus* 'fearing to' (VI. 203).
⁶ whales and monstrous beasts of Libya] Seemingly joining *Par pelagi monstris*, 'like the monsters of the sea', with *Libycae sic belua terrae*, 'so the beast of the Libyan land', i.e. the elephant. In modern and many early modern editions (including F.'s) there is a full stop between the two phrases, the second introducing a long simile, but some (e.g. Hortensius, sig. Bc5ʳ) did run the two together. M.'s 'whales' probably follows F.'s gloss *balaenis*.
⁷ it] i.e. its skin.

And kicked the shaft with his own eye away.¹
245 So, if a Libyan loopèd javelin pierce²
The side of a Pannonian bear, more fierce
Grown by her wound she wheels herself about,
Eager to catch the dart and pull it out,
Which still turns with her. Scaeva's looks now bore
250 No fierceness, all his face deformed with gore.
A shout that reached the sky the conquerors raise:
So little blood (though drawn from Caesar's face)³
Could not have joyed them more. But Scaeva now
In his great heart suppressing this deep woe,
255 With a mild look that did no valour show,⁴
'Hold, countrymen,'⁵ quoth he, 'forbear me now;   *spare me*
Wounds further not my death, nor now need I
More weapons in, but these pulled out, to die.
Into the camp of Pompey carry me:
260 Do't for your general's sake, let Scaeva be
Rather the example now of Caesar left,⁶
Than of a noble death.' Aulus beleft   *believed*
These feignèd words of his unhappily,
And did not the sword's point against him see:
265 But as to seize him and his arms he ventures,
His throat the lightning sword of Scaeva enters.
His valour then by this one death renewed
Waxed hot: 'Whoe'er dares think Scaeva subdued,
Thus let him rue', quoth he: 'if from this steel
270 Pompey seek peace, let him to Caesar kneel.⁷
Thought you me like yourselves, fearful and base?⁸

---

¹ kicked … away] *calcat*, 'stamps on' (VI. 219).
² if … pierce] *Cum iaculum parva Libys amentavit habena*, 'when a Libyan has hurled his javelin by means of a small thong' (VI. 221) — a common method of propelling spears in antiquity.
³ though drawn from Caesar's face] *conspectum in Caesare vulnus*, 'a wound glimpsed on Caesar' (VI. 227).
⁴ In his great heart … valour show] Heroizing *Ille tegens alta suppressum mente furorem | Mitis, & a vultu penitus virtute remota*, 'He, mild, covering up the fury concealed deep in his mind, and with virtue utterly removed from his expression' (VI. 258-59). See Introduction, pp. 16-17.
⁵ countrymen] *cives*, 'citizens' (VI. 230).
⁶ of Caesar left] i.e. of having deserted Caesar's command; 'noble death' (6. 262) translates *mortis honestae*, 'worthy death' (VI. 235).
⁷ to Caesar kneel] *adorato summittat Caesare signa*, 'Let him, having supplicated Caesar, lower his standards' (VI. 243).
⁸ fearful and base] Moralistically embroidering *segnemque ad fata*, 'sluggish to one's fate/

You love not Pompey and the Senate's cause
As I love death.' With that, the dust raised high
Gave them all notice Caesar's troops were nigh,
275 And from war's shame did the Pompeians free,
Lest a whole troop should have been thought to flee
From Scaeva only.[1] When the fight was done
He fell and died, for fight (when blood was gone)
Lent strength. His friends taking him as he falls
280 Upon their shoulders to his funerals
Are proud to bear him, and that breast adore
As if some sacred deity it bore,
Or valour's glorious image there did live.[2]
Then all from his transfixèd members strive
285 To pluck the piles, and therewithal they dressed
The gods themselves: on Mars his naked breast,
Scaeva, they put thy arms.[3] How great indeed
Had been thine honour, if those men that fled
Had been the warlike Celtiberians,
290 Germans long-armed or short Cantabrians.[4]
No triumphs now, no spoils of this sad war
Can deck the temple of the Thunderer.
With how great valour, wretch, hast thou procured
A lord?[5] Nor did great Pompey lie immured   [VI. 263][6]
295 And quiet from attempting fight again
At this repulse, no more than th'ocean
Is tired when lifted by strong eastern blast
'Gainst the repelling rocks, and eats at last
The rock's hard side, making, though late, a way.
300 Assaulting then (f)the fort that nearest lay
To th'sea, he takes it by a double war,

---

death' (VI. 244); F. glosses 'unwarlike and fearful of death'.

[1] With that ... Scaeva only] L. addresses Scaeva directly and shames Pompey only (*Magno*, VI. 248), but F. implicates 'the Pompeians' in general.

[2] valour's glorious image] *vivam magnae speciem Virtutis*, 'the living likeness of mighty Virtue' (VI. 254).

[3] they dressed ... thy arms] i.e. Scaeva's men adorn the gods' statues with weapons taken from his body, and that of Mars with Scaeva's own weapons.

[4] warlike Celtiberians ... Cantabrians] *durus Iber ... | Cantaber exiguis aut longis Teutonus armis*, 'the hardy Spaniard ... the German with long weapons and Cantabrian with short ones' (VI. 258-59).

[5] With how ... A lord?] A famous aphorism (VI. 262). L.'s *dominum*, 'master', is more biting, but *infelix*, 'unfortunate', more sympathetic, than M.'s 'lord' and 'wretch'.

[6] 6. 294-373] Pompey attacks; Caesar retreats and makes for Thessaly.

	And spreads his men over the fields afar,	
	Pleased with this liberty of changing ground.	
	So when full Padus swells above the bound	
305	Of his safe banks, and the near fields o'erflows,	
	If any land not able to oppose	
	That hill of water yield, that it o'erruns,	
	Opening t'itself unknown dominions;¹	
	Some owners must of force their lands forego,	
310	Some gain new lands, as Padus will bestow.	*the Po*
	Caesar, at first not knowing it, by light	
	From a tower's top had notice of the fight:	
	The dust now laid, he sees his walls beat down;	
	But when he found it past, and the foe gone,	
315	This rest his fury stirred, enragèd deep	
	That Pompey safe on Caesar's loss should sleep.²	
	Resolving (though to his own loss) to go	
	On and disturb the quiet of his foe,³	
	First he assaults Torquatus, who descries	*catches sight of*
320	As soon his coming as the sailor spies	
	Th'approach of a Circaean storm, and takes	
	Down all his sails when once the mainmast shakes;⁴	
	His men within the inner wall doth bring,	
	To stand more firmly in a narrow ring.	
325	O'er the ⁽ᵍ⁾first trenches' works Caesar was gone,	[VI. 290]
	When Pompey from the hills above sent down	
	All his whole troops upon th'enclosèd foe.	
	Th'inhabitants near Etna fear not so	
	Enceladus,⁵ when the fierce south wind blows,	
330	And Etna from her fiery caverns throws	
	Her scalding entrails forth,⁶ as Caesar's men,	
	By the raised dust o'ercome ere they begin	

---

¹ dominions] '-ions' is monosyllabic here, untypically for a line-ending.
² This rest ... sleep] Omitting L.'s contrast between Caesar's *Accendit*, 'he was inflamed', and the *Frigidaque ... signa*, 'chilly signs', of a combat opportunity gone cold (VI. 281–82).
³ Resolving ... of his foe] Omitting L.'s *minax*, 'menacing', of Caesar (VI. 285).
⁴ Torquatus] Lucius Manlius Torquatus. He was killed by the Caesarians while fleeing to Spain, and M. includes his name in Caesar's triumph in his *Continuation*, sig. H1ᵛ. Circaean storm] As F. notes, the town of Circeii juts into the Tyrrhene Sea: it was associated with Circe, the Colchian witch, who supposedly relocated to Italy.
⁵ near Etna] *Aetneis habitans in vallibus*, 'he who dwells in Etna's valleys' (VI. 293). Modern editions read *Henneis* for *Etnaeis*: Henna is a town in mid-Sicily.
⁶ And Etna ... forth] Embroidering *torrens in campos defluit Aetna*, 'and Etna flows down in torrents onto the plains' (VI. 295).

To fight; and in the cloud of this blind fear
Flying, they meet their foes; terror does bear
335 Them to their fate. Then might have been let out
The civil war's whole blood, and peace been brought.
Pompey himself their furious swords restrained.
O happy, Rome, still free had'st thou remained
With all thy laws and power,[1] if there for thee
340 Sulla had conquered.[2] 'Tis, and still shall be,
Caesar, our grief, thy worst of wicked deeds
(To fight with a good son-in-law) succeeds.
O luckless fates, for Munda's bloody day
Spain had not wept, Afric for Utica;[3]   *Africa*
345 Nor had Nile borne, her stream discolouring,
A carcass [(h)]nobler than th'Egyptian king;
Nor Juba [(i)]nak'd on Libyan sands had died,
Nor had the blood of Scipio pacified
Carthage dire ghosts, nor men's society
350 Had lost good Cato.[4] That day, Rome, to thee
Had been the last of ills; Pharsalia's day
In midst of fate had vanishèd away.
    Caesar this ill-possessèd place forsakes,[5]   [VI. 314]
And with his mangled [(k)]troops t'Emathia makes.
355 Pompey pursues his flying father-in-law,
Whom from that purpose his friends strive to draw,   *Pompey*
Persuading him to turn to Italy,
Now free from enemies. 'Never', quoth he,
'Will I like Caesar to my country come,
360 Nor never more unless with peace shall Rome[6]
See my return. In Italy I could
Have stayed at the beginning, if I would
Before Rome's temples this sad war have brought,

---

[1] free ... With all thy laws] Reading *libera legum*, 'free in thy laws' (VI. 301), as in F.; modern texts adopt Pieter Burman's emendation *libera regum*, 'free of kings'.
[2] if ... Sulla had conquered] For Pompey as Sulla's pupil see 1. 349-60.
[3] Munda's bloody day ... Utica] See 1. 43-46, 731-34.
[4] O luckless fates ... good Cato] A list of prominent deaths of Caesar's opponents, beginning with Pompey and moving on to Juba, Scipio (here pronounced disyllabically), whose ancestors conquered Carthage, and finally Cato. The final clause translates *nec sancto caruisset vita Catone*, 'nor would life [i.e. mankind] have lacked sainted Cato' (VI. 311).
[5] ill-possessèd place] *adverso possessam numine sedem*, 'a seat possessed by a hostile divine power' (VI. 314).
[6] unless with peace] *nisi dimisso ... milite*, 'unless I have dismissed my army' (VI. 321).

	And in the midst o'th'marketplace have fought.¹	
365	To draw the war from home, t'th'torrid zone,	
	Or Scythia's farthest cold I would be gone.	
	Shall I, a conqueror now, rob Rome of rest,	
	Who fled, lest she should be with war oppressed?	
	Let Caesar think Rome his, rather than she	
370	Should suffer from this war.'² Then easterly	
	He turns his course, paths devious marching over,	*remote, circuitous*
	Where regions vast Candavia does discover,³	
	And to Thessalia comes, which fate for this	
	Sad war ordained. Thessalia bounded is	[VI. 333]⁴
375	By the hill Ossa on the north-east side;	
	Pelion, when summer's in her height of pride,	
	His shade opposes 'gainst Sol's rising rays;⁵	*the sun's*
	The woody Othrys southward keeps away	
	The scorching Lion's heat; Pindus his height	*Leo's*
380	Keeps off the western winds and hastens night	
	By hiding the sun's set; those men ne'er feel	
	(That in the bottom of Olympus dwell)	
	The north wind's rage, nor all night long can see	
	The shining of the Bear. The fields, that lie	*Ursa Major*
385	A vale betwixt those hills, were heretofore	
	A standing pool with water covered o'er.	
	The fields kept in the rivers; Tempe then	
	Had no vent to the sea; to fill the fen	
	Was all the river's course. But when of yore	
390	Alcides Ossa from Olympus tore,	*Hercules*
	And Peneus suddenly the sea did fill,⁶	
	Sea-born Achilles' kingdom (that had still	

---

¹ midst o'th'marketplace] *medio ... foro*, 'in the middle of the Forum [at the centre of Rome]' (VI. 323–24). 'Sad war' (6. 364) is M.'s addition here and a refrain in books six and seven: see also 6. 291, 374; 7.28, 265.

² Shall I ... this war] L.'s Pompey directly addresses Rome here.

³ Where regions vast...] Lit. 'where Candavia opens up its great ravines' (*qua vastos aperit Candavia saltus*, VI. 333).

⁴ 6. 374–464] L. now offers an extended *ecphrasis*, painting Thessaly as a dangerous, sorcerous land.

⁵ the hill Ossa ... rising rays] L. makes Ossa Thessaly's south-east and Pelion its north-east limits, but in fact it is the other way around.

⁶ But when ... fill] *subitaeque ruinam | Sensit aquae Nereus*, 'Nereus [the sea] felt the ruin of sudden waters' (VI. 348–49), alluding to the myth that Thessaly (more precisely Pharsalus, as L. says, VI. 350) was revealed when Hercules tore apart the mountains of Olympus and Ossa to create the gorge of Tempe.

	Been better under water) first was shown,[1]	
	And Phylace, that landed first upon	
395	The Trojan shore her ship, and Dorion,	
	For the nine Muses' anger woe-begone,	
	Pteleos, and Trachis, Meliboea proud	
	Of great Alcides' shafts on her bestowed,	
	Base hire for Oeta's fire;[2] and where men now	*payment*
400	Over the once-renownèd Argos plough;	
	Larissa potent once; and where old tales	
	Describe the Echionian Theban walls;	
	Thither Agave banished, there the head	
	And neck of her dead Pentheus burièd,	
405	Grieved she had torn no more limbs from her son.[3]	
	The fens thus broke in many rivers run.	[VI. 360]
	On the west side, into th'Ionian Sea,	
	Clear but small Aeas runs: as small as he	
	Runs the Egyptian Isis' father's flood;[4]	
410	And Acheloüs, whose thick stream with mud	
	Soils the Echinades;[5] Evenus o'er	
	Meleager's Calydon, stained with the gore	
	Of Nessus, runs;[6] Sperchios swiftly slides	
	Into th'Maliac sea, whose channel glides	
415	Purely along Amphrysus' pasture fields,	
	Where Phoebus served;[7] Anauros, that ne'er yields	

[1] Sea-born Achilles' ...] M. nods to Achilles' mother, the sea-goddess Thetis. 'Sea-born' is lit. *aequorei*, 'watery' (VI. 350).

[2] Phylace ... Oeta's fire] Thessalian cities: Phylace was once ruled by Protesilaus, the first Greek to land on the shores of Troy, and the first to die in the Trojan War; Dorion was the birthplace of Thamyris, who challenged the Muses in poetry, and was blinded for his hubris. Meliboea was the home of Philoctetes, who received the arrows of Hercules as payment and reward for kindling his funeral pyre (on Mt Oeta).

[3] once renownèd Argos ... her son] Pelasgian Argos (not Argos of the Peloponnese); Larissa, home of Achilles; and the Thebes of southern Thessaly (not the city in Boeotia). For Agave, see 1. 613. 'Pentheus' (6. 404), like 'Pteleos' (6. 397), is disyllabic.

[4] as small ... flood] The river Inachus, on the plain of Argos: Inachus' daughter Io was transformed into the goddess Isis after several ordeals, as L.'s *avectae*, 'carried off', hints (VI. 363).

[5] Acheloüs] *tuus, Oeneu, | Pene gener*, 'almost your son-in-law, Oeneus' (VI. 363): Oeneus' daughter Deianeira was promised to the river-god Acheloüs, but became Hercules' bride.

[6] Evenus ... runs] Modern editions print *Euhenos*. The river is stained with the blood of Nessus, the centaur Hercules killed for trying to steal Deianeira, his wife; cf. 6. 411n, 442–43. Meleager (here pronounced to rhyme with 'eager') was a hero of Calydon.

[7] Sperchios ... Phoebus served] According to Greek myth, the god Apollo tended the herds of Admetus by the banks of the Amphrysus for a year as punishment for killing the Cyclops.

Nor fog, nor wind, nor exhalation;
And whate'er river, by itself not known
To th'sea, his waves on Peneus bestows;
420 Apidanos in a swift torrent flows;
Enipeus never swift unless combined,
Melas, and Phoenix with Asopos joined;[1]
Alone his stream pure Titaresus keeps,
Though in a different namèd flood he creeps,
425 And using Peneus as his ground, he flows
Above; from Styx (they say) this river rose,
Who (mindful of his spring) scorns with base floods
To mix, but keeps the reverence of the gods.[2]
 When first, these rivers gone, the fields appeared, [VI. 381]
430 Fat furrows the Boebician ploughshares reared;[3]
Th'Aeolian husbandmen then break the ground;
The Leleges and Dolopes then wound
Her fertile breast;[4] the skilled Magnetians
In horsemanship, the sea-famed Minyans.[5]
435 In Pelethronian dens t'Ixion there
A fruitful cloud did th'half-wild centaurs bear.[6]
Thee, Monichus, that couldst on Pholoë
Break hardest rocks; and furious Rhoecus, thee,
That up by th'roots could strong wild ashes tear
440 On Oeta's mount, which Boreas' blasts would bear;
Pholus, that did'st Alcides entertain, *Hercules*
Ravishing Nessus on the river slain
By venomed shafts, and thee, old Chiron, made
A constellation now, who seem'st t'invade
445 The Scorpion with thy Thessalian bow.[7] *Scorpio*

[1] Melas ... Asopos joined] Modern editions place this line (VI. 374) between VI. 368 (6. 415–16) and VI. 369 (6. 416–17).
[2] reverence of the gods] *timorem*, 'fear' (VI. 380): even the gods made (unbreakable) oaths by swearing upon the Styx.
[3] Boebician] From *Boebicio*, the early modern reading: modern editors print *Bebrycio* (VI. 382).
[4] Th'Aeolian ... fertile breast] In L., it is the Leleges who plough; the Aeolians and the Dolopes 'break the soil as colonist-farmers' (*solum fregere coloni*, VI. 384). 'Fertile breast' is M.'s phrase, reused for the Nile Delta in the *Continuation*, sig. C1ᵛ.
[5] Magnetians ... Minyans] Both pronounced with disyllabic rhymes.
[6] A fruitful cloud ... bear] 6. 437–46 lists famous centaurs, who according to myth were the offspring of Ixion and a cloud, and dwelt in Thessaly.
[7] Chiron ... A constellation now] The centaur Chiron, famously, was Achilles' tutor; he became the constellation Sagittarius.   Scorpion ... Thessalian] One of these two word-endings (probably 'Thessalian') is contracted to a single syllable, the other not.

> Fierce war's first seeds did from this country grow.   [VI. 395]
> Here the first horse for war sprang from a rock,
> Which mighty Neptune with his trident strock: *struck*
> To chew on the steel bit he not disdained,
> 450   And foamed, by his Thessalian rider reined.[1]
> From hence the first of ships the ocean ploughed,[2]
> And seas' hid paths to earth-bred mortals showed.
> Itonus first of all,[3] Thessalia's king,
> To form by hammer did hot metals bring,
> 455   Made silver liquid, stamped his coin's impress   *seal, stamp*
> In gold, and melted brass in furnaces.
> Hence did th'account of money first arise,
> The fatal cause of war and tragedies.[4]
> Here was that hideous serpent Python bred,
> 460   Whose skin the Delphian Tripos coverèd,
> Whence to those games Thessalian bays are brought.[5]   *laurels*
> Aloeus' wicked brood 'gainst heaven here fought,
> When Ossa on high Pelion's top was set,
> And the celestial orbs' swift motion let.[6]   *impeded*
> 465   When both the generals in this land (by fate   [VI. 413][7]
> Destined) encamped,[8] the war's ensuing state
> Fills all presaging minds. All saw at hand
> That hour, on which this war's last cast should stand.[9]

[1] Thessalian rider] *Lapithae domitoris*, 'a tamer who is a Lapith' (VI. 399).
[2] the first of ships … ploughed] Simplifying *Prima fretum scindens Pagasaeo litore pinus*, 'The first ship, carving the sea from Pagasaean [i.e. Thessalian] shore' (VI. 400). The ship is the Argo: see also 2. 213 ff., 768n.
[3] Itonus] *Ionos* in modern editions.
[4] The fatal cause of war and tragedies] *quod populos scelerata impegit in arma*, 'which has thrust mankind into wicked arms' (VI. 406); cf. 1. 736n.
[5] Here … brought] A reference to Apollo's founding of the Pythian games at Delphi. 6. 460 is added by M. from F.'s commentary; 6. 459 translates *Descendit Python, Cyrrhaeaque fluxit in antra*, 'Python descended, and slithered into Cyrrhaean caves' (VI. 408). Modern editions print *arva*, 'fields', for *antra*, 'caves'. 'Hideous' (6. 459) is disyllabic.
[6] Aloeus' wicked brood] The giants Otus and Ephialtes, children of Aloeus' wife Iphimedeia, but fathered by Neptune; they made war on the gods by piling up mountains, and obstructing the course of the planets.
[7] 6. 465–708] Sextus Pompey visits the witch Erictho.
[8] By fate | Destined] *damnata fatis tellure*, 'a land condemned by the fates' (VI. 413); F. glosses 'destined for civil war'.
[9] All saw … stand] *summique gravem discriminis horam | Adventare palam est*, '[they saw that] the grievous hour of the crisis point was arriving openly' (VI. 415–16). Modern editions join this clause to the next, *propius iam fata moveri*, '[and] that now fate was drawing nearer' (VI. 416; see 6. 469–70), but M. follows early modern punctuation. For M.'s (added) dice image in 'last cast', cf. 1. 200, 2. 277, 6. 8n.

	Cowards now trembled that war's fate so near	
470	Was drawn and feared the worst; both hope and fear	
	To this yet doubtful trial brought the stout.	
	But one (alas) among the fearful rout	*crowd*
	Was Sextus, Pompey's most unworthy son,	
	Who afterwards, a banished man upon	
475	Sicilian seas, turned pirate and there stained	
	The famed sea-triumphs his great father gained.	
	He, brooking no delay, but weak to bear	
	A doubtful state,¹ endeavours, urged by fear,	
	To find fate's future course. Nor does he crave	
480	From Delphian Phoebus, from the Pythian cave,	
	Or that famed oak, fruitful in acorns, where	
	Jove's mouth gives answer,² this event to hear;	*outcome*
	Nor seeks advice from them, to whom are known	
	Birds' flights, beasts' entrails, lightning's motion;	
485	Nor the Chaldaean, skilled astrologer,³	
	Nor any secret ways that lawful were;	
	But magic damned by all the gods above	
	And her detested secrets, seeks to prove,	
	Aid from the ghosts and fiends below to crave,⁴	
490	Thinking (ah, wretch!) the gods small knowledge have.	
	The place itself this vain dire madness helped.	[VI. 434]
	Near to the camp, th'Haemonian witches dwelt,	
	Whom no invented monsters can excel:	
	Their art's whate'er's incredible to tell.	
495	Besides, Thessalia's fields and rocks do bear	
	Strange killing herbs and plants and stones that hear	
	The charming witches' murmurs. There arise	
	Plants, that have power to force the deities.	

¹ weak to bear | A doubtful state] *venturisque omnibus aeger*, 'sick at all that was to come' (VI. 424).
² Jove's mouth] *ore Iovis* (VI. 427); modern editions read *aere Iovis*, 'Jove's cauldron'. A reference to the prophetic oak of Dodonian Jove, in Epirus.
³ the Chaldaean, skilled astrologer] *& Assyria scrutetur sidera cura*, 'nor he who examines the stars with Assyrian skill' (VI. 429) — part of a list of approved prophecies Sextus *doesn't* seek out.
⁴ But magic ... crave] *Ille supernis | Detestanda Deis saevorum arcana Magorum | Moverat, & tristeis sacris feralibus aras | Umbrarum, Ditisque fidem*, 'he had turned to [possibly 'practised'] the secrets of vicious sorcerers, secrets abominated by the gods above, and altars grim with savage rites, and the trust of ghosts and the god of hell' (VI. 430–33). M. follows F.'s paraphrase here, along with F.'s reading *Moverat* (Grotius's emendation), 'had moved', for the previously and today preferred *Noverat*, 'had known'.

	Medea there a stranger in those fields	
500	Gathered worse herbs than any Colchos yields.¹	
	Those wretches' impious charms turn the gods' ears,	
	Though deaf to many nations' zealous prayers;	
	Their voice alone bears through the inmost skies	
	Commands to the unwilling deities,	
505	Which not their care of heaven's high motions	
	Can turn away. When those dire murmurs once	
	Enter the sky, though the Egyptians wise	
	And Babylonians their deep mysteries	
	Should utter all,² th'Haemonian witch still bears	
510	From all their altars the gods' forcèd ears.	
	These witches' spells love's soft desires have sent	[VI. 452]
	Into the hardest hearts 'gainst fate's intent:³	
	Severe old men have burned in impious love,	
	Which tempered drinks and philtrums could not move,⁴	*philtres, potions*
515	Nor that, to which the foal his dam's love owes,	*mother's*
	The swelling flesh that on his forehead grows.⁵	
	Minds by no poison hurt have perishèd	
	By spells: those, whom no love of marriage bed	
	Nor tempting beauty's power could ere inflame,	
520	By magic knot-tied thread together came.	
	The course of things has stayed; to keep out day,	
	Night has stood still; the sky would not obey	
	The law of Nature;⁶ the dull world at their	
	Dire voice has been benumbed. Great Jupiter,	
525	Urging their course himself, admired to see	
	The poles not moved by their swift axle-tree.	
	Showers they have made, clouded the clearest sky,	
	And heaven has thundered, Jove not knowing why.⁷	

¹ Medea] Not named by L., although clearly intended by *hospita Colchis*, 'Colchian stranger' (VI. 441).
² the Egyptians wise | And Babylonians] Simplifying *Babylon Persea ... secretaque Memphis*, 'the Babylon of Perses [a Babylonian monarch, son of the legendary hero Perseus] and mysterious Memphis' (VI. 448).
³ love's soft desires] Simply *amor*, 'love', in L. (VI. 453). 6. 511–14 are quoted in John Weever's discussion of grave-robbing, *Ancient Funerall Monuments*, p. 43.
⁴ philtrums] *noxia ... pocula*, 'toxic potions' (VI. 454–55); M. translates F.'s *philtra*.
⁵ Nor ... grows] The *hippomanes*, a caul or membrane sometimes found on the forehead of a foal and believed to have aphrodisiac properties.
⁶ of Nature] M.'s addition, following F.: simply *legi*, 'its law' in L. (VI. 462).
⁷ And heaven ... why] See Jonson, *Masque of Queenes*, p. 198 (*Works*, III, p. 313): 'And that hath thundered, *Jove* not knowing why'.

By the same voice (with hair loose hanging) they
530　Moist swelling clouds and storms have chased away.
The sea without one puff of wind has swelled;
Again, in spite of Auster, has been stilled.　　　　　　　　*south wind*
Ships' sails have quite against the winds been swayed,
Steep waters' torrents in their fall have stayed,
535　And rivers have run back, Nile not o'erflown
In summer time, Maeander straight has run,
Arar has hastened, Rhodanus grown slow,　　　　　　　　　*Rhône*
High hills sunk down have equalled vales below.
Above his head the clouds Olympus saw;
540　In midst of winter Scythian snows did thaw
Without the sun; the tide-raised ocean
Haemonian spells beat from the shore again;　　　　　　　*Thessalian*
The ponderous earth, out of her centre tossed,
Her middle place in the world's orb has lost,
545　So great a weight struck by that voice was stirred,
And on both sides the face of heaven appeared.[1]
All deadly creatures and for mischief born,
Both fear and serve by death the witches' turn:
The tigers fierce and lions nobly bold
550　Fawn upon them; cold snakes themselves unfold
And in the frosty fields lie all untwined;
Dissected vipers by their power are joined;
Their poisoned breathings poisoned serpents kill.[2]
　　Why are the gods thus troubled to fulfil,　　　　　　　　[VI. 492]
555　And fearful their enchantments to contemn?[3]
What bargain has thus tied the gods to them?
Do they obey upon necessity
Or pleasure? Or some unknown piety
Deserves it? Or some secret threats prevail?
560　Or have they jurisdiction over all
The gods? Or does one certain deity fear[4]
Their most imperious charms, who, whatsoe'er

---

[1] *The ponderous earth ... appeared*] *Tantae molis onus percussum voce recessit, | Prospectumque dedit circumlabentis Olympi*, 'struck by the cry [of the witch], the weight of such a great mass has retreated, and granted a view of Olympus [i.e. the sky] revolving' (VI. 483–84). The meaning is that the earth has been knocked from its axis.

[2] *Their poisoned ... kill*] *Humanoque cadit serpens adflata veneno*, 'the serpent dies, breathed upon by human [i.e. witches'] venom' (VI. 491).

[3] enchantments] *cantus herbasque*, 'charms and herbs' (VI. 492).

[4] deity] Probably disyllabic, although typically M. gives it three syllables.

	Himself is forced to, can the world compel?	
	By them the stars oft from the pole down fell;	*heaven*
565	And by their voices' poison Phoebe turned,	*the moon*
	Grown pale with dark and earthly fires has burned,	
	No less than if debarred her brother's shine	*Phoebus, the sun*
	By interposal of the earth between	
	Her orb and his,[1] these labours undergone,	
570	Has she, depressed by incantation,	
	Until, more nigh, she foamed her jelly on	
	Their herbs.[2] These spells of this dire nation	[VI. 507][3]
	And damnèd rites dreadful Erictho scorns	
	As too too good, and this foul art adorns	
575	With newer rites: in towns her dismal head	
	Or houses' roofs is never coverèd.[4]	
	Forsaken graves and tombs (the ghosts expelled)	
	She haunts, by fiends in estimation held.[5]	
	To hear hell's silent counsels, and to know	
580	The Stygian cells and mysteries below[6]	*dwellings*
	Of Dis, her breathing here no hindrance was.	
	A yellow leanness spreads her loathèd face;	
	Her dreadful looks, known to no lightsome air,	
	With heavy hell-like paleness cloggèd are;	
585	Laden she is with long unkemmèd hairs.[7]	*uncombed*

[1] debarred ... Her orb and his] i.e. an eclipse of the moon.
[2] depressed by incantation] i.e. forced lower in the sky. M. reads *depressa* (VI. 505) rather than Grotius's recent conjecture, *deprensa* ('intercepted'), printed by F.; the reading is still contested. foamed ... Their herbs] *suppositas ... despumet in herbas*, 'deposits foam on the grass' (VI. 506). Thessalian witches were thought to draw down the moon and make love potions from its juices.
[3] dreadful Erictho] L. now turns to a specific witch, Erictho (6. 572-946).
[4] in towns ... coverèd] *Illi namque nefas urbis submittere tecto | Aut laribus ferale caput*, 'for it was an abomination to her to place her savage head beneath a roof or a home [lit. *Lares*, 'household gods'] within a city' (VI. 510-11). As later in this passage, M. draws on John Marston's *The Wonder of Women or The Tragedy of Sophonisba* (London: by John Windet for W. Cotton, 1606), where Erictho is a stage character described in passages lifted from L.: 'Here in this desert ... Dreadful *Erictho* lives, whose dismal brow | Contemns all roofs or civil coverture' (IV. i. 97-99).
[5] Forsaken ... estimation held] cf. Marston, *Sophonisba*, IV. i. 100-01: 'Forsaken graves and tombs, the ghosts forced out, | She joys to inhabit.' M.'s 'fiends' translates *deis Erebi*, 'gods of the Underworld' (VI. 513).
[6] To hear ... mysteries below] This couplet is used in Andrew Tooke's translation of François Pomey's *Pantheon* (London: Benjamin Motte for Robert Clavel, 1694), sig. P2^r (Ch. 7, section 3).
[7] A yellow leanness ... hairs] cf. Marston, *Sophonisba*, IV. i. 102-03, 107-10: 'A loathsome yellow leanness spreads her face, | A heavy hell-like paleness loads her cheeks ... *Erictho*

But when dark storms or clouds obscure the stars,
From naked graves then forth Erictho stalks
To catch the night's quick sulphur; as she walks,
The corn burns up and blasts where'er she tread,
590 And by her breath clear airs are poisonèd.
She prays not to the gods, nor humbly cries
For help, nor knows she pleasing sacrifice,
But funeral flames to th'altars she prefers,
Frankincense snatched from burning sepulchres.
595 The gods at her first voice grant any harm
She asks and dare not hear her second charm.¹
Live souls, that rule their limbs, she does entomb;
Death (though unwilling) seizes those to whom
The fates owe years; with a cross pomp men dead   *reverse procession*
600 Return from grave, corses from tombs have fled;   *corpses*
Young men's hot ashes and burnt bones she snatches
Out of the midst of funeral piles, and catches   *pyres*
The kindling brand in their sad parent's hand,
The funeral bed's black smoking fragments, and
605 Their ashy garments and flesh-smelling coals.
But when she finds a corse entombèd whole,
Whose moisture is drawn out, and marrow grown
Hard by corruption, greedy havoc on
Each limb she makes, and from their orbs doth tear
610 His congealed eyes, and sticks her knuckles there.
She gnaws his nails, now pale, o'ergrown and long;²
Bites halters' killing knots, where dead men hung;
Tears from the gibbets strangled bodies down,³
And from the gallows licks corruption.⁴

then | From naked graves stalks out, heaves proud her head | With long unkemmed hair loaden, and strives to snatch | The *Night*'s quick sulphur'.

¹ The gods ... second charm] cf. Marston, *Sophonisba*, IV. i. 123-24: 'To her first sound, the gods yield any harm, | As trembling once to hear a second charm.'

² But when ... and long] cf. Marston, *Sophonisba*, IV. i. 112-15: 'but when she finds a corse | New-graved, whose entrails yet not turn | To slimy filth, with greedy havoc then | She makes fierce spoil.'; IV. i. 117-18: 'then doth she gnaw the pale and o'ergrown nails | From his dry hand'.

³ Bites ... strangled bodies down] *laqueum, nodosque nocentes | Ore suo rupit: pendentia corpora carpsit*, 'she tore down the noose and guilty knots with her mouth and rent the hanging bodies' (VI. 543-44). M.'s 'gallows' and 'gibbets' reference seventeenth-century punishments: see also 7. 344-46. 'Strangled' may come from F.'s gloss *strangulati* to the alternative reading *nocentis* (VI. 543), '[the knots of] a guilty person'.

⁴ from ... corruption] *abrasitque cruces*, 'she scraped off the crosses' (VI. 545); F. infers *saniem*, 'the pus'.

615 She gathers dead men's limbs which showers have wet,
And marrow hardened in Sol's scorching heat.
She keeps the nails that pierced crucified hands,
And gathers poisonous filth and slime that stands
On the cold joints, and, biting with her fangs
620 The hardened sinews, up from ground she hangs.[1]
And wheresoe'er a naked carcass lie,
Before the beasts and ravenous fowls sits she,[2]
But tears or cuts no limb 'til it be bit
By wolves, from whose dry jaws she snatches it.
625 Nor spares she murdering, if life-blood she need,
That from a throat new opened must proceed.
She murders when her sacrifices dire
Life-blood and panting entrails do require,
And births abortive by unnatural ways
630 From wounded wombs she takes and burning lays
Them on her wicked altars. When she lacks
Stout cruel ghosts, such ghosts forthwith she makes:
All deaths of men serve for her action.
From young men's chins she pulls the growing down,
635 And dying striplings' hair she cuts away.
Erictho oft, when o'er the corse she lay   *corpse*
Of her dead kinsman and did seem to kiss,
Off from his maimèd head would bite a piece,
And, opening his pale lips, gellèd and clung   *congealed, jellied*
640 In his dry throat, she bites his cold stiff tongue,
And, whispering murmurs dire, by him she sends
Her baneful secrets to the Stygian fiends.[3]
 By general fame when Sextus notice had   [VI. 569]
Of her, in depth of night, when Titan made   *the sun*
645 At the Antipodes their noon of day,
Over the desert fields he takes his way.   *deserted*
The servants, waiting on his folly then,

---

[1] She keeps the nails ... hangs] *Insertum manibus chalybem nigramque per artus | Stillantis tabi saniem virusque coactum | Sustulit, et nervo morsus retinente pependit*, 'She took away the nail embedded in the hands, and the black gore of infection dripping over the limbs, and the clotted filth, and if a sinew resisted her biting, she hung from it' (VI. 547–49).
[2] ravenous] Probably contracted in pronunciation to 'rav'nous' (like 'poisonous', 6. 618, 761; 'opening', 6. 639 and 759).
[3] And, opening ... Stygian fiends] cf. Marston, *Sophonisba*, IV. i. 118–22: 'she bites his gellèd lips, | And sticking her black tongue in his dry throat, | She breathes dire murmurs, which enforce him bear | Her baneful secrets to the spirits of horror.'

Searching through broken tombs and graves of men,
Spied on a rock at last, where Haemus bends,[1]
650 And the Pharsalian lofty hills extends,
Erictho sitting. She was trying there
Spells, which ne'er witch nor magic god did hear,
And for new purposes was framing charms.
For fearing lest the civil war's alarms
655 Should to some other land be carried thence,[2]
And Thessaly should want that blood's expense,
Philippi fields, with incantations stained
And sprinkled with dire juice, she did command
Not to transfer the war, meaning t'enjoy
660 So many deaths, and the world's blood t'employ.
The carcasses of slaughtered kings to maim,
And turn the Roman ashes, was her aim;
To search for princes' bones, and each great ghost.
But what best pleased her, and she studied most,
665 Was what from Pompey's corse to take away,   *corpse*
Or upon which of Caesar's limbs to prey.
Whom first thus Pompey's fearful son bespake:[3]
'Wisest of all Thessalians, that can'st make   [VI. 589]
Foreknown all things to come, and turn away
670 The course of destiny, to me (I pray)
The certain end of this war's chance relate.
I am no mean part of the Roman state,
Great Pompey's son, now either lord of all
Or woeful heir of his great funeral.
675 My mind, though wounded now with doubtful fear,
Is well resolved any known woe to bear.
O take from chance this power, it may not fall   *that it may not*
Unseen and sudden on me. The gods call,
Or spare the gods, and force the truth out from
680 The ghosts below, open Elysium,
Call forth grim Death himself,[4] bid him relate
Which of the two is given to him by fate.
'Tis no mean task but labour worthy thee,
To search what end of this great war shall be.'[5]

[1] bends] *devexus*, 'sloping down' (VI. 576); Haemus is a mountain.
[2] civil war's alarms] *Mars … vagus*, 'wandering Mars/war' (VI. 578).
[3] bespake] 6. 667–84 are quoted by Weever, *Ancient Funerall Monuments*, pp. 43–44.
[4] grim Death himself] *ipsamque … Mortem*, 'Death herself' (VI. 601).
[5] what end … shall be] L. refers here to 'the die of fate' (*alea fati*, VI. 603).

685	The impious witch, proud of a fame so spread,	
	Replies.[1] 'Young man, wouldst thou have alterèd	[VI. 605]
	Some meaner fate, it had been easily done.[2]	
	I could have forced to any action	
	Th'unwilling gods. I can preserve the breath	
690	Of him, whom all the stars have doomed to death,[3]	
	And, though the planets all conspire to make	
	Him old, the midst of his life's course can break.[4]	
	But fates, and th'order of great causes all	
	Work downward from the world's original.	*cause, origin*
695	When all mankind depend on one success,	
	If there you would change aught, our arts confess	
	Fortune has greater power. But if content	
	You be alone to know this war's event,	
	Many and easy ways for us there be	
700	To find out truth; the earth, the sea, the sky,	
	The dead, the Rhodopeian rocks and fields	
	Shall speak to us.[5] But since late slaughter yields	
	Such choice of carcasses in Thessaly,	
	To raise up one of those will easiest be,	
705	That a warm, new-slain carcass with a clear	
	Intelligible voice may greet your ear,	
	Lest by the sun the organs parched and spilled,	
	The dismal ghost uncertain hizzings yield.'	*hissings*
	Then double darkness o'er night's face she spread,	[VI. 624][6]
710	And wrapping in a foggy cloud her head,	
	She searches where th'unburied bodies lie.	
	Away the wolves and hungry vultures fly,	
	Loosening their tallands, when Erictho comes[7]	*talons*
	To choose her prophet, griping with her thumbs	*clutching*
715	Their now cold marrows, seeking where a tongue	
	And lungs, with fillets whole, unwounded hung.	
	The fates of those slain men stand doubtful all	

---

[1] Replies] 6. 686–708 are quoted in Weever, *Ancient Funerall Monuments*, p. 44.
[2] easily] Probably disyllabic in pronunciation ('eas'ly').
[3] preserve the breath] *conceditur arti ... | Inseruisse moras*, 'my art is granted ... to have planted delays' (VI. 607–09).
[4] can break] M. omits *herbis* i.e. '[can break] with magic herbs' (VI. 610).
[5] the earth ... Shall speak to us] Omitting L.'s *chaos* (VI. 617) from this catalogue of potential objects of divination.
[6] 6. 709–946] Erictho brings a Roman soldier's corpse back to life, who tells of goings-on in the Underworld as a result of the civil war.
[7] Loosening] Probably disyllabic in pronunciation.

Which of their ghosts she from the dead would call.
Had she desired to raise th'whole army slain,
720 And to revive them for the war again,
Hell had obeyed; from Styx, by her strange might,
The people all had been drawn back to fight.[1]
When she a carcass fitting had espied,
An hook she fastened in his throat and tied
725 To it a fatal rope, by which the hag
O'er rocks and stones the wretchèd carcass drag,
That must revive. Under the hollow side
Of an high mountain, which to this black deed
The witch had destined, she the carcass lays.
730 A deep and vast descent of ground there was,
As low (almost) as the blind caves of Dis, *Pluto*
Which a pale wood with thick and spreading trees,
Barring the sight of heaven, and by Sol's light *the sun's*
Not penetrable, did o'ershadow quite.
735 Within the cave was bred by dreary night
Pale mouldy filth and darkness sad. No light
But light by magic made e'er shinèd there.
Within the jaws of Taenarus the air[2]
Is not so dull, that baleful bound 'twixt hell
740 And us: the princes in those shades that dwell
Send without fear their spirits hitherto;
For though this hag can force the fates to do
Whate'er she please, 'tis doubtful whether here
Or there those ghosts in their true place appear.[3]
745 She puts a various coloured clothing on,
And Fury-like her hair loose-hanging down
Was bound about with vipers, her face hid.
But when young Sextus and his train she spied
Shaking for fear, and his astonished eye
750 Fixed on the ground, 'Banish those fears,' quoth she,
'His life's true figure you shall see him take,

---

[1] And to revive ... to fight] *Cessissent leges Erebi, monstroque potenti | Extractus Stygio populus pugnasset Averno*, 'The laws of Erebus would have yielded, and in the face of such a powerful monster the people, extracted from Stygian Avernus, would have gone to war' (VI. 635–36). Lake Avernus in Italy was considered the entrance to the Underworld.

[2] the jaws of Taenarus] i.e. the entrance to the Underworld.

[3] For though this hag...] Lit. *Thessala vates*, 'Thessalian prophetess' (VI. 651). 'tis doubtful ... appear] *quod traxerit illuc | Aspiciat Stygias, an quod descenderit, umbras*, 'whether she hauled up Stygian ghosts there to see them, or whether she descended to do it' (VI. 652–53).

	That cowards need not fear to hear him speak.	
	But if the Furies to your eyes were shown,	
	The Stygian lakes, and burning Phlegethon,¹	
755	The giants bound, and Cerberus that shakes	
	His dreadful curlèd mane of hissing snakes,	
	Why should you fear, cowards, whilst I am by,	
	To see those fiends,² that shake at sight of me?'	
	Then with warm blood, opening fresh wounds, she fills	[VI. 667]
760	His breast, and gore to th'inward parts distils;	
	Of the moon's poisonous jelly-store she takes,	
	And all the hurtful broods, that nature makes:	
	Foam of mad dogs, which sight of water dread,	
	The pith of stags with serpents nourishèd,	*marrow*
765	Was mixèd there. The dire Hyena's knot,³	
	The spotted Lynx his bowels wanted not,	
	Nor that small fish, whose strength, though Eurus rise,	*east wind*
	Can stay the course of ships;⁴ the dragon's eyes;	
	The sounding stone, that brooding eagles make	
770	Warm in their nests; th'Arabian nimble snake,	
	The red sea-viper,⁵ precious gems that kept,	
	Skins from th'alive Libyan Cerastes stripped,⁶	
	The Phoenix' ashes laid in Araby.⁷	
	With these when vile and nameless poisons she	
775	Had mixed, and leaves filled with enchantments strong,	
	And herbs which her dire mouth had spit on young,	
	What poison she did on the world bestow!	
	Then adds a voice to charm the gods below	
	More powerful than all herbs, confounding noises	
780	Much dissonant, and far from human voices.	
	There was the bark of dogs, the wolves' sad howl,	
	The scritch's wailing, hollowing of the owl,	*screech-owl; shouting*
	All voices of wild beasts, hissing of snakes,	

---

¹ burning Phlegethon] *ripamque sonantem | Ignibus*, 'the riverbank crackling with fire' (VI. 662–63); M. deduces (like F. and other commentators) that this means the burning river of the underworld.
² fiends] *manes*, 'shades of the dead' (VI. 656).
³ dire Hyena's knot] Translating *nodus*, 'knot' (VI. 672), which probably in context means the hyena's hump; M. reads *dirae*, 'dire', instead of the now preferred *durae*, 'hard'.
⁴ small fish ... ships] L. specifies the *echineis* ('ship-sticker') or remora (VI. 675).
⁵ red sea-viper] So M.'s spelling, in all editions, although L.'s *rubris | Aequoribus ... vipera*, 'viper in the red seas' (VI. 678) and F.'s gloss, make clear that this is rather the Red Sea viper.
⁶ Libyan Cerastes] A horned snake: see 9. 821.
⁷ in Araby] *Eoa ... in ara*, 'on Eastern altars' (VI. 680).

	The sound that, beat from rocks, the water makes,	
785	The murmur of stirred woods, the thunder's noise	
	Broke from a cloud: all this was in her voice.	
	The rest Haemonian incantations tell,	
	And thus her voice pierces the lowest hell.	
	'Furies and Stygian fiends, whose scourges wound	[VI. 695]
790	All guilty souls;[1] Chaos, that wouldst confound	
	Unnumbered worlds; king of the earth beneath,	
	That griev'st to see the gods exempt from death;	
	Thou Styx, and fair Elysium, which no spirit	
	Of a Thessalian witch deserves t'inherit;	
795	Thou, that thy mother hat'st, Persephone,	
	And heaven; thou lowest part of Hecate,[2]	
	By whom the silent tongues of fiends with us	
	Have intercourse; hell's porter, Cerberus,	
	That currishness into our breasts dost put;[3]	*dog-likeness*
800	You Destinies, that twice this thread must cut;	
	And thou, the burning stream's old ferryman,	
	Tirèd with ghosts brought back to me again:	
	If I invoke you with a mouth profane	
	And foul enough, to hear these prayers deign;	
805	If with a breath fasting from human flesh	
	These incantations I did ne'er express,	
	If women's wombs' whole burdens upon you	
	And luke-warm brains I often did bestow,	
	If on your altars heads of infants slain	
810	I set, and bowels that must live again,	
	Obey my voice. No ghost, that long has felt	
	The Stygian shades, nor long in darkness dwelt,	
	But one that lately from the living went,	
	And is but yet at pale hell's first descent,	
815	And one, which (though obedient to this spell)	
	Could be but once transported o'er to hell,	
	I ask; let some known soldier's ghost relate	
	Before great Pompey's son his father's fate,	

---

[1] Stygian fiends ... souls] *Stygiumque nefas poenaeque nocentum*, 'the Stygian crime, and the punishments of the guilty' (VI. 695)

[2] lowest part of Hecate] Hecate had three incarnations: Moon in heaven, Diana on earth and Hecate below it.

[3] hell's porter ... dost put] *Ianitor & sedis laxae, qui viscera saevo | Spargis nostra cani*, 'And guardian of the broad abode, you who scatter our flesh to the savage dog' (VI. 702–03); as this dog is Cerberus the latter cannot be the guardian, as M. suggests.

	If civil war of you have merited.'¹	
820	Then lifting up her foaming mouth and head	[VI. 719]
	She saw hard by the ghost of that dead man	
	Trembling to enter his old gaol again,	
	Fearing those cold pale members, and into	
	That wounded breast and entrails torn to go.	
825	Ah wretch, from whom death's gift is ta'en away,	
	To die no more. That fates durst thus delay	
	Erictho wondered: wroth with death and fate,	
	The lifeless corse with living snakes she beat,	
	And through earth's crannies, which her charms had broke,	
830	Barked to the fiends,² and thus hell's silence shook.	
	'Megaera and Tisiphone,³ that slight	[VI. 730]
	My voice, through hell with your dire whips affright	
	Hither that wretched spirit,⁴ or from below	
	By your true names of Stygian bitches you	
835	I will call up, and to the sun's light leave:⁵	
	No dead men's graves shall harbour or receive	
	Your heads: I'll follow you, observing well,	
	And from all tombs and quiet urns expel.⁶	
	False Hecate, thee to the gods I'll show	
840	(To whom thou usest with bright looks to go)	*used*
	In thy pale rotten form, and so provide	
	Thou shalt not thy Tartarean visage hide.	*hellish*
	Under the earth's vast weight, I will relate	
	What food detains thee, in what wedlock's state	
845	Thou lov'st the night's sad king, with such a stain	*Pluto*
	That Ceres shall not wish thee back again.⁷	
	'Gainst thee, the world's worst judge,⁸ I will set free	
	The giants, or let in the day to thee.	
	Will you obey, or shall I him invoke,	

¹ of you have merited] i.e. has deserved well of you.
² fiends] *Manibus*, 'the shades of the dead' (VI. 729).
³ Megaera and Tisiphone] Two of the three Furies.
⁴ affright | Hither that wretched spirit] *non agitis ... animam?*, 'do you not drive hither that spirit?' (VI. 731-32). 'Spirit' is contracted to a single syllable here.
⁵ from below ... leave] A slightly imprecise version of *iam vos ego nomine vero* | *Eliciam, Stygiasque canes in luce superna* | *Destituam*, 'I will summon you by your true name and leave you as Stygian dogs [i.e. no longer Furies] in the upper light' (VI. 732-34).
⁶ quiet urns expel] M.'s adjective.
⁷ Under the earth's ... again] In L., 6. 843-46 (= VI. 739-42) address Persephone, but M. seemingly assumes it is still Hecate.
⁸ the world's worst judge] Dis/Pluto.

	Whose name the earth's foundations ever shook?	
850	Whose name the earth's foundations ever shook?	
	Who without hurt th'unveilèd Gorgon sees,	
	Of whose strong stripes Erinys fearful is,	
	Who keeps an hell unknown to you, and where	
	You are above, that dare by Styx forswear.'[1]	
855	Then straight the clotted blood grows warm again,	[VI. 750]
	Feeds the black wounds, and runs through every vein	
	And th'outward parts; the vital pulses beat	
	In his cold breast, and life's restorèd heat	
	Mixed with cold death through parts disusèd runs,	
860	And to each joint gives trembling motions.	
	The sinews stretch, the carcass from the ground	
	Rises not by degrees, but at one bound	
	Stands bolt upright; the eyes with twinking hard	*winking*
	Are oped; not dead nor yet alive appeared	*opened*
865	The face; his paleness still and stiffness stays.	
	He stands at this revival in amaze,	
	But his dumb sealed-up lips no murmur made,	
	Only an answering tongue and voice he had.	
	'Speak', quoth Erictho,[2] 'what I ask, and well	
870	Shalt thou rewarded be: if truth thou tell,	
	By our Haemonian art I'll set thee free	
	Throughout all ages, and bestow on thee	
	Such funerals, with charms so burn thy bones,	
	Thy ghost shall hear no incantations.	
875	Let this the fruit of thy revival be,	
	No spells, no herbs shall dare to take from thee	
	Thy long-safe rest, when I have made thee die.	
	The gods and prophets answer doubtfully,[3]	
	But he, that dares inquire of ghosts beneath,	
880	And boldly go to th'oracles of death,	
	Is plainly told the truth.[4] Spare not, but name	
	Plainly the things and places all, and frame	

---

[1] Who keeps an hell ... forswear] *Indespecta tenet vobis qui Tartara; cuius | Vos estis superi; Stygias qui peierat undas*, 'Who inhabits a Tartarus unseen by you, to whom you are the gods above, and who perjures the Stygian waters' (VI. 748–49). Erictho threatens to invoke the so-called *Demiurgus* or *Demigorgon*, a mysterious, powerful deity not constrained by the laws and frailties of normal gods.

[2] Erictho] 6. 869–86 are quoted in Weever's *Ancient Funerall Monuments*, pp. 44–45.

[3] The gods ... doubtfully] *tripodas, vatesque deorum | Sors obscura tenet*, 'an obscure outcome sways the tripods and prophets of the gods' (VI. 770–71); modern editions read *decet* for *tenet*, i.e. 'an obscure outcome befits'.

[4] But he, that dares inquire...] *discedit certus, ab umbris | Quisquis vera petit*, 'whoever seeks truth from ghosts, departs certain' (VI. 772–73); modern editions read *discedat*, 'let him depart'.

	A speech wherein I may confer with fate',	
	Adding a charm to make him know the state	
885	Of whatsoe'er she asked. Thus presently	
	The weeping carcass spake. 'I did not see	[VI. 777]
	The sisters' fatal threads, so soon (alas)	
	Back from those silent banks enforced to pass.	
	But what by speech from all the spirits I gained,	
890	Among the Roman ghosts fell discord reigned:	*bitter*
	Rome's wicked war disturbed hell's quiet rest.	
	Some captains from sad hell, some from the blessed	
	Elysian fields come forth,[1] and there what fate	
	Intends to do they openly relate.	
895	The happy ghosts looked sad.[2] The Decii then,	
	Father and son, wars-expiating men,	
	I saw;[3] the Curii, and Camillus wailing;	
	Sulla himself against thee, Fortune, railing;[4]	
	His issue's Libyan fate brave Scipio	
900	Bewailed,[5] and Cato, Carthage's great foe,	
	His nephew's bondage-'scaping death did moan.[6]	
	Among the blessèd spirits Brutus alone	
	Rejoiced, first consul, that Rome's king exiled.[7]	
	Fierce Catiline, stern Marius, and the wild	
905	Cethegi, breaking chains, o'erjoyèd were:[8]	
	The popular law-promulging Drusi there,	*promulgating*

---

[1] Some ... come forth] *Elysias alii sedes Tartaraque moesta | Diversi liquere duces*, 'various leaders left, some the Elysian fields and [others] sad Hell' (VI. 782–83). Modern editions follow Housman's conjecture *Elysias Latii sedes*, i.e. 'various leaders left the Elysian fields of Rome [a paradise reserved for Roman heroes] and sad Hell'.

[2] The happy ghosts] The 'blessed' spirits of Elysium.

[3] The Decii ... I saw] See 2. 325n, 7. 408; 'Decii' is disyllabic. M.'s 'wars-expiating' (6. 896) translates *Lustrales bellis animas*, 'their souls appeasing in wars' (VI. 786), using F.'s gloss *expiatores*.

[4] Sulla ... railing] Ironic: Sulla famously called himself *Felix*, 'fortunate' (see 2. 622n; book two, historical note (t)).

[5] brave Scipio] Either the conqueror of Hannibal or the final destroyer of Carthage, both ancestors to Q. Metellus Scipio, who dies in Africa in M.'s *Continuation*; see 2. 503.

[6] Cato ... moan] *non servituri maeret Cato fata nepotis*, 'Cato grieves the death of his descendant who would not be a slave' (VI. 790): a reference to M. Porcius Cato (234–149 BC), ancestor of L.'s Cato who — in events beyond L.'s extant text — committed suicide rather than surrender to Caesar.

[7] Brutus alone ... exiled] Legendary founder of the Roman republic who expelled Tarquin, and ancestor of the tyrannicide. 'Spirits' (6. 902) is once again contracted to a single syllable in pronunciation.

[8] Fierce Catiline ...] *Catilina minax ... Mariique truces*, 'threatening Catiline and the savage Marii...' (VI. 793, 794). This begins a list of Caesar's supporters in the underworld, many of whom were also champions of pro-plebeian reform. wild | Cethegi] Lit. *nudique Cethegi*, 'naked Cethegi' (VI. 794); see 2. 578.

  And daring Gracchi, shouting, clapped their hands,
  Fettered forever with strong iron bands
  In Pluto's dungeons.[1] Impious ghosts had hopes
910 Of blessèd seats: Pluto pale dungeons opes,   *opens*
  Prepares hard stones, and adamantine chains
  To punish the proud conqueror ordains.[2]
  Take you this comfort, in a blessèd room
  The ghosts expect your side and house to come,
915 And for great Pompey in Elysium
  Prepare a place.[3] The hour shall shortly come
  (Envy not then the glory of so small
  A life) that in one world shall lodge you all.[4]
  Make haste to meet your deaths, and with a mind
920 Haughty, though from small funerals, descend
  To tread upon the souls of Roman gods.[5]
  For burials is all this mortal odds,[6]
  And the Pharsalian fight must only try
  Who shall by Nile and who by Tiber lie.
925 But seek not thou thy destiny to hear,
  Which Fate,[7] though I be silent, will declare.
  A surer prophet shall thy father be
  In Sicily, although uncertain he
  Whither to call thee, whence to bid thee flee,
930 Or in what coast or climate safe to be.[8]
  Fear Europe, Asia, Afric: fates divide   *Africa*

---

[1] popular law-promulging Drusi ... dungeons] *popularia nomina Drusos | legibus immodicos*, 'the Drusi, those popular names, immoderate [in passing] laws' (VI. 795-96); in L. they, not the Cethegi as M. suggests (6. 905), are seen 'rejoicing', *laetantes* (VI. 795). M.'s line is irregular. daring Gracchi] *ausosque ingentia Gracchos*, 'the Gracchi, who dared enormities' (VI. 796); cf. 1. 288 and note.

[2] Impious ghosts...] *camposque piorum | Poscit turba nocens*, 'the guilty crowd demands the plains of the blessed [i.e. Elysium]' (VI. 798-99). L. goes on to assert that although hell's plebeian partisans and pro-Caesarians think the civil war will improve their conditions, in fact dire punishments are prepared for Caesar.

[3] In Elysium ... a place] *placido ... | ... sinu, regnique in parte serena*, 'a peaceful nook ... in the serene part of the kingdom' (VI. 803-04).

[4] The hour ... you all] *veniet quae misceat omnes | Hora duces*, 'the hour will come which will mingle all leaders' (VI. 806-07).

[5] the souls of Roman gods] i.e. the deified Julio-Claudian emperors.

[6] For burials ... odds] *& ducibus tantum de funere pugna est*, 'This fight among the leaders is only over a grave' (VI. 811).

[7] Fate] *Parcae*, 'the Fates' (VI. 812).

[8] A surer prophet ... to be] Pompey, after his death in Egypt, will come to Sextus in a vision. This event does not take place in L.'s extant poem, nor in M.'s *Continuation*.

Your funerals, as they your triumphs did.
O wretchèd house, to you the world shall yield
No place more happy than Pharsalia's field.'[1]
935 Thus having spoke the carcass did remain [VI. 820]
With a sad look, and begged for death again,
But could not die without a magic spell
And herbs; nor could the Fates restore to hell
His soul once sent from thence. With that, the witch
940 Builds up a lofty funeral pile, to which
The dead man comes: she lays him on the fires,
Leaves him and lets him die,[2] and then retires
With Sextus to his father's camp. And now
The welkin 'gan Aurora's light to show:[3] *sky; began; dawn's*
945 But to the camp 'til Sextus take his way,
The dark charmed night kept off approaching day.

FINIS.

---

[1] Fear Europe ... Pharsalia's field] Pompey will die in Egypt, his son Cneius in Spain, and his son Sextus in Asia (Miletus). Therefore the only place where a Pompey won't die, the 'safer' place (*Tutius*, VI. 820), is Thessaly.
[2] lets him die] Omitting *tandem*, 'at last' (VI. 827).
[3] welkin ... to show] *coelo lucis ducente colorem*, 'as the sky was taking on the colour of dawn' (VI. 828); F. mentions Aurora.

Annotations on the Sixth Book

(a) From their camps by the river Apsus, both generals at one time brought forth their armies, Pompey intending to intercept M. Antonius, and Caesar intending to join with Antony. Antony, certified by some Greeks of Pompey's ambushes, kept within his camp 'til the next day Caesar came to him. Pompey then, fearing to be enclosed by two armies, departing thence, marched to Asparagis near Dyrrachium, and there encamped. Thither also marched Caesar, and encamped not far from him.[1]

(b) Caesar, wanting provision, was desirous of battle, but Pompey, better provided of all necessaries, purposely delayed it.[2]

(c) Caesar, perceiving that Pompey would not be drawn out to fight, the next day by a great compass and difficult way went to Dyrrachium, hoping to exclude Pompey thence, where his corn and provision lay. Which Pompey perceiving, went thither also by a nearer way.[3]

(d) Caesar (that his own men might with the less danger forage and fetch in corn, as also to hinder Pompey from foraging, and to lessen his estimation among foreign nations) kept with garrisons all the tops of the hills, and fortified castles there, and drew strong trenches from castle to castle, so on every side enclosing Pompey. The work extended fifteen miles in compass, being so large that Pompey within wanted nothing, and Caesar could not man his works round.[4]

(e) Caesar's soldiers, wanting victual, besieged Pompey, abounding with all store of provision. Pompey, seeing the strange unheard-of food that Caesar's soldiers ate while they besieged him, said that he now made war against beasts.[5]

(f) Pompey, understanding by some renegados that Caesar's cross-trench between the two bulwarks toward the sea was not finished, sent a ship manned with archers and other soldiers to assault the defenders of the work behind. Himself about the end of night came thither also with his forces. Caesar's cohorts that watched there near the sea, seeing themselves assaulted both by land and sea, ran away, whom the Pompeians pursued with a great slaughter, 'til Mar[cus] Antonius with twelve cohorts coming down the hill made the Pompeians retreat again.[6]

---

[1] Translates F.'s note (a) on VI. 1.
[2] Translates F.'s note (b) on VI. 1.
[3] Translates/adapts F. on VI. 8 ff.
[4] Translates F. on VI. 328 ff.
[5] Largely M.'s note, summarising the situation as given by L. Pompey's comparison of Caesar's soldiers to wild beasts is recorded in F.'s note to VI. 113.
[6] Translates, with slight condensing, F.'s note to VI. 269. F. gives the identity of the 'renegados' (Latin *transfugis*, 'deserters') as the Allobrogians Aegus and Roscillus, and also

(g) Caesar, to repair that day's loss, assaulted with three and thirty cohorts the castle which Torquatus kept, and beat the Pompeians from the trench. Which Pompey hearing, brought his fifth legion to their succour. Caesar's horsemen, fearing to be enclosed, began first to fly, which the foot seeing, and seeing Pompey there in person, fled also. This victory if Pompey had pursued, he had utterly overthrown Caesar.[1]

(h) Pompey the Great slain upon the banks of Nile.[2]

(i) Juba, king of Mauretania, which had slain Curio and his legions before in the African war, was vanquished by Caesar, and, fearing to fall into Caesar's hands, he and Petreius slew each other.[3]

(k) For in these two conflicts Caesar lost nine hundred footmen, sixty-two horsemen, thirty centurions, ten tribunes and thirty-two ensigns of war.[4]

---

notes that Caesar's fleeing troops were reinforced by Antonius after reaching the camp of Marcellinus.

[1] The first three sentences follow closely F.'s notes on VI .290. The final point, summarising the complaint of 6. 335–52 (cf. VI. 299–313), was a commonplace observation of this moment in the war (and also mentioned by F. in his notes to this passage).
[2] This detail, though obvious, can be found in F.'s commentary.
[3] Taken loosely from F.'s note to VI. 309.
[4] Translates F.'s note to VI. 315.

To the Right Noble and Valiant General, Sir Horatio Vere, Baron of Tilbury.[1]

    Pharsalia's dreadful field, sung by a muse
    High as her subject was, this seventh book shows:
    Where Rome's vast power, her liberty, & laws,
    Great Pompey's fortune, and the better cause
5   Were all enforced to yield to Caesar's fate
    This book to you I chose to dedicate
    (Renownèd lord) whose prosperous sword did win
    (In the great'st[(a)] battle that this age hath seen)
    To Belgia liberty,[2] to England fame,
10 And to yourself a never-dying name.

    (a) Newport[3]

---

[1] To the Right Noble ...] Horace (Horatio) Vere, Baron Vere of Tilbury (1565–1635), celebrated commander in the wars against Catholic Spain and also, like the Earl of Warwick (dedicatee of book nine), of pronounced Puritan sympathies. He was knighted in 1596 by the Earl of Essex during the siege of Cádiz. Although England made peace with Spain in 1604, Vere continued to fight against her in the United Provinces, distinguishing himself at Sluys (1604) and Mulheim (1605), where he was credited with saving the Dutch army. He served as governor of Brill from 1609 until 1616. In 1620 Vere was chosen by the palatine envoy Count Dohna to command troops raised in England to defend the Palatinate for the Protestant cause, in the face of Buckingham's preferred candidate. He managed to hold almost the whole Lower Palatinate for a year, but in September 1622 was forced to surrender Mannheim and returned home to an enthusiastic welcome. In 1624–5 he helped in the (failed) relief of the siege at Breda in the Netherlands, again receiving praise for his heroic conduct in retreat. Vere was made a member of the Council of War in 1624 and on 24 July 1625 was created Baron Vere of Tilbury. He returned again to active service abroad in the late 1620s, retiring to England in 1632 and dying aged 70 in 1635; he was buried in Westminster Abbey.
[2] Belgia] The United Provinces (modern Netherlands).
[3] Newport] *sic*. At the battle of Nieuwpoort (2 July 1600), a celebrated victory over Spain, Vere commanded three hundred foot and famously rallied the vanguard after they were initially broken. M. chiefly parallels Dutch and Roman 'liberty' (the United Provinces were a republic) and their respective champions, Vere and Pompey, although the analogy between Nieuwpoort and Pharsalia might also associate Caesar with Vere as victors.

LUCAN'S
Pharsalia

The Seventh Book.

The Argument of the Seventh Book.[1]

Great Pompey's flattering dream; his soldiers all[2]
Eager of battle, urge their general;
Their wish (though rash and fatal) finds defence
In Cicero's unhappy eloquence.[3]
5 Against his will great Pompey's forced to yield:
The signal's given; Pharsalia's dreadful field
Is fought; Rome's liberty forever dies,
And vanquished Pompey to Larissa flies.[4]

Sad Titan later Thetis' lap forsook[5]   [VII. 1][6] *the sun*
Than nature's law required, and never took
A crosser way,[7] as if, borne back again
By the sphere's course, would eclipsèd fain,[8]
5 Attracting clouds, not food t'his flames to yield,[9]
But loath to shine upon Pharsalia's field.
    That night of Pompey's happy life the last,   [VII. 7]
Deceived by flattering sleeps, he dreamed him placed
In the Pompeian theatre,[10] among

---

[1] The Argument] See Argument to book one.
[2] his soldiers] *turba*, 'mob', in Sulpizio.
[3] unhappy eloquence] Sulpizio calls Cicero *cupidus facundo ore*, 'lustful in his eloquence'. This is M. Tullius Cicero, 106-43 BC, orator and statesman.
[4] Rome's liberty ... flies] M.'s emphasis on Rome's loss of liberty and Pompey's flight replaces Sulpizio's stress on L.'s condemnation of both Caesar and the tragic bloodshed of Pharsalus.
[5] Thetis' lap] *Oceano*, 'the ocean' (VII. 1). M.'s is common English poetic idiom, used also e.g. by Arthur Gorges (*Lucan's Pharsalia*, p. 114) to translate *pontus*, 'the sea' (at III. 633).
[6] 7. 1-49] Pompey's dream, the night before the battle of Pharsalus.
[7] never took | A crosser way] *numquam magis aethera contra | Egit equos*, 'never did he more drive his horses in a direction opposed to the heavens' (VII. 2-3), meaning heaven's rotating sphere, which in ancient astronomy imagined the sun to travel from west to east.
[8] eclipsèd fain] Paraphrasing *Defectusque pati voluit, raptaeque labores | Lucis*, 'and wanted to suffer failure, and the burden of light snatched away' (VII. 4-5).
[9] not food ... yield] Stoics believed the sun was fed by vapours from the earth.
[10] the Pompeian theatre] See 1. 145-46n; 'theatre' is trisyllabic.

10	Rome's people flocking in unnumbered throng,
	Where shouting to the skies he heard them raise
	His name, each room contending in his praise.
	Such were the peoples' looks, such was their praise,
	When in his youth and first triumphant days[1]
15	Pompey, but then a gentleman of Rome,
	Had quieted the west, and Spain o'ercome,
	Scatt'ring the troops' revolt Sertorius led, *rebel*
	And sat by th'Senate as much honourèd
	In his pure candid as triumphal gown.[2] *white*
20	Whether the doubtful fancy, fearful grown *imagination*
	Of future fate, run back to former joys,
	Or prophesying by such sights implies
	Their contrary and bodes ensuing woe,
	Or else on thee Fortune would thus bestow
25	A sight of Rome that could not otherwise:
	O, do not wake him from this sleep to rise,
	No trumpet pierce his ear; the next night's rest
	With the foregoing day's sad war oppressed
	Will nought but fights, blood and slaughter show.
30	Happy were Rome, could she but see (though so)
	Her Pompey, blessed with such a dream as this
	And happy night. O, would the deities
	Had given one day, Pompey, to Rome and thee,
	That both assured of your destiny
35	Might reap the last fruit of a love so dear!
	Thou goest, as if thy Rome should thee inter,[3]
	And she, still mistress of her wish in thee,
	Hopes that the fates lodge not such cruelty
	As to deprive her of thy honoured tomb.
40	To mourn for thee old men and young would come,
	Children untaught would weep; the matrons all
	With hair (as once at Brutus' funeral)[4]

---

[1] triumphant days] See 1. 135n.
[2] In his pure ... gown] After victory over Sertorius in Spain Pompey still wore the white toga of equestrian rank (M.'s 'gentleman'), rather than the purple of someone who had held a triumph; cf. 1. 339–41.
[3] goest] Pronounced 'go'st'.
[4] Brutus' funeral] According to Livy, II. 7 (*History of Rome, Volume I, Books 1–2*, trans. by B. O. Foster, Loeb Classical Texts (Cambridge, MA: Harvard University Presss, 1919), after the death of the regicide and founder of the Roman republic, the Roman women mourned for a year.

    Loose-hung, would beat their breasts. Now, though they fear
    The swords of the injurious conqueror,
45 Though he himself relate thy death,[1] they'll mourn
    At public sacrifice, as they adorn
    Jove's house with laurel:[2] wretched men, whose moan
    Concealed in sighs must vent itself alone,
    And dares not sound in public theatres.
50 Now had the rising sun obscured the stars,   [VII. 45][3]
    When all the soldiers murmuring up and down[4]
    (The fates now drawing the world's ruin on)
    Desire a signal of the fight. Poor men,
    Whose greater part should never see the end
55 Of that sad day, about their general's tent
    (Hast'ning the hour of their near death) they vent
    Their passions and complaints; and frantic grown,
    Their own and public fate they hasten on.
    They call great Pompey sluggish, timorous,
60 Patient of Caesar,[5] and ambitious
    Of sovereignty,[6] desirous still to reign
    O'er all those kings and fearing peace again.
    The kings and eastern nations all complained
    War was prolonged, and they from home detained.
65 The gods, when they our ruin had decreed,
    Would make it thus our own erroneous deed.[7]
    Ruin we sought, and mortal wars required:[8]
    In Pompey's camp Pharsalia is desired.
    Nor did this wish want Cicero's defence,
70 The greatest author of Rome's eloquence,
    In whose gown-rule fierce Catiline did fear
    The peaceful axes;[9] now turned soldier,

---

[1] himself] *victoris iniqui,* | ... *ipse* ... *Caesar*, 'the unjust victor, Caesar himself' (VII. 40–41).
[2] house] i.e. the temple of Jupiter Capitolinus.
[3] 7. 50–95] Pompey's soldiers, spoiling for a fight, are further inflamed by Cicero's speech (7. 75–95).
[4] up and down] M.'s idiom; simply *mixto murmure*, 'confused murmur', in L. (VII. 45).
[5] Patient of Caesar] i.e. too indulgent of Caesar.
[6] sovereignty] *orbis* [...] *regno*, 'monarchy of the world' (VII. 54–55); cf. 1. 5n, 1. 338n. The ending of 'ambitious' is disyllabic ('i-ous').
[7] The gods ... deed] L. addresses the gods directly here; modern editions often treat this as a question.
[8] mortal] i.e. fatal.
[9] gown-rule] *iure togaque*, 'by law and the toga', i.e. civil jurisdiction (VII. 63); cf. 1. 335n.

From bars and pleadings had been silent long,[1]
And this bad cause thus strengthens with his tongue.[2]
75 'Pompey, for all her gifts Fortune implores   [VII. 68]
That thou wouldst use her now:[3] thy senators,
Thy kings, and all the suppliant world entreat
Thy leave to conquer Caesar.[4] Shall he yet
So long a war against mankind maintain?
80 Well may the foreign nations now disdain
(Who suddenly were vanquished by thee)
That Pompey is so slow in victory.
Where's now thy spirit, thy confidence of fate?
Can'st thou now doubt the gods (ah most ingrate?)
85 Or fear'st thou to commit into their hand
The Senate's cause? Thy troops without command
Their eagles will advance: 'twere shame for thee
To be compelled to conquer. If thou be
Our general, and ours the war, to try
90 The hazard lies in our authority.[5]
Why hold'st thou the world's swords from Caesar's throat?[6]
They all are drawn almost, and tarry not   *wait not for*
Thy slow alarms: make haste, lest thy command
They all forsake;[7] the Senate does demand
95 If they thy soldiers or companions be.'
Great Pompey sighed to see how contrary   [VII. 85]
The gods were bent, and Fortune crossed his mind.[8]
'If you be all', quoth he, 'this way inclined:

M. omits L.'s description of Cicero as *iratus bellis*, 'angered by the wars' (VII. 65).

[1] From bars and pleadings...] *rostra forumque*, 'the rostra and the forum' (VII. 65). See 4. 879 for a similar change in idiom. 'Soldier' (7. 72) is trisyllabic.

[2] bad cause] *invalidae ... causae*, 'weak cause' (VII. 67).

[3] for all her gifts...] i.e. it is time for Pompey to return some of Fortune's many favours to him: *meritis*, 'deserts', in L. (VII. 68).

[4] entreat ... Caesar] *vinci socerum patiare rogamus*, 'we ask that you suffer your father-in-law to be defeated' (VII. 71).

[5] If ... authority] *Si duce te iusso, si nobis bella geruntur, | Sit iuris quocunque velint concurrere campo*, 'if you're leader by our command, if the wars are waged for us, it should be lawful for them to meet in battle wherever they want' (VII. 78–80). The idiom of hazarding battle is common in Renaissance English.

[6] throat] *sanguine*, 'blood' (VII. 81).

[7] They all are drawn ... forsake] M. retains the swords as the focus here, where L. switches between *tela*, 'missiles', *signa*, 'standards' and *classica*, 'trumpets' (VII. 82–83).

[8] Great Pompey ... mind] *Ingemuit Rector, sensitque deorum | Esse dolos, & fata suae contraria menti*, 'The ruler groaned, and sensed that this was the trickery of the gods, and that the fates were contrary to his own mind' (VII. 85–86).

	And me a soldier, not a general	
100	The time require, I'll be no let at all	*obstacle*
	To fate. Let fortune all these nations cast	
	Into one ruin: be this day the last	
	To the great'st part of men. But witness, Rome:	
	Pompey's enforced to this sad field to come.¹	
105	The war's whole work need not have cost one wound,	
	But Caesar, without blood subdued and bound,	
	Might have been brought to answer injured peace.	
	What fury's this (O blind in wickedness)?	
	To conquer without blood in civil war	
110	You are afraid.² Masters o'th'land we are:	
	The seas are wholly ours;³ the famished foe	
	To fetch in corn unripe is forced to go,	
	And 'tis become his wish by swords to die,	
	And with his ruin mix our tragedy.⁴	
115	In this some part is finished of the war,	
	That our freshwater soldiers do not fear	*novice*
	The fight (if that be in true valour done):⁵	
	Into extremest dangers many run	
	For fear of future ill. Valiant'st is he	
120	That fears not t'undergo a danger nigh,	
	Nor to defer it. Would you then commit	
	Your strength to Fortune's hand,⁶ and to one fight	
	The world's estate,⁷ desiring all that I	*condition, state*
	Should rather fight than get the victory?	
125	The rule of Rome's estate thou didst bestow,	
	Fortune, on me. Receive it greater now,	
	Protect it in this war's blind chance; to me	
	Nor crime nor honour shall this battle be.⁸	

---

¹ enforced ... to come] *quo cuncta perirent,* | *Accepisse diem,* 'has accepted the day on which all things perish' (VII. 91–92).
² You] M.'s apostrophe; *metuunt*, 'they're afraid', in L. (VII. 96).
³ Masters ... ours] *Abstulimus terras, exclusimus aequore toto,* 'we've taken the land from him and banished him from all the seas' (VII. 97).
⁴ And with ... tragedy] *mortesque suorum* | *Permiscere meis,* 'and mingle the death of his troops with mine' (VII. 100–01).
⁵ if that ... done] *Si modo virtutis stimulis, iraeque calore* | *Signa petunt,* 'if only through the goads of virtue and the heat of anger they demand the standards' (VII. 103–04).
⁶ Your strength] *tam prospera rerum,* 'such a favourable position' (VII. 107).
⁷ The world's estate] *mundi* | *Discrimen,* 'the world's critical moment' (VII. 108–09).
⁸ honour] *gloria,* 'glory' (VII. 112).

	Caesar, thy wicked prayers 'gainst mine prevail:¹	
130	We fight. How dismal to all people shall²	
	This day appear? How many lands undone³	
	Shall be? How crimson shall Enipeus run	
	With Roman blood? Would the first pile of all	
	This mortal war would light (if I could fall	
135	Without the ruin of our side) on me:⁴	
	For not more joyful can the conquest be.	
	Pompey a name shall be to everyone	
	Of hate or pity, when this fight is done.⁵	
	The conquered shall endure the worst of woe:	
140	The worst of crimes the conqueror shall do.'⁶	
	With that the reins he to their fury gives,	[VII. 123]⁷
	Suff'ring the fight. So th'artless sailor leaves	
	His helpless barque,⁸ when Corus' blasts are grown	*north-west wind*
	Too strong, to guidance of the winds alone.	
145	A fearful murmuring noise rose through all parts	
	Of th'camp:⁹ and diversely their manly hearts	
	Beat 'gainst their breasts.¹⁰ Upon the face of some	
	Appeared the paleness of a death to come,	
	And ghastly looks:¹¹ that day (they think) fate brings	
150	A lasting state of rule on earthly things,	
	And what Rome was, after this field is fought,	
	Be asked.¹² No man of his own danger thought,	

---

¹ prevail] Omitting *apud superos*, 'with the gods' (VII. 113).
² How dismal] *quantum scelerum, quantumque malorum*, 'how much crime, how much evil!' (VII. 114).
³ lands] *regna*, 'kingdoms' (VII. 115).
⁴ Would the first pile ...] *lancea*, 'javelin' (VII. 117); cf. 1. 7. Without ... on me] Omitting *momento rerum*, '[without] the shifting of the balance' (VII. 118); 'me' translates *caput hoc*, 'this head' (VII. 117).
⁵ this fight is done] *hac clade peracta*, 'this slaughter achieved' (VII. 120).
⁶ The conquered ... shall do] *Omne malum victi, quod sors feret ultima rerum; | Omne nefas victoris erit*, 'the conquered will have all the misery that the ultimate chance of things shall bring, the victor all the sacrilege' (VII. 123-24).
⁷ 7. 141-71] Pompey's troops prepare for battle.
⁸ artless sailor] Softening L.'s *arte relicta*, 'abandoning his skill [as a helmsman]' (VII. 126).
⁹ A fearful murmuring ... camp] See Textual Notes.
¹⁰ diversely ... their breasts] 'diversely' translates *Ictibus incertis*, 'with uncertain beats' (VII. 129), 'manly hearts' *animique truces*, 'savage wills' (VII. 128).
¹¹ ghastly looks] *facies simillima fato*, 'a face most resembling their fate' (VII. 130). M.'s phrase recalls Spenser's description of Fury's 'ghastly looks' (*Faerie Queene*, III. xii. 17) or Shakespeare, *Richard III*, III. 5. 8-9, 'Ghastly looks | are at my service, like enforcèd smiles'.
¹² that day ... Be asked] *Advenisse diem, qui fatum rebus in aevum | Conderet humanis, & quaeri Roma quid esset, | Illo Marte palam est*, 'it is clear the day had arrived which would

LUCAN'S PHARSALIA

Amazed with greater fears. Who, when he sees
All shores o'erflown, and th'uncurbed ocean rise
155 O'er mountains' tops, the firmament and sun
Fall down to earth, in such confusion
Could fear his own estate?[1] No private state
Has time to fear,[2] but Rome's and Pompey's fate.
    Nor did they trust their swords, unless sharp-set   [VII. 139]
160 On stones: the points of their dull piles they whet;
Each archer fits his bow with surest strings,
And choicest arrows in his quiver brings;
Horsemen sharp spurs provide, and strongest reins.[3]
So when earth's giants upon Phlegra's plains
165 (If with the acts of gods our human wars
We may compare) rebelled, the sword of Mars
In Etna's forge and Neptune's three-forked spear
Were scoured and sharpened;[4] Phoebus' arrows there
With Python dulled, made sharp;[5] the blue-eyed maid
170 Upon her shield Medusa's hairs displayed;[6]
Jove's lightning then the Cyclops moulded new.
    Fortune foretold the woes that should ensue   [VII. 151][7]
By many tokens: for the stormy sky
Withstood their marches into Thessaly.   *obstructed*
175 The clouds against their eyes did lightnings throw:[8]
Meteors like lamps, like fiery posts in show
And beams, cloud-breaking Typhons did arise,[9]   *whirlwinds*

establish the fate of human affairs forever, and in that battle pose the question: what would Rome be?' (VII. 131–33). See Textual Notes.

[1] in such confusion...] *Tot rerum finem, timeat sibi?*, '[given] the end of so many things, who could fear for himself?' (VII. 137).

[2] No ... fear] *non vacat ullos | Pro se ferre metus*, 'there is no opportunity to feel any fear for oneself' (VII. 137–38).

[3] Horsemen ... reins] In L. the cavalry enlarge their spurs and shorten their reins.

[4] So when earth's giants...] cf. 4. 55–60 and notes. Etna housed the forge of the Cyclopes, who made the thunderbolts of Jupiter and other weapons and armour for the Olympian gods.

[5] Phoebus' ... made sharp] *spiculaque extenso Paean Pythone recoxit*, 'Apollo re-forged [lit. 're-cooked'] his arrow tips, Python having been spread out [in death]' (VII. 148). For this myth, see 5. 92 ff. M.'s translation follows F.'s explanation.

[6] blue-eyed maid] *Pallas* (VII. 149), i.e. Pallas Athene or Minerva; M.'s detail.

[7] 7. 172–241] Portents and prognostications of disaster; cf. 1. 556 ff.

[8] The clouds ... throw] 7. 175 (= VII. 154) is considered spurious by modern editors of L.

[9] Meteors ... did arise] *Adversasque faces, immensoque igne columnas, | Et trabibus mistis avidos typhonas aquarum | Detulit* [sc. *aether*], 'the sky hurled down torches against them, and columns of immense fire, and greedy whirlwinds of waters with beams inmixed' (VII. 155–57). M.'s difficult syntax partly derives from a mistaken or overly compressed reading of

  And lightnings' flashes dimmed and closed their eyes.
  Their helmets' plumes were singed,[1] their piles did melt,
180 Sword-blades dissolved run down the hilts they felt.
  Their impious swords with sulphur from the skies
  Did smoke. Their ensigns hid with swarms of bees
  Could scarce be plucked from ground; the bearers bowed
  Themselves to get them up, which seemed o'erflowed
185 With tears from thence even to Thessalia.[2]
  The bull from th'holy altars ran away,[3]
  And to Pharsalia field directly flies,
  Whilst their sad altar wants a sacrifice.
   But what night-Furies, what Eumenides,
190 What Stygian powers, or gods of wickedness,
  What hellish fiends, Caesar, didst thou appease,
  Preparing for such wicked wars as these?
  Whether the gods or their own fears had wrought
  These wonders, doubtful 'tis, but many thought
195 They saw Olympus meet with Pindus' hill,
  And Haemus' fall th'adjoining valleys fill,
  That in the night Pharsalia sounded loud
  The noise of battle, that Baebeïs flowed
  Swiftly with blood.[4] But most admired they
200 To see each other's face show dark, the day
  Grow pale, and night their helmets overspread;
  Their fathers' ghosts and all their kinsmen dead
  T'appear before their eyes. But this alone
  Comforted their sick minds: knowing their own
205 Impious intents, brothers to kill and ope
  Their fathers' throats, they hence conceivèd hope,
  Thinking these monsters and portents t'imply
  Th'accomplishment of their impiety.[5]

F.'s paraphrases, which confusingly detach *trabibus mistis*, 'with beams inmixed', from the whirlwinds.

[1] were singed] M.'s invention; *Excussit cristas galeis*, '[lightning] knocked the crests off helmets' (VII. 158).

[2] With tears ... Thessalia] Underplaying the polemical edge of L.'s *rorantia fletu, | Vsque ad Thessaliam Romana, & publica signa*, 'standards drenched with tears, and until they reached Thessaly, Roman and public too [i.e. not serving one man's private interest]' (VII. 163–64).

[3] The bull ... away] Omitting *Admotus superis*, 'driven by the gods' (VII. 165).

[4] Baebeïs flowed | Swiftly with blood] Omitting *per Ossaeam*, 'through the region of Ossa' (VII. 176). Pindus, the vale of Haemus and the lake Baebeïs are all in Thessaly.

[5] they hence ... impiety] *gaudet monstris, mentisque tumultu | Atque omen scelerum*

LUCAN'S PHARSALIA 263

No wonder 'tis,[1] if men so near their end [VII. 185]
210 Trembled with frantic fear. If fates do lend
Presaging minds of future ills to men,[2]
Romans that sojourned in Armenia then
And Tyrian Gades and in what coast soe'er
Or climate they abode,[3] lamented there,
215 Blaming their causeless grief,[4] and did not know
Their losses in Pharsalia's overthrow.
An augur sitting on [(a)]th'Euganean mount,[5]
(If fame record a truth) where springs the fount *spring*
Of foggy Aponus, where Timavus does
220 First part and thence in several channels flows,
'This day', quoth he, 'the action's in the height:
Pompey and Caesar's impious armies fight.'[6]
Whether Jove's thunder and divining stroke
He had observed, or how thick air did choke
225 The jarring heavens, or on the poles did look,
Or in the firmament had found this fight
By the sun's paleness and stars' mournful light:
But nature sure did differently display
From other days the sad Thessalian day,
230 And if all men had skilful augurs been,
By all the world Pharsalia had been seen.
Greatest of men, whose fates through the earth extend,[7]

subitos putat esse furores, 'they rejoiced at these portents and mental turmoil, and believed this sudden madness to be an omen of their crimes' (VII. 183–84). Modern editions read *mentisque tumultum*, joining this phrase with *omen scelerum*: 'believed their sudden madness to be a disturbance of the mind and an omen of their crimes'. M.'s 'conceivèd hope' (7. 206) derives from F.'s wording.

[1] No wonder 'tis] *quid mirum* [...] *est*, 'what wonder is it?' (VII. 185–87).
[2] If fates ... to men] Modern editions add this clause to the preceding sentence; 'presaging minds of' = 'minds presaging of'.
[3] in what coast ... abode] *Sub quocunque die, quocunque est sidere mundi*, 'under whatever sun, or whatever star in the world' (VII. 189). Gades (7. 213) is probably anglicized, to rhyme with 'shades'.
[4] Blaming their causeless grief] i.e. grief whose causes they do not know (*& ignorat causas*, 'and doesn't know the causes', VII. 190).
[5] th'Euganean] Trisyllabic.
[6] An augur...] Alluding to accounts that an augur in Patavium, with which all the places L. mentions are associated, proclaimed on the day of Pharsalus that a battle was being fought and Caesar was victor (see e.g. Plutarch, *Caesar*, 47, trans. by Perrin, VII, p. 555). Lit. 'the impious armies of Pompey and Caesar fight', *inpia concurrunt Pompei et Caesaris arma*, VII. 196.
[7] through the earth] Here printed as in *1627* but conceivably elided, in pronunciation, to 'th'earth'; however, there are a number of irregular lines in this passage, the changing

Whom all the gods have leisure to attend,[1]
These acts of yours to all posterity
235 Whether their own great fame shall signify,
Or that these lines of mine have profited
Your mighty names[2] — these wars, when they are read,
Shall stir th'affections of the reader's mind,
Making his wishes and vain fears inclined[3]
240 As to a thing to come, not past, and guide
The hearts of all to favour Pompey's side.[4]
    Pompey descending down the hill displays   [VII. 214] *deploys*
His troops, reflecting rising Phoebus' rays,   *the sun's*
Not rashly o'er the fields:[5] in order good
245 And marshalled well the hapless army stood.[6]
The left wing first was Lentulus his care
With the first legion, then the best in war,
And fourth. Thou, stout Domitius, lead'st the right,
Valiant though still unfortunate in fight.[7]
250 In the main battle with his warlike bands
Brought lately from Cilicia, Scipio stands
Well fortified: here under a command,
A general first in Afric's scorched land.[8]   *Africa's*
But all along the swift Enipeus' side[9]
255 The loose-reined troops of Pontic horsemen ride,
And mountaineers of Cappadocia.
Upon the drier fields in rich array

rhythm perhaps deliberately stressing the gravity of the battle.
[1] Whom ... attend] *quorum fatis coelum omne vacavit*, 'at whose fates the entire sky was emptied' (VII. 206).
[2] lines of mine] *nostri ... cura laboris*, 'the care of my labour' (VII. 208).
[3] Shall stir ... inclined] *Spesque metusque simul, perituraque vota movebunt*, 'and the hope and the fear and at the same time the vain prayers [i.e. for the better side to win] will move [the reader]' (VII. 211).
[4] The hearts] M.'s addition.
[5] Pompey ... fields] *Miles, ut adverso Phoebi radiatus ab ictu | Descendens totos perfudit lumine colles, | Non temere inmissus campis*, 'The soldiers, gleaming from the rays of the sun, when in their descent they flooded the hills with light, were not sent rashly onto the plains' (VII. 214–16).
[6] marshalled well] M.'s addition.
[7] Lentulus ... Domitius] See 2. 493n and 2. 509 ff.
[8] a general first ... land] Scipio (see 2. 503; here pronounced with two syllables) holds a leadership position in the centre, but is not yet the commanding general of Roman forces, as he will be after Pharsalus, and a major character in May's *Continuation*.
[9] the swift Enipeus] *fluvios, & stagna undantis Enipei*, 'the currents and pools of churning Enipeus' (VII. 224); 'Enipeus' is trisyllabic.

>   Do the earth's monarchs, kings and tetrarchs stand,
>   And all the states that Roman swords command.[1]
> 260   Thither from Libya came Numidians,
>   Ituraea's archers, Crete's Cydonians;[2]
>   Fierce Gauls there fought against their wonted foe;
>   There warlike Spaniards their short shields did show.
>   The conqueror of all triumphs now deprive
> 265   And let no people this sad war survive.[3]
>   Caesar, that day dislodging to provide   [VII. 235]
>   For corn,[4] was marching out when he espied
>   The foes descending down the champion field,   *champaign, level.*
>   And that so often wished-for day beheld
> 270   That on one chance of war should set the main.[5]
>   Sick of delay and covetous of reign,
>   In this small tract of time condemned had he
>   The civil war as a slow villainy.
>   But when fate's falling ruin shake he saw,[6]
> 275   And both their fortunes to a trial draw:
>   His wondrous love of sword some languishment
>   'Gan feel.[7] His mind, though ever confident   *began to*
>   Of good success, now doubts: from fear his own,
>   As Pompey's fortunes from presumption,
> 280   Did keep his mind;[8] at last exiling fears,
>   With confidence he cheers his soldiers.[9]
>   'Brave soldiers, the world's awe, Caesar's estate,[10] [VII. 250]

[1] And all ... command] *atque omnis Latio quae servit purpura ferro*, 'And all royalty [lit. purple] in slavery under the Latian sword' (VII. 228).
[2] Ituraea's] Trisyllabic (probably 'Itur-yas' in pronunciation), allowing 'Cydonians' four syllables to rhyme with 'Numidians'.
[3] The conqueror ... survive] *Eripe victori gentes, & sanguine mundi | Fuso, Magne, semel totos consume triumphos*, 'Snatch all races from the victor [Caesar], Pompey, and by shedding the world's blood use up all triumphs [i.e. all opportunities for triumphs]' (VII. 233).
[4] dislodging] i.e. leaving his place of encampment, a military term (*OED*, 2†b). Lit. *statione relicta*, 'leaving his position' (VII. 235).
[5] the main] *omnia*, 'everything', i.e. the whole outcome of the war (VII. 239).
[6] fate's falling ruin] 'When he sensed that the tottering ruin of fate was swaying', *Casuram & fati sensit nutare ruinam* (VII. 244). Modern editions read *et fatis* or *fatis*, 'a ruin caused to totter by the fates'.
[7] wondrous love of sword] *rabies promptissima*, 'most ready frenzy' (VII. 245).
[8] from fear ... his mind] Awkwardly rendering *nec sua fata timere, | Nec Magni sperare sinunt*, 'his own fates didn't allow him to fear, nor Pompey's allow him to hope' (VII. 247–48).
[9] at last ... soldiers] Omitting *prosilit*, 'sprang forth' (VII. 249). The final '-iers' is disyllabic, as often in line-endings (cf. 7. 296, below); in the following line it is only one syllable.
[10] the world's awe, Caesar's estate] *O domitor mundi, rerum fortuna mearum*, 'O tamer of

That day of fight is come which we from fate
So oft have begged. O do not now desire,
But by your valours Fortune's aid acquire.[1]
What Caesar is lies in your hands alone.
This is the day which, passing Rubicon,
Was promised me, in hope of which we stirred[2]
And our forbidden triumphs have deferred.
This is the day that shall restore to you
Children and wives,[3] and shares of land bestow
Freed from war's duties:[4] this the day, that tries
(Witnessed by fate) whose cause the juster is.
This field the conquered side shall guilty make.
If you with fire and sword have for my sake
Assaulted Rome, now fight like soldiers,[5]
And free your swords from guilt. No hand in wars
Is pure in both sides' judgment, nor for me
Fight you alone, but that yourselves may be
Free lords of all the world.[6] I, for mine own
Content, could live in a plebeian gown,
Or be in any state, so you obtain
A perfect freedom:[7] by my envy reign.   *unpopularity*
Nor with much blood shall all the world be bought:[8]
But youths of Greece in schools of wrestling taught,
Base sluggish spirits that never arms did bear,
And mixed barbarian troops are standing there,
That, when the armies join, will ne'er abide
The trumpet's sound nor shouts of their own side.

---

the world, the very fortune of my affairs' (VII. 250).

[1] by your valours ... acquire] *iam fatum accersite ferro*, 'summon fate with your swords' (VII. 252).

[2] we stirred] *movimus arma*, 'took up arms' (VII. 255); the 'forbidden triumphs' (7. 289) are those denied to Caesar for his Gallic campaigns.

[3] Children and wives...] *pignora ... penates*, 'children and households' (VII. 257).

[4] shares of land ... duties] *et emerito faciat vos Marte colonos*, 'and by military service make you colonists' (VII. 258); cf. 4. 435n. M. follows F.'s paraphrase.

[5] fight like soldiers] *pugnate truces*, 'fight savagely' (VII. 262).

[6] Free lords of all the world] *ut libera sitis | Turba ... gentes ut ius habeatis in omneis*, 'so that you can be a free mob and have all peoples under your control' (VII. 264–65).

[7] I ... A perfect freedom] *Ipse ego privatae cupidus me reddere vitae, | Plebeiaque toga modicum conponere civem: | Omnia dum vobis liceant, nihil esse recuso*, 'I'm desirous of returning to private life and settling down as a modest citizen in a plebeian toga: but until everything is granted to you, I refuse to be nothing' (VII. 266–68).

[8] be bought] M.'s idiom; *petistis*, 'you seek' in L. (VII. 270).

310 In civil war few hands, alas, shall fight:[1]
Most of the blows upon Rome's foes shall light,
And rid the world of well-spared people. Go,
Break through those dastard nations, and o'erthrow   *cowardly*
The world at your first onset;[2] make it known
315 That all those nations, which so oft were shown
In Pompey's triumphs, are not worthy proved
Of one poor triumph. Are th'Armenians moved
Think you, what general shall Rome obtain?[3]
With least blood's loss would the barbarians gain
320 A sovereignty for Pompey?[4] They abhor
All Romans as their lords, and hate those more
Whom they have known. The trust of my affairs
To friends, whose valour through so many wars
In France I have beheld, does Fortune now
325 Commit: what soldier's sword do not I know?
And when through th'air a trembling pile is sent,
I'll truly tell you from what arm it went.
These signs I see that ne'er your general failed,
Fierce looks, and threat'ning eyes: you have prevailed.
330 Me thinks the rivers swelled with blood I see,
And at your feet the slaughtered bodies lie
Of kings and senators; nations today
Swim in this bloody field.[5] But I delay
My fortunes in detaining from the field
335 Your forward spirits:[6] pardon me though I yield
A while to pleasing hope.[7] I ne'er did see
The gods so liberal and so speedily:[8]
But one field's distance from our wish are we.

[1] alas] M.'s addition.
[2] Go ... first onset] *Ite per ignavas gentes, famosaque regna, | Et primo ferri motu prosternite mundum*, 'go through the cowardly races and realms known of by repute, and lay low the world with the first blow of your swords' (VII. 277–78).
[3] th'Armenians] Pompeian allies (cf. 3. 266–67).
[4] A sovereignty for Pompey] *Magnum praeponere rebus*, 'put Pompey in charge of things/ the state' (VII. 283). For M.'s idiom, see 1. 338n.
[5] bloody field] *immensa ... in caede*, 'massive slaughter' (VII. 294).
[6] Your forward spirits] *vos in tela ruentes*, 'you, rushing onto [your opponents'] spears' (VII. 295). 'Forward spirits', here pronounced 'sp'rits', is contemporary English idiom for courage in battle: see e.g. Shakespeare, *2 Henry IV*, I. 1. 183.
[7] though ... hope] *bella trahenti; | Spe trepido*, 'one bringing war — in anxious hope' (VII. 296).
[8] so liberal and so speedily] *tam magna daturos, | Tam prope me*, 'about to bestow such great rewards, so near to me' (VII. 298–99).

	That kings and nations are possessed of now,	*that which*
340	When this field's fought is Caesar's to bestow.	
	O gods, what stars, what influence of the sky	
	Has given so great a power to Thessaly?[1]	
	This day allots the punishment or gains	
	Of all our wars. Think upon Caesar's chains,	
345	His racks and gibbets; think you see this face,	
	These quartered limbs stand in the marketplace.[2]	
	Remember Sulla in the field of Mars,	
	For 'gainst a Sullan general are our wars.	
	My care's for you; this hand shall free mine own;[3]	
350	Whoe'er looks back before the day be won,	
	Will see me fall on mine own sword and die.	
	You gods, whose cares are drawn down from the sky	
	By Rome's dissensions,[4] let him conqueror be	
	That to the conquered means no cruelty,[5]	
355	And thinks his countrymen have not in aught	
	Misdone, because against his side they fought.	
	When Pompey in a narrow place had shut	
	Your helpless valour up, how did he glut	
	His sword with blood? But this I beg of you,	
360	Soldiers, let no man wound a flying foe;	
	Account him still your countryman that flies.	
	But while they stand in fight, let not your eyes	
	Be moved with piety, though in that place	
	Your fathers stood, but with your swords deface	
365	Their reverend looks. Whoe'er has sheathed his blade	
	In kinsman's breast, or by the wound he made	
	Has done no wrong to kindred, all as one	

---

[1] influence] Probably disyllabic ('infl-wence'), but an irregular meter cannot be ruled out.
[2] Think upon ... marketplace] *Caesareas spectate cruces, spectate catenas, | Et caput hoc positum rostris, effusaque membra, | Saeptorumque nefas et clausi proelia campi*, 'Look on the Caesarian crosses, look on the chains, and this head placed on the rostra [speakers' platform] and the limbs flung on the ground, and the wickedness of the *Saepta* [voting-places] and the battles of the closed Campus Martius' (VII. 304–06). M.'s vocabulary reflects seventeenth-century punishments and torture; see Introduction, pp. 16–17.
[3] this hand ... mine own] *nam me secura manebit | Sors quaesita manu*, 'for my lot will remain safely sought out by my own hand' (VII. 308–09).
[4] Rome's dissensions] *tellus, | Romanusque labor*, 'the earth and the labour of Rome' (VII. 311–12).
[5] to the conquered means no cruelty] *quicunque necesse | Non putat in victos saevum distringere ferrum*, 'whoever doesn't think it necessary to draw a violent sword upon his foes' (VII. 312–13).

Let him esteem kinsman and foe unknown.¹
Fill up the trenches, tear the rampires down,
370 That in full maniples we may come on.²
Spare not your camp: that camp shall be your own
From which yon dying army is come down.'
Scarce thus had Caesar spoke, when everyone
Fell to their charge and straight their armour don.   *duty*
375 A quick presage of happy war they take,
Of their neglected camp havoc they make;
Not ranked nor marshalled by the general³
Confused they stand, leaving to Fortune all.⁴
Had all been Caesars, had each soldier fought
380 For monarchy and Rome's sole empire sought,⁵
They could not all with more desire come on.⁶
    When Pompey saw them march directly down,   [VII. 337]⁷
That now the war admitted no delay
But this by heaven's appointment was the day,
385 He stands amazed and cold: the war to fear
'Twas fatal in so great a soldier.⁸
But cheering up his men, his own fears hiding,⁹
On a proud steed through every quarter riding,
'The time your valour's wished for,¹⁰ soldiers,
390 Is come,' quoth he, 'the end of civil wars.
This is the sword's last work, the judging hour
Of nations' fates:¹¹ now show your utmost power.

¹ all as one ... unknown] *ignoti iugulum tamquam scelus imputet hostis*, 'let him treat the throat of an unknown enemy as a crime [i.e. as that of a kinsman]' (VII. 325). See Textual Notes.
² in full maniples] Omitting the explanatory *acies non sparsa*, 'in ordered line of battle' (VII. 327). Maniples are small units of infantry.
³ nor marshalled by the general] *Arte ducis nulla*, 'by no art of their leader' (VII. 33): contrast 7. 242–45.
⁴ to Fortune all] *fatis*, 'the fates' (VII. 333)
⁵ Had all been Caesars ... sought] *si totidem Magni soceros, totidemque petentes | Vrbis regna suae funesto in Marte locasses*, 'had you placed as many fathers-in-law of Pompey there, as many people seeking the monarchy of their city in that fateful battle' (VII. 334–35). M. is influenced by F.'s paraphrase.
⁶ with more desire] *tam praecipiti ... cursu*, 'in such a headlong rush' (VII. 336).
⁷ 7. 382–434] Pompey rallies his troops for the battle.
⁸ the war ... soldier] *tantoque duci sic arma timere | Omen erat*, 'it was an omen in itself that such a great general feared to take arms in this way' (VII. 340–41); 'soldier' is once again trisyllabic.
⁹ cheering up his men] M.'s addition.
¹⁰ valour's wished for] i.e. valour *has* wished for.
¹¹ This is ... fates] Antonius in M.'s *The Tragedie of Cleopatra Queen of AEgypt*. Acted 1626

He that would see his household gods again,¹
His country, wife and children, must obtain
395 All by the sword: the gods have in this fight
Disposed them all. Our just cause does invite
To hope;² our swords the gods themselves shall guide
Through Caesar's breast, and in his blood provide
Th'establishment of Roman liberty.³
400 Had they to him decreed a monarchy,⁴
To my old age death might long since have come.
It was no sign the gods were wroth with Rome,⁵
Preserving Pompey for her leader now
And all helps else that conquest can bestow.⁶
405 Illustrious men such as old times did show,⁷
Do willingly these dangers undergo.
Should the Camilli, th'ancient Curii
Revive, or the devoted Decii,⁸
Here they would stand. Forces we have from th'east,
410 Numberless cities' aids: war never pressed⁹
So many hands. We use all nations
Of the whole world: people of all the zones,
Of all mankind 'twixt north and south that dwell,
Are here.¹⁰ We may enclose that army well
415 With our wide stretched-out wings.¹¹ The victory

(London: Thomas Harper for Thomas Walkly, 1639), sig. Cʳ: 'This is the sword's last work, the judging hour | Of Nations' fates, of mine and Caesar's power.' See 7. 695–97 and note.

¹ household gods] Omitting *carosque*, 'cherished' (VII. 346).
² invite | To hope] *iubet ... | Superos sperare secundos*, 'commands us hope for favourable gods' (VII. 349).
³ in his blood ... liberty] *ipsi | Romanas sancire volent hoc sanguine leges*, 'the gods themselves want to hallow Rome's laws with his blood' (VII. 350–51). F. glosses 'laws' as 'liberty'.
⁴ a monarchy] *regna ... mundumque*, 'kingdoms and the world' (VII. 352).
⁵ Rome] *populis urbique*, 'peoples and the city' (VII. 354).
⁶ And all ... bestow] *quae vincere possent | Omnia contulimus*, 'we have gathered everything together which may bring victory' (VII. 355–56).
⁷ Illustrious men ... show] Omitting *sacraque antiquus imagine miles*, 'and veteran soldiers, in their sacred resemblance [to ancient heroes]' (VII. 357). On these Republican examples cf. 1. 185–86, 6. 897.
⁸ devoted Decii] *Deciosque caput fatale voventes*, 'the Decii dedicating their lives to death' (VII. 359); see 2. 325n, 6. 895–96. 'Decii', like 'Curii' in the line above, is trisyllabic.
⁹ pressed] *Excivere*, 'summoned' (VII. 362); cf. 3. 249.
¹⁰ Are here] *sumus, arma movemus*, 'we are and make battle' (VII. 364).
¹¹ We may ... wings] A question in L. (VII. 365–66); 'wings' are the flanks of Pompey's army.

Asks not all hands: some need but shout and cry.¹
Caesar's small strength cannot employ us all.
Think that your mothers from the city wall,
Tearing their hair, entreat your valour now;
Think that the old unarmèd Senate bow
Their honoured hoary heads before your feet,
And Rome herself for liberty entreat.²
Think that this age and our posterity³
Do both entreat: one would in freedom die,
The other be free-born.⁴ And if there be
After these pledges a Rome left for me,⁵
I with my wife and sons before your feet
(If th'honour of a general would permit)
Would fall: unless you conquer here, your shame
And Caesar's mock is banished Pompey's name.
I crave in freedom my last age to spend,
And not be taught to serve so near my end.'⁶
This sad speech fired the Roman spirits anew:⁷
They wish to die, should what they fear be true.
    With equal fury then both armies meet;   [VII. 385]⁸
One for ambition, th'other freedom fight.⁹
These hands shall act what no succeeding year
Nor all mankind forever can repair
Though free from wars; this fight kills men to come,

---

¹ but shout and cry] *tantum clamore ... | Bella gerent*, 'make war by shouting alone' (VII. 367–68).
² unarmèd Senate...] *vetitumque aetate Senatum | Arma sequi*, 'the Senate, forbidden by age from marching to battle', VII. 371-72. And Rome ... entreat] *Atque ipsam domini metuentem occurrere Romam*, 'And that Rome herself, fearing a master, meets you' (VII. 373). F.'s gloss refers to 'liberty'. See Textual Notes.
³ this age and our posterity] *qui nunc est, populum, populumque futurum*, 'the current and future people' (VII. 374).
⁴ one would ... be free-born] *Haec libera nasci | Haec vult turba mori*, 'This throng wants to be born free; this to die [free]' (VII. 375-76).
⁵ a Rome left for me] See Textual Notes.
⁶ unless you conquer ... so near my end] *Magnus, nisi vincitis, exul, | Ludibrium soceri, vester pudor, ultima fata | Deprecor ac turpes extremi cardinis annos | Ne discam servire senex*, 'I, Magnus — who unless you win will be an exile, a thing of mockery to his father-in-law and your shame — lament my final fate, and the disgraceful years of my final stage of life, lest as an old man I must learn to be a slave' (VII. 379–82).
⁷ fired ... anew] *flagrant animi, Romanaque virtus | Erigitur*, 'their wills are inflamed, and Roman virtue stands tall' (VII. 383-4).
⁸ 7. 435–522] L. laments the epochal consequences of Pharsalia.
⁹ ambition ... freedom] *metus hos regni, spes excitat illos*, 'fear of monarchy inspires one army, the hope of it the other' (VII. 386); cf. 1. 95n.

440 And the next age before they enter womb.¹
All Latian names thence fabulous shall be,
And men in ruined dust shall scarcely see²
The Gabii, Veii, Cora, nor the room
Where Alba stood, nor fair Laurentium:
445 A country desolate, which none espies
But the forced consuls in night-sacrifice,
Blaming old Numa's institution.³
These monuments time's ruining hand alone
Has not defaced:⁴ war's civil crimes we see
450 In that so many cities emptied be.
To what small number is mankind reduced?
We all, whom the whole earth has since produced,
Are not enough the towns and fields to fill.
One town receives us all, and bondmen till⁵
455 Th'Italian lands: old houses stand alone
Rotten, and want a man to fall upon.
And wanting her old citizens there slain,
Rome with the dregs of men is filled again.⁶
This slaughter makes that Rome hereafter free
460 From civil war for many years shall be.
Pharsalia is the cause of all these ills.
Let Cannae yield, that our black annals fills,
And Allia damned in Roman calendars.⁷
Rome has remembered these as her small scars,
465 But would forget this day: O fatal time!
Those lives, that fortune had from every clime
Brought here to perish, might all loss repair
Mankind sustains by pestilential air,⁸

---

[1] before they enter womb] *Erepto natale*, 'their birth snatched away from them' (VII. 391).
[2] And men ... see] *Pulvere vix tectae poterunt monstrare ruinae*, 'ruins covered in dust can scarcely show' (VII. 393); L. and M. go on to list now desolate Latin towns.
[3] espies ... institution] 'espies' translates *habitet*, 'frequents' (VII. 395). For the rite discussed here, conducted by Rome's senior magistrates and supposedly instituted by Numa, second king of Rome, cf. 1. 584–87 and note.
[4] ruining] Disyllabic.
[5] bondmen] *vincto fossore*, 'chained labourers' (VII. 402).
[6] dregs of men] *mundi faece*, 'the dregs/sediment of the [rest of the] world' (VII. 405).
[7] Cannae ... And Allia] Cannae (216 BC) and Allia (390 BC), two disastrous defeats for Rome: M.'s added 'black annals' may derive from F.'s observation that Allia was marked among 'black days' in the Roman *Fasti*.
[8] all loss repair | Mankind sustains] i.e. 'repair all the loss that mankind sustains'.

Sickness, town-swallowing earthquakes or fire's rage.[1]
470 Here Fortune shows the gifts of many an age,
People and captains, robbing us of all
In one sad field, to show, when Rome did fall,
How great she fell.[2] The more thou didst possess
Of earth, the shorter was thy happiness.[3]
475 All wars before did land on thee bestow,
To both the poles Sol saw thy conquests go;   *the sun*
But that a little of the east remained,
Thou all the sky-encompassed globe hadst gained,
Thine had been night and day; the stars could shine
480 And planets wander o'er no land but thine.
But this one day thy fate as far back bears,
As 'twas advanced in all those former years.[4]
This bloody day is cause that India
The Roman fasces cannot keep in awe,
485 That consuls do not with their ploughs design
Sarmatian walls,[5] nor in their bounds confine
The Scythian Dahae, that still Parthians owe
For the blood lost in Crassus' overthrow,[6]
That liberty, ne'er to return again
490 And flying civil war, her flight has ta'en
O'er Tigris and the Rhene, and can be brought   *the Rhine*
No more, though with our bloods so often sought.[7]
Would we had ne'er that happiness possessed,[8]
Which Scythia and Germany has blessed:
495 Would Rome had ever served since that first light,[9]
When by the augury of vultures' flight,

---

[1] by pestilential air ... fire's rage] Omitting *insanamque famem*, 'maddened famine'; 'town-swallowing' paraphrases L.'s description of walls hurtling to the ground (VII. 414-16). Lines 469-70 appear to be a couplet of eleven syllables.

[2] when Rome ... How great she fell] L.'s apostrophe to Rome begins here: '[Fortune] shows you Rome, as you fall, how mighty you fall' (*tibi Roma ruenti | Ostendat quam magna cadas*, VII. 418-19); M. delays slightly, starting at 7. 473 (= VII. 419).

[3] The more ... happiness] A question in L. (VII. 419-20).

[4] this one day] *Emathiae funesta dies*, 'the tragic day of Pharsalia [lit. Emathia]' (VII. 427).

[5] That consuls ... walls] The walls of a new Roman colony would be marked by a consul driving a plough, his toga tucked up (*succinctus*, VII. 430, omitted by M.).

[6] Crassus' overthrow] See 1. 11-14.

[7] and can be brought | No more] *nec respicit ultra | Ausoniam*, 'and never looks back again to Italy' (VII. 435-36).

[8] that happiness possessed] i.e. liberty, which remains the subject in L.

[9] had ever served...] *servisses*, 'had been enslaved' (VII. 439). L. alludes to the legend that Romulus founded Rome on the Palatine after witnessing an omen of twelve vultures.

>
> Romulus filled with thieves his walls begun,
> Even 'til Pharsalia's woeful field was won.
> Brutus we tax:¹ Fortune, why did we frame   *blame*
> 500   Our freedom's laws or years by consul's name?
> Happy Arabians, Medes and eastern lands,
> That still have lived under their kings' commands:
> We last of all (though now ashamed to bow)
> A monarch's yoke are forced to undergo.²
> 505   No gods at all have we: when all things move
> By chance, we falsely think there is a Jove.³
> Can he down from the starry sky behold
> Thessalia's slaughter and his thunder hold?
> Can he with thunder cleave a senseless tree,⁴
> 510   Pholoë, Oete, harmless Rhodope?
> Must Cassius' hand rather this tyrant slay?⁵
> He at Thyestes' feast could shut up day,
> Involving Argos in a sudden night:⁶   *enveloping*
> And can he lend Thessalia his light,⁷
> 515   Where brothers fight and sons 'gainst fathers are?
> For mortal men no god at all takes care.
> But for this woe revenge we do obtain
> As much as fits that earth from heaven should gain:
> This war our emperors does equalize
> 520   To gods above and their souls deifies,
> Adorns their heads with thunder, rays and stars:⁸

---

¹ Brutus we tax] *De Brutis, Fortuna, queror*, 'I complain, Fortune, about the Brutuses' (VII. 440), i.e. the founder and avenger of the republic; see 6. 903n.

² We last of all ... undergo] *Ex populis, qui regna ferunt, sors ultima nostra est, | Quos servire pudet*, 'amongst those peoples who endure monarchies, ours is the ultimate lot, whom it shames to be slaves' (VII. 443-44).

³ when all ... Jove] *cum caeco rapiantur saecula casu, | Mentimur regnare Iovem*, 'since all ages are dragged along by blind chance, we lie that Jupiter reigns' (VII. 446-47).

⁴ a senseless tree] Condensing *Immeritaeque nemus Rhodopes, pinusque minanteis*, 'the groves of undeserving Rhodope and menacing pines' (VII. 450); M. instead refers to 'harmless Rhodope' on the next line. Modern editions print *pinusque Mimantis*, 'the pines of Mimas'.

⁵ Cassius' hand] Caius Cassius Longinus, Caesar's eventual murderer in 44 BC and a main character in M.'s *Continuation*; cf. 10. 658.

⁶ Thyestes' feast] See 1. 578.

⁷ Thessalia] Four syllables; contrast 7. 508, above.

⁸ our emperors...] Lit. *divos*, 'divine ones' (VII. 457) — but the emperors are meant, as F. indicates. their souls deifies | Adorns their heads] Translating *manes ... ornabit*, 'will adorn their shades' (VII. 458); probably influenced by F.'s gloss *animas Caes[areas]*, 'the souls of the Caesars'; cf. also M.'s 'men's souls' for *umbras*, 'shades, ghosts' at 7. 521 (VII. 459).

Rome by men's souls in her gods' temples swears.
    When both the armies marching on apace [VII. 460][1]
Near met,[2] stood parted but a little space,
525 They viewed each other's hands, striving to know
Each other's face, thinking which way to throw
Their piles, from whence their fates most threat'ning show,
What monstrous acts they were about to do.[3]
There they their brothers and their fathers spied
530 Against them stand, yet would not change their side.
But piety their breasts amazèd held,
And the cold blood in every limb congealed,
And every soldier his prepared pile
And ready stretched-out arm contained a while.
535 The gods send thee, O Crastinus, not death,
The common plague, but feeling after breath,[4]
Whose pile first thrown of all the fight began,
And Thessaly with Roman blood did stain.
O frantic violence, did Caesar stand
540 Quiet and was there a more forward [(b)]hand?
Shrill cornets then began the air to wound,
Th'alarums beat and all the trumpets sound,
The noise and shouts of soldiers pierce the sky
And reach the convex of Olympus high,
545 Above the thund'ring clouds.[5] The noise they make
The Thracian Haemus' sounding valleys take:
High Pelion's caverns echo back the sound,
Which Pindus and Pangaean rock rebound,
Th'Oetean mountains groan. The soldiers fear
550 Their shouts thus echoed from all hills to hear.

---

[1]   7. 523–74] The battle begins.
[2]   Near met] Compressing L.'s *fati suprema morantem | Consumsere locum*, 'swallowed up the space which delayed the climax of destiny' (VII. 460–61).
[3]   They viewed ... about to do] 7. 525–28 translate lines often rearranged in modern editions and with variant readings. The passage, as M. read it, is:
    Inde manum spectant, vultusque agnoscere quaerunt,
    Quo sua pila cadant, aut quae sibi fata minentur,
    Facturi quae monstra forent.   (VII. 462–64)
('Then they gaze at the band of men, and seek to identify faces, and where their spears will land, or what fates threaten them, and what atrocities they are going to commit').
[4]   the common plague] *quae cunctis poena paratur*, 'the punishment which awaits everyone' (VII. 470). Gaius Crastinus was a Roman centurion.
[5]   Above ... clouds] *Vnde procul nubes, quo nulla tonitrua durant*, 'where all clouds are far away, where no thunder lasts' (VII. 479).

	Numberless piles with different minds are thrown:	*intentions*
	Some wish to wound, others to light upon	
	The ground and keep their harmless hands from ill;	
	Chance rules them and makes guilty whom she will.¹	
555	But the least part of slaughter here was done²	
	With darts and flying steel:³ the sword alone	
	Was able civil quarrels to decide,	
	And Roman hands 'gainst Roman breasts to guide.	
	Pompey's great army narrowly disposed	
560	In a thick phalanx stand with bucklers closed	*shields*
	For fence, but wanted room (their ranks thus filled)	*defence*
	To throw their piles, their swords or arms to wield.⁴	
	But Caesar's loose-ranked troops all nimbly go⁵	
	And the thick-armèd wedges of the foe,	
565	Making their way through men and steel, assail,	
	And through the strongest jointed coats of mail	
	Pierce the ill-guarded breasts:⁶ each stroke finds out	
	A breast, though ne'er so fenced with arms about.	
	One army suffers, t'other makes the war:	
570	All cold and guiltless Pompey's weapons are,	
	All Caesar's impious swords are reeking hot.⁷	
	But Fortune here long doubting wavered not:	
	She swiftly bore (fitting so great a day)	
	A mighty ruin torrent-like away.⁸	
575	When Pompey's horse o'er all the fields at large	[VII. 506]
	Had spread their wings, the foes in flank to charge,⁹	*flanks*

---

¹ Chance] Conflating L.'s *casus* (chance) and *incerta ... Fortuna*, 'fickle Fortune' (VII. 487–88).

² 7. 555–582] Modern editions follow Housman's reordering, which inserts 7. 583–90 (= VII. 514–20) after 7. 554 (= VII. 488).

³ But the least part ... steel] A question in L: *Sed quota pars ...?*, 'but what little part...?' (VII. 489).

⁴ To throw ... wield] L. says they had no room to move their *dextra ac tela*, 'hands and spears' (VII. 494), and separately observes that *gladiosque suos compressa timebat*, 'crammed together, [Pompey's army] feared its own swords' (VII. 494).

⁵ all nimbly go] M.'s idiom: *Praecipiti cursu, vaesanum*, 'frenzied in headlong rush' (VII. 496).

⁶ ill-guarded] *tutoque ... sub tegmine*, 'beneath a safe covering' (VII. 499).

⁷ One army suffers ... hot] *Civilia bella | Vna acies patitur, gerit altera; frigidus inde | Stat gladius, calet omne nocens a Caesare ferrum*, 'One battle-line suffers civil war, the other wages it: on one side the cold sword stands motionless, but every guilty sword of Caesar's is hot' (VII. 501–03).

⁸ torrent-like] *fato torrente*, 'with rushing fate' (VII. 505).

⁹ in flank to charge] *bellique per ultima fudit*, 'and spread throughout the battle's furthest

	The light-armed soldiers scattered all attended,[1]	
	And 'gainst the foe their missile weapons bended.[2]	
	With their own weapons every nation fought,	
580	Yet by all hands the Roman blood was sought.	
	Arrows, stones, fire, lead-headed darts were thrown,	
	Which melted in the air's hot motion.[3]	
	There th'Ituraeans, Medes, Arabians shot	
	Their shafts: good archers all, yet levelled not;[4]	*aimed*
585	The air before their eyes was only sought[5]	
	By their wild aims, yet death from thence was wrought.	
	But no dire crime could stain the foreign steel:	
	Nought could work mischief but the Roman pile.	
	The air was darkened with thick arrows' flight,	
590	Which o'er the fields o'erspread a sudden night.	
	Then (c)Caesar, fearing lest his front should yield	[VII. 521]
	To their assault, obliquely cohorts held	
	Which suddenly from the right wing he sent,	*flank*
	Whither the wheeling horse their forces bent.[6]	
595	But Pompey's horse, unmindful now of fight	
	Nor stayed by shame at all, take speedy flight.	
	Unhappily (alas) were civil wars	
	Left to the trust of barbarous soldiers.[7]	

bounds' (VII. 506). M.'s tactical explication probably follows F.'s note, itself based on Caesar's *Commentarii*, III. 93. 3–4.

[1] scattered] *Sparsa per extremos levis armatura maniplos*, 'the light-infantry, scattered through the maniples on the extremities', i.e. on left and right (cf. 7. 370n).

[2] missile weapons bended] *saevasque manus*, 'their cruel bands [or hands]' (VII. 509). L. may mean they threw themselves into the fray in small companies, but M. follows F.'s explanation.

[3] lead-headed ... motion] *spatioque solutae | Aëris, & calido liquefactae pondere glandes*, 'gobbets dissolving by passing through an expanse of air and made liquid by their hot weight' (VII. 511–13). M.'s rendition depends on F.'s explanation.

[4] good ... levelled not] *Arcu turba minax, nusquam rexere sagittas*, 'a menacing crowd with their bows, but they nowhere controlled their arrows' (VII. 515). In the line above (7. 583), 'th'Ituraeans' has four syllables, with a stress on the first and third (contrast 7. 261); 'Arabians' has three syllables.

[5] before their eyes] *qui campis imminet*, 'which hung over the field' (VII. 516).

[6] Which suddenly ... bent] *inque latus belli qua se vagus hostis agebat, | Immittit subitum non motis cornibus agmen*, 'and without moving his wings sent a sudden column into [Pompey's] flank where the wandering enemy was fighting' (VII. 523–24). M. relies on F.'s commentary, itself based on Plutarch, *Life of Pompey*, 71. 3–4, trans. by Perrin, v. p. 300–01.

[7] alas] M.'s interjection. In 7. 598, the meter calls either for the contraction of 'barbarous', which would mean the expansion of 'soldiers' to three syllables (both quite typical for M.'s translation: see e.g. 7. 607, below), or leaving both as they would normally be pronounced today.

As soon as e'er some gallèd horse had thrown
600 Their riders and their limbs had trampled on,[1]
The horsemen fled and left the field each one,
Or turning reins upon their fellows run.
No fight ensues but execution hot;[2]
One side with sword, the other with bare throat
605 Made war; nor could Caesarian hands suffice
To execute their routed enemies.[3]
O would the blood that barbarous breasts did yield
Could have sufficed Pharsalia's mortal field,
And that no other blood thy streams might stain:[4]
610 Let those bones scattered o'er thy fields remain.
But if thou wouldst with Roman blood be filled,
Spare all the nations.[5] Let the Spaniards wild,
Th'Armenians, Syrians, and Cilicians,
Galatians, Gauls and Cappadocians
615 Survive: for when this civil war is done,
These people will be Romans every one.
These fears once raised through every quarter fly,
Sent by the fates for Caesar's victory.
    Then came the war to Pompey's Roman strength,   [VII. 545]
620 Which o'er the fields were now displayed in length.[6]
There stuck the war, there Caesar's fortune stayed.
No foreign kings fought there, no barbarous aid
From several nations to that place was brought:[7]
There their own brothers, there their fathers fought.
625 Mischief and fury raged: there, Caesar, are
Thy crimes. O fly from this sad part of war,
My soul, and leave it to eternal night:

---

[1] gallèd horse] *transfixus pectora ferro*, 'transfixed in the breast by iron' (VII. 528).

[2] execution hot] *Perdidit inde modum caedes*, 'then slaughter lost all moderation' (VII. 532). For M.'s idiom see e.g. Shakespeare, *Macbeth*, I. 2. 17–18: 'his brandished steel | which smoked with bloody execuṭion'.

[3] nor could ... enemies] L. is more aphoristic: *Nec valet haec acies tantum prosternere, quantum | Inde perire potest*, 'nor had this army the power to lay low so many as that [army] had to perish' (VII. 534–35).

[4] O would ... stain] Addressed to 'Pharsalia' in L. (VII. 535).

[5] all the nations] i.e. all those besides Rome.

[6] Roman strength ... length] Omitting *mediasque catervas*, 'and squadrons in the centre' (VII. 545). See Textual Notes.

[7] barbarous aid | From several nations] Expanding *manus ... rogatae*, 'requested forces' (VII. 549); *rogatae* is the preferred reading today; many Renaissance editions have *togatae*, 'Roman'; F. gives both.

LUCAN'S PHARSALIA

Let no succeeding age by what I write
Learn how much ill may be in civil fight.[1]
630 O rather let our tears and sorrows die:
What here thou didst, O Rome, concealed shall be.[2]
    Caesar, th'inciting fury of his men   [VII. 557]
And spur to their blind rage, lest his guilt then
Should wanting be at all,[3] rides through all parts
635 Adding new fury to their firèd hearts,
Viewing their swords, looking whose points with gore
Were lightly stained, whose blades were bloodied o'er,
Who falter in their blows, who hold their hand,
Who faintly strike, who fight as by command
640 And who with greediness,[4] who changes look
To see a Roman slain. Himself then took
Survey of bodies gasping on the ground,[5]
To let out all the blood crushing their wounds,
As fierce Enyo shakes her bloody lance,[6]
645 And Mars incites his warlike Thracians,[7]
Or drives with furious lashes o'er the field
His horses starting at Minerva's shield.
Black nights of slaughter, and dire deeds arise;
Like one great voice the dying soldiers' cries,
650 Clashing of armed breasts falling to ground,
And swords with swords meeting and breaking, sound.
He with fresh swords his soldiers still supplies[8]
To strike the faces of their enemies,
Forcing them on, still urging at their back,
655 And with his javelin beating on the slack.
Against the Senate, not plebeian foes
He guides their hands and swords:[9] full well he knows

---

[1] what I write ... civil fight] *me vate*, 'by me as a poet' (VII. 553); 'may be' translates *liceat*, 'may be permitted' (VII. 554).
[2] concealed shall be] *tacebo*, 'I will not tell' (VII. 556).
[3] lest ... at all] *Ne qua parte sui pereat scelus*, 'lest wickedness should fail in any part of his army' (VII. 558)
[4] who with greediness] *Quem pugnare iuvet*, 'whom it pleases to fight' (VII. 564).
[5] gasping on the ground] *proiecta*, 'lying outstretched' (VII. 565).
[6] Enyo] *Bellona*, the goddess of war (VII. 568); M. follows F.'s gloss in naming a Fury. 'Enyo' has three syllables.
[7] Thracians] *Bistonas* (VII. 569), a bellicose people often associated with Mars.
[8] with fresh swords ... supplies] Omitting *ac tela*, 'and missiles' (VII. 574).
[9] Against the Senate ... swords] *In plebem vetat ire manus, monstratque Senatum*, 'he forbids his forces to attack plebeians and shows them the Senate' (VII. 578).

	Where the laws live,¹ where the state's blood does flow;	
	Where he may conquer Rome, and overthrow²	
660	The world's last liberty. Together then	
	Fall senators with Roman gentlemen.³	
	Those honoured names Metelli, Lepidi,	
	Corvini and Torquati slaughtered die,	
	That oft commanders o'er great kings have been,⁴	
665	And, except Pompey, still the best of men.	
	In a plebeian helm disguisèd there	[VII. 586]
	What weapon, noble Brutus, ⁽ᵈ⁾didst thou bear?	
	The Senate's highest hope, Rome's greatest grace,	
	The last of all thy ancient honoured race?	
670	Through the armed foes rush not too rashly on,	
	Nor seek out thy Philippic fate too soon:⁵	
	Fate will to thee a Thessaly allot.	
	In vain thou aimest there at Caesar's throat:	
	He has not yet mounted the top of fate	
675	And reached that height that governs human state,⁶	
	To merit that brave death;⁷ no, let him reign,	
	That he, as Brutus' off'ring, may be slain.	
	Here all Rome's honour dies, here heaped on high	[VII. 597]
	The slaughtered Senate with plebeians lie.⁸	
680	But 'mongst those nobles that to Styx were sent,⁹	
	Warlike Domitius' ⁽ᵉ⁾death was eminent,	
	Whom fates had carried through all overthrows;	

---

¹ Where the laws live] Following Grotius's conjecture *viscera legum*, 'the vitals of the laws' (VII. 579), recorded by F.; modern editions read *rerum*, i.e. 'the vitals of the state'.
² overthrow] *petat*, 'search out, attack' (VII. 580).
³ senators with Roman gentlemen] *secundo | Ordine nobilitas*, 'the nobility with the second [i.e. equestrian] order' (VII. 581–82); M. omits *venerandaque corpora ferro | Vrgentur*, 'and hallowed bodies are beset by the sword' (VII. 582–83).
⁴ Those honoured names ...] Names of illustrious Roman nobility: the sense is general.   commanders o'er great kings] Translating *regum | Saepe duces*, 'often leaders of kings' (VII. 484–85), a common early modern reading noted by F., who nonetheless prefers a conjecture of Grotius, *legum*, '[leaders of] the laws'. Modern editions print *rerum*, '[leaders of] the state'.
⁵ Philippic fate] i.e. the battle of Philippi, in 42 BC, which Brutus (cf. 2. 247 ff., 6. 903) and Cassius (cf. 7. 511) fought and lost against forces led by Octavian and Mark Antony.
⁶ that height ... human state] *Iuri, & humani culmen, quo cuncta premuntur*, 'that pinnacle of human law by which everything is oppressed' (VII. 594).
⁷ brave death] *tam nobile letum*, 'so noble a death' (VII. 595).
⁸ with plebeians lie] *commista plebe*; modern editions read *non mixta plebe*, 'not mixed with plebeians' (VII. 598).
⁹ those nobles ... sent] *clarorum in strage virorum*, 'in that massacre of famous men' (VII. 599); on Domitius cf. 7. 248n.

Ne'er without him did Pompey's fortune lose;
Vanquished so oft by Caesar, yet dies now
685 With liberty and gladly falls into
A thousand wounds, proud that he shall no more
Be pardoned now. Him weltering in his gore
Caesar espied, with taunts upbraiding thus:
'Now my successor,[1] proud Domitius,
690 At length thou shalt forsake thy Pompey's side,
And war is made without thee.' He replied
With that last breath which in his dying breast
Struggled: 'Thou, Caesar, hast not yet possessed
The dire reward of all thy wickedness:
695 But yet art doubtful of thy fate, and less
Than Pompey, under whom secure I go   *carefree*
And a free ghost down to the shades below,[2]
And dying hope that thou subdued today
To us and him for thy misdeeds shalt pay.'
700 With this last speech away his spirit flies,
And night eternal closes up his eyes.
    We cannot in the world's sad funeral   [VII. 617]
Particular tears pay to the death of all,[3]
Nor search each private fate: whose breast a wound
705 Received; who spurned men's hearts upon the ground;[4]
Who through the mouth received his mortal wound
And thence breathed out his soul; who fell to ground
At the first stroke; who stood upright, the while
His lopped-off limbs fell down; who with a pile
710 Was fast nailed to the earth; whose blood spun out
And sprinkled all his foe's armed breast about;
Who kills his brother, and that then he may
Without shame rifle, throws his head away;   *pillage*
Who tears his father's face, that standers-by
715 Conjecture by his too much cruelty
'Twas not his father whom he robbed of life.
No death is worthy of particular grief,

---

[1] successor] Domitius had been due to take over the governorship of Gaul after Caesar's term of office ended.
[2] under whom secure ... shades below] The words also of the dying Antonius in M.'s *Cleopatra*, sig. D7ʳ; cf. 7. 392n.
[3] Particular] Probably shortened to 'partic'lar' in pronunciation (and in 7. 717, below).
[4] who ... upon the ground] *quis fusa solo vitalia calcet*, 'who tramples his vitals spilt on the ground' (VII. 620).

Nor have we time to weep for every wight.   *man*
No other loss was like Pharsalia's fight:
720 Rome there by soldiers, here by kingdoms dies:
There private men's, here nations' tragedies:[1]
Here flowed Assyrian, Grecian, Pontic blood;
But all these bloods the powerful Roman flood
Drove through the field away.[2] All people there
725 Are deeplier wounded than one age can bear:
Far more than life, than safety here is gone;
For all succeeding times we are o'erthrown.
These swords subdue all ages that shall serve.[3]
Alas what could posterity deserve
730 To be in thraldom born?[4] Fought we with fear?
Spared we our throats? The punishment we bear
Of others' flight.[5] To us that since do live
Fates should give war, if they a tyrant give.[6]

Pompey perceived Rome's fate and gods were gone,   [VII. 647]
735 In all this loss not movèd for his own
Ill-hap.[7] Ascending a small hill to see
The slaughters all that covered Thessaly,
Which while the war endured could not be spied,
He thence discerned how many people died,
740 How many swords reach at his destiny,
In how much blood he falls. Nor wishes he
(As wretches use) all with himself to drown   *are accustomed to do*
And mix the nations' ruin with his own,
But for survival of most part of men[8]
745 He deigns to think the gods worthy even then
Of prayers from him, and makes this to be

---

[1] Rome there … nations' tragedies] *illic per fata virorum, | Per populos hic Roma perit: quod militis illic, | Mors hic gentis erat*, 'in other battles Rome perished by the deaths of men, but here by whole peoples; there soldiers died, here a whole race' (VII. 633–35).

[2] Drove … away] *haerere … campisque vetat consistere*, 'forbade from clinging to and stopping on the battlefield' (VII. 636–37).

[3] that shall serve] i.e. and thereby condemn them to be enslaved forever.

[4] in thraldom born] *In regnum nasci*, 'to be born into a monarchy' (VII. 643); cf. 1. 5n.

[5] flight] *timoris*, 'cowardice' (VII. 644).

[6] To us … tyrant give] *post proelia natis | Si dominum, Fortuna, dabas, et bella dedisses*, 'If, Fortune, you gave a master to those born after the battle, you ought to have given wars too' (VII. 645–46).

[7] Pompey … not movèd] *vix clade coactus*, 'hardly moved by this catastrophe' (VII. 648); M. also omits L.'s adjective *infelix*, 'unfortunate', for Pompey.

[8] most part of men] *Latiae … pars maxima turbae*, 'the greatest part of the Roman throng' (VII. 656).

His sorrow's comfort. 'Spare, ye gods,' quoth he,
'To sink all nations: Pompey (if you list)   *desire*
Although the world remain and Rome subsist,
750 May be made wretched. If more wounds on me
You would inflict, a wife and sons have I:
So many pledges have we given to fate.
Is't nought for civil war to ruinate
Me and my house? Are we a loss so small
755 Without the world? Why wouldst thou ruin all,
Fortune? Now nought is mine.' With that he rides
Through his distressèd troops, and on all sides
Sounds a retreat, from death calling them back,[1]
Thinking himself not worth so great a wrack.   *disaster*
760 Nor lacked he spirit their weapons to defy
With throat or breast, but feared, if he should die,
No soldier then would fly but there would fall,
And all the world die with their general:
Or out of Caesar's sight a death he sought
765 In vain; thy head to Caesar must be brought,[2]
Where'er he please to see't. His wife's dear sight
Another reason was that caused his flight,
For in her sight the fates his death decreed.[3]
Then Pompey, mounted on a gallant steed,
770 Fled from the field, fearing no swords behind,
Bearing still a fate-unconquered mind;[4]
No sighs or tears he spent: with majesty
His grief was mixed, such as befitted thee,
Pompey, in Rome's calamity to shew.   *show*
775 With looks unchanged didst thou Emathia view.
That mind which war's success could ne'er erect
To pride, war's losses cannot now deject.
Fortune's as far below thy wretched fate,

---

[1] With that he rides … back] *sic fatur & arma, | Signaque, & afflictas omni iam parte catervas | Circuit, & revocat matura in fata ruentes*, 'thus he spoke and rode round the arms and standards and the squadrons afflicted in every part, and recalled them as they were rushing to their ripened fates' (VII. 666-68).

[2] thy head] L. doesn't address this remark clearly to Pompey; the next two (7. 766-68 = VII. 675-77) are addressed to Cornelia.

[3] the fates … decreed] M. follows the early modern reading *fatisque probatum*, 'approved by the fates' (VII. 676); modern editions read *fatisque negatum*, 'denied by the fates'.

[4] a fate-unconquered mind] *Ingentesque animos extrema in fata ferentem*, 'bearing his greatness of mind towards his ultimate fate' (VII. 679). The line is (probably knowingly) irregular.

              As she was false to thy triumphant state.¹
780   Securely now from empire's burden free   *unconcerned*
           Thou goest:² and on thy past prosperity
           Hast time to look; all boundless hopes are gone;
           And what thou wert may now be truly known.³   *were*
              Fly this dire battle, and to witness call   [VII. 689–727]
785   The gods that none for thy sake, Pompey, fall,
           That stay behind thee; in Thessalia,
           No more than Egypt, Munda, Africa,
           The battle's greatest part fought not for thee.⁴
           Nor shall the honoured name of Pompey be
790   War's quarrel now:⁵ the foes that still will be
           'Mongst us, are Caesar and Rome's liberty,
           And 'twill appear more plain after thy flight
           The dying Senate for themselves did fight.
           Let thy flight comfort thee: thou shalt not see
795   Those blood-stained troops nor their impiety;
           The rivers swelled with blood look back and see,
           And pity Caesar. With what heart can he
           Revisit Rome, made happier by this field?
           What banishment in foreign lands can yield
800   To thee, by thee whate'er can be endured
           Under th'Egyptian tyrant, rest assured
           The gods and favouring fates as best prefer:
           'Twere worse for thee to be the conqueror.⁶
           Let all the peoples wail and weep no more
805   But dry their tears, and let the world adore
           As well thy ruin as prosperity.

¹ triumphant state] L. mentions Pompey's three triumphs, *tres ... triumphos* (VII. 685).
² from empire's burden free | Thou goest] *iam pondere fati* | *Deposito*, 'having put down the weight of fate' (VII. 686–87). M. directly translates F.'s paraphrase. 'Goest is pronounced 'go'st'; cf. 7. 36.
³ all boundless hopes ... truly known] *spes nunquam implenda recessit,* | *Quid fueris nunc scire licet*, 'hope never to be fulfilled has vanished, and what you were you are now allowed to know' (VII. 688–89).
⁴ The battle's ... not for thee] *sic et Thessalicae post te pars maxima pugnae*, 'thus after you [i.e. your departure] the greatest part even of the Thessalian battle' (VII. 693). M. follows early modern punctuation in taking this clause with *nullum ... iam tibi Magne mori*, 'no-one dies for you Magnus' (VII. 690–91 = 7. 785), but modern texts join it to the next thought (7. 789–91 = VII. 694–96), i.e. after Pompey's departure the only struggle left was between Caesar and liberty.
⁵ be | War's quarrel now] Added to make sense of the syntax: see 7. 788n.
⁶ 'Twere worse ... conqueror] *Vincere peius erat*, 'it was worse to win' (VII. 706). On the 'Egyptian tyrant' (i.e. Ptolemy), see 8. 535 ff.

Look upon kings with a commanding eye,[1]
Egypt and Libya's kings whom thou hast crowned,
And cities built by thee,[2] and choose a ground
810 Where thou wilt die. Larissa town beheld
(First witness of thy fall) fled from the field
Thy noble self, unconquered by the fates.
Whose citizens all issuing forth the gates[3]
To meet thee (as if conqueror) they went,
815 And gifts from love and sorrow did present:
They ope their temples and their houses all.[4]
Much of his great name's left; in his own eye
He seems the least; nations would help him try
Once more his fortune and renew the war.
820 He cries, 'Be faithful to the conqueror:
What should the conquered do with towns and men?'
Thou, Caesar, in thy country's bowels then
Wert wading through Pharsalia's bloody field,
Whilst people's loves to thee he reconciled.[5]
825 Pompey rides thence; the people sigh, and cry,
And rail against each cruel deity.
The people's favour now is truly proved:
Whilst great, thou couldst not know thyself beloved.[6]
    When Caesar saw the field with Roman blood   [VII. 728]
830 Was overflowed enough, he thought it good
His swords from execution to refrain
And spare poor lives that would have died in vain.[7]
But lest the foes should to their camp in flight
Retire, and rest should banish terror quite,
835 He straight determines to assault their wall,
Whilst fortune's hot and terror works in all.

---

[1] commanding eye] *vultu non supplice*, 'with no submissive expression' (VII. 709).
[2] cities built by thee] *possessas urbes*, 'cities possessed', i.e. captured (VII. 710); F.'s note refers to Pompeiopolis, a city Pompey *did* build. Pompey had enthroned the Ptolemies and the client-king of Numidia.
[3] issuing] Probably disyllabic.
[4] all] Omitting *socios se cladibus optant*, 'they choose to be allies in his calamity' (VII. 716).
[5] Whilst ... reconciled] *At tibi iam populos donat gener*, 'yet your son-in-law bestows peoples on you' (VII. 723).
[6] The people's favour ... beloved] *Nunc tibi vera fides quaesiti, Magne, favoris | Contigit, ac fructus: felix se nescit amari*, 'Now the true loyalty and fruit of the favour you sought has touched you, Magnus: the fortunate man does not know he is loved' (VII. 726–27).
[7] His swords...] Omitting *manibusque suorum*, 'and [his soldiers] hands', VII. 729.
poor lives] *viles animas*, 'contemptible souls', VII. 730.

        Nor does he think that this command appears
        Too harsh to hot and wearied soldiers:
        Small exhortation leads them to the prey.[1]
840 'Our victory', quoth he, 'is full today,
        And for our blood nought is remaining now
        But the reward, which 'tis my part to show,
        I cannot say to give, what every man
        Shall give himself. Behold yon tents that stand
845 Full of all riches: there gold raked in Spain,   *gathered*
        There th'Eastern nations' treasuries remain.
        Pompey's and all those kings' estates do lack
        Possessors, soldiers: run and overtake
        Whom you pursue, and whatsoe'er to you
850 Pharsalia gives, take from the conquered now.'
        This speech of Caesar's and gold's impious love
        Over the swords the furious soldiers drove,
        To tread on senators and captains slain.
        What trench, what bulwark could their force sustain?
855 Seeking the price of all their wars and sin,
        To know for what they have so guilty been.[2]
          Spoiling the world they found a wealthy mass   [VII. 752]
        Which for war's future charges gathered was:
        But their all-coveting thoughts could not be filled
860 With what Spain's mines and Tagus' streams could yield,
        Or on their sands rich Arimaspians find;
        Though all the spoils be theirs, yet in their mind
        Their mischief at too cheap a sale they vent,
        And are bid loss in spoiling of these tents,
865 When to himself the conqueror Rome decreed,
        And in that hope whole mountains promisèd.[3]
        Patricians' tents impious plebeians keep,
        In kings' pavilions common soldiers sleep[4]
        On brothers' and on fathers' empty beds

---

[1] to the prey] *In praedam*, 'into plunder' (VII. 737). 'Soldiers' (7. 838) is trisyllabic.

[2] To know ... guilty been] *Scire volunt, quanta fuerint mercede nocentes*, 'they want to know at what price they were guilty' (VII. 749-51). Modern editions print *scire ruunt*, 'they rush to know'.

[3] And are bid loss ... promisèd] 'Bid loss' copies F.'s rare English gloss on *Decipitur*, 'are deceived' (VII. 760). While Caesar has promised *omnia*, 'everything' (VII. 759; M. translates as 'whole mountains'), in fact he reserves Rome (lit. *Tarpaeias ... arces*, 'Tarpeian citadels', VII. 758) to himself.

[4] common soldiers] *infandus miles*, 'sacrilegious soldiery' (VII. 762).

870	The killers lay their parricidal heads.
	But furious dreams disturb their restless rest:
	Thessalia's fight remains in every breast;
	Their horrid guilt still wakes, the battle stands
	In all their thoughts, they brandish empty hands
875	Without their swords. You would have thought the field
	Had groaned, and that the guilty earth did yield
	Exhaled spirits that in the air did move,
	And Stygian fears possessed the night above.
	A sad revenge on them their conquest takes:
880	Their sleeps present the Furies' hissing snakes
	And brands;[1] their countrymen's sad ghosts appear,
	To each the image of his proper fear.
	One sees an old man's visage, one a young,
	Another's tortured all the evening long
885	With his slain brother's spirit; their father's sight
	Daunts some. But Caesar's soul all ghosts affright.
	Orestes so, not purged in Scythia,
	Th'Eumenides' affrighting faces saw;
	Not more was Pentheus in Agave's fit
890	Dismayed, nor she when she was freed from it.[2]
	Him all the swords that dire Pharsalia saw
	And which the Senate in revenge should draw,
	Oppress that night, and hellish monsters scourge.
	But that which most his guilty soul did urge
895	Was this, that Styx, the fiends and Furies grim
	(Pompey being yet alive) had seized on him.
	But having suffered all, when day's clear light
	Displayed Pharsalia's slaughter to his sight,
	No dismal objects could avert his eyes
900	From thence: the rivers swelled with blood he sees,
	And heaps of bodies equalling high hills,
	And carcasses whence blood and filth distils.
	He numbers Pompey's people, and that place
	Ordains for banqueting from whence each face
905	He might discern and know them as they lie,

---

[1] The Furies' hissing snakes | And brands] *Sibilaque & flammas infert sopor*, 'sleep introduces hissing and flames' (VII. 772). M.'s expansion derives from F.'s gloss.

[2] Orestes so ... freed from it] Two famous examples of tragic madness. The Furies (Eumenides) pursued Orestes after he killed his mother Clytemnestra; he would eventually be purified in Scythian Tauros and released from their harassment. On Agave and Pentheus (here again disyllabic) see 1. 611, 6. 403–05.

	Proud that Emathia's earth he cannot see	
	Or scarce discern the slaughter-covered ground.	
	In blood his fortune and his gods he found.	
	And with that joyful sight to feed his eyes,	
910	To the wretch'd souls he funeral fire denies,	
	Making Emathia noisome to the air.	
	Carthage, that gave our consuls sepulchre	
	And Libyan fire on Cannae did confer,	
	Could not teach him his enemies t'inter:[1]	
915	Rememb'ring still (his anger not even then	
	With slaughter slaked) they were his countrymen.	
	We do not several fires or tombs desire:	
	Do but to all these nations grant one fire,	
	And let them not on piles distinct be brent;	*pyres; burned*
920	Or if thou aim at Pompey's punishment,	
	Piled up let Pindus' wood and Ossa be,[2]	
	That he from sea Pharsalia's fire may see.	
	This anger boots thee not, for 'tis all one	
	Whether the fire or putrefaction	
925	Dissolve them; all to nature's bosom go,	
	And to themselves their ends the bodies owe.	
	If now these nations, Caesar, be not burned,	
	They shall, when earth and seas to flames are turned.	
	One fire shall burn the world, and with the sky	
930	Shall mix these bones; where'er thy soul shall be	
	Their souls shall go; in air thou shalt not fly	
	Higher, nor better in Avernus lie.[3]	
	Death frees from fortune; earth receives again	
	Whatever she brought forth; and they obtain	
935	Heaven's coverture that have no urns at all.	*covering*
	Thou that deny'st these nations funeral,	
	Why dost thou fly these slaughter-smelling fields?	
	Breathe, if thou can'st, the air this region yields,	
	Or drink this water, Caesar, but from thee	
940	The rotting people challenge Thessaly,	
	And keep possession 'gainst the conqueror.	
	To the sad food of this Emathian war,	[VII. 825]

---

[1] his enemies t'inter] *hominum ritus ut servet in hostes*, 'to follow human custom in respect of enemies' (VII. 801). The reference is to Hannibal's ritual burning of the Roman dead, including their consuls, after his victory at Cannae (216 BC).

[2] Ossa be] Apparently misreading L.'s *Oetaeo*, 'Oetaean [wood]' (VII. 807).

[3] in Avernus lie] *Stygia sub nocte*, 'in Stygian night' (VII. 817).

　　　　Scenting from far the blood's corruption,
　　　　The Thracian wolves, Arcadian lions run;[1]
945　　Bears from their dens, dogs from their kennels come;
　　　　And all those ravenous creatures else on whom[2]
　　　　Nature bestows the strongest scents, full well
　　　　The air, by carrion putrified, to smell.
　　　　Hither all birds of prey assembled are,
950　　That long had waited on this civil war:
　　　　Birds that from Thrace to Nile in winter go,
　　　　Stayed longer then than they were wont to do;[3]
　　　　Ne'er did more birds of prey in one air fly,[4]
　　　　Nor did more vultures ever cloud the sky.
955　　From every wood came fowl: each tree was filled
　　　　With bloody birds that crimson drops distilled.
　　　　Down from the air blood and corruption rained　　　　　*rained on*
　　　　The conqueror's face, and impious eagles stained.
　　　　Birds from their weary tallands oft let fall　　　　　　*talons*
960　　Gobbets of flesh. Nor were the people all
　　　　Consumèd so, buried in bird or beast,
　　　　Which would not on their bowels fully feast
　　　　Nor suck their marrow all, but lightly taste.
　　　　The greatest part of Roman flesh is cast
965　　Disdained away, which by the sun and time
　　　　Dissolved, is mixèd with Thessalian slime.
　　　　　Unhappy Thessaly, what hast thou done　　　　　[VII. 847–72]
　　　　T'offend the angry gods,[5] that thee alone
　　　　So many deaths and impious fates should stain?
970　　What age, what length of time can purge again
　　　　The guilt that thou hast wrought?[6] What corn in thee
　　　　And grass with blood discoloured shall not be?
　　　　What ploughshare but some Roman ghost shall wound?
　　　　Before that time new battles on thy ground

---

[1] Thracian wolves, Arcadian lions run] L. refers to the more specific regions of Bistonia and Mount Pholoë (VII. 826–27).
[2] ravenous] Probably contracted to 'rav'nous'.
[3] Birds ... do] An apostrophe in L.: *vos ... aves* ('you birds', VII. 832–34); referring to cranes, who delay migration in order to feast.
[4] did ... fly] *presserunt aëra pennae*, 'feathers beat the air' (VII. 835).
[5] what hast ... angry gods] *quo tantum crimine ... | Laesisti superos*, 'with what crime so great have you wounded the gods' (VII. 847–48).
[6] purge again ... hast wrought] *quod sufficit aevum, | Inmemor ut donet belli tibi damna vetustas?*, 'what age is sufficient, that forgetful antiquity grant you pardon for the losses of this war?' (VII. 849–50).

975 Shall be, and impious civil wars shall stain
     Thy fields (before this blood be dry) again.¹
     If all the graves of our dead ancestors
     He should turn up² — their tombs that stand, and theirs
     Whose time-consumèd urns have cast abroad
980 Th'enclosèd dust — more ashes would be trod,
     And bones by harrows' teeth digged up and found
     In the sad furrows of Thessalia's ground.
     No mariners had sailèd from thy shore,³
     Nor husbandmen had ploughed thee anymore,
985 The Roman people's grave; thy ghostly field
     Had no inhabitant forever tilled;
     No herds of cattle on thy plains had run,
     Nor durst the shepherds feed their flocks upon   *dared*
     Thy pasture fields, with Roman blood manured;⁴
990 Nor habitable nor to be endured⁵
     (As in the torrid or cold icy zone),
     Shouldst thou have lyen, forsaken and unknown,⁶   *lain*
     If thou hadst been not first, but only seat
     Of wicked war. O give us leave to hate
995 This guilty land: ye gods, why do you stain
     The world, t'absolve it so? The blood in Spain,
     Sicilian seas, Mutina, Leucas spilt,
     Has quite absolved Philippi fields from guilt.⁷

FINIS.

---

¹ again] i.e. the battle of Philippi in 42 BC.
² He should] See Textual Notes.
³ had] = would have (a contrary-to-fact condition that continues in the subsequent clauses).
⁴ No herds of cattle ... manured] *gregibus dumeta carerent: | Nullusque auderet pecori permittere pastor | Vellere surgentem de nostris ossibus herbam*, 'the thickets would have lacked flocks, and no herdsman would dare to allow their cattle to pluck grass rising from our bones' (VII. 862–65).
⁵ Nor] Neither ... nor. In L. this and the following ideas are conjectures, beginning with *velut ... vel*, 'as if ... or' (VII. 866–67).
⁶ lyen] Pronounced 'line'.
⁷ O give us leave ... guilt] Future scenes of civil war. 'The blood in Spain' (*Hesperiae clades*, 'the Western slaughters', VII. 871) refers to the battles of Munda and Mylae. 'Sicilian seas' (*flebilis unda Pachyni*, 'the sorrowful water of Pachynus', VII. 871) evokes the battle of Naulochus in 36 BC. 'Mutina' is the battle of Mutina, 43 BC, waged between Antony and a senatorial coalition under Brutus; Leucas the battle of Actium, the final battle between Antony and Octavian, 31 BC. See 1. 43–46, 731–34, 6. 343–44.

Annotations on the Seventh Book

(a) The same day when this great Pharsalian field was fought, an Augur C. Cornelius being then at Patavium, observing his rules of augury, told unto them that stood by him the very instant when the battle began; and going again to his art, returned as it were inspired, and cries out with a loud voice, 'Caesar the day is thine'.[1]

(b) This Crastinus was an old soldier of Caesar's army, and now Emeritus, that is freed from the duties of the war, but for love of Caesar served in this war a voluntary. He, desiring to give the onset, spake this to Caesar: 'I hope, Caesar, this day so to behave myself, that thou shalt thank me either alive or dead'. He was slain run through the mouth.[2]

(c) When Caesar perceived that his horsemen could not withstand the force of Pompey's horsemen and archers, he drew forth 3000 men, which for that purpose he had placed in the right wing, they with such fury assaulted Pompey's horsemen, that they all fled; after whose flight all the archers wanting their defence were without resistance slain.[3]

(d) Marcus Brutus was there fighting in plebeian armour, and 'scaped the knowledge of Caesar's soldiers. This was that Brutus, that joining afterwards with Cassius was with him vanquished in the Philippian fields by Octavius and Antonius; after which battle all hope of Roman liberty was forever lost.[4]

(e) L. Domitius was by the Senate's decree to succeed Caesar in the government of France; in this war taking Pompey's side he was at Corfinium by his own soldiers brought bound to Caesar, and by him pardoned: afterward in Massilia he was vanquished by D. Brutus, Caesar's lieutenant, and fled.[5]

---

[1] Translating F.'s note to VII. 192.
[2] Translating F.'s note to VII. 471, itself drawing on Caesar, *Commentarii*, III. 91. 1, 99. 2.
[3] Compressing F.'s notes to VII. 521 and 524.
[4] Largely M.'s own note; one notes the emphasis again on liberty forever lost.
[5] This note translates two notes by F. on Domitius (notes to II. 479 and V. 220), both cross-referenced by F. himself in his note to VII. 600.

To the Right Honourable, Theophilus, Earl of Lincoln, &c.[1]

To you (most noble patriot), I present
Lucan's eighth book, a weeping monument
Of noble Pompey's death, where his great deeds,
In spite of Fortune's envy, find their meeds; *rewards*
5   And where life-giving lines, by times to come,
Shall make that little and unworthy tomb
That kept great Pompey's dust more honoured far
Than the great temples of the conqueror.[2]
Great men, as well the good as bad, may fall
10 By Fate's resistless power, but here lies all
The difference: the good (though fall'n) do lie
Great in their ruins, and posterity
Pays them their due; the bad (though great) man's name
Dies with himself, or leaves no heir but shame.[3]

---

[1] Theophilus, Earl of Lincoln] Theophilus Clinton, fourth Earl of Lincoln (c. 1600–1667): like most other dedicatees of *1627*, a peer of staunchly Puritan beliefs, who also raised and led troops on Protestant campaigns abroad in the early 1620s (James W. F. S. Hill, *Tudor and Stuart Lincoln* (Cambridge: Cambridge University Press, 2009), pp. 115, 117). M.'s dedication to him of a book commemorating a 'good (though fall'n)' hero and terming Lincoln 'patriot' is pointed: resistance to the Forced Loan in late 1626, which probably included complicity in a pamphlet circulated in Lincolnshire foreboding that 'we make ourselves and our posterity subject to perpetual slavery', saw Clinton imprisoned in the Tower at the time of *1627*'s publication (Richard Cust, *The Forced Loan and English Politics, 1626–1628* (Oxford: Oxford University Press, 1987), pp. 172–73). He was released in March 1628.

[2] a weeping monument ... conqueror] M. blends L.'s own defiant tribute to Pompey (see below, 8. 749–1006, esp. 1000–04 for the contrast with Caesar which M. echoes here) with the conventional language of early modern epitaphs, on which see e.g. P. Sherlock, *Monuments and Memory in Early Modern England* (Aldershot: Ashgate, 2008).

[3] Great men ... but shame] M.'s celebration of virtuous nobility in adverse circumstances has obvious topicality when applied to an imprisoned nobleman.

LUCAN'S
Pharsalia

The Eighth Book.

The Argument of the Eighth Book.[1]

Through devious deserts vanquished Pompey flies   *remote, circuitous; wilderness*
And sails to Lesbos, whence with weeping eyes
He takes his wife.[2] In several flying fleets
Sextus and other Roman lords he meets.[3]
5   Deiotarus the Gallogrecian king
Is sent to great Arsacides, to bring
To aid of Pompey's side the Parthian bows.[4]
The lords consult where to retire,[5] and chose   *choose*
Egypt's base shore. Th'unthankful king betrays
10   Old Pompey coming, and before the face
Of Sextus and Cornelia, ere he lands,
By base Achillas' and Septimius' hands
Great Pompey dies.[6] By night poor Codrus comes,
And on the shore his half-burnt trunk entombs
15   Without the head. The author doth inveigh
'Gainst treacherous Egypt, and base Ptolemy.[7]

O'er woody Tempe and th'Herculean straits,   [VIII. 1][8]
Following th'Haemonian woods' desert retreats[9]

---

[1] The Argument] See Argument to book one.
[2] weeping eyes] Echoing Sulpizio (*lachrymando*) but also corresponding to M.'s 'weeping monument', 8. Ded. 2.
[3] Sextus ... meets] Sextus Pompeius; cf. 6. Arg. 9.
[4] Deiotarus ... Parthian bows] Addition to Sulpizio. On Deiotarus, king of Galatia ('Gallogrecia') see 5. 63; Arsacides = Orodes II, king of the Parthians and responsible for the defeat of Crassus in 53 BC (see 1. 11–14).
[5] The lords] The Senate.
[6] Th'unthankful king ... Pompey dies] Ptolemy, king of Egypt. A pointed change to Sulpizio's *venientem regia prodit: | Coniugeque, & gnato coram confodit Achillas*, 'the palace betrays the one arriving: Achillas stabs him in front of his wife and son'.
[7] The author ... Ptolemy] Added by M.
[8] 8. 1–55] Pompey's flight from Pharsalia, finally arriving at the island of Lesbos.
[9] Following] Probably contracted to two syllables in pronunciation, eliding the middle vowel; cf. 'foll[o]wers', 8. 8 below.

(Though far about) great Pompey rode: his steed,
Quite spent past help of spur, had lost his speed.
5 Through devious ways he turns and leaves behind   *out-of-the-way*
No track of his uncertain flight:[1] the wind,
Filling the shaken woods with murmuring noises,
Made him afraid, and his own followers' voices
That rode behind and by him. For although
10 Fall'n from his height of former fortunes now,
He thinks his blood set at no vulgar rate,
But as high-prized, still mindful of his fate,
By Caesar, as himself for Caesar's head
Would give. But through the deserts as he fled,   *wilderness*
15 His presence and majestic face denied
A safe concealment:[2] many, as they hied   *hastened*
Unto his camp and had not heard his fall,
Stood in amaze to meet their general,
Wond'ring at fortune's turns, and scarce is he
20 Beleft, relating his own misery.[3]   *believed*
He grieves that any his low state should see,
And wishes rather in all lands to be
Unknown, and through the world obscurely go.[4]
But Fortune's ancient favour brings this woe
25 His present sinking state more to depress
By honour's weight and former happiness.
Now he perceives he did too early climb,
Blames his triumphant youth in Sulla's time,
And grieves to think upon, in these sad days,
30 His Pontic laurel or piratic bays.[5]
So too long age great'st happiness destroys,[6]

---

[1] devious ways] *Implicitasque errore vias*, 'ways criss-crossed by wandering' (VIII. 5). M.'s 'devious' may borrow from 8. Arg. 2, itself translating Sulpizio's *devia*; it also creates symmetry with Pompey's arrival in Thessaly, 'paths devious marching over', 6. 371 (*secutus | Devia*, VI. 329–30).

[2] his presence and majestic face] *Clara viri facies*, 'the man's famous face' (VIII. 14); cf. 2. 565–66n.

[3] scarce … misery] *cladisque suae vix ipse fidelis | Auctor erat*, 'and he himself was scarcely the trusted author of his own calamity' (VIII. 17–18).

[4] And wishes … obscurely go] *cunctis ignotus gentibus esse | Mallet, & obscuro tutus transire per urbes | Nomine*, 'he would prefer to be unknown to all nations and safely to go through the cities with an obscure name' (VIII. 18–19).

[5] Pontic laurel or piratic bays] *Corycias classes et Pontica signa*, 'the Corycian fleets and Pontic standards' (VIII. 26–27); for the references, see 1. 135n.

[6] great'st happiness] *ingentes animos*, 'great spirits' (VIII. 28).

And life surviving empire; former joys
Breed grief unless with them our end be sent
And timely death ensuing woes prevent.¹
35 Let none but with a mind prepared to die
Dare to adventure on prosperity.²
Now to the shore he came, where Peneus ran³
Red with Pharsalia's slaughter to the main.
There a ⁽ᵃ⁾small barque unfit for seas and winds,   *sea*
40 Scarce safe in shallowest rivers, Pompey finds,⁴   *sailing vessel*
And goes aboard. He, with whose navy's oars
Even yet Corcyra shakes, and Leucas' shores,
That tamed Sicilia and Liburnia,⁵
Goes fearful now in a small barque to sea.⁶
45 To Lesbos' shore his sails commanded are
By thee, Cornelia, conscious of his care,⁷
Where thou then lay'st, far more with sorrow filled,
Than if th'hadst been in dire Pharsalia's field.
Thy careful breast still sad presages shake,
50 And fears thy restless slumbers still awake.
Each night presents Thessalia: when night's done,
To th'shore, and sea-o'erhanging rocks begone   *gone*
With woe, to view the ocean's face she hies,⁸   *hurries*
And still all ships that come she first espies,
55 But dares ask nothing of her husband's state.
    Lo, now a ship that comes:⁹ alas, what fate   [VIII. 50]
It brings thou know'st not, but behold thy fears,
Thy care's whole sum; thy vanquished lord appears,

---

¹ former joys | Breed grief] *Dedecori est fortuna prior*, '[his] former fortune is a matter of shame' (VIII. 29–31); M. is probably thinking of the proverbial English 'false joys breed true grief'.
² Let none ... prosperity] A question in L. (VIII. 31–32).
³ Peneus] Disyllabic. The river Pineiós, in Thessaly.
⁴ shallowest] Contracted to two syllables in pronunciation; cf. 'following', above, 8. 2n.
⁵ That tamed Sicilia] In L., *Cilicum dominus*, 'master of the Cilicians' i.e. Cilician pirates (VIII. 38). An error (by M. or printers), never corrected. The first '-ia' here is monosyllabic, but the second disyllabic.
⁶ Goes fearful ... sea] *Exiguam vector pavidus correpsit in alnum*, 'a trembling passenger, [Pompey] crept aboard the tiny boat' (VIII. 39).
⁷ To Lesbos' shore ... By thee] Reading *iubes*, 'you order [Cornelia]' (VIII. 41); modern editions prefer *iubet*, 'he [Pompey] orders', which F. notes as a variant. M. omits *secreta*, 'hidden' shores (VIII. 40).
⁸ With woe] M.'s addition.
⁹ Lo ... comes] *en ratis ad vestras quae tendit carbasa portus!*, 'Behold a vessel which directs its sails to your port!' (VIII. 50).

296   Thomas May

	Himself the sad relater of war's crime.¹	
60	Why now lament'st thou not, thus losing time?	
	When thou may'st weep, thou fear'st. The ship drawn nigh,	
	She runs, and sees the crime of destiny:²	
	Pompey pale faced, his hoary hairs hung down	
	O'er his sad brow, his garments squalid grown.³	
65	Then grief contracts her soul: a sudden night	
	Invades her sense, and reaves her eyes of light;	*robs*
	Her nerve-forsaken joints all fail; cold is	
	Her heart; deceived with hope of death she lies.	
	But Pompey, landed, searches the shore's side,	
70	Whom when Cornelia's maids now near espied,	
	They durst not on fate's cruelty complain	*dared*
	More than with silent sighs,⁴ striving in vain	
	To lift their lady up: whom in his arms	
	Great Pompey takes and with embraces warms	
75	Her key-cold breast.⁵ But when the fled blood fills	
	Her outward parts, her husband's hand she feels	
	And better brooks his visage: he forbid	*bears*
	Her yield to fate, and thus her sorrow chid.	
	'Why is thy noble strength of courage broke	[VIII. 72]
80	(Woman descended from so great a stock)⁶	
	By the first wound of fate? Thou hast the way	
	To purchase fame that never shall decay:	
	Thy sex's praise springs not from war or state,⁷	
	But faithful love to an unhappy mate.	
85	Advance thy thoughts and let thy piety	
	Contend with fortune: love me now 'cause I	
	Am conquered, sweet;⁸ 'tis more true praise for thee	

¹ thy vanquished .... war's crime] Reading VIII. 51–52 as one syntactical unit, following early modern editions; modern editions separate *Nuntius armorum tristis rumorque sinister*, 'the sad messenger and sinister rumour of battle' (VIII. 51, compressed by M. into 'sad relater of war's crime') from *Victus adest coniunx*, 'your defeated husband is here' (VIII. 52).
² of destiny] *Deum*, 'of the gods' (VIII. 55).
³ Pompey ... squalid grown] *Deformem pallore ducem, vultusque prementem | Canitie, atque atro squalentes pulvere vestes*, 'the general, unsightly with pallor, concealing his face with his white hair, and his clothes squalid with black dust' (VIII. 56–57).
⁴ fate's cruelty] *fata*, 'the fates' (VIII. 64); M. is possibly inspired by F.'s 'lack of mercy', *inclementiam*.
⁵ key-cold breast] i.e. extremely cold. Lit. *astrictos ... artus*, 'rigid limbs' (VIII. 67).
⁶ so great a stock] Cornelia was of the famous Scipio family.
⁷ state] 'rights of laws' (*legum iura*, VIII. 75), a formula suggesting the legal order of a republican constitution. Some modern editions print *cura*, 'care', for *iura*.
⁸ sweet] M.'s added endearment; cf. 5. 857.

	To love me thus when all authority,	
	The sacred Senate, and my kings are gone.¹	
90	Begin to love thy Pompey now alone.	
	That grief extreme, thy husband yet alive,	
	Becomes thee not; thou shouldst that sorrow give	
	To my last funerals. Thou art bereft	
	Of nothing by this war: thy Pompey's left	
95	Alive and safe, his fortune's only gone;	
	'Tis that thou wail'st, and that thou lovd'st alone.'	
	Chid by her husband thus, by shame's constraint	[VIII. 86]
	She rose and uttered this most sad complaint.	
	'Would I to hated Caesar had been led	
100	A bride, since happy to no husband's bed.	
	Twice have I hurt the world: my bridal lights	
	Erinys, and th'unhappy Crassi's sprights	*spirits*
	Carrièd; accursèd by those ghosts, I bare	
	Th'Assyrian fortune to this civil war.²	
105	I was the cause that all these nations died,	
	And all the gods forsook the juster side.³	
	O greatest lord, worthy of better fate	
	Than my sad marriage, had dire Fortune's hate	
	Such power on thee? Why did I marry thee	
110	To make thee wretched? Take revenge on me,	
	Which willingly I'll pay. To make the sea	
	More passable, kings' faiths more firm to thee,	
	And all the world more hospitable, drown	
	Me by the way.⁴ O, would this life had gone	
115	Before to get thee victory, but now,	
	Dear Pompey, expiate thine overthrow.	

---

¹ when all ... are gone] Pompey invokes the *fasces*, M.'s 'authority' (cf. 1. 194n); 'the pious crowd of the Senate', *pia turba senatus*; and *Tantaque ... regum manus*, 'such a great band of kings' (VIII. 78–79).

² A bride ... in the civil war] Cornelia was previously married to Publius Crassus, who along with his father the triumvir died at Carrhae ('Th'Assyrian fortune'); cf. 1. 11–14. L. makes the Fury Erinys a *pronuba*, 'bridal attendant' (VIII. 90); M. adds reference to the 'bridal torches', perhaps assisted by F.'s note.

³ juster side] *causa meliore*, 'better cause' (VIII. 94).

⁴ O greatest lord ... by the way] M. adds the epithet 'sad' to Cornelia's marriage and 'dire' to Fortune, omits Cornelia's judgment that she is impious (*impia*, VIII. 97), and softens her final demand, *sparge mari comitem*, 'scatter your comrade on the sea' (VIII. 100). Modern and some early modern editions punctuate 8. 108–09 (= VIII. 95–96) as a question, F. and other early modern editions as an exclamation.

Where'er thou lyest, O cruel Julia,[1]
Revenged already in Pharsalia,
Come, wreak thine anger, let thy strumpet's death
120 Appease thy wrath and spare thy Pompey's breath.'[2]
This said, and sinking in his arms, her fall
Again drew tears from the spectators all.
Pompey's great heart relented,[3] and that eye
Wept there, that in Pharsalia's field was dry.
125   The Mytilenians then thus on the shore   [VIII. 109]
Bespake great Pompey: 'If forever more
It shall our honour be to have preserved
Thy dearest pledge,[4] if we have so deserved:
To grace the city of thy servants deign,[5]
130 And here with us, though but one night, remain;
Make this a place honoured forever more,
A place that Roman pilgrims may adore.[6]
Our town before all towns thou shouldst approve,
For all towns else may hope for Caesar's love.[7]
135 We have already trespassed; further yet
This is an isle, and Caesar wants a fleet;   *lacks*
Besides, thy nobles know this place, and here
Will meet. Thy fates on this known shore repair:
Take our gods' wealth, our temples' gold, and bands
140 Of our young men to serve by sea or land.
Take thou (though conquered) Lesbos' forces here,
Lest Caesar press them as the conqueror.[8]   *conscript*

---

[1] lyest] Monosyllabic; '-ia', in this line-ending and the next, is disyllabic.
[2] O, would this life ... Pompey's breath] i.e. Cornelia calls upon Julia to complete her vengeance by taking her life. For Cornelia as *paelice*, 'strumpet' (VIII. 104), cf. 3. 21–37.
[3] great heart] *duri pectora Magni*, 'the breast of hardened Magnus' (VIII. 107); *duri* suggests Stoic imperviousness to misfortune and passion, and also the elegiac conceit of the hard-hearted lover, but M. may choose to avoid the association of hard-heartedness, in Christian theology, with an unregenerate soul.
[4] Thy dearest pledge] i.e. Cornelia, *tanti pignus ... mariti*, 'the pledge/loved one of so great a husband' (VIII. 111).
[5] city of thy servants] *devotos sacro tibi foedere muros ... sociosque lares*, 'the walls vowed to you in sacred league, and allied Lares [household gods]' (VIII. 112–13).
[6] Roman pilgrims] *hospes Romanus*, 'Roman guest' (VIII. 115).
[7] Our town ... Caesar's love] L.'s Pompey is *victo*, 'conquered', and Caesar 'the conqueror', *victoris* (VIII. 116–17). 'Love' translates *favorem*, 'favour' (VIII. 117).
[8] Take thou ... the conqueror] *Accipe: ne Caesar rapiat, tu victus habeto*, 'Accept [our men]: in order that Caesar should not take them off, you, though conquered, should have them' (VIII .124). As F. notes, this line does not appear in some manuscripts and modern editions regard it as spurious. M. also omits *tota quantum valet*, 'as many [men] as the whole

O clear this faithful land of that foul crime,
That thou, which loved'st us in thy prosperous time,
145 Shouldst fear our faith in thy adversity.'
Glad of these men's so wondrous piety
For the world's sake, that some fidelity
Was left to wretched states, 'This land', quoth he,[1]
'That I of all the world most dear esteemed,
150 By this great pledge I left with you it seemed;
She was the hostage that my love was here,
That here my household gods and country were:
Here was my Rome. Fled from the field, before
I came to you, I touched upon no shore,
155 Knowing that Lesbos in preserving her
Had purchased Caesar's ire.[2] I did not fear
To give you cause your pardons all to plead:
Let it suffice that I your guilt have made.
I must through all the world my fates pursue.
160 O happy Lesbos,[3] ever famed, from you
People and kings shall learn fidelity
To us, or faithful you alone shall be.
Which lands are true, which false, I now must try.[4]   ascertain
Hear, O ye gods, if any gods with me
165 Remain, my last of prayers: grant us to find
A land like Lesbos, whose still faithful mind
Dares give safe landing to our conquered state,[5]
And parting safe, not fearing Caesar's hate.'   departure
His sad companion then aboard he took.
170 You would have thought all Lesbos had forsook
Their native soil, exiled, so great a cry
Was raised, and woeful hands heaved to the sky
All o'er the shore; for Pompey least of all,
(Though he deserved their sorrow by his fall),
175 But seeing her depart, whom they had seen
All this wartime as their own citizen,
The people wept. Of her the matrons dry

of Lesbos has' (VIII. 123).
[1] to wretched states] *in adversis*, 'in miserable circumstances' (VIII. 128).
[2] Caesar's] Omitting *saevi*, 'cruel' (VIII. 134).
[3] happy] '*too* happy' in L., *nimium felix* (VIII. 139).
[4] Which lands ... must try] *Fas quibus in terris, ubi sit scelus*, 'In what lands there is lawfulness, and where there is crime' (VIII. 142).
[5] our conquered state] *Marte subactum*, 'defeated in war' (VIII. 144).

	From tears could hardly have ta'en leave, though she	
	Unto her lord a conqueror had gone:¹	
180	She so had gained the love of everyone	
	By virtuous, courteous carriage, modesty	*deportment*
	Of a chaste look, proud to no company,	
	Lowly to all;² and such her life was seen	
	While her lord stood, as he had conquered been.³	
185	Now Titan's orb, half-drownèd in the seas,	[VIII. 159] *the sun's*
	Gave part to us, part to th'Antipodes,⁴	
	When care in Pompey's restless bosom runs,	
	Sometimes on Rome's confederate states and towns,	
	And kings' uncertain faiths; sometimes upon	
190	The south-scorched regions of the torrid zone.⁵	
	Sometimes, as too sad burdens, he lays by	
	His wearied cares of future destiny,⁶	
	Asking the master of each star, and where	
	He guesses land: what rules heaven gives to steer	
195	His ship at sea, what stars to Syria guide,	
	Which of Boötes' fires to Libya's side	*the ox-driver constellation*
	Directs.⁷ To this the master thus replies:	
	'We follow not those stars, which through the skies	
	Do slide and pass away: unconstant stars	
200	In the unfixed pole deceive the mariners;	*heavens*
	That pole that never falls, ne'er drowns in sea,	

¹ though she ... had gone] i.e. even if Pompey had returned as the victor of Pharsalus.
² By virtuous ... to all] M.'s early modern idiom: *Hos pudor, hos probitas, castique modestia vultus, | Quod submissa nimis, nulli gravis hospita turba*, 'Her modesty, integrity, the humility of her chaste expression [had attracted everyone], that she was exceedingly humble, a proud guest to no group' (VIII. 156–57). Some modern editions read *submissa animis* (after Heinsius) or *submissa animi*, both meaning 'humble in spirit'. M.'s 'virtuous' and 'courteous' (8. 181) are both disyllabic.
³ While her lord ... been] i.e. Cornelia had behaved as humbly at Lesbos as if Pompey had already been defeated.
⁴ Now Titan's orb ... th'Antipodes] i.e. the descending sun was half-visible, and therefore also half-visible to those on the other side of the world. M.'s 'Antipodes' derive from F.'s note at VIII. 160.
⁵ sometimes upon ... torrid zone] *nunc invia mundi | Arva super nimios soles Austrumque iacentis*, 'now upon the pathless tracts of the world beyond the excessive suns of the south' (VIII. 163–64); M.'s terminology derives from F.'s gloss.
⁶ Sometimes ... destiny] *Saepe labor moestus curarum, odiumque futuri | Proiecit fessos incerti pectoris aestus*, 'Often the sad toil of his cares, and hatred of the future, expelled the weary passions of his uncertain breast' (VIII. 165–66). M. here echoes Sulpizio's commentary in treating 'hatred of the future' as an object.
⁷ Which of Boötes ... Directs] i.e. which of the seven stars of the Plough [Ursa Major] constellation, *quotus in plaustro ... ignis* (VIII. 170).

	Famous for Cynosure and Helice,[1]	*Ursa Minor; Ursa Major*
	Doth guide our ships: whene'er that star's got up	
	Right vertical, just o'er the sailyard's top,[2]	
205	Then to the Bosporos we make apace	
	And seas, that Synthia's crooked shores embrace.[3]	
	But when more low and nearer to the sea	
	Artophilax and Cynosura be,	*Ursa Major; Ursa Minor*
	Then to the Syrian ports our course we steer:	
210	Canopus then is elevated there,	
	Which fears the north, and in the southern skies	
	Remains alone.[4] Who thence to th'left hand plies	
	(Pharos o'erpassed), into the Syrtes falls.[5]	
	But whither now shall we direct our sails?'	
215	To whom with doubtful thoughts Pompey replies:	
	'In all the course at sea observe but this,	
	To keep thy ship still far from Thessaly,	
	And to the heavens and seas leave Italy;	
	The rest trust to the winds. I now have ta'en	
220	My dear left pledge, Cornelia, in again.	
	I then was certain whither to resort,	*make for*
	But now let fortune find us out a port.'	
	Thus Pompey spake: the master straightway turns	
	About his sails, stretched out with equal horns,	
225	And to the left hand guides the ship, to plough	
	Those waves that 'twixt Chios and Asia flow;[6]	
	To the ship's length he turns his sails about.[7]	

[1] Cynosure and Helice] *Axis inocciduus, gemina clarissimus Arcto*, 'The never-setting pole, the brightest star in the twin Bears [Ursa Major and Minor]' (VIII. 175). M.'s names derive from F.

[2] that star's got up...] i.e. by aligning the sailyards so that Ursa Minor gradually 'rises' up them, the ship steers north for the territories north and east of the Black Sea.

[3] Synthia] *Scythiae*, 'Scythia' (VIII. 178), a never-corrected error.

[4] But when ... Remains alone] i.e. when Arctophilax and Cynosura sink in relation to the ship, it is steering south towards Syria. Canopus is the brightest star of the southern constellation and cannot be seen in the north. M.'s 'Artophilax' is a never-corrected misspelling.

[5] Who thence ... Syrtes falls] i.e. if the ship keeps Canopus on the left, and passes Pharos, it will end up on the north African coast.

[6] the master straightway ... Asia flow] i.e. the master sets the sails so that they hang equally and navigates the eastern Aegean. M. reads *Asiae cautes*, 'rocks of Asia' (VIII. 195), a reading supported by Grotius and F.; modern editions prefer *Asinae*.

[7] To ... about] *Hos dedit in proram, tenet hos in puppe rudentes*, 'he slackened these ropes at the prow, these ropes he holds in the stern' (VIII. 196). M. appears to respond to F.'s *alterum veli angulum protendit, reducto altero*, 'he stretches forth one corner of the sail, the

                    The sea perceives the change: her waves are cut
                    By the sharp stem with different motion.   *prow*
230   The skilful charioteer not half so soon
                    Reins round his horse, and doth with sudden change
                    About the goal his wheeling chariot range.¹

                        Sol hid the stars, and land discoverèd,   [VIII. 202]² *the sun*
                    When those that from Pharsalia's battle fled
235   To Pompey came: and first from Lesbos' shores
                    He met his son, then kings and senators.³
                    For Pompey yet (although at that sad time
                    Vanquished and fled) had kings to wait on him:⁴
                    Proud sceptered kings that o'er the east did reign,
240   Attended there in banished Pompey's train.   *retinue*
                    Then Pompey king Deiotarus commands
                    To go for aid to farthest eastern lands.⁵
                    'Most loyal king, since on Pharsalia's plains
                    This world was lost from Rome, it now remains
245   To try the east, those that by Tigris lie
                    And by Euphrates, yet from Caesar free.⁶
                    Grieve not, though to repair my fortunes lost
                    Thou to the Medes or farthest Scythians go'st,
                    Or quite beyond the day that this world sees.⁷
250   Bear my salutes to great Arsacides;⁸
                    And if our ancient league remain, which I
                    By Latian Jove, by his own deity

other having been drawn in'.
  ¹ charioteer ... chariot] Trisyllabic; likewise 'chariot' (8. 232) has two syllables in pronunciation.
  ² 8. 233-294] Pompey sends Deiotarus to seek help from the Parthians.
  ³ kings and senators] *procerum ... turba fidelis*, 'a loyal crowd of leaders' (VIII. 205).
  ⁴ For Pompey ... him] *Nam neque deiecto fatis, acieque fugato | Abstulerat Magno reges Fortuna ministros*, 'For, although cast down by fate and with an army put to flight, Fortune had not yet taken away servant-kings from Magnus' (VIII. 206-07).
  ⁵ Then Pompey ... lands] *Iubet ire in devia mundi | Deiotarum, qui sparsa ducis vestigia legit*, 'he orders Deiotarus, who picked out the scattered trail of his leader [Pompey], to go into the pathless world' (VIII. 210). For Deiotarus see 5. 63.
  ⁶ To try ... from Caesar free] *Eoam temptare fidem, populosque bibentes | Euphraten, & adhuc securum a Caesare Tigrim*, 'To test eastern loyalty and the peoples drinking the Euphrates and Tigris, still safe from Caesar' (VIII. 213-14).
  ⁷ Or ... sees] *Et totum mutare diem*, 'and change the entire day' (VIII. 217), an oblique phrase glossed by F. as 'to go to another clime', *subire aliud coeli clima*.
  ⁸ Arsacides] = Orodes II, King of Parthia. M., after L. (VIII. 218), uses the patronymic from Arsaces, founder of the Parthian empire. In L. 8. 251-54 (VIII. 218-21) are addressed to him.

He swore,[1] let the Armenian archers strong
Their well-bent bows and quivers bring along.[2]
255 If you, O Parthians,[3] undisquieted
I ever left when I pursued the fled
Unquiet Alans to the Caspian strait,
And forced you not for safety to retreat
To Babylon: marching o'er Cyrus' ground,
260 And the Chaldaean kingdoms' utmost bound,
Appearing nearer than the Persian
To the sun's rise, where into th'ocean[4]
Nysa's Hydaspes, and swift Ganges fall,
Suffered you only, when I conquered all,
265 To go untriumphed. Parthia's king alone   *escaped*
Of all th'east's monarchs 'scaped subjection.
Nor once alone do you your safety owe
To me: who, after Crassus' overthrow,[5]
Appeased the just incensèd wrath of Rome?
270 For all my merits now let Parthia come
Out of her bounds appointed and pass o'er
Greek Zeugma's walls and the forbidden shore.[6]
Conquer for Pompey: Rome will lose the day
Gladly.' The king refused not to obey,
275 Though hard were his command; laying aside
His kingly robes, and in a servant's weed
Attired he goes; in a distressèd time

---

[1] I | By Latian Jove...] Pompey swore by 'the Latian Thunderer', *Latium ... Tonantem* (VIII. 219), Arsacides by 'your wise men/wizards', *Per vestros astricta magos* (VIII. 220).
[2] let ... bring along along] *implete pharetras, | Armeniosque arcus Geticis intendite nervis*, 'Fill your quivers and bend your Armenian bows with Getic string' (VIII. 220-21).
[3] If you, O Parthians...] Pompey contrasts his harrying of other eastern peoples with his lack of aggression against the Parthians. He claims (lines 255-65) that he pushed the Alans (a group of Sarmatian tribes north of the Caspian Sea) to the Caspian strait (lit. *Caspia claustra*, VIII. 222), and that he went beyond the kingdom of Cyrus (i.e. Persia), marching as far east as Nysa (Nicaea, a city founded by Alexander after his victory near the river Hydaspes in 326 BC) and India's river Ganges.
[4] Persian ... th'ocean] As often in M.'s line-endings, '-ian' and '-ean' are disyllabic.
[5] Crassus' overthrow] *post vulnera cladis | Assyriae*, 'After the wounds of the Assyrian disaster' (VIII. 233-34); cf. 1. 11-14.
[6] For all my merits ... forbidden shore] *tot meritis obstricta meis, nunc Parthia ruptis | Excedat claustris vetitam per secula ripam, | Zeugmaque Pellaeum*, 'Let Parthia, contained by my achievements, with her bounds broken now cross the shore forbidden through the ages, and Pellaean Zeugma' (VIII. 235-37). Zeugma was a city on the Euphrates, founded by Alexander the Great (to whom L.'s Pompey implicitly compares himself here), and thus on the border between Parthian East and the Roman West.

'Tis safe for kings like poorest men to seem.
Therefore how much lives he, that's truly poor,
280 Safer than kings? The king took leave at shore.
And by the Icarion rocks great Pompey gone[1]
Leaves Ephesus and sea-calm Colophon;
Shaving small Samos' foaming rocks he goes.
A gentle gale blows from the shore of Cos:
285 Gnidon, and Phoebus-honoured Rhodes he leaves,   *Cnidus*
And sailing straight in the mid-ocean, saves
Telmessum's long and winding circuits.[2] First
Pamphylia greets their eyes, but Pompey durst
Commit his person to no town but thee,
290 Little Phaselis:[3] thy small company
And few inhabitants could not cause a fear;
More in the ship than in thy walls there were.
But sailing thence again, high Taurus shows
Itself, and Dipsas that from Taurus flows.[4]
295   Could Pompey think, when erst he cleared the seas   [VIII. 255][5] *first*
Of pirates' rage, it purchased his own ease?
He now flies safe along Cicilian shores[6]
In a small ship: there many senators,
Following, o'ertake their flying general
300 Within the haven of Celendrae small,[7]
Where in and out ships on Selinus passed.
In full assembly of the lords at last

---

[1] the Icarion rocks] A misprint for 'Icarian' (*Icariae scopulos*, VIII. 244), never corrected. Probably elided to 'th'Icarion' in pronunciation, and with '-ion' also contracted. The mistake is corrected in James Ussher's quotation of this passage in *The Annals of the World* (London: E. Tyler for J. Crook, 1658), p. 647.

[2] Shaving ... winding circuits] After sailing by Icaria and past the cities of Ephesus and Colophon on the Ionian coast, Pompey travels by the Dodecanese islands of Samos, Kos, the port city of Cnidus (M.'s 'Gnidon') on the Turkish coast and the island of Rhodes, then cuts across the ocean to avoid the winding bays of Telmessus (another west Lycian town).

[3] Pamphylia ... Phaselis] Respectively the plain-land and hilly region on the south-east coast of Asia Minor, and a port city on the eastern Turkish coast.

[4] Dipsas] *Dipsanta* (VIII. 255), glossed by F. as a river of Cilicia; modern editions print *Dipsunta*.

[5] 8. 295–530] The defeated Senate deliberates.

[6] Cicilian shores] A misspelling for Cilician, never corrected (*Cilicum*, VIII. 255); cf. 8. 306, below.

[7] Celendrae small] Early modern editions print *Celendris* or *Synedris* (VIII. 259). F. prints the latter but notes the former variant. Modern editions print *Syhedris* ('Syhedra', on the Cilician coast). In the preceding line (8. 299), 'following' is contracted to two syllables and 'general' extended to three.

Thus sadly Pompey spake. 'My lords, whose sight
(As dear companions both in war and flight)¹
305 I do esteem my country, though we stand
On a bare shore, in poor Cicilian land,
Attended with no force, advice to take
And new provision for a war to make,
Yet bring courageous hearts: I lost not all
310 In Thessaly, nor did my fortune fall
So low, but that this head again may rise.
Could Marius after all his miseries
In Libya rise to a seventh consulship?²
And me so lightly fall'n will fortune keep?³
315 A thousand captains on the Grecian sea,
A thousand ships I have: Pharsalia
Has rather scattered than quite overthrown
My strength; but me my actions' fame alone,
Which all the earth have seen, my name that now
320 The whole world loves, shall guard. Consider you
Th'Egyptian, Libyan, Parthian monarchies,
Both in their strength and faith, and then advise
Which fittest is to aid Rome's labouring state.
But I, my lords, will to your ears relate
325 Freely my secret'st cares, and tell the truth
How I incline.⁴ I do suspect the youth
Of Egypt's king, for true fidelity
Requires strong years;⁵ I fear the subtlety   *cunning*
And double heart of Mauritania's king;
330 Rememb'ring Carthage, whence his race did spring,
He gapes for Italy, and his vain breast   *eagerly desires*
Is much with thought of Hannibal possessed,
Whose blood co-mixed with th'old Numidian's

---

¹ My lords ... flight] *Comites bellique fugaeque | Atque instar patriae*, 'companions in war and flight, and representers of our country' (VIII. 262–63); F. suggests the latter phrase means those having their country's authority.

² rise to a seventh consulship] *an Libyae Marium potuere ruinae | Erigere in fasces, plenis & reddere fastis*, 'Could Libyan catastrophe lift Marius to the *fasces* [symbols of consular authority] and return him to the filled *Fasti*' (VIII. 269–70); the calendars (*fasti*) are 'filled' because of his many consulships (cf. 2. 688n). F. notes he had seven.

³ fortune] Most early modern editions capitalized and personified *Fortuna* here, but M. does not.

⁴ and tell ... incline] *Expromam, mentisque meae quo pondera vergant*, 'I will expound in what direction the weight of my mind inclines' (VIII. 280).

⁵ Egypt's king] cf. 8. 515 ff.

Obliquely Juba's pedigree distains.¹
335 He swelled to see Varus a suppliant grown,
And Roman fates inferior to his own.²
Therefore, my lords, to th'eastern world let us
Retire: Euphrates with a spacious
Channel divides the world; the Caspian straits
340 On t'other side yield safe and large retreats;
Another pole measures th'Assyrian days
And nights:³ another colour bear the seas
Severed from ours.⁴ Their aim is sovereignty;⁵
Their bows more strong, their steeds more fierce and high
345 Than ours; no boy nor agèd man wants skill
Or strength to shoot; deadly their arrows kill.
Their bows first broke Pellaean spears and won
Th'Assyrian wall-renownèd Babylon
And Median Bactra.⁶ Nor so fearful are
350 The Parthians of our piles, but that they dare
Come out to war against us: they have tried
Their shafts sufficiently when Crassus died.⁷
Nor are their trusty shafts armed at the head
With steel alone, but deadly venomèd:
355 Slight wounds are mortal, and the least blood drawn
Will kill. O would on the fierce Parthian
I were not forcèd to depend: their fate
Does too too much Rome's fortune emulate;⁸
Too many gods aid them. I'll draw from home

---

¹ I fear the subtlety ... distains] *anceps dubii terret solertia Mauri: | Namque memor generis Carthaginis impia proles | Imminet Hesperiae*, 'the double-edged cunning of the uncertain Moor scares me; for mindful of his Carthaginian race the impious offspring threatens Italy' (VIII. 283–85). Juba, king of Numidia, had Carthaginian ancestry (cf. 4. Arg. 12).
² He swelled ... own] A reference to the Roman general Varus' earlier request for aid from Juba: see 4. 632–908, 734n. 'Suppliant' (8. 335) is disyllabic.
³ Another pole] *polus ... alter* (VIII. 292); L. apparently means the 'other' southern hemisphere of the sky, but Parthia is in the northern hemisphere.
⁴ another colour bear the seas] *mare discolor*, 'differently coloured sea' (VIII. 293), probably the Red Sea, which L. seems to confuse with the northern Indian Ocean bordering Parthia.
⁵ Their aim is sovereignty] *regnandi sola voluptas*, 'their sole pleasure is to rule' (VIII. 294); cf. 1. 5n, 338n.
⁶ Their bows...] The Parthians defeated the armies of Alexander the Great and their *Pellaeas sarissas*, 'Macedonian lances' (VIII. 298).
⁷ Crassus] cf. 1. 11–14.
⁸ Rome's fortune] *fatis nostris*, 'our fates' (VIII. 307).

360	Some other nations of the east to come	
	To war. But if barbarians' leagues deceive	
	Our hopes, or else our scorned alliance leave,[1]	
	Let Fortune then our sad and shipwrecked state	
	Beyond the known and trafficked world translate;	*open to trade*
365	I will not sue to kings whom I have made,	*plead*
	But in my death this comfort shall be had:	
	Lying far off, this body shall not be	
	Subject to Caesar's rage nor piety.[2]	
	But there revolving my whole life's past fate	
370	Still honoured in those parts was Pompey's state.[3]	
	How great has eastern Tanaïs me seen?	*the river Don*
	How great beyond Maeotis have I been?	
	Into what lands did my victorious name	
	More sound, or whence in greater triumph came?[4]	
375	Favour my purpose, Rome: what happier	
	Can the gods grant thee, than in civil war	
	To use the Parthian arms to overthrow	
	That land, and mix their ruin with our woe?[5]	
	When the fierce Parthians have with Caesar fought,	
380	Crassus' revenge, or mine, must needs be wrought.'[6]	
	This said, he heard their murmur to condemn	
	His plot.[7] But Lentulus, 'mongst all of them	
	In spirit and noble grief the forward'st man,[8]	
	Thus (worthy his late consulship) began.	
385	'Has the Pharsalian loss so broke thy mind?	[VIII. 331]

---

[1] But if ... alliance leave] *Quod si nos Eoa fides & barbara fallunt | Foedera*, 'But if eastern trust and barbarous treaties deceive us' (VIII. 311–12). M. adds 'or else our scorned alliance leave'.

[2] this body ... piety] *nihil haec in membra cruente, | Nil socerum fecisse pie*, 'that my son-in-law has done nothing bloody, and nothing pious against these limbs' (VIII. 314–16).

[3] Pompey's state] L. uses the first person here.

[4] or whence ... came] Reading *redit* '[my name] returned' (VIII. 320); modern editions prefer *redi*, 'I returned'.

[5] to overthrow ... with our woe] *tantam consumere gentem | Et nostris miscere malis*, 'to consume that mighty race and embroil it in our woes' (VIII. 324–25).

[6] When ... be wrought] i.e. if the Parthians win, they avenge Pompey; if they lose, then Crassus is avenged.

[7] plot] *consilium*, 'plan' or 'advice' (VIII. 328). M's 'plot' may also mean 'scheme', but with 'murmur' and 'condemn' it may also imply unlawfulness and conspiracy (*OED*, 'plot', 4 and 5).

[8] But Lentulus ... man] *omneis | Virtutis stimulis & nobilitate dolendi | Praecessit*, 'ahead of all others in respect of his spurs to virtue and in nobility of his grief' (VIII. 328–30); cf. 5. 18. 'Spirit' is, as usual, contracted.

Has one day's fate the world so low declined?[1]
Doth that one battle our whole cause decide,
And no cure left to help our wounded side?
Is no hope left thee, Pompey, but to sue   *beg*
390   At the proud Parthians' feet?[2] Wouldst thou eschew
All lands and climes, and thither aim thy flight
Where cross poles reign and unknown stars give light,[3]
T'adore the Parthians and their deities,
Chaldaean fires and barbarous sacrifice?[4]
395   Why in this war pretend'st thou liberty?
Why is the wretched world deceived by thee,
If thou can'st serve?[5] Whose name they trembled at
As the chief ruler of the Roman fate,
Whom they have seen lead captive kings before
400   From wild Hyrcania and the Indian shore,[6]
Shall they now see cast down and broke by fate,
Measuring themselves by Pompey's begging state
With Rome, and Italy aspire t'inherit?[7]
Thou can'st speak nothing worth thy fate and spirit:
405   Their ignorance i'th'Roman tongue requires
That thou in tears shouldst utter thy desires.
Wouldst thou so wound our shame, that not from Rome
But Parthia the revenge of Rome should come?
She chose thee general of her civil war.
410   Why dost thou spread her loss and wounds so far
As Scythia, and teach Parthia to go
Beyond her bound?[8] Rome shall in her deep woe

---

[1] the world so low declined] *Vna mundi damnavit fata?*, 'Has one day condemned the fate of the world?' (VIII. 332).
[2] proud Parthians' feet] M.'s epithet, not in L. See 8. 494n.
[3] Where cross poles reign] *Adversosque polos* (VIII. 337), explained by F. as L. (inaccurately) placing Parthia beyond the equator; cf. 8. 341.
[4] T'adore ... sacrifice] *Chaldaeos culture focos & barbara sacra, | Parthorum famulus?*, 'To worship Chaldaean hearths and barbarous rites, a house-slave of the Parthians?' (VIII. 338–39). F. glosses *focos* as 'altars', perhaps suggesting M.'s 'sacrifice'.
[5] Why in this war ... can'st serve?] *quid causa obtenditur armis | Libertatis amor? miserum quid decipis orbem, | Si servire potes?*, 'Why is love of liberty held out speciously as a cause for war? Why do you deceive the wretched world, if you yourself can be a slave?' (VIII. 339–41).
[6] wild Hyrcania] *Hyrcanis ... silvis*, 'the Hyrcanian woods' (VIII. 343): a reference to Mithridates whom Pompey captured.
[7] Italy aspire t'inherit] *Extolletque animos Latium vesanus in orbem*, 'madly raise their spirits against the Latin world' (VIII. 345). Some modern editions follow Housman's reading *rex tollet*, 'the king raises', for *extollet*.
[8] Scythia ... Parthia] The meter requires one of these, but not both, to be trisyllabic.

This special comfort lose, of bringing in
No kings but serving her own citizen.¹
415 Can'st thou delight from farthest parts to come,
Leading fierce nations 'gainst the walls of Rome,
Following those eagles that slain Crassus lost?²
That only king, that from th'Emathian ⁽ᵃ⁾host   *Arsacides*
Was absent (fortune did his favour guide):
420 Will he provoke the conqueror's strong side³
And join with vanquished Pompey, think you? No,
We have no cause to trust that nation so.
The people all born in the northern cold
Are lovers of the war, hardy and bold,⁴
425 But in the east and southern climes, the heat
Of gentle air makes them effeminate.⁵
Their men soft clothing and loose garments wear.
Parthians upon the Median fields, and where
Along Sarmatian plains swift Tigris flows,
430 By liberty of flight can by no foes
Be vanquishèd; but where the earth does swell,
O'er craggy hills they cannot climb so well,
Nor in dark places can they use the bow,
Nor dare they swim torrents that swiftly flow,
435 Nor, in the field with blood all over dyed,⁶
Dare they the dust and summer sun abide.
No rams nor engines can the Parthian use,
Nor fill the trenches up: when he pursues,
Whate'er is arrow-proof serves for a wall.
440 Slight are their wars, their fights like flyings all:
They straggling fight, apter to fly than stand.⁷

---

¹ Rome shall...] *solatia tanti | Perdit Roma mali, nullos admittere Reges | Sed civi servire suo*, 'Rome loses the sole comfort of such a great evil, that she admits no kings, but is slave to her own citizen [i.e. Caesar]' (VIII. 354-56).
² that slain Crassus lost] *Signaque ab Euphrate cum Crassis capta sequentem*, 'and following standards captured with Crassus by the Euphrates (VIII. 358); cf. 1. 11-14.
³ fortune did ... strong side] *fato celante favorem ... nunc tantas ille lacesset | Auditi victoris opes...?*, 'Fate concealing its preference, now would he provoke the mighty resources of the reported winner?' (VIII. 360-61).
⁴ lovers of the war ... bold] *indomitus bellis, & Martis amator*, '[a people] untamed in wars and lovers of Mars' (VIII. 364). Modern editions read *mortis amator*, 'lover of death', a variant noted by F. but not followed by M. here.
⁵ makes them effeminate] *emollit*, 'softens' (VIII. 366).
⁶ with blood all over dyed] Referring to the combatants, not the field, as is clearer in L. (VIII. 375).
⁷ Slight are their wars...] *turmaeque vagantes | Et melior cessisse loco quam pellere miles,*

Their arrows venomed are,[1] nor close at hand
Dare they maintain a fight. Far off with bows
They shoot, and where it lists the wind bestows
445 Their wounds: but fight of sword does strength require;
All manly nations the sword-fight desire.[2]
At the first onset they'll disarmèd be,
And when their quivers are exhaust, must flee;   *exhausted*
Their trust in poison is, not in their hands.
450 Think'st thou them men, Pompey, that dare not stand
Without such helps the hazard of a fight?[3]
Can such base aid be worth so long a flight?
For thee so far from thine own land to die
And under barbarous earth entombed to lie
455 In a base monument, yet such a one
As will be envied, Crassus having none?
Thy state is not so pitiful, for death
(Not feared by men) ends all; but loss of breath
Under that wicked king Cornelia fears not.[4]
460 The Venus of those barbarous courts who hears not?[5]
Which like brute beasts all wedlock's rites exile,
And with wives numberless all laws defile.
Th'incestuous beds' abhorrèd secrets lie
Ope to a thousand concubines;[6] raised high
465 With wine and banqueting, the king refrains
No lawless lust though ne'er so full of stains;[7]

'their cavalry troops wander about and their soldiers are better at forsaking their station than routing [others]' (VIII. 380–81).
[1] venomed are] *Illita tela dolis*, 'Their weapons are smeared with trickery' (VIII. 382). F. glosses 'poison' (*veneno*).
[2] but fight of sword ... desire] Charles Cotton cites M.'s version of VIII. 385–86 in his translation of Montaigne's *Essays*, pp. 564–65 (I. 48). L.'s comment was well known among contemporary compilers of military maxims; see e.g. Robert Dallington, *Aphorisms ciuill and militarie* (London: for Edward Blount, 1613), sig. Cc4ʳ.
[3] that dare not ... a fight] *quos in discrimina belli | Cum ferro misisse parum est*, 'They for whom it is too little to commit to the hazard of war with steel alone' (VIII. 389–90).
[4] but loss ... fears not] *Sed tua sors levior ... At non Cornelia letum ...| timet*, 'But your lot will be easier ... It is not death that Cornelia will fear' (VIII. 395–97).
[5] The Venus ... hears not?] *num barbara nobis | Est ignota Venus*, 'Surely that barbarous lust (Venus) is not unknown to us' (VIII. 396–97). Note that this couplet is composed of eleven-syllable lines.
[6] Th'incestuous ... concubines] *thalamique patent secreta nefandi | Inter mille nurus?*, '[Are not] the secrets of the unspeakable bridal-chamber disclosed amongst a thousand young women?' (VIII. 400–01). 'Incestuous' is trisyllabic, as it also is at 8. 469.
[7] raised high ... full of stains] An innuendo-coloured version of *epulis vesana, meroque | Regia, non ullos exceptos legibus audet | Concubitus* (VIII. 402–03), 'the king, maddened with

	Th'embraces of so many women can
	Not all the night tire one insatiate man;
	In kings' incestuous beds their sisters lie
470	And mothers, which should names unstainèd be.[1]
	Oedipus' woeful tale condemns alone
	Thebes of a crime, though ignorantly done:[2]
	But there how often does the Parthian king
	Arsacides from such foul incest spring?
475	What can be wickedness to him, that may
	Defile his mother?[3] Shall Cornelia,
	Metellus' noble progeny, be led
	The thousand'th wife to a barbarian's bed?
	Yet none more often will the tyrant use
480	Than her: her husbands' titles will infuse
	A scornful lust,[4] and which will please him more,
	He'll know that she was Crassus' wife before,
	And comes (as fate did her to Parthia owe) *as if*
	A captive for that former overthrow.
485	Think on that slaughter:[5] 'twill not only bring
	Shame, to have begged aid from that fatal king,
	But to have made a civil war before;
	For what will Caesar and thyself be more
	Accused by all than that, while you two fought,
490	There could for Crassus no revenge be wrought?
	'Gainst Parthia all our armies should have gone,
	And that no strength might want, from garrison
	Our northern lands should have been freed each one,[6]

feasting and wine, dares sexual unions not legally specified'.

[1] incestuous beds ... unstainèd be] 'incestuous' is added by M., as at 8. 463 and 8. 474; 'names unstainèd', continuing the idiom of 8. 466, translates *sacrataque pignora*, 'sanctified relatives' (VIII. 405).

[2] Oedipus' woeful tale ... done] Oedipus, King of Thebes, unwittingly married his own mother Jocasta and had several children with her: his recognition of this and his downfall is the subject of Sophocles' *Oedipus Tyrannos*.

[3] Defile his mother] *implere parentem*, 'Impregnate [or simply 'fill'] his mother' (VIII. 409).

[4] her husbands' titles ... scornful lust] *Saevitiae stimulata Venus, titulisque virorum*, 'His lust will be stimulated by savagery, and her husbands' titles' (VIII. 413); cf. 8. 482.

[5] Think on that slaughter] *Haereat Eoae vulnus miserabile sortis*, 'Let that wretched wound to our Eastern fortunes stick [in your heart/mind]' (VIII. 417-19).

[6] Our northern ... each one] *vel Arctoum, Rhenique catervis | Imperii nudare latus*, 'the northern flank of our empire should be exposed to the Dacians and hordes of the Rhine' (VIII. 424-25).

'Til treacherous Susa and proud Babylon[1]
495 Had fall'n for tombs upon our slaughtered men.[2]
Of Parthian peace, Fortune, we beg an end,
And, if Thessalia end the civil war,
Against the Parthian send thy conqueror.
Of all the world I should rejoice alone   *only*
500 At Caesar's triumphs o'er that nation.
When thou the cold Araxis' streams hast crossed,
Shall not the slaughtered Crassus' mourning ghost
Upbraid thee?[3] Thou, whom our unburied ghosts
Long since expected with revenging hosts,
505 Com'st thou to sue for peace?[4] Besides, thine eyes
Sad monuments of Roman tragedies
Shall greet: the walls, on which our captains' heads
Were fixed, where bodies of our soldiers dead
Euphrates swallowed, and swift Tigris' stream
510 Rolled back again to earth. If thou to them
Can'st sue,[5] why, Pompey, dost thou scorn to pray
To Caesar sitting in Thessalia?
Look rather upon Rome's confederates,[6]
And if thou do suspect the southern states
515 And Juba's falsehood, go to Ptolemy;[7]
Egypt by Libyan quicksands westerly
Is guarded; on the east fall Nile's seven floods
To th'sea:[8] a land content with her own goods,

---

[1] treacherous Susa and proud Babylon] Parthian cities. M. adds 'proud' for Babylon (cf. 8. 390, 1. 12), evoking a conceit common to classical literature (cf. Martial, *Epigrammata*, VIII. 28. 17) and the Bible alike (e.g. 'prideful Babylon', *Genesis*, 11. 1–9, *KJV*).

[2] for tombs upon our slaughtered men] *In tumulos prolapsa ducum*, 'fallen upon the tombs of the leaders' (VIII. 426). This could be Rome's leaders or Parthia's; M. follows F.'s gloss, *Crassorum, tanquam illis rogi & inferiae*, '[the tombs] of the Crassi, as if [Babylon and Susa were] their funeral pyres and ritual sacrifices'.

[3] Crassus' mourning ghost] *Vmbra senis maesti Scythicis confixa sagittis*, 'The ghost of a gloomy old man, stuck full of Scythian arrows' (VIII .432).

[4] Thou … for peace?] Modern editions read this as inset-speech from Crassus' shade.

[5] If thou … Can'st sue] *ire per ista si potes*, 'If you can pass through such sights' (VIII. 439–40).

[6] Look … confederates] *quin respicis orbem* | *Romanum*, 'Why not turn your eyes to the Roman world' (VIII. 441–42); M. follows F.'s *amicos et socios* ('allies and confederates').

[7] go to Ptolemy] *petimus Pharon arvaque Lagi*, 'we head for Pharos and the lands of Lagus [the founder of the Ptolemaic dynasty]', VIII. 443.

[8] Egypt […] To th'sea] *hinc … inde*, 'on this side, on that' (VIII. 444); M.'s 'westerly' and 'the east' derive from F.

A land that needs nor rain nor merchandise,[1]
520 So much on only Nilus she relies.   *Nile*
Young Ptolemy reigns there, that owes his crown
To thee, once left to thy tuition.[2]
Fear not the shadow of a name; no hurt
Can be in tender years. In an old court
525 Let not religion, faith, or trust be sought:
Men used to sceptres are ashamed of nought;
The mildest government a kingdom finds
Under new kings.'[3] This speech quite turned their minds.
How are despairing states most free and bold?[4]
530 Pompey's opinion is by all controlled.[5]
   They leave Cilicia, and to Cyprus move   [VIII. 456][6]
Their course. No land does Venus better love,
Still mindful of her birth (if we at all
Think gods were born, or had original).[7]   *had a beginning*
535 Pompey, departing thence, his course 'gan bend
Round all the Cyprian rocks that southward tend,
And got into the interposèd main,
Nor by the night's weak light could he attain
Mount Casius, but, with struggling sails and strength,[8]
540 A lower port of Egypt reached at length,
Where parted Nilus' greatest channel flows,
And to the ocean at Pelusium goes.[9]

---

[1] nor rain nor merchandise] *non indiga mercis, | Aut Iovis*, 'Not in need of merchants or Jupiter' (VIII. 446-47): M. follows F. and other commentators in glossing the sky-god Jupiter here as 'rain'.
[2] tuition] *tutelae*, 'care, guardianship' (VIII. 449): Pompey was appointed his guardian after Ptolemy XII Auletes (his father) was restored to the throne in 55 BC.
[3] The mildest government] *mitissima sors*, 'The mildest lot' (VIII. 452).
[4] How are ... bold?] *quantum spes ultima rerum, | Libertatis habet!*, 'How much freedom does the final hope of things contain!' (VIII. 454-45). M. possibly responds to F.'s remark that desperate men adopt παρρησίας, free and bold speech.
[5] Pompey's ... controlled] *victa est sententia Magni*, 'Pompey's proposal was defeated' (VIII. 455): M. has perhaps added a pejorative sense of rebuke in 'controlled' (*OED*, s.v. †2 a and b).
[6] 8. 531-657] Pompey makes for Egypt; the Egyptians plot Pompey's death.
[7] of her birth] *undae ... Paphiae*, 'of the Paphian wave' (VIII. 458): Venus reputedly emerged from the sea at Paphos.
[8] Nor ... Mount Casius] Translating *Nec tenuit Casium nocturno lumine montem* (VIII. 463); modern editions read *gratum ... montem*, 'the mountain pleasing with its nocturnal light', and understand a reference to Pharos. Mount Casius rises on the Egyptian coast, east of Pelusium (cf. 8. 547).
[9] Where parted ... goes] *dividui pars maxima Nili | In vada decurrit Pelusia septimus amnis*, 'the largest part of the divided Nile, the seventh river to run into Pelusian seas' (VIII. 465-66).

That time was come wherein just Libra weighs
The hours and makes the nights equal with days;
545 Then pays the winter night's hours, which the spring
Had ta'en away.¹ They, hearing that the king
Was at Mount Casius, thither make repair:
The sun yet was not down, the wind blew fair.
The scouts along the shore post to the court,
550 And fill their fearful ears with the report
Of Pompey's coming.² Though their time were small
For counsel, yet th'Egyptian monsters all
Were met,³ 'mongst whom Achoreus began,
Whom age taught modesty, a mild old man
555 (Him superstitious Memphis, that observed
Th'increase of Nile, brought forth; while he had served
At the gods' altars, not one Apis lived
Five changes of the moon).⁴ His speech revived
The sacred league of Ptolemy's dead father,
560 And Pompey's merits,⁵ but Photinus rather,
A counsellor for tyrants, with base breath
Durst thus presume to counsel Pompey's death.⁶   *dared*

---

¹ That time ... away] i.e. the autumnal equinox. M. adds 'just' to Libra, a common classical and early modern epithet. M.'s 8. 535-42 and 543-46 are quoted (separately) to describe Pompey's arrival in Egypt in Ussher's *The Annals of the World*, pp. 649-50. M.'s 8. 543-44 also appear in Poole's *English Parnassus*, sig. Ll8ʳ.
² The scouts ... coming] *iam rapido speculator eques per litora cursu | Hospitis adventu pavidam compleverat aulam*, 'now the cavalry scout, with rapid course across the shore, had filled the trembling palace with the news of the arrival of a guest' (VIII. 472-73).
³ th'Egyptian monsters ... met] *tamen omnia monstra | Pellaeae coiere domus*, 'Yet all those wicked men gathered at the Pellaean house' (VIII. 474-75).
⁴ Achoreus began...] A fictitious priest and natural philosopher, who also appears in M.'s *The Tragedy of Cleopatra*; cf. x. 204 ff.   superstitious Memphis] *vana sacris*, 'empty in its rites' (VIII. 477); it held the Nilometer, a well measuring the Nile's waters.   not one Apis...] Achoreus' old age is expressed via reference to Apis, the sacred bull permitted to live for twenty-five years only.
⁵ The sacred league] See 8. 521-2 and note.
⁶ A counsellor ... death] *Sed melior suadere malis, & nosse tyrannos*, 'But better at counselling wickedness/the wicked and at knowing tyrants' (VIII. 482). The amoral advice of the eunuch Photinus (in other early modern and modern editions Pothinus) to have Pompey murdered was extremely well known in early modern England, and its gnomic opening (VIII. 484-95, 8. 562-77 in M.'s version) was often translated or adapted: see Paleit, *War, Liberty, and Caesar*, pp. 128-65. M. was seemingly aware of earlier adaptations (see notes below): 'with base breath', his addition, echoes the description of Pothinus as 'base' in Fletcher and Massinger's *The False One* (c. 1620, publ. 1647), e.g. 'the scorne of basenesse' (p. 196, v. 4. 77, in *The False One*, ed. by Robert Kean Turner, in *The Dramatic Works in the Beaumont and Fletcher Canon*, general ed. Fredson Bowers, vol. VIII (Cambridge: Cambridge University Press, 1992), pp. 113-221).

'Justice and truth have many guilty made:¹ [VIII. 484]
Faith suffers, Ptolemy, when it would aid
565 Whom fortune hates.² Join with the gods and fate,
And fly the wretched, love the fortunate;
Profit from honesty differs as far
As does the sea from fire, earth from a star.
Crowns lose their power, whilst only good they do:
570 Respect of right all strength does overthrow.³
'Tis mischief's freedom and th'uncurbèd sword
That does to hated crowns safety afford.⁴
No cruel actions, unless throughly done,   *thoroughly*
Are done secure.⁵ Let him from court be gone,
575 That would be good; virtue and sovereignty
Do not agree; nothing but fear shall he
That is ashamed a tyrant to be deemed.⁶
Let Pompey rue that he thy years contemned,
Thinking thou couldst not from thy shore drive back
580 A conquered man. Let not a stranger take
Thy sceptre: if thou wouldst resign thy reign,
Th'hast nearer pledges;⁷ give the crown again
To thy condemnèd sister. Let's keep free
Our Egypt from the Roman slavery.⁸
585 Shall we, that did not in the war adhere

---

¹ Justice and truth] *Ius, & fas*, 'Law, human and divine' (VIII. 484).
² Faith ... hates] *Dat poenas laudata fides, cum sustinet, inquit, | Quos Fortuna premit*, 'Praised faith pays the penalty, when it bolsters those whom Fortune crushes' (VIII. 485–86).
³ Crowns ... overthrow] *Sceptrorum vis tota perit, si pendere iusta | Incipit: evertitque arces respectus honesti*, 'The whole strength of sceptres perishes, if it begins to weigh what is just, and respect for what is right overthrows citadels [i.e. of kings]' (VIII. 489–90).
⁴ 'Tis mischief's freedom ... safety afford] M.'s couplet seemingly inspires Robert Baron's 'Tis mischifes freedom holds up Tyranny, | Which who so blushes t'own is no right King', in *Mirza* (London: for Humphrey Moseley, 1647), sig. B6ᵛ.
⁵ No cruel actions...] *facere omnia saeve non impune licet, nisi dum facis*, 'it isn't permitted to do everything violently unpunished, unless until you do it' (VIII. 492–93); cf. Jonson, *Sejanus*, II. 186–87 (*Works*, II, p. 275): 'TIBERIUS: Yet so we may do all things cruelly, | Not safely. SEJANUS: Yes, and do them thoroughly'
⁶ nothing but fear ... deemed] *semper metuet, quem saeva pudebunt*, 'He will always be afraid, whom savage deeds shame' (VIII. 495); cf. Jonson, *Sejanus*, II. 178–79 (*Works*, II, p. 275): '[SEJANUS]: The prince, who shames a tyrant's name to bear, | Shall never dare do any thing but fear'.
⁷ nearer pledges] Cleopatra, Ptolemy's sister. M.'s 'nearer pledges' (translating *pignora ... propiora*, VIII. 499), like 'resign' (8. 581), may be inspired by these terms in Fletcher and Massinger's *The False One*, I. i. 318 (during a paraphrase of Pothinus' speech).
⁸ Let's keep ... slavery] *Aegyptum certe Latiis tueamur ab armis*, 'Let's protect Egypt at least from Italian arms' (VIII. 501).

To Pompey, now provoke the conqueror?¹
Vagrant through all the world, hopeless of all,
He seeks with what land's ruin he may fall;
Haunted with civil war-slain ghosts he flies
590 Not only Caesar but the Senate's eyes,
Whose greater part feeds fowls in Thessaly.
He fears those nations whom he left to die
Mixed in one bloody field; he fears those kings
Whose hapless states his fall to ruin brings.
595 Now guilty of the loss, harboured by none,
To us, whom yet he has not overthrown,
He seeks. A greater cause, O Ptolemy,
Have we to accuse Pompey: why would he
Our quiet land stain with the crime of war,
600 And make us hated by the conqueror?
Why does thy misery choose our land alone
To bring Pharsalia's fortune and thine own
Feared punishment into? We bear a blame
Already (and our swords must purge the same),
605 In that because the Senate, moved by thee,
Gave us a crown, we wished thy victory.
This sword, now drawn by fate, we did provide
To wound not Pompey's but the conquered side,
And rather could we wish for Caesar's head:
610 But whither all are carried, we are led.²
Mak'st thou a doubt of our necessity
To kill thee, now we may? What strength have we
For thee to trust, wretch'd man? Thou saw'st our men
Unarmed, to plough soft mould scarce able, when   *soil*
615 Nile ebbed. Our kingdom's strength 'tis fit that we
Try, and confess: can'st thou, O Ptolemy,
Raise Pompey's ruin, under which great Rome
Itself is fall'n so low? Or dar'st thou come
To stir the ashes of Pharsalia,
620 And such a war upon thy kingdom draw?

---

¹ Shall we ... conqueror?] *Quicquid non fuerit Magni dum bella geruntur, | Nec victoris erit*, 'Whatever was not Pompey's while war was being waged, will not be the victor's either' (VIII. 502–03). M. takes the idea of provoking Caesar from F.

² But ... we are led] *rapimur, quo cuncta feruntur*, 'We are whirled away, whither all things are carried' (VIII. 522). L. alludes to Seneca's *Ducunt volentem fata, nolentem trahunt*, 'The fates lead the willing, drag the unwilling' (*Epistles*, 107. 11), a statement of Stoic determinism: see Introduction, pp. 7–9, 21–22.

	We to no side before the battle cleft:	*cleaved, adhered to*
	Shall we now cleave to Pompey's which is left	
	By the whole world? Provoking the known fates	
	And fearèd strength of Caesar? Wretched states	
625	Aid they, that did their prosperous times attend.[1]	
	No faith e'er chose a miserable friend.'	
	The mischief pleased them all. The young king, proud	[VIII. 536]
	Of this strange honour, that his men allowed	
	Him to command so wonderful a thing,[2]	
630	Chose out Achillas for the managing.[3]	
	Where the false land in Casian sands does lie	
	Stretched out, and fords witness the Syrtes nigh,	
	Weapons and partners of his murd'rous guile	
	He puts in a small boat. O gods, durst Nile,	
635	Durst barbarous Memphis, and th'effeminate men	
	Of soft Canopus harbour such a spleen?[4]	
	Has civil war depressed the world so low?	
	Or are the Roman fates dejected so?	
	Are Pharian swords admitted, and a room	
640	For Egypt left into this war to come?	
	In this at least, ye civil wars, be true:	
	Bring well-known hands, keep foreign beasts from you,	
	If Pompey's far-famed name deserve to be[5]	
	The crime of Caesar. Fears not Ptolemy	
645	The ruin of that name?[6] Or when the sky	
	Thunders, dar'st thou, effeminate Ptolemy,[7]	
	Insert thy profane hands? To terrify	
	Thee, king, a Roman's name enough should be,[8]	

---

[1] Wretched states … attend] i.e. only the state which has benefited from its ally's prosperity should aid it when it is in trouble.

[2] The young king … a thing] *laetatur honore | Rex puer insueto, quod iam sibi tanta iubere | Permittunt famuli*, 'the boy king rejoiced at an unaccustomed honour: his house-slaves permitted him to order such things' (VIII. 536–38). Modern editions print *permittant*, i.e. 'that his slaves *should* permit'.

[3] Achillas … managing] *Sceleri delectus Achillas*, 'Achillas was selected for the crime' (VIII. 538). Achillas was apparently once Ptolemy's tutor, and now his general.

[4] th'effeminate men … spleen] 'th'effeminate men' translates *tam mollis turba*, 'so soft a crowd' (VIII. 543); 'spleen' *hos animos*, 'these spirits' (VIII. 544).

[5] far-famed name] L. uses *Magnus*, 'the Great', for Pompey here (VIII. 549).

[6] that name] *tanti* … | *Nominis*, 'so great a name' (VIII. 550–51); cf. e.g. 1. 148.

[7] effeminate Ptolemy] *impure et semivir*, 'impure and half a man' (VIII. 552), traditional Roman slurs against eastern peoples. M.'s line is irregular. In *1627*, the spelling (and perhaps pronunciation) is 'effoeminate'.

[8] To terrify | Thee…] *Phario satis esse tyranno | Quod poterat, Romanus erat*, 'It should

318　Thomas May

<blockquote>

Without that worth that did the world control,
650　Rode thrice in triumph to the Capitol,
That governed kings, that led the Senate's war,[1]
And son-in-law was to the conqueror.
Why with thy sword our bowels dost thou wound?
Thou dost not know, proud boy, upon what ground
655　Thy fortunes stand; thou now can'st claim no right
To Egypt's sceptre, for in civil fight
He's fall'n, that Egypt's crown on thee bestowed.[2]
Now Pompey's ship took down her sails, and rowed   [VIII. 560][3]
Toward the shore.[4] The wicked band drew (b)near
660　In a small two-oared boat, with feignèd cheer[5]
Tell him the kingdom at his service stands,
And feigning that the shore for shelves and sands
Could not approachèd be by ships so great,
Into their little boat they do entreat
665　He would descend. If by the fates' decree
And everlasting laws of destiny
Pompey, condemnèd to that wretched end,
Had not been forced to shore, (c)none of his friends
Wanted presages of the dire event.
670　For had their faith been pure, if they had meant[6]
Their sceptre-giver truly t'entertain
In court, th'Egyptian king with all his train
And fleet had come. Pompey to fate gives way,
And, bid to leave his navy, does obey,
675　Preferring (d)death before base fear. Into
The enemy's boats Cornelia fain would go,[7]   *glad*
Now more impatient to be separate   *less tolerant*
From her dear lord, because she fears his fate.[8]
'Stay, wife and son, and far from shore', quoth he,
680　'Behold my fortune, and in this neck try
The tyrant's faith.' But, deaf to his commands,   *loyalty, trustworthiness*

</blockquote>

have been enough for an Egyptian tyrant that he was a Roman' (VIII. 555–56); M. then reverses the order of thought in L., who opens with Pompey's achievements (VIII. 553–56).

[1] that led the Senate's war] *vindexque Senatus*, 'avenger of the Senate' (VIII. 554).
[2] crown on thee bestowed] cf. 8. 572.
[3] 8. 657–832] The death of Pompey.
[4] Pompey's ship] In L. Pompey himself does the work (VIII. 560–62).
[5] with feignèd cheer] Added by M.
[6] their ... pure] Referring to Ptolemy's servants.
[7] The enemy's] Printed as in 1627; the meter demands a contraction (probably 'Th'enemy's').
[8] his fate] *clades*, 'disaster' (VIII. 579).

Frantic Cornelia wrings her woeful hands.[1]
'Whither without me goest thou, cruel man?[2]
Removed from Thessaly, must I again
Be left? Still fatal have our partings been.
In flight thou needed'st not to have touched in
At Lesbos, but there still have let me be,
If thou intend I ne'er shall land with thee,
Only at sea thy sad companion.'[3]
Thus all in vain Cornelia making moan,
Upon the ship's fore-deck stood looking o'er,
So full of grief and fear she could nor more
Look after him nor turn her eyes away.
Doubtful of his success, the fleet did stay,
Not fearing swords, nor force, nor treachery,
But lest great Pompey should submissively
Adore that sceptre that himself bestowed.
Septimius then, a Roman soldier, bowed,[4]
Saluting Pompey from th'Egyptian boat,
Who (O heaven's shame!) leaving his pile, had got
A barbarous partisan,[5] one of the guard
To Egypt's king: fierce unrelenting hard,
Bloody as any beast. Who would not then
Have thought that Fortune meant to favour men,
When she had kept this impious sword so far
From Thessaly, and stayed from civil war   *held back*
This hand?[6] But she disposed the swords (alas)
That civil mischief might in every place
Be done.[7] A tale the conquerors to shame

---

[1] woeful hands] *Tendebat geminas ... palmas*, 'She stretched forth her twin palms' (VIII. 583). M. swaps the ancient gesture of supplication for contemporary idiom; cf. e.g. Nathaniel Baxter, *Sir Philip Sydney's Ourania* (London: E. Allde for Edward White, 1616), sig. D3ʳ: 'They waile and wring their wofull hands for greife'.

[2] goest] Monosyllabic.

[3] sad companion] Epithet added. The line-ending '-ion' is disyllabic.

[4] Septimius ... bowed] Lucius Septimius, also described as 'revolted Roman villain' and Pothinus' 'creature' in Fletcher and Massinger's *The False One*, ed. by Kean Turner (1992), p. 123, I. 1. 185. The character was historical and mentioned also by Plutarch (*Life of Pompey*, 78–79, V, pp. 318–23).

[5] A barbarous partisan] M. updates — the partisan is a form of polearm used in the sixteenth and seventeenth centuries. Lit. *arma* ... | *Regia* ... *deformia*, 'misshapen royal weaponry' (VIII. 597–98), contrasted with the Roman military *pilum* or spear.

[6] Who would not ... This hand?] L. addresses Fortune here (VIII. 600–04); 'this impious sword' (8. 705) renders *tam noxia tela*, 'such harmful weapons' (VIII. 602).

[7] But she disposed ... Be done] *Disponis gladios, nequo non fiat in orbe*, | *Heu, facinus*

710 It was, the gods' eternal blush and blame:
A Roman sword should by a king be led,
And the Egyptian boy reach Pompey's head
With his own sword.¹ What fame shall future time
Give thee, Septimius? Or how style thy crime,
715 That Brutus' act as parricidal blame?²
And now the ending hour of Pompey came: [VIII. 610]
Putting himself into the monsters' ⁽ᵉ⁾hands,³
He went aboard their boat; the murd'rous bands
Straight draw; great Pompey seeing their drawn swords
720 Covers his face, disdaining to spend words
Or looks on such a fate,⁴ and shut his eyes,
Containing his great spirit, lest words might rise⁵
Or tears, his everlasting fame to taint.
But when Achillas' murd'ring weapon's point
725 Had pierced his side, scorning the villain's pride
No groans he gave;⁶ great, like himself, he died
With unstirred breast, and thus in secret spake.⁷
'All times that mention of Rome's labours make,
And future ages through the world, will see
730 This fact and Egypt's base disloyalty.⁸
Maintain thine honour now:⁹ the Fates to thee
Through thy whole life gave long prosperity,
And the world knows not (unless now they see)
How Pompey's spirit could bear adversity.

civile tibi, 'You (Fortune) place the swords, alas, in such a way that there may be no place in the world a civil crime is not committed for you' (VIII. 603–04).
  ¹ his own sword] i.e. Pompey's. In L. this sentence is addressed to Pompey (VIII. 607–08).
  ² act as parricidal blame] i.e. if it terms Brutus's assassination of Caesar *nefas*, 'an abomination' (VIII. 610). M.'s 'parricidal' is probably influenced by F.'s gloss *Parricidam*.
  ³ Putting himself .... hands] *Perdiderat iam iura sui*, 'He had already lost power over himself' (VIII. 612). M. omits L.'s pointed *regia*, 'royal [monsters]' (VIII. 613).
  ⁴ disdaining ... fate] *indignatus apertum | Fortunae praebere, caput*, 'Disdaining to show his revealed head to Fortune' (VIII. 615).
  ⁵ spirit] Almost certainly monosyllabic in pronunciation, as it is at 8. 734 below; contrast, however, 8. 745.
  ⁶ scorning ... he gave] *nullo gemitu consensit ad ictum | Respexitque nefas*, 'he submitted to the blow with no groan and took no heed of the crime' (VIII. 618–20).
  ⁷ great, like himself, he died] *seque probat moriens*, 'he tests himself in dying' (VIII. 621). M.'s idea of dying self-resemblance recalls Shakespeare, *Julius Caesar*, V. 4. 25, 'He will be found like Brutus, like himself'.
  ⁸ base disloyalty] *Phariamque fidem*, 'Egyptian fidelity' (VIII. 624). For the 'baseness' of Egypt see 8. Arg. 9, 13, 16.
  ⁹ Maintain ... honour now] *nunc consule famae*, 'Now be mindful of your reputation' (VIII. 624).

735	Blush not that such base hands thy death afford,[1]	
	But think, whoever strike, 'tis Caesar's sword.	
	Though they these limbs all torn and scattered leave,	
	Yet am I happy, gods. No god can reave	*rob (me of)*
	My happiness: my fortunes and my breath	
740	Expire at once, nor wretched is my death.[2]	
	Cornelia and my son this slaughter see:	
	So much more patient let my sorrow be.	*enduring*
	The more Cornelia and my son approve	
	My dying constancy, the more they'll love.'[3]	
745	So well could he his dying spirits guide,	
	Such strength of mind had Pompey when he died.[4]	
	But poor Cornelia, that had rather die	[VIII. 637]
	Than see that sight, with shriekings fills the sky.[5]	
	''Twas wicked I, dear lord, that murdered thee,	
750	For whilst at Lesbos thou turnd'st in to me,[6]	
	Caesar had entered Egypt's shore, for who	
	But he had power that horrid act to do?	
	Whate'er thou art, sent from the gods to kill,	
	Pleasing thine own revenge or Caesar's will,[7]	
755	Thou know'st not, wretch, where Pompey's bowels be:	
	Thou strik'st with fury there where conquered he	
	Desires thy stroke. Now let him suffer more	
	Than his own death and see my head before.[8]	

[1] Blush not ... afford] *Ne cede pudori | Auctoremque dole fati*, 'Don't yield to shame, and grieve at the author of your fate' (VIII. 627-28); cf. 8. 675, 730.

[2] my fortunes ... my death] *mutantur prospera vita*, 'my good fortunes change with my life' (VIII. 631).

[3] So much ... they'll love] *tanto patientus oro, | Claude dolor gemitus; natus, coniunxque peremptum, | Si mirantur, amant*, 'So much more patiently, grief, suppress your groans, I beg: my son and wife love me dead, if they marvel at my death' (VIII. 633-35). M.'s 'dying constancy' is a Stoic/neo-Stoic formula: see Introduction, pp. 7-9, 21-22.

[4] strength of mind] *ius ... animi morientis*, 'command of his dying will' (VIII. 636). M. continues the neo-Stoic patterning, possibly recalling Justus Lipsius's definition of constancy as *rectum et immotum animi robur animi*, an 'upright and unmoved force of mind', *De Constantia* (Antwerp: Christopher Plantin, 1584), sig. B^r.

[5] But poor Cornelia ... that sight] *At non tam patiens Cornelia cernere saevum | Quam perferre nefas*, 'but Cornelia, less tolerant of witnessing the savage crime than undergoing it' (VIII. 6 37-39). 'Poor' is M.'s epithet, a common one for Cornelia in the period: see e.g. Anon., *The Tragedie of Caesar and Pompey*, sigs B3^r, B4^r.

[6] For whilst ... to me] *Letiferae tibi causa morae fuit avia Lesbos*, 'out-of-the-way Lesbos was cause of your fatal delay' (VIII. 640).

[7] Pleasing ... Caesar's will] *vel Caesaris irae, | Vel tibi prospiciens*, 'either looking out for Caesar's rage or for you' (VIII. 643-44).

[8] and see ... before] i.e. let Pompey see Cornelia's death before his own.

I am not guiltless from the crime of war,
760 The only wife following my lord so far,
Fearless of camps or seas; and conquered too
I took him in, which monarchs durst not do.
Did I for this, husband, deserve to be
Left safe aboard? False lord, why spar'st thou me?
765 Or thought'st thou life (thou dying) fit for me?
I'll find a death, though not from Ptolemy.
O sailors, let me leap down from the deck,
Or with these twisted cables break my neck,[1]
Or let some worthy friend of Pompey's now
770 Here sheath his weapon, and for Pompey do
An act that he'll impute to Caesar's hate.
Why do you hinder my desirèd fate?[2]
Husband, thou liv'st, Cornelia has not power
Yet of herself; they hinder my death's hour',
775 And there she sounds, 'to be the conqueror's prey.' *swoons*
The fearful fleet hoist sails, and post away.[3]
    But when great Pompey fell, that sacred face [VIII. 663]
And honoured visage kept his former grace
Though angry with the gods;[4] death's utmost hate
780 Changed not his visage and majestic state,[5]
As they confess that his rent neck did see.
For stern Septimius in that cruelty
Finds out an act more cruel:[6] to uncover

---

[1] Or with ... break my neck] *Aut laqueum collo tortosque aptate rudentes*, 'or fashion twisted ropes as a noose for my neck' (VIII. 655). The early modern reading *aptate* is a command to the sailors; modern editions prefer *aptare* i.e. '[permit me] to fashion'. See Textual Notes.

[2] Why ... fate?] Addressed to sailors apparently restraining her; in L. she calls them *saevi*, 'savage' (VIII. 658).

[3] they hinder ... post away] *prohibent accersere mortem; | Servor victori. Sic fata, interque suorum | Lapsa manus, rapitur, trepida fugiente carina*, '"They forbid me to seek my death: I am being kept alive for the victor." Thus having spoken, having swooned among the hands of her people, she is carried off, as the trembling ship flees' (VIII. 660-63).

[4] that sacred face ... gods] *Permansisse decus sacrae venerabile formae | Iratamque Deis faciem*, 'The honoured shapeliness of his sacred figure remained, and face angered at the gods' (VIII. 664-65). Some modern editions read *placatam* for *iratam*, '[face] rendered serene by the gods'.

[5] majestic state] *habitu*, 'bearing' (VIII. 666).

[6] in that cruelty ... more cruel] *sceleris maius scelus invenit actu*, 'he found a crime greater than that act of crime' (VIII. 668). 'Stern' (8. 782) can mean 'merciless, cruel' in early modern English (see *OED*, s.v. †3). 'Cruel' is probably monosyllabic here, against M.'s normal practice.

His face, he cuts the cloth that was cast over,
785 Invading half-dead Pompey's breathing face.
His dying neck across the boards he lays,
Then cuts the nerves and veins, the twisted bones
He breaks; the art to whip off heads at once
Was not yet found.¹ But when the head was torn
790 Off from the trunk, 'twas by Achillas borne.²
Degenerate Roman, base Septimius,
Used in an under office, couldst thou thus
Basely cut off great Pompey's sacred head
To be (O shame) by another carrièd?³
795 Young Ptolemy to know great Pompey's face,
Those hairs that kings have honoured,⁴ whose curled grace
Adorned his noble front, strokes with his hands.⁵   *forehead*
Fixed on a pole the head of Pompey stands
Whilst yet his lips with throbbing murmurs shook,
800 His eyes unclosed, and lively was his look;
That head that still determined war and peace,⁶
That ruled the Senate, laws and suffrages;⁷   *votes*
Rome's fortune in that face took greatest pride.⁸
Nor was the wicked tyrant satisfied
805 With sight, but for memorial of the fact,⁹
Dire arts the head's corruption must extract.
The brain is taken out, dried is the skin,
The noisome moisture purgèd from within,
Medicines make solid and preserve the face.¹⁰

---

¹ the art ... found] *nondum artis erat caput ense rotare*, 'There was not yet the skill to send a head spinning with the sword' (VIII. 673).
² Achillas] *Pharius ... satelles*, 'the Egyptian henchman' (VIII. 675).
³ Basely ... by another carrièd] Omitting *diro ... ense*, 'with a dire sword' and condensing *o summi fata pudoris*, 'O destiny of utmost shame' into 'O shame' (VIII. 677, 678).
⁴ honoured] *verenda*, 'to be feared' (VIII. 679).
⁵ strokes with his hands] Understanding *coma, & ... | Caesaries compressa manu est* ('his hair and locks were seized by the hand', VIII. 680-81) as Ptolemy's hand, evidently following F.'s gloss that Ptolemy himself 'handled [*tractavit*]' his head. The hand in question is probably Achillas', however.
⁶ That head ... peace] *quo numquam bella iubente | Pax fuit*, 'at whose command for war there was never peace' (VIII. 684-85).
⁷ That ruled ... suffrages] *hoc leges campumque, & Rostra movebat*, 'This [head] which directed the laws, the Campus Martius, and the rostra' (VIII. 685); cf. 4. 879n.
⁸ Rome's ... pride] Addressed to Fortune in L. (VIII. 686).
⁹ for memorial of the fact] *sceleri superesse fidem*, 'that proof would outlive the crime' (VIII. 688); modern editions read *sceleris*, 'that proof of the crime would survive'.
¹⁰ Medicines] *veneno*, 'poison' (VIII. 829); 'medicines' is probably pronounced 'med'cines'.

810	Degenerate issue, last of Lagus' race,	[VIII. 692]¹
	Whom thy incestuous sister shall depose,²	
	When sacred vaults the Macedon enclose,	Alexander the Great
	When dust of kings in sumptuous buildings lies,	
	And the ignoble race of Ptolemies	
815	In pyramids and rich Mausolean graves³	
	Unjustly rest, must Pompey by the waves	
	An headless trunk against the shore be swept?	
	Was it too great a trouble to have kept	
	The carcass whole for Caesar? This sad date	duration
820	Did fortune give to Pompey's prosperous state,	
	By such a death as this to pull him down	
	From such an height, heaping all plagues in one	
	Sad day,⁴ which he so many years had been	
	Free from. Nor yet had Pompey ever seen	
825	Joy mixed with woe; no god his prosperous state	
	Did ere disturb, none helped his wretched fate;	
	But once for all with a deferring hand	
	Did Fortune pay him.⁵ Torn upon the sand,	
	Salt water playing in his wounds, the mock	
830	Of seas he lies, and beat 'gainst every rock:	
	No figure left of him; 'tis note enough	
	To know great Pompey, that his head is off.⁶	
	But fates, ere Caesar on that shore arrive,⁷	[VIII. 712]⁸
	A sudden funeral to Pompey give	
835	Lest he in none or in a better tomb	
	Should lie. To th'shore did fearful Codrus come	
	Out of his lurking hole, that was before	
	Great Pompey's quaestor, and from Cyprus' shore	
	Had followed him.⁹ He by the shades of night	

---

¹ 8. 810–32] An invective against Ptolemy.
² incestuous sister] Cleopatra.
³ Mausolean] Trisyllabic.
⁴ Sad day] *saeva die*, 'cruel day' (VIII. 704).
⁵ deferring hand] i.e. Fortune delayed the moment when she turned against him.
⁶ 'tis note enough...] *nullaque manente figura, | Vna nota est Magno capitis iactura revulsi*, 'with no figure remaining, the loss of his decapitated head is mark enough of Magnus' (VIII. 710–11).
⁷ fates] *Fortuna* in L. (VIII. 713).
⁸ 8. 833–1014] The burial of Pompey.
⁹ To th'shore ... followed him] Codrus (Cordus in modern editions) is Pompey's *infaustus ... comes*, 'inauspicious companion' (VIII. 717), and comes *ab Idalio Cinyreae litore Cypri*, 'from the Idalian shore of Cinyrean Cyprus' (VIII. 716).

840	Durst go (true love had vanquished terror quite)[1]	*dared to*
	To find his slaughtered lord along the sand	
	And through the waves, to bring the trunk to land.[2]	
	Faint light through dusky clouds sad Cynthia gave;	*the moon*
	But different coloured from the foamy wave	
845	The trunk appeared, which Codrus catching straight	
	When the waves ebbed, but tirèd with the weight,	
	Expects their flow to help him, and so bore	
	The trunk to land and placed it on the shore.	
	Then falling down, bathing the wounds in tears,[3]	
850	Thus to the gods he speaks and clouded stars.	
	'Fortune, no costly pile with odours filled	[VIII. 729] *pyre*
	Thy Pompey craves, nor that his hearse may yield	*bier*
	Precious Arabian fumes to fill the air,[4]	
	Nor that the pious Roman necks should bear	
855	Their country's father forth, nor to adorn	
	A funeral pomp old triumphs should be borne;	
	No funeral songs, nor that his troops the while	
	March a dead march about their general's pile:	
	Grant Pompey but a base plebeian bier	
860	That his torn limbs may carry to dry fire.[5]	
	Let him not want wood and a burner,[6] though	
	But mean, and let it be, O gods, enough	
	That with loose hair Cornelia does not stand	
	To take her last embrace and then command	
865	To fire the pile: from this last funeral rite	
	She is away, yet hardly out of sight.'[7]	
	This said, far off a little fire he kenned	*espied*
	Burn a neglected hearse, watched by no friend,[8]	*corpse*
	Thither he goes, and taking thence a part[9]	

---

[1] true love … terror quite] *victum pietate timorem | Compulit*, 'he contained a fear conquered by loyalty [to find…]' (VIII. 717–18).

[2] the trunk] In L. 'Magnus' (VIII. 720); cf. 8. 848.

[3] falling down] *incubuit Magno*, 'he lay down on Pompey' (VIII. 727).

[4] Precious Arabian fumes] *Eoos … odores*, 'eastern scents' (VIII. 731). F. glosses 'Arabian, Indian scents, the scents of Panchaean incense'; the association of Arabia with precious scents and other luxuries is widespread in Renaissance and classical literature.

[5] That his torn … fire] *Quae lacerum corpus siccos effundat in ignes*, 'to spread his mutilated corpse on dry [i.e. not scented] flames' (VIII. 737).

[6] him] *misero*, 'the wretched [Pompey]' (VIII. 738).

[7] She] *infelix coniunx*, 'the unhappy spouse [Cornelia]' (VIII. 742).

[8] neglected hearse] *corpus vile*, 'a base corpse' (VIII. 744). F. glosses *vile* as *neglectum*.

[9] taking thence] Reading, as in F. (following Grotius), *subducens* (VIII. 746); modern

870	Of fire and half-burned sticks, 'Whoe'er thou art,	
	Neglected ghost, dear to no friend,' quoth he,	
	'But happier than great Pompey, pardon me	
	(If any knowledge after death remains)¹	
	That by a stranger's hand thy hearse sustains	*pyre*
875	This wrong. I know thou yield'st, and can'st endure	
	For Pompey's sake this loss of sepulture,	*burial*
	And art ashamed of funeral rites, whilst he	
	Lies an unburied ghost.' Then speedily,	
	With his arms full of fire, poor Codrus ran	
880	To find the trunk, which to the shore again	
	The waves had beat. Then off the sand he wipes,	
	And gath'ring up the ribs of broken ships,	
	He lays them in a ditch. On no hewn trees	
	Or well-built pile the noble body lies:	*pyre*
885	Fire brought, not under-built, great Pompey takes.	
	Then sitting by the fire thus Codrus speaks.	
	'Rome's greatest lord, the only majesty²	[VIII. 759]
	Of Italy, if worse this burial be	
	Than none at all, than floating on the sea,	
890	Avert thy Manes and great ghost from me.³	*spirit*
	'Tis fortune's injury that makes this right:⁴	
	Lest fish or fowl or beasts or Caesar's spite	
	Might wrong thy corse,⁵ accept this little brand	*corpse*
	Of fire, since kindled by a Roman hand.⁶	
895	If fortune grant recourse to Italy,⁷	*return*
	Not here shall these so sacred ashes lie,	
	But from my hand Cornelia shall take,	
	And urn thy relics.⁸ Until then we'll make	*place in an urn*
	Thy burial's mark upon the shore, that who⁹	

editions read *subducit*, 'takes thence'.

1. knowledge] *sensus*, 'sense, feeling' (VIII. 749).
2. lord] *ductor*, 'leader, commander' (VIII. 760).
3. from me] *officiis meis*, 'from my ministrations' (VIII. 763).
4. fortune's] *fati*, 'fate's' (VIII. 763).
5. Lest ... thy corse] *ne ponti belua quicquam, | Ne fera, ne volucres, ne saevi Caesaris ira | Audeat*, 'lest any sea-beast, any wild animal, any birds, or the anger of savage Caesar dare something' (VIII. 764–65).
6. accept ... Roman hand] Omitting *quantum potes*, 'as far as you are able to' (VIII. 766).
7. Italy] *Hesperiam*, 'Land of the West' (VIII. 768); cf. 8. 888.
8. thy relics] Simply *te*, 'thee' in L. (VIII. 769).
9. we'll make ... the shore] Omitting L.'s informative *parvo saxo*, 'with a little rock' (VIII. 771).

900	Soe'er would pacify thy ghost, and do	
	Full right of funeral, may find out so	
	The body's ashes, and the sands may know[1]	
	Whither to bring thy head.' Thus having spoke,	
	He does with fuel the weak flame provoke.	
905	Pompey dissolved; his fat distilling fed	
	The little fire;[2] and now day promisèd	
	By bright Aurora dimmed the stars' weak lights.	*dawn*
	Codrus abruptly leaves the funeral rites	
	And runs, himself about the shore to hide.[3]	
910	What mischief fear'st thou (fool) for such a deed,[4]	[VIII. 781]
	Which long-tongued fame for ever shall renown?[5]	
	Caesar himself shall praise what thou hast done[6]	
	To Pompey's body. Go then, void of dread,[7]	
	Confess the funeral and require his head.	
915	An end of duteous works piety makes.	
	The bones half-burnt, not yet dissolved, he takes,	
	Still full of nerves and unconsumèd marrow;	
	Quenching them in sea-water, in a narrow	
	Piece of the earth together lays them down:	
920	Then, lest the ashes should abroad be blown	
	By the wind's force, he lays a stone above;	
	And lest some sailor should that stone remove	
	To tie his cable, with a coal-burnt staff	
	Upon the top he writes this epitaph:[8]	
925	'Here Pompey lies, Fortune, this stone we call	
	His tomb: in which, rather than none at all,	

---

[1] And the sands may know] i.e. 'and may know the sands'.

[2] Pompey ... The little fire] *Carpitur, & lentum Magnus destillat in ignem, | Tabe fovens bustum*, 'Magnus is kindled, and oozes into the slow fire, nourishing the pyre with his fat' (VIII. 777–78).

[3] abruptly leaves ... to hide] L. makes it clearer that he breaks off the rites prematurely (*rupto ordine*, VIII. 779), also calling Codrus 'amazed' or 'thunderstruck' (*attonitus*, VIII. 780).

[4] What mischief ... deed] *Quam metuis demens isto pro crimine poenam?*, 'What punishment do you fear, madman, for a crime like that?' (VIII. 781).

[5] long-tongued fame] *fama loquax*, 'talkative fame' (VIII. 782). M.'s epithet is a popular one for Fame in early modern literature — see. e.g. Fletcher, *The Loyal Subject* (1618), IV. 3. 252, 'I knew Fame was a liar, too long and long-tongued' (*The Loyal Subject*, ed. by Fredson Bowers, in *The Dramatic Works in the Beaumont and Fletcher Canon*, general ed. Fredson Bowers, vol. 5 (Cambridge: Cambridge University Press, 1982), pp. 151–288).

[6] Caesar himself] Omitting L.'s critical *socer impius*, 'the impious father in law' (VIII. 783).

[7] void of dread] *securus veniae*, 'assured of pardon' (VIII. 784).

[8] epitaph] *sacrum ... nomen*, 'his sacred name' (VIII. 792).

Caesar would have him lie.'¹ Why in a room
So small, rash hand, includ'st thou Pompey's tomb,   *confines, contains*
And shut'st up his great ghost?² As far he lies
930 As the earth's farthest shore extended is.
Rome's mighty name and empire's utmost bound
Is Pompey's tomb; this mark for shame confound
The shame of heaven.³ If Alcides lie   *Hercules*
Over all Oete, and all Nysa be
935 Great Bacchus' monument, why should one stone
In Egypt stand for Pompey's tomb alone?⁴
Did no one piece of earth thy name express,
All Egypt's land, Pompey, thou might'st possess.
Let us be still deceived, and still for fear
940 Of thee to tread on Egypt's land forbear.⁵
But if that sacred name must grace a stone,
Write his each deed, and glorious action:
The Alpine war of rebel Lepidus,⁶
The conquest of revolt Sertorius   *rebel*
945 (The consul being called home):⁷ those triumphs note
Which he but gentleman of Rome had got.⁸
Cilician pirates tamed, traffic made free,

---

¹ Here Pompey lies … lie] Although there are no quotation marks in *1627*, M. seems to have understood this epitaph as running to 8. 927 and incorporating an apostrophe to Fortune. As early modern editions show, however, the epitaph itself is only three words (*Hic situs est Magnus*, 'here lies Magnus') and the following lines are a question: *placet hoc, Fortuna, sepulchrum | Dicere Pompeii: quo condi maluit illum | Quam terra caruisse socer?*, 'Fortune, does it please you to say that this tomb is Pompey's, in which the father-in-law preferred he be buried, than lack any earth at all?' (VIII. 793–95).

² great ghost] *manesque vagantes*, 'his roaming spirit' (VIII. 796); cf. 8. 890. In L., 8. 927–29 (VIII. 795–97) continue the complaint to Fortune: the 'rash hand' (*temeraria dextra*) is not the addressee but the means whereby Fortune buries Pompey.

³ this mark … heaven] *obrue saxa | Crimine plena Deum*, 'Overturn these stones, replete with the criminality of the gods!' (VIII. 799–800). 'Heaven' is, untypically, disyllabic here.

⁴ Alcides … Bacchus' monument] cf. 3. 198; 1. 71 on Nysa and Bacchus (lit. *Bromius*, 'the Roarer', VIII. 801).

⁵ Of thee] *cinerumque tuorum*, 'of thy ashes' (VIII. 804) — i.e. in case of scattering them.

⁶ the Alpine war … Lepidus] On Lepidus, see 2. 583–84. In L. *truces Lepidi motus*, 'the savage rebellion of Lepidus', is not necessarily the same as *Alpinaque bella*, 'and the Alpine wars' (VIII. 808), but F.'s note that the action against Lepidus took place beyond the Alps may have encouraged this inference.

⁷ the conquest of revolt Sertorius] *Armaque Sertori … victa*, 'the conquered arms of Sertorius' (VIII. 809). M. recalls his own earlier translation, 7. 17. Pompey took over the campaign against Sertorius after the recall of the consul, Metellus Pius, to Rome.

⁸ those triumphs … had got] *et currus, quos egit eques*, 'and the chariot he drove as an *eques*' (VIII. 810). M. uses 'gentleman' for the Roman equestrian rank in both his translation and *Continuation*.

	Barbarian kingdoms conquered all that lie	
	Under the east and north. With this, make known	
950	How still from war he took a peaceful gown;[1]	
	Contented with three triumphs, he to Rome	
	His other conquests did forgive.[2] What tomb	
	Can hold all this? His ashes in this grave	
	No titles nor triumphant stories have.[3]	*inscriptions; chronicles*
955	That name that temples' lofty roofs and high	
	Triumphal arches, decked with victory,[4]	
	Were wont to bear, now near the lowest sand	
	A small grave shows, which strangers cannot stand	
	Upright to read; which (if it be not shown),	
960	The Roman travellers pass by unknown.	
	Egypt, whom civil fate has guilty made,	[VIII. 823][5]
	'Twas not in vain the Sibyl's verse forbade[6]	
	A Roman Nile's Pelusian mouth to touch,	
	Or once his summer-swellèd banks approach.	
965	How shall I curse thee for this impious deed?	
	May Nile run back and stay at his first head,	
	May thy unfruitful fields want winter rain,	
	And all like Ethiop's barren sands remain.	
	We let thy Isis in Rome's temples dwell,	
970	Thy deified dogs and sorrow-causing bell?[7]	
	Osiris whom thou showest while thou weep'st,	
	A man: our god in dust, thou, Egypt, keep'st.[8]	
	And thou that gav'st the tyrant temples, Rome,[9]	

---

[1] peaceful gown] *Civilem ... toga*, 'the citizen toga' (VIII. 814), i.e. Pompey gave up his commands and became a private citizen again.

[2] forgive] *donasse*, 'granted [many triumphs]' (VIII. 815), i.e. as gifts, by only claiming three.

[3] His ashes ... stories have] *surgit miserabile bustum | Non ullis plenum titulis, non ordine tanto | Fastorum*, 'a piteous tomb rises, full of no honorific inscriptions, nor any great sequence of the *Fasti*' (VIII. 816–18).

[4] with victory] *spoliis hostilibus*, 'with enemy spoils' (VIII. 819); a Roman custom.

[5] 8. 961–1114] The poet curses Egypt and commemorates Pompey's memory.

[6] the Sibyl's verse] *Cumanae carmine vatis*, 'the verse of the prophet of Cumae' (VIII. 823).

[7] Thy deified ... bell] *semideos canes*, 'demigod dogs' (VIII. 832), identified by F. as Anubis; 'bell' translates *sistra*, 'rattles' (VIII. 832), associated with eastern worship. F. says they were made of bronze and silver. 'Deified' may be disyllabic here.

[8] Osiris ... keep'st] Contrasting the annual death and resurrection of the Egyptian god Osiris, linked to the flooding of the Nile, with *nostros ... Manes*, 'Our ghost/shade' (VIII. 834); M.'s 'god' is possibly influenced by F.'s gloss that Pompey is 'the equivalent of a deity to us' (*nobis numinis instar*).

[9] thou ... Rome] M. implies this line is addressed to 'Rome', like the one below it, but L.

Hast not yet fetched thy Pompey's ashes home:
His ghost lies yet exiled. If Caesar's frowns
That first age feared, yet now thy Pompey's bones
Bring home, O Rome, if yet on that cursed land,
Not ruined by the waves, the marks do stand.
Who'll fear that grave? Who'll fear to take from thence
Ashes deserving temples?[1] That offence
Enjoin me (Rome) to do; my bosom use.
O too too happy I, if Rome would choose
My hand to open that base sepulchre,
And his dear ashes hither to transfer.
Perchance when Rome from oracles would crave
An end of dearth or pestilence to have,
Of too much fire or earthquakes, thou to Rome
Shalt by the gods' expressed appointment come,
Thy ashes borne by the high priest.[2] For who
To scorched Syene in June's heat can go
In view of Nile,[3] or Pharian Thebes descry
Under the show'ry Pleiades still dry;[4]
What eastern merchant, trafficking, resorts
To the Red Sea or rich Arabian ports,
But at thy grave's ever-adorèd stone
And ashes (though perchance scattered upon
The sands) will stay, thy ghost to pacify,
Before the Casian Jove preferring thee?[5]
This little grave can nothing hurt thy name;
Thy ghost would be of a far cheaper fame
Shrouded in gold and temples; fortune now
Bears more divinity, entombed so low;
This sea-beat stone is more majestic far

---

means Augustus here, who built a temple to the 'cruel tyrant' Caesar (*saevo ... tyranno*, VIII. 835).

[1] Who'll fear ... temples?] *Quis sacris dignam movisse verebitur urnam?*, 'Who will be afraid to move an urn worthy of sacred rites?' (VIII. 841). Modern editions read *umbram* ('ghost') for *urnam*, a variant acknowledged by F.

[2] high priest] i.e. the Pontifex Maximus, Rome's chief religious official. L. alludes to other times of crisis in Rome's history where catastrophe was averted by bringing a deity to Rome.

[3] scorched Syene] *adustam torrente Cancro Syenen*, 'Syene, burnt up by blazing Cancer' (VIII. 851).

[4] Under ... still dry] The arrival of the zodiacal sign the Pleiades normally signifies rain and the onset of winter: but even so it remains dry in Egyptian Thebes.

[5] Casian Jove] There was a temple of Jupiter on Mount Casius (cf. 8. 547).

Than the proud altars of the conqueror.[1]
1005 Some worship gods dwelling in dusky clay,
That to Tarpeian Jove refuse to pray.[2]
   'Twill vantage thee hereafter in thy grave   *benefit*
No polished marble's lasting works to have.
This little dust will quickly scattered lie,
1010 The tomb will fall, proofs of thy death will die.
And then a happier age will come, when none
Shall credit give to those that show the stone.
As false shall Egypt seem in times to come,
(As Crete of Jove's) to boast of Pompey's tomb.[3]

FINIS

---

[1] more majestic far ... conqueror] See 8. Ded. 7–8. M.'s 'more majestic' translates *augustius* (VIII. 861), an attack on imperial nomenclature.

[2] Some worship ... refuse to pray] *Tarpeiis qui saepe Deis sua tura negarunt, | Inclusum fusco venerantur caespite fulmen*, 'they who've denied their incense often to Tarpeian gods, worship a thunderbolt imprisoned in dusky turf' (VIII. 863–64). Modern editions print *Tusco*, 'Tuscan', for *fusco*, 'dusky' (VIII. 864), a reference to augurs consecrating the sites of lightning strikes.

[3] As Crete of Jove's] The islanders of Crete were proverbial 'liars' in antiquity, above all for their claim that the tomb of (immortal) Jove was on their island.

Annotations on the Eighth Book

(a) Pompey, in his flight from Larissa, came all along the Tempe to the shore, and lodged that night in the small cottage of a fisherman. About morning he went to sea in a little boat, and sailing along by the shore, met with a ship of greater burden, of which one Peticius a Roman was captain, who, knowing Pompey, received him, and transported him to Lesbos, where Cornelia lay. (Plutarch, Appian.)[1]

(b) When their boat drew near to Pompey, Septimius arose (who had once served as a tribune under Pompey) and in the Roman language saluted his general and welcomed him in the king's name. Achillas complimented with him in the Greek tongue, and desireth him to enter into his boat, by reason that the shelves and sands would not afford a passage to his ship.[2]

(c) Those that attended Pompey, seeing his entertainment not royal nor magnificent, but that a few only in a small boat were sent to meet him, began to suspect the treason and counselled Pompey to put to sea, and forsake that shore whilst yet he was free from danger.[3]

(d) Pompey, disdaining to appear fearful (although he were full of ill presages), came into Achillas his boat, as he was invited, and taking his leave of his wife and son, Sextus Pompeius, he repeated these two iambic verses of Sophocles:

Ὅστις δὲ πρὸς τύραννον ἐμπορεύεται,
κείνου 'στὶ δοῦλος, κἂν ἐλεύθερος μόλῃ.

These were the last words he spake to his friends, and so entered into the boat where Achillas was.[4]

(e) When Pompey was now far from his ship, and perceived no courteous entertainment in the boat, he looked upon Septimius and thus spake: 'have not I known thee heretofore, my fellow soldier?' Septimius, disdaining to answer him at all, only nodded his head to him, and when Pompey was rising out of the boat, Septimius first run him through with his sword.[5]

---

[1] Except for the phrase about Cornelia, translated entirely from F.'s note to VIII. 33, including the unspecific 'Plutarch, Appian (*Plutarch. & Appian.*)'.
[2] Translated entirely from F.'s note to VIII. 562, omitting only his reference to Plutarch.
[3] Translated entirely from F.'s note to VIII. 572, itself taken from Plutarch.
[4] Following F.'s notes to VIII. 576 and VIII. 577, themselves derived from Plutarch, *Life of Pompey*, 78–79. The citation from Sophocles — a fragment of an unknown play — means 'The man who travels to a tyrant is his slave, even if he goes as a free man'.
[5] Condensed from F.'s note to VIII. 610, derived from Plutarch, *Life of Pompey*, 79. 1–3. The lightly ironic idiom of 'courteous entertainment' and 'disdaining' is M.'s.

To the Right Honourable Robert, Earl of Warwick, &c.[1]

This book, which Cato's legend doth relate,
To you, most virtuous lord, I dedicate,
Whose worth securely may such stories love,   *unconcerned*
Whom great examples shame not but approve.
5 See here how hard to climb, how rough, and high
The paths that lead to true nobility
Virtue's best servants oft have found:[2] see here
Good Cato's strength o'ercome what task soe'er
His cruel mistress Virtue could command
10 And, marching o'er scorched Afric's desert sand,
Win (as our author thought) more honour far
Than any laurelled Roman conqueror
By lands subdued, or blood of nations shed,
When captived monarchs their proud chariots led.

---

[1] To the Right Honourable ...] Robert Rich, second Earl of Warwick (1587–1658): like many of M.'s aristocratic dedicatees a prominent Puritan and critic of Caroline absolutism, and military man. He opposed the Arminian (anti-Calvinist) party at the York House conference in 1626 and was among those who refused the Forced Loan of 1626–1627. He later served as lord high admiral for Parliament in the first civil war, until he was forced to surrender his commission in 1645. During 1627 he was preparing a voyage to plunder the Spanish treasure-fleets; however, the stress in M.'s dedication is on non-military virtue achieved through Stoic indifference to suffering (*apatheia*), which Cato exemplifies and which M. typically indicates with the epithet 'secure' (see Introduction, pp. 7–9, 21–22.).
[2] The doctrine of virtue being the true nobility recurs in M.'s dedications, but is particularly appropriate for Cato, a paragon of virtue not only in L.'s text but also in early modern England: see Jensen, '"Creating" Cato in Early Seventeenth-Century England'.

LUCAN'S
Pharsalia

The Ninth Book.

The Argument of the Ninth Book.[1]

Pompey's departed spirit to heaven ascends.[2]
His wife, and sons lament; Cato commends
His worthy life; checks the Cilicians,
And marching o'er the scorchèd Libyan sands
5   To Juba's kingdom, with strong patience
Endures the heat, the south wind's violence,
And killing serpents' venom. Caesar sees
Renownèd Troy's defaced antiquities,
To Egypt comes, and with dissembling breath
10 Complains and weeps for noble Pompey's death.[3]

    In Pharian coals his ghost could not remain,   [IX. 1][4]
Nor those few ashes his great spirit contain.
Out from the grave he issues, and forsakes
Th'unworthy fire and half-burnt limbs, and takes
5   Up to the convex of the sky his flight,
Where with black air the starry poles do meet.
The space betwixt the regions of the moon
And earth half-deified souls possess alone,[5]
Whom fiery worth in guiltless lives has taught
10 To brook the lower part of heaven, and brought   *bear, tolerate*
Them to th'eternal spheres, which not they hold
That are with incense buried, tombed in gold.
There fillèd with true light, with wond'ring eyes
The wand'ring planets and fixed stars he sees.

---

[1] See Argument to book one.
[2] spirit ... heaven] Both contracted to one syllable in pronunciation (as also at 9. 2 below). The beginning of this book has an unusual number of unmarked contractions and elisions.
[3] with dissembling breath] M.'s addition.
[4] 9. 1–58] Pompey's soul flies up into the heavens before taking residence in the hearts of Cato and Brutus; Cato gathers the republican remnants and makes his way to Africa.
[5] deified] Disyllabic.

15 He sees our day involved in midst of night,[1]
And laughs at his torn trunk's ridiculous plight.[2]
Then o'er the Emathian fields, his scattered fleet,[3]
And bloody Caesar's troops he took his flight:
And with revenge for these dire facts possessed
20 Cato's bold heart and Brutus' noble breast.[4]
Cato, while chance was [(a)]doubtful, and at stake
Whom civil war lord of the world would make,
Then hated Pompey, though with Pompey he
(Led by the Senate, and Rome's auspicy)
25 Had fought: but when Pharsalia's field was tried
He altogether favoured Pompey's side.[5]
His country wanting a protector then
He took, and cheered the trembling hearts of men,
And putting swords in fearful hands again,[6]
30 Made civil war neither for hope of reign
Nor fear of bondage. Nought at all in war
For his own sake did he: his forces are
Since Pompey's death alone for liberty,
Which lest the speed of Caesar's victory
35 Should seize upon, being dispersèd o'er
The coast, he sails unto Corcyra's [(b)]shore,
And in a thousand ships carries away
The conquered remnant of Pharsalia.
    Who would have thought so great a fleet had held   [IX. 34]
40 All flying men? That conquered ships had filled
The straitened seas? From thence they sail away
To ghost-filled Taenarus and long Malea,[7]

---

[1] our day ... night] *quanta sub nocte iaceret | Nostra dies*, 'under how great a night lies our day', i.e. when compared to Pompey's new illuminated location (IX. 13–14).

[2] ridiculous] Contracted in pronunciation to three syllables.

[3] the Emathian] Probably elided in pronunciation ('th'Emathian') for metrical purposes, although all editions print as here.

[4] Cato's bold heart, and Brutus' noble breast] *in sancto pectore Bruti ... et invicti ... mente Catonis*, 'in the sacred breast of Brutus and the mind of unconquered Cato' (IX. 17–18).

[5] but when Pharsalia's ...] *post Thessalicas clades*, 'after the Thessalian calamity' (IX. 23). Rome's auspicy] A reference to the drawing of omens from birds.

[6] and cheered ... again] *populi trepidantia membra refovit, | Ignavis manibus proiectos reddidit enses*, 'he cherished the quivering limbs of the [Roman] people, and returned swords cast away by cowardly hands' (IX. 25–26).

[7] ghost-filled Taenarus and long Malea] On Taenarus cf. 6. 740n. L.'s epithet for Malea (a promontory of the Peloponnese) is *Dorida*, 'Doric' (IX. 36). The meter calls for 'Malea' to be disyllabic, although the line could simply be irregular; 'Boreas' (9. 43, below) is certainly disyllabic.

	Thence to Cytherus; Boreas blowing fair	*north wind*
	Crete flies, and getting a good sea they clear	
45	The Cretan coast. Phycus, that durst deny	*dares to*
	Their men to land, they sack deservedly,	
	And thence along the deep, while fair winds blow,	
	Unto thy shore, O Palinurus, go	
	(For not alone doth our Italian sea	
50	Keep monuments of thee, but Libya	
	Can witness well calm harbours once did please	
	The Phrygian master):[1] when upon the seas	
	Descrying ships afar, they 'gan to fear	*catching sight of*
	Whether the men their foes or partners were:	
55	Caesar's known speed gave them just cause to fear	
	And still suspect his coming everywhere.[2]	
	But those sad ships brought grief and woes and cries,	
	Able to draw soft tears from Cato's eyes.	
	For after that Cornelia all in vain	[IX. 51][3]
60	(Lest Pompey's trunk beat from the shore again	
	Should float at sea) by prayers had strived to draw	
	From flight the sailors and her son-in-law,[4]	
	When from the shore that little fire descried	
	His most unworthy funeral, she cried,	
65	'Seemed I not worthy then, Fortune, to thee	
	To light my husband's funeral fire and lie	
	Stretched out on his cold limbs, burn his torn hairs,	
	And gathering his sea-scattered limbs, with tears	
	To bathe each wound? With bones and ashes hot	
70	To fill my lap, and in the temples put	
	The sad remainder of his funeral?[5]	
	That fire's no honour to his hearse at all.	*pyre*
	Besides, perhaps some hands of Egypt now	
	This loathèd office to his ashes do.	

[1] Palinurus…] Aeneas's Trojan helmsman ('Phrygian master') in Virgil's *Aeneid*, who perished off the coast of Italy; the land there was named for him, as was another promontory in Libya.

[2] Caesar's … everywhere] *praeceps facit omne timendum | Victor, & in nulla non creditur esse carina*, 'the fast-moving victor makes everything an object of fear, and he is not believed to be in no ship [i.e. is thought to be in every ship]' (IX. 47–48).

[3] 9. 59–134] Cornelia grieves and reports Pompey's message to his sons.

[4] son-in-law] *privignique*, 'step-son' (IX. 52). Sextus Pompey was the son of Pompey's third wife, Mucia.

[5] The sad … funeral] *Quicquid ab extincto licuisset tollere busto*, 'whatever it was lawful to salvage from his extinguished pyre' (IX. 61).

75	Well did the Crassi's ashes naked lie,	
	For by the gods' far greater cruelty	
	Is Pompey burnt.¹ Still shall my woes appear	
	In the same shape? And shall I ne'er inter	
	My slaughtered lords? And at full urns lament?	
80	What need'st thou tomb or any instrument	
	Of sorrow, wretch?² Doth not thy breast contain	
	Thy Pompey, and his image still remain	
	Within thee? Let those wives that mean to live	
	After their lords, urns to their ashes give.	
85	But yet the fire that lends yon envious light	
	From Egypt's shore brings nothing to my sight	
	Of thee, dear Pompey: now the flame is gone,	
	The vanished smoke bears to the rising sun	
	Pompey aloft; the winds unwillingly	
90	Bear us from thence, yet is no land to me	
	(Though triumphed by my lord as conqueror)	
	Nor chariot decked with laurel half so dear.³	
	My breast has quite forgot his happiness,⁴	
	And loves that Pompey whom Nile's shores possess.	
95	Fain would I stay under this guilty clime:	*gladly*
	The land's ennobled by so great a crime.⁵	
	I would not leave (believe me) Egypt's shore.⁶	
	Sextus, try thou the chance of war, and o'er	
	The spacious world thy father's colours bear.	*standards*
100	This his last will was trusted to my care:	
	"When me of breath death's fatal hour shall reave,	*rob*
	To you, my sons, this civil war I leave;	
	And let not Caesar's race in quiet reign,	
	Whilst any of our stock on earth remain.	

---

¹ far greater cruelty] *Invidia maiore*, 'greater hatred' (IX. 66). For 'the Crassi's ashes' (9. 75), see 8. 102–04 and note.

² wretch] L.'s epithet is *Impia*, 'impious one' (IX. 71).

³ Bear us from thence] *invisi tendunt mihi carbasa venti*, 'winds hateful to me stretch the sails' (IX. 77). chariot decked with laurel] *alta terens Capitolia currus*, 'chariot wearing out the lofty Capitol' (IX. 79).

⁴ My breast ... his happiness] *elapsus felix de pectore Magnus*, 'the fortunate Pompey has fled my breast' (IX. 80).

⁵ Fain would ... a crime] *terraeque nocenti | Non haerere queror: crimen commendat arenas*, 'I do not complain at clinging to this guilty land; the crime honours the sands' (IX. 81–82).

⁶ I would not leave ... shore] This line (IX. 83) is placed after IX. 77 (= 9. 90, after 'thence') in modern editions.

105	Solicit kingdoms and free powerful towns	
	By my name's fame:[1] these are the factions,	
	These are the arms I leave; what Pompey e'er	
	Would go to sea shall find a navy there.	
	My heirs may stir war in what land they will.	
110	Be but courageous, and remember still	
	Your father's lawful power. Serve under none	
	But Cato (whilst he fights for Rome) alone."[2]	
	I have performed thy trust, done thy behest,	
	Dear lord: thy cunning did prevail, and lest	
115	False I those words of trust should ne'er deliver,	
	Deceived I lived. Now Pompey, wheresoever	
	Th'art gone, through hell, if any hell there be,	
	Or empty chaos I will follow thee.	
	How long my life's decreed I do not know:	
120	If long, I'll punish it for lasting so;	
	For not expiring when it first did see	
	Thy wounds, with sorrow broken it shall die.	
	It shall dissolve in tears: no halter, sword,	
	Or precipice shall death to me afford.	
125	It were a shame for me, now thou art gone,	
	Not to have power to die with grief alone.'[3]	
	This said, and covering with a veil her head,	
	Under the hatches she resolved to lead	
	A life in darkness: nearly hugging woe	*closely*
130	She feeds on tears, and for her husband now	
	Embraces grief. The noise of stormy wind	
	Nor cries of fearful sailors move her mind;	
	Her hope contrary to the sailors is;	
	Composed for death and wishing storms she lies.	
135	They first arrived on Cyprus' foamy shore.	[IX. 117][4]
	From thence a mild east wind commanding bore	
	Their ships to Cato's Libyan camp. As still	
	A doubtful mind do sad presages fill,	
	Cneius, from shore spying his father's train,	
140	And brother running to the sea amain,	*at full speed*

[1] free powerful towns] *urbes | Libertate sua validas*, 'cities strong in their own liberty' (IX. 90–91).
[2] for Rome] *pro libertate*, 'for liberty' (IX. 97).
[3] with grief alone] i.e. of grief alone.
[4] 9. 135–94] Cornelia's ships join Cato's forces; Cato restrains Cneius Pompey (Pompey's eldest son) from his plans for immediate revenge.

'Where is our father, brother? Speak,' quoth he,
'Lives the world's head and honour, or are we
Undone, and Pompey to the shades below
Has borne Rome's fate?' He answers, 'Happy thou,
145 Whom fate into another coast dispersed;
Thou, brother, this dire mischief only hear'st:
Mine eyes are guilty of a father's death.
Nor did he lose by Caesar's arms his breath,
Nor of his fall a worthy author found.
150 By the false tyrant of Nile's impious ground,[1]
Trusting the gods of hospitality,
And his own bounty to old Ptolemy,[2]
In recompense of kingdoms given he died.[3]
I saw them wound our noble father's side,[4]
155 And thinking Egypt's king durst not have done
So much, I thought Caesar had stood upon
The shore of Nile. But not our father's wounds,
Nor blood so shed so much my heart confounds,
As that his head, which mounted on a spear
160 Aloft, we saw they through their cities bear,
Which (as they say) is kept for Caesar's eye:[5]
The tyrant seeks his guilt to testify.
For whether dogs or fowls' devouring maw
Consumed his trunk, or that small fire we saw
165 Dissolvèd it by stealth, I do not know.
Whate'er injurious fate to that could do,
I did forgive the gods that crime, and wept
For that part only which the tyrant kept.'
When Cneius heard these words, his inward woe [IX. 145]
170 In passionate sighs and tears he could not show,
But thus inflamed with pious rage 'gan speak:[6]
'Launch forth the fleet, sailors, with speed, and break
Through the cross-winds a passage with the oar.
Brave captains, follow me: never before

---

[1] By the false tyrant] *Rege sub impuro*, 'under [the rule of] an impure king' (IX. 130).
[2] to old Ptolemy] *In proavos*, 'to his [the present Ptolemy's] ancestors' (IX. 132).
[3] in recompense ... given] *donati victima regni*, 'a sacrifice of the kingdom he had bestowed' (IX. 132); cf. 8. 521.
[4] noble] *magnanimi*, 'great-minded' (IX. 133).
[5] Caesar's] *victoris iniqui*, 'the unjust victor's' (IX. 139).
[6] inflamed with pious rage] *iustaque furens pietate*, 'raging with a just sense of duty' (IX. 147).

175	Knew civil war more worthy ends than these,[1]	
	T'inter unburied Manes, and appease	*ghosts*
	Pompey with slaughter of th'effeminate boy.[2]	
	Why should not I th'Egyptian towers destroy?	
	And from the temples Alexander take,	
180	To drown his hearse in Mareotis' lake?[3]	*corpse*
	In Nile Amasis and those kings with him	
	Digged up from their Pyramides shall swim.[4]	
	All tombs shall rue Pompey's no sepulchre:	
	Isis (their goddess now) I'll disinter,	
185	Osiris' linen-covered shrine disperse,	
	And kill god Apis over Pompey's hearse.[5]	
	Upon a pile of gods I'll burn his head;	
	Thus shall the land by me be punishèd.	
	I will not leave a man to till those fields,	
190	Nor take the profit that Nile's flowing yields.	
	The gods and people banishèd and gone,	
	Thou, father, shalt possess Egypt alone.'	
	This said to launch the fleet forth he assays,[6]	
	But Cato stills the young man's wrath with praise.	
195	Now o'er the shore when Pompey's death was known	[IX. 167][7]
	The sky was pierced with lamentation:	
	A grief not seen, not parallelled at all,	
	That common people mourn a great man's fall.	
	But when Cornelia quite exhaust with tears	
200	Was seen to land with torn dishevelled hairs,	
	Their doubled lamentations sounded more.	
	Cornelia landed on a friendly shore;	
	Gathering the garments and triumphal weeds	
	Of hapless Pompey that expressed his deeds,	
205	And ancient trophies, painted robes and shield,	

---

[1] more worthy ends] *Tanta ... merces*, 'so great a price' (IX. 151).

[2] th'effeminate boy] *semiviri ... tyranni*, 'that half-man tyrant', i.e. Ptolemy (IX. 152).

[3] And from ... lake?] Alexander the Great was buried in Alexandria.

[4] In Nile Amasis ... swim] Amasis was a famous Pharaoh. 'Pyramides' is likely to have a Latinized pronunciation here, giving the word four syllables.

[5] And kill ... hearse] *et sacer in Magni cineres mactabitur Apis*, 'and sacred Apis will be sacrificed to the ashes of Magnus' (IX. 160).

[6] to launch ... assays] *& classem saevas rapiebat in undas*, 'and was pulling the fleet into the savage waves' (IX. 165). Modern editions read *saevus* for *saevas*, i.e. Cneius is savage, not the waves.

[7] 9. 195–342] An imaginary burial for Pompey; Cato's funeral oration; Cato's suppression of a near-mutiny.

	That thrice great Jove in triumph had beheld,	
	Into the funeral fire she threw them all;	
	Such was her lord's imagined funeral.¹	
	Example from her piety all take,	
210	And funeral fires all o'er the shore they make	
	T'appease the ghosts slain in Pharsalia.	
	So when the shepherds of Apulia	
	Make winter fires on their bare-eaten ground	
	To spring their grass again, a glistering round	*grow; brilliance*
215	The Vultur's arms and high Garganus yields,	
	And hot Matinus' bullock-pasture fields.²	
	But not more pleasing was't to Pompey's spirit³	[IX. 186–214]
	That all the people rail at heaven and twit	*reproach*
	The gods with Pompey, than what Cato spoke:	
220	Few words, but from a truth-filled breast they broke.	
	'A Roman's dead, not like our ancestry	
	To know the rule of right, but good', quoth he,	
	'In this truth-scorning age;⁴ one powerful grown	
	Not wronging liberty. The people prone	
225	To serve, he only private still remained:	
	He swayed the Senate but the Senate reigned.	
	Nought claimed he by the sword, but wished what he	
	Wished most, the Senate's freedom to deny.⁵	
	Great wealth he had, but to the public hoard	
230	He brought far more than he retained;⁶ the sword	
	He took, but knew the time to lay it down.	
	Armed he loved peace, though arms before the gown	

---

¹ imagined funeral] *Ille fuit miserae Magni cinis*, 'this, to wretched her, was Pompey's ash' (IX. 179); M. follows F.'s gloss *imaginarium bustum*, 'imaginary tomb'.

² Vultur's arms] Reading *Vulturis | Arma*, a misprint in F.'s text (IX. 184–85). The correct reading is *Vulturis | Arva*, 'the fields of Vultur' (a mountain in Apulia, like Matinus and Garganus).

³ spirit] Although typically disyllabic when ending a line, 'spirit' is contracted here to 'sp'rit' for reasons of rhyme and meter.

⁴ A Roman's dead...] *Civis obit*, 'a citizen has passed away' (IX. 190). not like our ancestry ... age] *multo maioribus inpar | Nosse modum iuris, sed in hoc tamen utilis aevo, | Cui non ulla fuit iusti reverentia*, 'far inferior to our ancestors in knowing the limit of lawful power, but of service in this age, in which there has been no reverence for justice' (IX. 190–92).

⁵ but wished ... deny] *Quaeque dari voluit, voluit sibi posse negari*, 'and what he wanted to be given, he wanted it to be possible for that to be refused to him' (IX. 196). See Textual Notes.

⁶ to the public hoard] M.'s addition, following F.'s gloss *in aerarium publ.*, 'the public treasury', at IX. 198.

He still preferred,¹ and ever pleased was he
Ent'ring or leaving his authority.
235 A chaste unrioted house,² and never stained
With her lord's fortune, to all lands remained
His name renowned, which much availèd Rome.
True liberty long since was gone, when home
Sulla and Marius came;³ but Pompey dead,
240 Even freedom's shadow is quite vanishèd.⁴
No Senate's face, no colour will remain
Of power;⁵ none now will be ashamed to reign.
O happy man, whom death when conquered caught,
And Egypt's guilt swords to be wished for brought.⁶
245 Perchance thou couldst have lived in Caesar's state.⁷
To know the way to die is man's best fate,
His next to be compelled: and such to me
(If captived now) Fortune, let Juba be;⁸   *captured*
Not to be kept to show the enemy
250 I do not beg, so headless kept I be.'⁹

More honour from these words the noble ghost   [IX. 215]
Received, than if the Roman bars should boast
His praise.¹⁰ Now mutinous the soldiers are,
Since Pompey's death grown weary of the war:
255 In which broils Tarcho, Cato's side to quit,¹¹
Took up the colours, who, prepared for flight   *standards*
With all his ships, was chid by Cato so.
'Never reclaimed Cilician, wouldst thou go   *pacified*

---

¹ Armed ... preferred] Reversing the emphasis of L.'s *praetulit arma togae, sed pacem armatus amavit*, 'he preferred arms to the toga, but when armed loved peace' (IX. 199).
² unrioted] Trisyllabic.
³ True liberty] *vera fides ... libertatis*, 'true faith in liberty' (IX. 204).
⁴ freedom's shadow] *ficta [libertas]*, 'the fiction of freedom' (IX. 206). M. may be echoing 3. 159.
⁵ No Senate's face ... Of power] *nec color imperii nec frons erit ulla Senatus*, 'nor will there be the pretext of lawful authority nor any façade of a Senate' (IX. 207): the implication of pretence in 'colour' is operative in both the Latin and early modern English.
⁶ And ... brought] i.e. and to whom [Pompey] Egypt brought the fate he wanted.
⁷ state] *regno*, 'monarchy' (IX. 210). See 1. 5n.
⁸ let Juba be] i.e. let Juba play towards Cato the part of Ptolemy towards Pompey.
⁹ Not to be kept ... I be] i.e. Cato is happy to be enslaved to his enemy, so long as it is as a headless corpse.
¹⁰ Roman bars] *rostra* (IX. 215): see 4. 879n.
¹¹ Tarcho] Following Grotius's 1614 conjecture *Tarcho in motu*, 'Tarcho in rebellion' (IX. 219), recorded by F.; previous editions had *Tarchon motus*, 'Tarchon rebelling'. Modern editions read *Tarchondimotus*, the name of this Cilician leader.

To thy old theft at sea? Is Pompey slain
260 And thou returned to piracy again?'
Then round about he on each man 'gan look,   *began to*
'Mongst whom one boldly thus to Cato spoke,
Not hiding his intent: ''Twas not the love
Of civil war but Pompey first did move
265 Our arms (excuse us Cato): we adhered
By favour. Now he, whom the world preferred
Before her peace, is dead, our cause is gone:
Now let's return to our left mansion,   *home*
Our household gods and children dear to see.
270 For what can civil war's conclusion be,
If not Pharsalia's field nor Pompey's death?
Our time of life is spent: now let us breathe
Our last in peace; let our old age provide
Our funeral piles, which civil war denied   *pyres*
275 Two greatest captains. For no barbarous
Or cruel yoke will fortune lay on us,
No Scythian nor Armenian tyranny.
The subjects of Rome's gownèd state are we.[1]
He that was second, Pompey being alive,
280 Is first with us: the highest place we give
His sacred name. He whom war's fortunes make
Shall be our lord, no general we'll take.[2]
Unto the war we followed thee alone:
We'll follow fate, Pompey, now thou art gone.
285 Nor have we cause to hope for good success,
Since Caesar's fortune now doth all possess.
Th'Emathian strength is by his victory
Dispersed; we lose his mercy; only he
Has power and will to spare the conquerèd.
290 Our civil war's a crime now Pompey's dead,
'Twas duty while he lived. If, Cato, thou
Will serve thy country still, let's follow now
Those eagles which the Roman consuls keeps.'
Thus having spoke, aboard the ship he leaps
295 With all his company. Rome's fate had gone,

---

[1] The subjects ... we] *sub iura togati | Civis eo*, 'I become subject to [lit. I go beneath] the laws of a toga-ed citizen [i.e. Caesar]' (IX. 238–39).
[2] He whom ... we'll take] In L. a direct address to Pompey: *dominum, quam clades cogit, habebo | Nullum, Magne, ducem*, 'I will have the master which calamity forces, but no general, Magnus [i.e. no general except Pompey]' (IX. 241–42). 'General' is here trisyllabic.

The people bent to slavery upon
The shore exclaim.[1] But from a sacred breast
Cato to them at last these words expressed.
'Fought you, young men, with Caesar's army's hopes,
300 (No more true Roman, but Pompeian troops)
To gain a lord? Since for no lord you fight,
But live to do yourselves, not tyrants right,
Since your spent bloods can no man's rule procure
But your own safety,[2] you'll not now endure
305 The wars; to live in bondage you desire
And for your slavish necks a yoke require.[3]
Your danger's worthy now,[4] the cause is good:
Pompey perhaps might have abused your blood.
And will you now, when liberty's so nigh,
310 To aid of Rome your swords and throats deny?
Of three lords fortune now has left but one.
Egypt's base king, and Parthian bows have done
More for the laws than you (O shame). Go, ye
Base men and scorn the gift of Ptolemy.
315 Who will believe your hands could guilty be
Of any blood? He'll rather think that ye
Were the first men that from Pharsalia fled.
Go then securely: you have merited
Pardon in Caesar's judgment, not subdued
320 By siege or open force. O servants lewd,[5]
When your first master's dead, his heir you'll serve.
Why would you not more than your lives deserve
And pardons? Ravish with you for a prey
Metellus' daughter, Pompey's wife away
325 And his two sons;[6] the gift of Egypt's king
Surpass. Or could you to the tyrant bring
My head, no small reward't would render ye;

---

[1] The people … exclaim] *& omnis | Indiga servitii fervebat litore plebes*, 'and all the people, needing slavery, thronged the shore' (IX. 253–54).

[2] But live … procure] *quod tibi, non ducibus, vivis, moriensque quod orbem, | Acquiris nulli*, 'because you live for yourselves not your leaders, and by your death acquire a world for no man' (IX. 259–60). Modern editions read *morerisque* for *moriensque*, i.e. 'because you live and die for yourselves not your leaders, and acquire a world for no man.'

[3] to live in bondage you desire] *nescis sine rege pati*, 'and don't know how to endure without a king' (IX. 262).

[4] worthy now] *Digna viris*, 'worthy of men' (IX. 263).

[5] O servants lewd] *O famuli turpes*, 'O disgraceful slaves' (IX. 274).

[6] Metellus' daughter, Pompey's wife] Cornelia.

Then to good purpose have you followed me.
On then, and in our bloods your merit make;
330 'Tis slothful treason a bare flight to take.'[1]
This speech of Cato straight recalls from seas
Their flying ships, as when a swarm of bees
Their honeycombs and barren wax forsake,
Nor hang in clusters now but singly take
335 Their flight i'th'air, and taste not (slothful grown)
The bitter thyme; at sound of brass alone
Amazed they leave their flight, again approve
Their flowery tasks, again their honey love:
Glad is the shepherd on sweet Hybla's hill
340 To keep the riches of his cottage still.[2]
So Cato's speech on their affections wrought,
And them to patience of a war had brought.[3]
   And now their restless minds with toil t'inure, [IX. 294][4]
And teach them warlike labours to endure,
345 With weary marches first their strength he tries
Along the sands; their second labour is
To scale Cyrene's lofty walls. On whom
Cato no vengeance took, when overcome
(Though they against him shut their gates): to him
350 Revenge sufficient did their conquest seem.[5]
He thence to Libyan (c)Juba's kingdom goes,[6]
But there the Syrts did nature interpose,   *Syrtes*
Which Cato's dauntless virtue hopes to pass.
These Syrts, when all the world's first structure was,[7]
355 Nature as doubtful left 'twixt sea and land
(For neither sink they quite like seas to stand,[8]

---

[1] slothful treason] *Ignavum scelus*, 'a cowardly crime' (IX. 283).
[2] at sound of brass ... Hybla's hill] According to Virgil (*Georgics*, IV. 70–72), bees congregate at the sound of a brass cymbal. Hybla, a Sicilian mountain, was famous for its honey.
[3] patience of a war] *iusti patientia Martis*, 'endurance of a just war' (IX. 293).
[4] 9. 343–476] Cato prepares to lead his troops to an ally, Juba king of Numidia; however, the fleet is destroyed and they decide to cross over the Libyan sands.
[5] Revenge ... seem] *Poenaque de victis sola est, vicisse, Catoni*, 'for Cato, the conquered's sole punishment is that he beat them' (IX. 299).
[6] goes] *peti placuit*, 'pleased him to seek' (IX. 300): he does not arrive there for many hundreds of lines.
[7] the world's first structure was] *primam mundo natura figuram | Cum daret*, 'when nature was giving initial shape to the world' (IX. 303–04).
[8] quite like seas to stand] *quo stagna profundi | Acciperet*, 'whereby to receive the still waters of the deep' (IX. 305–06).

                Nor yet like land with shores repel the main,
                But doubtful and unpassable remain,
                A shelf-spoiled sea, a water-covered land,
360   Where sounding waves let in by sands command.
                This part of nature Nature's self disclaimed,
                As a vain work and to no purpose framed).
                Or once the deep-drowned Syrts were seas entire,
                But burning Titan thence to feed his fire   *the sun*
365   Drew up those waves so near the torrid zone,
                And now the water holds contention
                With Phoebus' drought; which by continuance spent,[1]   *the sun's*
                The Syrts will grow a solid continent.
                For now their tops but shallow waters hide,
370   The fading sea decays at every side.
                    When first the fleet began to launch from shore,   [IX. 319]
                In his own kingdom did black Auster roar,   *south wind*
                Whose blasts the sea from ships' invasion keep,
                And from the Syrts far roll the wavy deep,
375   Or flat the sea with thrown-in heaps of sand.
                Now the resistless winds the seas command,
                Whose blasts of all spread sails, that fastened were
                To the mainmast, quite robbed the mariner.
                In vain the shrouds to wind so violent
380   Deny their sails: beyond the ship's extent,
                Beyond the prow the swellèd linen's blown.
                But where a man more provident was known,
                That did his linen to the sail-yard tie,
                He quite despoiled of tackling presently
385   Was overcome. That fleet had far more ease
                Which on the deep was tossed with certain seas.
                But all those ships which had cut down their masts
                T'avoid the fury of strong Auster's blasts,   *the south wind's*
                (As then the wind against the tide did strive)
390   Against the wind the conquering tide did drive.
                Some ships the sea forsakes, whom straight the sands
                Unseen surprise, whose state now doubtful stands:[2]

    [1]   continuance] Trisyllabic.
    [2]   whom straight ... doubtful stands] Translating *interrupta profundo | Terra ferit puppes*,
    'the land interspersed with sea bears the ships' (IX. 335–36). M. includes the next clause,
    dubioque obnoxia fato, 'and submitting to a doubtful fate', though the punctuation of early
    modern and modern editions makes clear that this describes 'Part of the ship' in the next
    sentence.

	Part of the ship upon firm ground doth rest,	
	Part swims in water. Now the sea's oppressed	
395	With flats, the sands assault the ocean,	*sand-flats*
	And though strong Auster drive the waves amain,	*violently*
	They cannot master these high hills of sand:	
	On th'ocean's back far from all countries stand	
	Heaps of dry dust not by the ocean drowned.	
400	The wretched sailors, though their ship's on ground,	
	No shores can see. Part of the fleet this shallow	
	Detains; the greater part their rudders follow,	
	And safe by flight, by skilful pilots' aid	
	Are to Tritonia's standing pool conveyed.	
405	This pool (they say) that god esteemeth dear	
	Whose shrill shell-trumpet seas and shores do hear.[1]	
	This Pallas loves, born of the brain of Jove,	
	Who first on Libya trod.[2] (The heat doth prove	
	This land next heaven.) She, standing by the side,	
410	Her face within the quiet water spied,	
	And gave herself from the loved pool a name,	
	Tritonia.[3] Here doth the silent stream	
	Of dark oblivious Lethe gently fall	
	That from hell's Lethe takes original.[4]	*derives its source*
415	The waking dragon's charge is near to these,	*sleepless*
	The once robbed orchard of th'Hesperides.[5]	
	To rob old times of credit, the desire	
	Is spite, or truth from poets to require.	
	A golden wood there was whose yellow trees,	
420	Laden with wealthy fruit, stood bowed: of these	
	A dragon guardian was, which never slept,[6]	
	And the bright wood a troop of virgins kept.	
	Hither Alcides coming, did surprise	*Hercules; capture*
	The wealth and burden of those laden trees,	

[1] that god ... hear] i.e. Triton, the sea-god.
[2] Pallas loves] According to Greek myth Pallas was born from the head of Jupiter after he had eaten her mother Metis.
[3] Tritonia] Here pronounced with four syllables, for emphasis; contrast 9. 404, above.
[4] Lethe] Disyllabic. L. claims that the source of Libyan Lethe is the underworld river that brings oblivion; cf. 3. 31.
[5] The waking dragon's ... th'Hesperides] 9. 415–26 recount one of the twelve tasks of Hercules, to take the golden apples belonging to the Hesperides (a group of Libyan nymphs, M.'s 'virgins'), guarded by a dragon, and bring them back to Eurystheus, tyrant of Argos.
[6] which never slept] Omitting *Robora complexus rutilo curvata metallo*, 'winding itself round the trunks bowed by the metal [of the golden fruit]' (IX. 364).

	And leaving light their robbèd boughs did bring	
425	Those glittering apples to th'Argolian king.	
	Part of the fleet got off from hence again,	
	And from the Syrtes driven, did remain	
	Under great Pompey's eldest son's command	
430	On this side Garamantis in rich land.	*of Garamantis*
	But Cato's virtue brooking no delay,	*tolerating*
	Through unknown regions led his troops away,	
	T'encompass round the Syrts by land, for now	
	The stormy seas unnavigable grow	
435	In winter time, but storms desirèd are	
	To cool the temper of the swelt'ring air.	
	They fear no cold in Libya's scorchèd clime,	
	Nor too much heat, because in winter time.	
	Ent'ring these barren sands thus Cato spake:	
440	'You that have followed me, soldiers, and make	
	Freedom your only safety,[1] settle now	
	Your minds with constancy to undergo	
	Virtue's great work. We march o'er barren fields,	
	O'er sunburnt regions, where no fountain yields	
445	Water enough, where Titan's heat abounds,	
	And killing serpents smear the parchèd grounds.	
	Hard ways: but whom their falling country's cause	
	Through paths unknown and midst of Libya draws,	
	Who make no vows for their returning home,	
450	But think of going only, let them come.	
	I would deceive no soldier nor keep close	
	My fears to draw them on. Let only those	
	My followers be, whom dangers do invite,	
	Who think it brave and Roman in my sight	
455	T'endure the worst of ills.[2] He that would have	
	A surety for his safety and fain save	*gladly*
	His lovèd life,[3] let him be gone from me,	

---

[1] You ... only safety] *O quibus una salus placuit mea castra secutis | Indomita cervice mori*, 'O you, whom one safety alone has pleased in following my camps, to die with unmastered neck' (IX. 379–80).
[2] Who think it ... of ills] *Qui, me teste, pati, vel quae tristissima, pulcrum, | Romanumque putant*, 'Who, with me as witness, think that it is beautiful and Roman to suffer even the most dreadful things' (IX. 391–92).
[3] fain save ... life] *capiturque animae dulcedine*, 'and is captivated by the sweetness of life' (IX. 393).

And find an easier way to slavery.[1]
Upon the sands whilst I first footing set,
460 Let me first suffer th'air's annoying heat:
Let serpents' poisoned teeth first seize on me,
And in my fate do you your dangers try.
Let him that sees me drinking, water crave,
And plain of heat, when I a shelter have,   *complain*
465 Or when I ride before the foot, straight grow   *infantry*
Weary, if any by endurance know
Whether I go soldier or general.
The sands, heat, thirst and poisonous serpents,[2] all
Are sweet to virtue: hard things patience loves,
470 And sweetest still, when dearest, goodness proves.
These Libyan dangers only justify
The flight of men.' Thus their hot spirits he
With labour's love and virtue strived to fire;[3]
Marching o'er deserts never to retire
475 Secure, he goes to Libya, gracing there
With his great name a little sepulchre.[4]
 If th'old account we follow, Libya is   [IX. 411–510][5]
The world's third part:[6] following the winds, and skies,
A part of Europe.[7] For not distant more
480 Than Scythian Tanaïs is Nilus' shore
From western Gades, where Europe Afric flies
And makes the ocean room;[8] but greater is
Asia than both. For as they both send forth —
Libya from south, and Europe from the north[9] —

---

[1] to slavery] *Ad dominum*, 'to a master' (IX. 394); 'easier' is disyllabic.
[2] poisonous] Probably contracted, in pronunciation, to 'pois'nous'.
[3] strived to fire] *incendit*, 'did fire' (IX. 407).
[4] great name a... little sepulchre] Foreshadowing Cato's eventual death by suicide in Utica in 46 BC, as described in book four of M.'s *Continuation* (1630); 'great name' renders *sacrum ... nomen*, 'sacred name' (IX. 409).
[5] 9. 477–585] A description of Libya and an account of the dust-storm which envelops Cato's men.
[6] th'old account] *famae*, 'rumour' (IX. 411). In early modern England, 'the old account' usually referred to the Julian calendar, replaced by the Gregorian in Catholic countries in 1582, but not in Protestant ones until the eighteenth century, or sometimes (as seemingly by M. here) to ancient, pre-Copernican ideas of geography and astronomy.
[7] following ... Europe] i.e. if the world is divided into two only.
[8] For not ... room] i.e. Europe and Africa are the same breadth, from Gades (Cádiz) in the far west, to Tanaïs (the river Don) in the east, where that river borders with Asia. 'Gades' is monosyllabic, as elsewhere: see e.g. 3. 303, 4. 740, 7. 213.
[9] Libya ... north] M. simplifies, avoiding L.'s references to northern and southern winds (IX. 417–20).

485	The western wind, the eastern wind alone	
	From Asia blows. That part that's fertile known	
	Of Libya, westward lies, but moisture lacks:	
	The north wind dry with us, there stormy, takes	
	His flight but seldom thither.¹ The rich soil	
490	No wealthy growing minerals do spoil:²	
	The earth corrupts into no brass nor gold,	
	But keeps her natural and perfect mould.	*soil*
	The Mauritanian men are rich alone	
	In citron-wood, of which no use was known	
495	To them of old, contented with the shade.³	
	Our axes first did that strange wood invade;⁴	
	From far we fetch our tables, as our meat.⁵	
	But in those parts about the Syrts, whose heat	*Syrtes*
	Is violent, and scorching Sol too near,⁶	*sun*
500	No corn can grow, no vines can prosper there,⁷	
	Nor trees deep rooting take; the sandy ground	
	Wants vital temper, and no care is found	*temperateness*
	Of Jove in that at all;⁸ the barren land	
	Through every season doth unchangèd stand	
505	By nature's negligence. Yet this dull earth	
	Unto a few small herbs affords a birth,	
	Which are the hardy Nasamonians' fare.	
	Near the sea coast they bleakly seated are,	
	Whom barbarous Syrts with the world's loss maintain:	*Syrtes; maintains*
510	For spoil they still upon the sand remain.⁹	

¹ The north wind … thither] *Arctoos raris Aquilonibus imbres | Accipit, & nostris reficit sua rura serenis*, 'it receives northern rains from scarce north winds, and refreshes its fields with our untroubled weather' (IX. 422–23). M. relies on F.'s explanation here.

² the rich soil … spoil] *In nullas vitiatur opes*, 'there is no spoiling for the sake of wealth' (IX. 424); M.'s idea of minerals comes from F. Untypically, 'minerals' is here trisyllabic, like 'natural' at 9. 492, below.

³ The Mauritanian men … shade] Although preserving L.'s sense, M.'s wording translates F.'s gloss for IX. 426–27.

⁴ strange] In the sense of 'hitherto unknown'; L.'s word is *ignotum* (IX. 429).

⁵ From far we fetch…] *Extremoque epulas, mensasque petivimus ab orbe*, 'We've sought both our meals and our tables from the ends of the earth', IX. 430.

⁶ violent] Trisyllabic.

⁷ No corn … there] *exurit messes et pulvere Bacchum | Enecat*, '[the climate] burns the crops and strangles the vine with dust' (IX. 433–34).

⁸ Jove … at all] Jupiter as weather-god.

⁹ the world's loss maintain … remain] M. relies on F.'s gloss: lit. *nam litoreis populator arenis | Imminet, & nulla portus tangente carina, | Novit opes*, 'for the plunderer is at hand on the sandy shore, and while no vessel touches a port, knows wealth' (IX. 441–43). As the

And though no merchant trade with them, yet gold
They have, and still by shipwreck traffic hold
With all the world. This way did virtue bear
Cato along:[1] the soldiers could not fear
515 A storm by land, or think of blust'ring wind,
But there (alas) the ocean's dangers find.
For more on land than sea the south winds roar
About the Syrts, and hurt the land much more.
No rocks nor mountains stand opposèd there
520 To break his force and turn him into air;[2]
No well-grown oaks, no wood opposèd stands;
The ground lies open all, free are the sands
To Aeol's rage, which violently strong[3]   *Aeolus'*
Hurries through th'air a sandy cloud along.
525 Their greatest part of land the winds do bear
Into the air, which hangs not fixèd there.
His house and land the Nasamonian sees[4]
Fly in the wind, their little cottages
Blown o'er their heads into the air as high
530 As from a fire the smoke and sparkles fly;[5]
The mounted dust like smoke obscures the sky.
And then more strong than usual did the blast
Assault our men;[6] no soldier could stand fast,
No, nor the ground on which they stood could stay.
535 'Twould shake the earth and bear that land away
If Libya hollow were, or harder mould   *soil*
The southern winds in caverns to enfold,[7]
But since composed of loose and fleeting sands
Resisting not, it bides; the lowest stands
540 Because the highest yields.[8] Helmets of men,

passage goes on to explain, L. means that the rest of the world provides sustenance through the loot of shipwrecks.
[1] virtue] *Dura iubet virtus*, 'hard virtue orders [Cato to go]' (IX. 445). See 9. Ded. 7 and note.
[2] his ... him] i.e. the south wind.
[3] Aeol's rage] = the rage of the winds; cf. 2. 487n. 'Violently' has four syllables.
[4] land] *regna*, 'kingdoms' (IX. 458).
[5] their little cottages ... the air] *volitantque a culmine raptae | Detecto Garamante casae*, 'and cottages ripped away at the roof fly into the air, leaving the Garamantian [a local inhabitant] uncovered' (IX. 459–60).
[6] our men] *Romanum ... agmen*, 'the Roman column' (IX. 463).
[7] or harder ... to enfold] i.e. were the harder soil to enfold.
[8] the lowest ... yields] *imaque tellus | Stat, quia summa fugit*, 'and the lowest part of the

352   THOMAS MAY

  Their shields and piles, the wind with fury then
  Bereft them of, and through the welkin tossed,   *robbed; sky*
  That in some foreign far-removèd coast
  Perchance by men was deemed a prodigy,
545 And nations feared arms falling from the sky,
  Thinking those weapons wrest from men did fall   *wrenched*
  Down from the gods. So once I think that all
  Our sacred shields to holy Numa were,   *shields sacred to*
  Which now our choice patrician shoulders bear.[1]
550 The southern wind or northern robbed of yore
  Some foreign people that those bucklers wore.[2]
  The land thus plagued with wind, the soldiers all
  Down to the ground, their clothes fast-girded, fall,[3]
  Hold fast the earth, yet sure they scarcely lay
555 By weight nor strength from being blown away.[4]
  Mountains of dust the south wind's furious hand
  Rolls o'er their heads; drownèd in heaps of sand
  The soldiers scarce can stir. Some, though upright,
  With rising earth are overwhelmèd quite,
560 And, though the earth remove, want motion.[5]
  Vast stones of ruined walls from far are blown,
  And (strange to tell) in some far region fall:[6]
  They ruins see, that see no house at all.
  No paths nor difference now of ways are known:
565 Their course is guided by the star alone
  Like navigators;[7] not all stars to us
  In that horizon are conspicuous,
  For to earth's face (there bowèd) many be
  Obscured from sight.[8] But when the air was free

ground remains because the highest part is flying away' (IX. 470–71).
[1] So once ... bear] Numa, an early king of Rome, once witnessed a shield falling from the sky and made eleven more shields to conceal its identity; the shields were later carried in a yearly ritual by the Salii, a priesthood of patrician Romans.
[2] those bucklers wore] *ancilia nostra*, 'our shields' (IX. 480).
[3] fall] Omitting *metuensque rapi*, 'fearing to be snatched away' (IX. 482); modern editions print *timuitque*, 'and feared', for *metuensque*.
[4] being] Untypically disyllabic.
[5] And ... want motion] *immoti terra surgente tenentur*, 'and are held motionless by the rising earth' (IX. 489).
[6] (strange to tell) ... region] *Effuditque procul miranda sorte malorum*, 'and pour out by wondrous lot far from these evils' (IX. 491).
[7] Like navigators] Not in L.; M. reproduces F.'s *vel navigantibus*.
[8] not all ... from sight] *nec sidera tota | Ostendit Libycae finitor circulus orae, | Multaque devexo terrarum margine celat*, 'nor does the horizon, the limit of the Libyan country, show

570	From the wind's rage, dissolved again by heat
	And scorching day, their bodies flowed with sweat,
	Their mouths with thirst were parched: a little stream
	They spied which from a muddy fountain came,
	From whence with much ado a soldier got
575	His helmet full of water, and straight brought
	The same to Cato. Their dry throats were all
	With dust besmearèd, and the general
	Himself was envied for that little draught.
	'Base soldier', answers he, 'in thy poor thought
580	Seemed I alone so worthless? None but I
	Tender and weak in all this company?
	This punishment thou more deserv'st than I,
	To drink thyself while all the army's dry.'
	Then stirred with wrath he struck the helmet down:
585	The water spilt sufficed them everyone.
	And now to Libya's only temple, placed [IX. 511][1]
	In Garamantis rude, they came at last.
	Jupiter Ammon is adorèd there,
	Not armed with thunder like our Jupiter,
590	But crooked horns, to whom the Libyans build
	No sumptuous fane; no orient-jewels filled[2] *temple*
	The house with lustre. Though the Indians,
	The Ethiops, and rich Arabians[3]
	Jupiter Ammon's name do all adore
595	And no god else, yet still that god is poor.
	No wealth corrupts his fane: a god of th'old
	Pureness his temple guards from Roman gold.[4]
	That place of all the country only green[5]
	Shows a god's presence. All that lies between
600	Leptis and Berenicis is dry sand
	And barren dust; no part of all the land
	But Ammon's seat bears trees. The cause of it

all the stars, and it conceals many by the sloping margin of the earth' (IX. 495–97), i.e. as one travels south, the celestial pole descends. M.'s rendition depends heavily on F.'s gloss.

[1] 9. 586–676] Cato's army arrives at the shrine of Jupiter Ammon on the north African coast. Cato refuses his soldiers' demand to consult the oracle, instead expounding Stoic ideas of virtue and fate.
[2] sumptuous … filled] Here 'sumptuous' and 'orient' are disyllabic.
[3] Though … Arabians] 'Ethiops' is disyllabic, as are the two '-ians' ending lines in this couplet.
[4] th'old | Pureness] *morumque priorum*, 'ancient customs' (IX. 520).
[5] only green] L. specifies a wood, *silva* (IX. 522).

A neighbouring fountain is, whose waters knit
The moistened earth and make fertility.¹
605 But when the sun at noon is mounted high,
Those trees no shadow can diffuse at all:
Their boughs scarce hide their trunks. No shade or small
The sunbeams make, since perpendicular.²
It is perceived this is the region where
610 The summer tropic hits the zodiac.³   *tropic of Cancer*
The signs obliquely rise not, but direct.   *constellations*
Nor more direct the Bull than Scorpio,
Moist Capricornus than hot Cancer go,
Nor Gemini than Sagittarius,
615 Nor Leo than opposed Aquarius,
Virgo than Pisces, Libra's motion
Than Ariës. But whom the torrid zone
Divides from us, those people ever see
The shadows southward which here northward be:⁴
620 You slowly seeing Cynosure, suppose⁵   *Ursa Minor*
Her undrenched car into the ocean goes,
And that no northern sign from seas is free.
You stand far distant from each axle-tree;
Your signs in midst of heaven converted be.⁶
625   The eastern people standing at the door   [IX. 544–86]
The oracles of hornèd Jove t'implore,
Gave place to Cato, whom his soldiers ply   *urge*
That of that Libyan far-famed deity
His future fate's event he would be taught.⁷

---

¹ make fertility] *& domitas unda connectit arenas*, 'and binds together the tamed sands with a stream' (IX. 527).
² since perpendicular] *tam brevis in medium radiis compellitur umbra*, 'so short is the shadow contracted into the centre by the sun's rays' (IX. 528); M. uses F.'s *perpendiculariter*.
³ It is ... the zodiac] *deprensum est hunc esse locum qua circulus alti | Solstitii medium signorum percutit orbem*, 'it is understood that this is the place where the course of the high solstice bisects the mid-orb of the constellations' (IX. 531–32). The following passage (9. 611–24) describes the constellations at the equator, where the signs of the zodiac are visible for equal periods of time. M. relies heavily on F. to construe and simplify L.'s allusive astronomy. Modern editions place 9. 617–24 (= IX. 538–43) before 9. 611–17 (= IX. 533–37).
⁴ But whom ... be] L. addresses this observation to the people in question, the addressees of 'you' and 'your' (9. 620, 622, 624), thus describing the constellations from *their* perspective.
⁵ seeing] Disyllabic.
⁶ And that no ... be] A rare triple rhyme.
⁷ That of ... would be taught] *exploret Libycum memorata per orbem | Numina, de fama tam longi iudicet aevi*, 'that he test the divine power celebrated throughout the Libyan

630 Him Labienus most of all besought:[1]
'Chance and the fortune of our way', quoth he,
'Lend us the mouth of that great deity
And his sure counsels: we may now implore
His powerful guidance through this war and o'er
635 The dangerous Syrtes.[2] For to whom should I
Believe the gods would trulier certify
Their secret wills, than Cato's holy breast?
Whose life to heavenly laws was still addressed
And followed god? Behold we now have here
640 A freedom given to talk with Jupiter:
Cato, enquire of wicked Caesar's fate
And know what shall be Rome's ensuing state,[3]
Whether this civil war be made in vain,
Or shall our laws and liberties maintain.[4]
645 Let Ammon's sacred voice thy breast inspire.
Thou lover of strict virtue,[5] now desire
To know what virtue is, seek from above
Approvement of the truth.'[6] He full of Jove,   *approval*
Whom in his secret breast he carried ever,
650 These temple-worthy speeches did deliver:
'What, Labienus, should I seek to know?
If I had rather die in arms than bow
Unto a lord? If life be nought at all?[7]
No difference betwixt long life and small?[8]
655 If any force can hurt men virtuous?

world, and pass judgment on a reputation of such longevity' (IX. 547–48). M.'s version may be influenced by F.'s not particularly accurate gloss that Cato should find out *de huius belli eventu*, 'about this war's outcome'.

[1] Labienus] See 5. 396–98 and note.
[2] His ... this war] *bellique datos cognoscere casus*, 'and to know the decreed outcomes of the war' (IX. 553).
[3] Rome's ensuing state] *patriae venturos ... mores*, 'the future customs of our country' (IX. 559).
[4] our laws and liberties maintain] *Iure suo populis uti legumque licebit*, '[whether] peoples will be permitted to use their own right [i.e. to govern themselves freely] and laws' (IX. 560); cf. 2. 334. For M.'s 'laws and liberties', see Introduction, pp. 25–26.
[5] strict virtue] *durae ... virtutis*, 'hard virtue' (IX. 562).
[6] Approvement of the truth] *exemplar honesti*, 'a model of good conduct', i.e. in these circumstances (IX. 563).
[7] rather die in arms ... under a lord] *an liber in armis | Occubuisse velim potius, quam regna videre?*, 'whether I'd prefer to fall in battle, a free man, than witness a monarchy?' (IX. 566–67).
[8] difference] Untypically trisyllabic.

If Fortune lose, when virtue doth oppose,
Her threats?[1] If good desires be happiness,
And virtue grow not greater by success?
Thus much we know, nor deeper can the skill
Of Ammon teach. The gods are with us still
And, though their oracles should silent be,
Nought can we do without the god's decree,
Nor needs he voices: what was fit to know
The great Creator at our births did show.[2]
Nor did he choose these barren sands to shew   *show*
(Hiding it here) his truth but to a few.
Is there a seat of god, save earth and sea,
Air, heaven, and virtue? Why for god should we
Seek further? Whate'er moves, whate'er is seen
Is Jove. For oracles let doubtful men
Fearful of future chances troubled be:
Sure death, not oracles ascertain me.   *make me confident*
The coward and the valiant man must fall.[3]
This is enough for Jove to speak to all.'
Then marching thence the temple's faith he saves,   *credibility*
And to the people untried Ammon leaves.
    Himself afoot before his wearied bands   [IX. 587]
Marches with pile in hand, and not commands
But shows them how to labour; never sits
In coach or chariot; sleeps the least anights;
Last tastes the water. When a fountain's found,
He stays afoot 'til all the soldiers round
And every cullion drink. If fame be due   *base fellow*
To truest goodness, if you simply view
Virtue without success, whate'er we call
In greatest Romans great was fortune all:
Who could deserve in prosperous war such fame,
Or by the nations' blood so great a name?
Rather had I this virtuous triumph win

---

[1] If fortune lose ... Her threats] While closely translating *Fortunaque perdat | Opposita virtute minas* (IX. 569), M. seemingly echoes here Ben Jonson, *Sejanus*, III. 324-25 (*Works*, II, p. 305), 'she herself [Fortune] | when virtue doth oppose, must lose her threats' (the speech of Silius to the Senate before killing himself); cf. 9. 673 and note.

[2] The great Creator] *auctor*, 'author' (IX. 575).

[3] The coward ... fall] *pavido fortique cadendum est* (IX. 583). M.'s translation, though close to L.'s Latin, echoes Silius before his suicide in Jonson's *Sejanus*, III. 334 (*Works*, II, p. 305); cf. 9. 657n.

690 In Libya's desert sands, than thrice be seen
In Pompey's laurelled chariot or to lead
Jugurtha captive.¹ Here behold indeed,
Rome, thy true father by whose sacred name²
(Worthy thy temples) it shall never shame
695 People to swear; whom, if thou e'er art free,³
Thou wilt hereafter make a deity.
Now to a torrid clime they came, more hot
Than which the gods for men created not.⁴
Few waters here are seen, but in the sands
700 One largely-flowing fountain only stands,
But full of serpents as it could contain.
There on the banks hot killing asps remain,
And dipsases in midst of water dry.⁵
When Cato saw his men for thirst would die,
705 Fearing those waters, thus he spake to them:
'Fear not to drink, soldiers, this wholesome stream;
Be not affrighted with vain shows of death.
The snakes' bite deadly, fatal are their teeth,
When their dire venom mixes with our blood:
710 The water's safe.' Then of the doubtful flood
He drinks himself; there only the first draught
Of all the Libyan waters Cato sought.
    Why Libya's air should be infested so   [IX. 619]⁶
With mortal plagues, what hurtful secrets grow
715 Mixed with the noxious soil by nature's hand,
Our care nor labour cannot understand,   *nor = or*
But that the world, in the true cause deceived,
Instead of that a common tale received.⁷
In Libya's farthest part, whose scorchèd ground
720 The ocean warmed by setting Sol doth bound,   *the sun*

---

¹ In Pompey's … captive] Jugurtha, king of Numidia, was captured and led in triumph in Rome in 104 BC by Marius; cf. 2. 74n.
² thy true father] *parens verus patriae*, 'true father of his country' (IX. 601); a dig at the emperors who adopted this title.
³ if thou e'er art free] *si steteris unquam cervice soluta*, 'should you ever stand with a neck unyoked' (IX. 603).
⁴ more hot … not] i.e. the gods created no land hotter for mortals.
⁵ dipsases … dry] Dipsases were snakes whose bite caused the victims to die of thirst; cf. 9. 825n.
⁶ 9. 713–804] The myth of Medusa, the snake-haired Gorgon who petrified with her gaze, is used to tell the origin of Libya's poisonous snakes.
⁷ a common tale] *Fabula*, 'fable/myth' (IX. 623).

Medusa's country lay, whose barren fields
No trees do clothe, whose soil no herbage yields:
Changed by her look all stones and rocks they grow.
Here hurtful nature first those plagues did show:
725 First from Medusa's jaws those serpents grown
Hissed with forkèd tongues, and hanging down[1]
Like woman's hair upon her back, gave strokes
Unto her pleasèd neck. Instead of locks
Upon her horrid front did serpents hiss;
730 Her comb combed poison down, no part but this
Safe to be seen about Medusa was.
For whoe'er feared the monster's mouth and face?
Whom, that had viewed her with an eye direct,
Did she e'er suffer sense of death t'affect?[2]
735 She hastened doubting fate, preventing dread;
Their bodies died before their souls were fled,
Enclosèd souls with bodies turned to stone.[3]
The Furies' hairs could madness work alone:
Cerberus hissing Orpheus' music stilled,
740 Alcides saw that Hydra which he killed,[4]   *Hercules*
But this strange monster even her father who
Is the sea's second god, her mother too
Cetos and Gorgon sisters fearèd:[5] she
Could strike a numbness through the sea and sky
745 And harden all the world into a stone.
Birds in their flight have fall'n congealèd down,
Running wild beasts to rocks converted were,
And all the neighbouring Ethiopians there[6]
To marble statues. Not a creature brooks   *bears*
750 The sight of her: t'avoid the Gorgon's looks

---

[1] Hissed with forkèd] The meter calls for 'Hissed' to have two syllables but this seems somewhat awkward before 'forkèd'; one possible solution is that it is double the normal length, quantity here substituting for accent.

[2] sense of death t'affect] *mori*, 'to die' (IX. 639); M. translates F.'s paraphrase.

[3] Enclosèd ... stone] *nec emissae riguere sub ossibus umbrae*, 'and their ghosts, not departing, hardened beneath their bones' (IX. 641).

[4] Cerberus ... killed] In legend the great poet Orpheus tamed Cerberus to gain entrance to the Underworld; on the Hydra, see 4. 697–99n. 'Cerberus' is three syllables and 'Orpheus' two.

[5] her mother too | Cetos] Following the Renaissance reading *Cetosque* for Medusa's mother (IX. 646); modern editions call her Ceto and correct to *Cetoque*. The meter demands that 'feared' is disyllabic, but this would be unusual; cf. 9. 726n.

[6] neighbouring Ethiopians] Two syllables and four, respectively.

Her snakes themselves backward themselves invert.
She near Alcides' pillars could convert
Titanian Atlas to an hill,[1] and those
Giants with serpents' feet that durst oppose
755 The gods themselves, those wars in Phlegra field
Her face could end, but showed in Pallas' shield.[2]
Thither the son of shower-raped Danaë,[3]
Borne on th'Arcadian wings of Mercury,
Inventor of the harp and wrestling game,
760 Flying through th'air with borrowed Harpe came,[4]
Harpe, whom monster's blood before did stain
When he that kept Jove's lovèd cow was slain.[5]
Aid to her wingèd brother Pallas gave,
Conditioning the Gorgon's head to have.   *stipulating, upon condition*
765 She bids him fly to Libya's eastern bound,
His face averted, o'er the Gorgon's ground.
In his left hand a shield of shining brass,
Wherein to see the stone-transforming face
Of stern Medusa, Pallas bade him keep,
770 Then laid Medusa in an endless sleep,
But yet not all: part of her snaky hair
Defends her head, some snakes still waking are,
Some o'er her face and sleeping eyelids glide.
Minerva doth th'averted Perseus guide,
775 And with a trembling hand directs the stroke
Of his Cyllenian Harpe,[6] which quite broke

---

[1] near Alcides' pillars] *sub Hesperiis ... columnis*, 'beneath western pillars' (IX. 654), i.e. the rocky promontories flanking the Strait of Gibraltar; cf. 3. 302.

[2] and those ... Pallas' shield] *coeloque timente | Olim Phlegraeo stantes serpente gigantes | Erexit montes bellumque immane Deorum | Pallados e medio confecit pectore Gorgon*, 'and once, when heaven feared [them], the Gorgon erected the giants standing with snakes for legs into mountains at Phlegra, and finished the dreadful war of the Gods from the middle of Pallas' breast [i.e. from her position on Minerva's shield]' (IX. 655-58). M.'s paraphrase derives from F.; Minerva's shield is his own touch. On Phlegra and gigantomachy see 4. 655 ff., 7. 164-70; on the shield, 7. 169-70, 647.

[3] the son ... Danaë] Perseus, slayer of Medusa, was born after Jupiter visited the Greek princess Danaë in the form of a shower of gold. In the following passage, following M.'s usual practice, 'Perseus' is disyllabic.

[4] Harpe] Disyllabic (*harpē*, in Greek 'curved blade', IX. 662): the word is often capitalized in Renaissance editions and M. clearly took it to be the name of Perseus' weapon. 'Flying' is monosyllabic.

[5] he ... cow] A reference to the myth of Io and the death of Argus: while Argus guarded Io (who was in the form of a cow) Mercury killed him.

[6] Cyllenian] Mercury's (Cyllene was the god's birthplace).

Her large snake-covered neck. How strange a look
Had Gorgon's head cut off by Perseus' stroke
And tow'ring blade?¹ What poison did arise
780 In her black mouth? What death shot from her eyes?²
Which not Minerva durst to look upon;
And Perseus sure had been congealed to stone,
Had not Minerva hid that dismal face
With those snake-hairs. Now Perseus flies apace
785 To heaven with Gorgon's head, but in his mind
Considering how the nearest way to find,
Over the midst of Europe means to fly.
But Pallas straight forbids that injury
To Europe's fruitful fields, and bids him spare
790 The people there: for who can in the air
Refrain to gaze when such a bird he spies.³
Perseus converts his course,⁴ and westward flies
O'er desert Libya, whose unfruitful seat
Untilled lies ope to nought but Phoebus' heat,   *the sun's*
795 Who runs his burning course straight o'er their heads.⁵
No land than this a larger shadow spreads
'Gainst heaven, nor more the moon's eclipse doth cause
When, straying not in latitude, she draws
Neither to north nor south but still is found
800 In signs direct.⁶ Yet this unfruitful ground,
Barren in all that's good, a seed could yield
From venom which Medusa's head distilled.
From those dire drops mixed with the putrid earth
Sol's aiding heat did give new monsters birth.⁷   *the sun's*
805   First from that dust so mixed with poison bred   [IX. 700]⁸

---

¹ tow'ring blade] *lunati ... ferri*, 'crescent-shaped weapon' (IX. 678): see 7. 759n. Modern editions read *hamati* ('hooked') for *lunati*.
² 9. 780–81] Questions in M., but exclamations in most Renaissance editions.
³ 9. 790–91] A statement in M., but a question in most Renaissance editions.
⁴ Perseus ... course] Omitting *Zephyro*, '[with the aid of] the west wind' (IX. 689).
⁵ Who runs ... heads] *premit orbita solis | Exuritque solum*, 'the sun's course oppresses and burns the soil' (IX. 691–92).
⁶ 9. 796–800] A problematic passage of Roman astronomy, suggesting that in equatorial regions such as Libya both the sun and (at night) the earth's shadow cast by the sun beneath it, are directly overhead, in the latter case interfering with the moon when it moves straight across the sky ('in signs direct', *per recta ...| Signa*, IX. 694–95, refers to the zodiac).
⁷ dire drops ... birth] 'dire drops' omits L.'s *fero de sanguine*, 'from her beastly blood' (IX. 698), '[which] the heat helped [i.e. helped breed] and boiled into the putrid sand', *Quos calor adiuvit, putrique incoxit arenae* (IX. 699).
⁸ 9. 805–1016] Cato and his troops encounter a terrifying variety of poisonous snakes. M.

          Rose the sleep-causing asp with swelling head,
          Made of the thickest drop of Gorgon's gore,[1]
          Which in no serpent is compacted more.
          She wanting heat seeks not a colder clime,
810   Content to live in her own Libya's slime.[2]
          But O how shameless is our thirst of gain?
          Those Libyan deaths are carried o'er the main,[3]
          And asps at Rome are sold as merchandise.
          In scaly folds the great haemorrhus lies,
815   Whose bite from all parts draws the flowing blood.[4]
          Chersidros then, that both in land and flood
          Of doubtful Syrtes lives; chelydri too,
          That make a reeking slime where'er they go;
          The cenchris creeping in a tract direct,   route, path
820   Whose speckled belly with more spots is decked
          Than e'er the various Theban marble takes;
          Sand-coloured ammodytes;[5] the hornèd snakes[6]
          That creep in winding tracks; the scytale —
          No snake in winter casts her skin but she —
825   The double-head;[7] dipsas, that thirsty makes;[8]
          The water-spoiling newt; the dart-like snakes.[9]
          The pareas, whose way his tail doth guide;
          The prester too, whose sting distendeth wide
          The wounded's foamy mouth;[10] the seps, whose bite
830   Consumes the bones, dissolves the body quite;[11]

relies heavily on commentaries for serpent lore to assist his translation, especially F., who himself often cites L.'s chief source, Nicander's *Theriaca* (second century BC). Often the snake's name hints at its method of death: see notes below.

[1] thickest ... gore] *Plenior ... sanguis, & crassi gutta veneni*, 'the fullest blood and drop of viscous poison' (IX. 703).
[2] slime] *arenas*, 'sands' (IX. 705). On the asp's effects see 9. 931–36.
[3] carried o'er the main] *inde petuntur | Huc*, 'are thence sought hither' (IX. 706–07).
[4] Whose ... blood] *non stare suum miseris passura cruorem*, 'not allowing their own blood to stay in its wretched victims' (IX. 708). See 9. 921–30.
[5] Sand-coloured] *Concolor exustis, atque indiscretus arenis*, 'of the same colour as the parched sands and indistinguishable from them' (IX. 715); 'ammodytes' has three syllables, rhyming with 'lights'.
[6] hornèd snakes] *cerastae* (IX. 716); the detail of horns may come from F., although Greek *cerastos* means 'horned'.
[7] double-head] *gravis in geminum surgens caput Amphisboena*, 'the heavy amphisboena, rising into twin heads' (IX. 719).
[8] that thirsty makes] *torrida*, 'parched' (IX. 718). In Greek *dipsa* = thirst; see 9. 846–71.
[9] dart-like snakes] *iaculi*, 'javelin-[snakes]' (IX. 720); see 9. 937–43.
[10] The prester ... mouth] See Textual Notes. In Greek *prēstēr* = 'inflater'; see 9. 904–19.
[11] the seps] In Greek *sēps* = 'putrifying sore'; see 9. 875–903.

The basilisk, whose hiss all snakes doth scare[1]
(Hurtful before the venom touch), who far
All vulgar serpents from his sight commands,
Reigning alone upon the emptied sands.
835 You dragons too, glist'ring in golden pride,
Who hurtless wander through all lands beside,
Hot Afric mortal makes:[2] aloft you fly
Through the air on wings, and follow speedily
The herds. Your strokes the mightiest bulls destroy,[3]
840 Great elephants not 'scape you: all you kill,
Nor need you poison's help to work your will.
 This thirsty way among these venomed snakes   [IX. 734]
Cato amidst his hardy soldiers takes:
Where many losses of his men he found,[4]
845 And deaths unusual from a little wound.
A trodden dipsas, turning back his head,
Did bite young Aulus, ensign-bearer bred
Of Tyrrhene race. No grief nor pain ensued:[5]
His wound no pity found, no danger shewed,   *showed*
850 But in (alas) did fiery venom deep
Into his marrow and scorched entrails creep,
Which quite drunk up all moisture that should flow
Into his vital parts. His palate now
And tongue is scorched and dry: no sweat could go
855 To his tired joints, from's eyes no tears could flow.   *from his*
His place nor his sad general's command   *neither his place*
Could stay this thirsty man:[6] out of his hand
He throws his eagle, water runs to have
Which the dry venom in his heart did crave.
860 Though he in midst of Tanaïs did lie,   *the Don*
Padus, or Rhodanus, he would be dry,   *the Po; Rhône*

---

[1] The basilisk …] See 9. 945–49.   scare] Spelt 'scarre' (and presumably so pronounced) in *1627*, thus rhyming more closely with 'far' than the modern variant; see note to 1. 301.

[2] Hot Afric mortal makes] i.e. hot Africa makes you [dragons] mortal. Mortal here means 'lethal'; L.'s term is *Pestiferos*, 'plague-bringing' (IX. 729). Modern editions print *letiferos*, 'death-bringing'.

[3] 9. 837–39] Another rare triple rhyme; cf. 9. 622–24. 'Mightiest' is disyllabic. The meter calls for a contraction in the previous line, probably of 'the air' to 'th'air'.

[4] many losses] *tot tristia fata*, 'so many woeful deaths' (IX. 735).

[5] No grief nor pain ensued] *Vix dolor, aut sensus dentis fuit*, 'there was scarcely any pain or sense of the bite [lit. of a tooth]' (IX. 739).

[6] place] *decus imperii*, 'the dignity of his command' (IX. 747): to carry the eagle-standard was a special honour. 'Generals' is trisyllabic.

	Or drink the streams wherever Nilus flows.	
	The soil adds to his drought: the worm doth lose	*snake*
	Her venom's fame, helped by so hot a land.	
865	He digs and seeks each vein in all the sand.	
	Now to the Syrts he goes, and in his mouth	*Syrtes*
	Salt water takes, which could not quench his drought	
	Although it pleased. He did not know what kind	
	Of death he died, nor his disease could find,	
870	But thinks it thirst; and now full fain he would	*gladly*
	Rip open all his veins and drink his blood.	
	Cato commands them (loath his men should stay	
	To know what thirst was) straight to march away.	
	But a more woeful death before his eye	
875	Appeared: a seps on poor Sabellus' thigh	
	Hung by the teeth, which he straight with his hands	
	Cast off, and with his pile nailed to the sands.	
	A little snake, but none more full than she	
	Of horrid death: the flesh falls off, that nigh	
880	The wound did grow, the bones are barèd round,	
	Without the body naked shows the wound.[1]	
	His shanks fall off, matter each member fills,[2]	
	His knees are bared, his groin black filth distils,	
	And every muscle of his thighs dissolves:	
885	The skin that all his natural parts involves,	
	Breaking lets fall his bowels. Nor doth all	
	That should remain of a dead body, fall:	
	The cruel venom, eating all the parts,	
	All to a little poisonous filth converts.[3]	
890	The poison breaks his nerves, his ribs doth part,	
	Opens his hollow breast, there shows his heart,	
	His vitals all, yea all that man composes,	
	And his whole nature this foul death discloses;[4]	

[1] Without the body ... wound] *Iamque sinu laxo nudum sine corpore vulnus*, 'and now as the hole gapes, [he is] a naked wound without a body' (IX. 769).
[2] matter ... fills] *Membra natant sanie*, 'his limbs swim with filth' (IX. 770).
[3] poisonous] Contracted to two syllables in pronunciation.
[4] there shows ... discloses] Reading *abstrusum fibris vitalibus, omne | Quidquid homo est, aperit pestis. natura profana | Morte patet*, 'the plague lays bare what is hidden beneath vital entrails, everything that makes a man; his nature is disclosed by the foul death' (IX. 778–80, in early modern editions). Modern editions treat IX. 779 as a single unpunctuated sentence, meaning 'the plague lays bare by its foul nature what makes a man', and place it before IX. 777 (= 9. 890). The effects on the different parts of the body listed in 9. 890–92 then follow and are summarized as *omne | Morte patet*, 'everything is laid bare in death' (IX. 779–80, in modern editions).

His head, neck, shoulders and strong arms do flow
895 In venomous filth;[1] not sooner melts the snow
By hot south winds, nor wax against the sun.
This is but small I speak: burnt bodies run
Melted by fire in filth,[2] but what fire e'er
Dissolved the bones? No bones of his appear.
900 Following their putrid juice, they leave no sign[3]
Of this swift death. The palm is only thine[4]
Of all the Libyan snakes: the soul take they,
But thou alone the carcass tak'st away.
    But lo a death quite contrary to it: [IX. 789]
905 Marsian Nasidius an hot prester bit,
Whose face and cheeks a sudden fire did roast:[5]
His flesh and skin was stretched, his shape was lost.
His swelling body is distended far
Past human growth, and undistinguished are
910 His limbs: all parts the poison doth confound,
And he lies hid, in his own body drowned,
Nor can his armour keep his swoll'n growth in.
Not more doth boiling water rise within
A brazen cauldron, nor are sails more swelled
915 By western winds. No limb he now can wield:
A globe deformed he is, an heap confused,[6]
Which rav'ning beasts did fear, which birds refused,
To which his friends durst do no obsequy,
Nor touch, but from the growing carcass fly.
920   But yet these snakes present more horrid sights: [IX. 805]
A fierce haemorrhus noble Tullus bites,
A brave young man that studied Cato's worth,
And as in pouncing of a picture, forth
Through every hole the pressèd saffron goes,[7]

---

[1] In venomous filth] M.'s addition; 'venomous' is probably pronounced as two syllables.
[2] filth] Omitting L.'s *Hoc et flamma potest*, 'this a flame can do too' (IX. 784).
[3] putrid juice] *putresque ... medullas*, 'putrid marrow' (IX. 785); 'following' is contracted to two syllables.
[4] palm] i.e. sign of victory in a competition.
[5] Marsian Nasidius ... bit] i.e. a prester bit Nasidius.   sudden fire] *rubor igneus*, 'fiery redness' (IX. 791).
[6] an heap confused] *confuso pondere truncus*, 'a trunk of confused weight' (IX. 801).
[7] And as in pouncing ... saffron goes] *Vtque solet pariter totis se effundere signis | Corycii pressura croci*, 'and as a spout of Corycian saffron is wont to spray out from all images at once' (IX. 808–09); as F. explains, probably referring to statues in Roman theatres. M. switches the idiom to contemporary painting: 'pouncing' is a process of tracing using pin-

925	So from his every part red poison flows	
	For blood.¹ His tears were blood: from every pore,	
	Where nature vented moisture heretofore,	
	His mouth, his nose, flows blood; his sweat is red;	
	His running veins all parts be bloodièd,	
930	And his whole body's but one wound become.	
	An asp's sharp bite did Laevus' heart benumb.²	[IX. 815]
	No pain he felt: surprised with sudden sleep	
	He died, descending to the Stygian deep.³	
	Not half so sudden do those poisons kill	
935	Which dire Sabaean sorcerers distil	
	From off the falsely seeming Sabine tree.⁴	
	On an old stump a dart-like snake did lie,⁵	[IX. 822–27]
	Which, as from thence herself she nimbly threw,	
	Through Paulus' head and wounded temples flew.	
940	'Twas not the poison wrought his fate; the blow	
	Itself brought death. To her comparèd, slow	
	Fly stones from slings, and not so swift as she	
	From Parthian bows do wingèd arrows flee.⁶	
	What helped it wretched Murrus that he did	[IX. 828–36]
945	Kill a fierce basilisk? The poison slid	
	Along his spear, and fastened on his hand,	
	Which he cut off, and then did safely stand	
	With that hand's loss, viewing securely there	
	The sad example of his death so near.	
950	Who would have thought the knotty scorpion had	
	Such power in killing or a sting so bad?	

pricks, before powder is pressed through the holes to leave an outline of the image.
¹ For blood] i.e. instead of blood.
² An asp's ... benumb] Translating *Niliace serpente*, 'serpent of the Nile' (IX. 816), as 'asp', following most commentaries. L. addresses the victim here: *tibi, Laeve miser*, 'But in your case, unhappy Laevus' (IX. 815).
³ to the Stygian deep] *Stygias ... ad umbras*, 'to the Stygian shades' (IX. 818); modern editions use the variant *socias*, 'comradely [shades]'.
⁴ 9. 935-36] A complex and still disputed passage. M. appears to follow F.'s text, itself indebted to a conjecture and explanation of Grotius: *Stipite quae diro virgas mentita Sabinas | Toxica fatilegi carpunt matura Sabaei* (IX. 821-22): '[poison] which death-collecting Sabaeans seize when toxic and ripe, and falsely resembling Sabine wands, from the evil trunk'. Roman magistrates used twigs from Sabine trees for ceremonial purposes; the Sabaeans are an Arabian people, famous traders in perfumes; the trees from which they harvest incense resemble the Sabine yew-tree.
⁵ a dart-like snake] *iaculum vocat Africa*, 'Africa calls it the javelin' (IX. 823).
⁶ From Parthian ... flee] *Quam segnis Scythicae strideret arundinis aër*, 'how slowly the air of a Scythian arrow whistles' (IX. 827); M. follows F.'s paraphrase.

	Her straight stroke won, when she Orion slew,	
	A trophy which the constellations shew.¹	*show*
	Who, small solpuga, from thy hole would flee?	[IX. 837–38]
955	Yet the three sisters give their power to thee.²	
	So that no rest they found by night nor day,	[IX. 839–64]
	They feared the ground itself on which they lay.	
	For neither heaps of leaves nor reeds they found	
	To make them beds, but on the naked ground	
960	Exposed their bodies, whose warm vapour's steam	
	By night attracted the cold snakes to them,	
	Whose harmless jaws, whilst night's astringent cold	
	The poison freezed, unhurt their bosoms hold.	
	Nor by the guidance of the stars their way	
965	Can they discern, but oft complaining say,	
	'Restore, O gods, to us those wars again,	
	From which we fled: restore Pharsalia's plain.	
	Why should we die, whose lives devoted were	
	And sworn to war, the death of cowards here?	
970	The dipsases on Caesar's party are,	
	And hornèd snakes help end our civil war.³	
	O let us go where the hot zone doth lie:⁴	
	'Twould ease our grievèd hearts that to the sky	
	We might ascribe our deaths. In nought do we	
975	Accuse thee, Africa, or, Nature, thee:	
	For thou this monster-bearing country, ta'en	
	From men's plantation,⁵ didst for snakes ordain;	
	This land all barren, where no corn could thrive,	
	Thou mad'st that men might from these serpents live,	
980	But we are come into their dwellings here.	
	Take punishment on us, thou god whoe'er,	
	Hating our journey, didst the world divide,⁶	
	Placing the doubtful Syrtes on one side,	

---

¹ Orion ... shew] An allusion to the death of Orion, killed by a scorpion: they were immortalized as the constellations Orion and Scorpio.

² Yet ... to thee] *et tibi dant Stygiae ius in sua fila sorores*, 'and yet the Stygian sisters grant you power over their threads' (IX. 838), i.e. the Fates, responsible for the life-span of mortals. The solpuga is a venomous ant.

³ hornèd snakes] *cerastae*: see 9. 822n.

⁴ hot zone] *zona rubens*, 'reddened zone' (IX. 852); M. omits *atque axis inustus | Solis equis*, 'and the sky burnt by the sun's horses' (IX. 852–53).

⁵ men's plantation] *Gentibus*, 'peoples' (IX. 856).

⁶ journey] *commerciam*, 'interchange, traffic, trade' (IX. 860). F. glosses *iter hoc et transitum vetitum*, 'this journey and forbidden crossing'.

The torrid zone on t'other, death's sad seat
985 Placed in the midst. To thy most hid retreat
Our civil war dares go: to the world's end
Our ways, through nature's secrets prying, tend.¹
    Worse things, perchance, must be endured than this.   [IX. 865]
The pole declines, the setting sun doth hiss
990 Drenched in the sea. No land doth further lie
This way than Juba's woeful monarchy,
Known but by fame. We shall perchance again
Wish for this serpents' land: th'air doth contain
Some comfort yet, some things are living here.
995 Alas, we wish not for our country dear,
Europe nor Asia, different suns which see:
Under what pole, O Afric, left we thee?   *Africa*
'Twas winter at Cyrene when we lay:
Is the year's course changed in so small a way?
1000 The south is at our backs: to th'adverse pole
Our journey tends; about the world we roll.
We are, perchance, Antipodes to Rome.²
Let this our comfort be, let Caesar come,
O let our foes pursue where we have fled.'
1005 Thus they in sad complaints unburdenèd
Their loaded patience. Cato's virtue keeps
Them proof 'gainst any labour,³ who still sleeps
Upon the naked sands and every hour,
Present at every fate, tempts fortune's power,
1010 Comes at all calls. His presence doth bestow
Far more than health, a strength to undergo
Even death itself. Whilst Cato's standing by
They are ashamed impatiently to die.⁴
What power o'er him had any misery?⁵
1015 Whose presence grief in others breasts subdued,

---

¹ Our civil war ... tend] *per secreta tui bellum civile recessus | Vadit: & arcani miles tibi conscius orbis | Claustra petit mundi*, 'civil war walks the secret places of your retreat; and the soldier, aware of your hidden region, seeks the boundaries of the world' (IX. 864–66).
² Antipodes to Rome] *nunc forsitan ipsa est | Sub pedibus iam Roma meis*, 'now perhaps Rome herself is already beneath my feet' (IX. 877–78); M.'s idea of the 'Antipodes' is taken from F.'s gloss.
³ keeps ... labour] *cogit tantos tolerare labores*, 'compels them to endure such labours' (IX. 881).
⁴ impatiently to die] *gementem*, 'groaning' (IX. 886).
⁵ misery] *lues*, 'plague, pestilence' (IX. 888).

And what small power can be in sorrow shewed.¹
    Some ease at last did tired Fortune give   [IX. 890]²
To their long suff'rings: there a nation live,
Marmarian ⁽ᵈ⁾Psylls from serpents' biting free.³
1020 They armed with powerful incantations be:
Their blood's secure, and, though they did not charm,
By touch of poison cannot suffer harm.
The place's nature this did justly give,
That serpent-free they might with serpents live.
1025 'Twas well that in this poisonous air they breathe,⁴
For peace is made betwixt themselves and death.
Of their own broods such certain proofs have all,
That when to ground a new-born child doth fall,
Fearing strange Venus hath their beds defiled,
1030 By deadly asps they try the doubted child.
As th'eagle when her eaglets are disclosed,⁵   *exposed*
Lays them against the rising sun exposed:
Those that with steady eye can view his beams,
And boldly gaze, those only she esteems,
1035 The other scorns; the Psylls so count it there
Their nation's pledge, if infants do not fear
The serpents' touch or freely play with snakes.
They, not content with their own safety, take
For strangers care: and following th'army then⁶
1040 Against those serpents aided Cato's men.
For when the camp was pitched, those sands that lay
Within the compass of the trenches they
Did purge with snake-expelling charms throughout,
And med'cinable fires made round about.
1045 There wallwort cracks, and fennel gum doth fry,
Thin tamarisk, Thessalian centory,
Strong panace, Arabian pepperwort,⁷

---

¹ And what ... shewed] *Spectatorque docet magnos nil posse dolores*, 'and by watching taught that great sufferings have no power' (IX. 889).
² 9. 1017–80] Cato's troops encounter the Psylli, an African people immune to snakebite, who escort them to Leptis.
³ from serpents' biting free] *a saevo serpentum innoxia morsu*, 'uninjured by the cruel bite of serpents' (IX. 892). See Textual Notes.
⁴ poisonous] Contracted to two syllables in pronunciation.
⁵ are disclosed] *calido cum protulit ovo*, 'when [she] has carried them out of the warm egg' (IX. 902).
⁶ following] Pronounced 'foll'wing'.
⁷ Strong panace...] 'panace' has three syllables; 'Arabian' is also trisyllabic.

Sicilian thapsos burned with sulphurwort,
Larch trees and southernwood, which serpents dread
1050 And horns of stags far off from Afric bred.¹
So night was safe: if stung by day they were,
That magic nation's miracles appear,
For 'gainst the Psylls the taken venom strives:
Marks to the wounded place their spittle gives,
1055 Whose force the poison in the wound doth stay.
Then with a foaming tongue dire charms they say
In ceaseless murmurs. For no time to breathe
The danger gives: approaching speedy death
Admits no silence. Oft hath poison ta'en
1060 In th'inmost parts been charmed away again.
But, when called out by their commanding tongue,
If any poison dare to tarry long,
Then falling down they lick the pallid wound,
And with a gentle bite squeezing it round
1065 Suck with their mouths the poison out, and it
Extracted from the key-cold body spit,
And in their mouths tasting the poison well
What serpent deepest bit the Psylls can tell.
Now o'er the fields encouraged by their aid
1070 The Roman soldiers wandered less afraid.
Thus Cato treading sands of Libya²
The moon twice waning and twice wexing saw.   *waxing*
    Now more and more the sands to harden 'gan,   *began*
And Afric's thickened ground grew glebe again.   *became soil*
1075 Trees here and there began t'extend their shade
And cottages of reeds and sedges made.
How great an hope of better ground had they,
When first they saw fierce lions cross their way?
Leptis was near'st, which quiet harbour lent.
1080 Their winter free from heat and storms they spent.
    Now Caesar with Pharsalia's slaughter cloyed,   [IX. 950]³
Leaving all other cares, his thoughts employed

---

¹ 9. 1045–50] A catalogue of plants with medicinal properties (= IX. 917–21). M.'s English variants of L.'s Latin terms are almost certainly taken from an upmarket English herbal, e.g. Rembert Dodoens, *A New Herbal, or History of Plants*, trans. by Henry Lyte (London: Ninian Newton, 1619).
² Libya] Trisyllabic.
³ 9. 1081–end] The narrative switches to Caesar, who crosses the Hellespont and visits the ruins of ancient Troy, before travelling to Egypt and receiving Pompey's head.

In the pursuit of Pompey, and was brought
(When he his steps by land had vainly sought)
1085 By fame's report to sea, and passed o'er
The Thracian straits, and that love-famed shore[1]
Where once fair Hero's woeful turret stood;
Where Helle's tragedy new named the flood.[2]
No arm of sea bounds with a stream so small
1090 Asia from Europe, though Propontis fall
Narrow into the Euxine sea, and from
Purple Chalcedon part Byzantium.[3]
Thence goes to see renowned Sigaean sands,   = *Caesar goes*
The stream of Simois[4] and Rhoetean lands
1095 Famed for the Grecian worthy'stomb, where lie
Great ghosts so much in debt to poetry.[5]
Sacked Troy's yet honoured name he goes about,
To find th'old wall of great Apollo out.[6]
Now fruitless trees, old oaks with putrefied
1100 And rotten roots the Trojan houses hide
And temples of their gods: all Troy's o'erspread
With bushes thick, her ruins ruinèd.[7]
He sees the bridal grove Anchises lodged,[8]
Hesione's rock, the cave where Paris judged,
1105 Where nymph Oenone played, the place so famed
For Ganymedes' rape; each stone is named.[9]

---

[1] passed o'er … love-famed shore] Conceivably both 'passed' and 'famed' have two syllables here, as required by the meter, but this could also be a couplet of nine lines each.
[2] Where once…] The lovers Hero and Leander were separated by the narrow channel of the Hellespont, a sea that gained its name from Helle; on her fate see 4. 62n.
[3] and from … Byzantium] i.e. divides (*dirimat*, IX. 959) Byzantium from 'purple Chalcedon'. L.'s epithet is *ostriferam*, 'oyster-bearing' (IX. 959); oysters have purple dye. The meaning is that the Hellespont was narrower than the Euxine sea or Propontis dividing Europe from Asia at Byzantium (modern Istanbul).
[4] Simois] Normally 'Simoïs' but here disyllabic ('Sim-wis'); a river of Troy.
[5] Thence goes … poetry] The 'Grecian worthy' is Ajax son of Telamon, buried at Rhoeteum; Achilles was supposedly buried in Sigeum.
[6] th'old wall … out] Apollo and Poseidon reputedly built the walls of Troy.
[7] her ruins ruinèd] *etiam periere ruinae*, 'even the ruins have perished' (IX. 969).
[8] He sees … lodged] i.e. where Anchises lodged; *silvasque latentes | Anchisae thalamos*, 'the secret woods which were the marriage-chamber of Anchises' (IX. 970–71). Anchises and Venus were Aeneas' parents.
[9] Hesione's rock … named] Hesione was a daughter of Laomedon king of Troy, exposed on a rock to a sea-monster (but saved by Hercules); Paris judged the beauty contest between Venus, Juno and Athena; the nymph Oenone (trisyllabic) was Paris' first wife; the boy Ganymede was stolen by Jupiter, to become his cup-bearer on Olympus. 'Hesione' must be three syllables here, either by contracting 'io' into one syllable or — the less likely option

	A little gliding stream which Xanthus was	[IX. 974]
	Unknown he passed, and in the lofty grass	
	Securely trod; a Phrygian straight forbid	
1110	Him tread on Hector's dust. With ruins hid,	
	The stone retained no sacred memory.	
	'Respect you not great Hector's tomb?'[1] quoth he.	
	O great and sacred work of poësy,	
	That freest from fate, and giv'st eternity	
1115	To mortal wights! But Caesar, envy not	*men*
	Their living names:[2] if Roman muses aught	
	May promise thee, whilst Homer's honourèd,	
	By future times shall thou and I be read.[3]	
	No age shall us with dark oblivion stain,	
1120	But our Pharsalia ever shall remain.[4]	
	Then Caesar, pleased with sight of these so praised	[IX. 987]
	Antiquities, a green turf-altar raised	
	And by the frankincense-fed fire prepared	
	These orisons not vain: 'You gods, that guard	
1125	These heroes' dust,[5] and in Troy's ruins reign;	
	Aeneas' household gods, that still maintain	
	In Alba and Lavinia your shrines,[6]	
	Upon whose altars fire yet Trojan shines;	
	Thou sacred temple-closed Palladium,[7]	
1130	That in the sight of man didst never come:	
	The greatest heir of all Iulus' race	
	Here in your former seat implores your grace,[8]	
	And pious incense on your altars lays.	

— by rhyming with 'bone'. 'Ganymedes' is here pronounced in ancient fashion, with four syllables, rather than to rhyme with 'screeds'.

[1] great Hector's tomb] See Textual Notes. Hector, prince of Troy and their preeminent warrior, was killed by Achilles: his burial is the subject of *Iliad*, XXIV (see H. van Thiel, ed. *HomeriIlias*, Bibliotheca Weidmanniana, 2 (Hildesheim, Zurich, and New York: Georg Olms, 1996).

[2] living names] Following F.'s prosaic *vitalitatem* over L.'s *sacrae ... famae*, 'sacred fame' (IX. 982).

[3] shall thou and I be read] *Venturi me teque legent*, 'those to come will read me and you' (IX. 985), i.e. my poem about you. M. used this motto as the epigraph to his *Supplementum*.

[4] our Pharsalia] *Pharsalia nostra* (IX. 985); L. may mean the battle only, but many early modern readers, including F. and M., take this to mean the title of the poem (IX. 985).

[5] dust] *cinerum*, 'ashes' (IX. 990).

[6] Alba and Lavinia] Locations near Rome; cf. 1. 215, 7. 444. L.'s *Lavinia sedes*, 'Lavinian seat' (IX. 991) means the town of Lavinium; M.'s 'Lavinia' has four syllables.

[7] Palladium] See 1. 633–34 and note.

[8] The greatest heir...] *clarissimus*, 'most renowned' (IX. 995).

	Prosper my course, and thankful Rome shall raise	
1135	Troy's walls again, your people I'll restore,	
	And build a Roman Troy.' This said, to shore	
	He hastes, takes shipping, and to Corus lends	*north-west wind*
	His full-spread sails, with haste to make amends	
	For these delays, and with a prosp'rous wind	
1140	Leaves wealthy Asia and fair Rhodes behind;	
	The west winds blowing still, the seventh night	
	Discovers Egypt's shore by Pharian light.	
	But ere they reach the harbour, day appears	
	And dims the nightly fires, when Caesar hears	
1145	Strange tumults on the shore, noises of men,	
	And doubtful murmurings, and fearing then	
	To trust himself at land,[1] stays in his fleet,	
	Whom straight Achillas launches forth to meet,[2]	
	Bringing his king's dire gift, great Pompey's head,	
1150	With an Egyptian mantle coverèd;	
	And thus his crime with impious words to grace:	
	'Lord of the world, greatest of Roman race,[3]	[IX. 1014]
	And now secure (which yet thou dost not know)	
	In Pompey's death, my king doth here bestow	
1155	What only wanted in Pharsalia's field,	*was lacking*
	And what thy wars and travel's end will yield:	
	We, in thy absence, finished civil war.	
	For Pompey, here desiring to repair	
	Thessalia's ruins, by our sword lies slain.	
1160	By this great pledge, Caesar, we seek to gain	
	Thy love, and in his blood our league to make.[4]	
	Here, without bloodshed, Egypt's kingdom take,	
	Take all Nile's fertile regions and receive	
	Whatever thou for Pompey's head wouldst give.	
1165	Think him a friend worthy thine arms to have,[5]	
	To whom the fates such power o'er Pompey gave.	

[1] To trust himself at land] *dubiis veritus se credere regnis*, 'fearing to put his trust in wavering/fickle monarchies' (IX. 1009).

[2] Achillas ... to meet] *satelles*, 'an attendant' (IX. 1010). In identifying Pompey's murderer, M. contradicts most early modern commentators, including F., who followed Plutarch and Appian in saying it was Theodotus of Chios (sometimes called 'Theodorus' in the Renaissance), Ptolemy's teacher of rhetoric. Of previous commentators, only Hortensius suggests Achillas (col. 1034).

[3] Lord of the world] *Terrarum domitor*, 'subduer/tamer of the earth' (IX. 1014).

[4] our league] i.e. with Caesar: *tecum*, 'with you' in L. (IX. 1021).

[5] friend ... to have] *clientem*, 'client' (IX. 1024), i.e. Ptolemy.

Nor think his merit cheap,[1] since brought to pass
With easy slaughter; his old friend he was,[2]
And to his banished father did restore
1170 The crown of Egypt. But why speak I more?
Find thou a name for this great work of his,
Or ask the world; if villainy it is,
The more thou ow'st to him, that from thee took
This act of villainy.' Thus having spoke,
1175 Straight he uncovers and presents the head,
Whose scarce-known looks pale death had alterèd.
    Caesar at first his gift would not refuse,[3]   [IX. 1035]
Nor turn his eyes away, but fix'dly views
'Til he perceived 'twas true, and plainly saw
1180 'Twas safe to be a pious father-in-law,[4]
Then shed forced tears, and from a joyful breast
Drew sighs and groans, as thinking tears would best
Conceal his inward joy; so quite o'erthrows
The tyrant's merit,[5] and doth rather choose
1185 To weep than owe to him for Pompey's head.
He that on slaughtered senators could tread[6]
And see the blood-stained fields of Thessaly
Dry-eyed, to thee alone durst not deny
The tribute of his eyes.[7] Strange turn of fate![8]
1190 Weep'st thou for him, whom thou with impious hate,[9]
Caesar, so long pursued'st? Could not the love
Of daughter, nephew, not alliance move?
Think'st thou among those people that bewail
Great Pompey's death, these tears can aught avail?[10]

---

[1]   his merit cheap] The deserved reward for the deed in L., not Ptolemy's personal merit (IX. 1026–27).
[2]   his old friend he was] *hospes*, 'guest' (IX. 1028).
[3]   would not refuse] *non damnavit*, 'did not condemn' (IX. 1035).
[4]   pious] Possibly contracted to one syllable in pronunciation, as elsewhere with '-ious' (e.g. 'impious', 9. 1190 below; contrast, however, 9. 1200); alternatively 'be a' could be elided into a single syllable.
[5]   quite o'erthrows ... merit] i.e. Ptolemy's recompense for killing Pompey; M. chooses F.'s gloss *evertit*, 'overthrows', over L.'s *Destruit*, 'destroys' (IX. 1042).
[6]   slaughtered senators] *membra Senatus*, lit. 'the limbs of the Senate' (IX. 1043). M. omits *duro ... vultu* (IX. 1043-44), 'with a hard face', i.e. lacking expression or feeling.
[7]   The tribute of his eyes] *gemitus*, 'groans' (IX. 1046).
[8]   Strange turn of fate!] *O sors durissima fati*, 'O hardest lot of fate!' (IX. 1046).
[9]   impious hate] *scelerato Marte*, 'criminal war' (IX. 1047).
[10]   can aught avail?] *castris prodesse tuis*, 'will be beneficial to your camp', i.e. military cause (IX. 1051).

1195	Perchance thou envy'st Ptolemy's dire fact,[1]
	And griev'st that any had the power to act[2]
	This but thyself; that the revenge of war
	Was lost and taken from the conqueror.[3]
	What cause so ever did thy sorrow move,
1200	It was far distant from a pious love.[4]
	Was this the cause that thy pursuit did draw
	O'er land and sea, to save thy son-in-law?[5]
	'Twas well sad fortune took the doom from thee,
	And spared so far a Roman modesty
1205	As not to suffer thee, false man, to give
	Pardon to him, or pity him alive.[6]
	Yet to deceive the world and gain belief,[7] *credence, faith*
	Thou add'st a language to thy feignèd grief.
	'Thy bloody present from our presence bear, *[IX. 1064–1108]*[8]
1210	For worse from Caesar than slain Pompey here
	Your wickedness deserves. The only meed *reward*
	Of civil war, to spare the conquerèd,
	We lose by this; and did not Ptolemy
	His sister hate, I could with ease repay
1215	This gift of his, and for so black a deed
	Return his sister Cleopatra's head.
	Why waged he secret war, or why durst he
	Thus thrust his sword into our work? Did we
	By our Pharsalian victory afford
1220	Your king this power, or license Egypt's sword?
	I brooked not Pompey to bear share with me *tolerated*
	In rule of Rome, and shall I Ptolemy?
	All nations joinèd in our war in vain,[9]
	If any other power on earth remain

---

[1] Ptolemy's dire fact] In L. simply *tyranni*, 'the tyrant' (IX. 1051), not his crime.
[2] the power to act] *captique in viscera Magni ... licuisse*, 'permission [to proceed] against captured Pompey's vitals' (IX. 105–23).
[3] the conqueror] Omitting *superbi*, '*proud* conqueror' (IX. 1054).
[4] from a pious love] *a vera pietate*, 'from true piety' (IX. 1056).
[5] Was this ... ?] The Latin begins with *scilicet*, 'doubtless this was the reason' (IX. 1057).
[6] to give | Pardon ... or pity him] Expanding *miserere*, 'to take pity on' (IX. 1051).
[7] to deceive the world] Simply *fallere*, 'to practice deception', in L. (IX. 1052).
[8] 9. 1208–260] Caesar feigns grief at Pompey's death. The Lucanian passage forms the model for Octavius's response to Antonius's death in M.'s *The Tragedy of Cleopatra*, sigs D9^{r-v}.
[9] All nations ... in vain] *frustra civilibus armis* | *Miscuimus gentes*, 'vainly we immersed all nations in civil conflict' (IX. 1076–77).

1225	But Caesar now, if any land serve two.
	We were determined from your shore to go,[1]
	But fame forbid us, lest we should seem more
	To fear than hate dire Egypt's bloody shore.[2]
	And do not think you have deceivèd me —
1230	To us was meant such hospitality,
	And 'twas our fortune in Thessalia's war
	That frees this head. With greater danger far
	Than could be feared, we fought. I feared the doom
	Of banishment, the threats of wrathful Rome
1235	And Pompey's force:[3] but had I fled, I see
	My punishment had come from Ptolemy.
	We spare his age, and pardon his foul fact,
	For let your king for such a deed expect
	No more than pardon. But do you inter
1240	This worthy's head,[4] not that the earth may bear
	And hide your guilt; bring fumes and odours' store
	T'appease his head, and gather from the shore
	His scattered limbs; compose them in one tomb.
	Let his dear ghost perceive that Caesar's come,
1245	And hear my pious grief. Whilst he prefers
	All desperate hazards before me,[5] and dares
	Rather to trust his life with Ptolemy,[6]
	The people all have lost a joyful day,
	The world our peace. The gods my prayers denied
1250	That, laying these victorious arms aside,
	I might embrace thee, Pompey, and request
	Our former life and love, and think me blessed[7]
	After this war thy equal still to be.
	Then had my faithful love persuaded thee,[8]
1255	Though conquered, to excuse the gods and make
	Thee, Rome, to pardon me.' Though thus he spake,

---

[1] determined … to go] *vertissem Latias … proras*, 'I would have turned our Latin prows' (IX. 1079).

[2] fame forbid us…] *famae cura*, 'concern for fame' (IX. 1080). than hate … shore] *damnasse*, 'to have condemned' (IX. 1080); M. adds 'dire'.

[3] the threats … force] *generique minas Romamque*, 'my son-in-law's threats and Rome' (IX. 1086).

[4] This worthy's] *tanti ducis*, 'so great a leader's' (IX. 1090).

[5] All desperate hazards] *omnia*, 'everything' (IX. 1095).

[6] Ptolemy] Omitting *clienti*, '[Pompey's] client Ptolemy' (IX. 1096).

[7] love] *Affectus*, 'affections' (IX. 1200).

[8] faithful love] *pace fideli*, 'faithful peace [or amity]' (IX. 1202).

He found no partners in his grief: the rest
Believed not his and their own tears suppressed,
And durst (O happy freedom) with dry eye,[1]
1260 Though Caesar wept, behold this tragedy.

FINIS.

---

[1] with dry eye] The grotesque spectacle, familiar under tyrants, of sycophants publicly smiling while inwardly grieving, knowing their ruler's official mourning conceals inward glee — the observation that this amounts to freedom is sarcastic and desperate. M. downplays the subordinates' contortions, omitting *hilares*, 'merry, smiling', and *laeta fronte*, 'putting on a happy expression'; 'happy freedom' renders *bona libertas*, 'good liberty' (IX. 1206–07).

Annotations on the Ninth Book

(a) Whilst the event of the civil war was yet doubtful, and both the generals were possessed of their full strengths, Cato was fearful of both their intents, and hated them both, as fearing that the conqueror would captive his country. But after the battle of Pharsalia was fought, and Caesar had conquered, he was then wholly of Pompey's side, desiring to uphold the party vanquished.[1]

(b) Pompey the Great, pursuing Caesar into Thessalia, had left Cato with a great strength to guard Dyrrachium, who, hearing the overthrow and flight of Pompey, marched away to take shipping at Corcyra, and follow Pompey to join his strength with him.[2]

(c) Cato at Cyrene, hearing that Lucius Scipio, the father-in-law of Pompey the Great, was joined in Africa with Juba King of Mauritania, and that Atius Varus, whom Pompey had deputed his Lieutenant in Africa, was there also, marched over land thither, in which march being thirty days upon those desert sands, and with admirable patience, and magnanimity enduring the journey; forsaking his horse always and marching afoot in the head of his army, to teach his soldiers rather than command them to endure hardness. He arrived at last at Juba's court where, though the soldiers with one voice elected him general, he refused the charge, and chose rather to serve under Scipio, than command himself in chief.[3]

(d) These Psylli are a people inhabiting those parts of Africa fortified by nature with an incredible privilege against the strength of poison, and sustain no harm by the biting of serpents. The serpents (saith Pliny) are afraid of them, and when others are bitten, these Psylli, by sucking the wounds and muttering some charms, do easily cure them. They have a custom (as writers report) when their children are born. If the father suspect his wife's chastity, he exposes the infant to all kinds of serpents: if begotten by a stranger, the child dieth; but if lawfully begotten, the privilege of his father's blood protecteth him against the venom.[4]

---

[1] Mostly M.'s note.
[2] Adapted from F.'s note (on IX. 30).
[3] Mostly M.'s note.
[4] Drawing on F.'s notes (at IX. 912), which themselves refer to Pliny's *Natural History* (first century AD) and the *Collectanea* of Solinus (c. 300 AD).

LUCAN'S
Pharsalia

The Tenth Book.

The Argument of the Tenth Book.[1]

Caesar in Egypt fearless walks and sees
Their temples, tombs and famed antiquities.[2]
Before his feet fair Cleopatra kneels,[3]
Whom to her brother king he reconciles.
5   With sumptuous feasts this peace they celebrate;
To Caesar's ear Achoreus doth relate[4]
Nile's ebbs and flows, and long concealèd spring.
Within the palace Caesar and the king
By stern Achillas are besieged by night.[5]
10 Caesar to Pharos takes a secret flight;
There from his ship he leaps into the waves,
And his endangered life by swimming saves.[6]

When Caesar first, possessed of Pompey's head,   [x. 1][7]
Arrivèd there, and those dire sands did tread,
His fortune strove with guilty Egypt's fate,
Whether that Rome that land should captivate,[8]   *capture, conquer*
5   Or Egypt's sword take from the world the head
Both of the conqueror and the conquerèd.[9]

---

[1] The Argument] See Argument to book one.
[2] temples ... antiquities] Expands Sulpizio's *templa* (temples).
[3] fair Cleopatra] M.'s adjective.
[4] Achoreus] Here pronounced with three syllables, although later (at 10. 205 and 10. 226) with four.
[5] Within the palace ... night] M. removes the detail of Photinus ordering Achillas to besiege Caesar; 'stern' is his added epithet.
[6] Caesar to Pharos ... saves] M.'s final line refers to his continuation of L.'s narrative: see 10. 623-72, below, and notes. L.'s narrative ends with Caesar surrounded and in doubt (X. 546); Sulpizio's *argumentum* with him *metuens*, 'afraid', and plunging into the water.
[7] 10. 1-62] Caesar visits Alexandria, founded by Alexander the Great, and Alexander's tomb.
[8] Whether ... captivate] *regnum Lagi Romana sub arma | Iret*, '[whether] Lagus' kingdom should submit to Roman arms' (x. 5-6).
[9] Both ... conquered] Thus all early modern editions, leading to an extra syllable; possibly the second 'the' is a mistaken addition or there is an unprinted elision, most likely 'th'conqueror'.

	Pompey, thy ghost prevails; thy Manes free	*ghost*
	Caesar from death lest Nile should after thee	
	Be by the Romans loved.¹ He goes from thence	
10	To Alexandria, armed with confidence²	
	In this dire mischief's pledge, following along	
	His fasces.³ But, perceiving that the throng	
	Of people murmured that in Egypt he	
	Bore th'ensigns up of Rome's authority,	
15	He finds their wav'ring faiths,⁴ perceiving plain	
	That for his sake great Pompey was not slain.	
	Then with a look still hiding fear, goes he⁵	
	The stately temple of th'old god to see	
	Which speaks the ancient Macedonian greatness.	
20	But there, delighted with no object's sweetness,⁶	
	Not with their gold, nor gods' majestic dress,	
	Nor lofty city walls, with greediness	
	Into the burying vault goes Caesar down.⁷	
	There Macedonian Philip's mad-brained son,	[x. 20]⁸
25	The prosperous thief,⁹ lies buried, whom just fate	
	Slew in the world's revenge; vaults consecrate	*consecrated vaults*
	Contain those limbs, which through the world 'twere just	
	To cast abroad. But Fortune spared his dust,	
	And to that kingdom's end his fate remained.	

¹ loved] M. adopts *amaret*, 'loved' (x. 8), the preferred reading of modern editions and known by the late sixteenth century; most early modern editions, however, including F.'s, read *haberet*, 'possessed'.
² Alexandria] *Paraetoniam ... urbem*, 'the Paraetonian city' (x. 9); the port of Paraetonium was near Alexandria.
³ armed with confidence ... fasces] *securus ... | Pignore tam saevi sceleris sua signa sequutus*, 'secure thanks to that savage crime's pledge, Caesar followed his own standards [into the city]' (x. 9-10). Modern editions read *secutam*, thus making Alexandria, rather than Caesar, bound by the pledge of Pompey's murder. M.'s 'fasces', translating L.'s *signa*, '[military] standards', derives from L.'s use of *fasces* (symbols of Roman political authority) in the next line (x. 11), which he there translates as 'ensigns ... of Rome's authority' (10. 14); cf. 1. 194n. 'Following' (10. 11) is likely pronounced 'foll'wing'.
⁴ wav'ring faiths] i.e. faiths were wavering; *discordia ... | Pectora, & ancipites animos*, 'discordant breasts and wavering wills' (x. 12-13).
⁵ goes he] Omitting *intrepidus*, 'boldly' (x. 15); L.'s Caesar is undeterred by his own fear.
⁶ 10. 19-20] A couplet of eleven-syllable lines.
⁷ burying] Disyllabic.
⁸ 10. 24-56] An attack on Alexander the Great, a prototype of the global conqueror Caesar aspires to be. John Weever quotes L.'s lines and M.'s translation when discussing people's desire to visit the graves of 'eminent worthy persons', *Ancient Funerall Monuments*, pp. 40-41.
⁹ There ... thief] Quoted in Poole's *English Parnassus*, sig. Q5ᵛ, under 'Alexander'.

	380	Thomas May	

30	If e'er the world her freedom had attained,	
	He for a mock had been reserved, whose birth	
	Brought such a dire example to the earth,¹	
	So many lands to be possessed by one.	
	Scorning the narrow bounds of Macedon,²	
35	And Athens which his father had subdued,	
	Through Asian lands with human slaughter strewed,	
	Led by too forward fates he rushes on,³	
	Driving his sword through every nation.	
	Rivers unknown, Euphrates he distains	*stains, discolours*
40	With Persians' blood, Ganges with Indians';⁴	
	Th'earth's fatal mischief, lightning dire, that rent	
	All people, and a star malevolent	
	To nations.⁵ To invade the south-east sea	
	He built a fleet. Not barren Libya,⁶	
45	Water, nor heat, nor Ammon's desert sands	
	Could stop his course. Upon the western lands	
	(Following the world's devex) he meant to tread,⁷	*declivity*
	To compass both the poles and drink Nile's head.	
	But death did meet his course: that check alone	
50	Could nature give this king's ambition,⁸	
	Who to his grave the world's sole empire bore,	
	With the same envy that 'twas got before;	
	And, wanting heirs, left all he did obtain	*lacking*
	To be divided by the sword again.⁹	
55	But feared in Parthia and his Babylon	
	He died. O shame, that eastern nation	

---

¹ such a dire example to the earth] *non utile mundo | ... exemplum*, 'a profitless example [or lesson] to the world' (x. 26-27) — as no-one heeded it.

² narrow bounds] M. omits *latebras suorum*, 'his kinsmen's lurking places' (x. 28); *latebrae* is often used of robbers and outlaws.

³ too forward fates] *fatis urguentibus*, 'with the fates urging him on' (x. 30).

⁴ he distains | With Persians' blood] *miscuit*, 'he mingled' (x. 32). M. often uses this verb when blood is spilled (cf. 1. 2, 103, 356, 2. 208).

⁵ malevolent | To nations] *iniquum | Gentibus*, 'unjust/unfair to nations' (x. 33-35).

⁶ Libya] Trisyllabic.

⁷ the world's devex] The downward curve of the earth's surface. M. imports the Latin *devexa* (x. 39); his use of English 'devex' as a noun in this sense is unprecedented and unparalleled. 'Following' is again disyllabic; cf. 10. 12n.

⁸ that check ... ambition] *Hunc potuit finem vesano ponere regi*, '[nature] could place only this limit on the maddened king' (x. 42). 'Ambition' (here four syllables, as a line-ending) is a keynote of M.'s vocabulary: see 1. 95n.

⁹ left all ... again] *lacerandas praebuit urbes*, 'he proffered the cities to be torn apart' (x. 45).

>   Then trembled at the Macedonian spear
>   Far more than now the Roman pile they fear!
>   Though all the north, the west and south be ours,[1]
> 60 In th'east the Parthian king contemns our powers.[2]   *despises*
>   That which to Crassus proved a fatal place
>   A secure province to small Pella was.[3]
>   Now the young king come from Pelusium   [x. 53][4]
>   Had pacified the people's wrath, in whom,
> 65 As hostage of his peace in Egypt's court,
>   Caesar was safe; when lo, from Pharos' port,
>   Bribing the keeper to unchain the same,
>   In a small galley Cleopatra came,
>   Unknown to Caesar entering the house:[5]
> 70 The stain of Egypt, Rome's pernicious[6]
>   Fury, unchaste to Italy's disgrace;
>   As much as Helena's bewitching face
>   Fatal to Troy and her own Greeks did prove,
>   As much Rome's broils did Cleopatra move.[7]
> 75 Our Capitol she with her sistrum scared,
>   With Egypt's base effeminate rout prepared   *crowd*

[1] the north, the west and south] *sub Arcton | ... Zephyrique domos, terrasque ... | Flagrantis post terga Noti*, 'beneath the Great Bear ... the dwellings of the west wind and the lands behind the burning South wind' (x. 48-50).

[2] the Parthian ... powers] *cedemus in ortus | Arsacidum domino*, 'we will yield in the east to the master of the Arsacids' (x. 50-51); cf. 8. 250.

[3] fatal place] *non felix*, 'not fortunate' (x. 51). Pella] The original capital of Macedon's kings.

[4] 10. 63-200] Cleopatra's seduction of Caesar, followed by a lavish banquet. L.'s antagonistic portrait was a source for many early modern representations of Cleopatra. M.'s *The Tragedy of Cleopatra*, though modelled on L. in other respects, draws on Dio and Plutarch to fashion a more balanced picture, but book two of M.'s *Continuation*, sigs C4^r-8^v, appropriates details from L.'s account in a hostile retelling of the later stages of Caesar and Cleopatra's affair. James Ussher quotes L. (x. 54-60) and May (10. 63-71) in his *Annals of the World*, p. 656.

[5] the house] *Emathiis tectis*, 'Emathian [i.e. Macedonian] house' (x. 58).

[6] The stain of Egypt] *dedecus Aegypti*, 'the shame of Egypt' (x. 59); cf. Samuel Daniel, 'A Letter from Octavia to Marcus Antonius', in *The poeticall essayes* (London: P. Short for Simon Waterson, 1599), sig. B2^r: 'that incestious Queene | The staine of *Aegypt*, and the shame of *Rome*'.

[7] As much as ... move] *quantum inpulit Argos, | Iliacasque domos facie Spartana nocenti, | Hesperios auxit tantum Cleopatra furores*, 'As much as Helen moved Argos and the Trojan homes with her harmful Spartan face, so much did Cleopatra increase Italian furies' (x. 60-62). L.'s lines appear on the title-page of M.'s *The Tragedy of Cleopatra*. They were also paraphrased in Anon., *The Tragedie of Caesar and Pompey*, sig. E4^r, which like M.'s *Continuation* (1630), sig. C4^v, uses the term 'bewitch' to describe Cleopatra's seductive effect.

To seize Rome's eagles, and a triumph get
O'er captived Caesar,[1] when at Leucas' fleet[2]
It doubtful stood whether the world that day
80 A woman, and not Roman should obey.
Her pride's first spring that impious night had been,   *origin*
That with our chiefs mixed that incestuous queen.
Who would not pardon Antony's mad love,
When Caesar's flinty breast desires could move
85 In midst of war, when heat of fight raged most,[3]
And in a court haunted by Pompey's ghost?
Imbrued with blood from dire Pharsalia's field,
Could he unto adult'rous Venus yield?[4]
And mix with warlike cares (O shameless head)
90 A bastard issue and unlawful bed,
Forgetting Pompey, to beget a brother
To thee, fair Julia, on a strumpet mother.[5]
Suff'ring the forces of his scattered foes
To join in Afric, basely he bestows   *Africa*
95 Time in Egyptian love, a conqueror
Not for himself but to bestow on her;[6]
Whom, trusting to her beauty, without tears,
Though gesture sad, with loose, as if rent hairs,
Dressed in a beauteous and becoming woe[7]
100 Did Cleopatra meet, bespeaking so:
'If, mighty Caesar, nobleness there be,   [x. 85]

---

[1] Our Capitol ... captived Caesar] 10. 75–78 (x. 63–67) are paraphrased in M.'s *Cleopatra*, sig. C3ᵛ. Cleopatra's 'sistrum' (10. 75) is an Egyptian rattle, associated by many Roman writers with Cleopatra's oriental witchcraft (cf. 8. 970); 'effeminate' translates *imbelli*, 'unwarlike' (x. 64). 'Effeminate' (10. 76) is pronounced 'effem'nate'.

[2] Leucas' fleet] *Leucadioque ... sub gurgite*, 'in the Leucadian gulf' (x. 66) i.e. the battle of Actium, where Octavius Caesar defeated Antony and Cleopatra in 31 BC.

[3] could move ... raged most] In L. Caesar's breast *hauserit*, 'has drunk', the fire of love *in media rabie medioque furore*, 'in the midst of his frenzy and midst of his madness' (x. 71–72).

[4] unto adult'rous Venus yield] i.e. have extra-marital sex; L.'s Caesar is explicitly *adulter*, 'the adulterer' (x. 74).

[5] A bastard issue ... strumpet mother] Caesarion, the love-child of Caesar and Cleopatra. 'Strumpet mother' translates *Obscaena ... matre*, 'obscene mother' (x. 78); cf. 3. 23.

[6] but to bestow on her] i.e. bestow Egypt (*Pharon*, 'Pharos', x. 81) on Cleopatra.

[7] with loose ... woe] *simulatum comta dolorem | Quem decuit, veluti laceros dispersa capillos*, 'adorned in the pretended grief which was seemly, her hair in disarray, as if torn' (x. 83–85). *Dolorem | Quem decuit*, 'grief which was seemly', is Grotius's conjecture, replacing *quam decuit*, 'which became her'; modern editions read *qua decuit*, 'as far as was becoming'. 'Beauteous' is disyllabic. Poole includes M.'s 'beauteous and becoming woe' in his *English Parnassus*, p. 378.

       Egyptian Lagus' royal issue I,
       Deposed and banished from my father's state,
       If thy great hand restore my former fate,[1]
105   Kneel at thy feet a queen. Unto our nation
       Thou dost appear a gracious constellation.[2]
       I am not the first woman that hath swayed
       The Pharian sceptre:[3] Egypt has obeyed
       A queen, not sex excepted. I desire
110   Thee read the will of my deceasèd sire,
       Who left me there a partner to enjoy
       My brother's crown and marriage bed.[4] The boy
       (I know) would love his sister, were he free:
       But all his power, will, and affections be
115   Under Photinus' girdle.[5] To obtain
       The crown I beg not. Caesar, from this stain
       Free thou our house: command the king to be
       A king, and free from servants' tyranny.[6]
       Shall slaves so proud of Pompey's slaughter be,[7]
120   Threat'ning the same (which fates avert) to thee?
       Caesar, 'tis shame enough to th'earth and thee,
       His death Photinus' gift and guilt should be.'
         Her suit in Caesar's ears had found small grace,[8]   [x. 104]
       But beauty pleads and that incestuous face

---

[1] If ... fate] Reading *si*, 'if'; modern editions print *ni*, 'unless' (x. 88).

[2] 10. 105–06] Conceivably an alexandrine couplet, if '-ion' is disyllabic, as it usually is in M.'s line-endings; otherwise a rare feminine rhyme.

[3] hath swayed ... sceptre] *Non urbes prima tenebo* | *Femina Niliacas*, 'Nor will I be first to hold the cities of the Nile' (x. 91). M. uses 'sway' in the sense of 'to wield as an emblem of sovereignty or authority' (*OED*, s.v. 8).

[4] crown and marriage bed] *iura communia regni,* | *Et thalami*, 'shared right of rule and of the marriage-bed' (x. 93–94); modern editions read *thalamos*, separating the marriage bed from the rights of rule.

[5] But all his ... girdle] *habet sub iure Pothini* | *Affectus, ensesque suos*, 'but he holds his feelings and his swords [i.e. soldiery] at Pothinus' command' (x. 95–96); cf. *OED*, 'girdle', s.v. 1.c: '(to have, hold) under one's girdle: in subjection, under one's control', with overtones of effeminacy.

[6] To obtain ... tyranny] *nil ipsa paterni* | *Iuris habere peto: culpa, tantoque pudore* | *Solve domum: remove funesta satellitis arma* | *Et regem regnare iube*, 'I myself seek no part of my father's authority: free this house from such guilt and shame, remove the pernicious weapons of a henchman, and order the king to reign' (x. 96–98).

[7] Shall slaves so proud] *quantosne tumores* | *Mente gerit famulus*, 'what swellings of pride one house-slave bears in his mind' (x. 99–100).

[8] Her suit ... small grace] *Nequicquam duras temptasset Caesaris aures*, 'fruitlessly had she assailed the tough ears of Caesar' (x. 104); M.'s 'suit' and 'pleads' (10. 124) accentuate the legal analogy.

125	Prevails; the pleasures of a wanton bed	
	Corrupt the judge. The king had purchasèd	
	His peace with weighty sums of gold, which done,[1]	
	With sumptuous feasts this glad accord they crown.[2]	
	Her riot forth in highest pomp (not yet	*debauchery*
130	Transferred to Rome) did Cleopatra set.[3]	
	The house excelled those temples which men build	
	In wicked'st times: the high-arched rooves were filled	
	With wealth, high tresses golden tables bore,[4]	
	Nor did carved marble only cover o'er	
135	The house; alone th'unmixed Achates stood,[5]	
	And pillars of red marble;[6] their feet trod	
	On pavements of rich onyx; pillars there	
	Not covered with Egyptian eben were;[7]	*ebony*
	Eben was timber there, and that rich wood	
140	Not to adorn but prop the palace stood.	
	The rooms with ivory glistered,[8] and each door	
	Inlaid with Indian shells, embellished o'er	
	With choicest emeralds; the beds all shone	
	With richest gems and yellow jasper stone;[9]	
145	Coverlids rich, some purple dyed in grain,	*coverlets; fast-dyed*
	Whose tincture was not from one cauldron ta'en,	
	Part wove of glittering gold, part scarlet dye,	
	As is th'Egyptian use of tapestry.[10]	

[1] The king ... sums of gold] *Pax ubi ducis parta, donisque ingentibus emta est*, 'when the leader's peace was made, and bought with great gifts' (x. 107). M. follows F. in interpreting the leader as Ptolemy; modern interpreters prefer Caesar.

[2] With sumptuous ... crown] *Excepere epulae ... gaudia*, 'feasts maintained the joy' (x. 108).

[3] Her riot ... set] Luxury on the Egyptian scale was still unknown in Rome at this date, but not, by implication, in L.'s time: see 1. 175 ff. On 'riot', see 1. 179n.

[4] high tresses] See Textual Notes.

[5] unmixed Achates stood] Agate, a semi-precious crystalline rock (M. prefers the Latin word); 'unmixed', translating *non segnis*, 'not lazy', because it supports itself (x. 115), is inspired by F.'s gloss.

[6] red marble] *purpureus lapis*, 'purple stone' (x. 116).

[7] pillars ... were] *Hebenus Mareotica vastos | Non operit postes*, 'Egyptian ebony did not cover the vast door-posts' (x. 117–18), i.e. was not a purely cosmetic finish.

[8] ivory] Pronounced 'iv'ry'.

[9] the beds all shone ... stone] Reading *Fulget gemma toris, & Iaspide fulva supellex: | Strata micant* (x. 122–23). The meaning of *supellex* is ambiguous (possible translations include 'furniture', 'bedspread', 'tableware'). Modern editors now assume a missing line, printing *fulva supellex | <Stat mensas onerans, variaque triclinia veste> | Strata micant*, after Housman.

[10] As is ... tapestry] *Vt mos est Phariis miscendi licia telis*, 'As is the custom of mingling

	The servitors stood by, and waiting pages,[1]	
150	Some different in complexions, some in ages;	
	Some of black Libyan hue, some golden hairs,	
	That Caesar yields in all his German wars	*concedes*
	He ne'er had seen so bright a yellow hair.[2]	
	Some stiff-curled locks on sun-burnt foreheads wear.	
155	Besides th'unhappy strength-robbed company,	
	The eunuched youths,[3] near these were standing by	
	Youths of a stronger age, yet those so young	
	Scarce any down dark'ning their cheeks was sprung.	
	Down sat the princes, and the higher power,	[x. 136]
160	Caesar: her hurtful face all painted o'er	
	Sat Cleopatra, not content alone	
	T'enjoy her brother's bed nor Egypt's crown,	
	Laden with pearls; the Red Sea's spoilèd store	
	On her rich hair and wearied neck she wore.[4]	
165	Her snowy breasts their whiteness did display	
	Thorough the thin Sidonian tiffany[5]	*through; transparent silk*
	Wrought and extended by the curious hand	
	Of Egypt's workmen.[6] Citron tables stand	
	On ivory trestles,[7] such as Caesar's eyes	
170	Saw not when he king Juba did surprise.[8]	
	O blind ambitious madness, to declare	
	Your wealth to him that makes a civil war,	
	And tempt an armèd guest! For though that he	

threads in Egyptian looms' (x. 126).
[1] The servitors ... pages] *tum famulae numerus turbae, populusque minister*, 'then the multitude of the house-slave crowd, and the mass of attendants' (x. 127).
[2] yellow hair] *rutilas ... comas*, 'red hair' (x. 131); possibly based on F.'s observation that Germans have blonde not red hair.
[3] strength-robbed ... youths] *ferro mollita iuventus | Atque execta virum*, 'youth softened by the blade and emasculated' (x. 133-34).
[4] On ... wearied neck she wore] Condensing L.'s description of her head-dress, *cultuque laborat*, 'labours under her decoration' (x. 140).
[5] Her snowy breasts ... Sidonian tiffany] *Candida Sidonio perlucent pectora filo*, 'her white breasts shone through Sidonian thread' (x. 141).
[6] Wrought ... workmen] Simplifying *Quod Nilotis acus compressum pectine Serum | Solvit et extenso laxavit stamina velo*, 'thread/fabric which, compressed by the comb of the Seres [a region in Africa], the Egyptian needle has unpicked, and loosened the threads by stretching the fabric' (x. 142-43). 'Curious' here means 'expert, ingenious' (*OED*, s.v. †2.4).
[7] Citron ... trestles] *Dentibus hic niveis, sectos Atlantide silva | Imposuere orbes*, 'here on snowy teeth they placed circles cut from the woods of Atlas' (x. 144-45), i.e. round tables using tusks as legs.
[8] Juba did surprise] L. means the capture of Juba (*capto*, x. 146), as described in book three of M.'s *Continuation*.

Sought not for wealth by war's impiety
175 And the world's wreck,[1] suppose our chiefs of old
Were there, composed of that poor age's mould,
Fabricii, Curii grave, or that plain man
That consul from th'Etrurian ploughs was ta'en,
Were sitting at those tables, whom to Rome
180 With such a triumph he would wish to come.[2]
    In golden plate they fill their feasting boards   [x. 155]
With what the air, the earth or Nile affords,
What luxury with vain ambition had
Sought through the world, and not as hunger bade;
185 Beasts, fowls, the gods of Egypt are devoured.[3]
From crystal ewers is Nile's water poured
Upon their hands. Studded with gems that shine,
Their bowls contain no Mareotic wine,
But strong and sparkling wines of Meroë,
190 To whom few years give full maturity.
With fragrant nard and never-fading rose   *spikenard (aromatic plant)*
Their heads are crowned, their hair anointed flows
With sweetest cinnamon that has not spent
His savour in the air nor lost his scent
195 In foreign climes; and fresh amomum brought   *cardamom*
From harvests near at hand. There Caesar's taught
The riches of the spoilèd world to take,
And is ashamed that he a war did make
With his poor son-in-law, desiring now
200 Some quarrel would 'twixt him and Egypt grow.
When wine and cates had tired their glutted pleasure,   [x. 172][4] *dainties*
Caesar begins with long discourse to measure
The hours of night, bespeaking gently thus
The linen-vested grave Achoreus:

---

[1] For though that he | Sought not] *non sit licet ille*, 'Even if he were not that man [i.e. Caesar] who ...' (x. 149).

[2] suppose our chiefs ... to come] M.'s syntax is unnecessarily difficult: the meaning is that even Rome's most famously frugal families would want to bring back Egypt's spoils in triumph to Rome. 'That plain man' ('plain' translating *sordidus*, 'dirty', x. 153) probably means the famously virtuous Q. Cincinnatus (*c.* 519–*c.* 430 BC), who returned to his small farm after saving Rome. The generalising 'Fabricii' and 'Curii' (10. 177) are trisyllabic and disyllabic respectively; cf. 3. 177, 1. 186, 6. 897, 7. 407.

[3] gods ... are devoured] *Aegypti posuere deos*, '[they] put the gods of Egypt on the table' (x. 158).

[4] 10. 201–380] Caesar prompts Achoreus to speak of the origins of the Nile, one of the great natural-philosophical mysteries of the ancient world.

205	'Old man devoted to religion,	
	And (which thine age confirms) despised by none	
	Of all the gods, to longing ears relate	
	Egypt's original, her site and state,	*origin*
	Worship of gods, and what doth ere remain[1]	*still*
210	In your old temples charactered, explain.	*engraved*
	The gods that would be known, to us unfold.	
	If your forefathers their religion told	
	Th'Athenian Plato once, when had you e'er	
	A guest more worthy or more fit to hear?[2]	
215	Rumour of Pompey drew our march thus far	
	And fame of you, for still in midst of war	
	I leisure had of heaven and gods to hear	
	And the stars' course; nor shall Eudoxus' year	
	Excel my consulship.[3] But though so much	
220	My virtue be, my love of truth be such,	
	There's nought I more desire to know at all	
	Than Nile's hid head and strange original,	
	So many years unknown. Grant but to me	
	A certain hope the head of Nile to see,	
225	I'll leave off civil war.' Caesar had done,	
	When thus divine Achoreus begun:[4]	
	'Let it be lawful, Caesar, to unfold	[x. 194]
	Our great forefathers' secrets hid of old	
	From the lay people.[5] Let whoe'er suppose	
230	It piety to keep these wonders close:	*hidden*
	I think the gods are pleased to be made known,[6]	
	And have their sacred laws to people shown.	
	Planets which cross and slack the tenth sphere's course,[7]	*hold back*

---

[1] and state, | Worship of gods] *vulgique ... mores, | Et ritas, formasque Deum*, 'the manners of her common people and the rites and shapes of her gods' (x. 178–79).

[2] Plato ... to hear?] The Greek philosopher (fifth century BC) is supposed to have visited Egypt.

[3] Eudoxus' year ... consulship] Eudoxus of Cnidus (fourth century BC) supposedly brought back the Egyptian calendar and calculation of the year to Greece. M. assumes *meus annus*, 'my year' (x. 187), means the length of Caesar's consulship: in fact, as most commentaries explained, it refers to Caesar's revision of the Roman (now 'Julian') calendar.

[4] divine Achoreus begun] *sacer*, 'sacred' (x. 193); M. may allude to the English noun 'divine' (clergyman).

[5] lay people] *populis ... profanis*, 'the profane masses' (x. 195).

[6] to be made known] Omitting *hoc opus* (x. 198): in L., the gods welcome the disclosing of 'this work' (the Nile's source), not themselves.

[7] Planets ... course] *Sideribus, quae sola fugam moderantur Olympi, | Occuruntque polo*, 'the stars which alone regulate the flight of the heavens and move in opposition to the sky'

       Had from the world's first law their different powers.
235 The Sun divides the years, makes nights and days,
       Dims other stars with his resplendent rays,[1]
       And their wild courses moderates; the tides
       Of Thetis, Phoebe's growth and waning, guides.   *the moon's*
       Saturn cold ice and frozen zones obtains,
240 Mars o'er the winds and wingèd lightning reigns,[2]
       Quiet, well-tempered air doth Jove possess,
       The seeds of all things Venus cherishes,[3]
       Cyllenius rules o'er waters which are great —   *Mercury*
       He, when he enters where the Dog Star's heat   *Sirius*
245 And burning fire's displayed, there where the sign
       Of Cancer hot doth with the Lion join,   *Leo*
       And where the Zodiac holds his Capricorn
       And Cancer, under which Nile's head is borne —
       O'er which when Mercury's proud fires do stand,[4]
250 And in a line direct (as by command
       Of Phoebe the obeying ocean grows)   *the moon*
       So from his opened fountain Nilus flows,
       Nor ebbs again 'til night have from the sun
       Those hours recovered which the summer won.
255   Vain was the old opinion, that Nile's flow   [x. 219]
       Was caused or helped by Ethiopian snow.[5]
       For on those hills cold Boreas never blows,   *the north wind*
       As there the natives' sun-burnt visage shows,
       And moist hot southern winds. Besides, the head
260 Of every stream that from thawed ice is bred,
       Swells then when first the spring dissolves the snows.
       But Nile before the dog-days never flows,[6]
       Nor is confined within his banks again
       'Til the autumnal equinoctian:[7]   *equinox*

(x. 199–200); M. follows F.'s paraphrase.

[1] Dims other stars ... rays] *ire vetat*, '[the sun] forbids [the stars] to move' (x. 203); M.'s change of idiom may reflect F.'s observation (derived from Joseph Scaliger's commentary on Manilius) that L.'s astronomical claim is false.

[2] wingèd lightning] M.'s epithet: lit. *incerta*, 'unpredictable' (x. 206).

[3] Jove ... Venus cherishes] Referring to the planets; M.'s 'cherishes', translating *Possidet*, 'possesses' (x. 209), alludes to Venus as love goddess.

[4] Mercury's proud fires] A change of idiom from L.'s *dominus ... aquarum*, 'the master of waters' (x. 215).

[5] Ethiopian] Four syllables ('Eth-i-o-pian'); 'Boreas' in the next line is disyllabic.

[6] the dog-days] *Canis radios*, 'the sun-beams of Sirius' (x. 226), which rises in July.

[7] autumnal equinoctian] *ante parem nocti Libra sub iudice Phoebum*, 'before the sun

265	Thence 'tis he knows no laws of other streams,	*this is why*
	Nor swells in winter, when Sol's scorching beams	*the sun's*
	Are far remote, his waters want their end.	= *and his waters*
	But Nile comes forth in summer time to lend	
	A cooler temper to the swelt'ring air	
270	Under the torrid zone; lest fire impair	
	The earth, unto her succour Nilus draws	
	And swells against the Lion's burning jaws.	*Leo's*
	And when hot Cancer his Syene burns,	
	Unto her aid implorèd Nilus turns,	
275	Nor 'til the sun to autumn do descend	
	And that hot Meroë her shades extend,	
	Doth he restore again the drownèd field.	
	Who can the causes of this flowing yield?	
	Even so our mother nature hath decreed	
280	That Nile should flow, and so the world hath need.	
	As vainly doth antiquity declare	[x. 239]
	The west winds cause of these increases are,	
	Which keep their seasons strictly, and long stay	
	And bear within the air continued sway.	
285	These from the western parts all clouds exile	
	Beyond the south, and hang them over Nile,	
	Or else their blasts the river's current meet,	
	And will not let it to the ocean get;	
	Prevented so from falling to the main,	*sea*
290	The stream swells back and overflows the plain.	
	Some through the caverns of earth's hollow womb[1]	[x. 247]
	In secret channels think these waters come,	
	Attracted to th'equator from the cold	
	North clime, when Sol his Meroë doth hold;	
295	The scorchèd earth attracting water, thither	
	Ganges and Padus flow unseen together:	*Po*
	Venting all rivers at one fountain so	
	Within one channel Nilus cannot go.	
	From th'ocean swelling, which begirts about	[x. 255]
300	All lands, some think increasèd Nile breaks out;	
	The waters lose, ere they so far have ran,	

is equal with night under the sign of Libra' (x. 227); M. translates F.'s gloss *aequinoctium autumnale*.

[1] earth's hollow womb] *magnosque cavae conpagis hiatus*, 'great gaps in [earth's] hollow frame' (x. 248).

Their saltness quite. Besides, the ocean
Is the stars' food, we think, which Phoebus draws   *the sun*
When he possesseth fiery Cancer's claws;
305 More than the air digests, attracted so,
Falls back by night and causes Nilus' flow.
   I think if I may judge so great a case,   [x. 262]
Some waters since the world created was
In after ages from some broken vein
310 Of earth have grown; some god did then ordain,
When he created all the world, whose tides
By certain laws the great Creator guides.
   Caesar's desire to know our Nilus' spring   [x. 268]
Possessed th'Egyptian, Persian, Grecian king.¹
315 No age but strived to future time to teach
This skill; none yet his hidden nature reach.
Philip's great son, Memphis' most honoured king,
Sent to th'earth's utmost bounds to find Nile's spring
Choice Ethiops: they trod the sunburnt ground   *selected*
320 Of the hot zone, and there warm Nilus found.
The farthest west our great Sesostris saw,
Whilst captive kings did his proud chariot draw,²
Yet there your Rhodanus and Padus spied
Before our Nile's hid fountain he descried.
325 The mad Cambyses to the eastern lands
And long-lived people came:³ his famished bands
Quite spent, and with each other's⁽ᵃ⁾ slaughter fed,
Returned thou, Nile, yet undiscoverèd.
No tale dares mention thine original:
330 Th'art sought wherever seen. No land at all
Can boast that Nile is hers. Yet I'll reveal,
As far as that same god that doth conceal
Thy spring inspires me. From th'Antarctic pole
Under hot Cancer do thy surges roll

---

¹ th'Egyptian ... king] Other famous seekers of the source of the Nile: Sesostris, king of Egypt; Cambyses, king of Persia; and Alexander the Great.
² Whilst captive ... draw] *et Pharios currus regum cervicibus egit*, 'and drove his Egyptian chariots over the necks of kings' (x. 276). M. possibly recalls a famous scene from Marlowe's 2 *Tamburlaine*, IV. 3, which has kings pulling the protagonist's chariot, as well as imagery in *Edward II* (I. 1. 174) and *The Massacre of Paris* (21. 51–53) (all in *The Complete Works*, ed. by Bowers).
³ mad Cambyses ... came] Cambyses was *vesanus*, 'insane' (x. 279), for marching into the desert: the 'long-lived' people are the Macrobii, an Ethiopian people who supposedly lived for 120 years.

335 Directly north, winding to east and west.
Sometimes th'Arabians, sometimes Libyans blessed
With fruitfulness thou mak'st. The Seres spy[1]
Thee first and seek thee too, thy channel by
The Ethiopians as a stranger flows,[2]
340 And the world knows not to what land it owes
Thy sacred head, which Nature hid from all,[3]
Lest any land should see thee, Nilus, small.
She turned away thy spring and did desire [4]
No land should know it, but all lands admire.[5]
345 Thou in the summer solstice art o'erflown,
Bringing with thee a winter of thine own,
When winter is not ours; nature alone
Suffers thy streams to both the poles to run.[6]
Not there thy mouth, not here thy spring is found.
350 Thy parted channel doth encompass round
Meroë, fruitful to black husbandmen
And rich in eben wood whose leaves though green[7]   *ebony*
Can with no shade assuage the summer's heat,
Under the Lion so directly set.[8]   *Leo*
355 From thence thy current with no water's loss
O'er the hot zone and barren deserts goes,
Sometimes collected in one channel going,
Sometimes dispersed and yielding banks o'erflowing.
His parted arms again collected slide
360 In one slow stream where Philas doth divide
Arabia from Egypt.[9] O'er the sand,
Where the Red Sea by one small neck of land
From ours is kept, thou, Nile, dost gently flow.
O, who would think thou e'er so rough couldst grow
365 That sees thee gentle here? But when thy way

---

[1] The Seres] An African people.
[2] as a stranger flows] *feris alieno gurgite campos*, 'you [the Nile] strike the plains with a foreign flood' (x. 293).
[3] sacred head] *Arcanum ... caput*, 'secret head/source' (x. 295).
[4] spring...] *sinus*, 'folds, coils' (x. 297).
[5] land ... lands] Translating *populis* and *gentes*, 'peoples, races' (x. 297-98).
[6] nature alone...] M.'s interpolation; L. (x. 300-01) doesn't specify who is responsible.
[7] And rich ... though green] *Laeta comis hebeni, ... arbore multa | Frondeat*, 'happy in its ebony fronds, it is in leaf with many a tree' (x. 304-05).
[8] Under the Lion ... set] *Linea tam rectum mundi ferit illa Leonem*, 'the line of the world [i.e. the equator] strikes Leo so upright' (x. 306); M. follows F.'s gloss.
[9] Arabia] Four syllables.

	Steep cataracts and craggy rocks would stay,	
	Thy never-curbèd waves with scorn despise	
	Those petty lets, and foaming lave the skies;	*obstacles; wash*
	Thy waters sound; with noise the neighb'ring hills	
370	Thy conquering stream with froth grown hoary fills.	
	Hence he with fury first assaults that isle,	
	Which our forefathers did Abatos style,	
	And those near rocks which they were pleased to call	
	The river's veins, because they first of all	
375	His swelling growth did show. Hence nature did	
	His straggling waves within high mountains hide,	
	Which part thee, Nile, from Afric; betwixt those	*Africa*
	As in a vale thy pent-up water flows.	
	At Memphis first thou run'st in fields and plains,	
380	Where thy proud stream all banks and bounds disdains.'	
	Thus they secure, as if in peace, a part	[x. 332]¹
	Of night discoursed. But base Photinus' heart,²	
	Once stained with sacred blood, could ne'er be free	
	From horrid thoughts.³ Since Pompey's murder he	
385	Counts nought a crime: great Pompey's Manes bide	*spirit*
	Within his breast, and vengeful Furies guide	
	His thoughts to monsters new, hoping to stain	*unnatural acts*
	Base hands with Caesar's blood which fates ordain	
	Great senators shall shed.⁴ Fate to a slave	
390	That day almost the Senate's vengeance gave,	
	The mulct of civil war. O gods defend,	*penalty; prevent*
	Let none that life, in Brutus' absence, end.⁵	
	Shall th'execution of Rome's tyrant be	
	Base Egypt's crime, and that example die?⁶	
395	Bold man, he makes attempt against fate's course,	
	Nor at close murder aims.⁷ By open force	

---

¹ 10. 381–500] Photinus, who counselled Pompey's murder, now urges his accomplice Achillas to kill Caesar.
² But base Photinus' heart] *vesana Pothini | Mens*, 'the insane mind of Pothinus' (x. 333); for 'base' see 8. 562n.
³ horrid thoughts] *scelerum motu*, 'motion to wickedness' (x. 335).
⁴ Great senators] *victos Patres*, 'defeated senators' (x. 339).
⁵ O gods defend ... end] *procul hoc avertite, fata, | Crimen, ut haec Bruto cervix absente secetur*, 'Ward this crime far off, fates, that in Brutus' absence this [Caesar's] neck be sliced' (x. 341–42).
⁶ Shall ... die?] Not a question in L: the sense is that if this death happens in Egypt, it loses its exemplary function.
⁷ Nor at close murder aims] *occultae caedem committere fraudi*, '[nor aims] to entrust the

	A most unconquered captain he assaults:	
	So much are minds emboldened by their faults.¹	
	He durst the death of Caesar now command,	*dares*
400	As Pompey's once,² and by a faithful hand	
	To stern Achillas this dire message send,³	
	Who shared with him in murdered Pompey's end,	
	Whom the weak king against himself and all	
	Trusts with a strength, his force's general.⁴	
405	'Thou on thy downy bed securely snort,⁵	[x. 354] *snore*
	Whilst Cleopatra hath surprised the court.	*attacked*
	Pharos is not betrayed, but given away.	
	Haste thou (though all alone) this match to stay?⁶	
	Th'incestuous sister shall her brother wed;⁷	
410	Caesar already has enjoyed her bed;⁸	
	'Twixt those two husbands Egypt is her own,	
	And Rome her hire for prostitution.⁹	*payment*
	Have Cleopatra's sorceries beguiled	
	Old Caesar's breast, and shall we trust a child?¹⁰	
415	Who, if one night incestuously embraced,	
	The beastly pleasures of her bed he taste	

slaughter to hidden deception' (x. 345).
¹ So much ... faults.] In L., 10. 398 (= x. 347) begins a new sentence, *Tantum animi delicta dabant, ut* ..., '[Pothinus'] crimes gave him such confidence that...'; M. transforms this into a gnomic observation.
² He durst ... once] *colla ferire | Caesaris, & socerum iungi tibi, Magne, iuberet*, 'he gave the order to strike Caesar's neck, and that his father-in-law be joined to you, Magnus' (x. 347–48).
³ dire message send] *haec dicta*, 'these words' (x. 349). M. adds the epithet 'stern' to Achillas; cf. 10. Arg. 9.
⁴ Whom ... general] *Quem puer imbellis cunctis praefecerat armis, | Et dederat ferrum, nullo sibi iure retento, | In cunctos, seque simul*, 'Whom the unwarlike boy had put in charge of all his forces, and keeping no authority for himself, had granted the sword against everyone and himself alike' (x. 351–53).
⁵ Thou ... snort] *Tu mollibus ... | ... incumbe toris, & pingues exige somnos*, 'you lie in your soft bed and enjoy rich slumber' (x. 353–54).
⁶ Haste thou ... to stay?] *Cessas accurrere solus | Ad dominae thalamos?*, 'Do you alone delay speeding to your mistress' bedroom?' (x. 356–57).
⁷ Th'incestuous sister] 'incestuous' (pronounced with three syllables) translates *impia*, 'impious' (x. 357), which perhaps means her relationship to Caesar not Ptolemy.
⁸ Caesar ... bed] *Nam Latio iam nupta duci est*, 'for she is already bride to the Latian general' (x. 358).
⁹ prostitution] Following M.'s usual practice, the final '-ion' here is disyllabic.
¹⁰ Have Cleopatra's ... a child?] *Expugnare senem potuit Cleopatra venenis. | Crede, miser, puero*, 'Cleopatra could conquer the old man with her poisons. Trust a boy, wretch' (x. 360–61). 'Incestuously' has four syllables here, the middle 'uous' treated as one syllable.

Clothed with the name of marriage,[1] 'twixt each kiss
He gives my head and thine; the gibbet is
Our fortune if he find his sister sweet.[2]
420 Hope we no aid from any side to meet:
The king's her husband, her adulterer
Caesar; and we (I grant), both guilty are
In Cleopatra's sight,[3] where 'twill appear
Crime great enough that we are chaste from her.[4]
425 Now by that crime which we together did,
And lost,[5] and by the league we ratified
In Pompey's blood, I pray be speedy here:
Fill on the sudden all with war and fear.
Let blood break off the marriage night and kill
430 Our cruel queen, whose arms soe'er she fill
In bed tonight.[6] Nor fear we Caesar's fate:
That which advanced him to this height of state,[7]
The fall of Pompey, was our glory too.
Behold the shore, and learn what we can do,
435 Our mischief's hope; behold the bloodied wave,
And in the dust great Pompey's little grave
Scarce covering all his limbs.[8] He whom we fear
Was but his peer. But we ignoble are
In blood: all one; we stir no foreign state   'tis all one
440 Nor king to aid, but our own prosperous fate
To mischief bring.[9] And still into our hands

---

[1] The beastly pleasures .... marriage] *Hauserit obscoenum titulo pietatis amorem*, 'he has drunk obscene love, under the name of piety' (x. 363).

[2] the gibbet ... sweet] *crucibus, flammisque luemus, | Si formosa soror*, 'We pay by crucifixion and burning, if he finds his sister shapely' (x. 365–66); cf. 7. 344–46.

[3] In Cleopatra's sight] *tam saeva iudice*, 'before so savage a judge' (x. 368).

[4] where ... chaste from her] *Quem non e nobis credit Cleopatra nocentem | A quo casta fuit?*, 'Which of us won't she believe guilty, by whom she was chaste [i.e. who failed to have sex with her]?' (x. 369–70).

[5] And lost] i.e. failed to profit from (*Perdidimus*, x. 371).

[6] and kill ... tonight] L.'s Pothinus urges them to slaughter Cleopatra *together with* whatever man is in bed with her (x. 374–75).

[7] Caesar's fate ... height of state] *Hesperii Fortuna ducis. Quae sustulit illum, | Imposuitque orbi*, 'the fortune of the Western general, which raised him up and imposed him on the world' (x. 376–77).

[8] And in the dust ... grave] In L., Pompey's grave is made *out of* dust (x. 380).

[9] But we ignoble ... mischief bring] *Non sanguine clari: | Quid refert? nec opes populorum, ac regna movemus, | Ad scelus ingentis fati sumus*, 'We are not of distinguished blood: what does it matter? Nor do we mobilise the wealth of peoples, or kingdoms, but we have a mighty destiny when it comes to crime' (x. 383).

Fortune delivers them: see, ready stands
Another nobler sacrifice than he;
This second blood appeases Italy.
445 The blood of Caesar will those stains remove
Which Pompey's murder stuck,¹ and make Rome love
Those hands she once thought guilty. Fear not then
His fame and strength: he's but a private man,²
His army absent. This one night shall end
450 The civil war, and to whole nations send
A sacrifice t'appease their ghosts below
And pay the world that head which fates do owe.³
Go confidently then 'gainst Caesar's throat:
For Ptolemy let Egypt's soldiers do't,
455 The Romans for themselves. But stay not thou:
He's high with wine and fit for Venus now.
Do but attempt, the gods on thee bestow
Th'effect of Brutus' and grave Cato's vow.'⁴
Achillas, prone to follow such advice, [x. 398]
460 Draws out his army straight in secret wise.
Without loud signals given, or trumpet's noise,
Their armèd strength he suddenly employs.
The greatest part were Roman soldiers there,
But so degenerate and ⁽ᵇ⁾changed they were
465 With foreign discipline that, void of shame,⁵
Under a barb'rous slave's command they came,
Who should disdain to serve proud Egypt's king.⁶
No faith nor piety those hirelings bring
That follow camps: where greatest pay is had,
470 There's greatest right; for money they invade,
Not for their own just quarrel, Caesar's throat.

---

¹ The blood of Caesar] *iugulus ... Caesaris haustus*, 'the drained throat of Caesar' (x. 387).
² but a private man] *miles*, '[a mere] soldier' (x. 391); M. (misleadingly) alludes to Caesar's claimed right to military authority.
³ A sacrifice ... do owe] *Inferiasque dabit populis, & mittet ad umbras | Quod debetur adhuc mundo, caput*, '[this night] will bestow a sacrifice on the peoples, and send to the shades that head which is still owed to the world' (x. 393). In the final line of M.'s *Continuation*, Caesar dies 'a sacrifice t'appease th'offended gowne' (sig. L3ʳ); cf. 10. 444.
⁴ Th'effect ... vow] *tot vota Catorum, | Brutorumque*, 'the many prayers of the Catos and Brutuses' (x. 397–98), i.e. for Caesar to die.
⁵ so degenerate ... discipline] *sed tanta oblivio mentes | Cepit, in externos corrupto milite mores*, 'such forgetfulness [of being Roman] captured the minds of a soldiery that had been corrupted into foreign ways' (x. 402–03).
⁶ void of shame ... king] 'void of shame', 'barbarous' and 'proud' are all M.'s additions.

O wickedness, within what land has not
Our empire's wretched fate found civil war?
Those troops removed from Thessaly so far
475 Rage Roman-like here upon Nilus' shore.
What durst the house of Lagus venture more   *dared*
Had they received great Pompey? But each hand
Performs that office which the gods command,
Each Roman hand help to this war must lend;
480 The gods were so disposed Rome's state to rend.[1]
Nor now doth Caesar's or great Pompey's love
Divide the people or their factions move.
This civil war Achillas undertakes:
A barb'rous slave a Roman faction makes,[2]
485 And had not fates protected Caesar's blood,
This side had won. In time both ready stood:[3]
The court in feasting drowned did open lie
To any treason,[4] and then easily
Might they have ta'en at table Caesar's head,
490 His blood amidst the feasting goblets shed.
But in the night tumultuous war they fear,
Promiscuous slaughter ruled by chance,[5] lest there
Their king might fall. So confident they are
Of their own strength, they hasten not but spare
495 So great an action's opportunity.
Slaves think deferring Caesar's death to be
A reparable loss. 'Til day-break light
His execution is put off. One night
To Caesar's life Photinus power could give,
500 'Til Titan show his rising face to live.[6]   *the sun*
  Now on Mount Casius Lucifer appeared,   [x. 433][7] *the morning star*
With hot though infant day had Egypt cheered;
When from the wall they viewed those troops afar

---

[1] Rome's state] *Latium corpus*, 'the body of Latium' (x. 416).
[2] barbarous slave] *satelles*, 'attendant, henchman' (x. 418).
[3] both ready stood] i.e. Photinus and Achillas.
[4] To any treason] *ad cunctas ... | Insidias*, 'to every ambush' (x. 422–23).
[5] Promiscuous ... chance] *caedes confusa manu permissaque fatis*, 'a confused mêlée of slaughter, and one permitted by the fates' (x. 426). 'Tumultuous' and 'promiscuous' are both trisyllabic.
[6] 'Til Titan ... to live] See Textual Notes.
[7] 10. 501–622] The final episode of the unfinished tenth book. Caesar is besieged in Alexandria by Egyptian forces and Roman deserters.

March on well-ranked and marshalled for a war,[1]
505 Not in loose maniples, but ready all
To stand or give a charge. The city wall
Caesar distrusts, and shuts the palace too,
So poor a siege enforced to undergo.[2]
Nor all the house can his small strength maintain:
510 One little part great Caesar can contain.[3]
Whilst his great thoughts both fear and anger bear,
He fears assaults and yet disdains to fear.[4]
So in small traps a noble lion caught
Rages and bites his scornèd gaol with wrath;[5]
515 So would fierce Vulcan rage, could any stop
Sicilian Etna's fiery cavern's top.[6]
He that in dire Pharsalian fields of late[7]
In a bad cause presumed on prosperous fate,[8]
And fearèd not the Senate's host, nor all
520 The Roman lords, nor Pompey general,
Feared a slaves' war.[9] He, here assaulted, took *escaped to*
A house, whom Scythians bold durst ne'er provoke,[10]
Th'Alani fierce, nor Mauritanians hot
Which fast-bound strangers barbarously shoot.[11]

---

[1] March on ... war] *sed iustos qualis ad hostes | Recta fronte venit*, 'the battle-line came with squared front, like one against an equal enemy' (x. 437–39).

[2] So poor ... undergo] *Degeneres passus latebras*, 'suffering so degenerate a hiding-place' (x. 441).

[3] Nor all the house ... contain] *Nec tota vacabat | Regia compresso: minima collegerat arma | Parte domus*, 'nor hemmed in, did the whole palace remain available to him: he had gathered his forces in a tiny part of the palace' (x. 441–42). M.'s approving 'great Caesar' may acknowledge F.'s reference to Florus, *Epitome of Roman History*, II. 13. 58, who refers to Caesar's *mira virtute*, 'wondrous virtue', here (see *Epitome of Roman History*, trans. by Edward S. Forester (Cambridge, MA: Harvard University Press, 1984)).

[4] disdains to fear] *indignaturque timere*, 'and scorns *that he is* afraid' (x. 444). M. adds 'great' to Caesar's 'thoughts', *animos* (x. 443).

[5] Rages ... wrath] *Et frangit rabidos praemorso carcere dentes*, 'and breaks his rabid teeth on his bitten prison' (x. 446).

[6] So would ... top] Addressed to Vulcan (*Mulciber*, x. 448), in L.

[7] in dire ... of late] *Thessalici qui nuper rupe sub Aemi*, 'he who recently beneath the crag of Thessalian Haemus' (x. 449).

[8] In a bad cause] *causa sperare vetante*, 'though the cause forbade him to hope' (x. 451); cf. 7. 64.

[9] Roman lords ... slaves' war] Translating *Hesperiae cunctos proceres*, 'all the leaders of the West' (x. 450), and *servile nefas*, 'the crime of slaves' (x. 453).

[10] He ... took | A house] *intraque penates | Obruitur telis*, 'within the shrine of the palace's household gods he came under a barrage of missiles' (x. 453–54).

[11] whom Scythians ... shoot] M. adds the epithets 'bold', 'fierce', 'hot' and 'barbarously shoot'; 'barbarously' is pronounced with four syllables.

525 He whom the Roman world could not suffice,
Nor all that 'twixt the Gades and India lies,[1]
Like a weak boy seeks lurking holes alone[2]
Or woman in a late surprisèd town,   *attacked*
Nor hopes for safety but in keeping close[3]
530 And through each room with steps uncertain goes,
But not without the king. Him he retains
About his person still; his life he means
Shall the revenge and expiation be
Of his own fate.[4] Thy head, O Ptolemy,
535 He means to throw, for want of darts or fire
Against thy servants: as Medea dire,[5]
When her pursuing sire's revenge she fled,
Stood armed against her little brother's head
To stay her sire. But desperate fate so nigh
540 Enforcèd Caesar terms of peace to try.
A courtier from the absent king is sent
To check his men and know this war's intent.[6]
But there the law of nations could obtain
No power:[7] their king's ambassador is slain[8]
545 Treating of peace, to add one horrid crime,
O monstrous Egypt, to thy impious clime.[9]

---

[1] Nor all that ... lies] *Parvaque regna putat Tyriis cum Gadibus Indos*, 'and thinks that India, together with Tyrian Cádiz [i.e. a territory stretching from the far east to the far west] to be but a small realm' (x. 457).

[2] lurking holes alone] *tuta domus*, 'safe home' (x. 459).

[3] keeping close] i.e. staying concealed (*OED*, s.v. 4c); *spem vitae in limine clauso | Ponit*, 'he puts his life's hope in a closed threshold' (x. 459).

[4] his own fate] i.e. death (*morti*, x. 462).

[5] as Medea dire] *barbara*, 'barbarous' (x. 464); cf. 4. 613, 6. 499. Medea fled Colchis with Jason in the Argo; to detain her pursuing father, she killed and dismembered her brother Absyrtus, scattering the limbs behind the vessel.

[6] A courtier ... intent] *missusque satelles | Regius ut saevos absentis voce tyranni | Corriperet famulos, quo bellum auctore moverent*, 'a royal attendant was sent to rebuke the savage slaves with the voice of their absent tyrant [and ask] by whose authority they waged war' (x. 468–70).

[7] the law of nations] *ius mundi ... nec foedera sancta | Gentibus*, 'universal law and compacts sacred among nations' (x. 471–72). Embassies had been considered worthy of special protection in antiquity, but M. may be considering early modern discussions of the law of nations in e.g. Alberico Gentili's 'On Embassies' (*De Legationibus Libri Tres*, 1585) or Grotius' 'On the Law of War and Peace' (*De Iure Belli ac Pacis*, 1624).

[8] is slain] Implied but not stated by L. F. records Grotius's conjecture of some missing words in x. 472–73; modern editions sometimes print Housman's conjecture of a supplementary line.

[9] to thy impious clime] Not in L.

Impious Pharnaces, Pontus, Thessaly,[1]
Nor Spain, nor Juba's far-spread monarchy,[2]
Nor barbarous Syrtis durst attempt to do
550 What here effeminate Egypt reaches to.[3]
The war on every side grows dangerous,
And showers of falling darts even shake the house.
No batt'ring ram had they to force the wall,
Nor any engine fit for war at all,
555 Nor used they fire: the skill-less people run[4]
Through the vast palace scattered up and down,
And use their joinèd strength nowhere at all:
The fates forbid, and Fortune's Caesar's wall.[5]
 But where the gorgeous palace proudly stands   [x. 486]
560 Into the sea, from ships the naval bands
Assault the house; but Caesar everywhere
Is for defence at hand and weapons here,
There wildfire uses.[6] Though besieged he be,
Doth the besiegers' work (such strength had he   = *he does*
565 Of constant spirit):[7] wildfire balls he threw
Among the joinèd ships, nor slowly flew
The flame on pitchy shrouds and boards that drop
With melted wax; at once the sailyard's top
And lowest hatches burn. An half-burnt boat
570 Here drowns in seas, there foes and weapons float,
Nor o'er the ships alone do flames prevail,
But all the houses near the shore assail.
The south winds feed the flame and drive it on

---

[1] Impious Pharnaces, Pontus] Compressing *Pontus, & impia signa | Pharnacis*, 'Pontus and the impious standards of Pharnaces' (x. 475–76).

[2] Spain] *gelido circumfluus orbis Ibero*, 'the world that is lapped around by cold Iber [modern Ebro]' (x. 476).

[3] durst attempt ... reaches to] *Tantum ausus scelerum, ... quantum | Deliciae fecere tuae*, '[none of these other nations] have dared such enormities as your allurements have' (x. 477–78). M.'s 'effeminate' (pronounced 'effem'nate'), not in L., may reflect F.'s comment on the 'in no way virile monsters', the eunuchs Photinus and Ganymedes.

[4] the skill-less people] *coeca iuventus | Consilii*, 'blind youth, devoid of a plan' (x. 482–83).

[5] The fates ... wall] *Fata vetant, murique vicem fortuna tuetur*, 'the fates forbid (their entry) and in place of a wall fortune protects [Caesar]' (x. 485).

[6] weapons here ... wildfire] *hos aditus gladii, hos ignibus arcet*, 'He defends these attacks with the sword, these with fire' (x. 488). For M.'s 'wildfire', see 3. 737n.

[7] such strength ... constant spirit] *tanta est constantia mentis*, 'so great was his steadfastness of mind' (x. 490). M.'s idea of strength may echo early modern neo-Stoicism here, esp. Justus Lipsius's definition of *constantia* as a *rectum et immotum animi robur*, 'an upright and immovable force of will': *De Constantia*, sig. B^v.

	Along the houses with such motion,	
575	As through the welkin fiery meteors run,	*heavens*
	That wanting fuel feed on air alone.	*lacking*
	This fire awhile the court's besieging stayed,	[x. 504]
	And drew the people to the city's aid.	
	Caesar that time would not in sleep bestow,[1]	
580	Who well could use occasions, and knew how	
	In war to take the greatest benefit	
	Of sudden chances,[2] ships his men by night,	
	Surprises Pharos.[3] Pharos heretofore	*attacks*
	An island was, when prophet Proteus wore	
585	That crown, but joined to Alexandria now.	
	Two helps on Caesar doth that fort bestow:	
	Commands the sea, the foe's incursions stayed,	
	And made a passage safe for Caesar's aid.	
	He now intends no longer to defer	
590	Photinus'(c) death, though not enough severe.[4]	
	Not fire, nor beasts, nor gibbets reave his breath;[5]	*take*
	Slain with a sword he dies great Pompey's death.	
	Arsinoë,(d) from court escapèd, goes	
	By Ganymedes' help to Caesar's foes,	
595	The crown (as Lagus' daughter) to obtain,[6]	
	By whose just sword was stern Achillas slain.[7]	
	Another to thy ghost is sacrificed,	
	Pompey, but Fortune is not yet sufficed.	

---

[1] time] *tempora cladis*, 'time of/for destruction' (x. 505).

[2] Who well ... chances] *semper feliciter usus | Praecipiti cursu bellorum, tempore rapto*, 'always fortunate in using high-speed moves in war, and seizing opportunity' (x. 507–08). M.'s translation registers F.'s full stop after *tempore rapto*; modern editions join these words to Caesar's next action, 'and having seized the opportunity, he ...'.

[3] Surprises Pharos] Omitting *claustrum pelagi*, '[Pharos] the gateway to the sea' (x. 509).

[4] He now intends ... severe] *fatum meriti poenasque, | Distulit ulterius: sed non, qua debuit, ira*, 'he put off no longer the death and punishment of deserving Pothinus: but not with the wrath which it merited' (x. 515–16).

[5] Not fire ... breath] *non cruce, non flammis, non rabido non dente ferarum*, 'not the cross, nor flames, nor the rabid teeth of wild beasts' (x. 517); cf. 10. 419n. Some modern editions find x. 517–20 (= 10. 590–91) problematic and conjecture a missing line.

[6] The crown ... obtain] *quae castra carentia rege | Vt proles Lagea tenet*, 'as Lagus' daughter, she takes charge of the camp lacking its king' (x. 521–22). M.'s attribution of regal ambition to Arsinoë, Cleopatra's younger sister, is not in L.: it derives from Caesar, *Commentarii*, III. 112. 10, a passage quoted by F. 'Ganymedes' is pronounced with four syllables here, as it is also at 10. 605 below; cf. 9. 1106n.

[7] stern Achillas] *famulumque ... terribilem*, 'terrible slave' (x. 522–23). 'Stern' is M.'s habitual epithet for Achillas: see 10. Arg. 9, 10. 401.

LUCAN'S PHARSALIA

      Far be it, gods, that these two deaths should be
600 His full revenge: the fall of Ptolemy
      And Egypt's ruin not enough is thought,
      Nor ere can his revenge be fully wrought,
      'Til Caesar by the Senate's swords be slain.
      But though the author's dead, these broils remain:
605 For Ganymedes, now commander, moved
      A second war, which full of danger proved.
      So great the peril was, that day alone
      Might Caesar's name to future times renown.
         While Caesar strives, pent up so closely there,
610 To ship his men from thence, a sudden fear
      Of war did his intended passage meet.
      Before his face the foe's well-riggèd fleet,
      Behind their foot from shore against him fight.   *infantry*
      No way of safety's left: valour nor flight,
615 Nor scarce doth hope of noble death remain.
      No heaps of bodies, no whole armies slain
      Are now required to conquer Caesar there:
      A little blood will serve. Whether to fear
      Or wish for death he knows not. In this same
620 Sad strait, he thinks of noble Scaeva's fame,[1]   *time of hardship*
      Who at Dyrrachium, when his works were down,   *ramparts, walls*
      Besieged all Pompey's strength himself alone: [x. 546][2]
      Th'example raised his thoughts, resolved to do
      What Scaeva did, but straight a scorn to owe
625 *His valour to examples checks again*
      That high resolve: great thoughts great thoughts restrain.
      Yet thus at last: 'Scaeva was mine, 'twas I
      Nurtured that spirit: if like him I die,
      I do not imitate, but Caesar's feat
630 *Rather confirms that Scaeva's act was great.*[3]
      In this resolve had Caesar charged them all

---

[1] noble Scaeva's fame] On Scaeva and Dyrrachium, see 6. 153 ff.

[2] 10. 623–72] M.'s narrative continuation, italicised in 1627–1635 but not 1650. In outline M. imitates Giovanni Sulpizio's often-reprinted eleven-line supplement in Latin hexameters of the late fifteenth century, which likewise has Caesar swimming to safety with his men (see Appendix A). His version is longer, however, weaving in echoes of L.'s own bitter protests against historical causality. This continuation, and its tone, anticipate M.'s seven-book *Continuation* of 1630.

[3] *Th'example ... was great*] Caesar's concern with his own heroic exemplarity is prompted by Sulpizio's continuation (see Appendix A, lines 1–2), but also recalls the dying Pompey's interest in his self-image, 8. 716 ff.

>   *Himself alone, and so a glorious fall*
>   *(Slain by a thousand hands at once) had met,*
>   *Or else ennobled by a death so great*
> 635   *Those thousand hands, but Fortune was afraid*
>   *To venture Caesar further than her aid*
>   *Could lend a famous rescue and endear*
>   *The danger to him. She discovers near*
>   *Ships of his own: thither when Caesar makes,*
> 640   *He finds no safety there, but straight forsakes*
>   *Those ships again, and leaps into the main.*
>   *The trembling billows feared to entertain*
>   *So great a pledge of fortune, one to whom*
>   *Fate owed so many victories to come,*
> 645   *And Jove (whilst he on Caesar's danger looks)*
>   *Suspects the truth of th'adamantine books.*[1]
>   *Who could have thought but that the gods above*
>   *Had now begun to favour Rome and love*
>   *Her liberty again? And that the fate*
> 650   *Of Pompey's sons, of Cato and the state*
>   *'Gainst Caesar's fortune had prevailèd now?*[2]
>   *Why do the powers celestial labour so*
>   *To be unjust again?*[3] *Again take care*
>   *To save that life they had exposed so far,*
> 655   *That now the danger, even in Caesar's eye,*
>   *Might clear their doom of partiality?*
>   *But he must live until his fall may prove*
>   *Brutus and Cassius were more just than Jove.*[4]

---

[1] *Suspects ... th'adamantine books*] i.e. doubts Caesar's supposedly destined victory. M.'s 'adamantine books', used also in *The Tragedy of Cleopatra*, sig. C^v, and *Edward III*, sig. E^v, to describe the book of the Fates, probably derives from Ovid, *Metamorphoses*, xv. 810, where Jupiter refers to the tablets of the Fates, 'made of bronze and solid iron (*ex aere et solido ... ferro*)'. M.'s use of adamant — a mythical, ultra-hard substance sometimes associated with diamond or lodestone (see *OED*, s.v. 1) — to describe the implacable laws of the Fates or Destiny can also be found, for example, in Dekker's *News from Hell* (London: R. B[lower, S. Stafford, and Valentine Simmes] for V. V. Ferebrand, 1606), sig. F3^v, and William Drummond's *Poems* (Edinburgh: Andrew Hart, 1616), sigs D3^v, K2^r.

[2] *Who could have thought ... prevailèd now?*] cf. 1. 138–40, 'Who justlier took | Up arms, great judges differ: heaven approves | The conquering cause, the conquered Cato loves' (*Quis iustius induit arma, | Scire nefas: magno se iudice quisque tuetur; | Victrix causa deis placuit, sed victa Catoni*, 1. 128).

[3] *Why do the powers ... unjust again*] cf. Virgil, *Aeneid*, 1. 19: *tantaene animis caelestibus irae?* ('Can there be such anger in celestial beings?'). The emphasis on injustice, however, is M.'s.

[4] *more just than Jove*] M. completes the thought driving 10. 647 ff.: that the assassins of

Now all alone on seas doth Caesar float,
Himself the oars, the pilot and the boat;
Yet could not all these offices employ
One man's whole strength; for his left hand, on high
Raisèd, holds up his papers and preserves
The fame of his past deeds; his right hand serves
To cut the waves, and guard his life alone
'Gainst th'ocean's perils and all darts, which thrown
From every side do darken all the sky,
And make a cloud, though heaven itself deny.[1]
 Two hundred paces thus alone he swam
'Til to the body of his fleet he came.
His o'erjoyed soldiers shouting to the skies
Take sure presage of future victories.[2]
FINIS.

Caesar are morally superior to Jupiter, i.e. destiny. In M.'s *Continuation*, there is a similar emphasis on justice, though the morality of the actions of Brutus and Cassius is presented in more complex fashion.

[1] *Yet could not all ... deny*] Caesar's swim to safety, carrying papers in one hand, ultimately derives from Suetonius, *Divus Julius*, 64, in *Suetonius*, I, pp. 114–15, and Plutarch, *Life of Caesar*, 49. 4–5, VII, pp. 560–61, although it also forms the climax of Sulpizio's brief continuation. M. adds the tableau of him prevailing, Scaeva-like, against a hail of missiles.

[2] *His o'erjoyed ... victories*] M. takes the huzzahs of Caesar's soldiers from Sulpizio (Appendix A, lines 11–12), but adds the detail of victories to come, which he will go on to narrate in his *Continuation* of 1630.

Annotations on the Tenth Book

(a) Cambyses, the son of Cyrus and king of Persia, added to his monarchy the kingdom of Egypt; he intended a further war against the Ethiopians, which are called Macrobii by reason of the extraordinary length of their natural lives. But by reason of the tediousness of the march, and want of provision, there was in his army a great famine, [so] that they killed by lot every tenth soldier, and fed upon them.[1]

(b) Achillas, coming to assault Caesar, had an army of twenty thousand. They were many of them Roman soldiers, which had served before under Gabinius, but had changed their manner of life and, corrupted with the riot of Egypt, had quite forgotten the Roman discipline.[2]

(c) Photinus, the king's tutor, remaining with Caesar, sent secret encouragements to Achillas to go forward with his siege, which being discovered by interception of his messengers, he was slain by Caesar.[3]

(d) Ganymedes, an eunuch, and tutor to Arsinoë the younger sister of the King of Egypt, assaulted Achillas by treachery and slew him, and being himself made general of the army, he continued the siege against Caesar.[4]

FINIS.

---

[1] Paraphrases F. on x. 280, 281. The term 'Macrobii' is also taken from F. (who renders it in Greek); its explanation as 'long-lived', which may derive from Seneca, *De Ira*, III. 20, was proverbial in the early modern period.
[2] Loosely translates F.'s note to x. 402 (itself taken from Caesar's *Commentarii*, III. 110. 1–2).
[3] A translation of Caesar, *Commentarii*, III. 112. 12, probably taken from F.'s note to x. 515.
[4] Following [Hirtius], *The Alexandrian War*, 4, as recorded in F.'s notes to this passage: modern readers may consult A. G. Way, trans., *Caesar: Alexandrian War. African War. Spanish War*, Loeb Classical Texts (Cambridge, MA: Harvard University Press, 1955), pp. 14 ff.

Appendix A: Giovanni Sulpizio's Continuation[1]

Erexit mentem trepidi tam fortis imago
Et facturus erat memorandi nobile leti
Exemplum, sed fata vetant, & fida salutis
Ostendit fortuna viam. Nam laevus amicas
5 *Prospexit puppes, nando quas ausus adire,*
Ecquid stamus, ait, vel iam per tela, fretumque
Eripiar, iuguli vel non erit ulla potestas
Eunucho concessa mei. Tunc puppe relicta
Prosilit in pontum. Siccos fert laeva libellos,
10 *Dextra secat fluctus, tandemque illaesus amico*
Excipitur plausu clamantis ad aethera turbae.

Translation:
[1] So brave an image roused the fearful man's spirit, and he was prepared to leave the noble example of a death worth remembering. But the fates forbid it, and faithful Fortune shows a way to safety. For on the left friendly vessels he espied, which daring to attain by swimming, he said, [6] 'Shall I indeed stand still? Either now I will make it safe through the weapons and the waves, or at least no power over my throat will be granted to a eunuch.' Then, abandoning the prow, he leaps into the sea. His left hand holds his books dry, his right cuts the waves. At last, uninjured, he is received with the friendly applause of a crowd shouting to the skies.

---

[1] Printed as in *M. Annaei Lucani Cordubensis ... Pharsaliae Libri X*, ed. by Hortensius (Basle: Henricus Petrus, 1578), sig. Zx4[r], where it is called 'A Supplement to the Tenth Book [*Supplementum Decimi Libri*]'. It was first printed in 1493, in Sulpizio's own edition of Lucan.

TEXTUAL NOTES

Frontispiece Verses] *only in 1627–1635; not 1626 (where there was no title page engraving) or 1650 (when there was a new title page).*

To the True Lover … Devonshire, &c.] *1627–1650; not 1626.*
To the True Lover … Rank] *1627;* To the Right Honourable *1627–1650.*[1]
(saith learned Heinsius)] *1627; not 1631–1650.*

THE LIFE OF MARCUS ANNAEUS LUCANUS] *1627–1650; not 1626.*
which is more likely:] *1627; not 1631–1650.*

To my Chosen Friend] *1627–1650; not 1626.*
25 in Judgment] *1627;* to Judgment *1631–1650.*

To his All-Deserving Friend] *1627–1650; not 1626.*

Upon this Unequalled Work] *1627–1650; not 1626.*
28 infamy] *1627, 1635–1650;* infancy *1631.*

Book 1

16 what] that *1626, 1631–1650.*
16 had] have *1626, 1631–1650.*
21 Araxis] Araxes *1635.*
51 whether] *1626, 1631–1650;* whither *1627.*
70 Not Phoebus I'll from Cirrha's shades desire] *1626–1627;* Phoebus from Cirrha's shades I'll not desire *1631–1650.*
70 Cirrha's] *1631–1650;* Cyrtha's *1626–1627.*[2]
89 growing] *1626–1627, 1635;* groaning *1631, 1650.*[3]
110 does] *1626–1635;* do *1650.*
209 general's veins] *1626–1627, 1635;* general veins *1631, 1650.*[4]
237–40 The horsemen first passed o'er the violent stream, | And take the water's fury; after them, | The current's violence being broke before, | The footmen find the earlier passage o'er.] *1626–1627;* The horsemen first are placed against the stream | To take the waters' fury; under them | The footmen sheltered, found a

---

[1] 'The Right Honourable' is an honorific used of peers below the rank of Marquis. The second Earl of Devonshire inherited his earldom on his father's death (3 March 1626), and the identically named third Earl on 20 June 1628.
[2] 'Cyrtha's' is probably a misprint: even though Cyrtha was a city in Africa, all known Renaissance editions read *Cirrhea* at 1. 64.
[3] The misprint in *1650* indicates the text was set from a copy of *1631.*
[4] See textual note to 1. 89.

passage o'er | More calm, the current being broke before. *1631–1650*.[1]
294 would] *1626–1627*; could *1631–1650*.
307 thy] *1626, 1631–1650*; they *1627*.
322 A thousand dangers, now the tenth year free] *1626–1627*; A thousand storms in ten years' victory *1631–1650*.
326 had come] *1627–1650*; were come *1626*.
354 diffused] *1626–1627*; effused *1631–1650*.
375 the strongest] *1627–1650*; the conqueror *1626*.
377 these] *1626–1627*; those *1631–1650*.
391 While life-blood keeps this breathing body warm] *1626–1631*; While blood of life these breathing bodies warms *1635–1650*.[2]
392 this agile arm] *1626–1631*; these agile arms *1635–1650*.[3]
413 ram] *1626–1631, 1650*; rams *1635*.
423 dispersed] *1626–1631, 1650*; dispierced *1635*.
436 Circius] *1626–1627*; Cirtius *1631–1635*; Circus *1650*.
459 Nemasus] *1626–1631*; Nemossus *1635–1650*.[4]
488–89 Death long life's middle is (if you maintain | The truth): the Northern people happy are] *1627*; The midst twixt long lives (if you truth maintain) | Is death. But those wild people happy are *1631–1650*.[5]
498 lofty] *1626, 1631–1650*; loftly *1627*.
560 adorn] *1626–1631*; possess *1635–1650*.
606 threat'ning] *1635–1650*; threating *1627*; threatnings *1631*.
620 *new paragraph in 1626*.
636 Cybel] *1626, 1631–1650*; Sybel's *1627*.
637 Septemviri] *1626–1627, 1635–1650*; Septemvirs *1631*.
637 sacred] *1626, 1631–1650*; sacrest *1627*.

Book 2

Dedic. 12 flatter] *1626, 1631–1650*; flarter *1627*.

---

[1] See note to 1. 240.
[2] L.'s wording here is *spirantia corpora*, 'breathing bodies' (1. 363).
[3] *fortes lacerti*, 'brave hands' (1. 364); M.'s change, as at 1. 387 (see textual note, above) indicates that L.'s Laelius is talking about his fellow soldiers, not just himself.
[4] Nemasus] M. may be attempting to solve a textual crux at 1. 419. Most Renaissance texts read *Nemetis* or *Monethis* here, both Germanic peoples (the Nemeti living near modern Speyer), but this reading makes the geographic sequence of L.'s catalogue awkward; he seems to cross the Rhine only to veer back again. *1635–1650* correct to 'Nemossus', capital city of the Arverni in central Gaul (now Clermont), from the reading *Nemossi* originally proposed by Jakob Moltzer in 1551 and accepted by Grotius and F. (in *M. Annaei Lucani, de bello civile, libri decem. Cum scholiis ... I. Sulpitii Verlani, certis autem locis Omniboni. Una cum annotationibus ... I. Micylli* (Francofurti: apud Chr. Egenolphum, 1551).
[5] L. here refers to *populi, quos despicit Arctos*, 'peoples on whom the North star looks down' (1. 458).

Arg. 12 Brundusium] *1626–1635*; Brundosium *1650*.
16 When] *indented paragraph 1626–1627; no paragraph 1631–1650*.
45 that to each] *1626, 1631–1650*; that each *1627*.
151–54 now guilty men are slain | So long, 'til none but guilty men remain; | Anger not curbed by law breaks forth; they wreak | Their private hatreds now: for Sulla's sake] *1626–1627*; first guilty men are slain, | At last when none but guilty could remain | Their hates take greater freedom; forth they break | Without the curb of any law; they wreak | Their private angers now: for Sulla's sake… *1631–1650*.[1]
162 beasts' dens] *1626, 1631–1650*; beast dens *1627*.
184 and Marius … made?] *1626–1627*; how Marius … made *1631–1650*.
185 Who, mangled, sacrificed] *1627*; A mangled sacrifice *1626*; And wretched sacrifice *1631–1650*.
202 so spoil] *1627–1650*; to spoil *1626*.
207 sadly] *1627–1650*; sladly *1626*.
255 'Banished…] *no paragraph this ed.; indented paragraph 1626–1650*.
257 reave thee of] *1635*; reave thee off? *1626–1631*; reave thee off; *1650*.
297 country's laws] countries, laws, *1627–1650*.
300 from an inside clear] *1626, 1635*; for an inside clear *1627–1631, 1650*.
367 Nor] *1626, 1631–1650*; Not *1627*.
429 seas'] *1631–1650*; sea's *1626–1637*.
446 greet] *1626–1635*; great *1650*.
449 Night-air infecting] *1627–1650*; Night-air-infecting *1626*.
532 t' other] *1626–1635*; th' other *1650*.
574 now let Rome] *1626–1627, 1635–1650*; new let Rome *1631*.
578 Nak'd armed] *1626–1631*; Mad-brained *1635–1650*.[2]
585 Beheaded, buried] *1626–1627*; Beheaded then, that *1631–1650*.
616 horns] *1626–1631*; horn, *1635–1650*.
635 do I leave?] *1627–1650*; did I leave? *1626*.
713 lofty] *1626–1631*; loftly *1635–1650*.
755 they run] *1627–1650*; run *1626*.
761 In sight] *1627–1650*; In field *1626*.

Book 3

1–7 Now had … he sees] *1626–1627*; The wind-stuffed sails had forth the navy

---

[1] As well as re-wording this passage (II. 143–46), M.'s later revision adds a translation of *Tunc data libertas odiis*, 'then liberty was given to hatreds' (II. 145), omitted from his original version.
[2] L.'s full phrase is *exertique manus vesana Cethegi*, 'the insane hand of uncovered Cethegus' (II. 543).

sent | Into the main, the sailors looks were bent | Upon th'Ionian waves [wants, *1631*]; but Pompey's eye | Was ne'er turned back from his dear Italy, | His native coast, and that beloved shore | Which Fate ordains he ne'er shall visit more, | 'Til the high cliffs no more for clouds he sees *1631–1650*.
14 ghosts] *1626, 1631–1650*; ghost *1627*.
131 Through this] *1635–1650*; Though this *1626–1631*.
163 Th'excuse t'our shame] *1631–1650*; Th'excuse our shame] *1626–1627*.
225 Pitane] *1626, 1631–16–50*; Pirane *1627*.
299 worlds] *1626, 1631–1650*; words *1627*.
432 lofty] *1626, 1631–1650*; loftly *1627*.
483 Losing their leaves are forced t'admit the day] *1626–1627*; Then first cut down, admit the sight of day *1631–1650*.[1]
520 fly] *1626–1627*; flew *1631–1650*.
558 ship] *1626–1631*; ships *1635–1650*.
583 Ploughing the seas, soldiers] *1626–1631*; Of those that ploughed the seas *1635–1650*.
687 on] *1626–1631*; in *1635–1650*.
694 vital] *1626, 1631–1650*; viral *1627*.
779 lit] *this ed.*; light *1626–1650*.
784 feats of chivalry] *1626–1627*; feats of soldiery *1631–1650*.

Annotations on the Third Book

The following notes were added from 1631 onwards. Note (a) in 1627 became note (g), not included here: see p. 146.

(a) The usual time of mourning, among the Romans, for the loss of husband or wife, was ten months; within which space of time it was accounted infamous to marry; and therefore Cornelia daughter to Lucius Scipio, and widow of Pub. Crassus, who was married to Pompey the Great within that time, is here styled by Julia strumpet.[2]

(b) Caesar, although it much concerned him to pursue Pompey, and overtake him before his strength were too much increased by foreign aid, yet partly for want of ships, and partly fearing lest in his absence there might happen some new commotion in Italy, and withal fearing the Pompeian army, that was then in Spain under the conduct of Afranius and Petreius, he resolved first to go and settle things at Rome, and afterwards to go fight against those armies in Spain.[3]

---

[1] Translating *posuere comas, & fronde carentes | Admisere diem*, 'laid down their foliage, and lacking leaves admitted the day' (III. 443–44).
[2] M.'s note, using details in the commentaries. This note must refer to 'Strumpet Cornelia' (3. 23), but is not signalled in the texts of *1631–1650*.
[3] Translating verbatim F.'s note to III. 52, itself rewording previous commentaries. The

(c) Valerius was sent into Sardinia to fetch corn, and Curio into Sicily as propraetor with three legions; those countries were two of the greatest granaries of the Roman empire.[1]

(d) Caesar assembled the senators into Apollo's temple, and there with courteous language excused himself concerning this war, as a thing undertaken only to preserve his own dignity against the envy and injury of a few, he entreateth them to take care of the commonwealth, and join with him in it: likewise to send ambassadors to Pompey and the consuls concerning peace.[2]

(e) The tribunicial power was held so sacred, that whoso did offer any violence unto it, they thought the gods would take revenge, and conceived the reason of that great and miserable overthrow, which Marcus Crassus received in Parthia, to be because Atticus the tribune had cursed him as he went away.[3]

(f) Caesar passing through the further Gallia, and understanding that Domitius, whom he had lately taken prisoner at Corfinium, and released again was come into Massilia, a city that favoured Pompey's faction, he called out some of the chief of the city, and admonished them not too much to obey one man, and so draw a war upon themselves; they shut the gates against Caesar, but requested him gently to pass by them, hoping by that means to have kept themselves in safety, and to have remained as neuters in the war; but that drew this heavy siege upon them. 'Unhappy Massilia', saith Florus, 'which desiring too much to preserve her peace, for fear of war fell into a war'.[4]

(h) The story in the place concerning the firing of these works which Caesar's soldiers had raised, and the actions of the Massilians is not rightly related by Lucan; but differs much from the relation of true histories.[5]

---

note belongs at 3. 56, but is not signalled in the texts.

[1] Combining F.'s notes to III. 59, III. 64 and III. 66. The note probably belongs at 3. 63, although it is not signalled in the texts.

[2] Translating verbatim F.'s note to III. 103, which combines several historical sources and commentaries; implicitly it contests L.'s hostile portrait of Caesar's treatment of the Senate. The note (not signalled in the actual texts) belongs at 3. 109.

[3] M.'s note, closely following the wording of F., itself echoing previous commentaries on III. 125. The note, not signalled in the texts, belongs at 3. 134 and perhaps supplies important context for M.'s rather bland 'office wronged'; L.'s term is *violata potestas*, 'violated authority' (III. 125).

[4] Mostly following verbally F.'s note to III. 298; the section 'hoping by that ... drew this heavy siege upon them' is M.'s addition. The quotation from Florus, cited by F. and M., is to *Epitome*, II. xiii. 23. M.'s note is signalled from *1631* onwards at 3. 128.

[5] This note, which is signalled at 3. 541 from *1631* onwards, appears to be M.'s own. It does not correspond verbally to any specific remark in the commentaries, although F.'s commentary on the final section of this book does remark frequently on L.'s historical inaccuracy and anti-Caesarian partisanship.

Book 4

9 Vectones] *1627*; Vestones *1631–1650*.
61 wexèd] *1627–1635*; waxed *1650*.
99 vittle] *1627–1635*; victual *1650*.
109 joined] *1627* joyning *1631–1650*.
144 left] *1627, 1635–1650*; let *1631*.
173 whether *1627–1631, 1650*] whither *1635*.
204 now confessed] *1627–1650*; *see note in commentary*.
303 foe] *1631–1650*; for *1627*.
328 Drives] *1627*; Dives *1631–1650*.[1]
330–32 No springs appeared, opening the pumice stone, | No bubbling brook rolls little pibble stones, | Nor sweating cave makes distillations] *1627–1631*; No springs, soft gliding on the pumice stone, | Among the gravel no cool vein at all | Is found, no drops from sweating caverns fall. *1635–1650*.[2]
359 Breathings *1627–1635*] Breathing *1650*.
364 on] *1627, 1635–1650*; no *1631*.
371 starvèd bands *1627–1635*] stormed bands *1650*.
454 dried] *1627–1631*; dry *1635–1650*.
479 farther *1631–1650*] father *1627*.
491 They come *1627–1635*] The come *1650*.
514 The master of the ship] *1627*; the captain of the ship *1631–1650*.
744 Autololes] *1627*; Autolodes *1631–1650*.
810 eagles] *1627–1631*; ensigns *1635–1650*.
834 far] *1627–1635*; for *1650*.
857 not secure] *1627–1635*; nor secure *1650*.
867 Fortune *1627–1631*] fortune *1635–1650*.
875 And the dust] *1627–1631*; For the dust *1635–1650*.
888–89 *as printed, 1635–1650*; *new paragraph at line 889, 1627–1631*.

Annotations on the Fourth Book

(f) Lieutenants] *1635–1650*; Lieutenant *1627–1631*.
(f) across the sea *this ed*; cross the sea] *1627–1650*.
(f) possibly] *1635–1650*; possible *1627–1631*.

---

[1] The Latin *Merserit* (IV. 298) suggests that 'Dives' is the more likely reading.
[2] Translating *Aut micuere novi, percusso pumice, fontes:* | *Antra nec exiguo stillant sudantia rore,* | *Aut impulsa levi turbatur glarea vena*, 'Nor did new springs glisten after the pumice stone was broken, nor sweating caves drip with a tiny stream, nor was gravel disturbed by a light vein [i.e. of water]' (IV. 300–02). F.'s gloss of the final line, *Nec minutissimi lapilli crepitant vena i. meatu fluentis aquae*, 'Nor did the tiniest stones rustle with the vein i.e. movement of flowing water', may have influenced M.'s translation.

In all editions from 1631 onwards the insertion of 3 extra historical notes created considerable confusion in their alphabetization, never corrected. We explain these changes as follows.

– *The following note was inserted and identified as note (e) in the text at 4. 162:*

Afranius and Petreius, when Caesar's horsemen had stopped their ways of foraging and fetching in corn, and withal frighted because many cities in that part had revolted to Caesar, and the rest were like to follow their example, resolved to transfer the war into Celtiberia, which remained yet in the friendship of Pompey, as having received great benefits from him in the Sertorian war; besides, they supposed that the fame of Caesar was yet more obscure among those barbarous peoples.[1] Therefore, at the third watch, they secretly dislodged, and passing over the river Sicoris, they marched with speed toward Iberus.[2] When Caesar by his scouts understood this, and hearing that beyond there were mountainous, strait, and rugged passages, which if the enemy should first enter, they might with ease keep him back and carry the war into Celtiberia and those far countries,[3] he commanded his horsemen with speed to prevent them; and himself marching through devious and rough ways, arrived first at those places and encamped himself between Afranius and the river Iberus, which Afranius was marching to. The two camps were here[4] fortified so near to each other, that the soldiers distinctly knew each other's faces, and talked with their kindred, and ancient acquaintances.[5]

– *The following note was inserted and identified as note (f) in the text at 4. 285:*

In this appeared a strange clemency of Caesar, that, after he had heard the cruelty of Petreius towards his soldiers — how, taking them from their friends' company (that had upon promise secured them) he caused them to be murdered (as the poet relates plainly) — Caesar notwithstanding seeking out Petreius his soldiers in his camp, spared their lives all and suffered as many of them as would to depart. But many tribunes, centurions and others would not

---

[1] Translating F.'s note to IV. 143, itself taken from Caesar, *Commentarii*, I. 61.
[2] Translating F.'s note to IV. 148.
[3] Translating F.'s note to IV. 157.
[4] between Afranius and the river Iberus, which Afranius was marching to. The two camps were here ...] *This ed.*; which Afranius was marching to the two camps were here ... *1631*; between Afranius and the river Iberus. The two camps were here ... *1635–1650*. The 1631 printing is a clear mistake derived from a page break.
[5] He commanded ... ancient acquaintances] M.'s summary, from F.'s notes to IV. 167, 169.

return, but stayed and served after under Caesar.[1]

– *The following note was inserted and identified as note (h) in the text at 4. 396:*

These two generals, Afranius and Petreius, though they were here pardoned by Caesar upon promise to serve no more against him, did notwithstanding afterwards in the African war follow Scipio against Caesar, where they were again overthrown. Afranius was taken prisoner, and by Caesar's command was slain.[2] Petreius, despairing of pardon (as is afterwards shown) slew himself upon King Juba's sword.[3]

The historical annotations printed after the text were re-alphabetized, (a) to (k), to reflect their revised order of appearance. However no similar re-alphabetization occurred within the text. Thus the old note (e) was still indicated as (e) in the text at 4. 351, although in the notes themselves it had become note (g). The old note (f) was still indicated as (f) in the text at 4. 442 although in the notes themselves it now appeared as (i). Finally the old note (g) was still indicated as (g) in the text at 4. 644 but in the notes themselves as (k).

Book 5

36 vacation] *1631–1650*; vocation *1627*.
50 your] *1631–1650*; you *1627*.
158 Make] *1627–1635*; Made *1650*.
243 he] *1627–1631*; she *1635–1650*.
251 breast] *1631, 1650*; breasts *1627, 1635*.
274 his] *1627–1631*; this *1635–1650*.
315 bloodless] *1627–1635*; bootless *1650*.[4]
318 choose] *1627–1635*; chose *1635*; close *1650*.
334 his] *1627–1631*; this *1635–1650*.
377 vanquished] *1627–1631*; vanished *1635–1650*.[5]
395 fly] *1627–1631*; flee *1635–1650*.
433 Salapian] *1627–1631*; Salapanian *1635–1650*.

---

[1] Loosely based on F.'s note to IV. 255. The phrase 'strange clemency' and the stress on how L. 'clearly relates' Caesar's generosity is M.'s.
[2] was slain] *1635–1650*; and was slain *1627–1631*.
[3] Petreius, despairing...] M.'s observation. For his treatment of Petreius' death in his *Continuation* and its debt to the account of the *Bellum Africum* (94. 1; Way, trans., *Caesar*, pp. 294–95); see Backhaus, pp. 380–81.
[4] translating *inanes ... lacertos*, 'useless arms' (v. 275).
[5] Both 'vanquished' and 'vanished' are M.'s additions.

434 Sypus] *1631–1650*: Syprus *1627*.
435 lands] *1627–1635*; land *1650*.
437 Calabrian *1631–1650*; Calabria *1627*.
471–72 pace | Of war] *this ed.*; space *1627–1650*.[1]
480 *this ed.*; *new paragraph 1627–1650*.
624 her] *1627–1635*; the *1650*.
646 does] *1627–1635*; doth *1650*.
931 Is] *1631–1650*; And *1627*.

Annotations on the Fifth Book

(o) Augurers] *1627*; Augurs *1631–1650*.

Book 6

4 towns] *1627, 1635–1650*; towes *1631*.
4 owe the destinies] *1627, 1635–1650*; owne *1631*.
74 Kentish] *1631–1650*; Rentish *1627*.
77 *new paragraph 1631–1650*.
84 account] *1627–1631*; accounts *1635–1650*.
86 Mischief's oft done] *1627*; Mischiefs oft done *1631–1650*.
218 struck full] *1627*; stuck full *1631–1650*.
219 *1627–1631*; *no new paragraph 1635–1650*.
240 Gortinian] *1627*; Gortyan *1631–1650*.
241 struck] *1627*; stuck *1631–1650*.
262 beleft] *1627*; be left *1631*; beleeft] *1635–1650*.
267 one death] *1627–1631*; one's death *1635–1650*.
298 and eats] *1627–1631*; but eats *1635–1650*.
312 of the fight] *1627*; from the fight *1631–1650*.
448 strock] *this ed.*; stroke *1627–1650*.
469 Cowards] *1627–1635*; Coward *1650*.
488 detested] *1627–1635*; detected *1650*.[2]
685 so spread] *1627, 1635–1650*; to spread *1631*.
769 brooding] *1631–1650*; broodings *1627*.
845 detains] *1627*; destains *1631–1650*.

---

[1] 'space' is almost certainly an uncorrected printer's error; the Latin is *rapiendi tempora belli*, 'time of seizing war' (v. 409).
[2] The Latin, *detestanda* (VI. 431), suggests many of the *1650* changes in this part of M.'s text reflect errors introduced during printing.

Book 7

53 of the fight] *1627*; to the fight *1631–1650*.
56 Hastning] *1627*; Hasting *1631–1650*.
72 axes] *1627–1631*; ax *1635–1650*.
145–46 A fearful murmuring noise rose through all parts | Of th'camp] *1627–1631*; A fearful murmuring noise through all parts | Arose' *1635–1650*.
151–52 And what Rome was, after this field is fought, | Be asked] *1627–1631*; And doubt what Rome, after this field is fought | Shall be *1635–1650*.
191 fiends] *1626–1631*; fiend *1635–1650*.
198 Baebeïs] *this ed.*; Baebai's *1627–1650*.
229 day] *1627–1635*; days *1650*.
268 champion] *1627–1631*; champaigne *1635–1650*.
368 Let him esteem] *1627*; Shall I esteem *1631–1650*.[1]
380 Rome's sole empire sought] *1627–1635*; Rome; whole empire sought *1650*.
416 Asks] *1627, 1635–1650*; Asked *1631*.
422 for liberty entreat] *1627*; for freedom doth entreat *1631–1650*.
426 a Rome] *1627*; a room *1631–1650*.[2]
476 conquests] *1627–1631*; conquest *1635–1650*.
518 from heaven] *1627*; 'gainst heaven *1631–1650*.[3]
548 rock] *1627*; rocks *1631–1650*.
597 were civil wars] *1627–1631*; where civil wars *1635–1650*.
619–21 Then came the war to Pompey's Roman strength, | Which o'er the fields were now displayed in length. | There stuck the war, there Caesar's fortune stayed] *1627*; Then came the war to Pompey's Roman power | The war, that variously had wandered o'er | The fields, there stuck, there Caesar's fortune stayed *1631–1650*.[4]
630 O rather] *1627, 1635–1650*; Or rather *1631*.
658 does] *1627–1635*; doth *1650*.

---

[1] Translating *ignoti iugulum tamquam scelus imputet hostis*, 'let him treat the throat [i.e. homicide] of an unknown enemy as if it were a crime' (VII. 329), i.e. as if it was a kinsman's. M.'s change from *1631* almost certainly derives from the explicatory paraphrase of Hugo Grotius, recorded by F., which has Caesar talking of how *he* will treat such actions as of great service, *tanto beneficio*, to him.

[2] An evident correction in later editions; the Latin here is *locus*, 'place, room' (VII. 373).

[3] The correction suggests some form of revenge on the gods, and cannot be ruled out as implicit in L.'s sarcastically sanctimonious *Vindictam, quantam terris dare numina fas est*, 'as much vengeance as it is lawful for gods to give to mortal lands' (VII. 455).

[4] M.'s correction recognizes *hic bellum*, 'this war' (VII. 547), as governing VII. 546, *quod totos errore vago perfuderat agros* ('which had spread in aimless wandering through the whole battlefield'); however, in *1627* it seems he followed the punctuation of many editions, including F.'s, which place VII. 546 with the preceding line, *Ventum erat ad robur Magni, mediasque catervas*, 'They arrived now at Pompey's strength and his squadrons in the centre'.

665 still the best of men] *1627*; all the best of men *1631–1650*.
719 No other] *1627–1631*; No other's *1635–1650*.
745 worthy even then] *1627*; even worthy then *1631–1650*.
773 befitted] *1627–1631*; befitteth *1635–1650*.
859 all-coveting] *1627, 1635–1650*; all-covering *1631*.
950 had] *1627–1631*; hath *1635–1650*.
978 He should turn up] *1627*; He should *1631–1650*.[1]

Book 8

Arg. 5 Gallogrecian] Gallogracian *1627-1635*; Gallogrecian *1650*
98 rose] *1635–1650*; rise *1627–1631*.
196 fires] *1627–1635*; guides *1650*.[2]
267 Nor] *1627–1631*; Not *1635–1650*.
285 Gnidon] *1627*; Gindon *1631–1650*.
291 a fear] *1627–1635*; fear *1650*.
292 the ship] *1627–1635*; thy ship *1650*.
335 Varus] *1631–1635*; Varrus *1627*; Tarus *1650*.
483 fate did her to] *1627–1631*; fate to her did *1635–1650*.
537 interposèd] *1635–1650*; enterposed *1627–1631*.
561 A] *1627–1631*; And *1635–1650*.
571 'Tis] *1627–1635*; This *1650*.
738 gods] *1627*; god *1631–1650*.
768 cables] *1627*; shrouds to *1631–1650*.
788 whip off] *1631–1650*; whip of *1627*.
817 An] *1627, 1635–1650*; And *1631*.
865 rite] *1627–1635*; cite *1650*.
875 can'st] *1635*; cast *1627–1631*.
893 thy] *1627–1635*; my *1650*.
896 not yet] *1627*; and yet *1631*; scarce yet *1635–1650*.
974 Hast] *1635–1650*; Has *1627–1631*.
995 ever-adorèd] *1627–1635*; ever-adornèd *1650*.
997 pacify] *1635–1650*; pacificy *1627–1631*.
1003 This] *1627, 1635–1650*; The *1631*.

Book 9

14 fixed stars] *1635–1650*; first *1627–1631*.[3]

---

[1] A clear mistake in *1627*: the Latin is *vertamus*, 'we should turn' (VIII. 855).
[2] *1650*'s reading is possibly a mistaken read-across from 8. 195, 'guide'.
[3] The Latin here is *astra* | *Fixa polis*, 'stars affixed to the heavens' (IX. 12–13); 'first' is

TEXTUAL NOTES

30 war] *1627–1635*; wars *1650*.[1]
52 The Phrygian master] *1635–1650*; Thy *1627–1631*.[2]
62 the sailors] *1627–1631*; her sailors *1635–1650*.
100 my care] *1627–1635*; thy care *1650*.[3]
178 towers] *1627–1635*; row'rs *1650*.
201 doubled] *1627*; troubled *1631–1650*.[4]
227–98] *Due to a printing error (the transposition of pages) 263–98 follow 261 in 1627; 227–62 follow 298. From 1631 on this is corrected.*
359 water] *1631–1650*; water't *1627*.
450 going only, let] *1627–1631*; going, only let *1635–1650*.[5]
512 shipwreck] shippwacke *1627*.
519–20 No rocks ... air:] *1627–1650 punctuate as a question.*
546 wrest] *1627–1631*; reft *1635–1650*.
566 not all] *1627*; nor all *1631–1650*.
580–81 None ... company?] *1635–1650: 1627–1631 punctuate as a statement.*
641 enquire] *1635–1650*; enquires *1627–1631*.[6]
645 breast] prest *1627*.
667 god] *1627–1631*; gods *1635–1650*.[7]
828–29 The prester too, whose sting distendeth wide | The wounded's foamy mouth;] *1627–1631*; The greedy prester too distending wide | His venom-foaming mouth *1635–1650*.[8]
882 member] *this ed.*; members *1627–1650*.
985 most hid] *1627–1631*; moist hid *1635–1650*.
1019 Marmarian Psylls] *1635–1650*; Marinarian Psylls *1627–1631*.[9]

probably a misprint for 'fixed'.
[1] The Latin here is *civilia bella*, 'civil wars' (IX. 28).
[2] *Phrygio ... magistro* (IX. 44) clearly means Palinurus himself in L.; 'thy', which suggests a reference to someone else, is nonsensical, and clearly a misprint for 'the' in *1627–1631*. See textual note to 9. 14.
[3] As with the correction at 9. 178 (see below), this alteration in *1650* is almost certainly a printer's error: the Latin (IX. 86) reads *nostra cura*, 'my care', and is required by the sense.
[4] The Latin, *geminato verbere plangunt*, 'they mourned with doubled scourge' (IX. 173), suggests *1627* is the right reading and the later ones a printer's error.
[5] The later *1631* and *1635* punctuation is probably simply a misplaced comma, but it's difficult to be sure: M.'s 'let them come' is only implicit in L., whose precise wording is *quibus ire sat est*, 'for whom to go is enough' (IX. 388).
[6] The later correction is clearly intended even in *1627*: the Latin reads *inquire in fata nefandi | Caesaris*, 'search into the fates of evil Caesar' (IX. 558–59).
[7] Probably a later misprint; L.'s *Dei*, 'God's' (IX. 578), is emphatically singular and refers to Stoic ideas of a divinely infused universe.
[8] *oraque distendens avidus spumantia prester*, 'the prester, eagerly opening wide foaming jaws' (IX. 722), probably means the snake's jaws, but M. seemingly initially followed F., who refers to a prester's bite 'stretching out' the skin of a victim later in the narrative (see 9. 905 ff.), before later changing his mind.
[9] The Latin (IX. 894) is *Marmaridae Psylli*; the change (possibly a printer's error) in *1635*

1045 There] *1635–1650*; Their *1627–1631*.[1]
1068 bit] *1627–1631*; bite *1635–1650*.
1082 thoughts] *1627–1631*; thought *1635–1650*.
1089 arm] *1627–1631*; arms *1635–1650*.
1106 *no new paragraph 1631–1650.*
1112 Respect you not great Hector's tomb?] *1627–1635*; Jove's Hercian altar seest thou not? *1650*.[2]
1115 wights!] *1635–1650*; wights; *1627–1631*.
1117 whilst] *1627*; while *1631–1650*.
1141 west winds] *1627*; west wind *1631–1650*.

Book 10

41 Th'earth's] *1627, 1625–1650*; Th'earth *1631*.
58 fear!] fear. *1627–1650*.
78 O'er captived] *1627–1631*; Or a captiv'd *1635–1650*.
89 shameless] *1631–1650*; harmless *1627*.[3]
128 feasts] *1627–1635*; feast *1635–1650*.
133 high tresses] *1627–1631*; high tressles *1635–1650*.[4]
164 rich hair] *1627–1631*; red hair *1635–1650*.
173 guest!] *1635–1650*; guest. *1627–1631*.
186 water] *1631–1650*; mater *1627*.
201 cates] *1627, 1650*; cares *1631*; cakes *1635*.
243 Cyllenius] *1627–1631*; Cyllerius *1635*; Mercurius *1650*.
254 won.] *1627, 1635–1650*; wor *1631*.
282 these] *this ed.*; this *1627–1650*.
308 since the world created was] *1627–1631*; since the great creation was *1635–1650*.
309 broken vein] *1627–1631*; earthly vein *1635–1650*.[5]

also regularizes the meter.
 [1] The Latin *hic*, 'here' (IX. 917), indicates that 'their' is a misprint for 'there'.
 [2] The usual reading here (IX. 979) is *Herceas aras*, referring to the altar of Hercian Jove where Priam, King of Troy, was assassinated. Most Renaissance editors give this reading; some (including F.) note the variant *Hectoreas aras*, 'Hector's altars', also followed by Gorges.
 [3] Both the sense and the Latin (*Pro pudor!*, 'for shame!', X. 77) show that *1627* is a printer's error.
 [4] The meaning is obscure. In *1627–1631* it may be a simple misprint; *1635–1650* amend to 'tressles', and M. uses this word later (10. 169); but while the sense of 'framework' or 'beam' fits the milieu of architectural description, it does not accurately render L.'s *crassumque trabes absconderat aurum*, 'a thick layer of gold hid the beams' (X. 113). Perhaps, prompted by F.'s gloss *laminae aureae*, 'gold-leaf', we should assume that M. meant 'tress' in the sense of 'layer' or strand.
 [5] The full Latin is *concussis terrarum ... venis*, 'the veins of the earth having been broken' (X. 264).

310 Of earth have grown; some god did then ordain] *1627–1631*; Have broke: some other god did then ordain *1635–1650*.[1]
365 here?] *this ed.* here, *1627–1650*.
408 stay?] *1627–1650 punctuate as a statement; other early modern editions as a question.*
451 below] *1635–1650*; bestow *1627–1631*.[2]
500 Til Titan ... to live] *1627–1631*; And till Sol rises grant him leave to live *1635–1650*.
502 With hot though infant day had] *1627–1635*; And with hot day though infant *1635–1650*.
504 well-ranked] *1627–1631*; well-rack'd *1635–1650*.
590 Photinus] *this ed.*; Protinus *1627–1631*; Photenus *1635–1650*.

Annotations on the Tenth Book

(b) They were] *1627–1635*; There were *1650*.

---

[1] 'Then' in *1627–1631* may be a mistake for 'them' (*quasdam*, x. 265), but is retained despite the revision in *1635–1650*.

[2] Obscure. *1627–1631* may be attempting '[this night] will bestow a sacrifice on the peoples, and send to the shades that head which is still owed to the world', *Inferiasque dabit populis, & mittet ad umbras | Quod debetur adhuc mundo, caput* (x. 392–93). But M.'s English is awkward, hence the correction to the more intelligible 'ghosts below' from 1635.

GLOSSARY:
MOST IMPORTANT NAMES AND PLACES

We are indebted to the *OCD* and *New Pauly* in compiling these entries.

Abatos: an island or rock in the Nile, near Philae.

Abydos: city at the narrowest part of the Dardanelles, opposite Sestos; the two are kept apart by the Hellespont, the narrow strait separating Europe and Asia.

Achaea: a region comprising the north-east of the Peloponnese, between the Corinthian Gulf and the Chelmos and Panachaikon mountains.

Achillas: once the boy-king Ptolemy's tutor; commander of the Egyptian army. Responsible for Pompey's assassination.

Achoreus: a member of Ptolemy's court, probably fictitious. A natural-philosopher/priest.

Actium: see 'Leucas'.

Adrian: = 'Adriatic', part of the Mediterranean, the waters between the Balkan coast and Italy.

Aegean: part of the Mediterranean, the waters between the mainlands of Greece and Turkey.

Aeniochs: = the Heniochi, a tribe living on the north-eastern shores of the Black Sea, and according to L. excellent horsemen. They claimed descent from the Spartan brothers Castor and Pollux.

Agave: in Greek myth, queen of Thebes and mother of Pentheus. Driven mad by Bacchus, she killed and dismembered her son.

Aeolus: in Greco-Roman myth, the king of the winds. His kingdom was an island with a cave-prison, reputedly in the region between Italy and Sicily.

Afranius: Lucius Afranius, consul 60 BC. Along with Petreius he was sent by Pompey as a legate to administer Hispania ulterior 53–49 BC. He joined forces with Petreius at Ilerda and was defeated by Caesar, then granted permission to withdraw. Afranius later fought at the battle of Pharsalus against Caesar, before fleeing to Dyrrachium, then Africa; he also fought at the battle of Thapsus (46 BC), where he was captured and killed.

Agamemnon: major character in Homer's *Iliad*; commander of the Greek forces in the war against Troy, an expedition which had been prompted by the Trojan Paris' ravishment of Helen.

Alani: see 'Sarmatia'.

Alba: Alba Longa, the Latin city founded by Aeneas' son Ascanius. The location of the sanctuary of Jupiter Latiaris, the god of the league of Latin cities and the location for celebration of the *Feriae Latinae*, a ritual undertaken by the consuls

GLOSSARY

and other magistrates of Rome annually.

Alcides: see 'Hercules'.

r. Albis: the Elbe, flowing from the modern Czech Republic to the North Sea.

Alexander: Alexander the Great, son of Philip II of Macedon, global conqueror. He founded Alexandria; his general Ptolemy founded the Ptolemaic dynasty.

r. Alpheus: river of the Peloponnese (southern Greece).

Alps: mountain range stretching across Europe from south-east France through north-western Italy.

Ambracia: see 'Epirus'.

Ammannus: mountains, part of the Taurus range between Syria and Cilicia.

Ammon: name for Jupiter, worshipped in the form of a ram, at an oracular shrine in Libya.

Amphissia: a city in Phocis.

Amyclas: fictitious; a poor fisherman.

Ancona: harbour town of Picenum, on the central east coast of Italy.

Antaeus: in Greco-Roman myth the Libyan son of Tellus: a giant who forced all visitors to wrestle with him, and gained strength from contact with his mother. Killed by Hercules.

Antonius:

(2. 128) Marcus Antonius 'Orator': 143–87 BC, consul 99 BC. A leading orator of the day and grandfather of Marcus Antonius the triumvir. At first a friend of Marius, he served as a legate in the Social War, but later became his enemy and victim, after Marius's return to Rome in 87 BC.

(4. 445) Gaius Antonius, younger brother of Marcus Antonius the triumvir. A legate of Caesar in 49 BC and naval commander, blockaded by Pompey and a participant in Lucan's Ilerda episode. He was captured by Brutus in Apollonia in 43 BC and executed in 42 BC.

(5. 546) Marcus Antonius: 83–31 BC. Member of the second triumvirate, Roman statesman and general. Famously loyal to Caesar, he had served as his legate in Gaul in the 50s, and, after Pompey had fled Italy in 49 BC, was placed in charge while Caesar fought in Spain. After Caesar's assassination he shared power with Lepidus and Octavian. When this arrangement broke down, he ended up in protracted military conflict with Octavian in western Greece. Forming an alliance with Cleopatra, after the naval loss of the Battle of Actium (31 BC) to Octavian, he committed suicide.

Anxur: now Terracina, approx. 35 miles south-east of Rome, directly connected by the Via Appia.

Apis: bull-god worshipped at Memphis, Egypt.

Appius: Appius Claudius Pulcher, d. 48 BC. Consul 54 BC. Valerius Maximus (1. 8. 10) and Orosius (6. 15. 11) record that he consulted the Delphic Oracle about the outcome of the civil war (Paulus Orosius, *Seven books of history against the pagans: the apology of Paulus Orosius*, trans. by Irving W. Raymond (New York: Columbia University Press, 1936).

Apollo: also 'Paean' (a cult-name), god of prophecy and poetry; and (as sun-god) 'Phoebus' or 'Sol'.

r. Apsus: modern Crevata, a river on the Illyrian coast.

Apulia: region of south-east Italy. Geographically diverse, with marshy coastal regions and a high plateau in the north. Its mountains, according to L., include Garganus and Matinus. Towns include Luceria (modern Lucera), Salapia and Sypus. Its most infamous town was Cannae, the location of a catastrophic defeat to the Carthaginians in 216 BC.

Aquilon: Aquilo, the north wind.

r. Arar: modern Saône. Tributary of the Rhône, river of eastern France.

r. Araxis: modern Aras, it rises in Turkey and is the main river of Armenia.

Argo: the first ship, commanded by Jason and crewed by the Argonauts. Its mission was to voyage to Colchis (surviving the Clashing Rocks) in order to retrieve the Golden Fleece.

Argos: city of the Peloponnese; home to Eurystheus and Agamemnon.

Arian: the Arians lived in the south-east of Parthia.

Aricia: a city of Latium, on the Via Appia (modern Ariccia). It included a grove or wood sacred to 'Scythian Diana', so called because the grove's cult statue originated from Tauris (and, according to legend, was brought to Italy by Orestes).

Arimaspian: a mythical people of the extreme north, associated in legend with wealth in gold.

Arisbe: a town in the northern Troad, Asia Minor.

Armenia: the highland region south and south-west of the Caucasus. In 188 BC it was divided into Greater Armenia (east) and Lesser Armenia (west).

Arsinoë: sister of Ptolemy and Cleopatra.

Asculum: = Ascoli Piceno, a town in the Marche region of Italy, in the province of Ancona.

Assyria: Bronze age empire, centred in northern modern Iraq. Its cities included Babylon. L. associates Assyria with skill in astrology and magic.

Astures: a people who lived on the Atlantic coast, northern Spain.

r. Atax: modern Aude, rising in the Pyrenees and discharging into the Mediterranean south of Narbonne.

Athamas: the home of the Athamanes, a people of Epirus.

Athens: chief city of Attica.

Auximum: modern Osimo, a town of the Marche region of Italy, in the province of Ancona.

Athos: a densely forested peninsula of north-eastern Greece.

Atlas: mountain in north Africa; originally a giant son of Iapetus. In myth conceived of as holding up the heavens.

r. Aufidus: modern Ofanto, which flows east from its source in Campania through Apulia, to the sea.

Aulis: port town of Greek Boeotia, facing Chalcis.

GLOSSARY

Auster: south wind.

Autololes: a Gaetulian tribe of north-west Africa.

Avernus: the deep lake connected to the sea near Baiae, and reputedly an entrance to the Underworld.

Babylon: capital city of the Parthian empire, ruled previously by the Persians and Alexander.

Bacchus: god of prophecy, wine and poetry. His devotees the Bacchae experienced divine madness.

Bactra/Bactria: land east of Parthia, roughly modern-day Afghanistan. Bactra is one of its cities.

r. Bactros: river of Bactria north-east of Parthia.

Baebius: Marcus Baebius Tamphilus, a victim of Marius who died in 87 BC.

r. Baetis: the Guadalquivir, which flows into the sea at Cádiz in Spain.

r. Bagradas: modern Ksar Baghai, the longest river in north-eastern Africa.

Basilus: L. Minucius Basilus served under Caesar in Gaul 53–52 BC, then as a legate in the Adriatic in 49–48. In 45 BC Caesar awarded him the praetorship, but he later joined the conspirators against Caesar. He was killed in 43 BC by his own slaves.

Berenice, Berenicis: modern Benghazi, Libya.

Bessians: (Bessi) a nomadic Scythian tribe who travel on the frozen Sea of Azov.

Boeotia: region of south-eastern central Greece.

Boötes: the 'ox-driver' (the constellation ahead of Ursa Major/The Plough).

Boreas: the north wind.

Bosporus: narrow waters between Propontis and the Black Sea.

Brundisium: modern Brindisi, on the south-eastern peninsula of Italy, facing east towards Greece.

Brutus:

(6. 903) Lucius Junius Brutus: assassin of Tarquinius Superbus and founder of the Roman Republic. First consul of Rome, 509 BC.

(2. 247) Marcus Junius Brutus (85–42 BC). In 49 BC he joined the Republican cause. After Pharsalus he was pardoned and favoured by Caesar. In 44 BC, he took the lead in Caesar's assassination. Together with Cassius, he fought Antony and Octavian at Phillippi in 42 BC, and after the battle was lost, he committed suicide.

(3. 558) Decimus Junius Brutus Albinus: Caesarian naval commander at Massilia in 49 BC. Later he took part in the conspiracy against Caesar. He was abandoned by his army, captured by a Gallic chief and put to death at the order of Marcus Antonius in 43 BC.

Byzantium: Greek city at the western entrance of the Bosporus.

Caesar: Gaius Julius Caesar (100–44 BC), warlord, statesman and triumvir: the eventual winner of the first civil war. A nephew of Marius. His daughter Julia, born in 83 BC, married Pompey: her death in 54 BC severed their bond. Appointed consul in 59 BC, he pushed through a number of populist laws: he was then awarded the provinces of Gallia Cisalpina, Illyricum and Gallia Transalpina. He undertook several campaigns in Gaul, achieving its near total conquest by 56 BC. He also embarked on other exploratory ventures, crossing the Rhine in 55 and 53 BC, and making an invasion of Britain in 54 BC. In 49 BC the Senate ordered Caesar to demobilize his legions: instead he marched on Rome, crossing the Rubicon in January. After a series of successes in the civil war, he finally returned to Rome, having defeated the sons of Pompey at Munda in March 45 BC. In 44 BC he was appointed dictator for life. He was assassinated on 15 March by a group of senators led by Brutus and Cassius.

Calabria, Calabrian: peninsula of south-east Italy.

Calpe: Gibraltar, commonly described as the westernmost point of the world by the Romans.

Cambyses: son of Cyrus and king of Persia: died 552 BC. Conqueror of Egypt, he made an expedition to find the source of the Nile.

Camillus: celebrated and ancient Republican family. Its most famous member was M. Furius Camillus, *c.* 446–365 BC, conqueror of Veii in 396 BC, saviour of Rome after the Gauls' invasion in 387 BC and rebuilder of the city.

Candavia: a mountain range in the district of Illyricum, beginning in Epirus.

Cannae: see 'Apulia'.

Canopus: a port city east of Alexandria (8. 636); the brightest star of the southern constellation (8. 210).

Cappadocia: central and eastern Asia Minor (now eastern Turkey). Pompey installed Ariobazarnes II as a client king there in 64 BC.

Capua: a city on the western coast of Italy, north of modern Naples.

Carbo: Gnaeus Papirius Carbo, ally of Marius and Cinna against Sulla. He was captured off Sicily in 82 BC and Pompey had him put to death.

Carmanians: a people living east of the Persians in southern Iran.

Carrhae: see 'Crassus'.

Carthage: city of north Africa, and Rome's chief enemy in the middle republic: its most famous general was Hannibal. Finally destroyed in 146 BC.

Carystus: a town in Euboea.

Casius: mount Casius rises on the Egyptian coast, east of Pelusium.

Caspian strait: the Caspian Gates, modern Darial Pass.

Castalian springs: the spring at Delphi sacred to Apollo and the Muses.

Catiline: Lucius Sergius Catilina, responsible for an attempted coup on Rome, foiled by Cicero in 63 BC. Cornelius Cethegus and P. Cornelius Lentulus Sura (consul 71 BC), were his associates in the conspiracy.

Cato:

(2. 252) Marcus Porcius Cato, also known as Cato Uticensis or Cato the Younger (95–46 BC), a leader of the patrician faction in the lead-up to the war. He fought under Pompey for the republic against Caesar, and was later celebrated as a Stoic saint by Seneca, Lucan's uncle: he committed suicide at Thapsus in 46 BC rather than surrender to Caesar.

(1. 336) Marcus Porcius Cato, also known as Cato the Censor or Cato the Elder (234–149 BC). Great grand-father to Cato the Younger, stern moralist and exemplar of Republican virtue.

Catulus: Quintus Lutatius Catulus *c.* 121–61/60 BC. Consul in 78 BC with M. Aemilius Lepidus: when Lepidus rebelled in 77 BC he defeated him.

Cayci: the Caici (or Chauci) were a Germanic tribe living on the North Sea coast, on both banks of the lower Weser.

Celenae: a town in Phrygia, Asia Minor.

Celendrae: town of Epirus and location of the Senate's meeting after the defeat at Pharsalus.

Celtiberians: Celts who had migrated to Spain: they inhabited the middle Ebro valley.

r. Cephisus: beginning near Delphi, this river runs through Phocis and Boeotia.

Ceraunia: the mountain range which rises close to the shore of Epirus, and runs along the Albanian coast to the Strait of Otranto.

Cerberus: in myth, snake-maned dog with three heads, guardian of the entrance to the Underworld.

Ceres: goddess of corn and the harvest: mother of Persephone.

Cethegus: see 'Catiline'.

Chalcis: town of Euboea, situated at the narrowest point of the Euripus channel between Euboea and Attica.

Chaonia: see 'Epirus'.

Charybdis: whirlpool in the straits of Messina, opposite the monster Scylla.

Cicero: Marcus Tullius Cicero (106–43 BC); consul 63 BC. Roman orator and statesman. Responsible, during his consulship, for suppressing the 'Catilinarian conspiracy' (see 'Catiline'). Absent from Rome in the eighteen months before the outbreak of civil war (serving as Governor of Cilicia, 51–50 BC), he was unable to broker peace between Caesar and Pompey; invited by Caesar to take his place in the Senate at Rome in 49 BC, he instead joined the camp of Pompey. After Pompey's defeat at Pharsalus he was pardoned by Caesar, but in the wake of Caesar's assassination (in which he had no part, though he approved) he returned to a leading role in politics, soon attempting to have Marcus Antonius (see 'Antonius') declared an enemy of the state. When Antony and Octavian formed the second triumvirate in 43 BC, Antony demanded that Cicero be killed, and he became one of the first victims of the proscriptions.

Cilicia: the south coastal region of Asia Minor; its Taurus mountain range, lying to the north of Cilicia, was the seat of the pirates subdued by Pompey in 67 BC: thereafter it was added to the numerous colonies established by Pompey in Greece and Asia Minor. Corycus, Mallos and Aegae are coastal cities of Cilicia.

Cimbrians: the Cimbri, a Germanic tribe from Jutland, finally defeated in 101 BC.

r. Cinga: (now Cinca) a Spanish river flowing from the Pyrenees into the Iberus.

Cinna: Lucius Cornelius Cinna (d. 84 BC), a supporter of Marius, who occupied the vacuum left by Marius' death and served as consul four consecutive times (87–84 BC). This period of time, the *dominatio Cinnae*, was considered by later Romans an age of tyranny and terror. While re-arming to deal with Sulla's return from the east, Cinna was killed in a mutiny of his own troops.

Cirrha: city of (and used as synonym for) Delphi.

Cleopatra: daughter of Ptolemy XII and sister-wife of the boy-king Ptolemy (70–31 BC). She had an affair with Caesar (producing the son Caesarion) and was given sole command of Egypt in 47 BC. In 41 BC she allied with Marcus Antonius, ruling large parts of the east, and also had three children with him. After the battle of Actium in 31 BC she fled to Alexandria and committed suicide.

Clupea: modern day Kèlibia, north-east Tunisia.

Coastrae: a little-known tribe of the Taurus mountain range.

Cnidon: Cnidus, port city on the Turkish coast.

Codrus: (Cordus) a quaestor of Pompey and, according to L., responsible for his hasty burial in Egypt.

Colchos: (Colchis) a city on the east coast of the Black Sea, home of the famed Golden Fleece.

Colline Port: gate. Site of the final battle (82 BC) between Sulla and Marius, won by Sulla.

Colophon: city on the Ionian coast, in modern Turkey.

Cone: island in the Danube.

Cora: Latin city, finally destroyed by Sulla.

Corcyra: Corfu, northernmost of the Ionian islands.

Corinth: isthmus separating the Peloponnese from mainland Greece.

Corfinium: = Corfinio, in the province of L'Aquila: in antiquity a major town.

Cornelia: wife of Pompey (m. 52 BC). Daughter of Aemilia Lepida and Q. Caecilius Metellus Pius Scipio (consul 52 BC). Previously married to Publius Licinius Crassus, son of the triumvir, who perished at the Battle of Carrhae in 53 BC.

Corus: north-north-west wind.

Corvinus, Corvini: Roman Republican family. Most prominent was Marcus Messalla Corvinus (64 BC –AD 8).

Cotta:

(1. 459) Aurunculeius Cotta, d. 54 BC. A legate of Caesar in his campaigns in Gaul; ambushed and killed during the Gallic uprising led by Ambiorix.

(3. 156) Lucius Aurelius Cotta: consul in 65 BC. According to L., a supporter of Caesar in the civil war (other accounts suggest that he remained neutral). After Caesar's death he withdrew from politics.

Cotys: King of the Astae and Odrysae (Thrace), client-king of Rome and ally of Pompey: in 48 BC he sent his son Sadalas (in M. Sadalis) with cavalry to fight at the battle of Pharsalus.

Crassus:

Marcus Licinius Crassus (115–53 BC), general and triumvir, consul (with Pompey) in 70 and 55 BC. In 72 BC he suppressed the slave revolt led by Spartacus which had broken out in 73, defeating Spartacus in 71. In 55 BC he instituted a campaign against the Parthians, and crossed the Euphrates in April 53 with seven legions:

he was defeated at Carrhae in May 53, in a catastrophic defeat for Rome that also broke up the first triumvirate.

Publius Licinius Crassus: son of the above, and husband to Cornelia until his death at Carrhae.

r. Crustumium: (the Conca) flowing east through the Marche, the region around Ancona.

Curii: A celebrated Republican family. The most famous of the Curii, Manlius Curius Dentatus, consul in 290 BC, defeated the Sabines, ended the third Samnite War and defeated Pyrrhus in 275 BC. He was also eulogized in Roman exemplary texts for resisting corruption.

Curio: Caius Scribonius Curio (c. 90–49 BC). He had been elected tribune of the plebs in 50 BC as an opponent to Caesar, but then — apparently bribed by Caesar — began to speak on Caesar's behalf. During the war, Curio served Caesar in Italy, Sicily and Africa, where he defeated Varus but was then killed by the pro-Pompeian Numidian King Juba.

Cyanean Isles: see 'Argo'.

Cydonia, Cydonians: north-west Crete.

Cyllene, Cyllenian: birthplace of Mercury, Arcadia, Greece.

Cynosura, Cynosure: Ursa Minor.

Cynthia: also 'Phoebe'; the moon-goddess, the moon.

Cyrene: the most important city of the Cyrenaica, colonized by the Greeks c. 630 BC, situated on the north-eastern coast of modern Libya.

Cyrrha: see 'Phocis'.

Cyrus: founder of the Persian empire and conqueror of Croesus.

Cytherus: the island of Cythera, south of Cape Malea.

Dacia/Daci: a people dwelling to the west of the Black Sea, in the region north of the Lower Danube.

Dahae: Scythian people, dwelling east of the Caspian Sea.

Dalmatia: Roman province, lying on the eastern shore of the Adriatic Sea.

Damascus: major city of Syria.

Decius, Decii: the Decii Mures were a famous Republican family associated above all with the Roman ritual of *devotio* (a ritual of self-sacrifice in battle). In 340 BC, Publius Decius Mus charged into the enemy Latini and was killed, but the Romans won the battle (Livy, *History of Rome*, 8. 6–11): his son died in the same manner (Livy, *History of Rome*, 10. 26–30) against the Celts in 295 BC.

Deiotarus: king of the Galatians (modern central and north-east Turkey); an ally of the Romans against Mithridates of Pontus. After Caesar's assassination, he made himself king of all Galatia, and died c. 40 BC.

Delphian, Delphos: Delphi, shrine of Apollo on Parnassus.

Destinies: Clotho, Lachesis and Atropos, the Fates (*Parcae*). Responsible for spinning and cutting the thread of a human life-span.

r. Dirce: river of Thebes (Greece).

Dis: see 'Pluto'.

Domitius: L. Ahenobarbus Domitius, consul 54 BC, Pompeian commander and opponent of Caesar. The emperor Nero's great-great-grandfather. In February 49 he attempted to resist Caesar's advance at Corfinium and was captured by Caesar, then pardoned. He continued to fight with Pompey and led a wing at Pharsalus: he was killed in the battle.

Druids: a sector of Gallic society: in charge of religious matters, tutors to young Celtic nobility and part of tribal leadership. L. thinks they are philosophers who believe in metempsychosis, a belief-system guaranteeing the careless attitude to death of the Celts.

Drusi: M. Livius Drusus (d. 109 BC) and his son of the same name, both tribunes of the plebs, were associated by L. with plebeian agitation and reform in the late second and early first centuries BC.

Dyrrachium: also called Epidamnus. Modern Durrës in Albania, a town on the Illyrian coast. Harbour for ships bound from Italy (Brundisium). Pompey's forces were besieged by Caesar there in 48 BC.

Echinades: islands opposite the mouth of the r. Achelous, Thessaly.

Elysium: portion of the Underworld, the 'Isles of the Blessed'.

Emathia: the location of the battle of Pharsalus, and often in L. cognate with Thessaly.

Encheleae: an Illyrian tribe (the 'Eel-people'): descendants of Cadmus, who with his wife Harmonia was transformed into a snake at the end of his life and went to Illyria.

r. Enipeus: river of Thessaly. The battle of Pharsalus was fought on its northern bank.

Ephesus: city on the Ionian coast (modern Turkey).

Epidamnus: see 'Dyrrachium'.

Epirots: see 'Epirus'.

Epirus: the coastal region in north-west Greece (now shared between Greece and Albania). Its towns include Chaonia, Oricum (founded by the Trojans Helenus and Andromache), and the seaports Ambracia and Palaeste.

Erebus: the Underworld.

Erictho: night-witch of Thessaly.

r. Eridanus: = Po, the largest river of Italy, flowing east through northern Italy to a delta south of Venice.

Erinys: a Fury, hellish pursuer of vengeance and inciter of frenzy. In pl. sometimes 'Eumenides', 'the kindly ones'. Megaera and Tisiphone are named Furies in L.

Eryx: a mountain of Sicily.

Ethiop, Ethiopian: the lands and peoples south of Egypt.

Etna: a volcano of Sicily.

Euboea: island opposite Boeotia and Attica. Its cities included Chalcis and Carystus.

Euboean channel: see 'Euripus'.

Eumenides: see 'Erinys'.

r. Euphrates: along with Tigris, famous rivers of Mesopotamia, believed in antiquity to come from a common source. L. puts the rising of the river in Persis, the Parthian region of south-west Iran.

Euripus: the channel between the Greek island of Euboea and Attica.

Eurus: the east wind.

Euxine: the Black Sea.

Fabricius: Caius Fabricius Luscinus, consul in 282 and 278 BC, and a famous example of frugal virtue: Plutarch records the unsuccessful attempt of Pyrrhus, King of Epirus, to bribe Fabricius (*Pyrrhus*, 20. 1).

Gabii: See 'Latium'.

Gaetuli: a Berber tribe, inhabiting the east coast of modern Tunisia. According to L. they rode without saddles.

Gades: Cádiz. Often in L. synonymous with the westernmost point of the world.

Ganymedes: (9. 1106) Trojan boy, stolen by Jupiter to become his cup-bearer; (10. 594ff.) Eunuch and tutor to Arsinoë.

r. Ganges: river of India: in L. specifically the limit of the advances east of Alexander the Great, and more generally the easternmost point of the known world.

Garamantes, Garamantis: a Berber tribe of the Libyan interior: Garamantis is their land.

Garganus: see 'Apulia'.

Gaul, Gallic: Celtic peoples, spanning modern France, Belgium, Germany and Italy. L. names the Lingones, Ruteni, Santoni, Leuci, Remi, Bituriges, the Suessones, Sequani, the Belgae (who fought in war-chariots, which had scythes attached to their axles) and the Aedui (M.'s Hedui), allies of Rome since 121 BC. Also the Nervii (who took part in the 54 BC uprising led by Ambiorix of the Eburones), the Batavi, Pictones, Turoni and Andes/Andecavi (M.'s Andian), Treviri (M.'s Trever), and Ligures.

Gaurus: a mountain in Campania, in southern Italy.

Gaza: Babylonian, then a Persian garrison town; under Roman rule, part of the province of Syria and declared a free city by Pompey.

Gebenna: Cebenna, the modern Cévennes mountain range.

Genabos: (Genabum/Cenabum) the capital of the Carnutes, who lived between the Seine and Loire.

Gelonian: a people who lived east of the Tanaïs.

r. Genusus: modern Skumbi, a river on the Illyrian coast.

Germany: along with the Celts, the subject of Caesar's campaigns in the 50s BC: the peoples east of the Elbe and across the Rhine.

Getes: a people dwelling to the west of the Black Sea, in the regions south of the Lower Danube.

Gnossos: city of Crete.

Gortyna: city of Crete.

Gracchi: A family-name that became a byword both for advocacy of the common people, and for overstepping traditional boundaries to power. Several Gracchi served as tribunes of the plebs. Tiberius Gracchus (tribune 133 BC) proposed agrarian reforms which were strongly contested by the Senate; and when he illegally attempted to serve a second term in office, he was killed by a senatorial faction. His brother Caius (tribune 123–121 BC) carried on the reform movement, but when he was not re-elected in 121 he turned to armed rebellion, and was executed.

Haemonian: another term for Thessalian.

Haemus: a mountain-range of Thrace.

Hannibal: Carthaginian general in the second Punic War and Rome's greatest foe. After inflicting several defeats in Italy, he was compelled to return to Carthage, and finally defeated: see 'Scipio'.

Helice: the constellation Ursa Major. In myth Helice was originally the girl Callisto, a princess of Parrhasium in Arcadia. She was transformed into a bear, then translated to the heavens as a star-sign.

Hellespont: the narrow sea dividing Europe and Asia, modern Dardanelles.

Hercules: hero of Greek myth, son of Jupiter, and target of his step-mother Juno's jealousy. Famous for completion of the 'twelve labours' set by the tyrant Eurystheus; tragic madness (with the result that he murdered his wife Deianira and children); and death on Mt Oeta, after which he was translated to heaven. Important as a Stoic model in both antiquity and the early modern era.

r. Hermus: a river in western Asia Minor into which the Pactolus flows. The rivers and land alike in this area were famed for their gold.

Hortensius: Quintus Hortensius Hortalus, 114–49 BC. Consul 69 BC: husband of Marcia until his death, after which she re-married Cato the Younger.

r. Hydaspes: a major river of the Punjab, flowing into the Indus.

r. Hydrus: a river running through modern Otranto.

Hyrcania: the region of Iran on the south-east corner of the Caspian Sea, famed for its forests.

Icarion: the island Icaria.

Idalia: the land around Mount Ida, located in the southern Troad, Asia Minor.

Idumaea: the region of southern Judaea.

Ilerda: modern Lérida, Spain.

Inarime: Ischia, the largest island in the Bay of Naples.

r. Indus: the Indus, the largest river of India.

Iolchos: town of Thessaly; home of Jason and departure point of Argo, the first ship.

Ionian Sea: bay of the Mediterranean, south of the Adriatic Sea.

r. Isapis: Umbrian river.

r. Isara: modern Isère, left tributary of the Rhône.

r. Isaurus: Umbrian river.

r. Ister: modern Danube.

Ituraea: the region of north Palestine and south Syria famed for its archers.

r. Jader: see 'Salona'.

Janus: double-faced god of door and gate, associated with beginnings. The door of his temple in the Roman forum was ritually closed in peacetime.

Jove: see 'Jupiter'.

Juba: king of Numidia and Pompeian supporter (*c.* 85–46 BC). He trapped and killed Curio at Utica in June 49 BC. After the battle of Pharsalus, he brought large forces to Africa; after Caesar's victory at Thapsus, Juba fled without his army; arriving at the city of Zama, however, he was denied entry. He died with Petreius near Zama.

Julia: (b. *c.* 83 BC) the daughter of Julius Caesar and (fourth) wife of Pompey the Great, whom she married in 59 BC. She died in childbirth in 54 BC.

Jupiter: ruler of Olympus and king of the gods. Sometimes also in L. in his guise as a weather-god of storms and rain. God of Rome, Latium and the Latin League, with important temples on the Capitoline and Mount Alba.

Labienus: Titus Labienus (*c.* 100–45 BC) one of Caesar's most important commanders in Gaul, 58–50 BC. But in 49 Labienus crossed to Pompey's side, fought with him at Pharsalus, and campaigned in Africa in 47. After the battle of Thapsus in 46 he fled to Spain and was killed at Munda in 45.

Lacinia: southernmost promontory of Italy, modern Capo delle Colonne.

Lagus: father of Ptolemy Soter I, founder of the Ptolemaic dynasty.

Larissa: Thessalian city on the south bank of the river Peneus.

Latium: area around early Rome, roughly modern Lazio. Bounded by the rivers Tiber and Anio to the north-west, by the Apennines and the Monti Lepini to the east, and Campania in the south. Its cities included Gabii, Praeneste and Sacriportum.

Laurentium: Laurentum, Latin city ruled by King Latinus according to Virgil.

Lemanus' lake: = Lake Geneva.

Lentulus:

(2. 499) Publius Cornelius Lentulus Spinther, consul 57 BC and Pompeian commander in the civil war. According to Caesar (*Commentarii*, 3. 4. 1) he formed two legions at the outbreak of war; according to L., commander of the left flank at the battle of Pharsalus. Escaping after Pharsalus via Rhodes and Cyprus to Egypt, he was killed.

(2. 579) see 'Catiline'.

(5. 16) Lucius Cornelius Lentulus Crus (d. 48 BC), consul 49 BC. Brother of Lentulus Spinther, above. Ally of Pompey. After the battle of Pharsalus he fled to Egypt, and died there shortly after Pompey.

(2. 583) Marcus Aemilius Lepidus, consul 78 BC, with Q. Lutatius Catulus. After strong disagreements during their consulship, Lepidus formed a faction that marched on Rome in 77 BC. He was defeated near Rome by Pompey and fled to Sardinia, where he died in 77.

Lepidus, Lepidi: prominent Republican family of the *gens Aemilia*.

Leptis: Leptis Magna is modern Lebda in Libya, about 160 kilometres south of Cyrene; Leptis Minor is modern Lamta in Tunisia.

Lesbos: Aegean island, capital city Mytilene.

Lethe: river of the Underworld, whose waters induce forgetfulness in the souls that drink from it.

Leucas: modern Leuca, the promontory off which the battle of Actium between Octavian and Antony/Cleopatra was fought (31 BC). Often used metonymically for 'Actium' in M. and L.

Libo: Lucius Scribonius Libo (b. c. 90 BC, consul 34 BC). Pompeian supporter and naval commander in the Adriatic, 49–48 BC. Survived the civil war then joined Antony in 35 BC.

Liburnia: on the north-eastern Adriatic, modern Croatia.

Libya: in L. catch-all term for north Africa.

r. Liger: modern Loire.

Lilybaeum: modern Marsala, on the western coast of Sicily.

r. Liris: modern Garigliano and its tributary the Liri.

Lissus: a city with a harbour on the Illyrian coast.

Luceria: see 'Apulia'.

Lucifer: the Morning Star.

Luna: Etrurian town near the coast of Liguria.

Macedon: region between the Balkans and the Greek peninsula, home of the kings of Macedon, birth-land of Alexander the Great and the Ptolemies. Its capital city was Pella: M. often uses 'Pellaean' as synonymous with 'Ptolemaic' or 'Egyptian'. After its fall to the Romans in 146 BC it was established as the Roman province of Macedonia.

r. Macra: modern Magra, a river in north-west Italy, which flows into the sea near Luna, a port abandoned since Roman times.

r. Maeander: modern Büyük Menderes, Turkey.

r. Maendar: river of Phrygia, Asia Minor.

Maenalus: mountain in Arcadia.

Maeotis: modern Sea of Azov, which flows into the Black Sea and is, according to L., often frozen over.

Malea: south-east cape of the Peloponnese.

Marcellus: Caius Claudius Marcellus, consul 49 BC. A Pompeian supporter, and army commander. He died in 48, probably before Pharsalus.

Marcia: daughter of Lucius Marcius Philippus, wife of Cato, and then in 56 BC of Quintus Hortensius Hortalus (consul 69 BC), in order to bear him an heir. After his death in 50 BC Marcia returned to Cato.

Mareotis: modern lake Mariut in northern Egypt.

Marica: the mother of Latinus, first king of Latium. Her name was commemorated in the forests near Minturnae (modern Minturno).

Marius:

Gaius Marius (157–86 BC). A 'new man', he held the consulship seven times and celebrated two triumphs, over the Numidian king Jugurtha (104 BC) and the Teutones/Cimbri (101 BC). He lost influence in the 90s BC and became embroiled in strife with Sulla. Plutarch records Marius' efforts to hide in marshland at the mouth of the Liris after being forced to flee Rome in 86 BC, and his confrontation with a Cimbrian sent to execute him after his capture and imprisonment at Minturnae (*Life of Marius*, 40, in *Lives*, vol. IX. pp. 575ff.).

Marius, Gratidianus, d. 82 BC. Nephew of Gaius Marius. After Sulla's victory he was killed at the tomb of Quintus Lutatius Catulus in grisly fashion.

Marmaric: the Marmarica is the region on the north coast of Africa between Egypt and Cyrene.

Mars: Roman god of War, and father of Romulus, founder of Rome.

Marsians: a people living east of Rome, in central Italy.

Massagetes: a nomadic people beyond Scythia. According to L. they subsisted on the blood of their horses, as well as using them for travel.

Massilia: modern Marseilles, an old colony of Phocaea, Asia Minor.

Massylians: a people of eastern Numidia.

Mauritanians: a people from the area of Morocco and western Algeria.

Medea/Media: Iranian people: in L., synonymous with 'Parthian'.

r. Medua: modern Mayenne, western France.

Megaera: see 'Erinys'.

Memphis: city of Egypt.

Meroë: on the eastern bank of the Nile River, near present-day Shendi, in North Sudan.

r. Metaurus: modern Metauro, flowing east through the Marche, the region around Ancona.

Metellus, Metelli: a famous conservative family, particularly prominent from the second century BC. They included Metellus Balearicus, b. 170 BC and consul 123 BC, and Metellus Numidicus (c.160–91 BC), consul 109 BC and enemy of Marius. The following Metelli are characters or specifically named in Lucan:

(3. 120ff.) Lucius Caecilius Metellus, tribune of the plebs in 49 BC. On his attempts to resist Caesar cf. Plutarch, *Pompey*, 62. 1. 2.

(3. 181) Quintius Caecilius Metellus Creticus (consul 69 BC), who conquered Crete and made it a Roman province in 67 BC.

For the Pompeian commander Metellus, see 'Scipio'.

Mevania: modern Bevagna, town of Perugia.

Minerva: also 'Pallas': one of the Olympian gods, whose aegis, containing the figure of Medusa, induced panic in war.

Mithridates: Mithridates VI of Pontus (*c.* 120–63 BC), king of Pontus and Armenia and great antagonist of Rome. For his defeat see 'Pompey'. Under his rule the kingdom of Pontus reached as far east as the Tauric Chersonesos and into the Roman province of Asia. Warring against the Romans through the 80s BC, he was finally defeated by Pompey in 66 BC.

Moschi: a people who lived south of the northern Sarmatians, near Colchis, on the east coast of the Black Sea.

Munda: town of Spain and location of the last battle of the civil war, in March 45 BC.

Mutina: modern Modena, location in April 43 BC of the civil war battle between

Octavian and Antony, and Decimus Brutus; a defeat for the tyrannicide forces.

Mysia: region in the north-west of Asia Minor. Caicus is its main river, which flows into the sea near the town Pitane.

Mytilene: see 'Lesbos'.

Nabathaean: of north-west Arabia.

r. Nar: (modern Nera) runs through Sabina and Umbria before reaching the Tiber.

Nasamonians: a Libyan tribe living on the bank of the Great Syrtis.

Nasis: modern Nisita a (formerly volcanic, and therefore vaporous) island in the gulf of Naples.

Nile, Nilus: famous Egyptian river: its source was the subject of natural-philosophical enquiry throughout antiquity.

Niphates: according to L. a river (3. 267); actually mountains, part of the Taurus range in Armenia.

Notus: the south wind.

Numa: second king of Rome. Believed by the Romans to have brought religious law to Rome.

Nymphaeum: Shëngin, a few miles north of Lissus (modern Lezhë in Albania).

Nysa: birthplace of Bacchus, somewhere in the east.

Oeta / Oete: mountain of Thessaly.

Olostrians: apparently an Indian people.

Olympus: mountain of Thessaly, thought to be the home of the gods.

Oricum: see 'Epirus'.

Orion: constellation, 'the Hunter': in myth translated to the stars after being killed by a scorpion sent by Artemis.

r. Orontes: the main river of Syria (approx. 450 km long, also known as the Asi). It begins in Lebanon and flows through Syria and Turkey into the Mediterranean.

Ossa: mountain of Thessaly.

Paean: see 'Apollo'.

r. Pactolus: river of western Asian Minor, which flows into the Hermus. The rivers and land alike in this area were famed for their gold.

r. Padus: modern Po, the largest river of Italy.

Palaeste: see 'Epirus'.

Pallas: see 'Minerva'.

Pamphylia: the plain-land and hilly region on the south-east coast of Asia Minor, set between the high Taurus in the east, north and west.

Pangaea: a mountain south-west of Philippi, Thessaly.

Pannonia, Pannonian: area north and east of the Danube.

Parnassus: a mountain of Phocis in Greece, which overlooks Delphi and is the home of Apollo's oracle and the Muses.

Parthia, Parthian: In the first century BC/AD Rome's main foreign foe, an empire incorporating central Asia to eastern Iran. Susa (now Shush in western Iran) was its capital.

GLOSSARY

Pelion: mountain of Thessaly.

Pella, Pellaean: see 'Macedon'.

Pelorus: a mountain of Sicily, on its north-eastern promontory.

Pelusium: Egyptian city at the mouth of the Nile delta.

r. Peneus: modern Pineiós; main river of Thessaly, reaching the Aegean near modern Stomio.

Pentheus: see 'Agave'.

Perseus: mythological hero, who wore winged sandals and carried a shield bearing the emblem of Medusa, which turned all who saw it to stone. For the historical Perseus (4. 174) see under 'Philip'.

Perusia: the siege of Perusia was part of the conflict between Marcus Antonius and Octavian, 41–40 BC. Octavian besieged Lucius Antonius, brother of Marcus, who surrendered: Octavian then took a drastic revenge on the inhabitants of the town.

Petreius: Marcus Petreius, c. 110–46 BC, praetor c. 64 BC. Sent by Pompey as legate to administer Hispania ulterior 55–49 BC. He joined forces with Afranius at Ilerda: there they were defeated by Caesar, who granted them permission to withdraw. After Ilerda, Petreius was wounded at Ruspina in 48 and defeated at Thapsus in 46. Refused entry to Zama, he and fellow Pompeian Juba, King of Numidia, killed each other in a suicide pact.

Petra: mountain fortress on the border between Thessaly and Macedonia.

Peuce: island in the Danube.

Phaethon: in myth, son of Phoebus Apollo: he attempted to drive the chariot of the Sun, but crashed, killing himself and scorching the whole earth.

Pharnaces: Pharnaces II (c. 97–47 BC), king of Pontus. He rebelled against his father Mithridates and made peace with Pompey, who installed him as client-king and ruler of the Bosporus.

Pharos, Pharian: Egyptian; more specifically the island housing the famous lighthouse opposite Alexandria.

Pharsalia, Pharsalus: town of Thessaly which gave its name to the major battle of the civil war between Pompey and Caesar in August 48 BC. Pharsalia refers to the region more generally.

Phaselis: a port-city on the eastern Turkish coast near present-day Tekirova.

r. Phasis: modern Rioni, in western Georgia, flowing west into the Black Sea. In L. often associated with Pompey's defeat of Mithridates. Also Colchis, the location of the mythical Golden Fleece stolen by Jason and the Argonauts.

Phemonoë: priestess of Apollo at the oracle of Delphi.

Philas: Philae, an island in the Nile in southern Egypt.

Philip: Philip V of Macedon, defeated by Titus Quinctius Flamininus in 197 BC; Philip's son Perseus was defeated by Aemilius Paulus in 168 BC.

Philippi: town of east Macedon, location for the final battle of the civil war between Brutus and Cassius, and Antony and Octavian in 42 BC. Often conflated with Pharsalus by L.

Phlegra: location of the battle between the giants and Olympian gods: sometimes placed in Thessaly, sometimes on the west coast of Italy.

Phocis: region of central Greece. Its eastern and western plains are divided by the Parnassus mountain range. Cities include Amphissia and Cirrha: according to L., the Massilians (modern Marseilles) claimed their descent from Phocis.

Phoebe: see 'Cynthia'.

Phoebus: see 'Apollo'.

Pholoë: a Thracian mountain often associated in literature with centaurs.

Photinus: eunuch counsellor to the boy-king Ptolemy and responsible for Pompey's assassination.

Phrygia, Phyrgian: region of Asia Minor; Trojan.

Pindus: mountain range of western Thessaly.

Pisa: Pisa, Italy (2. 425): city of Tuscany, central Italy; Pisa, Greece (3. 194): region and city of the western Peloponnese.

Pleiades: the 'Seven Sisters' star-sign, found in the constellation of Taurus. In myth originally daughters of Atlas and Pleione, translated to the stars.

Plough: see 'Wagon'.

Pompey:

Gnaeus Pompeius Magnus (106–48 BC), warlord, statesman and triumvir. Pompey attained the epithet Magnus ('Great') through his military exploits: L. frequently mentions his triple triumphs. The first, over Iarbas of Numidia (81 BC), was technically illegal on the grounds that he was not of sufficient rank, since, at 25, he was too young to enter the Senate. He celebrated further triumphs over Spain (71 BC) and, with the defeat of Mithridates, Asia (62 BC); and he was famous for clearing the Mediterranean of pirates in 67 BC and conquering Jerusalem in 63 BC. In 57 BC, in response to a food shortage at Rome, the Senate gave Pompey a five-year curatorship of the grain supply (cf. 1. 343). In addition to leading the senatorial forces, he was able to draw on colonists and clients loyal to him from Spain, Gaul, Africa and the East, as well as parts of Italy.

Pompey, Cneius: 'Pompey the Younger' (75–45 BC), eldest son of Pompey the Great, born to Pompey's third wife Mucia Tertia. After his father's death, Cneius Pompey continued to fight, escaping after the defeat of Pompeian forces at Thapsus (46 BC), and finally being defeated at the battle of Munda in Spain (45 BC). He was executed by Lucius Caesennius Lento.

Pompey, Sextus: younger son of Pompey the Great (76/70?–35 BC), by Pompey's third wife, Mucia. Sextus survived the major battles of the civil war, and in the wake of Caesar's death he continued to war against the second triumvirate, holding Sicily with a strong sea-force, attempting a sea blockade of Italy, and challenging Octavian for power. He was finally executed in 35 BC in Miletus.

Pontine Marshes: now the Agro Pontino, an area of marshland in central Italy, from just east of Anzio to Terracina.

Pontus, Pontic: see 'Mithridates'.

Praeneste: see 'Latium'.

Ptolemy: Ptolemy XIII, c. 62–44 BC, son of Ptolemy XII and brother of Cleopatra.

Responsible for Pompey's assassination and, after Caesar's arrival, a plot to defeat the latter militarily.

Pyrrhus: king of Epirus (306–302 and 297–272 BC); also king of Macedonia (288–284 BC). One of Rome's greatest foes and an outstanding general, repeatedly defeating the Romans in the 270s BC.

Rhamnus: town on the east coast of Attica which overlooked the Euboean strait. Closely associated with the goddess Nemesis.

Rhodes: island sacred to Apollo, the largest of the Dodecanese islands of Greece.

r. Rhodanus: the Rhône.

Rhodope: mountain of Thrace.

Riphaean: a mountain range in the far north of Scythia.

Romulus: legendary founder and first king of Rome and killer of his twin brother Remus. Responsible for expanding the population via the rape of the Sabine women. Later translated to heaven in a mysterious whirlwind and worshipped as the god Quirinus.

r. Rubicon: river of north-eastern Italy marking the boundary between the Roman province of Cisalpine Gaul and Italy.

r. Rutuba: a tributary of the Tiber, the river of Rome.

Sabellians: a people of south and central Italy.

Sabine women: abducted by Romulus' Romans to become brides, these women interceded in the war between their new husbands and their Sabine fathers, preventing bloodshed.

Sacriportum: see 'Latium'.

Sadalis: see 'Cotys'.

Salapia: see 'Apulia'.

Salona: a city stretching along the Dalmatian coast, above the mouth of the river Jadro (L.'s Jader), situated north and west of modern Solin, Croatia.

Salerne: modern Salerno, a port city south-east of Naples.

Samnis, Samnite: of Samnium, a region of southern Italy.

Sarmatia, Sarmatian: catch-all term for Iranian nomadic tribes including the Alani and Iazyges, who invaded Scythia, and settled in the Caucasus and west as far as the Danube.

r. Sarnus: river dividing Picenum from Campania, the southernmost Italian region.

Sason: modern Saso, an island mid-way between the Greek coast and Brundisium.

Scaevola: Q. Mucius Scaevola (c. 140–82 BC), consul 95 BC, Pontifex Maximus; assassinated in the shrine of Vesta, a victim of Marius.

Scipio:

Publius Cornelius Scipio 'Africanus': in 204–203 BC Scipio Africanus' siege of Utica in Africa forced the Carthaginian general Hannibal to forsake Italy. Roman general and consul 205 BC; credited with defeating Hannibal at the battle of Zama (202 BC) and winning the second Punic war.

Q. Caecilius Metellus Pio Scipio (95–46 BC), son of P. Cornelius Scipio Nasica and co-consul with Pompey in 52 BC: it was his motion in the Senate, directing

Caesar to disband his army, that provoked the civil war. Scipio was granted command of the province of Syria for 49 BC, and he took the leadership of the centre at Pharsalus. He escaped to Africa after the battle and was defeated near Thapsus.

Scylla, Scyllean: mythical monster guarding the straits of Messina, opposite the whirlpool Charybdis.

Scythia: territory east and north-east of the Black Sea. Often used in general terms to denote the 'untamed' peoples of the east. In L. Scythians are associated with hardy living amidst frost and snow, and a nomadic life-style.

Scythian Ocean: the Black Sea.

Selinus: port city of Cilicia.

Senones: the Gallic tribe that sacked Rome 387 BC.

Septimius: Lucius Septimius. Caesar mentions him as a military tribune, and as a centurion under Pompey in 67 BC (*Commentarii*, 3. 104). He served with Aulus Gabinius in Egypt in 55 BC, remaining in Egypt as part of the garrison securing Ptolemy XII Auletes' throne.

Seres: people of north-east Asia, associated with the silk trade; however, L. believes that they inhabit the upper reaches of the Nile.

Sertorius: Quintus Sertorius (123–73 BC). A Marian supporter, in 80 BC he raised a band of anti-Sullan Roman exiles in Spain, and held most of Spain for several years in the conflict known as the 'Sertorian War'. After some initial success against Pompey (who had been placed in charge of Hispania Ulterior) he suffered several military defeats and, as a result of his tyrannical behaviour, lost the support of his Spanish and Roman faction. He died in 73 BC, assassinated by fellow Roman Marcus Perpenna Vento.

Sesostris: an ancient king of Egypt (and according to Herodotus, Diodorus Siculus and Strabo, another world-conqueror in Alexander's mode).

Sestos: see 'Abydos'.

Sextus: see 'Pompey'.

r. Sicoris: modern Segres, tributary of the Ebro, whose basin comprises parts of France, Andorra and Spain.

Sibyl: the Sibyl of Cumae was a priestess of Apollo, apparently responsible for creating the Sibylline Books, works of prophetic value entrusted to a priestly college.

Sidon: town in northern Judaea.

r. Siler: = Sele, a river of Campania, which flows through the territories of Salernum (Salerno), a port on the Tyrrhenian sea.

r. Sonna: M.'s misspelling of Senna, an Umbrian river.

Sophene: a region of Armenia, forced to accept client-king status in 66 BC after Pompey's expedition to Artaxata.

Spartacus: leader of a slave revolt in 73 BC; finally defeated by Pompey and Crassus in 71 BC.

Staechas: the Stoechades, modern Îles d'Hyères, islands off the coast east of Marseilles.

r. Strymon: the river between Thrace and Macedon.

Suevia, Suevians: catch-all term for the Germanic peoples living east of the Elbe and Rhine.

Sulla:

Lucius Cornelius Sulla Felix (c. 138–78 BC), Roman general and statesman of the conservative faction. Consul twice (in 88 and 80 BC). His antagonism with Marius exploded in the 'Social Wars' of the 80s BC; after marching on Rome in 81 and defeating Marius he made himself dictator and was responsible for the proscriptions, a series of political killings. After his second consulship he retired to Puteoli and lived as a private citizen.

Faustus Cornelius Sulla (d. 46 BC): son of the above and ally of Pompey. He fought at Pharsalus but after the defeat at Thapsus he was captured and killed.

Susa: see 'Parthia'.

Syene: modern Aswan, a town on the borders of Egypt and Ethiopia.

Sypus: see 'Apulia'.

Syrtes, Syrts: notoriously treacherous sandy shallows around the Libyan coast.

Taenarus: Cape Tainaron, a promontory of the southern Peloponnese; understood in antiquity to be an entrance to the underworld.

r. Tagus: the longest river in the Iberian peninsula, famed for its gold-bearing properties.

r. Tanaïs: modern Don, the river dividing Scythians and Sarmatians and, according to L., originating in the Riphaean mountains in the far north. It was often designated as the border between Asia and Europe, and flows into the Sea of Azov.

r. Taras: a river by Tarentum (modern Tarento).

Tarpeian Rock/Hill: a cliff on the Capitoline hill of Rome, from which traitors and murderers were thrown; by metonymy, the Capitol itself.

Tarsus: a town in the south of Cilicia; according to L. founded by the Greek hero Perseus.

Tartarean, Tartarus: the area of the Underworld devoted to the punishment of sinners.

Taurus: a mountain range along the northern border of Cilicia.

Telmessus, Telmessum: town of west Lycia, near present-day Fethiye, Turkey.

Tempe: a gorge in northern Thessaly between Olympus and Ossa.

Tethys: in L. metonymy for the sea: wife of Oceanus.

Themis: Titan goddess of justice; according to Greek myth the original inhabitant of the oracle of Delphi before being expelled by Apollo.

Thermus: Quintus Minucius Thermus, praetor 49 BC and Pompeian commander.

Theseus: Greek hero of Athens, slayer of the Cretan Minotaur. According to legend he forgot to put white sails on his ships when returning from Crete, the sign that he had succeeded: his father Aegeus, believing him to be dead, jumped to his death from cliffs on seeing the black sails.

Thesprots: the Thesprotes are a tribe of Epirus.

Thessalia, Thessaly: region of north-west Greece and theatre for the major civil war battle of Pharsalus in 48 BC.

r. Tiber: river associated above all with Rome. Rising in the Apennine Mountains and flowing through Tuscany, Umbria and Lazio, it flows into the Tyrrhenian Sea near Ostia.

Tigranes: son-in-law of Mithridates and king of Armenia. He was awarded rule of Armenia by Pompey, after capitulation to him in his eastern campaign.

r. Tigris: along with the Euphrates, a famous river of Mesopotamia, believed in antiquity to come from a common source. L. puts the rising of the river in Persis, the Parthian region of south-west Iran. It is approximately 1850 km long.

Tisiphone: see 'Erinys'.

Titan: in L., metonymy for the sun.

Torquatus, Torquati: prominent Roman Republican family of the *gens Manlia*.

Trachis: a city of Thessaly.

Trebia: a town in the province of Piacenza and location for the first major battle of the Second Punic War, in December 218 BC: a disastrous defeat for the Romans.

Tyre: a town in northern Judaea.

Tyrrhene: part of the Mediterranean Sea off the western coast of Italy.

Umbria, Umbrians: non-coastal region of Italy straddling the Apennines, east of Tuscany and north-east of Rome.

Utica: town near Carthage and location near to the civil war battle of Thapsus, June 46 BC, between Caesarian forces and the remaining Republican forces; location of Cato's suicide.

Varus: Publius Attius Varus, Pompeian commander. Varus had been propraetor of the province of Africa in 52 BC, and usurped control of the province again after defeat at Picenum. Though defeated by Curio, he was saved by the Numidian king Juba, and continued to fight against Caesar, finally dying at the battle of Munda in 45 BC.

Veii: ancient city of Etruria, annexed by Rome in 386 BC.

Veneti: a tribe of north-east Italy, who gave their name to modern Venice.

Vesta: protector goddess of Rome and goddess of the hearth. Her shrine with its flame was tended by the Vestal Virgins.

Vestine rivers: i.e. rivers of the Vestine region of Italy, roughly the modern Abruzzo region.

Vettones: Spanish people of central Iberia.

Vogesus: modern Voges mountains, bordering Germany on the uplands of eastern France.

r. Vulturnus: Campanian river flowing into the Tyrrhenian sea near Capua.

Wagon: (also 'Wain', 'Plough') part of the constellation of Ursa Major.

Wain: see 'Wagon'.

Xerxes: Persian King. In 480 BC as part of an attempted invasion of Greece, he joined Sestos and Abydos (towns on either side of the Hellespont, the sea dividing Europe and Asia), with a bridge of ships in order to join the continents.

BIBLIOGRAPHY

Accius, *Remains of Old Latin*, ii, ed. and trans by E. H. Warmington, Loeb Classical Texts, (Cambridge, MA: Harvard University Press, 1936)
Ahl, Frederick, *Lucan: An Introduction* (Ithaca, NY: Cornell University Press, 1976)
D'Alessandro Behr, Francesca, *Feeling History: Lucan, Stoicism, and the Poetics of Passion* (Columbus, OH: Ohio State University Press, 2007)
Alexander, Sir William, *Doomes-Day, or, the Great Day of the Lords Judgement* (London: Andro Hart, 1614)
Anon., *The Tragedie of Caesar and Pompey, or Caesar's Revenge* (London: George Eld for John Wright, 1607)
Appian, *Roman History, Volume III: The Civil Wars, Books 1–3.26*, trans. by Horace White, Loeb Classical Texts (Cambridge, MA: Harvard University Press, 1913)
Appian, *Roman History, Volume IV: The Civil Wars, Books 3.27–5*, trans. by Horace White, Loeb Classical Texts (Cambridge, MA: Harvard University Press, 1913)
Arber, Edward, ed., *A Transcript of the Registers of the Company of Stationers of London, 1554–1640 AD*, 5 vols (London: privately printed, 1875–1894)
Aubrey, John, *Brief Lives*, ed. by John Buchanan-Brown (London and New York: Centaur Press, 1972)
Augustine, St, *Of the City of God*, trans. by John Healey (London: George Eld, 1610)
Backhaus, Birger, ed., *Das Supplementum Lucani von Thomas May: Einleitung, Edition, Übersetzung, Kommentar* (Trier: WVT, 2005)
Barclay, John, *Barclay his Argenis: or the Loves of Poliarchus and Argenis*, trans. by Kingsmill Long and Thomas May (London: George Purslowe for Henry Seile, 1625)
Baron, Robert, *Mirza* (London: for Humphrey Moseley, 1647)
Bartsch, Shadi, *Ideology in Cold Blood: A Reading of Lucan's Civil War* (Cambridge, MA: Harvard University Press, 1997)
—— 'Lucan and Historical Bias', in *Brill's Companion to Lucan*, ed. by Paolo Asso (Leiden: Brill, 2010), pp. 303–16
Baxter, Nathaniel, *Sir Philip Sydney's Ourania* (London: E. Allde for Edward White, 1606)
Bentley, Gerald E., *The Jacobean and Caroline Stage*, 6 vols (Oxford: Oxford University Press, 1941–1968)
Bernard, F., '*Fatum* and *Fortuna* in Lucan's *Bellum Civile*', *Classical Philology*, 62 (1967), 235–42
Bernard, S., and Sowerby, R., eds, *The Plays and Poems of Nicholas Rowe vol. IV: Poems and Lucan's Pharsalia (Books I–III)* (London: Routledge, 2017)
Boccalini, Traiano, *The new-found politicke*, trans. by John Florio et al. (London: Eliot's Court Press for Francis Williams, 1626)
Bramble, J. C., 'Lucan', in *The Cambridge History of Classical Literature ii: Latin Literature*, ed. by E. J. Kenney and W. V. Clausen (Cambridge: Cambridge University Press, 1982), pp. 533–57

BRAUND, SUSANNA, 'Lucan', in *Oxford Bibliographies in Classics*, https://www.oxfordbibliographies.com/view/document/obo-9780195389661/obo-9780195389661-0033.xml. Accessed 14 October 2019
—— 'Violence in Translation', in *Brill's Companion to Lucan*, ed. by Paolo Asso (Leiden: Brill, 2011), pp. 507–24
BROWN, C. A., and MARTINDALE C., eds, *Lucan: The Civil War. Translated as Lucan's Pharsalia by Nicholas Rowe* (London: Everyman, 1998)
BUCKLEY, EMMA, and DINTER, MARTIN T., eds, *A Companion to the Neronian Age* (Oxford: Wiley-Blackwell, 2013)
CAMBRIDGE, UNIVERSITY OF, *Epicedium Cantabrigiense* (Cambridge: Cantrell Legge, 1612)
CAESAR, G. JULIUS, *Commentarii de Bello Ciuili*, ed. by Renatus du Pontet (Oxford: Clarendon Press, 1908)
—— *Caesar: Alexandrian War. African War. Spanish War*, trans. by A. G. Way, Loeb Classical Texts (Cambridge, MA: Harvard University Press, 1955)
CHALK, BRIAN, *Monuments and Literary Posterity in Early Modern Drama* (Cambridge: Cambridge University Press, 2015)
CICERO, MARCUS TULLIUS, *De Oratore: Books I–II*, trans. by E. W. Sutton, ed. by H. Rackham, Loeb Classical Texts (Cambridge, MA: Harvard University Press, 1948)
—— *The Polytyque Book Named Tullius De Senectute*, trans. by William Caxton (London: William Caxton, 1481)
—— *De Senectute, De Amicitia, De Divinatione*, trans. by W. A. Falconer, Loeb Classical Texts (Cambridge, MA: Harvard University Press, 1923)
—— *Philippics*, trans. by Walter C. A. Ker, Loeb Classical Texts (Cambridge, MA: Harvard University Press, 1926)
CHENEY, PATRICK G., *Marlowe's Republican Authorship: Lucan, Liberty, and the Sublime* (Basingstoke: Palgrave MacMillan, 2009)
CHESTER, ALLAN G., 'Thomas May: Man of Letters, 1595–1650' (Pennsylvania, PA: University of Pennsylvania Press, 1932)
COKAIN, ASTON, *A Chain of Golden Poems* (London: William Godbid, 1658)
COLVIN, SIDNEY, *Early Engraving & Engravers in England (1545–1695): A Critical and Historical Essay* (London: British Museum, 1905)
COOPER, JOHN M., 'Justus Lipsius and the Revival of Stoicism in Late Sixteenth-Century Europe' in *New Essays on the History of Autonomy*, ed. by Natalie Brender and Larry Krasnoff (Cambridge: Cambridge University Press, 2004), pp. 7–29
COURTNEY, EDWARD, *The Fragmentary Latin Poets* (Oxford: Oxford University Press, 1993)
CRINITO, PIETRO, *Libri de Poetis Latinis* (Florence: Filippo I Giunta, 1505)
CUST, RICHARD, *The Forced Loan and English Politics, 1626–1628* (Oxford: Oxford University Press, 1987)
DALLINGTON, ROBERT, *Aphorisms ciuill and militarie* (London: for Edward Blount, 1613)
DANIEL, SAMUEL, *The poeticall essayes of Sam. Danyel* (London: P. Short for Simon Waterson, 1599)
DAY, HENRY J. M., *Lucan and the Sublime: Power, Representation and Aesthetic Experience* (New York: Cambridge University Press, 2013)

DEKKER, THOMAS, *Nevves from hell brought by the Diuells carrier* (London: R. B[lower, S. Stafford, and Valentine Simmes] for V. V. Ferebrand, 1606)

DICK, BERNARD F., 'Fatum and Fortuna in Lucan's *Bellum Civile*', *Classical Philology*, 62 (1967), 235-42

DINTER, MARTIN T., *Lucan's Epic Body: Anatomizing Civil War* (Ann Arbor: University of Michigan Press, 2012)

DODOENS, REMBERT, *A New Herbal, or History of Plants*, trans. by Henry Lyte (London: Ninian Newton, 1619)

DRAYTON, MICHAEL, *The Battaile of Agincourt* (London: Augustine Mathews for William Lee, 1627)

DRUMMOND, WILLIAM, OF HAWTHORNDEN, *Poems* (Edinburgh: Andrew Hart, 1616)

DU BARTAS, GUILLAUME DE SALLUSTE, *Bartas his Divine Weeks and Works Translated*, trans. by Joshua Sylvester (London: Humphrey Lownes, 1608)

DUPPA, BRIAN, ed., *Jonsonus Virbius* (London: E. Purslowe for Henry Seile, 1638)

'DWALPHINTRAMIS' [possibly Richard Bernard or John Bernard], *The Anatomie of the Service Book, Dedicated to the High Court of Parliament* (location and printer unknown, 1641)

ESPOSITO, P., and WALDE, C., eds, *Letture e lettori di Lucano: Atti del Convegno internazionale di studi, Fisciano, 27-29 marzo 2012* (Pisa: ETS, 2015)

EVANS, ROBERT C., *Jonson, Lipsius, and the Politics of Renaissance Neo-Stoicism* (Durango: Longwood, 1992)

EVELYN, JOHN, *Sylva, or a Discourse of Forest Trees, and the Propagation of Timber in His Majesty's Dominions*, 2nd ed. (London: John Martyn and James Allestree, 1670)

FANTHAM, ELAINE, 'The Angry Poet and the Angry Gods: Problems of Theodicy in Lucan's Epic of Defeat', in *Ancient Anger. Perspectives from Homer to Galen*, ed. by Susanna Braund and Glenn W. Most (*Yale Classical Studies* 32) (Cambridge: Cambridge University Press, 2004), pp. 229-49

FEENEY, DENIS C., *The Gods in Epic: Poets and Critics of the Classical Tradition* (New York: Oxford University Press, 1991)

FISCHLI, WALTER, *Studien zum Fortleben der Pharsalia des M. Annaeus Lucanus* (Luzern: E. Haag, 1944)

FLETCHER, JOHN, *The Loyal Subject*, ed. by Fredson Bowers, in *The Dramatic Works in the Beaumont and Fletcher Canon*, general ed. Fredson Bowers, vol. 5 (Cambridge: Cambridge University Press, 1982), pp. 151-288

—— AND MASSINGER, PHILIP, *The False One*, ed. by Robert Kean Turner, in *The Dramatic Works in the Beaumont and Fletcher Canon*, general ed. Fredson Bowers, vol. 8 (Cambridge: Cambridge University Press, 1992), p. 113-222

FLORUS, *Epitome of Roman History*, trans. by Edward S. Forester (Cambridge, MA: Harvard University Press, 1984)

FULLER, THOMAS, *The History of the Worthies of England* (London: J. Grismond, W. Leybourne and William Godbid for Thomas Williams, 1662)

GALTIER, F., and POIGNAULT, R., eds, *Présence de Lucain* (Clermont-Ferrand: Centre de Recherches A. Piganiol-Présence de l'Antiquité, 2016)

GÄRTNER, THOMAS, 'Objektives Fatum und Subjektive Fatumsgläubigkeit im Bürgerkriegsepos des Lucan', *Acta Antiqua*, 45 (2005), 51-84

GOLDSCHMIDT, NORA, *Afterlives of the Roman Poets: Biofiction and the Reception of Latin Poetry* (Cambridge: Cambridge University Press, 2019)
—— 'Lucan: A Guide to Selected Sources', in *Living Poets* (Durham, 2015), https://livingpoets.dur.ac.uk/w/Lucan:_A_Guide_to_Selected_Sources?oldid=4787. Accessed 29 October 2019
GORGES, SIR ARTHUR, *Lucan's Pharsalia: containing the ciuill warres between Caesar and Pompey* (London: Nicholas Okes for Edward Blount, 1614)
GREVILLE, FULKE, *Certaine learned and elegant vvorkes of the Right Honorable Fulke Lord Brooke written in his youth, and familiar exercise with Sir Philip Sidney* (London: E[lizabeth] P[urslowe] for Henry Seyle, 1633)
GROTIUS, HUGO, *M. Annei Lucani Pharsalia ... ex emendatione H. Grotii, cum eiusdem ad loca insigniora notis* (Leiden: ex officina Plantiniana Raphelengii, 1614)
HADFIELD, ANDREW, *Shakespeare and Republicanism* (Cambridge: Cambridge University Press, 2005)
HARDIE, PHILIP, 'Lucan in the English Renaissance', in *Brill's Companion to Lucan*, ed. by Paolo Asso (Leiden: Brill, 2011), pp. 491–506
—— *Virgil's 'Aeneid': Cosmos and Imperium* (Oxford: Clarendon Press, 1986)
HENDERSON, JOHN, 'Lucan/The Word at War', *Ramus*, 16 (1987), 122–64
HEYWOOD, THOMAS, TRANS., 'The Conspiracy of Cateline' in [G. Sallustius Crispus,] *The Two Most Worthy and Notable Histories which Remain Unmained to Posterity* (London: W. Jaggard for J. Jaggard, 1609)
HILL, JAMES W. F. S., *Tudor and Stuart Lincoln* (Cambridge: Cambridge University Press, 2009)
HORACE (Horatius Flaccus, Q.), *Odes of Horace the Best of Lyrick Poets*, trans. by Sir Thomas Hawkins (London: Augustine Mathews for William Lee, 1625)
—— *Opera*, ed. by Edward Wickham and H. Garrod (Oxford: Clarendon Press, 1901)
HULSE, CLARKE, *Metamorphic Verse: The Elizabethan Minor Epic* (Princeton: Princeton University Press, 1981)
HYDE, EDWARD, EARL OF CLARENDON, *The Life of Edward Earl of Clarendon ... Written by Himself*, 2 vols (Oxford: Clarendon Press, 1827)
JACKSON, THOMAS, *A Treatise Concerning the Original of Unbelief, Misbelief or Mispersuasions* (London: John Dawson for John Clark, 1625)
JENSEN, FREYA COX, '"Creating" Cato in Early Seventeenth-Century England', in *Concepts of Creativity in Seventeenth-Century England*, ed. by R. Herissone and A. Howard (Cambridge: Boydell and Brewer, 2013), pp. 233–52
—— *Reading the Roman Republic in Early Modern England* (Leiden: Brill, 2012)
JOHNSON, SAMUEL, *Prefaces Biographical and Critical to the Works of the English Poets* (London: J. Nichols, 1779–1781)
JOHNSON, W. R., *Momentary Monsters: Lucan and His Heroes* (Ithaca, NY: Cornell University Press, 1987)
JONSON, BEN, *The Cambridge Edition of the Works of Ben Jonson*, ed. by David Bevington, Martin Butler and Ian Donaldson, 7 vols (Cambridge: Cambridge University Press, 2012)
—— *The Complete Masques*, ed. by Stephen Orgel (New Haven & London: Yale University Press, 1969)

KENDAL, GORDON, ed., *Gawin Douglas: The Aeneid (1513)* (London: Modern Humanities Research Association, 2013)
KLINGER, F., ed., *Horatius Flaccus, Q., Opera* (Leipzig: Teubner, 1959)
LEIGH, MATTHEW *Lucan: Spectacle and Engagement* (Oxford: Clarendon Press, 1997)
LILBURNE, JOHN, *The Innocent Man's First Proffer* (London: printer unknown, 1649)
LINTOTT, ANDREW W., 'Lucan and the History of the Civil War', *The Classical Quarterly*, 21 (1971), 488–505
LIPSIUS, JUSTUS, *De Constantia Libri Duo* (Antwerp: Christopher Plantin, 1584)
LIVY, *History of Rome, Volume I, Books 1-2*, trans. by B. O. Foster, Loeb Classical Texts (Cambridge, MA: Harvard University Press, 1919)
LUCANUS, MARCUS ANNAEUS, *Pharsalia*, ed. by Thomas Farnaby (London: Richard Field, 1618)
—— *Pharsaliae Libri X*, ed. by Lambertus Hortensius (Basle: Henricus Petrus, 1578)
—— *De bello civile, libri decem. Cum scholiis ... I. Sulpitii Verlani, certis autem locis Omniboni. Una cum annotationibus ... I. Micylli* (Francofurti: apud Chr. Egenolphum, 1551)
LUCIAN OF SAMOSOTA, *Complete Works*, ed. by A. M. Harmon, K. Kilburn, M. D. Macleod and H. C. Hofheimer (Cambridge, MA: Harvard University Press, 2000)
MACLEAN, GERALD, *Time's Witness: Historical Representation in English Poetry, 1603-1660* (Madison: Wisconsin University Press, 1990)
MAES, YANICK, 'Translating Lucan in the Early Seventeenth Century', in *A Companion to the Neronian Age*, ed. by Emma Buckley and Martin T. Dinter (Oxford: Wiley-Blackwell, 2013), pp. 405-424
MARLOWE, CHRISTOPHER, *The Complete Works*, ed. by Fredson Bowers, 2 vols, 2nd ed. (Cambridge: Cambridge University Press, 1981)
MARSTON, JOHN, *The Wonder of Women or The Tragedie of Sophonisba as it hath beene sundry times acted at the Blacke Friers* (London: John Windet for W. Cotton, 1606)
MARTIALIS, MARCUS VALERIUS, *Epigrammata*, ed. by W. M. Lindsay, 2nd ed. (Oxford: Clarendon Press, 1902)
MARVELL, ANDREW, *The Poems*, ed. by Nigel Smith, revised ed., Longman Annotated Poets (Edinburgh: Pearson, 2007)
MASSINGER, PHILIP, *The Roman Actor* (London: Bernard Alsop and Thomas Fawcett for Robert Allot, 1629)
MASTERS, JAMIE, *Poetry and Civil War in Lucan's 'Bellum Civile'* (Cambridge: Cambridge University Press, 1992)
MAY, THOMAS, *A Breviary of the History of the Parliament of England* (London: Robert White for Thomas Brewster and Gregory Moule, 1650)
—— *A Continuation of Lucan's Historicall Poem till the death of Julius Caesar* (London: J. Haviland for James Boler, 1630)
—— *A Discourse Concerning the Success of Former Parliaments* (London: for I. H. and H. White, 1642)
—— *The Heire An Excellent Comedie as it was Acted by the Company of the Revels* (London: Bernard Alsop for Thomas Jones, 1622)
—— *The Heire An Excellent Comedie as it was Acted by the Company of the Revels.*

1620 (London: Augustine Mathews for Thomas Jones, 1633)
—— *Historiae Angliae Parliamenti Breviarium* (London: Charles Sumptner for Thomas Bruster, 1650)
—— *The History of the Parliament of England: which began November the third, M.DC.XL.* (London: Moses Bell for George Thomason, 1647)
—— *Lucan's Pharsalia: or the Civil Wars of Rome, between Pompey the Great and Julius Caesar* (London: Augustine Mathews for Thomas Jones and John Marriot, 1627)
—— *The Old Couple, A Comedy* (London: J. Cottrel for Samuel Speed, 1658)
—— *Supplementum Lucani* (Leiden: Willem Christiaens van der Boxe, 1640)
—— *The Victorious Reign of Edward III* (London: John Beale for T. Walkley and B. Fisher, 1635)
—— *Virgil's Georgicks Englished* (Britain's Burse: Humphrey Lownes for Thomas Walkley, 1628)
McCREA, A., *Constant Minds: Political Virtue and the Lipsian Paradigm in England, 1584-1650* (Toronto: University of Toronto Press, 1997)
MILTON, JOHN, *Complete Shorter Poems*, ed. by John Carey (New York and London: Longmans, 1968)
—— *A Variorum Commentary on the Poems of John Milton. Vol. 4: Paradise Regained*, ed. by Walter MacKellar (London: Routledge and Kegan Paul, 1975)
MONTAIGNE, MICHAEL SEIGNEUR DE, *The Essays*, trans. by Charles Cotton (London: for T. Basset, M. Gilliflower and W. Hensman, 1685)
VON MOOS, PETER, 'Lucain au Moyen Âge', in *Entre histoire et littérature: Communication et culture au Moyen Âge*, ed. by Peter von Moos (*Millennio medievale*, 58) (Firenze: Sismel, 2005), pp. 89-204
MORFORD, MARK, *Stoics and Neostoics: Rubens and the Circle of Lipsius* (Princeton: Princeton University Press, 1991)
MORRILL, JOHN, 'Devereux, Robert, Third Earl of Essex (1591-1646)', *ODNB*
NARDUCCI, EMANUELE, *La provvidenza crudele. Lucano e la distruzione dei miti augustei* (Pisa: Giardini, 1979)
—— *Lucano: un'epica contro l'impero* (Roma-Bari: Laterza, 2002)
NEWSTOK, S., *Quoting Death in Early Modern England: The Poetics of Epitaphs Beyond the Tomb* (Basingstoke: Palgrave Macmillan, 2015)
NORBROOK, DAVID, 'Lucan, Thomas May, and the Creation of a Republican Literary Culture' in *Culture and Politics in Early Stuart England*, ed. by Kevin Sharpe and Peter Lake (Stanford: Stanford University Press 1993), pp. 45-66
—— 'May, Thomas (b. in or after 1596, d. 1650)', *ODNB*
—— *Poetry and Politics in the English Renaissance* (Oxford: Oxford University Press, 2009)
—— *Writing the English Republic: Poetry, Rhetoric and Politics, 1627-1660* (Cambridge: Cambridge University Press, 2000)
OESTREICH, GERARD, *Neostoicism and the Early Modern State* (Cambridge: Cambridge University Press, 1982)
OROSIUS, PAULUS, *Seven books of history against the pagans: The apology of Paulus Orosius*, trans. by Irving W. Raymond (New York: Columbia University Press, 1936)
OVIDIUS NASO, PUBLIUS, *Metamorphoses*, ed. by W. S. Anderson (Stuttgart & Leipzig: Teubner, 1991)

PALEIT, EDWARD, *War, Liberty, and Caesar: Responses to Lucan's 'Bellum Ciuile'*, ca. 1580-1650 (Oxford: Oxford University Press, 2013)
PELTONEN, MARKKU, *Classical Humanism and Republicanism in English Political Thought, 1570-1640* (Cambridge: Cambridge University Press, 1995)
PERKINS, WILLIAM, *A Golden Chain, or the description of Theology* (Cambridge: John Leggat, 1600)
PHILLIPS, EDWARD, *Theatrum Poetarum, or a Compleat Collection of the Poets, especially the most eminent, of all ages* (London: for Charles Smith, 1675)
PLUTARCH, *Plutarch's Lives*, trans. by Bernadotte Perrin, 11 vols, Loeb Classical Texts (London: W. Heinemann, 1914)
POCOCK, J. G. A., *The Machiavellian Moment: Florentine Political Thought and the Atlantic Republican Tradition*, 2nd ed. (Princeton and Oxford: Princeton University Press, 2003)
POMEY, FRANÇOIS, *Pantheon*, trans. by Andrew Tooke (London: Benjamin Motte for Robert Clavel, 1694)
POOLE, JOSHUA, ed., *The English Parnassus: or, a help to English Poesy* (London: for Thomas Johnson, 1657)
PUGH, SYRITHE, *Herrick, Fanshawe and the Politics of Intertextuality: Classical Literature and Seventeenth-Century Royalism* (Farnham/Burlington, VT: Ashgate, 2010)
RADICKE, JAN, *Lucans poetische Technik. Studien zum historischen Epos. Mnemosyne Supplement 249* (Leiden: Brill, 2004)
RIDER, JOHN, *Rider's Dictionary Corrected and Augmented* (London: Adam Islip, 1606)
ROCHE, PAUL, *Lucan: De Bello Ciuili Book 1* (Oxford: Oxford University Press, 2009)
RUTGERS, JOHANNES, *Variarum Lectionum Libri Sex* (Leiden: Elzevir, 1616)
RUTZ, WERNER, ed., *Lucan* (Wege der Forschung, 235) (Darmstadt: Wissenschaftliche Buchgesellschaft, 1970)
SCALIGER, JULIUS CAESAR, *Poetices Libri Septem*, ed. by Gregor Vogt-Spira and Luc Deitz, 6 vols (Stuttgart: Frommann Holzboog, 1994-2011)
SELDEN, JOHN, *The Duello, or Single Combat* (London: George Held for I. Helm, 1610)
SENECA, LUCIUS A., *Epistles*, trans. by Richard M. Gummere, 3 vols, Loeb Classical Texts (Cambridge, MA: Harvard University Press, 1917)
—— *Moral Essays, Volume I: De Providentia. De Constantia. De Ira. De Clementia*, trans. by John W. Basore, Loeb Classical Texts (Cambridge, MA: Harvard University Press, 1928)
SHAKESPEARE, WILLIAM, *The Complete Works: Modern Critical Edition*, ed. by Gary Taylor, John Jowett, Terri Bourus, Gabriel Egan, et al., The New Oxford Shakespeare (Oxford: Oxford University Press, 2016)
SHERLOCK, PETER, *Monuments and Memory in Early Modern England* (Aldershot: Ashgate, 2008)
SHIFFLETT, ANDREW, '"By Lucan Driv'n About": A Jonsonian Marvell's Lucanic Milton', *Renaissance Quarterly*, 49 (1996), 803-23
SIDNEY, SIR PHILIP, *The Countess of Pembroke's Arcadia* [1593], ed. by Maurice Evans (London: Penguin, 1977)
SKINNER, QUENTIN, *Liberty before Liberalism* (Cambridge: Cambridge University Press, 1998)

SKLENÁR, R., *The Taste for Nothingness: A Study of Virtus and Related Themes in Lucan's 'Bellum Civile'* (Ann Arbor: University of Michigan Press, 2013)

SMITH, NIGEL, *Literature and Revolution 1640-1660* (New Haven and London: Yale University Press, 1994)

SMITH, THOMAS, *Certain Additions to the book of Gunnery, with a Supply of Fireworks* (London: Humphrey Lownes for W. Ponsonby, 1627)

SOWERBY, R., ED. *The Plays and Poems of Nicholas Rowe vol. V: Poems and Lucan's Pharsalia (Books IV-X)* (London: Routledge, 2016)

SPENSER, EDMUND, *Complaints. Containing sundrie small poemes of the worlds vanitie.* (London: for William Ponsonbie, 1591)

—— *The Faerie Queene: Disposed into Twelue Books, Fashioning 12 Morall Vertues* (London: for William Ponsonbie, 1590)

STATIUS, PUBLIUS PAPINIUS, *Silvae*, ed. and trans. by D. R. Shackleton Bailey, revised by Christopher A. Parrott (Cambridge, MA: Harvard University Press, 2015)

SUETONIUS, *Lives of the Caesars*, trans. by J. C. Rolfe, Loeb Classical Texts, 2 vols (Cambridge, MA: Harvard University Press, 1914)

SYDENHAM, CUTHBERT, ATTRIB., *An Anatomy of Lieut. Col. John Lilburn's Spirit and Pamphlets* (London: John Macock for Francis Tryton, 1649)

TACITUS, CORNELIUS, *Annalium Ab Excessu Divi Augusti Libri*, ed. by C. D. Fisher (Oxford: Clarendon Press, 1906)

TESORIERO, CHARLES, ed., *Oxford Readings in Classical Studies: Lucan*, assisted by Frances Muecke and Tamara Neal with an Introduction by Susanna Braund (Oxford: Oxford University Press, 2010)

VAN THIEL, H., ED. *Homeri Ilias*, Bibliotheca Weidmanniana, 2 (Hildesheim, Zurich, and New York: Georg Olms, 1996)

THOMAS, RICHARD F., *Virgil and the Augustan Reception* (Cambridge: Cambridge University Press, 2001)

TRACY, JONATHAN, *Lucan's Egyptian Civil War* (Cambridge: Cambridge University Press, 2014)

USSHER, JAMES, *The Annals of the World* (London: E. Tyler for J. Crook, 1657)

VALERIUS MAXIMUS, *Memorable Doings and Sayings*, ed. and trans. by D. R. Shackleton Bailey, 2 vols (Cambridge, MA: Harvard University Press, 2000)

VIRGIL, ED., P. *Virgili Maronis Opera*, ed. by R. A. B. Mynors, (Oxford: Oxford University Press; Oxford Classical Texts, 1969)

WALDE, CHRISTINE, ed., '*Fortuna* bei Lucan — Vor- und Nachgedanken', in *Götter und menschliche Willensfreiheit von Lukan bis Silius Italicus*, ed. by Thomas Baier (*Zetemata. 142*) (München: C. H. Beck, 2012), pp. 57-74

—— 'Lucan (Marcus Annaeus Lucanus), Bellum Civile', in *The Reception of Classical Literature: Brill's New Pauly Supplements I, vol.5*, ed. by Christine Walde (Leiden: Brill, 2012) http://dx.doi.org/10.1163/2214-8647_bnps5_ID_0030. Accessed 27 March 2020

—— *Lucans 'Bellum Civile'. Studien zum Spektrum seiner Rezeption von der Antike bis ins 19. Jahrhundert* (Bochumer Altertumswissenschaftliches Colloquium, 78) (Trier: Wissenschaftlicher Verlag Trier, 2009)

WARMINGTON, ERIC H., *Remains of Old Latin: In Four Volumes* (Cambridge, MA: Harvard University Press, 2006)

WARREN, CHRISTOPHER N., *Literature and the Law of Nations, 1580–1680* (Oxford: Oxford University Press, 2015)

WEEVER, JOHN, *Ancient Funerall Monuments within the United Monarchy of Great Britain, Ireland, and the islands adjacent* (London: Thomas Harper, 1631)

WOLF-HARTMUT, FRIEDRICH, 'Cato, Caesar, and Fortune in Lucan', in *Lucan: Oxford Readings in Classical Studies*, ed. by Charles Tesoriero, assisted by Frances Muecke and Tamara Neal with an Introduction by Susanna Braund (Oxford: Oxford University Press, 2010), pp. 369–410

WOOD, ANTHONY À, *Athenae Oxonienses*, ed. by Philip Bliss, 4 vols (London: for F. C. and J. Rivington, 1813–1820)

WORDEN, BLAIR, 'Ben Jonson Among the Historians', in *Culture and Politics in Early Stuart England*, ed. by Peter Lake and Kevin Sharpe (Stanford: Stanford University Press 1993), pp. 67–90

—— 'English Republicanism', in *The Cambridge History of Political Thought*, ed. by J. H. Burns with Mark Goldie (Cambridge: Cambridge University Press, 1991), pp. 443–78

—— *Literature and Politics in Cromwellian England* (Oxford: Oxford University Press, 2007)

WYMER, ROWLAND, *Suicide and Despair in the Jacobean Drama* (Brighton: The Harvester Press, 1986)

INDEX

Note: only Lucan's major characters and some of his locations are included here; for others, please consult the Glossary. References by book and line number are to May's translation.

Alexandria, siege of, 5, 10.9–672
Ambition, 24, 26n, 82, 1.95, 1.163, 7.436, 10.50
Appius Claudius, 5.78–270

Bertie, Robert, Earl of Lindsey, 24, 181
Brutus, Marcus Junius, 6, 7, 43, 82n, 291, 2.247–344, 5.237–9, 7.499, 7.666–77
Buckingham, see Villiers

Caesar, Gaius Julius, 5, 6, 17, 1.156–72, 2.467–560, 2.694–726, 3.49–186, 3.325–492, 4.1–439, 5.271–831, 6.1–152, 6.311–376, 7.189–208, 7.265–381, 7.591–665, 7.829–941, 9.1081–1260, 10.1–672
Cato, Marcus Porcius, 6, 2.247–414, 9.186–1080
Carew, Thomas, 2
Cavendish, William, 2nd Earl of Devonshire, 14, 27, 38–39, 218
Charles I, 2, 23, 25, 82n, 147n, 2.103n
Civil war (40s BC), 5, *passim*
Civil War (1640s), 4–5, 22–23
Cleopatra, 6, 10.63–200, 10.409–31
Clinton, Theophilus, Earl of Lincoln, 24, 292
Cornelia, 5.832–939, 8.45–184, 8.675–97, 8.746–776
Cotton, Charles, 2, 4.303n, 8.446n
Cowley, Abraham, 11
Curio, 147, 1.289–317, 3.63, 4.643–906

Daniel, Samuel, 10, 11, 21, 10.70n
Digby, Sir Kenelm, 2, 3
Delphic oracle, 182, 5.78–270
Devereux, Robert, 2nd Earl of Essex, 24, 147

Erictho, 7, 218, 6.472–946

Faction, 24, 26n, 38, 80, 82, 410, 1.737, 2.398n, 4.781n, 5.16n, 5.402, 9.106, 10.482, 10.484
False One, The, 16, 19, 8.562n, 8.582n, 8.698n
Farnaby, Thomas, 14–15, *passim*
Fate and Fortune, 7–8n, *passim*

Gorges, Sir Arthur, 1, 17, 21, 418n, 1.8n, 1.477n, 3.25n, 7.1n
Grotius, Hugo, 10–11, 14–15, 407n, 415n, 3.271n, 4.271n, 6.489n, 6.572n, 7.658n, 7.664n, 8.226n, 8.869n, 9.255n, 9.936n, 10.99n, 10.544n

Heinsius, Daniel, 38n,
Herbert, William, Earl of Pembroke, 25, 82
Hortensius, Lambertus (early modern scholar), 15, 405n, 1.240n, 2.18n, 3.78n, 5.115n, 6.232n, 9.1148n
Hulsen, Friedrich, 13, 21, 27, 28, 37
Hyde, Edward, Earl of Clarendon, 2, 3n, 13n, 23, 26, 45n

Jonson, Ben, 2–3, 15–16, 19, 20–22, 23, 43, 45n, 82n, 218n, 2.252n, 7.528n
Sejanus, 19, 82n, 8.574n, 8.577n, 9.657n, 9.673n
Catiline, 21–22

Liberty, 8, 11, 13, 14, 20, 24, 25, 26, 36, 43, 254, 255, 291, 1.188, 1.292n, 1.715n, 2.318, 3.121–2n, 3.148, 3.383, 4.253, 4.637, 4.639–40n, 4.890, 5.236–9n, 6.152n, 7.399n, 7.422n, 7.489–92n, 7.660, 7.685, 7.791, 8.395, 8.396–7n, 9.33, 9.105n, 9.112n, 9.224, 9.238–40n, 9.309, 9.1259n, 10.649
Lipsius, Justus, 19, 21, 8.746n
Lucan (Marcus Annaeus Lucanus)
    Life, 9
    Suicide, 9, 36–37, 39

Index

Bellum Civile, 4–8
    Early modern reception, 9–12
    Political context and attitudes, 6–9
    Relationship to history, 7–8
    Style, 10

Marlowe, Christopher,
    translation of Lucan, 1, 16, 1.8n, 1.42n, 1.106n, 1.199n, 1.200n, 1.206n, 1.240n, 1.274n, 1.279n, 1.456n, 1.477n, 1.478n, 1.614n, 10.322n
Marston, John
    The Tragedy of Sophonisba, 16, 6.576n, 6.578n, 6.585n, 6.596n, 6.611n, 6.642n
Marvell, Andrew
    'Tom May's Death', 4, 22
Massilia, siege of, 3.325–824
May, Thomas
    Continuation of Lucan, 2, 3, 4, 5n, 8n, 21n, 27–28, 36n, 1.95n, 1.360n, 1.545n, 2.252n, 4.233n, 4.286n, 5.398n, 6.322n, 6.433n, 9.476n, 10.63n, 10.74n, 10.452n
    History of the Long Parliament, 3–4, 1.545n
    Life and career, 1–4
    Lucan's Pharsalia
        afterlife, 26–28
        attitude to history, 20–21
        dedications, 14, 24–25
        'the life of Marcus Annaeus Lucanus'
        political and literary context, 19–26
        publication, 12–14
        prosody, 34–5
        sources, 14–15
        style, 15–19
        title page, 36–37
    Supplementum Lucani, 3, 27, 36n, 4.286n, 9.1118n
    The Tragedy of Cleopatra 2, 3, 20, 8.558n, 9.1209n, 10.63n, 10.74n, 10.646n
    The Victorious Reign of Edward III, 218n, 1.318n, 2.75n, 10.646n

Nedham, Marchamont, 4, 22
Nero, 5, 9, 36, 37n, 38–9, 1.35–72

'Patriot', 23, 26, 82n
Pharsalus, battle of, 5, 7, 1.1n, 7.1–998
Pompey (Gnaeus Pompeius Magnus), 5, 6–7, 13, 15, 17, 24, 37, 38–9, 43, 44, 1.555–6, 2.415–422, 2.561–786, 3.1–48, 3.187–324, 5.1–77, 6.1–199, 294–471, 7.7–188, 7.242–65, 7.382–434, 7.460–665, 7.734–828, 8.1–1014, 9.1–20

Republicanism, 5, 11–12, 25–26
Rich, Robert, 2nd Earl of Warwick, 24n, 218n, 254n, 333

Scaeva, 7, 16, 219, 6.153–294, 10.620
Seneca, Lucius Annaeus, 9, 17, 21, 40, 41, 404n, 2.304n, 8.610n
Shakespeare, William, 16, 115n, 1.231n, 1.625n, 2.26n, 2.218n, 2.529n, 2.746n, 5.797n, 7.149n, 7.335n, 7.603n, 8.727n
Scaliger, Joseph, 10, 10.236n
Scaliger, Julius Caesar, 10, 4.655n
Selden, John, 2, 17n
Sextus Pompeius, 219, 6.472–946
Sheffield, Edmund, Earl of Mulgrave, 25, 115
Spenser, Edmund, 16, 36n, 1.231n, 2.647n, 5.277n, 7.149n
Sulpizio, Giovanni, 15, 40n, 42n, 47n, 116n, 219n, 255n, 293n, 378n, 405, 8.6n, 8.192n, 10.623–72n
Stoicism and neo-Stoicism, 10–11n, 19, 21–22, 25, 219, 8.744n, 8.746n, 10.565n

Vaughan, John, 2, 13, 23, 45
Vere, Sir Horatio, 254
Villiers, George, Duke of Buckingham, 23–25, 82n, 147n, 181n, 218n, 254n
Virgil (Publius Vergilius Maro), 2, 4, 5, 7–8, 36, 2.647n, 4.431n, 5.109n, 9.52n, 9.330n, 10.653n
Vulteius, 7, 16–17, 24, 147, 4.512–642

Willoughby, Lord, see Bertie

www.ingramcontent.com/pod-product-compliance
Lightning Source LLC
Chambersburg PA
CBHW071434300426
44114CB00013B/1423